HUMAN RESOURCE MANAGEMENT

SECOND EDITION

P. JYOTHI

Reader
School of Management Studies
University of Hyderabad
Hyderabad

D.N. VENKATESH

HR and OD Consultant

OXFORD
UNIVERSITY PRESS

OXFORD
UNIVERSITY PRESS

Oxford University Press is a department of the University of Oxford.
It furthers the University's objective of excellence in research, scholarship,
and education by publishing worldwide. Oxford is a registered trademark of
Oxford University Press in the UK and in certain other countries.

Published in India by
Oxford University Press
22 Workspace, 2nd Floor, 1/22 Asaf Ali Road, New Delhi 110 002

First Edition published in 2006
Second Edition published in 2012
10th impression 2023

ISBN-13: 978-0-19-807411-3
ISBN-10: 0-19-807411-5

Typeset in Garamond
by iPlus Knowledge Solutions Private Limited, Chennai
Printed in India by MP printers (A Unit of Dainik Bhasker group)

For product information and current price, please visit www.india.oup.com

To

the Almighty,

our parents, and our gurus

Preface to the Second Edition

The study of human resource management (HRM) helps in developing a clear understanding of the concepts, methods, techniques, and issues involved in managing human resources in an organization. This understanding is helpful in employing, maintaining, and developing a motivated workforce in an organization.

Human resource management and its study have assumed greater importance in the global economy as employees with diverse backgrounds and cultural values work together successfully and resourcefully. It has become imperative for organizations to attract and retain the right talent in this new dynamic business environment. HRM has become a crucial part of every business, and the role of the human resource (HR) manager has moved from the back end to being a strategic partner in the organization's long-term goals. It is in this context that we present this second edition.

Since the publication of the first edition, we have been receiving encouraging feedback about the book from students as well as faculty members. This edition improves upon the coverage of the original edition, making the text much more comprehensive and better structured. We hope that it will further aid students in understanding the basic principles of this subject.

KEY FEATURES

- Contains classroom-tested cases from Indian and international business organizations
- Includes examples and exhibits in key areas of HRM
- Provides chapter-end exercises with concept review questions, objective type questions, and project work

NEW TO THIS EDITION

- Three new chapters on strategic HRM, e-HRM, and international HRM
- New sections on HRM, recruitment, and selection practices in India and major HRM functions
- New case studies in all chapters
- Multiple choice questions and fill in the blanks in all chapters

COVERAGE AND STRUCTURE

With its expanded coverage, the book now contains 22 chapters. Chapters 1 and 2 discuss the scope and definition of HRM and explain it in the context of a dynamic business environment. Chapter 2 includes new sections on cultural diversity and work–life balance.

Chapter 3, which is a new chapter on strategic HRM, establishes the linkages between organizational-level strategies of the firm and HRM.

Chapter 4 deals with planning the supply of human resources and its role in strategic planning, while Chapter 5 describes the use of job analysis and design, especially in determining the important tasks, skills, and procedures required to perform a job effectively.

Chapter 6 describes the various methods of recruitment and processes related to retaining employees. This chapter includes a new section on recent trends and practices in India.

Chapter 7 explains the process of employee selection and its methods, while Chapter 8 discusses the key concepts, processes, and procedures related to placement and induction.

Chapter 9 discusses career planning and career management from the individual and organizational perspectives. Chapter 10 covers the importance and methods of employee training in organizations. This chapter includes a section on new methods of training and identification of training needs. Chapter 11 discusses executive and management development programmes.

Chapter 12 describes the design of a performance appraisal system and the methods adopted to assess the performance of employees. This chapter includes a new section on potential appraisal. Chapter 13, which is a new chapter on e-HRM, throws light on the increasing usage of technology in HR functions.

Chapter 14 discusses the various theories of employee motivation, and the relationship between employee benefits and motivation, which leads to a discussion on the various concepts, objectives, and guidelines related to compensation packages, in Chapter 15.

Chapter 16 explains the HR perspective of industrial relations and the role and characteristics of trade unions, particularly in the context of globalization, while Chapter 17 describes the processes of collective bargaining and workers' participation in management.

Chapter 18 covers the issues and concerns related to employee safety and health. Chapter 19 discusses knowledge management and HR issues related to managing the knowledge worker, and Chapter 20 explains the various HR audit and accounting procedures.

Chapter 21 discusses the various styles of leadership and the HR practices related to the promotion of organizational values and ethics. Chapter 22, a new chapter on international HRM, focuses on the increasing number of employees in multinational companies and the existence of cultural diversity.

ACKNOWLEDGEMENTS

We would like to thank Dr Anamika Pandey, Galgotia Business School, Greater Noida for contributing the chapter on e-HRM and Prof. Arindam Saha, Jaipuria Institute of Management, Indore for contributing the chapters on strategic HRM and international HRM.

We also received many suggestions for improving the content of the book. We are thankful to Dr R.K.S. Mangesh Dash, Institute of Management and Information Science (IMIS), Bhubaneswar; Prof. K.V. Ganpathy, Chetana Institute of Management and Research, Mumbai; and Mr T.K. Goon, TAG Solutions, New Delhi for their valuable feedback.

P. Jyothi
D.N. Venkatesh

Foreword to the First Edition

Today we are living in a changed world, which is also a new world for many. The older generation finds it new and feels that it does not belong to this world any more. For the younger generation it is a new world anyway. Many rules are being rewritten. Technology and money have ceased to provide competitive advantage; technology is available to all across the world and money is now globally sourced.

Many financial institutions are suffering because there are no borrowers, and interest rates have fallen down drastically in the last few years. Both technology and finance are available to talented people. Systems are ceasing to provide competitive advantage as most corporations and countries are becoming systems driven. In this changed world, people seem to have become the focal point. It is people who make things happen. With the realization that it is people who provide competitive advantage, employees have assumed pivotal importance in organizations now.

The future of corporations is in the hands of the people who work as their employees. The search for talent is on. In such a world, getting talented people and nurturing, developing, and utilizing them to achieve organizational goals gain a strategic perspective. The rules of the game have to be rewritten; some of them may not be entirely new, but their relevance has to be re-established in the changed context. The authors have done precisely this in this book on human resource management. They have discussed the changing scenario and rewritten the rules of the game to meet its challenges.

In the various chapters of this book, the authors cover in detail the principles, practices, benchmarks, trends, and various other aspects of human resource management (HRM), supported by case studies. In the initial chapters, they have appropriately covered the role of HRM in the dynamic environment. Besides all the important topics normally covered in an HRM book, such as HR planning, recruitment, induction, performance measurement and management, training, and career development, the authors have also discussed the new skills required by HR managers, the identification of business trends and HR competencies, workforce diversity, the forces acting on HRM, such as corporate objectives, HR planning, the rapidly evolving technology, etc. Organizational restructuring, work analysis and design, global placement, cultural adaptation, and handling separations, downsizing, and rightsizing are some of the other important topics covered in this book.

In discussing the important topic of compensation, concepts regarding pay systems, factors influencing compensation, the levels, principles, components, methods, and theories of executive remuneration, and reward programmes to encourage performance have also been dealt with.

In the last part, the authors have covered in detail the contemporary issues and emerging trends in HRM. The chapter on knowledge management, which discusses the management of knowledge workers, HRM in a knowledge economy, and technology management, and the one on HR accounting and auditing procedures, which discusses the balanced scorecard approach, are refreshingly new subjects for students and professionals of HRM. The scope of the coverage is also fairly large, including studies on non-government organizations, public sector undertakings, multinational companies, small and big corporations, and individuals and groups.

This book is rich with concepts, experiences, case studies, and research findings. The authors have done a wonderful job of putting together a rich and contemporary text for all managers, HR professionals, and faculty and students of HRM.

The text interspersed with various cases and anecdotes makes this book an enjoyable reading experience. It has been a pleasure to read this book and I congratulate the authors for their wonderful contribution to the HR profession through this book.

T.V. Rao

Preface to the First Edition

The human resource of an organization constitutes its entire workforce. Human resource management (HRM) is responsible for selecting and inducting competent people, training them, facilitating and motivating them to perform at high levels of efficiency, and providing mechanisms to ensure that they maintain their affiliation with the organization.

Human resource management is also an art of developing people and their potentialities for their personal growth and for the growth of the organization. It is a process of bringing people and organizations together to ensure that individual and collective goals are closely aligned. People have always been considered as critical in an organizational set-up. Unlike other resources, such as technology, finance, and materials, which can be purchased, human resource is a critical and sensitive element, and it needs to be handled with care. Often, organizations are concerned not only about employee productivity but also about employee commitment and harnessing their potentialities for maximum growth.

Since people constitute the cornerstone of any organization, HRM assumes central importance in most organizations. Any decision or process in an organization must be implemented through its people. In a competitive situation, it is the ingenuity, zeal, enthusiasm, and commitment of its people that makes all the difference for an organization. Therefore, the study of HRM forms an important part of the curriculum of any management course.

The concepts and practice of employer–employee relationships have undergone a change over the last decade. In a globally competitive economy, efforts to boost productivity and quality are a continuous process. To be more responsive to a dynamic business environment, organizations are increasingly adopting an approach to HRM that emphasizes redistribution of power, greater participation by individuals, and teamwork. It has been observed that the only sustainable competitive advantage an organization can have in today's environment is its people. Effective management of human resource is not an issue of competence only; it is also an issue of survival. Therefore, while being aware of the established practices in HRM, human resource managers must also be able to understand and apply innovative techniques to successfully and productively manage human resources. The importance of HRM, therefore, would become even more crucial in the years ahead.

Industrial revolution and large-scale production in the eighteenth and nineteenth centuries gave rise to the practice of 'personnel management', which started as a voluntary movement in the US and the UK. Traditionally, the role of the 'personnel manager' was to maintain records of personnel and act as a liaison between the employee and the employer. Taylor's scientific management, Fayol's principles of management, Maslows' hierarchy of needs, MCGregor's Theory X and Theory Y, the Hawthorne experiments, and the human relations movement, all contributed significantly to the concept and practice of personnel management. Recognizing that human beings are the most important assets of an organization, the term 'personnel' was replaced with 'human resource'. Also, as developing human resource is crucial for productivity and growth, HRM is now increasingly focusing on the development function.

ABOUT THE BOOK

The book is designed to meet the requirements of management students at the postgraduate level by explaining the key concepts of HRM through numerous examples of managerial applications. Given its practical, application-oriented approach, it will also be a useful resource for practising managers and other professionals active in training and consultancy. The book discusses HRM in the context of the recent trends in the globalized economy and presents a comparative perspective of HR practices in different societies. It also discusses HRM in international organizations and the impact of the emergence of knowledge management and the knowledge worker on HRM.

PEDAGOGICAL FEATURES

The book discusses HRM in the Indian context, taking examples from world-class organizations, such as TCS, IBM, SmithKline Beecham, Vysya Bank, Woolworths Group, Novo Nordisk, etc. It also discusses contemporary HR practices in organizations such as Reliance Energy Limited, ICICI Bank Limited, Premier Chemicals, HCL Perot Systems, and Unilever.

Additional features of the book include end-chapter questions and interesting practicals, such as group discussions and outdoor projects, to promote self-learning. An Instructor's Manual is available on demand for instructors using the book.

COVERAGE AND STRUCTURE

The book contains 20 chapters. Chapters 1 and 2 discuss the scope and definition of HRM and explain HRM in the context of a dynamic environment. Chapter 3 deals with planning the supply of human resources and its role in strategic planning, while Chapter 4 describes the use of job analysis and design, especially in determining the important tasks, skills, and procedures required to perform a job effectively. The various methods of recruitment and process related to retaining employees are described in Chapter 5. Chapter 6 explains the process of employee selection and examines its methods. The key concepts, processes, and procedures related to placement and induction are discussed in Chapter 7. Chapter 8 discusses career planning and career management from individual and organizational perspectives. While Chapter 9 covers the importance and methods of employee training in organizations, Chapter 10 discusses the executive and management development programmes. Chapter 11 describes the design of a performance appraisal system and the methods adopted to assess the performance of the employees. Chapter 12 discusses the various theories of employee motivation and the relationship between employee benefits and motivation, which leads on to a discussion on the various concepts, objectives, and guidelines related to compensation packages in Chapter 13. Chapter 14 explains the HR perspective of industrial relations and the role and characteristics of trade unions, particularly in the context of globalization, whereas Chapter 15 describes the processes of collective bargaining and workers' participation in management. Chapter 16 covers the issues and concerns related to employee safety and health. Chapter 17 discusses knowledge management and HR issues related to managing the knowledge worker, and Chapter 18 explains the various HR audit and accounting procedures. Finally, Chapter 19 discusses the various styles of leadership and the HR practices related to promoting organizational values and ethics.

ACKNOWLEDGEMENTS

We would like to express our sincere thanks to our gurus, who nurtured and groomed us through our formative years and continue to motivate us to keep learning throughout the journey of life. We would like to thank our parents, without whom we would not have been what we are today. We also take this opportunity to thank the Almighty, without whose blessings and grace this challenging task could not have been accomplished.

Every author owes a great deal to others and the authors of this book are no exception. First and foremost, we are indebted to Prof. T.V. Rao, who kindly agreed to write the Foreword for this book. We greatly appreciate his contribution. We are indebted to our friends in Oxford University Press who constantly guided and motivated us in our endeavour. Without their continuous moral support, the book would not have seen the light of the day.

We acknowledge the contributions and support of Mr Krishna Sagar Rao and Mr Dayal Anubhuti at various stages of preparing the manuscript. We would also like to acknowledge the interactions we had with our industry colleagues, which helped in shaping the cases of the book. The authors also appreciate the patience and diligence of Ms Subhashini in typing the manuscript, making corrections in it, and delivering it on time.

We are thankful to the University of Hyderabad, especially the School of Management Studies, for providing us the necessary infrastructure and support for speedy completion of the book. Finally, we are thankful to our respective family members, particularly P. Jyothi's daughter Bhavani, for kindly bearing with us during the writing of the book.

P. Jyothi
D.N. Venkatesh

Features of the Book

Strategic Human Resource Management

Objectives

After studying this chapter, you will be able to understand
- the concept of strategic human resource management (SHRM)
- the linkages between organizational strategy and HRM strategy
- SHRM models and strategies

INTRODUCTION

The developments in the field of HRM over the last four to five decades (well-documented in management literature) have brought about significant changes in the nature of the HR function as we see today.

LEARNING OBJECTIVES

Each chapter begins with learning objectives that focus on the knowledge that you will acquire after studying the chapter.

EXHIBITS

The chapters contain exhibits that help in understanding the application of the theory discussed in the chapter.

EXHIBIT 19.1 Pharmaceutical firms

Research scientists in the R&D units of pharmaceutical firms are given a totally free work environment. The chief executive/head of R&D does a periodic review of the focus areas of research, that is, diseases related to diabetes, cancer, etc., and provides information about the current treatment available and the trend of research (molecular/drug) being done elsewhere in the world. Based on these inputs, the scientists start their molecular research in groups. When they feel that enough work has been done and the results need to be tested, the head

Job design concern and approaches are considered to have begun with the scientific management movement.

Job designing evolved into what is popularly known as job en The industrial engineering approach is basically concerned with process, tool design, plant layout, operating procedures, work me standards, and human–machine interactions. It has also been closely with sophisticated computer applications involving computer assi (CAD). These computer systems had a positive impact by reducin

SIDEBARS

Important concepts appear as sidebars throughout the text for quick recapitulation. This will help you in revision before an exam.

FIGURES AND TABLES

All chapters contain figures and tables to illustrate the topics discussed in the chapter.

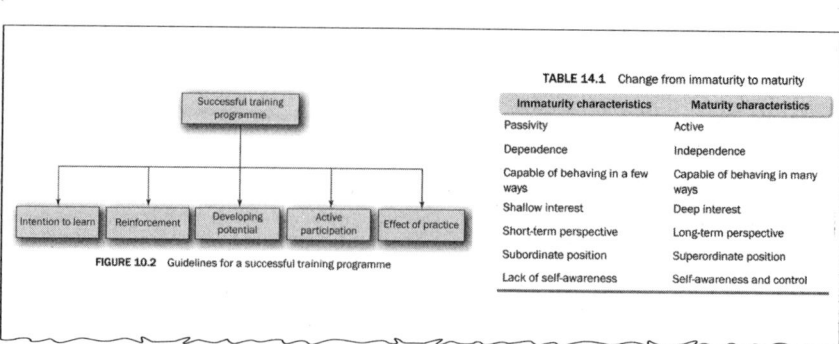

FIGURE 10.2 Guidelines for a successful training programme

TABLE 14.1 Change from immaturity to maturity

Immaturity characteristics	Maturity characteristics
Passivity	Active
Dependence	Independence
Capable of behaving in a few ways	Capable of behaving in many ways
Shallow interest	Deep interest
Short-term perspective	Long-term perspective
Subordinate position	Superordinate position
Lack of self-awareness	Self-awareness and control

SUMMARY

In this chapter, an important function of HR—performance appraisal—has been discussed. An employee's growth, personal development, and job satisfaction are all dependent on his/her performance. Similarly, an organization's growth, future planning, and employee development are all contingent upon employee performance. Further, an employee's performance is also used as an indicator for compensation packages, career counseling, and identifying training needs. This chapter discusses both traditional and modern methods of performance appraisal. It also relates performance to aspects such as strategy, change management, and learning. The process of appraisal usually involves comparing the performance with a standard. An employee's performance against these standards is judged by using different methods. There are a few raters' biases, which might interfere in the rating process. This can be overcome effectively. Further, the data obtained from the appraisal process may be utilized effectively for performance planning and improvement, thereby establishing a performance management system in the organization.

SUMMARY

The summary at the end of each chapter draws together the main concepts discussed in the chapter. This will help you to remember and revise important concepts.

KEY TERMS

All important terms have been explained at the end of each chapter as key terms. This will help you in quick recapitulation of all the new terms that you have learnt in the chapter.

■ ■ ■ | KEY TERMS

360 degree feedback An effective means of gathering information about employees' behaviour and performance at work, including employees' relationships with others

Compensation Something, such as money, given or received as payment or reparation, as for a service or loss

Correlation A causal, complementary, parallel, or reciprocal relationship, especially a structural, functional, or qualitative correspondence between two comparable entities

Holistic Emphasizing the importance of the whole and the interdependence of its parts

Incentive An additional payment (or other remuneration) to employees as a means of increasing output

Prerequisites Things or conditions that are required or necessary as a prior condition

Quantifiable To determine or express the quantity

Stratified sampling Sampling done in strata or layers

SWOT analysis A very effective way of identifying strengths and weaknesses, and of examining the op-

---

3. On-the-job training does not include
   (a) job rotation
   (b) coaching
   (c) job enlargement
   (d) action learning

Concept Review Questions

1. Outline the factors contributing to the evolution of IHRM.
2. Why do you think organizations would require managers with multicultural experience?
3. How do you see cultures affecting business decisions/actions?

Fill in the Blanks

1. Continuous learning and _____ inform mould managers, and also help them gain the spect of their subordinates.
2. The analysis of the _____ helps

Project Work

1. An MNC may face numerous problems because of the huge cultural and legal differences between the countries that it operates in. Visit websites, gather data from secondary sources, and analyse them. Prepare a report with your findings on how these MNCs manage op

EXERCISES

A series of objective and concept review questions as well as project assignments highlight the major topics covered in the chapters. These exercises enhance your learning and can be used for review and class-room discussion.

END-OF-CHAPTER CASES

Each chapter ends with case studies that are designed to consolidate your understanding of the chapter subject and broaden your decision-making skills.

CASE STUDY 1

Induction Issues in an Indian BPO—Firstnet

Firstnet is a domestic BPO operating out of eight major cities in the country. They support customers in the telecom and insurance verticals. The total employees working across all the centres in the country is close to 10,000. The company has been recruiting close to 1,000 employees every month for expansion and replacement of outgoing employees.

- The trainers conducting the induction and orientation programmes were not effective in terms of communication and imparting the skills required for performing on the job.
- The training content was quite contradictory to what the joinees were doing on the job.
- The training was too theoretical with very little hands-on training.

Brief Contents

Detailed Contents

List of Case Studies

Nature and Concept of HRM

INTRODUCTION

The advent of the era of liberalization and globalization along with the advancements in information technology (IT) has transformed the world around us. It has brought to centre stage the importance of human resources, more than ever before. The purpose of human resource management (HRM) is to enable appropriate deployment of human resources.

In a competitive scenario, effective utilization of human resources has become necessary and the primary task of organizations is to identify, recruit, and channel competent human resources into their business operations for improving productivity and functional efficiency. Several authors have tried to explain the meaning of human resources and one of the comprehensive definitions was given by Leon C. Megginson, who described human resources as the sum total of the knowledge, abilities, and attitudes of all the employees of an organization. Effective utilization of human resources would lead to both accomplishment of individual and organizational goals and creation of assets at the national level. It is in this context that development of human resources, which involves continuous honing of employee skills, has become vital for the very survival of organizations, let alone growth and development.

Definitions

Management has been defined as control and creation of a technological and human environment that can support optimal utilization of resources and competencies for achieving organizational goals. Management has also been variously defined as development of people; the process of decision-making and control over actions of human beings; planning, organizing, and controlling of people and resources; the process of accomplishing the desired organizational objectives; effective utilization of available resources for delivery of services and goods, etc.

It is in this backdrop that we will try to understand the broad definitions of HRM given by various experts.

Process consisting of four functions—acquisition, development, motivation, and maintenance of human resources.

–David A. Decenzo and Stephen P. Robbins

Personnel management is the planning, organizing, directing, and controlling of the procurement, development, compensation, integration, maintenance, and separation of human resources to the end that individual, organizational, and societal objectives are accomplished.

–Edward Filippo

Recent literature on knowledge management and creation of people-centric partnership suggests that there is a need to increasingly integrate information technology (IT) with human competence for optimum utilization of both kinds of resources. An analysis of various definitions indicates that HRM includes the following activities:

- Aligning the HR strategy with the corporate strategy of the organization
- Working for the well-being of all the employees
- Developing employee competencies
- Sourcing, deploying, and developing human resources for optimal utilization
- Empowering employee
- Managing performance

HRM can be defined as a strategic and coherent approach to the management of the most valued assets of an organization, that is, people, who individually and collectively contribute to the organizational objectives. Storey (1989) has made a distinction between *hard* and *soft* versions of HRM. The hard approach focuses on the quantitative and strategic aspects of managing the human resources. It is a rational approach, which deals with human resources like any other economic factor. It emphasizes the need for managing people to enhance their contribution to improving the quantitative advantage of the organization. It aims at protecting the interests of the management and building a strong corporate culture by internalizing the mission and value statements of the organization.

The soft approach to HRM, whose roots can be traced to the human resource school, emphasizes factors such as communication, motivation, and leadership. It treats employees as the essential means of realizing organizational objectives rather than mere objects. It focuses on engendering commitment among employees by winning their hearts. The functions of HRM include the following:

- Facilitating the retention of skilled and competent employees
- Building the competencies of human resources by facilitating continuous learning and development

- Developing and implementing high performance work systems
- Developing management practices that engender high commitment
- Developing practices which foster team work and flexibility
- Making the employees feel that they are valued and rewarded for their contribution
- Facilitating management of workforce diversity and availability of equal opportunities to all

HUMAN RESOURCE MANAGEMENT—HISTORY

> ■ ■ ■
> The evolution of HRM can be traced back to the HR movement in the ancient period.

The evolution of HRM can be traced back to the HR movement in the ancient period. However, in the modern age, that is, up to 1930s, it was referred to as personnel management and the focus was on the employer–employee relations. Studies on HR were initially guided by Taylor's scientific management principles and then graduated through the Hawthorne studies to the behavioural school based on the theories of Abraham Maslow, Herzberg, and Douglas McGregor.

Various developments in the 21st century heralded the arrival of the knowledge and IT era. During the initial phases, IT was perceived as an all-pervasive phenomenon and attempts were made to tune all organizational processes to this development. However, the experience of a large number of organizations both at the global and the national level has led to the realization that IT has to play only a supportive role in achieving organizational objectives and for this purpose an organization has to focus on its three core areas, that is, people, processes, and performance (Figure 1.1).

HRM and the 3 Ps

Let as discuss an organization's three core areas in this section.

People   It is now an established fact that the core strength of an organization lies in its human resources and it would not be an exaggeration to say that all other resources can be replaced except human resources.

Processes   Organizational processes evolve over a period of time and often these are treated as sanctimonious. The justification for doing so is the belief that what has worked so well in the past would work in the future as well. However, in the fast changing world, much emphasis is laid on flexibility and adaptability. In the past, it would have been a Herculean task to reengineer the processes, but in an IT-enabled environment, reengineering of processes at the server level would simultaneously and effortlessly lead to reengineering across the organization.

Performance   The existence of an organization is primarily dependent on its ability to create value and continuously increase the rate of return on investment (ROI). The two pillars supporting the performance of an organization are people and IT. The integration of these two factors plays the pivotal role in improving the performance of an organization at both individual and organizational levels. IT helps in documenting the knowledge pool in an organization and

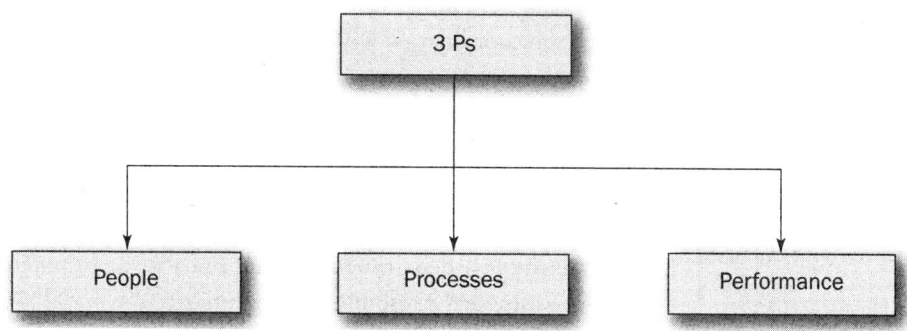

FIGURE 1.1   HRM and the 3 Ps

making it available to the employees through intranet and similar means. Further, management of knowledge workers is different from that of conventional employees as the level of intelligence and maturity of knowledge workers is higher and, hence, they expect greater levels of flexibility and freedom in their work area.

HRM and Its Evolution in India

The history of HRM in India dates back to the early 1980s when Mr Udai Pareek and Mr T.V. Rao championed the cause of the HRM movement. The early adopters of the HRM movement include public sector enterprises such as Bharat Heavy Electricals Limited (BHEL), State Bank of India, etc. Initially, Indian organizations used to have an industrial relations (IR) department, which was subsequently re-christened as the personnel and IR department, and made part of with the welfare department as one of its sub-departments. The personnel department predominantly suited the blue-collar employees since their general awareness and educational levels were low and the approach was more of administrative nature. The growing importance of the service sector in the Indian economy has also highlighted the importance of change in approach by the personnel and administrative departments. The profile of an employee in the new scenario has the following features:

> ■ ■ ■
> The growing importance of the service sector in the Indian economy has also highlighted the importance of change in approach by the personnel and administrative departments.

- Employees are mostly in their mid-twenties or early thirties.
- All employees are educated and their level of general awareness is high.
- Employees are more committed to the profession than to the organization.
- The rates of attrition and the level of mobility of employees among the organizations are high.

The organizations have to compete for scarce resources, the most important among them being the human resources, more so in the case of the service sector. This has called for the radical transformation of personnel and administrative departments into human resource departments to reflect the human facet of organizations. A glance at the structure of various Indian organizations indicates that the majority of the organizations have rechristened their personnel and administrative departments as human resource development (HRD) departments. However, this transformation into the HRM mode is at various stages in different organizations. The progressive players and market leaders, especially in the IT and service sectors, have fully adopted this approach while other players are in the process of adoption.

The transformed HR department performs the following functions:

- Participating in the strategizing sessions of business policy
- Preparing the HR strategies in coordination with the corporate strategies

> ■ ■ ■
> The HR department has outgrown its mere functional role and has come to assume the responsibility of building the brand for the company.

- Implementing the various HR policies and practices including HR planning, recruiting and inducting, compensation structuring, career planning, competence mapping, managing performance etc.

The flow of activities in the HRM function is diagrammatically represented in Figure 1.2.

Overall, the HR department has outgrown its mere functional role and has come to assume the responsibility of building the brand for the company

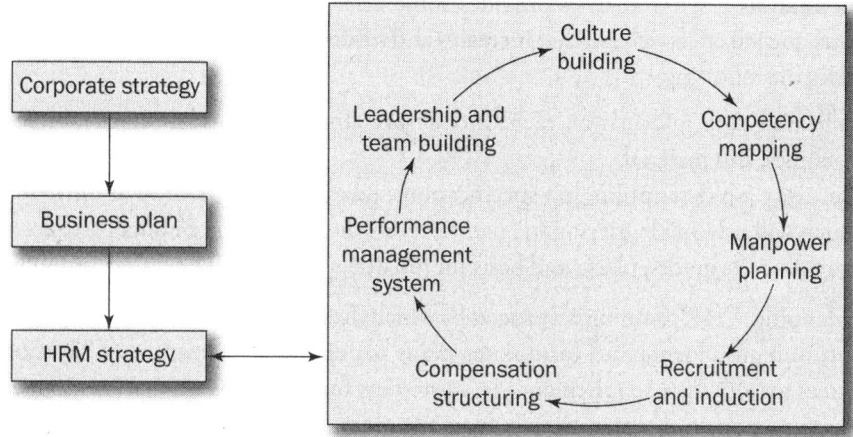

FIGURE 1.2   Flow of activities in the HRM function

to attract the best available talent in the market and also to retain the existing talent. This helps in reducing the recruitment cost and the replacement cost apart from reducing the attrition rates, which helps the organization to complete its projects in time.

MAJOR FUNCTIONS OF HUMAN RESOURCE MANAGEMENT

Human resource may be defined as the total knowledge, skills, creative abilities, talents, and aptitudes of an organization's workforce as well as the values, attitudes, approaches, and beliefs of the individuals involved in the affairs of the organization. It is a sum total or aggregate of inherent abilities, acquired knowledge, and skills possessed by the employees of an organization. HRM is concerned with getting better results through efficient management of employees.

The process oriented nature of HRM brings people and organizations together so that the goals of each are met. It has a pervasive nature and helps people to realize their potential fully. It encourages employees to give their best and be dynamic rather than being dogmatic. It facilitates the organization by providing competent and motivated employees. It has a cohesive role to play by unifying all the departments in an organization.

The functions of HRM are related to specific activities of personnel management, which include staff development, compensation, and employee relations. These functions are directly linked to objectives and strategies of the organization. An organization comes into existence for the realization of its objectives. The objectives determine the structure, and the structure determines the different roles and positions in an organization. This is the starting point for the functions of HRM. We will now discuss the various functions of HRM:

Staffing

Organizational design defines the different positions in the staff hierarchy. Staffing is one of the primary functions of HRM and involves work analysis, HR planning, recruitment, selection, placement, induction, and orientation. The following paragraphs discuss these functions:

Work analysis Work analysis provides some basic information on various skills required to perform the job effectively, so that it creates and sustains organizational capability. Work analysis includes the following:

- Collecting data, information, facts, and ideas relating to various aspects of jobs, including men, machines, and material
- Preparing job description, job specifications, job requirements, and employee specifications, which will help in identifying the nature, levels, and quantum of human resources
- Providing the guides, plans, and basis for job design and for all operative functions of HRM

HR planning HR planning is a process by which the management of an organization determines its future requirements and formulates plans for effective utilization of the existing human resources to fulfil these requirements. It is a strategy for the acquisition, utilization, improvement, and preservation of an enterprise's human resources. It relates to establishing job specifications, determining the number of personnel required, and developing sources of human resources. The HR planning function involves the following:

- Estimating present/future requirements, and supply of human resources based on objectives and long-term plans of the organization
- Forecasting HR requirements based on the present inventory of human resources
- Suggesting steps to meet the future HR requirements

Recruitment Recruitment is the process of acquiring applications for specific positions to be filled in the organization. In other words, it is a process of searching for and pooling of applications for jobs, so that the right people may get selected. The process involves the following:

- Sourcing of applications from internal and external sources
- Strategizing to attract the best talent from the market
- Screening the applications and preparing for the selection process

Selection Selection is the process of differentiating between applicants in order to identify (and hire) those with a greater likelihood of success in a job. The selection function includes the following:

- Preliminary screening interview
- Application blanks
- Psychological tests
- Interview
- Hiring decision

Placement Placement is a process of assigning the selected candidates with the most suitable job. It is the matching of employee specifications with job requirements.

Induction and orientation of employees Induction is the process of integration attempted by the organization to introduce the organizational policies and programmes to new employees. The orientation programme involves the following:

- Acquainting the employee with company philosophy, objectives, policies, growth opportunities, etc.
- Introducing the employee to the people with whom they will work

Performance Appraisal

Performance appraisal may be defined as the systematic evaluation of an individual with respect to his/her potential for development. The appraisal process involves the following:

- Developing appraisal policies and procedures
- Conducting performance appraisal
- Evaluating appraisal and performance management

Training and Development

Training is a process of enhancing the efficiency, capacity, and effectiveness at work. The function includes the following:

- Identifying training needs at the individual, group, and organizational levels
- Designing training programmes
- Evaluating the effectiveness of training programmes

Career Planning and Management

Career management is an organizational process that implements and monitors career plans within the organization's career systems. The function includes the following:

- Providing career guidance and support to the employees
- Counselling and assisting employees on transfers and promotions

Compensation Management

Compensation is a systematic approach to provide monetary benefits to employees in exchange for work performed. The function includes the following:

- Conducting job evaluation process
- Developing suitable wage and salary programmes
- Formulating incentives and other fringe benefits

Human Resource Accounting, Audit, and Research

In today's organizations, HRM is measured and evaluated by auditing and accounting procedures. The function includes the following:

- Performing HR accounting, which is a measurement of the cost and value of HR in the organization
- Conducting HR audit, which evaluates policies and procedures to determine the effectiveness of HRM
- Conducting research, developing a database, and evaluating the existing HR practices for better functioning

These functions constitute the strategic approach to manpower management in an organization. Managing people involves employing people, and designing and developing the related resources to enhance their performance. More importantly, it involves utilizing and compensating their service to optimize business profitability through employee performance. The human capital within various departments needs to kept motivated to enable the company to benefit from employee skills and experience.

ORGANIZATIONAL STRUCTURE

An organization is a closely coordinated social entity with an identifiable boundary that functions on a relatively continuous basis to achieve common objectives and goals. The objectives determine the structure. Organizational structure defines how tasks and relationships are allocated and coordinated. In other words, it refers to the defined relationships between the elements of the organization—people, tasks, information, and control processes. The management of people in organizations constantly raises questions such as the following:

- Who does what?
- How should activities be grouped together?
- What lines of communication need to be established?
- How can the roles and objectives be aligned together?

HR managers and practitioners should be able to contribute to the process of organizational design as they understand the factors affecting organizational behaviour. The process of organizing can be understood as the design, development, and maintenance of a system of coordinated activities in which individuals and groups of people, guided by a leader, work towards organizational objectives. The key term here is 'system'. Organizations are considered as open systems, which are affected by internal and external environments, and have a structure of their own. Organizational design is the process of developing an organizational structure.

Organizational structure may be explained with the help of variables such as the following:

- *Centralization*—the number of people participating in decision-making with respect to major policies and planning
- *Autonomy*—the freedom experienced by the top management in decision-making
- *Differentiation*—the number of specialized functions represented in different departments
- *Formalization*—the extent to which an employee's role is defined by formal documentation
- *Span of control*—the number of subordinates that a manager can and should supervise
- *Specialization*—the number of specialized functions identified and formalized in the organization

These components may not be exhaustive, but serve our purpose of understanding the organizational structure (Figure 1.3 depicts the organizational chart of the HR department of a company). An organization may have functional structure, divisional structure, or matrix structure. We will now discuss these organizational structures.

Functional Structure

It is a typical type of organizational structure where positions are grouped according to their main or specialized functions. It is most widely used for basic functional areas such as marketing, finance, HR, operations, and production. In an organization where a functional structure is adopted, it becomes easier to identify the key result areas (KRAs). The terminology might differ

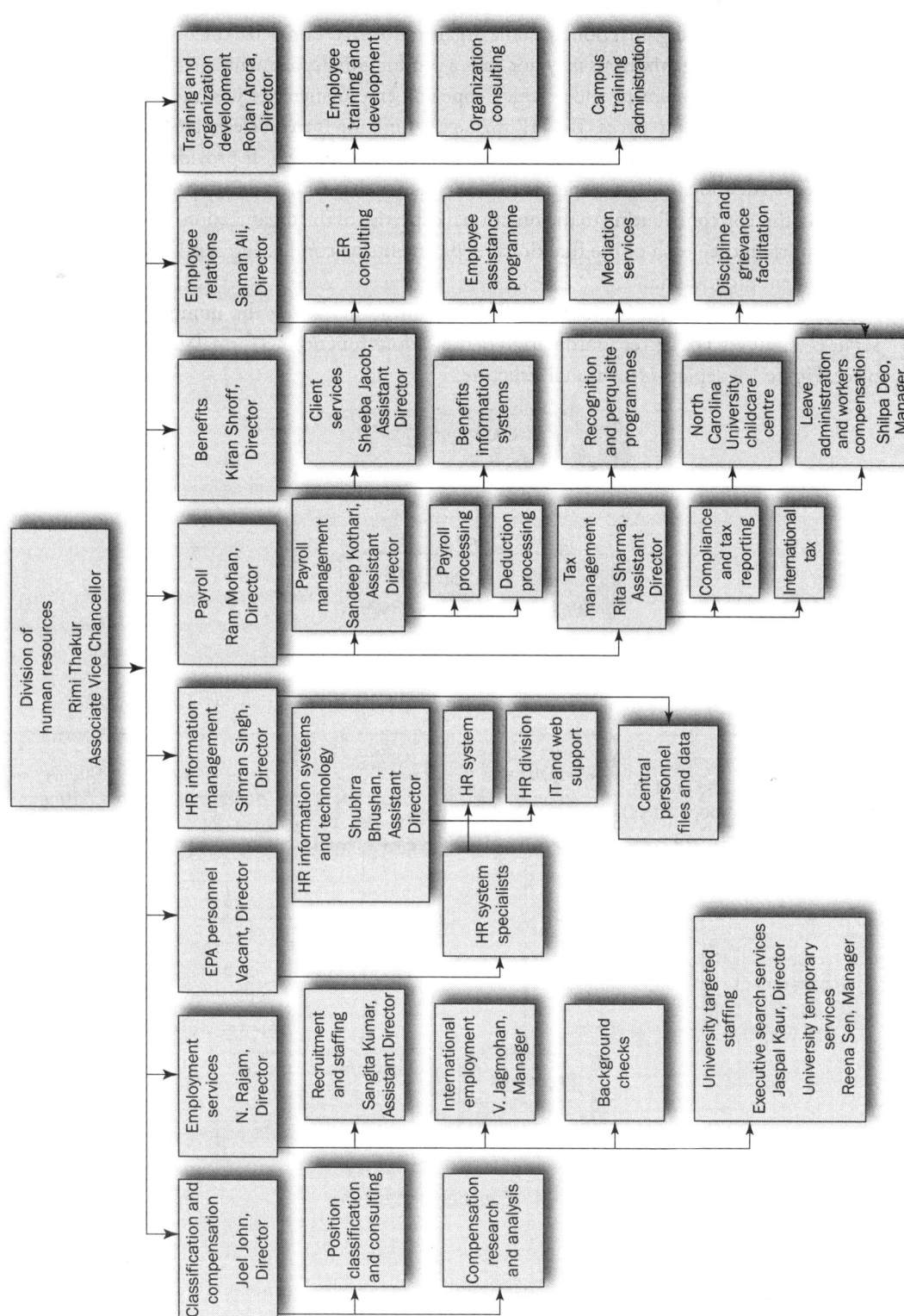

FIGURE 1.3 Example of the organizational chart of the HR department of a company

from organization to organization. In some organizations, certain departments may not exist. For example, religious organizations may not have a production department.

A functional structure provides large scope for employment as it seeks diverse skills and knowledge from the employees. The HR manager's function is to set clear career paths within the specialized function and allow for the career growth of employees. It provides opportunities to employees to develop in-depth expertise. There is clarity that each position specializes in a specific function, thereby contributing to the functional expertise of the organization. The HR manager's role is to strengthen each of the functional departments by conducting continuous training and development programmes.

A functional structure is more suited to organizations where the number of products or services is limited. For better coordination of the various functions, a formal structure has to be in place. Figure 1.4 depicts a functional structure.

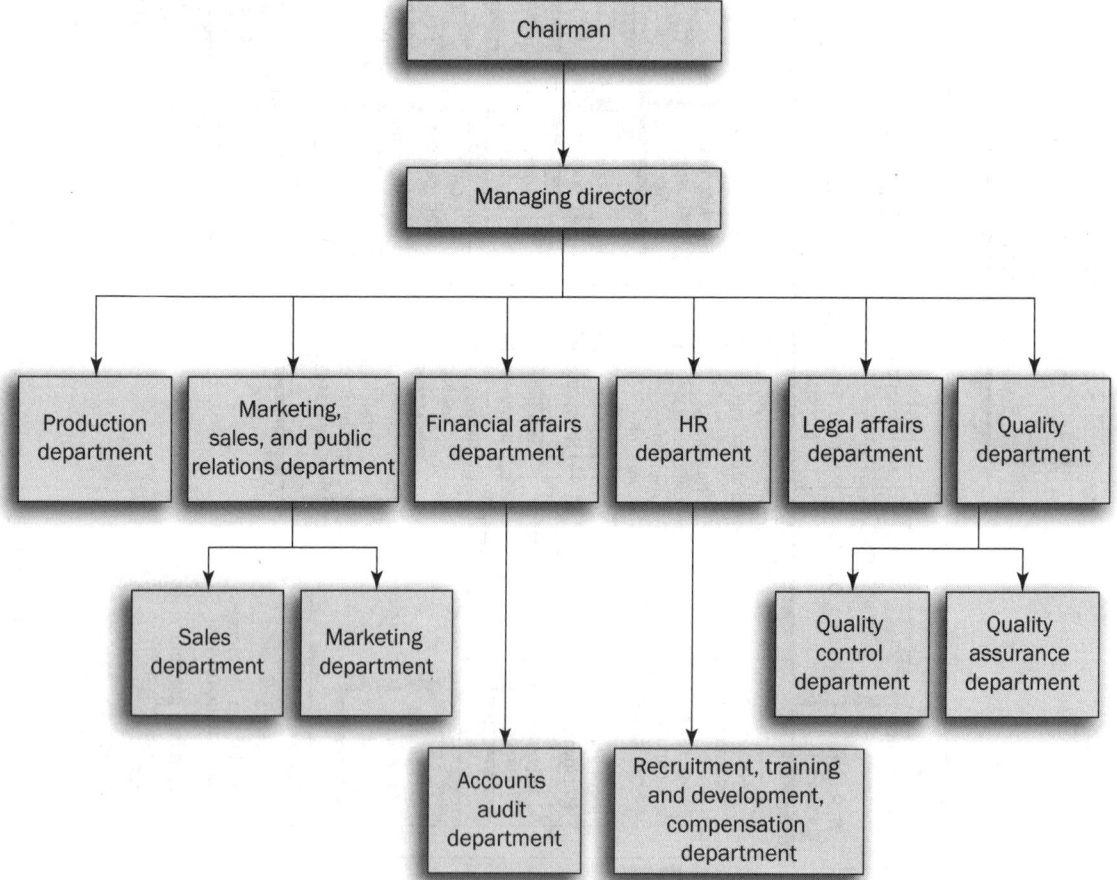

FIGURE 1.4 Functional structure

Divisional Structure

A divisional structure is a type of departmentalization in which positions are grouped based on similarity of products, services, or geographical areas. Divisional structure refers to the division of large functional pyramids into smaller, more flexible, administrative units. It is designed to promote self sufficiency and efficiency in the units. The more popular forms of divisional structure are the product divisions and geographical divisions. Product divisions are more suitable for large, multi-product organizations. In this form of organizational structure, the large functional units are further divided into small units, and each such unit is grouped in terms of products manufactured and sold. Each division is responsible for its own performance and profitability. Each unit has a functional structure within it, such as personnel, manufacturing, and marketing departments. Functional managers perform the tasks associated with the products of their own division.

Each division needs to perform the HR functions. For example, product development and specialization demand expertise from the research and development (R&D) wing. The process of recruitment needs to identify such individuals. At times, certain groups of the workforce such as sales personnel may be increased based on the performance of the company. In other words, the HR functions need to be customized in accordance with the performance of the organization and demand from the market. A divisional structure is represented in Figure 1.5.

Matrix Structure

A matrix structure is a type of departmentalization wherein function and division patterns are superimposed and are combined in the same structure. Essentially, a matrix structure has two chairs of command—vertical and horizontal. As shown in Figure 1.6, the functional departments such as human resources, marketing, finance, R&D, production, and engineering constitute the horizontal hierarchy. The managers of different products represent the divisional units, which operate vertically across the structure. In a matrix structure, an employee has to report to two matrix bosses. For example, an employee of the marketing department may report to the Vice-President–Marketing horizontally and to the manager of a particular product vertically. Therefore, the structure is more complicated and overrules the unity of command. Thus, the matrix structure facilitates decentralization of decision-making.

The role of an HR manager is complicated as it includes a range of functions from training of employees in interpersonal skills and decision-making to handling critical incidents.

HRM AND IT

The advent of information technology has changed the competitive landscape of the corporate world. IT influences the corporate world through three factors:

- *IT practices:* It denotes the capabilities of a company to effectively utilize IT applications and infrastructure to support its business processes and operations.

■ ■ ■
HR managers have to initiate an organizational-culture building exercise for internalization and adoption of the desired values.

- *Information management practices:* It denotes the organizational capabilities to manage the entire information life cycle, that is, sensing, collecting, organizing, processing, and maintaining information.
- *Information behaviours/values (IBV):* It indicates the organizational capabilities to promote behaviours and values that facilitate the effective use of information.

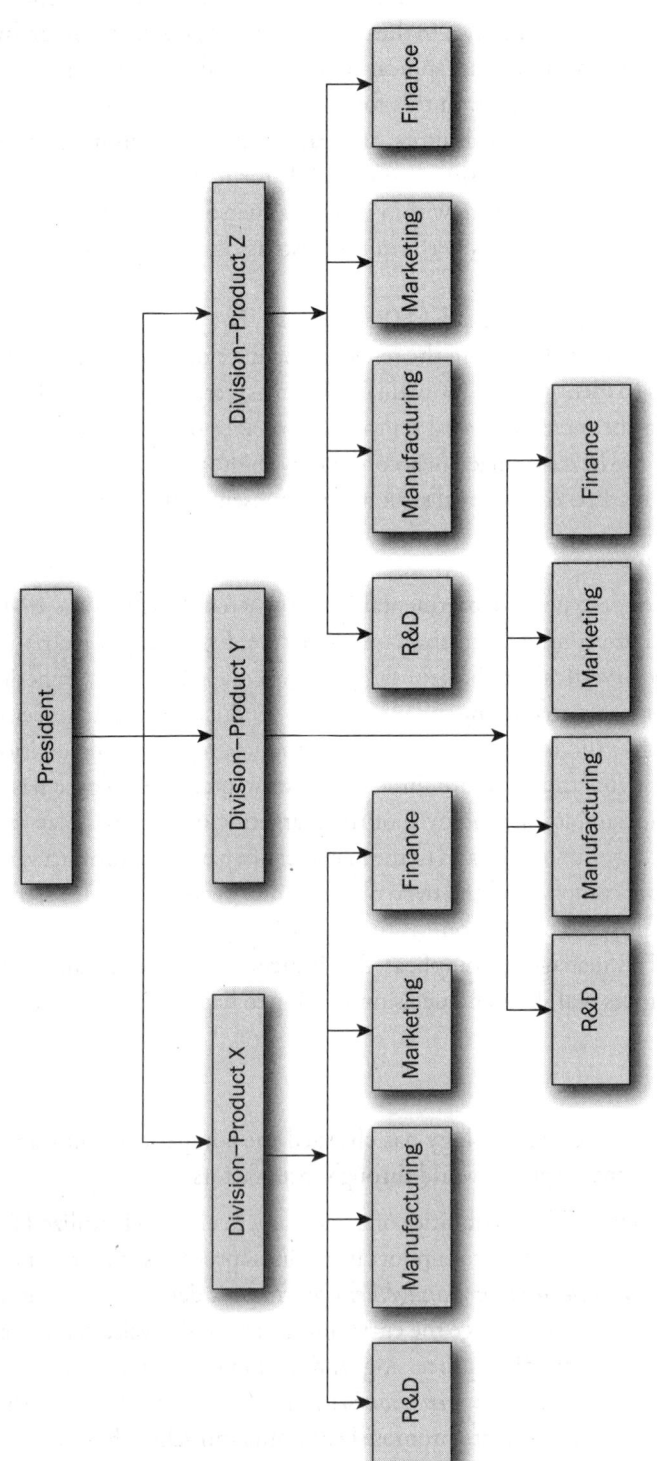

FIGURE 1.5 Divisional structure

Source: http://sameh.files.wordpress.com/2006/05/Organization%20Structure2.jpg

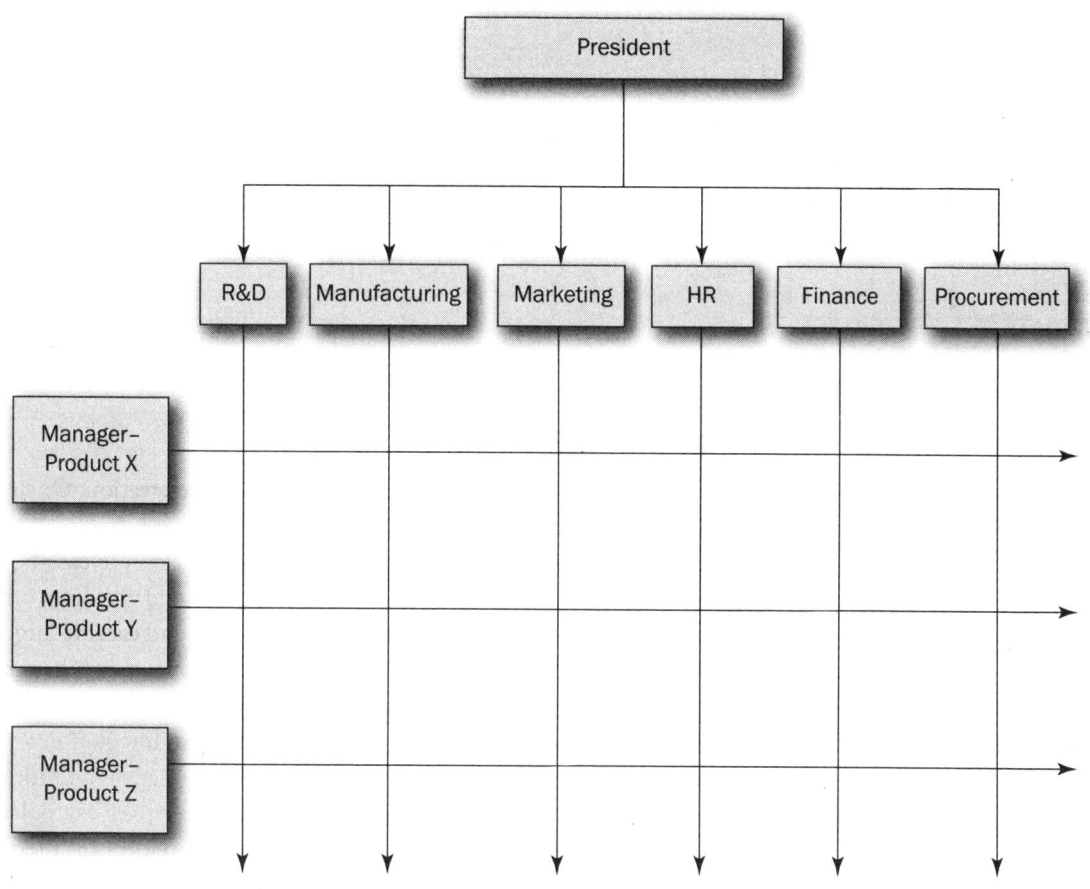

FIGURE 1.6 Matrix structure

Source: http://sameh.files.wordpress.com/2006/05/Organization%20Structure3.jpg

> ■ ■ ■
> HR managers have to initiate an organizational-culture building exercise for internalization and adoption of the desired values.

The first one, that is, IT practices, is more in the domain of IT specialists, while the HR department has to deal with the second and the third, respectively. HR managers have to work in close coordination with the IT head for creating awareness about the information management practices. The key challenge is to define and communicate the information behaviours/values expected from the employees. More importantly, HR managers have to initiate an organizational-culture building exercise for internalization and adoption of the desired values.

HRM AND COMPETENCY BUILDING

Two of the recent and widely used terms among HRM professionals are 'competency building' and 'competency mapping' among the employees. Beginners in the subject would wonder what could be the importance of the so called 'competence' in organizational context and more so from the HRM perspective. Michael Porter, who shared his pathbreaking research findings through his book *Competitive Advantage*, has proposed that the competitive advantage for an organization is

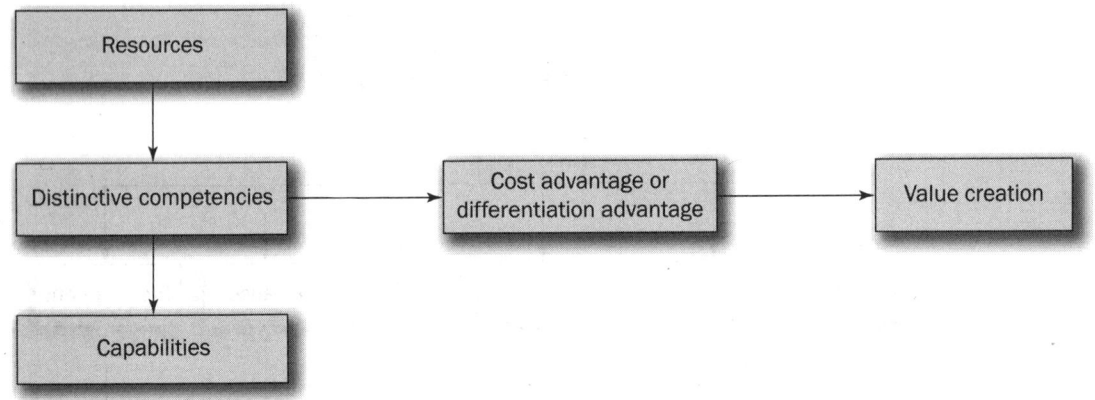

FIGURE 1.7 Model of competitive advantage

dependent on its distinctive capabilities to use the available resources for value creation. One of the fundamental and generic models of competitive advantage is shown in Figure 1.7.

The model shown in Figure 1.7 indicates that the activities of an organization are based on various resources, such as material, human, financial, etc., and the capabilities would vary from one company to another. For instance, L&T Ltd has the capabilities to undertake and execute large-scale construction projects in a time-bound manner. Its distinctive capabilities are those that are unique to the company. In the same way, Reliance has the capabilities to undertake and complete large-scale petrochemicals projects as a strategy towards forward and backward integration and gaining economies-of-scale over its rivals. Depending on its distinctive capabilities, an organization can have cost advantage or differentiation advantage. Indian IT companies are typical examples, as they started with a cost advantage and are gradually moving towards differentiation advantage to meet the competition in American and European markets. At the end of the entire process, an organization should be able to create value for all its stakeholders, that is, employees, shareholders, investors, etc.

HRM AND PERFORMANCE MANAGEMENT

In the present competitive scenario, one of the foremost challenges for the organizations, and more specifically for the HR department, is to facilitate performance of individuals to realize the organizational objectives. Planning for performance is the first step towards performance management.

■ ■ ■
Planning for performance is the first step towards performance management.

Performance planning can be defined as systematic outlining of tasks/activities to be carried out by the employees during the specific period so that they are able to contribute towards accomplishment of organizational goals. The planning process involves aspects such as the time frame, activities/area-wise targets, tasks to be coordinated, etc. In short, performance planning emphasizes individual contribution vis-à-vis the organizational goals. The scope of performance planning in an organization covers its entire set of employees. Further, there has been an eternal debate as to whether performance planning should be top-down, bottom-up, or both ways. The process

■ ■ ■
The scope of performance planning in an organization covers its entire set of employees.

■ ■ ■
Often, employees are found lacking in performance due to lack of clarity about their roles and responsibilities.

of performance planning involves various activities such as task analysis and/or activity analysis, analysis of key performance areas (KPAs), analysis of key result areas (KRAs), tasks and target identification, preparation of activity plans/action plans, goal setting exercises, etc.

Practitioners and researchers after prolonged debate have come to the conclusion that there is no generic and universally applicable performance management model and the approach would depend on the specificities of individual organizations. The various aspects of devising the performance management system (PMS) of an organization are as follows:

- *Results and output:* The foremost aspect is measurability of the output; for instance, the results achieved have to be defined clearly in terms of number, figures, etc. It is important for the appraiser as well as the appraisee to state clearly the yardsticks for measurement.
- *Input dimensions:* They indicate the activities/tasks to be carried out by individual employees for achieving the tasks set or defined. The other aspects to be considered are time frame and input quality. As it is said, a task well planned is half the success achieved, and the ability of an employee lies in accurately assessing and arranging the requirements for successful completion.
- *Time dimension:* Apart from the objectives/goals/targets, in a competitive environment, it is critical for employees to complete the jobs assigned to them in time. Often, people tend to evaluate performance without taking into account the time aspect, but for a comprehensive and objective analysis, performance has to be assessed against time. Further, while evaluating performance, it is essential to analyse the time taken by the same employee or another employee to complete a similar job under similar circumstances.
- *Focus dimension:* Performance also has a focus dimension and it would depend upon the area of focus, which varies from job to job. For instance, in case of a trainer, the areas of focus would be self-learning as well as facilitating the learning of the trainees. In case of marketing managers, the focus area would be gaining market share in the existing as well as new markets, etc.
- *Input–output relationship:* It indicates the effort vis-à-vis performance. In this sense, the measure for performance would be whether an employee could deliver higher levels of performance for the same input, which would imply improved levels of efficiency.
- *Role clarity and performance facilitation:* Often, employees are found lacking in performance due to lack of clarity about their roles and responsibilities. In other words, they lack clear understanding of their job profile and the responsibilities. The immediate superior is also responsible for such a situation since it is his or her responsibility to see that the employees concerned have a clear idea of their job profile and responsibilities.

HRM AND LEADERSHIP BUILDING

Many successful organizations are of the view that the success, to a large extent, is dependent on having the right leaders at the right time. The debate here is whether leadership should emerge on its own in an organization or the organization should make a conscious attempt to build leaders for its future growth. Prima facie, both the approaches are equally valid for building successful leadership. For instance, when we look at some of the successful enterprises such as Reliance, Infosys, etc., it is observed that the growth and development of the these organizations is mainly because of the foresight and leadership capabilities of their founders, that is, Dhirubhai Ambani and Narayana Murthy, respectively.

Similarly, when we analyse the emergence of great historical leaders, we find that they did not establish their leadership overnight, but through a sustained and long-term process. For instance, in our country, we have had leaders such as Mahatma Gandhi, who from his humble background rose to become one of the all-time great leaders of the world. Mrs Indira Gandhi, who belonged to one of the most influential political families of the country, also became a great leader over a period of time.

Some of the key issues in the emergence of leaders are as follows:

Knowledge   Socrates thought that professional or technical competence is a prerequisite for holding the position of leadership. It is a general tendency of people to follow somebody who knows what to do in a crisis. The three important qualities that attract people towards leaders are authority of position/rank, authority of personality, and authority of knowledge. Socrates clearly emphasized the latter. Kautilya, one of the renowned ancient Indian strategists, has given an extensive description of successful leaders and their essential traits.

Experience   Leaders are born rarely and often are products of their times. It would not be an exaggeration to say that the times of trials and tribulations in history have provided excellent opportunities for the emergence of leaders. Nelson Mandela had to struggle for about three decades to emancipate himself and other fellow compatriots in South Africa.

Action-orientedness   Mere intellectual thought and foresight would not make a good leader since the followers constantly look forward to their leader for command and orientation. As the saying goes, a leader should lead by example first and then, after developing the followers, adopt the approach of leading from behind.

People management capability   One of the essential qualities of successful leaders is to convince and carry along their subordinates on an identified course of action to realize the collective objectives. The prolonged freedom struggle did not deter the people of India from continuing to believe in the leadership of Mahatma Gandhi. Similar is the case of Nelson Mandela. In Myanmar, Aung San Sui Kyi, the leader who had been fighting for democratic rights of people in her country for many years, had many loyal followers in spite of the oppression by the military junta.

> ■ ■ ■
> The three important qualities that attract people towards leaders are authority of position/rank, authority of personality, and authority of knowledge.

> ■ ■ ■
> A leader should lead by example first and then, after developing the followers, adopt the approach of leading from behind.

Foresight and acumen   Leaders should be able to predict the future with conviction so that the followers remain patient and persistent till the end. Moses in ancient Christian mythology was one such leader, who led his followers on the path of truth in spite of many a struggle.

Leaders should learn from the above historical examples, while establishing leadership-building practices in an organization. A proactive HR strategy, which attempts to build good leaders, would have the following features:

- Recruitment policies that attract and retain the best talent in the country
- Job postings that provide challenging and learning assignments to prospective organizational leaders

- Career planning that facilitates growth of youngsters into organizational leadership positions
- Organizational culture-building exercise that can promote parameters such as openness, transparency, honesty, and integrity of employees

According to Socrates, a successful leader should have the following six skills:

- Selecting the right man for the right job
- Punishing the bad and rewarding the good
- Winning the goodwill of subordinates
- Attracting alliance and helpers
- Keeping what they have gained
- Working diligently and efficiently to fulfil their own responsibilities

HR managers, while grooming prospective leaders, should attempt to inculcate the aforementioned skills in them. Lao Tzu, in his writings on leadership, has envisaged a humble leader who is neither self-assertive nor talkative. Alexander the great, the Greek emperor known for his charismatic leadership, used to march along with his soldiers on foot even in deserts and adverse conditions to maintain the unity and team spirit of his soldiers. This quality holds equally good in the organizational context, as the actions of leaders should speak for themselves.

HRM AND CHANGE MANAGEMENT

Change is inevitable in life and yet we feel comfortable and secure in an environment that is steady and where the future does not appear uncertain. In case of organizations, the general tendency is to be complacent with policies and practices that have been successful in the past. Often, organizations and individuals at the helm of affairs get into the delusion that past success is a guarantee of future success and one has to continue to adhere to policies and practices that have been successful in the past. It is for this reason that the list of Fortune 500 companies of the world keeps changing every decade.

A cursory glance at the history of many of the successful organizations indicates that organizations that have been adaptive and change-oriented continue to be successful, while those otherwise become a part of history. Adaptability and change orientation cannot be inculcated overnight, but organizations have to build practices to facilitate and nurture change management processes. In the contemporary scenario, organizations are faced with multi-faceted challenges, such as changes in technology, competition, etc., and increasingly face new challenges on account of change. It is important to note that though change has been prevalent in all times, of late the pace of change has become very rapid.

Some of the new challenges for organizations are as follows:

- Customers and global operations demand 24 × 7 service.
- Technology facilitates any-location work possibilities.
- Geographical borders have been blurred and a virtual world has been created.

These developments make the challenges of HR even more difficult. Human resource, which has been a staff function, has now assumed a strategic function, as it has to coordinate with other functional areas in forecasting the future and gearing up the human resources to meet the future challenges. Simultaneously, HR has the onerous task of convincing the top management to initiate and sustain change management programmes, which usually have initial debacles. Some of the challenges for HR personnel as regards change management are as follows:

- Facilitating the work–life balance for employees
- Facilitating the culture change for employees
- Competence mapping and building
- Preparing career plans
- Managing attritions
- Managing cultural diversity
- Sustaining and improving the productivity and creativity
- Reorienting the organizational practices and policies to suit the new generation employees

In the context of work–life balance, the employees have to balance among work, home, and community, and HR personnel have responsibilities such as the following:

- Facilitating pragmatic awareness programmes
- Facilitating their thinking both about work and non-work life streams
- Educating managers to counsel and coach employees
- Providing professional counselling directly to employees who are struggling to adjust

One of the important challenges in change management vis-à-vis HR functions is making organizations and employees adapt to jobs and careers that have short life cycles. For this purpose, organizations as well as employees will have to frequently reinvent themselves through continuous learning and skill upgradation. The learning processes have to be synchronized in the sense that organizations and employees have to work in sync in the same direction. In the present context, employees have a greater responsibility to continuously learn and upgrade themselves if they want to remain useful to the organization and progress in their careers.

All said and done, there is no universal approach to change management, as the success of change initiatives is dependent on various factors such as organizational culture, determination of the top management, and proactiveness of the HR personnel.

VALUE-BASED HUMAN RESOURCE STRATEGY

Organizations in the competitive scenario are continuously faced with the necessity to create and sustain practices that facilitate value creation. The existence of organizations is largely dependent on creating outputs that mathematically outweigh the value of inputs, which in turn gives it the competitive advantage over its rivals. The human resources has a key role in the entire process, which includes the following responsibilities:

- Developing the competitive advantage of organizations by proactively updating the business strategy
- Contributing to creation and catering of shareholder value and for this purpose, creating short-, medium-, and long-term strategies to facilitate cash generation
- Developing the HR strategy as an integral part of the business strategy
- Taking the top management or CEO of the organization into confidence while formulating the HR strategy
- Reorienting the processes, priorities, and skills of the HR department to facilitate and support the HR strategy for value creation

The essential components of an HR strategy are plans and programmes related to HR projects, intentions that crystallize into specific plans/projects, formal and informal arrangements in organizations to facilitate work processes, economic value creation, etc. Often, HR professionals tend to author the HR strategy independently. However, for the success of the strategy, HR professionals must create acceptance and credibility for it by taking inputs from the various functional departments.

HOLISTIC FACET OF HRM

HR personnel are increasingly expected to involve themselves in business planning and execution to understand the business requirements and tune the HR strategies to the emerging business realities. Any holistic HRM approach would include the following dimensions:

- Participating in business strategy planning
- Tuning HR strategies to business strategy requirements
- Undertaking change management programmes to bring in cultural transformation
    - Coordinating with the business heads to implement HR strategies and policies
    - Promoting active ownership of HR policies by business heads to improve credibility of the policies and successfully implement them

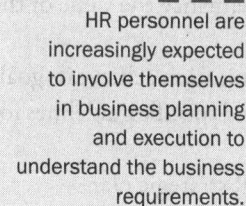

HR personnel are increasingly expected to involve themselves in business planning and execution to understand the business requirements.

Thus, it is clear that the HR function has become more demanding and is no longer restricted to be just a personnel, training, or administrative function, but is a hybrid of all these functions, which calls for new skills and attitude from the HR personnel.

ESSENTIAL SKILLS FOR AN HR MANAGER

From these discussions, it is clear that the HR manager has to totally reorient himself before attempting to address the organizational challenges. Some of the skills required in an HR manager in the emerging context are discussed as follows (Figure 1.8):

Strategic planning   A broad review of global human resource development shows that HR managers have been increasingly participating in the strategic planning process, and this evidence suggests that the strategic planner is an emerging role in HR.

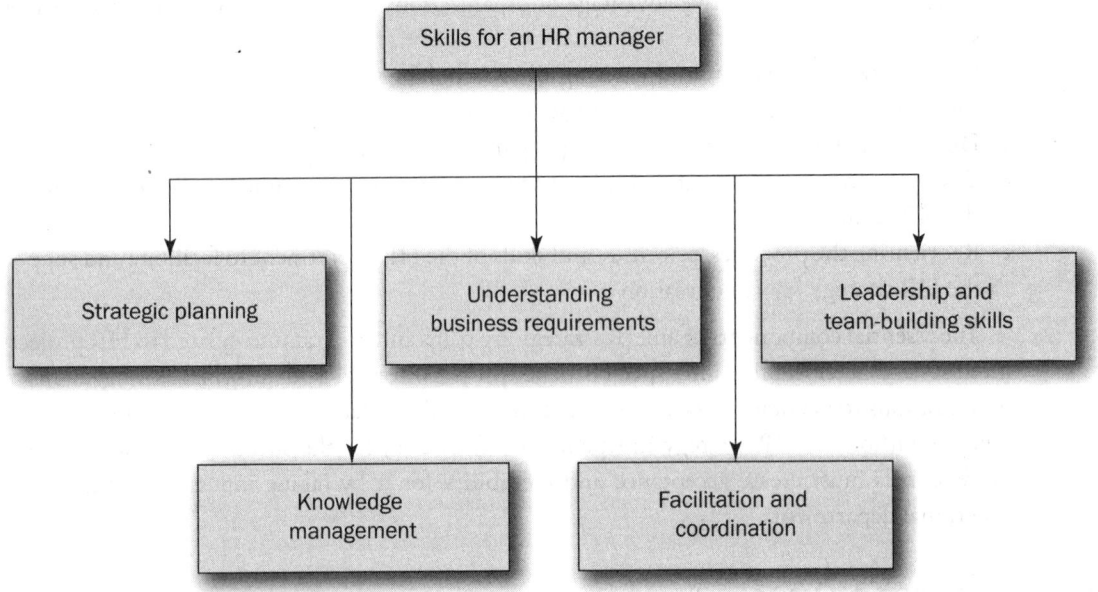

FIGURE 1.8 Essential skills for an HR manager

Simply put, strategic planning determines where an organization is headed for over the next year or more, how it is going to get there, and how it would know if it got there or not. An HR strategic plan helps in defining goals and strategies for achieving them. It enables the department to go beyond day-to-day tasks to see its larger purpose and function within the organization. Additionally, having a strategic plan can help show HR executives, the business rationale for its decisions by demonstrating how HR actions fall into the organization's overall goals.

An organization-wide business plan outlines the organization's current situation and where it intends to go. In its simplest form, the plan is a goal statement. We can enhance the value of the HR by linking it with the organization's goals.

An HR strategic plan describes what the HR must do to help the organization achieve its goals by listing the steps for meeting those goals, target dates for completion, and specific guidelines for measuring performance.

The following steps are key to the successful implementation of an HR strategic plan:

- Set measurable goals.
- Involve the right people in the planning process.
- Communicate after the planning.

The HR managers need to be conscious of the above aspects and should have the expertise and capability to take part in strategic planning, to understand its linkage to HR goals, and more importantly to translate the organizational strategic plans into HR action plans and ensure their implementation.

> ■ ■ ■
> An HR strategic plan describes what the HR must do to help the organization achieve its goals.

Understanding business requirements and realities   HR managers need to have an understanding of the business requirements and realities. Often, HR managers become unmindful of the business context while pursuing their own

> ■ ■ ■
> It is essential for HR managers to understand the business jargon to be able to relate their ideas better to the business/technical heads.

agenda. For instance, if the top management is trying to achieve the annual targets and the HR manager comes up with an innovative HR practice unconcerned with the business targets, it is likely to be rejected by the top management. In addition, it is essential for HR managers to understand the business jargon to be able to relate their ideas better to the business/technical heads.

Leadership and team-building skills   Often an effective supervisor turns out to be an ineffective manager since he or she does not possess the required leadership and team-building skills. Managers need to be highly motivated themselves, and proficient in motivating and carrying their teams along with them. In the process of goal setting and project execution, team commitment is a critical requirement. Thus, leadership and team-building skills are more pronouncedly required in project-based work environments and matrix hierarchy systems.

Knowledge management capabilities   Pooling of the available intellectual capital, and making it available among the employees at large are considered as critical factor for the success of an organization. Though there are various IT tools such as intranet, learning management system, etc., the efficacy of a manager lies in motivating the people to share their knowledge and expertise with their peers, etc. HR managers have to be adept not only in soft skills, but also in building and sustaining knowledge management systems in an organization.

Facilitation and coordination   Technical experts and project leaders are often lost in their own world, which leads to gaps and mismatch in organizational performance. It is here that the role of HR managers assumes critical importance, as they have to facilitate inter-team and inter-project coordination for achieving the desired goals or level of performance.

SUMMARY

The chapter begins with an introduction to the current and emerging challenges for organizations, and various definitions and perspectives of human resource management (HRM). It also discusses the major functions of HRM. Further, it discusses the evolution of HRM, 3 Ps of HRM, interrelationship between HRM and IT, competency building, performance management systems and components, role of HRM in leadership building, HRM and change management, value-based human resources strategy, holistic facet of HRM, and, finally, the skills required for an HR manager.

■ ■ ■ | KEY TERMS

Attrition   The ratio of employees who leave/resign from the organization to the total number of employees, calculated on an annual basis

Blue-collar workers   Employees working in manufacturing environments with low-pay jobs, usually manual labourers

Channelization   The process of directing the inputs for the purpose of obtaining desired outputs

Coherent approach   The approach that holistically considers all factors affecting a particular decision

Competency building   The process of building capabilities of employees to improve their productivity

Competency mapping   The process of identifying the competencies of all the employees of the organization

Performance management system (PMS)   A system designed to manage and improve the performance of the employees in an organization

■ ■ ■ EXERCISES

Multiple Choice Questions

1. The purpose of HRM is to
   - (a) restructure
   - (b) enable appropriate deployment of HR
   - (c) minimize medical claims from retirees
   - (d) achieve most output with least input
2. The HRM approach focuses on
   - (a) designing the contents of the training to be delivered
   - (b) the compensation system
   - (c) the quantitative and strategic aspects of managing HR
   - (d) none of these
3. Which of the following is not included in the 3 Ps of HRM?
   - (a) Price
   - (b) People
   - (c) Processes
   - (d) Performance
4. Which of the following is not a concern of HRD?
   - (a) Employee training
   - (b) Employee orientation
   - (c) Employee rights
   - (d) Employee appraisals
5. Which of the following is a process that significantly affects organizational success by having managers and employees work together to set expectations, review results, and reward performance?
   - (a) Management by objectives
   - (b) Performance appraisal
   - (c) Performance management
   - (d) Organizational planning

Fill in the Blanks

1. _____ is defined as systematic outlining of activities to be carried out by the employees during a specific period.
2. HR managers play a vital role in _____.
3. _____ has shared his pathbreaking research findings through his book *Competitive Advantage*.
4. Performance also has a _____ and it would depend upon the area of focus, which varies from job to job.
5. Leadership cannot be established overnight, but only through a sustained and _____.

Concept Review Questions

1. Explain the importance of HRM in the emerging scenario.
2. Explain the contrast between the hard and soft approaches of HRM.
3. Describe the evolution of HRM in the Indian scenario.
4. Explain the transformation of HRM into a management function.
5. Distinguish between the personnel and HRM functions.
6. Describe the various facets of HRM.
7. What is the holistic facet of HRM?
8. Does HRM have a role in leadership building in organizations?
9. What are the essential skills for an HR manager?

Project Work

1. Analyse the challenges for HR personnel in the IT industry.
2. Prepare the activity report of an HR manager of a company, known for his/her proactive HR practices.

■ ■ ■ REFERENCES

Adair, J. 2003, *Learning from Great Leaders—Inspiring Leadership*, Thorogood Publishing, London, pp. 153–71.

Armstrong, M. 2003, *Handbook of Strategic Human Resource Management*, Crest Publishing House, New Delhi, pp. 65–89.

Boulter, N., Dalziel, M., and Hills, J. 2004, *People and Competencies—A Handbook*, Crest Publishing House, New Delhi, pp. 26–35.

Clutterbuck, D. 2004, *The HR Guide to Organizational Change—Managing Work–Life Balance*, Chartered Institute for Personnel and Development, London, pp. 109–18.

Grundy, T. and Brown, L. 2003, *Value-based Human*

Resource Strategy—Developing Your Consultancy Role, Elsevier Butterworth Heinemann, Oxford, pp. 15–36.

Marchand, D.A., Kiettinger, W.J., and Rollis, J.D., *Information Orientation—The Link to Business Performance*, Oxford University Press, Oxford, pp. 173–90.

Rao, T.V. 2004, *Performance Management and Appraisal Systems—HR Tools for Global Competitiveness*, Sage

Publications, London, UK, pp. 173–99.

http://sameh.files.wordpress.com/2006/05/Organization%20Structure2.jpg, accessed on 16 September 2011.

http://sameh.files.wordpress.com/2006/05/Organization%20Structure3.jpg, accessed on 16 September 2011.

Diva Skin Clinic

CASE STUDY 1

Diva Skin Clinic was founded by Dr Mourya, who is a dermatologist. Dr Mourya, who hails from an industrial and entrepreneurial family, identified skin clinics as an emerging opportunity for business. He has seen the success of leading chains such as 'Kaya', which has ventured into beauty and skin clinics across the country. Kaya, which started with two clinics, four years ago, has now grown to over 100 clinics across India.

Dr Mourya engaged a reputed consultant to do a study on the business potential of skin and wellness products in the country. The consultant, after an extensive study, came back with the feedback that this business could clock in about ₹5,000 crores in a decade. In the report, the consultant suggested separation of the skin and wellness aspects, as combining the two was leading to confusion in brand equity in the minds of potential customers.

Armed with this feedback, Dr Mourya decided to start the 'Diva' Skin Clinic chain, as he wanted the brand to project the image of a confident and modern woman, who is self-conscious and strives to look good.

For commencing the operations, Dr Mourya hired a core team comprising a CEO and heads of HR, finance, branding, and administration to prepare a blueprint for rolling out the chain of clinics.

Dr Mourya, in his brief to the core team, stated that he believed in having a structured and professional interaction with them, and would like to give them the freedom to formulate business plans. However, the team must seek his approval before executing plans.

The HR head, Mr Satish, had a series of discussions with the core team, about the quality and quantity of manpower that could support them in building the brand. The core team suggested the following to Mr Satish:

- Recruit the best dermatologists from across the city.
- Hire excellent paramedical staff.
- Encourage and support staff who strive to ensure service excellence.

Questions
1. Analyse whether Dr Mourya has a structured and professional approach towards HRM at Diva.
2. Discuss and suggest the approach to be taken by Mr Satish to place the HRM practices in the organization on a firm footing.

Aditya Communications Ltd

CASE STUDY 2

Aditya Communications Ltd is one of the top IT firms operating at various locations both within the country and abroad. The average age of employees is around 25 years and the average rate of attrition in the company is around 18%. The company currently has an organizational culture rooted in traditional values and practices such as bureaucracy, dogmatic procedures and practices, respect for hierarchy, functional orientation, and comparatively rigid compensation structure. The HR head, in a review meeting with the SBU heads, has identified the following issues:

- Building and sustaining the motivation levels of employees
- Recruitment and retention of talented youngsters
- Making the job assignments challenging
- Providing learning opportunities to employees
- Fast track career paths for star performers

To tackle these issues, the HR head has developed an action plan to be implemented over a period of one year to accomplish the following:

- Mapping the competencies of the employees
- Evaluating human resources vis-à-vis the current and forecasted business strategies
- Creating recruitment plans to meet the competency gaps

- Retraining and redeployment plans
- Framing and implementing a flexible compensation structure
- Developing and implementing a comprehensive performance management system that can facilitate employee motivation, identify the training needs, provide for career progression, and more importantly, revise the compensation annually

Questions

1. Discuss this case with your friends and analyse the action plan vis-à-vis the challenges faced by the organization.
2. Enact a role-play for the case study and discuss its outcomes.

Regal Pharmaceuticals

Regal Pharmaceuticals is a reputed company, known for its proactive HR policies and practices. The vision and the mission statements of the company also reflect the corporate social responsibility of undertaking environment-friendly manufacturing activities. Some of the innovative HR practices of the company are as follows:

- Creating change management plans for preparing the company in the GATT scenario
- Culture building exercises that support self-initiation, openness, honesty and integrity, team-work, etc.
- Career planning for good performers
- Challenging and learning assignments for grooming future leaders
- Sharing of knowledge management infrastructure, such as intranet, which nurture and support shared learning

However, the chairman and managing director (CMD) of the company received a show cause notice from the Pollution Control Board on account of pollution created by one of the manufacturing units. The notice was well publicized in the print as well as electronic media and the company's image of being socially responsible was tainted. The PR managers carried out extensive campaigns clarifying the company's

concern for the environment. The employees of the company were perplexed with the external information and started doubting the company's holy vision and mission statements and also the credibility of the top management. The HR head met with the PR managers and decided the course of action. He also organized personal meetings of the CMD and top executives with the employees in the corporate office as well as the manufacturing locations, apart from interviews to the media. The HR head in consultation with the PR managers created employee awareness groups (EAGs), which were empowered to inspect the pollution control mechanism being implemented by the company. The members of the EAG were counselled to tour the neighbouring villages to create awareness about the responsible actions taken by the company.

Questions

1. Do you think that the company believes in practising what it preaches?
2. Is the HR department proactive and does it display leadership capabilities in the crisis situation?
3. Would you suggest any additional steps to the HR department to address the challenges?
4. What steps should the HR department adopt to reinforce value-based management?

HRM in a Dynamic Environment

INTRODUCTION

In today's intensely competitive and globalized business environment, it has become extremely difficult for a company to maintain its competitive advantage in the market by becoming a low-cost leader or a product differentiator. In order to create a niche for itself in the market, a firm requires a highly committed and competent workforce. Competitive advantage lies not only in product differentiation or cost leadership, but also in being able to tap a company's core competencies and to rapidly respond to customers' needs and competitors' moves. In other words, an organization's competitive advantage lies in its ability to consolidate corporate-wide technologies and skills into competencies that empower it to adapt quickly to a changing environment.

In an increasing number of organizations, human resources are now viewed as a source of competitive advantage. It is now widely accepted that distinctive competencies can be obtained through highly developed employee skills, distinctive organizational culture, and efficient management processes and systems. This is in contrast to the traditional emphasis on transferable resources such as equipment. Competitive advantage, which can be obtained with a high-quality workforce, enables organizations to compete on the basis of market feedback, product and service quality, differentiated products, and technological upgradation.

Strategic HRM has been defined as 'the linking of human resources with strategic goals and objectives in order to improve business performance and develop an organizational culture that fosters innovation and flexibility'. Strategic HR means incorporating the HR function as a strategic partner in the formulation of a company's strategies as well as in the implementation of those strategies through various HR activities such as recruiting, selecting, training, and rewarding personnel. The term 'HR strategies' refers to specific HR actions that a company plans to undertake to achieve its aims.

■ ■ ■
In an increasing number of organizations, human resource is now viewed as a source of competitive advantage.

UNDERSTANDING THE PRESENT-DAY SCENARIO

> ■ ■ ■
> The term 'HR strategies' refers to specific HR actions that a company plans to undertake to achieve its aims.

Human resource management can play a vital role in environmental scanning, that is, identifying and analysing external opportunities and threats that may play a crucial role in a company's success. It is in a unique position to supply competitive intelligence that may be useful in the strategic planning process. HRM also participates in the strategy formulation process by supplying information regarding the company's internal strengths and weaknesses. The strengths and weaknesses of a company's human resource can have a determining effect on the viability of the firm's strategic options.

By design, this perspective demands that HR managers become strategic partners in business operations, playing prospective roles rather than being passive administrators reacting to the requirements of other business functions. Strategic HR managers need a change in their mindset, from seeing themselves as relationship managers to resource managers who know how to utilize the full potential of their human resources.

The new breed of HR managers should be able to measure the monetary impact of their actions in order to demonstrate better, the value added by their functions. HR professionals become strategic partners when they participate in the process of defining business strategies, when they help in converting a strategy into action, and when they design HR practices that align with the overall business strategy. By fulfilling this role, HR professionals increase the capacity of a business to execute its strategies.

The primary role of a strategic HR manager is to translate business strategies into HR priorities. In any business setting, whether corporate, functional, business unit, or product line, a strategy exists explicitly in the formal process, in the form of documents, or implicitly in a shared agenda on priorities. As strategic partners, HR professionals should be able to identify those HR practices that put the strategy into action. The process of identifying such HR practices is called organizational diagnosis. It is a process through which an organization is audited to identify and determine its inherent strengths and weaknesses.

Translating business strategies into HR practices helps a business in three ways. First, the business can adapt to change because the time taken from the conception to the execution of a strategy is shortened. Second, the business can meet the customer demands better because its customer service strategies are translated into specific policies and practices. Third, the business can achieve optimum financial performance through effective execution of its strategy.

Therefore, a strategic perspective of HRM, which requires simultaneous consideration of both external (business strategy) and internal (consistency) requirements, leads to superior performance by a firm.

> ■ ■ ■
> The primary role of a strategic HR manager is to translate business strategies into HR priorities.

Performance advantage is achieved through the following:

- Marshalling resources that support the business strategy and implementing the chosen strategy efficiently and effectively
- Utilizing the full potential of the human resources to the firm's advantage
- Exploiting other resources such as physical assets and capital, to complement and augment the HR-based advantage.

■ ■ ■
Research methodology
techniques and
statistical tools can be
applied to establish
the effectiveness of HR
interventions on sound
scientific grounds.

The HR function often takes up the role of a strategic business partner. In order to achieve this distinction, HRM has to contribute to the bottom line. It is ultimately the profit that matters. However, how do we go about achieving it? The problems faced in the process are that, unlike core line functions, HR initiatives are too intangible to be noticed and have a reasonably long gestation period in pay-off.

Therefore, the challenge is to quantify HR interventions in tangible terms (Ulrich and Huselid 2001). Further research work on the topic has been done by Andrew Mayo in his book *The Human Enterprise*. The idea is to work out a cost–benefit analysis of every HR project, be it regarding recruitment and selection or training and development. It is rightly said that what can be measured can be monitored. Indian companies have of late realized the importance of human capital. Companies such as Infosys and SAIL also show the value of human assets in their balance sheets.

Research methodology techniques and statistical tools can be applied to establish the effectiveness of HR interventions on sound scientific grounds. However, the fact remains that there is always a bit of subjectivity associated in gauging any human characteristic. Therefore, the mission of HR is to reduce the subjectivity part and incorporate as much objectivity as possible into the HR process and at the same time preserve its human face.

The new role has to be viewed from a strategic perspective, where HR plays an important and vital role in designing and implementing the HR strategy for an organization. The approach to HR planning activity is no more in isolation, but very much aligned to the overall business strategy of the organization. In order to deliver a strategic impact, HR strategy needs to be in sync with the business objectives, and the systems and processes incorporated must also support the required results. Some of the successful models/strategies used by the companies are generalist strategy, personnel strategy, e-HR strategy, performance culture, etc. These strategies or models have their own advantages and disadvantages. Some of the evaluation parameters taken into consideration while planning a suitable strategy are priority and focus, likely impact, size and structure of the organization, benefits and risks involved, budget and time constraints, technology usage, etc. More than the new strategic role adopted by the HR fraternity, the contribution of the HR function has also seen a radical change in the recent past.

The performance assessment methodology and measures, introduction of HR scorecard, and use of return on investment (ROI) concept in measuring HR performance of this function in terms of financial outputs have allowed the HR function to identify strategic business units akin to other functions. With the advent of the knowledge management era, HR professionals have to now deal with more empowered and informed business associates. This makes it necessary for the HR managers to be competent on the professional front and have sound business knowledge. They should also be proactive and innovative in their approach towards HR strategies.

■ ■ ■
It is the responsibility of
an HR manager to define
the qualities expected
in the prospective
employees and enable
the company to attract
suitable talent for its
requirements.

Managing change and diversity has become a crucial part of the HR agenda. Today, we find that the workforce in any organization has become highly diverse and cross-cultural. In such a scenario, the HR division often plays a consulting role within an organization and tries to build an employee-oriented culture. Combating the acute attrition rate prevalent in the knowledge industry, HR professionals are forced to think out of the box to make their retention strategies successful. It is the responsibility of an HR manager to define the qualities expected in the prospective employees and enable the company to attract suitable talent for its requirements. Thus, the HR function enhances the value proposition of the corporation.

HRM PRACTICES IN INDIA

As discussed in the previous section, Indian companies have now realized the importance of human capital, and some companies are even indicating the value of the human assets in their balance sheets. As such, HR is now viewed from an investment perspective as well. However, the shift from traditional approach to investment perspective presents challenges such as the use of new performance measurement techniques and indicating performance in financial terms. In addition to these challenges, there are number of other trends, which influence how organizations manage their employees. While some of the trends pertain to changes in external environment, others pertain to ways in which organizations respond to changes internally. Three major internal challenges faced by organizations are technological changes, work-force diversity, and increase in the number of women in organizations.

By its very nature, HRM is a highly complex, contextual, and an evolutionary management function. India is a country with rich history, diverse cultures, and institutional framework. Post liberalization, the country has witnessed a number of contrasts in educational levels, economic progress, social attitudes, and policies on integration with the global economy. Today, India is widely recognized as one of the most attractive economies in the world. Capital and labour, the two important aspects of productivity, caused growth and development that attracted multinational companies (MNCs). By 2020, India is expected to add about 250 million to its labour pool at the rate of 18 million per year. By 2030, India is expected to have a greater workforce than China. With the emergence of the services sector in India, there has emerged a demand for highly qualified employees possessing job relevant skills. Organizations have become increasingly strategy driven, with the HR playing a major role. The success of the Indian companies, especially those from sectors such as software services, pharmaceuticals, and biotechnology, highlight the talent and capabilities of human resources in India. These relativities were demonstrated in a recent study of three global Indian companies with 235 managers, where the evidence presented, positively linked HRM practices with organizational performance (Khandekar and Sharma 2005).

The Indian IT/ITES industry with revenues of US $39.6 billion has emerged as the largest private sector industry in the country. The industry provides direct employment to 1.6 million professionals, and indirect employment to over 6 million people. According to a National Association of Software Services Companies (NASSCOM) survey, as reported in *The Economic Times* (May 2009), India has a workforce of around 400 million, out of which 30% to 35% are female. However, only one-fifth of these women work in urban areas. The same survey reported that the number of women in the BPO sector grew to 6.7 lakhs in 2008. There are different types of work profiles in BPOs including those of customer service/call centre executives, email help providers, medical transcribers, and insurance claim processors. Generally, women still do not occupy management and decision-making positions in the IT industry. According to an International Labour Organization (ILO) report (2008), women in most developing countries have a passive attitude towards technology. Socialization patterns and unequal access to education and training hinder the access and use of technology. Table 2.1 illustrates some of the key HRM practices in Indian organizations.

The emergence of the IT/ITES industry has led to the redesigning of the existing HR practices. Issues of retention, attrition, and organizational commitment have posed challenges for the organizations necessitating adoption of new HR practices. Job-hopping and frequent employee turnover have become common across organizations. Therefore, traditional HR policies need to be revisited in the present context.

TABLE 2.1   Key HRM practices in Indian organizations

HRM practice	Observable features
Job description	• Percentage of employees with formally defined work roles is very high in the public sector
Recruitment	• Strong dependence on formal labour market
	• Direct recruitment from institutions of higher learning is very common amongst management, engineering and similar professions
	• Amongst other methods, placement agencies, the Internet, and print media are the most popular.
Compensation	• Strong emphasis on security and long-term employment in public sector including a range of facilities such as healthcare, housing, and schooling for children
Training and development	• Poorly institutionalized
	• Little research on popularity of training programmes and their effect on skill and value development
Performance appraisal	• A very low coverage of employees under formal performance appraisal
Promotion and reward	• Moderately variable across industries
	• Seniority systems still dominate the public sector enterprises
	• Use of merit and performance limited mostly to MNCs
Career planning	• Limited in scope
	• The seniority-based escalator system in the public sector provides stability and progression in career
	• Widespread use of voluntary retirement scheme (VRS) in public sector by high performing staff
	• Cross-functional career paths uncommon
	• The seniority-based escalator system in the public sector provides stability and progression in career
	• Widespread use of voluntary retirement scheme (VRS) in public sector by high performing staff
	• Cross-functional career paths uncommon
Gender equity	• Driven by proactive court rulings, ILO guidelines, and legislature provisions
Reservation system	• Lack of strategic vision and inclusive approach
	• The central government has fixed 15% reservations for scheduled castes, 7.5% for scheduled tribes, and 27% for backward communities
	• Reservations policies vary among states

Source: Chatterjee (2007)

The issue of retention is much more critical in the high value-adding BPO sector such as R&D activities. This $40 billion industry has one of the highest attrition rates of around 20% to 25%. Many companies are developing innovative incentive packages to counter this job-hopping phenomenon. Table 2.2 illustrates some of these initiatives taken by leading companies in India.

Indian MNCs and their global technical services rivals have made India a battlefield for recruitment of the best workers. Consequently, there has been a dramatic shift in the recruitment practices. For example, IBM's workforce in India has more than doubled in two years to 53,000. This outcome has come with the elimination of 20,000 jobs in high-cost markets such as the US, Europe, and Japan. The R&D centre of IBM is staffed with 3,000 world-class engineers and is being recognized for its ability to innovate on all areas from simple processes and software to semiconductors and supercomputers. It is interesting to note that IBM had dominated the recruitment market in technical services in India during 2006. This leading company recruited

TABLE 2.2 Examples of retention strategies for young professionals in India's BPO and services sectors

Name of the company	Retention strategy	Impact
Tata Consulting Services (TCS)	• A choice of working in over 170 offices across 40 countries in a variety of areas • Paternity leave for adoption of a girl child • Discounts on group parties	• Significant reduction in job hopping achieved
ICICI Bank	• Identification of talented staff • Alternative stock options • Quicker promotion	• Higher retention rate achieved
Wipro	• 'Wings Within' programme where existing employees get a chance to quit their current job role and join a different firm within Wipro	• Higher retention rate achieved
Infosys	• Fostering a sense of belongingness, creative, artistic, and social activities for the employees and their families. • Initiating one of the best corporate universities in the world	• Moderate increase in retention rate achieved
Microsoft India	• Excellent sporting and wellness facilities • Employees allowed to choose from flexible working schedules • Moving people across functions and sections to assist employees find their area of interest	• Struggling to minimize job hopping
Mahindra and Mahindra	• Culture change valuing innovation and talent over age and experience • Institutionalizing a practice called 'reverse mentoring' where young people are given an opportunity to mentor their seniors	• Stabilized job hopping significantly

Source: Chatterjee (2007)

10,000 employees out of a total of 25,000 people, who were recruited to the technical services industry. The prominence of IBM as an employer of technically qualified personnel has been acknowledged in the press as well (*Business Week* 2007).

In Pune, the company has been dispatching vans with signs saying, 'IBM is hiring', at the gates of the rivals at lunch time. 'Their hit rate is pretty good', laments a manager at a tech firm that has lost employees to IBM.

Talent management, competency mapping, and career management are the focus areas of employees while engaging in a job. Organizations which have recognized these factors are able to retain talent.

Government policies on HR issues are changing with the changing trends. Even in government and public sector organizations, the trend is towards contractual employment coupled with rightsizing and downsizing. Earlier, the public sector organizations were characterized as being low in performance standards, soft in deviations, over staffed, and unionized. Today, some of the departments such as transport, canteens, and horticulture, as well as some HR functions are outsourced. Organizations are focusing on employee engagement practices and welfare measures to retain talent.

CULTURAL DIVERSITY

Cultural diversity is a phenomenon that organizations may leverage for developing wider business vision and introducing profitable business activities and policies. People of different cultures may have different perspectives, which may appear to others as irrational or contrary. To a certain extent, reactions of people from some countries could be managed. However, even in countries which are currently witnessing rapid political and economic change such as China, Russia, and Poland, deep-rooted attitudes and beliefs will be resisted during sudden transformation of values. Corporate cultures vary widely within the country and national business styles are markedly more diverse. For example, in a Japanese–USA joint venture, the Americans are usually profit-oriented, whereas the Japanese are more interested in increasing their market share. The different perspectives may cause conflict on the way forward for the company. When a capitalistic country sets up business in a socialist country, the areas of conflict are even more obvious.

As globalization of business brings executives together, there is a growing realization that we need to examine concepts and values in a more detailed manner. For example, the word 'contract' translates easily from language to language, but notionally it has many interpretations. To a Swiss, German, Scandinavian, American, or British person, it is something that has been signed and adhered to. Signatures give it a sense of finality. However, Japanese regard a contract as a starting document, which may be rewritten and modified as circumstances require. A South American sees it as an ideal, which is unlikely to be achieved, but which is signed to avoid argument (Lewis 1999).

A growing number of progressive organizations are realizing the impact of valuing diversity in the workplace on an organization's success. Valuing differences was seen as an important business case initiative by many organizations in the 1990s. The North Americans opine that effective HR strategies may help organizations to utilize diversity to enhance their competitive advantage. The benefits of successful diversity management programmes are increasingly obvious (e.g., better decision-making, greater creativity and innovation, and more successful marketing to different types of customers). Successful organizations need to move from treating everyone alike, to recognizing employee differences and responding to these differences in ways that ensure employee attraction, retention, and greater productivity, while at the same time not encouraging discrimination. Workers do not set aside their cultural values and lifestyles when they work; it affects their attitudes toward work, the way they work with others, and ultimately their productivity. If properly managed, diversity can increase creativity and innovation, and improve decision-making. A high-performance work culture is based on the synergies that accrue from diversity in the work team and task success. When not managed properly, there is increased potential for high turnover, difficulty in communication, increased levels of destructive conflict, higher rates of absenteeism, stress, burnout, and similar negative consequences (Cahoon and Rowney 1988, Golembiewski 1996).

The key to success in any diversity initiative lies with the leaders of the organization. Among other attributes, successful leaders must do the following:

- Make a visible and credible commitment to strategic human resources development, provide promotional opportunities for women and minorities
- Implement policies and procedures that equip all employees with the tools and processes necessary for career planning, development, and diversity training
- Implement techniques and processes that measure the impact of diversity efforts
- Establish compensation and reward systems that reinforce diversity initiatives

By focusing on the cultural roots of national behaviour in business, we can foresee and predict how employees from different cultures will respond. A working knowledge of the basic traits of other cultures will minimize cultural shocks and enable us to interact successfully with international business partners.

WORK–LIFE BALANCE

Work may be defined as activities carried out by human beings for varying purposes. Activity is an important aspect of life, essential for growth and health. It is through activities that human beings adjust to the environment. Sometimes activity is engaged in for its own sake, sometimes it is reflexive, and often it is purposive with an end, object, or purpose in view. Purposive activities are termed as work.

Over the last few years, the concept of work has gained significance with increasing research in industry and education. To describe work, the elements of responsiveness, purpose, adjustment, habit, interest, motive, drive, intelligence, aptitude, self-direction, and adaptive behaviour along with minor complexities must be introduced. Hence, work is an activity directed towards the accomplishment of purpose. Human work is an activity with an end in view (Cleeton 1949).

The economic purpose of work is the means by which we provide the goods and services needed by our society. The type of work performed, has always conferred a social status on the workers and their families. Much attention has been placed on the economic and societal aspect of work. Far less attention has been paid to the personal meaning of work, yet it is clear from the recent research that work plays a crucial and perhaps an unparalleled psychological role in the formation of self-esteem, identity, and a sense of order (Organ 1978).

Some functions served by work have been summarized (Sofer 1970) as follows:

- Work is instrumental for survival.
- Work provides opportunities for interaction with others.
- Work provides scope for personal achievement, meeting and surpassing goals recognized as praise worthy.
- Work assures oneself of one's capacity to deal effectively with one's environment.
- Work provides one with opportunities to relate oneself to the society and to contribute by providing the needed goods and services.

Hence, it is obvious that work provides a means for the satisfaction of various needs. Purposive work is carried out in organizational settings. An organization comes into existence to accomplish its objectives. The objectives determine the structure, which in turn determines the positions and the hierarchy in the organizations. The positions clarify the roles to be executed by the personnel in the organization.

The phrase 'work–life balance' is relatively new to the research and corporate policy lexicon, and reflects issues raised by changes in the workforce demographics, family patterns, women's employment, attitudes toward work and family, and changes in the traditional employee–employer contract.

Women CEOs of the Fortune 1000 (March 2009), published by Catalyst (the US firm working to expand opportunities for women and business), identifies the women CEOs of the Fortune 500 and 1000 companies. Of the Fortune 500 companies, only 15 CEOs are women, including one Indian, Indra K. Nooyi of PepsiCo Inc. Workforce has grown by around 12%, but is only expected to grow 4% between 2010 and 2020 (Benko and Weisberg 2007).

The percentage of women occupying management positions in India is roughly 3% to 6%, and only around 2% of Indian women serve as managers in Indian corporations. However, most statistics focus on labour in the organized sectors (96% of the women workers are in the organized sector), leaving out many workers in unorganized (informal) sectors of the economy. According to the 2001 Indian census, the work participation rate of female workers in rural areas in 31% and in urban areas is 11.6%. Out of India's 397 million workers, 123.9 million are women, 106 million women are in the rural areas and 18 million in the urban areas (www.cpiml.org/liberation/year 2004/febraury/WomenWorkers.htm). However, only 7% of India's labour force is in the organized sector (including workers on regular salaries in registered companies), with the remaining workers (93%) in the unorganized or informal sectors.

Furthermore, long hours are spent in transit to the office, and driving for other non-work-related obligations such as dropping off and picking up children at school or day care, running household errands, and visiting extended family. This means less time for leisure and domestic tasks that require routine attention. Consequently, there is a growing dependence on private services to compensate for increased hours spent at work and on the road. Coordinating and managing these many services points to yet another dimension of the organization and time management challenge, that is, the work–family balance issue.

For a long time, work and family were considered as two different entities which demanded different skills and mindsets from the individuals. However, the increasing number of women in the workforce has shifted focus on the balance that women are trying to achieve. Traditional research on the work–family interface has focused on the negative outcomes associated with work and family roles (Hanson, Colton, and Hammer 2003; Wayne, et al. 2004). That is, most researchers have focused on the conflict associated with the management of these two roles (e.g., Frone, Russell, and Cooper 1992). The widely accepted and used term work–family conflict focuses on the fact that engaging in one role makes participation in the other role more difficult (Greenhaus and Beutell 1985). It is defined as a type of inter-role conflict in which the competing demands of work and family roles are incompatible (Greenhaus and Beutell 1985).

Work–family conflict has been related to significant individual and organizational problems such as absenteeism, intentions to leave work, low organizational commitment, and low satisfaction in job, family, and life (Allen, Herst, Bruck, and Sutton 2000; Aryee 1992; Bedeian, Burke, and Moffet 1988; Higgins, Duxbury, and Irving, 1992; Kossek and Ozeki 1998; Lyness and Thompson 1997; Netemeyer, Boles, and McMurrian 1996; Thomas and Ganster 1995). In addition, negative mental and physical health outcomes (e.g., depression, stress, and job burnout) have been associated with high levels of work–family conflict (Boles, Johnstone and Hair, 1997; Frone 2000; Parasuraman, Purohit, Godshalk, and Beutell 1996). In the recent times, scholars have called for a more balanced approach that recognizes the positive effects of combining work and family roles (Barnett and Hyde 2001; Frone 2003). Experiences in one role can produce positive experiences and outcomes in the other role. (Greenhaus and Powell 2006) refer to this mechanism as work–family enrichment.

The potential benefits of engaging in work and family roles have been overlooked (Brockwood, Hammer, and Neal 2003; Hanson, et al. 2003). Researchers who have studied the positive side of the work–family interface have listed the positive correlates of work–family conflict as 'enrichment' (Rothbard 2001), 'facilitation' (Grzywacz and Bass 2003), and 'positive spillover' (Brockwood, et al. 2003). In contrast to the difficulties associated with work–family conflict, enrichment occurs when having multiple roles provides benefits to the individual (Rothbard 2001).

Research on engagement in work and family roles often focuses on environmental influences (e.g., supervisor, organizational climate, social policy) on an individual's emotion, cognition, and behaviour. Several researchers (Carlson 1999; Lockwood, Casper, Eby, and Bordeaux 2002; Sumer and Knight 2001; Wayne, Msisca, and Fleeson 2004) have suggested that personality be given greater consideration in understanding how an individual views and experiences the multiple roles in life.

Caligiuri and Nicole Givelekian researched on the strategic HR perspective and emphasized on the need to focus on employees who occupy critical or core positions in the organization and excel in them. As core positions are central to a firm's success, they tend to be associated with high stress, long working hours, and constant spillover from work to personal life. In order to reduce the risk of stress and burnout, prevent job dissatisfaction and low occupational commitment, and ultimately improve the firm's productivity, the researchers encouraged work–life balance among core employees. The researchers also affirmed the importance of taking into account individual differences and personal characteristics as they affect employees' perceptions of their status of work–life balance, that is, when they feel out of balance, the amount of spillover they are comfortable with, etc. As core employees tend to be achievers and high-performers, it is crucial for the company not to over-utilize them, and hence, avoid causing stress, etc. The researchers suggested several ways to promote greater work–life balance among core employees such as introducing services that help reduce the non-work hassles, initiating wellness programmes to increase employees' physical and psychological well-being, and organizing recreational activities.

EVOLUTION OF HRM INTO STRATEGIC HRM

Over the years, organizations' expectations from their HR departments have changed considerably. The function was, and still is, expected to ensure that its policies, practices, and procedures shape the culture of the organization in a way that is consistent with its values and vision. There has been a change in the way these responsibilities are discharged. In today's corporate world, HR, like other functions, is expected to have a clear-cut plan, which would drive an organization towards its goal. As individuals, HR practitioners are now under increasing pressure to be credible in the eyes of their client groups.

Some Important Questions Faced by HR

Many tough questions have plagued the HR function since its conception such as the following:

- What are the functions of HR?
- How does the work of HR benefit the business?
- What drives the HR agenda?

Similar questions are rarely asked about the sales and marketing groups or even the finance departments. The contributions made to the business by other functions are generally valued more highly as those are better articulated, better planned, better analysed, and better understood than those of the HR department. It is ironical that even the people working in the HR department are clueless about the role they play in the larger scheme of the organization. Therefore, HR departments have generally failed to establish a strong and consistent cross-company, cross-industry image.

Examining the Functions and Practices

The HR division of the Institute for Development and Research in Banking Technology (IDRBT), Hyderabad, established by the RBI, spent a lot of time understanding what it does as a function, how clear it is about its agenda, how it measures its work, how it makes and communicates preferences, how it presents itself, how it manages customer expectations, and how it distributes responsibilities within its own department.

The entire exercise led to the conclusion that the department could help itself by making a drastic change in how it plans, communicates, and manages the HR initiatives that make up its annual and three-year plans. It wanted to reposition itself so that it was respected and considered to be valuable for its business partners. As a first step, it set about changing its planning process.

Identifying the Criteria

In the first phase of the project, it identified the criteria to evaluate the work it was asked to do. Having a set of logical criteria would help it to evaluate ideas generated by both line and HR managers throughout the company and would also discourage it from carrying out its own pet projects or giving in to pressure from the line managers. This would help the department to prioritize its initiatives. Bearing in mind its desire to build relationships, it decided against establishing the criteria itself. It asked all its directors and Vice-Presidents as to what criteria they would use to determine the relative importance of the various functions undertaken by the HR.

They suggested contribution to the following:

- Improving business performance
- Early delivery of business benefits
- Maximizing employee engagement
- Improving or simplifying people management activities
- Supporting legal or regulatory compliance

This is an example of how organizations today are expecting more and more from the HR function. Pressure on the HR function also stems from a lacklustre business environment and the need to control costs, both within HR and across the workforce. However there is a growing expectation that HR should be a strategic function and should play a more significant role in helping a corporation succeed. Most HR professionals agree with that expectation. The problem is in determining what it precisely means. What does a strategic HR function do? How does an HR division make the fundamental shift or transform from being a traditional staff management function to strategic player in the business?

Starting with a Vision

In making any transformation, the best way to begin is to have a clear picture of the goal—a vision of what a strategic HR function is. In essence, a strategic HR division's central purpose boils down to 'improving the performance of the company's workforce to support the overall corporate goals.' Accenture, a global management consulting, technology services, and outsourcing company, believes that the HR must play three distinct roles to fulfil this central purpose.

Business advisor/consultant   HR managers must be able to sit as peers with executives from other divisions of the company and actively participate in strategic decision-making. They must also advise, coach, and educate senior executives on how workforce issues can affect the overall performance of the business, and offer solutions to support the execution of business plans. This means that HR professionals must thoroughly understand the capabilities of the company's people and how the enterprise operates, and bring those insights together to identify the best way to deploy people to deliver business objectives.

Change leader   HR professionals must play an active role in shaping the workforce to support a company's long-term business objectives. They must have a firm grasp of organizational behaviour, communication, and change management, and should be prepared to plan and lead large-scale change programmes and leadership development initiatives that would improve workforce performance.

HR functional expert   HR professionals should update themselves on the HR practices being followed in the industry as well as the new developments occurring in the field and apply that knowledge to create effective business solutions. The HR field is evolving, which means that an effective HR department needs to stay in touch with the new range of tools and techniques available, including advanced technologies in e-learning, web-based workspace portals, and innovative organizational approaches such as the outsourcing of its various functions.

> ■ ■ ■
> HR groups should establish clear service-level agreements with the business units in order to gauge their effectiveness.

It is important for an HR department to operate like a business concern while undertaking the various roles otherwise it will fail to achieve its objectives. This means regularly measuring how well it is serving its customers, that is, business units that rely on its services. HR groups should establish clear service-level agreements with the business units in order to gauge their effectiveness. They should measure their effectiveness in terms of business results and improvements that have taken place in the performance of the workforce, and base rewards on those measurements. HR executives should create a concise scorecard that lets them keep track of the improvements and highlight HR's business value to the senior-level management.

Preparing a Framework for Action

> ■ ■ ■
> The roles played by a strategic HR function are quite different from the administrative tasks.

The roles played by a strategic HR function are, of course, quite different from the administrative tasks traditionally associated with HR. In order to fulfil them, HR needs to undergo a fundamental shift from the traditional back-office, transaction-handling focus to proactive decision-making for the benefit of the business.

That is a big change. HR organizations will typically have to work on many fronts to create an environment that will enable the HR professionals to perform in a different and a more strategic manner. It means changing the HR processes, procedures, policies, and performance measures as well as equipping the HR professionals with new skills and new information-access tools.

For example, a company once worked with Accenture to create an Internet recruiting application that uses intelligent-agent technology to identify potential candidates and route profiles to the appropriate people. Another company established a 'business partnership' programme that paired specific HR executives with key segments of the business, such as sales and marketing and IT, which enabled the HR division to participate in business strategy sessions at those units.

When a major medical technology company teamed up with Accenture to transform its HR division, the effort involved creating a new strategy and organizational structure for HR, streamlining HR governance, improving communication across the company's HR groups worldwide, and developing of continuous improvement processes. This comprehensive effort opened the door to an integrated, enterprise-wide HR function with faster decision-making and greater strategic impact.

Changing the HR environment can be quite complex because there are a variety of factors

> ■ ■ ■
> Changing the HR environment can be quite complex because there are a variety of factors that drive and enable improved performance.

that drive and enable improved performance. It requires a number of separate initiatives that have to be identified, prioritized, and planned and in the end, these various efforts have to come together like the pieces of a puzzle to create a coherent whole. It can be difficult for executives to get a hang of it all, but there are ways to organize and simplify their efforts.

To simplify the process, HR managers can use a 'workforce performance model' that takes into consideration the entire performance-enabling environment. With the help of the model, the managers can understand the various factors that enhance workforce performance and their interrelationship, and address them in an integrated and coordinated fashion. This helps ensure that all the factors needed for success are addressed; that individuals are motivated and properly skilled; that the workforce as a whole has the right resources, processes, and systems; and that all initiatives ultimately work together to support enterprise-wide business strategies.

While tackling the transformation initiatives, the HR groups should undertake the following:

- Create thorough implementation and project plans that include clear milestones and measurements of progress.
- Actively market HR's strategic capabilities to the rest of the organization to overcome the business units may have about HR and its role.
- Take action on the findings of assessments of the HR function, and work with all HR stakeholders to gain their support and involvement.
- Provide the learning opportunities that will enable employees to work and succeed as a strategic function.
- Work proactively to overcome the hesitation and resistance to change that employees are likely to feel.
- Communicate with and manage the expectations of the HR workforce and other executives in the organization so that everyone understands what is being undertaken and why.

It is clear that the transformation of HR into a truly strategic function is not a simple task. However, with the right tools and expertise, it can be done and the pay-off for doing it right can be quite significant. Today, a company's workforce is its critical asset and a strategic HR function is the key to making the most of that asset. By taking on a strategic role, HR can meet the rising expectations of the senior-level management, and actively derive path breaking improvements in human performance to help the company succeed in the market.

STRATEGIC CORPORATE SUSTAINABILITY

Reconciling organizational effectiveness with current economic realities creates an inevitable paradox.

Demands on Managers

- Think strategically and invest in the future, but keep the numbers up
- Be entrepreneurial and take risks, but do not cost the business anything by failing
- Become passionately dedicated to 'visions' and committed to carrying them out, but be flexible and responsive

Demands on Organizations

- Get 'lean and mean' through restructuring, but be a great company to work for and offer employee-centred policies such as job security
- Communicate a sense of urgency and push for faster execution and faster results, but take more time to plan for the future
- Decentralize to delegate profit and planning responsibilities to small, autonomous business units, but centralize to capture efficiencies and combine resources in innovative ways

The corporate need to embrace the paradox inherent in these dilemmas is unquestionable. This so requires the motivation and creative input from the entire organization and not merely of the selected few. Our economy is dynamic, moving, complex, and sophisticated to support a simple response mechanism that existed prior to the electronic age. The establishment of an identified set of corporate values that has people's development at its epicentre is vital for the sustained development of an organization that depends fundamentally on the ideas, commitment, and motivation of its workforce.

Increased profit and revenue no longer remain the key motivators of corporate success. The level of employee motivation, customer engagement, product innovation, and customer service are the other vital factors that play a crucial role in a firm's success. Figure 2.1 demonstrates the evolution of corporate culture, which incorporates these and many other changes.

A shared knowledge base and a common purpose have now become the fundamental tenets of corporate success. However, what do we mean by the term 'purpose'? The term 'purpose' incorporates the identity of the organization and the features that make it different from the other

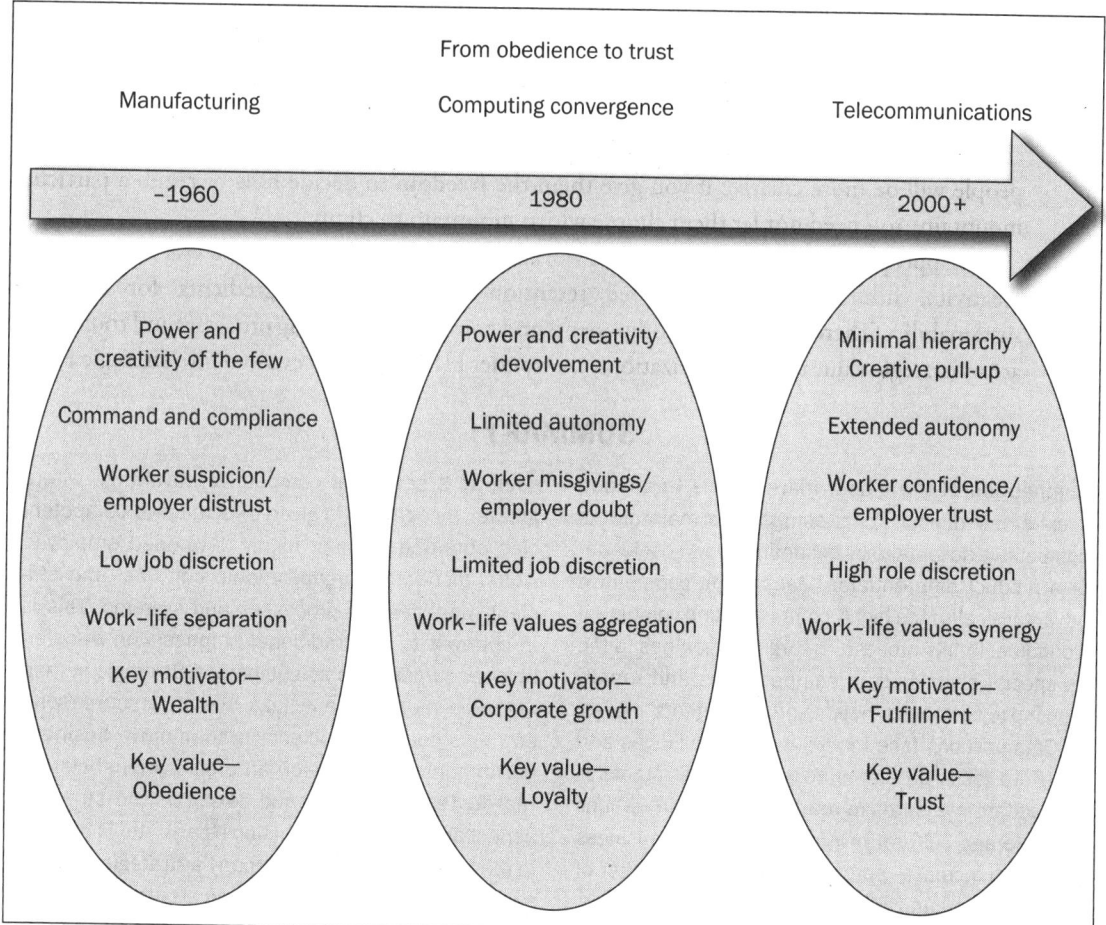

FIGURE 2.1   Three stages of corporate cultural evolution

companies. It is what a company wants to achieve and what it is willing or unwilling to do to achieve it. However, in its pursuit of exceptional performance and sustained growth, there are certain organizational values and financial restrictions it should not violate. The values concern ethics, health, safety, environment, and the way a company treats its employees and external relations.

To achieve corporate distinction, there should be a feeling of uniqueness and collective engagement, free flow of information within the organization, transparency between the goals and efforts of the employer and the employee, a sense of belongingness to corporate values, a sense of self-worth, and a collective purpose.

There are three key elements that create an environment of raised personal aspirations and extraordinary collaborative efforts: first, development of shared ambitions that energize the organization; second, the need to establish unifying values to reinforce an individual's commitment to the organization; and third, the ability to give employees a sense of personal fulfilment by linking their individual contributions directly to the larger corporate-wide agenda.

The fundamental aspect of this process is trust. Trust equates to credibility, respect, fairness, pride, and camaraderie. The 'psychological contract' between an employer and employee is uncomplicated, when there is a stable alignment between the corporate goals and employee expectations.

Value, purpose, and direction take centre stage, so do employability and corporate attraction. However, trust and empowerment require a sophisticated control mechanism.

When it comes to granting creative freedom, the key is to grant the employees autonomy concerning the means, that is, concerning the process, but not necessarily the ends. In other words, people will be more creative if you give them the freedom to decide how to climb a particular mountain. You need not let them choose which mountain to climb.

An appropriate value set that binds a workforce together for increased levels of motivation, creativity, fulfilment, and employee retention—the essential ingredients for corporate sustainability. There are multiple components and complex monitoring processes and tools which are of strategic value to the organizations; no wonder HRM has now evolved into strategic HRM.

SUMMARY

Competition in the global marketplace has made it extremely difficult for a company to maintain its competitive advantage by becoming a low cost leader or a product differentiator. Maintaining competitive advantage calls for a highly committed and competent workforce. In this process, an organization has to tap its special skills or core competencies and rapidly respond to customers' needs and competitors' moves.

Organizations face many internal challenges and therefore focus on employee engagement practices and welfare measures to retain talent. Organizations can leverage cultural diversity to develop business vision and increase profitability. A growing number of progressive organizations are realizing the positive impact of diversity in the work place.

In many organizations today, human resource is seen as a source of competitive advantage where greater recognition is given to distinctive competencies obtained through highly developed employee skills, distinctive organizational cultures, and efficient management processes and systems. This is in contrast to the traditional emphasis on transferable resources such as equipment. Strategic human resource management links human resource with strategic goals and objectives to improve business performance and develop an organizational culture that fosters innovation and flexibility. The strategic aspect accepts the HR function as a strategic partner in the formulation of the company's strategies as well as in the implementation of those strategies through various HR activities such as recruiting, selecting, training, and rewarding personnel.

■ ■ ■ | KEY TERMS

Human resource evolution   Gradual or rapid transformation of the concept of human resource management

Human resource strategy   Designing of a process or a model to implement an HR policy for measurable outcomes

Strategic human resources   Strategic components of the HR process needed for organizational sustenance and growth

Strategic human resource management   Human resource management model that is guided by planned outcomes and effects

■ ■ ■ | EXERCISES

Multiple Choice Questions

1. Which of the following management functions is applicable to HRM?
   (a) Planning, organizing, leading, and controlling
   (b) Planning and organizing only
   (c) Leading and controlling only
   (d) None of these

2. Which of the following functions of HRM deals with collective bargaining?
   (a) Staffing
   (b) Forecasting
   (c) Employee assistance management
   (d) Employee relations management

3. The primary role of a strategic HR manager
   (a) is to study the impact of societal behaviour on an organization
   (b) is to move people across functions and sections
   (c) is to translate business strategies into HR priorities
   (d) is to generate organizational reports

4. All of the following are vital factors that play a crucial role in a firm's success except
   (a) employee motivation
   (b) customer engagement
   (c) product innovation
   (d) increased pay packages

5. Workforce today has become
   (a) highly diverse and cross-cultural
   (b) demanding
   (c) interfering in management decisions
   (d) all of these

Fill in the Blanks

1. _____ and revenues no longer remain the key motivators of corporate success.

2. HR professionals are forced to think out of the box to make their _____ successful.

3. Pressure on the HR function also stems from a lacklustre business environment and the need to _____, both within HR and across the workforce.

4. The _____ between an employer and employee is an uncomplicated document when corporate goals and employee expectations are in sync with each other.

5. To achieve corporate distinction, there should be a feeling of uniqueness and _____.

Concept Review Questions

1. Explain the role of HR in the formulation of strategies in an organization.

2. Bring out the differences between HR and strategic HR.

3. What is the role of HR in formulating the vision of an organization?

4. How do we align strategic HR objectives with the objectives and strategy of an organization?

5. How is an HR vision evolved?

6. Explain the concept of planning. What is the importance of planning?

7. How are the HR dimensions of small-scale business plans integrated with the HR strategy?

8. How is the HR strategy communicated, implemented, and reviewed in an organization?

Project Work

1. Identify a company known for its proactive HR department and prepare a report on its HR strategies.

2. Prepare a discussion paper on the cultural diversity of an HR department in a multi-location IT company. Discuss the challenges it faces in the changed business scenario.

■ ■ ■ REFERENCES

Allen, T.D., Herst, D.E.L., Bruck, C.S., and Sutton, M. 2000, 'Consequences associated with work-to-family conflict: A review and agenda for future research', *Journal of Occupational Health Psychology*, 5, pp. 278–308.

Aryee, S. 1992, 'Antecedents and outcomes of work–family conflict among married professional women: Evidence from Singapore, *Human Relations*, 45, pp. 813–37.

Balaji, C., Chandrasekhar, S., and Dutta, R. 1996, *Leading Change Through Human Resources: Towards a Globally Competitive India,* Tata McGraw-Hill, New Delhi, pp. 11–35.

Barnett, R.C. and Hyde, J.S. 2001, 'Women, men, work, and family', *Americal Psychologist*, 56, pp. 781–96.

Bartnett, Rosalind Chait 2001, 'Work–Family Balance', *Encyclopedia of Women and Gender*, Vol.11, Academic Press.

Bedian, A.G., Burke, B.G., and Moffett, R.G. 1988, 'Outcomes of work–family conflict among married male and female professionals', *Journal of Management*, 14, pp. 475–91.

Boles, J.S., Johnston, M.W., and Hair, J.F. 1997, 'Role stress, work–family conflict and emotional exhaustion: Inter-relationships and effects on some work-related consequences', *Journal of Personal Selling and Sales Management*, 1, pp. 17–28.

Brockwood, K.J., Hammer, L.B., and Neal, M.B. 2003, *An Examination of Positive Work–family Spillover Among Dual-earner Couples in the Sandwiched Generation*, Presented at the annual meeting of the Society for Industrial and Organizational Psychology, April, Orlando.

Budhwar, P.S., Saini, D.S., and Bhatnagar, J. 2005, 'Women in management in the new economic environment: The case of India', *Asia Pacific Business Review*, 11(2), June, pp. 179–193.

Cahoon, A.R. and Rowney J.I.A. 1988, 'Individual and organizational characteristics of women in managerial leadership roles', *Proceedings of Women in Management Research Symposium,* Mount Saint Vincent University, Halifax.

Chatterjee, S.R. 2007, 'Human Resource Management in India: "Where From" and "Where To?"', *Research and Practice in Human Resource Management*, 15(2), pp. 92–103.

Frone, M.R. 2003, 'Work–family balance'. In J.C. Quick and L.E. Tetrick (Eds), *Handbook of Occupational Health Psychology*, American Psychological Association, Washington, DC, pp.143–62.

Frone, M.R., Russell, M., and Cooper, M.L. 1992, 'Antecedents and outcomes of work–family conflict: testing a model of the work–family interface', *Journal of Applied Psychology*, 77, pp. 65–78.

Golembiewski, R.T. 1996, *Managing Diversity in Organizations*, The University of Alabama Press, Tuscaloosa.

Goodstein, L.D., Pfeiffer, J.W., and Nolam, T.H.1985, Applied Strategic Planning: *A New Model for Organizational Growth and Vitality,* University Associates Inc., San Diego, pp. 162–89.

Greenhaus. J.H (2002), 'Industrial and organizational psychology: career dynamics'. In Borman, W.C., Ilgen D.R., and Klimoski, R.J. (Eds), *Comprehensive Handbook of Psychology*, Volume 12, pp. 519–40, Wiley, NewYork.

Greenhaus, J.H. and Beutell, N.J. 1985, 'Sources of conflict between work and family roles', *Academy of Management Review*, 10, pp. 76–88.

Greenhaus, J.H. and Powell, G.N. 2006, 'When work and family are allies: A theory of work–family enrichment', *Academy of Management Review*, 31(1), pp. 72–92.

Grzywacs, J.G. and Bass, B.L. 2003, 'Work, family, and mental health: Testing different models of work–family fit', *Journal of Vocational Behaviour*, 34, pp. 133–53.

Hanson, G.C., Colton, C.L., and Hammer, L.B. 2003, *Development and Validation of a Multidimensional Scale of Work–Family Positive Spillover*. Paper presented at the annual meeting of the Society for Industrial and Organizational Psychology, April, Orlando.

Higgins, C.A., Duxbury, L.E., and Irving, R.H. 1992, 'Work–family conflict in the dual-career family', *Organizational Behaviour and Human Decision*

Processes, 51, pp. 51–75.

Khandekar, A. and Sharma, A. 2005, 'Managing human resource capabilities for sustainable competitive advantage: An empirical analysis from Indian global organization', *Education and Training,* 47(47/48), pp. 628–639.

Kossek, E.E. and Ozeki, C. 1998, 'Work–family conflict, policies, and the job-life satisfaction relationship: A review and directions for organizational behaviour-human resources research', *Journal of Applied Psychology*, 83, pp. 139–49.

Lewis, C.P. 1997, *Building a Shared Vision: A Leader's Guide to Aligning the Organization,* Productivity Press, Portland.

Lewis, Richard D. 1999, *When Cultures Collide—Managing Successfully Across Cultures,* Nicholas Brealey Publishing, London.

Lockwood, A.L., Casper, W.J., Eby, L.T., and Bordeaux, C. 2002, *A Review of Work–Family Literature: Where We've Been and Where We Need to Go,* Paper presented in W.J. Casper (chair) and J. Barling (discussant) symposium, Emerging Directions in Work and Family Research, at the annual American Psychological Association Conference, Chicago.

Lyness, K.S. and Thompson, D. 1997, 'Above the glass ceiling? A comparison of matched samples of female and male executives', *Journal of Applied Psychology*, 82, pp. 359–75.

Mintzberg, H. 1994, *The Rise And Fall of Strategic Planning,* The Free Press Macmillian Inc., New York, pp. 72–97.

Netemeyer, R.G., Boles, J.S., and McMurrian, R. 1996, 'Development and validation of work–family conflict and family–work conflict scales', *Journal of Applied Psychology*, 81, pp. 400–10.

Parasuraman, S., Purohit, Y.S., Godshalk, V.M., and Beutell, N.J. 1996, 'Work and family variables, entrepreneurial career success, and psychological well-being', *Journal of Vocational Behaviour*, 48, pp. 275–300.

Pareekh, U. 1992, 'Managing Transition: The HRD Response', Conference paper for the National HRD Network Symposium at Bangalore, Tata McGraw Hill, New Delhi, pp. 111–45.

Pettigrew, A. 1991, *Managing Change for Competitive Success,* Blackwell, Oxford, pp. 54–69.

Rothbard, N.P. 2001, 'Enriching or depleting? The dynamics of engagement in work and family roles', *Administrative Science Quarterly*, 46, pp. 655–84.

Saini, D.S. 2006, 'Labour law in India,' In H.J. Davis, S.R. Chatterjee, and M. Heur (Eds) *Management in India: Trends and transition*, Response Books, New Delhi, pp. 60–94.

Schein, E.H 1978, 'Career Dynamics: Matching Individual and Organizational Needs, Addison-Wesley, Reading.

Schwartz, F.N. 1992, 'Women as a business imperative', *Harvard Business Review,* 70(2), pp. 105–113.

Srivastava, P. 1994, *Strategic Management: Concept and Practices,* South-western Ohio, pp.135–42.

Sumer, H.C. and Knight, P.A. 2001, 'How do people with different attachment styles balance work and family? A personality perspective on work–family linkage', *Journal of Applied Psychology*, 86, pp. 653–63.

Thomas, L.T. and Ganster, D.C. 1995, Impact of family-supportive work variables on work–family conflict and strain: A control perspective', *Journal of Applied Psychology*, 80, pp. 6–15.

Ulrich, D. and Huselid, M.A. 2001, *The HR Scorecard: Linking People, Strategy, and Performance,* Harvard Business School Press, Harvard.

Wayne, J.H., Musisca, N., and Fleeson, W. 2004, 'Considering the role of personality in the work–family experience: Relationships of the big five to work–family conflict and facilitation, *Journal of Vocational Behaviour*, 64, pp. 108–30.

http://vecam.org/article565.html, accessed on 12 January 2012.

Office of the Registrar General, India. (n.d.), *Total Workers in India—2001 Census; Statistical Profile on Women Labour,* http://labourbureau.nic.in/WL%202K5-6Table%201.1.htm, accessed on 14 April 2009.

Women workers in India in the 21st century—Unemployment and Underemployment, www.cpiml.org/liberation/year_2004/febraury/WomenWorkers.htm, accessed on 30 April 2009.

IndTel India Pvt. Ltd

Sumanth Bandaru is from the family of an industrial house (SBR Group) based in South India. He completed his bachelors from the London School of Economics (LSE) and masters from the Harvard Business School (HBS). Later, he worked with McKinsey in New York for four years and returned to India in the year 2007. When he returned, the telecom sector was in its growth phase and had reached a subscriber base of 80 million customers. Sumanth felt that though the group had lost the opportunity in the first phase of telecom revolution, they could still make an attempt, as the Government of India was toying with the idea of issuing additional licences to new players to introduce fresh competition and to lower the tariff further.

Sumanth had a detailed discussion with the group's core team and sought their approval to venture into telecom space. After getting their approval, he started identifying suitable foreign partners, who could bring in the technical expertise to the proposed venture. After exploring a number of global players, the group, zeroed in on a Netherlands-based telecom major, which operates across Europe and Africa for joint venture. After discussions, it was decided that the SBR group will have 60% equity, whereas the foreign partner will have 40% equity in the proposed venture.

After finalizing the agreement, the organization applied to the Government of India for licences and was awarded licences in six states to launch its telecom operations. The group, IndTel India Pvt. Ltd, named Sumanth as the chief executive officer (CEO) of the company. Sumanth wanted to quickly get into action and roll out telecom operations. The action plan developed by the company includes the following:

- Creating a core team
- Recruiting experienced professionals from the telecom space so that they bring in domain expertise
- Exploring tie-ups with existing players on sharing the tower infrastructure with the twin objectives of reducing capital expenditure and shortening timelines for rolling out IndTel across the six states
- Hiring an HR manager for drafting the HR policies and practices; hiring required professionals as per the projected timelines, and for commencing the operations within six months

Questions
1. Prepare a draft organization structure for IndTel based on a study of organization structures of existing telecom players in India.
2. What should be the key differentiators for an organization in terms of attracting and retaining talent?

Zentech Limited

Zentech Limited was established by a first-generation entrepreneur Aditya Chauhan during the early 1980s when the IT industry was just beginning to evolve. The company was started with an initial corpus of ₹5 lakhs to assemble and market computers. The foresight of the entrepreneur made the company one of the top manufacturers in the country in a few years time. During the early 1990s, with the advent of software development, the company also ventured into software service area and by the late nineties, it grew to become one of the top software service providers in the country with over 20,000 employees worldwide. However, after 2000, the company's business went down drastically and its

CEO Chauhan realized the need to de-link the ownership from professional management. He recruited two top professionals as the CEO (chief executive officer) and the COO (chief operating officer) respectively, while he himself chose to become the chairman of the board. The new CEO and COO, with a view to recast the company, recruited a new and dynamic HR manager, and after discussions they decided to place before the board the outlines of the new organizational structure, which proposed to have strategic business units (SBUs). After the approval by the board, a new core group consisting of the CEO, COO, SBU heads, and HR head was constituted to review and operationalize the following HR strategies:

- Map the competencies of all the employees in the organization.
- Identify the competency and manpower gaps vis-à-vis the business forecast.
- Prepare a training schedule for the competency development of the existing manpower.
- Prepare a career plan for all employees.

- Prepare recruitment plans keeping in view the attrition rates of the company and industry.

Questions
1. Do you feel the HRM in the company is dynamic?
2. Is the HR strategy responsive and in sync with the corporate strategy?
3. Is the HR department proactive and professional?

Akarsh Electronics

Akarsh Electronics is an electronics company that started in the late 1970s to manufacture and market black and white and colour televisions in the country. The company initially found it very tough to market the televisions in the country as Doordarshan only started its telecast in 1982 coinciding with the ASIAD games. The ASIAD games gave impetus to television sales in the country. The company, due to its innovative marketing strategies, was able to garner second position in the market.

Over the years, with the advent of liberalization, the rules of the game have changed dramatically. The market, which was restricted to domestic players, has been opened to the foreign players, who enjoy the pull effect. The Indian TV consumers, who were struggling for long to get a foreign brand, now easily find international brands in the domestic market. Further, the foreign players are able to aggressively advertise their products and are successful in projecting their products as premium brands in the market. All these factors have led to the following changes in the television market in the country:

- Indian brands have been relegated to fifth and sixth positions.
- Black and white TV has become outdated.
- Colour TV market has become highly competitive.
- Foreign brands use dealer margins, etc., to push their brands.

Due to these factors, Akarsh Electronics faces the following problems:

- Negative sales growth
- High employee loss to foreign companies

- Reduced profits
- Low employee morale

For overcoming these problems, the CEO decided to restructure the organization and initiate the following measures:

- Recruit HR head, Vice-President–Marketing, and Vice-President–Finance to head the respective functions
- Strengthen the marketing team by recruiting young MBA graduates
- Strengthen the product development and market research departments
- Build the competencies of employees across all functional areas

For implementing these strategies, an action team consisting of the HR head, Vice-President–Marketing, and Vice-President–Finance was constituted by the CEO. They were asked to submit a weekly report. During a course of one year, they have achieved/implemented the following:

- Appointment of a consultant on change management
- Identification of competencies and implementation of competency-building plans
- Recruitment of fresh talents

Questions
1. Do you think that the HR department is proactive?
2. Will the intiated steps change the company's profile for the better?
3. Can you suggest any additional measures for improving the functional efficiency of the organization?
4. Conduct a role-play on the case study.

Strategic Human Resource Management

Objectives

After studying this chapter, you will be able to understand
- the concept of strategic human resource management (SHRM)
- the linkages between organizational strategy and HRM strategy
- SHRM models and strategies
- the linkages between SHRM and organizational performance

INTRODUCTION

The developments in the field of HRM over the last four to five decades (well-documented in management literature) have brought about significant changes in the nature of the HR function as we see today. From being reactive and laden with administrative responsibilities, HRM today is proactive and is considered to be strategic for organizational growth. The contribution of HRM in improving a firm's performance as well as the overall success of any organization (alongside other factors) is well established now.

TABLE 3.1 Traditional vs emerging HR functions

Traditional	Emerging
Reactive	Proactive
Employee advocate	Business partner
Task focus	Task/enablement focus
Operational issues	Strategic issues
Qualitative measures	Quantitative measures
Stability	Constant change
How? (Tactical)	Why? (Strategic)
Functional integrity	Multifunctional
People as expenses	People as assets

Source: Holbeche (1999)

The present day HR and its strategic role in the organization is the result of this marked shift in the understanding of HR. Table 3.1 outlines the traditional and emerging HR functions.

■ ■ ■
An internal and external fit between a firm's external environment, business strategy, and HR strategy is very crucial.

There has to be an internal and external fit between a firm's external environment, business strategy, and HR strategy. This implies that business strategies and HRM policies interact, and determine business performance. Gratton (1999) suggests that this integration needs to take place at two levels—horizontal (integration between the various HR interventions) and vertical (integration between business strategy and HR strategy).

This leads us to the discussion of the strategic HR approach, where the priorities of HR are the same as those of the overall business. Strategic HR would not only include managing talent, but also developing suitable policies and procedures to enable good performance. The HR attributes that are crucial to the implementation of a firm's competitive strategy, such as a capable and committed workforce, the development of employee competencies, and excellent training systems, are precisely the sort of qualities that are difficult to imitate, and enhance the sustainable competitive potential (Ulrich 1997).

When we talk about the hard and soft approaches to HR (Storey 1989), we are perhaps distinguishing strategic HRM from technical HRM. The hard approach posits that people are important resources that help organizations to achieve competitive advantage. Therefore, these resources have to be acquired, developed, and deployed in ways that will benefit the organization (Armstrong and Baron 2002). The soft approach lays emphasis on a high commitment and high performance approach to the management of people (Holbeche 1999). The development of such an approach requires a strong focus on organizational culture, and can only be achieved through increased involvement, communication, and commitment. Table 3.2 highlights the multiple roles of the HR function. One of the key roles is being a strategic partner.

TABLE 3.2   Ulrich's multiple role model for HRM

Role	Deliverable/Outcome	Metaphor	Activity
Managing strategic human resources	Executing strategy	Strategic partner	Aligning HR and business strategy: Organizational diagnosis
Managing firm infrastructure	Building an efficient infrastructure	Administrative expert	Reengineering organization processes: Shared services
Managing the employee contribution	Increasing employee commitment and capability	Employee champion	Listening and responding to employee: Providing resources to employees
Managing transformation and change	Creating a renewed organization	Change agent	Managing transformation and change: Ensuring capacity for change

Source: Ulrich (1997)

WHAT IS STRATEGIC HRM?

The emergence of strategic human resource management (SHRM) is an outcome of the concerns on integration of HRM into the business strategy and adaptation of HRM at all levels of the organization (Guest 1987, Schuler 1992). Let us first look at the term *strategy* in Exhibit 3.1, which explains its meaning in an organizational context.

EXHIBIT 3.1   Strategy in an organizational context

The origin of the term *strategy* can be traced to the Greek word 'strategos', which means a military general who organizes, leads, and directs his forces to the most advantageous position (Bracker 1980, Legge 1995, Lundy and Cowling 1996). In an organizational context, the top management team or the CEO could fulfil the role of a strategist.

In business, strategy would consist of a series of steps such as formulating business objectives, conducting SWOT analysis, setting organizational goals, identifying strategic alternatives, and conducting regular evaluation (Mello 2006).

SHRM is about systematically linking people with the organization and integrating HRM strategies into corporate strategies. HR strategies relate to the management of human resources in an organization to achieve the desired objectives. The focus is on aligning the organization's HR practices and policies with corporate plans. This helps organizations to achieve competitive advantage by creating unique HRM systems that cannot be imitated by others (Barney 1991, Huselid, et al. 1997).

There are numerous areas that have been the focus of SHRM. These include areas such as HR accounting, HR planning, responses of HRM to strategic changes in the business environment, and matching human resources to organizational requirements.

The level of integration of HRM into the corporate strategy can be evaluated by factors such as representation of specialist people managers on the board, the presence of a written people management strategy emphasizing the importance and priorities of human resources in all parts of the business (in the form of a mission statement, guidelines, or rolling plans), nature of consultation with people management specialists in the development of corporate strategy, translation of the people management strategy into a clear set of work programmes, proactive nature of people management departments through the creation of rolling strategic plans (emphasizing the importance of human resources in all parts of the business), mission statements, alignment of HR policies with business needs through business planning processes, use of participative management processes and committee meetings, and HR audits. (Budhwar and Sparrow 1997, 2002).

LINKAGES BETWEEN STRATEGY AND HRM

Purcell (1989) has talked about a two-level integration of HRM into the business strategy—*upstream or first-order decisions* and *downstream or second-order decisions*:

- First-order decisions address issues related to the organizational mission and vision statement. These decisions are related to the direction of the business, actions needed to guide the future course of action, and broad HR issues that will have an impact in the long term.
- Second-order decisions deal with scenario planning at both strategic and divisional levels in the short term, say, 3–5 years. These decisions are also related to HR policies linked to each core HR function (such as recruitment, selection, development, and communication).

Guest (1987) proposes integration at three levels:

- First, the *fit* between HR policies and business strategy
- Second, the principle of *complementary* (mutuality) of employment practices aimed at generating employee commitment, flexibility, improved quality, and internal coherence between HR functions
- Third, the *internalization* of the integration of HRM and business strategies by the line managers (also see Legge 1995)

SHRM MODELS

There are quite a few theoretical models that highlight the nature of linkage between HRM strategies and organizational strategies:

- Matching model of Fombrun, et al. (1984)
- Harvard model of Beer, et al. (1984)
- Warwick model (1990)
- Guest's model (1989)

The models proposed by Fombrun, Beer, Warwick, and Guest highlight the nature of linkage between HRM strategies and organizational strategies.

Matching Model

Fombrun, et al.'s (1984) 'matching model' emphasizes the efficient utilization of human resources to accomplish organizational objectives. According to this model, like other resources of the organization, human resources have to be obtained at low cost, used sparingly, and developed to their potential. The matching model is based on Chandler's (1962) argument that an organization's structure is the outcome of its strategy. Fombrun, et al. emphasized a *tight fit* between the organizational strategy, organizational structure, and HRM system. The main aim of the matching model is to develop an appropriate human resource system characterizing those HRM strategies that contribute most to the efficient implementation of the business strategies.

Fombrun's matching model provided a framework for subsequent development of theories in the field of SHRM.

The matching model provided a framework for subsequent development of theories in the field of SHRM.

Harvard Model of SHRM

The 'Harvard model' (Figure 3.1) of SHRM was first articulated by Beer, et al. (1984). When compared to the matching model, this model is considered soft HRM (Storey 1992, Legge 1995, Truss, et al. 1997). It lays emphasis on the 'human' aspect of HRM, and is concerned with the employer–employee relationship. The model highlights the interests of different stakeholders in the organization, and how their interests are related to the objectives of the management.

The model allows for analysis of various outcomes at both the organizational and societal levels. However, this model has been criticized for not explaining the complex relationship between strategic management and HRM (Guest 1991).

The matching model and the Harvard analytical framework represent two very different theories, the former being closer to the strategic management literature, and the latter to the human relations tradition. The Harvard model helps determine the nature of SHRM in different contexts, which include the following:

- The influence of different stakeholders and situational variables on HRM policies of an organization
- The extent to which communication with employees is used to maximize commitment
- The level of emphasis given to employee development

Warwick Model

Warwick model recognizes the changing nature of the business environment.

The warwick model recognizes the changing nature of the business environment. It takes care of the shift in the business scenario (from stable to turbulent or vice versa) in an increasingly globalized workforce. The model gives full recognition to the external context of SHRM and identifies a two-way rather than a one-way relationship with the organizational strategy.

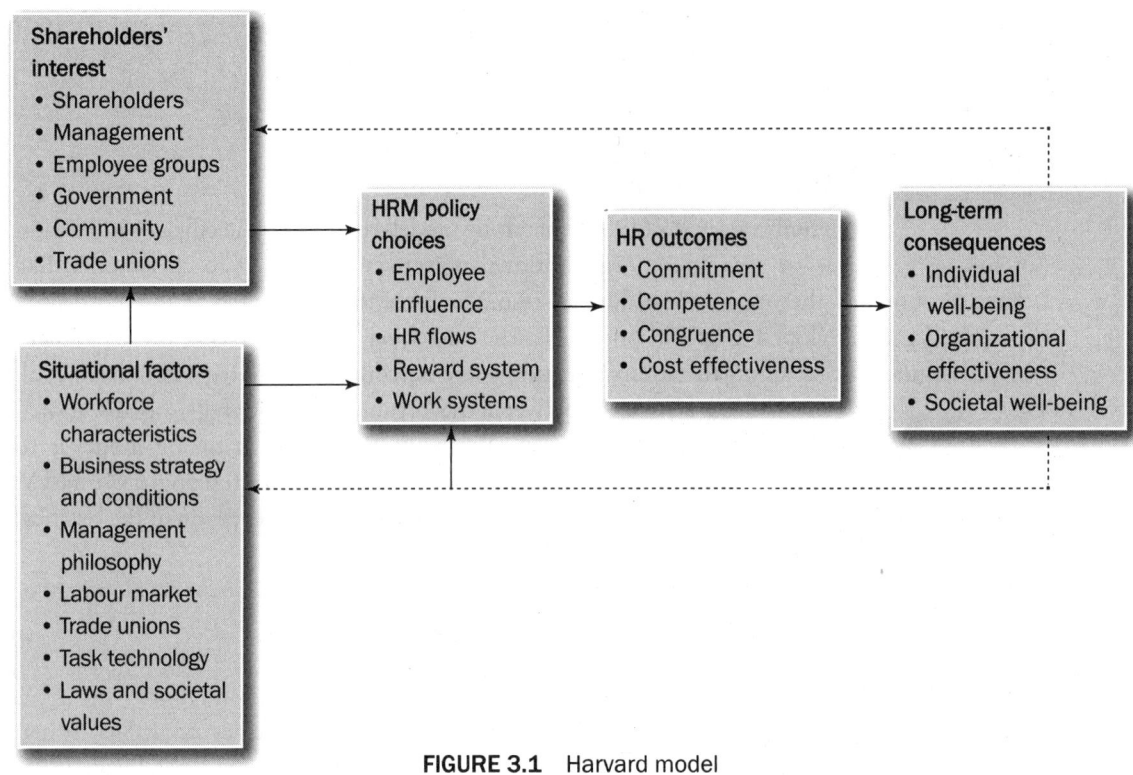

FIGURE 3.1   Harvard model

Source: Beer, et al. (1984)

Guest's Model

Guest's model is based on the following four HR outcomes:

- Strategic intent
- Commitment
- Flexibility
- Quality

He sees these outcomes as a package necessary to accomplish the desired organizational outcomes.

SHRM PROCESS

As discussed earlier, the purpose of SHRM is to ensure that HRM is fully integrated with the business strategy of the firm. This would imply that HR policies are coherent both across policies and across hierarchies, and HR practices are adjusted, accepted, and used by line managers and employees as part of their everyday work (Schuler 1992).

The SHRM process includes outlining mission and goals, environment analysis, strategy formulation, strategy implementation, and strategy evaluation.

A typical process flow chart of SHRM is provided in Figure 3.2. The process starts with outlining the vision, mission, and goals of an organization. The analysis of internal and external environments forms the next stage. These two initial steps lead to the core steps of SHRM.

SHRM has many different components, including HR policies, culture, values, and practices.

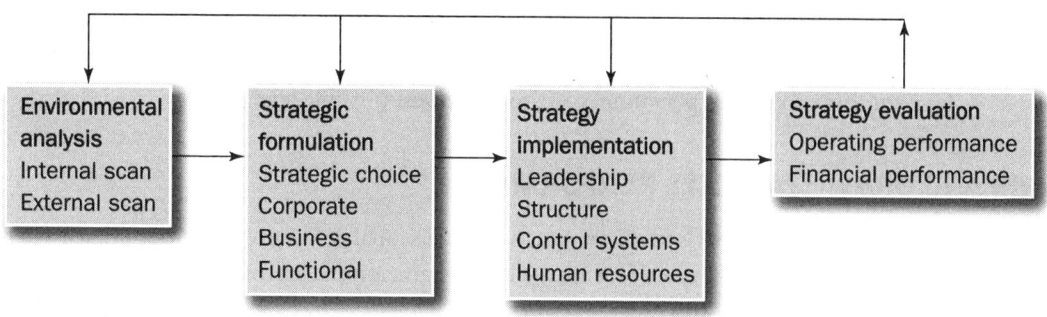

FIGURE 3.2 SHRM process flow chart

PORTER'S GENERIC BUSINESS STRATEGIES AND HRM

Michael Porter (1980, 1985) identified three possible generic strategies for competitive advantage in business—*cost leadership* (when the organization reduces costs by producing a product or a service at less expense than its competitors); *innovation* (when the products/services of the organization are unique); and *quality* (when the organization is delivering high quality goods and services to customers). A number of HRM combinations can be adopted by firms to implement Porter's model (Figure 3.3) of business strategies. Schuler (1989) proposes corresponding HRM philosophies of *accumulation* (careful selection of good candidates based on their personalities rather than technical fit), *utilization* (selection of individuals on the basis of technical fit), and *facilitation* (the ability of employees to work together in collaborative situations). The effectiveness of individual HR practices is contingent on firm strategy. The performance of an organization that adopts HR practices appropriate to its strategy will then be higher.

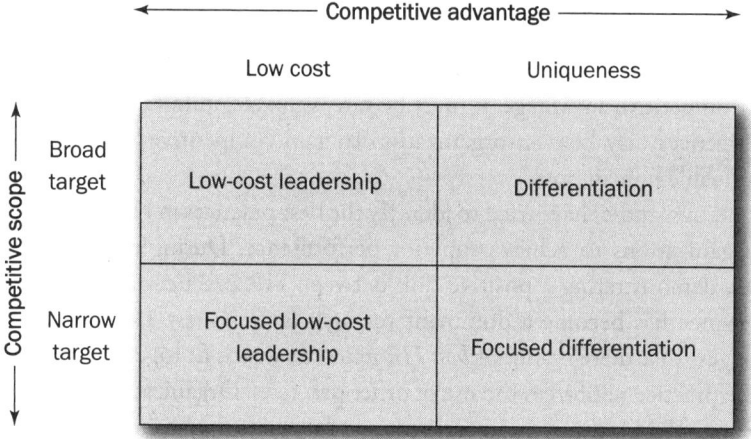

FIGURE 3.3 Porter's competitive strategies

Source: Porter (1985)

GENERIC HR STRATEGIES

Various generic HR strategies pursued by organizations in different contexts have been outlined by Budhwar and Sparrow (2002):

- *Talent acquisition* to attract the best human talent from external sources
- *Effective resource allocation* to maximize the use of existing human resources by always having the right person in the right place at the right time

- *Talent improvement* to maximize the talent of existing employees through continuous training and guidance in their jobs and career
- *Cost reduction* to reduce personnel costs to the lowest possible level

SHRM AND ORGANIZATIONAL PERFORMANCE

The eventual goal of SHRM is to contribute to organizational performance, that is, the accomplishment of the firm's goals. There are four areas where organizational performance could be measured:

- HR outcomes (turnover, absenteeism, job satisfaction)
- Organizational outcomes (productivity, quality, service)
- Financial outcomes (return on assets (ROA), profitability)
- Market share (stock price, growth, returns)

HR strategies directly impact HR outcomes, followed by organizational, financial, and capital market outcomes.

HRM models tend to assume that an alignment between business strategy and HR strategy will improve organizational performance and enhance competitiveness. A number of studies (Guest 1997, Pfeffer 1998) have found that, in spite of the methodological challenges, HRM practices are positively associated with superior organization performance.

Many studies focus on (a) the human resources (skills, knowledge, and potential), (b) HR processes (recruitment, development, reward, and work systems), and (c) job design and empowerment strategies, through which HR practices impact on business performance. For a resource to be a source of competitive advantage, it must be rare, valuable, inimitable, and non-substitutable. Thus, HR practices may help an organization to gain competitive advantage by developing a unique and valuable human pool.

> ■ ■ ■
> HRM models assume that an alignment between business strategy and HR strategy will improve organizational performance and enhance competitiveness.

Numerous studies have tried to identify the best practices in HR that could help organizations to achieve superior performance. During the past two decades, demonstrating a positive link between HR practices and business performance has become a dominant research issue (Guest 1997). Studies also suggest that there is a set of *best HR practices*, which fit together in a way that one practice reinforces the use of other practices. Organizations develop a range of HRM policies and practices that deal with the business strategies outside the area of HRM. This implies that a fit between business strategy and HRM policies/practices will improve performance.

SUMMARY

The chapter begins by emphasizing the strategic role of HRM. It defines strategic human resource management (SHRM) as the process of linking the HR function with strategic objectives of the organization to improve performance. It outlines the concept, nature, and process of SHRM. It discusses the various developments in the field of SHRM. The chapter highlights the importance of interrelatedness of business strategies and HR strategies for improving organizational performance.

The chapter also discusses various areas where the matching of HRM and organizational strategy is crucial. It discusses various SHRM models proposed by Fombrun, Beer, Warwick, and Guest, and explains Porter's model of competitive strategies. The chapter concludes with a discussion on SHRM and organizational performance.

■ ■ ■| KEY TERMS

Concept of 'fit' Synchronization (internal and external fit) between a firm's external environment, business strategy, and HR strategy

Hard vs soft aspects The hard approach of HRM posits that people are important resources that help organizations achieve competitive advantage. Soft HRM focuses on a high commitment and high performance approach to the management of people.

HR strategy process Includes outlining mission and goals, environment analysis, strategy formulation, strategy implementation, and strategy evaluation

Organizational performance Refers to achievement of organizational goals and includes HR outcomes (turnover, absenteeism, job satisfaction, etc.), organizational outcomes (productivity, quality, service, etc.), financial outcomes (ROA, profitability, etc.), and market share (stock price, growth, returns, etc.)

SHRM Process of linking human resource function with the strategic objectives of the organization to improve performance

■ ■ ■| EXERCISES

Multiple Choice Questions

1. Creating a unique HRM system helps organizations to achieve
   - (a) monopoly
   - (b) competitive advantage
   - (c) locus of control
   - (d) mission statements

2. The Harvard model of SHRM is concerned with
   - (a) manager–subordinate relationship
   - (b) industrial relations
   - (c) employer–employee relationship
   - (d) customer relationship

3. The SHRM process includes all of the following except
   - (a) outlining mission and goals
   - (b) environment analysis
   - (c) strategy formulation
   - (d) strategic intent

4. The eventual goal of SHRM is to contribute to
   - (a) organizational performance
   - (b) profitability
   - (c) customer satisfaction
   - (d) employee satisfaction

5. Organizational performance could be measured in all of the following areas, except
   - (a) HR outcomes
   - (b) organizational outcomes
   - (c) financial outcomes
   - (d) brand equity

Fill in the Blanks

1. Michael Porter identified three possible generic strategies for competitive advantage in business: _____, _____, and quality.

2. Organizations develop a range of HRM policies and practices that deal with business strategies _____ of HRM.

3. For a resource to be a source of competitive advantage, it must be rare, _____, inimitable, and non-substitutable.

4. There has to be an _____ and external fit between a firm's external environment, business strategy, and _____.

5. 'Hard' and 'soft' approaches to HR distinguish strategic HR from _____.

Concept Review Questions

1. Define SHRM. What are the main factors that have contributed to the growth of SHRM?

2. What are the benefits of strategic integration of HRM into the business strategy?

3. Analyse the main models of SHRM.

4. Establish linkages between SHRM and organizational performance.

■ ■ ■| REFERENCES

Armstrong, M. 1987, 'A case of the emperor's new clothes', *Personnel Management*, 19(8), pp. 30–35.

Becker, B.E. and Gerhart, B. 1996, 'The impact of human resource management on organizational performance: Progress and prospects', *Academy of Management Journal*, 39, pp. 779–801.

Beer, M., Spector, B., Lawrence, P.R., Quinn Mills, D., and Walton, R.E. 1984, *Human Resource Management*, Free Press, New York.

Bracker, J. 1980, 'The historical development of the strategic management concept', *Academy of Management Review*, 5(2), pp. 219–24.

Budhwar, P. and Sparrow, P.R. 1997, 'Evaluating levels of strategic integration and devolvement of human resource management in India', *The International Journal of Human Resource Management*, 8(4), pp. 476–94.

Budhwar, P. and Sparrow, P.R. 2002, 'An integrative framework for determining cross-national human resource management practices', *Human Resource Management Review*, 12, pp. 377–403.

Chandler, A. 1962, *Strategy and Structure*, MIT Press, Cambridge.

Delaney, J.T. and Huselid, M.A. 1996, 'The impact of human resource management practices on perceptions of organizational performance', *Academy of Management Journal*, 39, pp. 949–69.

Delery, J. and Doty, D.H. 1996, 'Modes of theorizing in strategic human resource management: Test of universalistic, contingency, and configurational performance predictions', *Academy of Management Journal*, 39, pp. 802–35.

Fombrun, C.J., Tichy, N.M., and Devanna, M.A. 1984, *Strategic Human Resource Management*, Wiley, New York.

Gratton, L. 1999, 'People processes as a source of competitive advantage' In L. Gratton, V.H. Hailey, P. Stiles, and C. Truss (Eds) *Srategic Human Resource Management*, Oxford University Press, Oxford.

Guest, D.E. 1991, 'Personnel management: The end of orthodoxy?', *British Journal of Industrial Relations*, 29(2), pp. 147–75.

Guest, D.E. 1997, 'Human resource management and performance: A review and research agenda', *International Journal of Human Resource Management*, 8(3), pp. 263–76.

Hendry, C. and Pettigrew, A.M. 1990, 'Human resource management: An agenda for the 1990s', *International Journal of Human Resource Management*, 1(1), pp. 17–43.

Hendry, C. and Pettigrew, A.M. 1992, 'Patterns of strategic change in the development of human resource management', *British Journal of Management*, 3, pp. 137–56.

Hendry, C., Pettigrew, A.M., and Sparrow, P.R. 1988, 'Changing patterns of human resource management', *Personnel Management*, 20(11), pp. 37–47.

Higgs, A.C., Papper, E.M., and Carr, L.S. 2000, 'Integrating selection with other organizational processes and systems' In J.F. Kehoe (Ed.) *Managing Selection in Changing Organizations*, Jossey-Bass, San Francisco.

Holbeche, L. 1999, *Aligning Human Resources and Business Strategy*, Butterworth-Heinemann, Oxford.

Huselid, M.A. 1995, 'The impact of human resource management practices on turnover, productivity and corporate financial performance', *Academy of Management Journal*, 38, pp. 635–70.

Huselid, M.A. and Becker, B.E. 1996, 'Methodological issues in cross-sectional and panel estimates of the human resource—firm performance link', *Industrial Relations*, 35, pp. 400–22.

Huselid, M.A., Jackson, S.E., and Schuler, R.S. 1997, 'Technical and strategic human resource management effectiveness as determinants of firm performance', *Academy of Management Journal*, 40, pp. 171–88.

Katou, A. and Budhwar, P. 2006, 'Human resource management systems on organizational performance: A test of mediating model in the Greek manufacturing context', *International Journal of Human Resource Management*, 17(7), pp. 1223–53.

Katou, A. and Budhwar, P. 2007, 'The effect of human resource management policies on organizational performance in Greek manufacturing firms', *Thunderbird International Business Review*, 49(1), pp. 1–36.

Legge, K. 1995, *Human Resource Management: Rhetorics and Realities*, MacMillan Business, Chippenham.

Lundy, O. and Cowling, A. 1996, *Strategic Human Resource Management*, Thompson, London.

Mello, J.A. 2006, *Strategic Human Resource Management*, South-Western, Thompson.

Miles, R.E. and Snow, S.S. 1978, *Organizational Strategy, Structure, and Process*, McGraw-Hill, New York.

Miles, R.E. and Snow, S.S. 1984, 'Designing strategic human resources systems', *Organization Dynamics*, 16, pp. 36–52.

Pfeffer, J. 1994, *Competitive Advantage through People*, Harvard Business School Press, Boston.

Pfeffer, J. 1998, *The Human Equation*, Harvard Business School Press, Boston.

Porter, M.E. 1980, *Competitive strategy: Techniques for analyzing industries and competitors*, Free Press, New York.

Porter, M.E. 1985, *Competitive advantage: Creating and sustaining superior performance*, Free Press, New York.

Purcell, J. 1989, 'The impact of corporate strategy and human resource management' In J. Storey (Ed.) *New Perspectives on Human Resource Management*, Routledge, London, pp. 67–91.

Quinn, J.B., Mintzberg, H, and James, R.M. 1988, (Eds.) *The Strategy Process: Concepts, Context, and Cases*, Prentice-Hall International, Englewood Cliffs.

Richardson, R. and Thompson, M. 1999, *The Impact of People Management Practices on Business Performance: A Literature Review*, IPD, London.

Schuler, R.S. 1989, 'Strategic human resource management and industrial relations', *Human Relations*, 42(2), pp. 157–84.

Schuler, R.S. 1992, 'Linking the people with the strategic needs of the business', *Organizational Dynamics*, pp. 18–32.

Storey, J. 1992, *Developments in the Management of Human Resources*, Blackwell Business, London.

Truss, C., Gratton, L., Hope-Hailey, V., McGovern, P., and Stiles, P. 1997, 'Soft and hard models of human resource management: A reappraisal', *Journal of Management Studies*, 34, pp. 53–73.

Ulrich, D. 1997, Human Resource Champions: *The Next Agenda for Adding Value and Delivering Results*, Harvard Business School Press, Boston.

Youndt, M., Snell, S., Dean, J., and Lepak, D. 1996, 'Human resource management, manufacturing strategy, and firm performance', *Academy of Management Journal*, 39, pp. 836–66.

Reducing Costs at BizTech

CASE STUDY

BizTech provides voice automation technology and services to its clients across the globe. With a strong network across 17 countries, it enjoys a steady list of clients. Notwithstanding the economic recession, the annual turnover grew steadily by 18% during the last three years. While competitors (local players) took away a slice of BizTech's market share, especially in developing economies, the company still has a stronghold on the multinational clients.

The top management team encourages fair practices and appropriate workforce development measures. Over the last two years, the company has seen a steep rise in costs associated with outsourcing of its payroll functions. The HR department focuses mainly on training and development activities, organization development (OD) interventions, and appraisals, whereas the administration and payroll-related activities are outsourced to an HR consultancy. The HR team at BizTech feels that the existing HR software lacks flexibility and necessary key features to support future growth and to attract top talent. They have recommended that the company implement an IT solution that would not only help its future activi-ties/expansion plans, but also help analyse historical employee data to retain talent.

One of its competitors has implemented an enterprise-wide human capital management (HCM) solution to improve HR capabilities and conduct payroll operations. The new solution has helped the competitor achieve considerable operational benefits (e.g., negligible errors). It has enabled the competitor to not only improve day-to-day administration-related activities, but also to streamline HR planning and recruitment.

BizTech is wondering whether taking back the payroll to its in-house team would put extra pressure on the HR team. The proposed IT solution seems highly beneficial, but apprehensions do exist among the top management team.

Questions

1. What could be the reasons for the apprehension among the top management team of BizTech about implementing the new system?
2. Would you recommend BizTech to go for the new system? Justify your answer.
3. Can you identify the connection between HR functions and business strategy in this case?

Human Resource Planning

Objectives

After studying this chapter, you will be able to understand
- the nature and concept of human resource planning (HRP)
- the objectives of HRP
- the various factors affecting HRP
- the process of HRP
- forecasting internal and external human resource supply
- computer simulation and regression analysis

INTRODUCTION

Human resources undoubtedly play the most important part in the functioning of an organization. The term 'resource' or 'human resource' signifies potentials, abilities, capacities, and skills, which can be developed through continuous interaction in an organizational setting. The interactions, interrelationships, and activities performed all contribute in some way or other to the development of human potential. Organizational productivity, growth of companies, and economic development are to a large extent contingent upon the effective utilization of human capacities. Hence, it is essential for an organization to take steps for effective utilization of these resources. In the various stages in the growth of an organization, effective planning of human resources plays a key role. Matching the requirements of the job with the individual is important at all stages, including the recruitment procedures, in this endeavour. When organizations

■ ■ ■
Organizational plans, goals, and strategies require effective HRP.

contemplate diversification or expansion, or when employees have to be promoted, human resource planning (HRP) plays an important role. Further, the organizational plans, goals, and strategies also require effective HRP.

Definition

Human resource planning is a process by which the management of an organization determines its future human resource requirements and how the existing human resources can be effectively utilized to fulfil these requirements. In the process of HRP, the management strives to have the

■ ■ ■
Human resource planning is a process by which the management of an organization determines its future HR requirements.

appropriate number and the appropriate kind of people at the appropriate place. It is a system of matching the supply of existing people with openings or opportunities the organization expects over a given period of time.

HRP is a futuristic form of assessment. It tries to assess human resource requirements in advance keeping the organizational objectives, production schedules, and demand fluctuations in the background. It forms an integral part of the overall corporate strategy and reflects the broad thinking of the management about human resource needs.

Coleman has defined human resource planning as 'the process of determining human resource requirements and the means of meeting those requirements in order to carry out the integrated plan of the organization'.

Stainer defines human resource planning as a 'strategy for the acquisition, utilization, improvement, and preservation of an enterprise's human resources. It relates to establishing job specifications or the quantitative requirements of the jobs determining the number of personnel required and developing sources of human resource'.

According to Wickstrom, human resource planning consists of a series of activities:

- Forecasting future human resource requirements, either in terms of mathematical projections of trends in the economic environment and development in industry or in terms of judgement estimates based upon the specific future plans of a company
- Making an inventory of present human resources and assessing the extent to which these resources are employed optimally
- Anticipating human resource problems by projecting present resources into the future and comparing them with the forecasts of requirements to determine their adequacy, both quantitatively and qualitatively
- Planning the necessary programmes of requirement, selection, training, development, utilization, transfer, promotion, motivation, and compensation to ensure that future human resource requirements are properly met

Thus, HRP aims at getting the right number of qualified people into the organization at the right time. The process involves assessing current human resources, estimating the supplies and demand for labour, and matching demand with current supplies of labour.

OBJECTIVES OF HUMAN RESOURCE PLANNING

The basic purpose of having a human resource plan is to have an accurate estimate of the number of employees required with the matching skills to meet the organizational goals. It is a database where one can easily identify the existing skills and matching positions held. It is close to a flow chart wherein we also try to estimate the future requirements of human resource and the existing movement of the workforce towards it. It also provides us a time estimation and to select and train the required number of additional human resources.

The objectives of HRP (Figure 4.1) may be summarized as follows:

- *Forecasting human resource requirements*: HRP is essential to determine the future human resource needs in an organization. In the absence of such a plan, it would be difficult to have the services of the right kind of people at the right time.
- *Effective management of change*: Proper planning is required to cope with changes in market conditions, technology products, and government regulations in an effective way. These changes call for continuous allocation or reallocation of skills as lack of planning may result in underutilization of human resource.
- *Realizing organizational goals*: Planning is essential to meet the needs of expansion programmes and growth strategies of the organizations.

■ ■ ■
The objective of HRP is to maintain and improve the organization's ability to achieve its goals by developing strategies that will result in optimum contribution of human resources.

- *Promoting employees:* The database available provides a comprehensive skill repertoire, which facilitates for decision making as to the promotional opportunities to be made available for the organization.
- *Effective utilization of human resource*: This database is also useful for identifying surplus and unutilized human resources. In times of downsizing or in estimating the cost–benefit analysis of human resources would add value to the process.

The objective of HRP is to maintain and improve the organization's ability to achieve its goals by developing strategies that will result in optimum contribution of human resources. For this purpose, Stainer recommends the following nine strategies for the human resource planners:

- They should collect, maintain, and interpret relevant information regarding human resources.
- They should report periodically human resource objectives and requirements, existing employees, and allied features of human resource.
- They should develop procedures and techniques to determine the requirements of different types of human resource over a period of time from the standpoint of organizational goals.
- They should develop measures of human resource utilization as components of forecasts of human resource requirements along with independent validation.
- They should employ suitable techniques leading to effective allocation of work with a view to improving human resource utilization.
- They should conduct research to determine factors hampering the contribution of the individuals and groups to the organization with a view to modifying or removing these handicaps.
- They should develop and employ methods of economic assessment of human resources to reflect its features as income generator and cost and accordingly improve the quality of decisions affecting the human resource.
- They should evaluate the procurement, promotion, and retention of the effective human resources.
- They should analyse the dynamic process of recruitment, promotion, and loss to the organization and control these processes with a view to maximizing the individual and group performance without involving high cost.

It is usually the top management that formulates the vision and translates the vision into objectives. Further, these objectives get translated into strategies and long-term plans. These plans

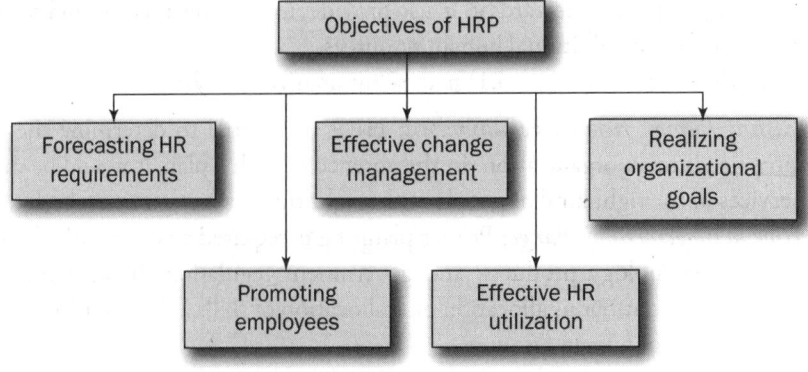

FIGURE 4.1 Objectives of HRP

usually form the guidelines for the human resource department to plan for human resource requirements. Besides, various functional and departmental heads periodically furnish information to the HR department about their human resource requirements. The HR department coordinates the above information and prepares the human resource plan. Professor Geisler outlined the responsibilities of HR department in respect of HRP as follows:

- Assist and counsel operating managers to plan and set objectives.
- Collect and summarize human resource data keeping long-run objectives and broad organizational interests in mind.
- Monitor and measure performance against the plan and keep top management informed about it.
- Provide proper research base for effective human resource and organizational planning.

FACTORS AFFECTING HUMAN RESOURCE PLANNING

Human resource planning is affected by the following factors.

Lack of skilled resources   This is a major problem faced by the organizations today. Lack of appropriate skills, abilities, and capacities to execute the task is a general problem experienced by the managers. Sometimes it is lack of skills and often it is obsolescence of skills that prompts for HRP. Separation of employees: At times employees leave and separate from the organization due to factors such as resignation, death, premature retirement, ill health, termination, etc. In all such instances, HRP becomes a necessity.

Change in organizational objectives   Whenever organizational plans take different forms such as expansion, growth, diversification, etc., different skill sets become necessary and that requires HRP.

Change in policies   Technological changes, impact of globalization, or changes in fiscal and trade policies might also affect organizational functioning and result in employee planning.

PROCESS OF HUMAN RESOURCE PLANNING

The general definition of human resource planning suggests several interrelated activities that together constitute an HRP system. An effective HRP closes the gap between the current situation and the desired state of affairs in the context of an organizational strategy. Thus, an HRP system may include

- *a talent inventory* to assess current human resources and to analyse how they are currently being used,
- *a human resource forecast* to predict future HR requirements such as the number of workforce needed, number expected to be available, skills required, and labour supply,

- *action plans* to enlarge the pool of people qualified to fill the projected vacancies through actions such as recruitment, selection, training, placement, promotion, development, etc., and
- *review and monitoring* to provide feedback on the overall effectiveness of the HRP by monitoring the degree of attainment of HR objectives.

The steps involved in HRP may be summarized as follows: (a) linking organizational strategy to HR planning, (b) forecasting, (c) gap analysis, and (d) implementation of HRP.

Linking Organizational Strategy to Human Resource Planning

Environmental scanning helps HR planners identify and anticipate sources of problems, threats, and opportunities that should drive the organization's strategic planning. Scanning provides a better understanding of the context in which HR decisions are/will be made. Both an external and internal environment scan are critical for effective planning.

Amazon's downsizing in 2001 is an example of the use of environmental scanning to drive strategy and HR planning in a situation of uncertainty. Their sales and growth projections drove their downsizing efforts although there was great uncertainty about the state of the American economy.

While there can be (and often are) situations with ambiguous problems, threats, and opportunities, the probability of reducing or eliminating the ambiguity is increased by a more thorough environmental scan. The idea is to attempt to turn a threat into an opportunity with relevant information. In general, the greater the amount of relevant information that managers have about a problem, the more likely that the problem can be turned into an opportunity. Both external and internal environmental scans are critical for this information. Amazon is a good example here. They closed a large and costly customer service centre in Seattle despite projections of 20% to 30% sales growth because their study of global telecommuting told them they could meet their sales growth projections with a far less costly customer service centre in India.

The biggest benefit of strategic planning is its emphasis on growth for it encourages managers to look for new opportunities rather than simply downsizing. However, the main problem in strategic planning is planning in times of uncertainty. Since the future is unpredictable, the burden of strategic planning need not rest only with the top management, but be shared by the line managers, customers, and suppliers.

Lewisplatt, the former chief executive officer (CEO) of Hewlett-Packard (HP), typified this approach: 'My role is to encourage discussion of the wide spaces, the overlap and gaps among business strategies, and the important areas that are not addressed by the strategies of individual HR businesses.' To bridge these gaps, HP brings all its customers and suppliers together with managers in its many business units in strategy sessions aimed at creating new market opportunities.

HRP parallels the plans for the business as a whole. HRP focuses on issues such as what the proposed business strategies imply with respect to human resources, and the internal and external constraints an organization faces, for example, the work rules stipulating the working conditions and age specifications. The questions that need to be addressed are as follows:

- What are the implications in staffing, compensation practices, training and development, etc.?
- What can be done in the short term to prepare for long-term needs?

> The biggest benefit of strategic planning is its emphasis on growth, for it encourages managers to look for new opportunities rather than simply downsizing.

A variety of HR planning applications arise from the linkage to business strategy. While both the strategic planning and the long-range perspective might highlight the organization's philosophy, environmental scanning helps in determining the objectives, goals, strengths, and constraints of the organization. The HRP process might directly focus on

- vision of the business
- external factors
- internal supply analysis

At the level of operational planning, the focus is on action plans, availability of resources, plans for acquisition, mergers, diversifications, etc. The direct linkage to HR planning arises in terms of forecasting requirements such as creating a database of human resources and planning for the projected requirements.

The recruitment process, promotions and transfers, training and developmental programmes, etc., are framed based on the availability of budget, programme scheduling, and performance goals.

One critical component at this stage is to understand the relevant labour market. Labour market conditions definitely influence HR planning in terms of both number and types of available employees. There is increased demand or shortage of supply for certain types of skilled workforce. For example, there is a great demand for doctors, nurses, teachers, scientists, and other skilled personnel. Certain laboratories lack competent people who will be able to execute their tasks. The student–teacher ratio is pathetic.

On the other hand, scarce availability of workforce with certain categories of skills forces the organizations to engage not so competent workforce. To a certain extent, availability or non-availability of the workforce is affected by geographical factors. To a certain extent, technology is facilitated to bridge the gap caused by geographical factors. For example, global telecommuting is having a significant impact on the definition of labour market.

Another factor is the role of competing employers. The number and type of employers seeking similarly qualified personnel or offering similar compensation in the same geographical location also can serve to define the labour market.

The entire world is now the labour market for many skilled and unskilled jobs. The outsourcing of the manufacturing or assembly process to a foreign location is now commonplace in many industries. According to the National Association of Software Service Companies in India, the export of IT services is expected to increase to $69 billion by 2012. One call centre in Bangalore, 24 × 7customer.com, founded in 2000, includes a Fortune 500 financial services company and a major telecommunications company. General Electric and British Airways have large customer service centers in India and are expanding this function due to low cost and low turnover of personnel and high quality of the work. Entry-level customer service representatives in India earn between $2,000 and $3,000 per year, a good salary by India's standards. The total savings estimates for US companies for this critical work is between 20% and 40%.

What is also becoming more common is that skilled labour is being farmed out to lower paid, overseas workers as well. HP, IBM, Texas Instruments, and Siemens in Bangalore, India, employ skilled workers, many of whom write software packages for these companies. Dallas-based software company 12 Technologies runs software centres in Bangalore and Mumbai. The programming costs are estimated to be about one-third of the cost of an American programmer. However, this difference could change rapidly as the demand for Indian programmers grows. The consulting firm McKinsey and Company reports that in the next few years, new jobs in accounting, software development, and transcribing will generate more than 10 lakh new jobs and billions in revenue for India.

According to Joel Kotkin, the author of *Tribes*, Indians will emerge as a leading economic force following China. It is estimated that millions of Indians who live in other countries constitute the best-educated and most affluent group in the world. Even though Asia has seen its cultural influence for millennia, only in the last few years the diaspora reached significant levels.

Mr P.V. Nair, the former Indian High Commissioner to Singapore stated, 'Liberalization in India has not only made Indians abroad willing to invest in India, it has also liberated the India-based entrepreneur from past inertia.'

In 1989, according to some estimates, the combined overall global real estate investment of Indians totalled over US$ 100 billion. In Britain, the Hindujas are among the wealthiest families.

Forecasting

■ ■ ■
The purpose of HR forecasting is to estimate labour requirements for a future time period.

The purpose of HR forecasting is to estimate labour requirements for future time period. HR forecasts are of two types: (a) demand forecasting and (b) supply forecasting.

We may consider both of them separately as each rests on different assumptions and depends on different sets of variables.

Demand Forecasting

■ ■ ■
Estimates of labour requirements are carried out through demand and supply forecasting of human resources.

Many times businesses reported shortage of skilled or qualified workers. Technological changes, demands of consumers, etc., are also responsible for preparing a demand forecast. A forecast of labour demand derives from a projection of how business needs will affect HR. Hence, the HR manager should be in a position to anticipate the needs and set priorities from among conflicting goals. The forecasting methods may be broadly classified under two categories: (a) qualitative and (b) quantitative.

Qualitative A simple method of demand forecast is to identify the future plans of the organization and assess its human resource requirement vis-à-vis its current human resource. With current trends in cost cutting, each unit's requirements or objectives may change or differ. Hence, instead of a centralized approach, a decentralized one catering to each functional unit is recommended. These suggestions are then pooled to arrive at an aggregate or composite forecast for companies. Other popular methods include the Delphi technique and the nominal group technique to arrive at unanimity in the decisions. Though originally these were designed as problem-solving methods, the usage of these would to a large extent minimize interpersonal differences and conflicts. In the Delphi technique, individuals give the projections independently to a mediator. The mediator then passes on these projections to other members of the group. Each member has the opportunity to look into what the others' projections are. Until a consensus is reached, the procedure continues. Since the members do not interact face-to-face, difference of opinions does not result in interpersonal problems. Experts make revisions independently and anonymously. The technique can be more standardized by using network computers to give their preferences and opinions. Its main advantage is that it is quite futuristic and includes future plans.

However, it has two disadvantages:

- It is time consuming.
- It is subjective and sometimes may not include past data.

The nominal group technique is somewhat similar to the Delphi technique, but the main difference is that experts join in a conference and have face-to-face discussions and share their opinions. All the opinions of the members are presented either on a big screen or boards so that they can freely and immediately rank them and arrive at a consensus. The advantages are that it facilitates group thinking and exchange of ideas. However, this technique is also prone to subjectivity.

Quantitative Quantitative methods are based on the assumption that the future can be extrapolated from the past. Trend analysis incorporates certain business factors that include units produced, revenue generated, and a productive ratio. For example, Pratt & Whitney calculated 16 jet engines per factory worker and almost 20 support, marketing, and management personnel for every 100 factory workers. Their external environmental scanning data indicated ratios that are more favourable for General Electric, Pratt's chief competitor. In the labour demand, changes can be forecasted by projecting changes in the business factor and/or the productivity ratio. Trend analysis includes six steps:

- Determine the appropriate business factor that relates to the size of the workforce.
- Identify the historical record of that in relation to the size of the workforce.
- Calculate the productivity ratio (average output per worker per year).
- Determine the trend.
- Make necessary adjustments in the trend, past and future.
- Project to the target year.

If the trend analysis is to be successful, there must be a critical use of the appropriate business factor. There is an assumption in the learning curves that the average number of units produced per employee will increase as more units are produced. Since the workers learn to perform their tasks more efficiently over time, an increase is expected. Learning curves are evident in virtually all industries. For example, in the automotive industry, learning curves of new models improve by over 50% through the life of the model. Hence, the business factor should be directly related to the essential purpose of the business. Universities typically use student enrolment by discipline, hospitals use patient-days, manufacturers typically use output needs, and retailers use sales adjusted by inventory.

Regression analysis This analysis uses information from the past relationship between the organization's employment level and some criteria known to be related to employment. For example, companies can establish a statistical relationship between sales or work output and level of employment. The learning curve also influences behaviour. More complicated quantitative methods can improve accuracy by incorporating operational constraints (e.g., budgets, mix of labour) into the models. Under varying business scenarios, it is possible to forecast demand through this elaboration. Ideally, HRP is as comprehensive as possible to provide a leeway for a wide variety of business activities.

Supply Forecasting

A good starting point for projecting the firm's future supply of labour is assessing its current supply of labour. The simplest method of internal supply forecast is succession planning or the career plans orchestrated by the organization. This step is vital as it conveys an inventory of the firm's current and projected competencies. The database can be generated with the help of payrolls, skill inventories, job profiles, job families, age distributions, or qualification and experiences. This data needs to be updated frequently and should also include data on employees' career aspirations and goals. Internal supply forecasts help a company's hiring, firing, transfer, promotion, and development practices. If this is ignored, that is, if the present employees are overlooked for any new job openings within the organization, it might lead to dissatisfaction and frustration among them. Yet, another aspect that might form an integral part of the skill inventory is the performance appraisal system and results.

The above database provides inputs for succession planning and replacement charts to identify individuals who may fill the gap when an incumbent leaves. Succession plans may be developed for employees, non-management employees, or both. The process of development includes development of a planning horizon, identifying replacement candidates for each key position, assessing their current performance and readiness for promotion, identifying career development needs, and integrating the career goals of individuals with company rules. The overall objective is to keep people ready in case of a vacancy during emergency.

There are over 300 computerized human resource information systems (HRIS) available now, many of which include skills inventories. The General Electric Company, Dunn and Bradstreet, Bharat Heavy Electricals Limited (BHEL), etc., are some examples that use electronic data files for projecting successions, early retirements, future openings, and overstaffing problems.

More complicated transition models such as Markov analysis are used for long-range forecasts in large companies. Markov analysis uses historical information from movements of internal labour supply to predict what will happen in the future. An estimate is made of the likelihood that persons in a particular job will remain in that job or be transferred, promoted, demoted, terminated, or retired using data collected over a number of years. Probabilities are used to represent a historical flow of personnel through the organization; a 'transition matrix' is formed from these probabilities, and future personnel flows are estimated from this matrix.

Exhibit 4.1 presents Markov data from one division of Progressive Tools, one of the largest tools companies serving the automotive industry. The transition probability matrix presents percentages or probabilities of employee movement through four positions within the division. These data were retrieved from personnel records and averaged over a five-year period. The matrix shows that 80% of the more skilled machinist jobs are retained after one year with only 5% turnover rate. These data were used by Progressive to plan their recruiting strategy based on their projected contracts. The data indicated a strong need to evaluate the assembler job to determine the causes of the high turnover rate and the need to concentrate recruiting at that level in anticipation of shortages of assemblers in the coming year when contracts were expected to expand.

EXHIBIT 4.1 Markov analysis at Progressive Tools

	A	M	F	S	Exit
Assemblers (A)	.70	.10			.20
Machinists (M)	.05	.80	.10		.05
Foreman (F)		.10	.75	.05	.10
Supervision (S)			.05	.90	.05

(Contd)

EXHIBIT 4.1 (Contd)

	Staffing levels	A	M	F	S	Exit
Assemblers (A)	250	175	25			50
Machinists (M)	120	6	96	12		6
Foreman (F)	40		4	30	2	4
Supervision (S)	20			1	18	1
Forecast		181	125	43	20	61

Skills Inventory Pro Forma

Personal factors

Name.........	Birth place.........
Age.........	Occupation of parents.........
Sex.........	Present address.........
Dependants.........	Permanent address.........
Marital status.........	Telephone number.........
	E-mail id.........

Education and training

School attended with years.........
Degree/diplomas obtained.........
Training received.........

Experience and Skills

Job areas.........	Special skills (such as ability to speak/write foreign languages).........
Job titles.........	Reasons for leaving supervisory responsibilities ....
Job dates.........	....

Additional information

Salary.........	Test results.........
Grade.........	Performance ratings.........
Absenteeism record.........	Location of relatives.........
Disciplinary record.........	Appraisal data.........
Career plans.........	Any other information.........

Source: Benardin, H.J. 2002, *Human Resource Management: An Experiential Approach*, McGraw-Hill/Irwin, USA, p. 89.

Eaton Corporation and Weyerhaeuser have also used Markov analysis successfully in their forecasts. However, available research data in the use of Markov analysis is meagre. Variables such as unemployment rate, environmental changes, competitive status, business plans, and customer demand, which differ significantly in the situation when the probabilities were established will have a profound effect on the usefulness of the Markov projections for the future.

External supply   External supply consists of those individuals in the labour force who are potential recruits of the firm. The skill levels determine the relevance of the labour in a global way. For example, for a highly skilled job, the entire country may be relevant. For an unskilled job, the relevant labour market is usually the local community. Several governmental and industrial reports, such as reports by the Bureau of Labour Statistics and the Institute of Labour, provide statistics, which regularly forecast the supply of labour and make estimates of available workers, in general, for each job category.

Computer simulation   Computers are used in a most sophisticated forecasting approach. Various mathematical models are used in computer and simultaneously used in extrapolation, indexation, and survey results, to compute future human resource needs. Over a period of time, the models are updated to meet the human resource demands.

Gap Analysis

The existing number of personnel and their skills (from HR inventory) are compared with the forecasted human resource needs (demand forecasting) to determine the qualitative and quantitative gaps in the workforce. A reconciliation of demand and supply forecasts gives us the number of people to be recruited or made redundant as the case may be. This forms the basis for preparing the human resource plan.

Exhibit 4.2 illustrates the people policies at CMC, a Tata group company.

EXHIBIT 4.2   People policies at CMC

A company is known by its people. CMC, a Tata group company, has a significant number of the best skilled people in cutting-edge technologies, with knowledge about a panoply of domains, working together to create customer delight.

Spread across its four strategic business units (SBUs)—customer services, systems integration, IT-enabled services, and education and training—more than half of its employees have more than five years of experience, more than 21% have postgraduate degrees, and more than 46% are engineers.

People Policies

The company has aligned its HR policies with its strategy of sustaining a high-technology business. These policies have been designed to enable scalability of business and processes, while achieving a high level of ownership and involvement in employees.

All its HR endeavours are built around its core values and beliefs:

- Trust and faith
- Flexibility
- Inculcating a culture of openness
- Nurturing the talent of employees at the company level
- Concern for individuals

CMC's initiatives, policies, and procedures have evolved through a consultative process with a high degree of employee involvement. This has helped CMC create a non-hierarchical, flexible, and informal work environment. The company believes that the development of its people is its prime responsibility. To create this environment, the company formulated a number of unique policies to develop individual potential.

Working at the cutting edge, keeping abreast of new technologies, and acquiring new skills are not options; these are a must. That is why CMC lays so much emphasis on training and development.

(Contd)

EXHIBIT 4.2   (Contd)

No matter the sector it operates in or the industry where it functions, every Tata group company sets aside a significant amount of resources to train and develop its people. CMC is no exception. Training and development are a critical component of its HR policy.

All new recruits are inducted into the organization through a structured training programme involving technical training at its staff training college and training in soft skills by a qualified HR team. The learning process does not stop once the induction phase is complete; it rather gets intensified, and continuously so.

The HR policy provides for a minimum of six days of training a year for all its employees. Non-executive employees are trained in personal and professional effectiveness, engineers are trained in developing good communication skills, and frontline executives are trained in making incisive business presentations.

Executive development courses are held for staff with supervisory responsibilities; managerial employees undergo training for management, development, project management, and interviewing skills; and senior managers are sponsored for advanced management development programmes in leading institutions.

Employee Development

CMC has an online, web-enabled performance management system called 'Speed' or a system for performance evaluation and employee development, which evaluates and develops the potential of its employees. Speed helps everybody at CMC move ahead fast.

CMC utilizes Speed as a tool for managing performance, planning and motivating, and evaluating and enhancing the performance of its employees. This system seeks to establish and maintain an environment that supports its business processes and ensure that employee performance is evaluated against the achievement of objectives that are aligned to the company's goals. With Speed, the goal of taking CMC to a higher plane is being realized at a brisk pace.

Implementation of Human Resource Planning

■ ■ ■

Action programmes help organizations adapt to changes in the environment.

Labour demand forecasts affect a firm's progress in many different areas including recruitment, selection, performance appraisal, training, transfer, and other career enhancement activities. These activities all constitute action programmes. Action programmes help organizations adapt to changes in the environment. Some activities included in the action programmes are as follows:

- *Recruitment plans*: Recruitment plans indicate the number and type of people required at the specified time period. The recruitment plan will have a direct link with human resource plan and the management will develop strategies accordingly.
- *Selection and promotion plans*: Organizations' strategy will always be to select employees who have already developed the skills necessary to perform competently.
- *Training plans*: Training plans indicate the number of employees at all levels who will undergo training and identify the need for training. This is directly linked to organizational growth plans and future strategies.
- *Retention plans*: Retention plans indicate reasons for employee turnover and show strategies to avoid wastage through compensation policies or changing working conditions.
- *Appraisal plans*: An appraisal system can be strengthened when the selection process selects competent employees and the system of functioning motivates the employee for enhanced performance.
- *Redeployment plans*: Redeployment plans identify the employees who need to be transferred, trained, or relocated because of technical obsolescence or overstaffing.

- *Downsizing plans*: Downsizing is a step taken by the management to offload overstaff by identifying redundancies and resorting to voluntary retirement schemes, golden handshake, layoff, etc.

In essence, HRP is usually done both for a short-term and long-term period. Short-term planning usually aims at meeting exigencies, arising out of sudden deaths or resignations. Keeping the replacement charts ready is one way to handle the short-term requirements. Little training at certain levels or times might take care of inadequacies in the short-term planning process.

Long-term planning is usually done for a period of about five years. In the long run, it is possible to develop management systems for existing as well as new jobs.

LIMITATIONS

However, the planning process has some inherent limitations and problems.

- *Problems of accuracy*: It may be an ambitious venture to predict workforce demands for the future, as it is linked to many uncontrollable factors. Changing trends, as we are witnessing now, is a good example of such factors, which involves a complete shift in the nature of work plans, etc.
- *Emphasis on quantitative aspects*: The forecasting methods are highly dependent on quantitative methods, and the work-related human aspects such as motivation, morale, career goals, etc., are ignored.

SUMMARY

This chapter begins with an overview of the nature and concept of human resource planning (HRP), discusses the objectives of HRP, and recommends various strategies for human resource planners to achieve the organizational goals and objectives.

Further, the chapter explains in detail the step-by-step procedure involved in an HRP system, such as linking organizational strategy to employment planning, demand forecast, labour demand forecast, gap analysis, and action plans.

■ ■ ■ KEY TERMS

Forecast To estimate or calculate in advance, especially to predict

Human resource Employees or workers available to a particular group or required for a particular task

Planning A scheme, programme, or method worked out beforehand for the accomplishment of an objective

Qualitative Relating to, or involving, comparisons based on qualities

Quantitative Relating to, or involving, the measurement of quantity or amount

Regression analysis The measurement of change in one variable that is the result of changes in other variables

■ ■ ■ EXERCISES

Multiple Choice Questions

1. The objective of human resource planning (HRP) is to
   (a) develop strategies that result in optimum

   contribution by human resources
   (b) assist and advice line managers in accomplishing the basic goals
   (c) demonstrate that women or minorities are

employed in proportion to their representation in the firm's relevant labour market

(d) make an employment decision, but not on the basis of legitimate job-related factors

2. Downsizing by companies such as Amazon is an example of
   (a) lay-off
   (b) environment scanning
   (c) retrenchment
   (d) job enrichment

3. HRP in terms of both number and types of available employees is influenced by
   (a) executives
   (b) trade unions
   (c) downsizing
   (d) labour market conditions

4. An HRP system includes review and monitoring to
   (a) enlarge the pool of people qualified to fill the projected vacancies
   (b) provide feedback on the overall effectiveness of HRP
   (c) predict future HR requirements
   (d) assess current human resources

5. The biggest benefit of strategic planning is
   (a) data storage
   (b) quality of life
   (c) resource allocation
   (d) emphasis on growth

Fill in the Blanks

1. _____ is used for long-range forecasts in large companies. It uses historical information from movements of internal labour supply to predict what will happen in the future.

2. A reconciliation of _____ forecasts gives the number of people to be recruited or made redundant.

3. _____ identify the employees who need to be transferred, trained, or relocated because of technical obsolescence or overstaffing.

4. _____ usually aims at meeting exigencies arising out of sudden death or resignation.

5. _____ uses information from the past relationship between the organization's employment level and some criteria known to be related to employment.

Concept Review Questions

1. Why is HRP more common among large organizations than among small ones?

2. What are the advantages of HRP for a large organization?

3. Outline the steps involved in the HRP process.

4. Discuss the problems in HRP. How can you plan for human resource requirements in an effective manner?

Project Work

1. Study the human resource and employment planning practices in an IT company and a non-IT company.

2. Prepare a case study on employment planning scenario based on the data collected for an IT company and a non-IT company.

3. Compare and contrast the challenges in employee planning in the IT sector vs the manufacturing sector.

4. Conduct a role-play on the case studies developed with your fellow students.

5. Prepare a brief write-up on the efficacy of employee planning and its relation to the organization's business roles.

■ ■ ■ | REFERENCES

Bacharach, S. 1989, 'Organizational theories: Some criteria for evaluation', *Academy of Management Review*, pp. 496–515.

Barney, J. 1991, 'Firm resources and sustained competitive advantage', *Journal of Management*, pp. 99–120.

Guest, D. 1989, 'Personnel and HRM: Can you tell the difference?', *Personnel Management*, pp. 48–51.

Miles, R. and Snow, C. 1984, 'Designing strategic human resources systems', *Organizational Dynamics*, pp. 36–52.

Milliman, J., Von Glinow, M., and Nathan, M. 1991, 'Organizational life cycles and strategic international human resource management in multinational companies: Implications for congruence theory', *Academy of Management Review*, pp. 318–39.

Schmidt, F., Hunter, J., McKenzie, R., and Muldrow,

T. 1979, 'Impact of valid selection procedures on workforce productivity', *Journal of Applied Psychology*, pp. 609–26.

Schuler, R. and Walker, J. 1990, 'Human resources strategy: Focusing on issues and actions', *Organizational Dynamics*, pp. 5–19.

Schuler, R.S. and MacMillan, I. 1984, 'Gaining competitive advantage through human resource practices', *Human Resource Management*, pp. 241–56.

Smith-Cook, D. and Ferris, G.R. 1986, 'Strategic human resource management and firm effectiveness in industries experiencing decline', *Human Resource Management*, pp. 441–58.

Ulrich, D. 1991, 'Using human resources for competitive advantage'. In R. Kilmann and Kilmann, I. et al. (Eds), *Making Organizations Competitive*, pp. 129–55.

Wernerfelt, B. 1984, 'A resource based view of the firm', *Strategic Management Journal*, pp. 171–80.

Wright, P.M. and Snell, S.A. 1991, 'Towards an integrative view of strategic human resource management', *Human Resource Management Review*, pp. 203–25.

Neo Ventures BPO

CASE STUDY 1

Neo Ventures is a mid-sized BPO operating in three south Indian cities—Chennai, Hyderabad, and Bengaluru with headquarters in Bengaluru. The company operates in both international and domestic arenas in the following verticals:

- Banking and finance
- Telecom
- Internet service provider (ISP) and information technology (IT)

The banking and finance vertical (international) contributes to 70% of the business, while the rest comes from other verticals. With a headcount of 1,500 full-time employees (FTEs) in Chennai, 1,200 FTEs in Hyderabad, and 2,000 FTEs in Bengaluru, the company is headed by a chief executive officer (CEO). Figure 4.2 depicts the organization structure of Neo Ventures.

The company took a serious hit during the recent financial crisis as its customers included leading commercial banks in the US and Europe. As a consequence, the company had to rightsize its employees by about 1,200 FTEs across the three centers. Prashant Khurana, the CEO, called for an urgent meeting of the chief operating officer (COO), site directors, and functional heads to discuss an action plan to deal with the situation. The action points that emerged from the meeting were as follows:

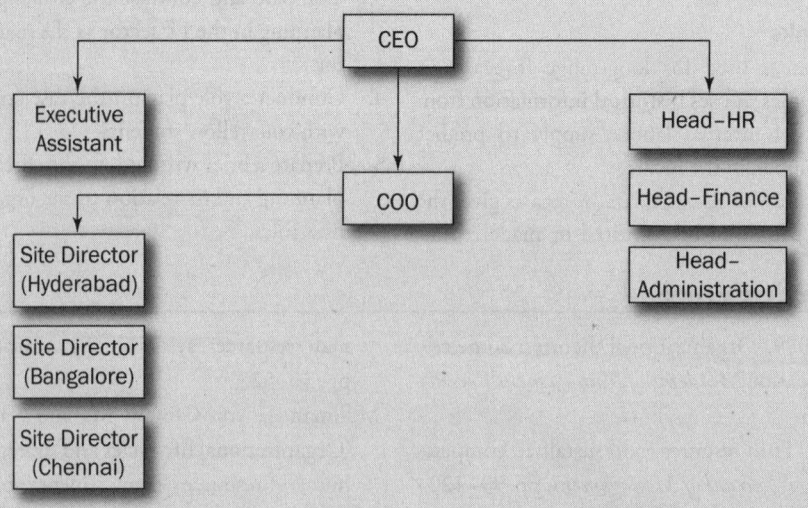

FIGURE 4.2 Organizational structure of Neo Ventures

- Avoid retrenchment unless there are no other alternatives.
- Plan for migration of employees to other business areas.
- Consider salary cost implications, while planning manpower movement.
- Constitute a committee consisting of site directors and heads of HR and finance to work on various alternatives to address the situation and give recommendations within 15 days.

The committee held a series of discussions to carry forward the mandate and submit the recommendations to the corporate board for its approval. Some of the recommendations of the committee on the issue are as follows:

- Classify the affected employees into three broad categories, that is, high performers, good performers, and bad performers.
- Place the bad performers on notice for two months for retrenchment.
- Identify the opportunities in other areas, that is, the telecom and ISP verticals, and redeploy all the high performers and some of the good performers.
- Explore the option to redeploy the remaining good performers in domestic operations with reduced pay through a fresh temporary contract.

Questions

1. Analyse the human resources planning at Neo Ventures.
2. Review the action plan prepared by the committee and suggest an alternative action plan with changes.

CASE STUDY 2 — Reliance Energy Ltd

Careers at Reliance Energy Ltd (REL) are built on the concept of forming a team of people or individuals who are made responsible for specific functions, from concept to development and implementation, with concomitant empowerment.

REL provides employees seamless merging of functional roles to provide a sharper business focus and groom employees for larger responsibility across the industry sector. The company believes that working smarter would mean not just doing a given job well, but also stretching it into a mini profit-making project. As the transition from the old HRD to the new people management has materialized, the HR function at REL has begun to play a role much broader in scope, stronger in impact, and more permanent in effect.

Career Development

Employees have various opportunities to develop their careers at REL:

- Exposure to latest technological know-how
- World-class management practices
- Multifunctional skills
- Customer relationship management
- Exposure to regulatory, legal, and contractual aspects of business
- Fast growth

Recruitment

Woven into strategic planning, recruitment in REL does not involve short-term vacancy or the annual ritual of campus recruitment. Translating corporate strategies into a manpower plan and developing a long-term programme accordingly, REL is tracking down people with the combination of knowledge, experience, skills, and behaviour best suited to achieving the company's objectives. The focus of the recruitment process is to

- attract people with multidimensional experiences and skills
- induct talent with a new perspective to lead the company
- develop a culture that attracts people to the company
- locate people whose personalities fit the company's values
- devise methodologies for assessing psychological traits
- seek out unconventional development ground for talent
- design entry pay that competes on quality as well as quantum
- anticipate and find people for positions proactively

Induction

A formal induction programme is organized for all the new employees. A structured induction programme is carried out in the following cases:

- Lateral inducts
  - This provides a general overview of the organization to the new recruits and familiarizes employees with various business processes, culture, and business practices of the company.
  - It also covers soft skills modules such as team building, change management, and communication.
- Graduate engineer trainees (GETs)
  - The induction programme contains technical training (on the job and classroom training), functional training, and managerial skill development.

Performance Management

To ensure that the talent that REL attracts can help it achieve its goals, we create appropriate working conditions by adopting the following steps:

- Evaluating all jobs so as to assign them to the individuals best suited for them
- Designing customized jobs, if necessary, using techniques drawn for behavioural sciences and industrial psychology
- Creating manpower configurations to boost the ability of the individuals
- Balancing corporate and employee interests by designing individual career paths

Objectives of REL's performance management system (PMS)

The following are the objectives of REL's PMS:

- Create a culture of excellence that inspires every employee.
- Match organizational objectives to individual aspirations.
- Equip people with the skills necessary to perform their duties.
- Clear growth paths for specially talented individuals.
- Provide new challenges to rejuvenate stagnant careers.
- Forge a partnership with people for managing their career.
- Empower employees to take decisions without fear of failing.
- Imbibe teamwork in all operational process.

Performance Appraisal System

The performance appraisal system in REL provides for
- recognition of individual performance
- continual learning and development
- better skills and employability
- monetary and other rewards
- the achievement of the organization's goals
- increased productivity and profitability
- a motivated workforce

Training and Development

With the changing business environment becoming more and more dynamic, a need on a continual basis for improved domain expertise is the need of the hour. The core function of our training department is to bridge the gap between the changing requirements of the job and the abilities that individuals need to perform these tasks such as self-directed leadership, self-motivated teams and self-generated creativity to excel in their respective areas of performance.

Objective of the training and development department

- Make learning one of the fundamental values of the company.
- Commit major resources and adequate time to training.
- Use training to bridge the gap with the external work.
- Integrate training into initiatives for change management.
- Use training as a developmental tool for individuals.
- Link organizational, operational, and individual training needs.
- Install training systems that substitute work experience.
- Ensure that training allows the staff skills to bloom.
- Use retraining to continuously upgrade employees' skills.
- Create a system to evaluate the effectiveness of training.

Questions

1. Critically analyse the HR practices of REL.
2. Evaluate the linkage between the career plan and recruitment practices.
3. Analyse the performance management systems and suggest the changes, if any.
4. Evaluate the approach towards training and development in REL.

Job Analysis and Design

Objectives

After studying this chapter, you will be able to understand

- the nature, process, and methods of job analysis
- the uses of job analysis
- the methods of job designing
- the nature, methods, and uses of job description and job specifications
- job analysis in the broad context of HR functions

INTRODUCTION

After the employee planning process, the next logical step is that of work analysis and design. Job analysis is a systematic process of gathering information about work, jobs, and relationships between jobs. For effective corporate performance, certain HR prescriptions, such as use of validated test and formal performance appraisal are required. These prescriptions necessitate work analysis or job analysis. Corporate restructuring process, quality improvement programmes, human resource planning, job design, recruitment strategies, training programmes, and succession planning are among the other HR activities that are based on job analysis.

Work analysis provides some basic information about the various jobs and skills required to perform the job effectively so that it creates and sustains organizational capability. Job descriptions and job specifications are needed to attract and select qualified employees and evaluate the compensation systems and particular compensation decisions. Job standards are required for performance evaluation and to determine the wage and compensation structure.

Whatever be the changing nature of the work, work analysis increases the possibility of deliverables to both internal and external customers. Today, even though various terms such as project and role are used for the concept of job, work analysis forms the basis of all important HR functions.

Job analysis is the systematic analysis of an existing or proposed position or group of positions within an organization. Understanding and being able to perform good job analysis is an essential HR function forming the basis of selection, promotion, training, etc. It is the best way to establish what exists, what is good, and what should be changed. Work analysis examines major work processes to identify results required, the documents, activities and persons involved, and the sequence of activity.

While one must not overuse this technique (i.e., go into such detail that you do not see the forest for the trees), it has proven time and again to be

■ ■ ■
Job standards are required for performance evaluation and to determine the wage and compensation structure.

> **■ ■ ■**
> Job analysis is defined as the process of identifying and determining particular job duties and requirements and the relative importance of these duties for a given job.

a critical analytical tool in the continual pursuit of improved organizational quality and productivity.

In addition, the process of work analysis is particularly useful to assess your organization and job accountabilities. As you make decisions to effect work improvements, you will be able to reassign accountabilities to better accommodate effective work flows and to gain better utilization of your human and other resources.

Definition

Job analysis is a process that identifies and determines in detail the particular job duties and requirements and the relative importance of these duties for a given job. Job analysis is a process where judgments are made about data collected on a job. An important concept of job analysis is that the analysis is conducted of the job, not the person. While job analysis data may be collected from incumbents through interviews or questionnaires, the product of the analysis is a description or specifications of the job, not a description of the person.

OBJECTIVES OF JOB ANALYSIS

The purpose of job analysis is to establish and document the 'job-relatedness' of employment procedures such as training, selection, compensation, and performance appraisal. One of the important uses of job analysis is to produce a basic description of the job that can facilitate selection of appropriate human resource. Another is to provide employees and supervisors with a basic description of jobs describing duties and characteristics of each incumbent in common with and different from other positions or jobs. When compensation is closely associated with levels of difficulty, these descriptions will help foster a feeling of organizational fairness related to compensation. Other important uses that job analysis can be put to are as follows:

- Indicate training needs
- Put together work groups or teams
- Provide information to conduct salary surveys
- Provide a basis for determining a selection plan
- Provide a basis for putting together recruitment
- Describe the physical needs of various positions to assess discrimination complaints
- Provide inputs for organizational analysis
- Provide inputs for strategic planning
- Provide inputs for any human relations needs assessment
- Provide a basis for coordinating safety concerns

Let us discuss some of the important objectives of job analysis in detail.

Determining Training Needs

Job analysis can be used in training or 'needs assessment' to identify or develop

- training content
- assessment tests to measure effectiveness of training

- equipment to be used in conducting the training
- methods of training (i.e., small group, computer-based, video, classroom)

Compensation

Job analysis can be used in compensation to identify or determine

- skill levels
- compensable job factors
- work environment (e.g., hazards, attention, physical effort)
- responsibilities (e.g., fiscal, supervisory)
- required level of education (indirectly related to salary level)

Selection Procedures

Job analysis can be used in selection procedures to identify or develop

- job duties that should be included in advertisements of vacant positions
- appropriate salary level for the position to help determine what salary should be offered to a candidate
- minimum requirements (education and/or experience) for screening applicants
- interview questions
- selection tests/instruments (e.g., written tests, oral tests, job simulations)
- applicant appraisal/evaluation forms
- orientation materials for applicants/new hires

Performance Review

Job analysis can be used in performance review to identify or develop

- goals and objectives
- performance standards
- evaluation criteria
- length of probationary periods
- duties to be evaluated

Quality and Productivity

Many organizations overlook an important technique in achieving the goal of continuous improvement. Work analysis is the examination of the way work is done. Work analysis focuses on shortening work periods, removing redundant or low-value steps, and simplifying interfaces between groups or individuals involved in the work process.

This process of changing what we do, how we do it, and the organization's structure to support it is sometimes called 'reengineering'.

This technique also aids in the analysis and documentation of procedures. Even if the work process does not change, a new understanding of it will be gained by the participants, bringing the procedures in use into focus and providing an opportunity for continuous improvement. Therefore, the staff members are involved in the analysis, they are trained for future analysis, and are committed to the opportunities for change that have been identified.

> **Work analysis is the examination of the way work is done.**

Effectively developed, the job description is a communication tool that is significant for an organization's success. A poorly written job description, on the other hand, adds to workplace confusion, hurts communication, and makes people feel as if they do not know what is expected of them.

PROCESS OF JOB ANALYSIS

> **The process of job analysis is an elaborate one involving job descriptions, specifications, and evaluations.**

The process of job analysis is an elaborate one involving job descriptions, specifications, and evaluations. Each of these steps involves a meticulous way of collecting information and preparing job descriptions so that there can be a clear idea of the jobs and duties to be performed. The job specification process identifies the type of skills, knowledge, and qualifications the candidates need to possess in order to execute the task efficiently.

According to the Boston Consulting Group, job analysis is undertaken to collect or obtain one or more of the following types of information regarding the job:

Work activities   This includes information about the actual work activities performed, such as cleaning, selling, teaching, or painting. Such a list may also indicate how, why, and when the worker performs each activity.

Human behaviour   Information about human behaviour, such as sensing, communicating, deciding, and writing, may also be collected. This will give clear indication regarding job demands such as lifting weights, walking long hours, or sitting for a long time in front of a computer.

Performance standard   Information regarding the performance standards is collected keeping in view the quantity of work done or quality of each duty performed. These standards help in evaluating the employees.

Machines, tools, equipment, and work aids   The kinds of product made, materials processed, knowledge dealt with or applied (e.g., finance, law), and services offered (e.g., counselling, repairing) come under this category of information.

Job context   This includes information about matters such as working conditions, work schedule, and the organizational and social context, for example, the number of people with whom the employee would normally interact. Information regarding incentives for doing the job might also be included in this category.

Human requirements   Finally, information is usually compiled regarding human requirements of the job, such as job-related knowledge or skills (e.g., educational qualification, training, work experience) and required personal attributes (e.g., aptitudes, physical characteristics, personality, interests).

Steps in Job Analysis

Work analysis follows a systems approach. It involves the following steps:

- Identify the work process of concern.
- Select and train a team to conduct the analysis.
- Identify the main results required.

- Identify the participants in the work process, and list them by name and position in the vertical columns of the work analysis chart.
- Track the work process, often using document trails or information flows, from the first person to each and every other person, recording the activity conducted.
- Subsequent to identifying the overall work process, add to the work analysis the documents or information added or created, and results produced, for each activity.
- Then use the work analysis form to assess beneficial actions such as
  - whether activities and functions could be effectively combined;
  - how interfaces might be simplified;
  - how documents might be combined;
  - where critical delays or possible quality problems might arise; and
  - where skills may be needed.

METHODS OF JOB ANALYSIS

Job analysis is a systematic exposition of the activities within a job. It is a scientific method to define the duties, responsibilities, and accountabilities of a job. It involves the identification and description of what is happening on the job and also of the skills and qualifications of personnel needed for the job.

Review previous job analysis, if any, and read any recruitment information such as newspaper advertisements and brochures/information given to past applicants. Gain a basic understanding of the current and possible reporting and working relationships between this job and other jobs. In case of a new job or position that has not existed in the organization before, make sure you understand the reasons for the position from the person in highest authority over the position (this will save you a lot of trouble with regard to office politics). Always begin by asking a job incumbent or supervisor to list the duties of the position and then to indicate the most important tasks by ranking them beginning with one. Then ask them to indicate the task ranked five or the duties on which they spend the most time (these are not necessarily the same). Some people stop here. In the hands of a good analyst, job analysis can support several personnel decisions.

Data Gathering

This section discusses the various data gathering methods used in organizations (Figure 5.1).

Observation　Stand and watch one employee work. This method is best used for manufacturing jobs and jobs that are easily discernible by merely seeing what a person physically does.

Desk audit　Go to an employee's work location and ask them to take you through their most important and most frequent tasks. This is a good way to analyse clerical and technical positions.

Individual or group interviews　Get a group of your best performers together in a room where they cannot receive telephone calls. Ask them to explain why certain tasks are more important than others and how tasks are performed. This approach is best used for managerial and supervisory positions or in conjunction with a desk audit when there are several positions and you want to make sure you do not miss anything. It tends to yield very good selection (criteria for choosing new employees) information.

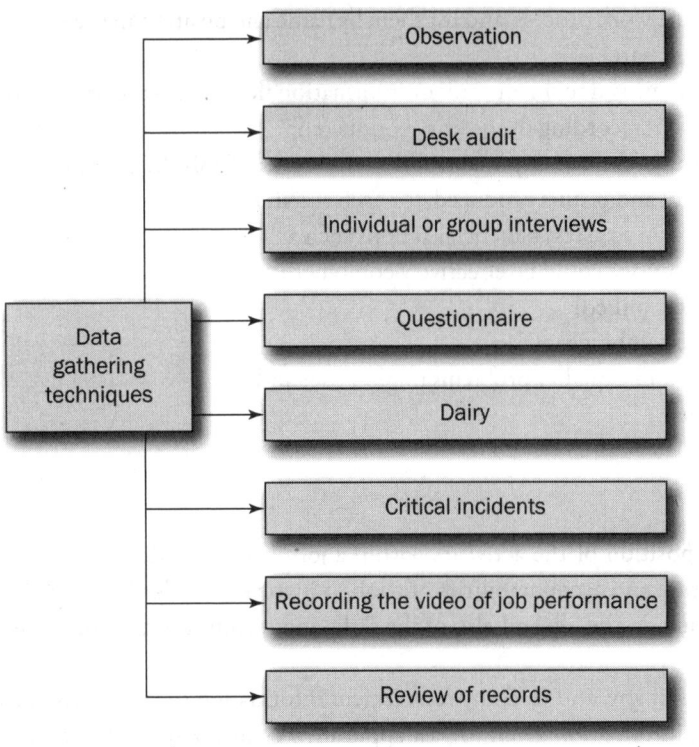

FIGURE 5.1 Data gathering methods

Questionnaire Use this approach when there are several positions and it is not feasible to bring several employees together for an interview. One should prepare the questionnaire by conducting one or more desk audits, brainstorming sessions, or interviews. Because questionnaires can be designed to gather different kinds of information, they are also good at clarifying information gathered during brainstorming, desk audits, or previous job analysis.

Diary Ask one or more incumbents to keep a diary of duties noting the frequency of the tasks performed.

Critical incidents Ask one or more incumbents to brainstorm (if there is only one person, you will have to participate in brainstorming with that person) about critical incidents that happen routinely and infrequently while working. Separate these into two lists. Generate one list of incidents indicating good or excellent performance and another indicating poor performance. This approach is excellent for determining training and selection strategies. The results lend themselves to meeting discrimination complaints concerning selection choices where the person chosen clearly possesses the skill and knowledge to perform the most critical duties indicating success on the job. The analyst will have to extrapolate a list of duties to be performed from the incidents.

Recording the video of job performance This is a good approach because it can be watched over and over again to perform analysis and because it can be pulled out later to re-evaluate.

Review of records Review records of work such as maintenance requests and make a list of requested repairs. It is important to take representative samples so that seasonal variations in work requests do not mislead. This is a good approach for jobs such as those of mechanics or electricians. The kinds of repairs being performed and, thus, the duties being performed most often can be itemized. However, this approach could also be used for computer programming and computer troubleshooting jobs in which incumbents have records of work requests or works completed.

The following are the various other methods used for obtaining job analysis information:

- US civil procedure
- Quantitative job analysis techniques
- Positional analysis questionnaire: Here a structured list of work activities is given to the employee. He allots a score from 0 to 5 to each activity. These scores bring out a quantitative

score for five basic job activities of any employee: (a) having decision making/communication/ social responsibilities, (b) performing skilled activities, (c) being physically active, (d) operating vehicles/equipment, and (e) processing information. These scores help one to analyse a job based on other jobs, giving each job a relative grading.

- Department of labour (DOL) procedure: This procedure gives the worker three categories dealing with data, people, and things, respectively. Each category has some listed activity. The worker has to select from these activities and thus a specific job profile is created from this method. This method aims to standardize the job description of the various jobs.

- Functional job analysis (FJA): This method is a combination of both the aforementioned methods. This method has two advantages.
  - This method rates the job not only on data, people, and things, but also four other factors, namely, (a) the extent to which specific instructions are necessary to perform the job, (b) the extent to which reasoning and judgment are required to perform the task, (c) the mathematical ability required to perform the task, and (d) the verbal and language facilities required to perform the task.
  - It identifies the performance standards and training requirements.

Considering these methods, there is a need to bring stability to the procedure. That is why it is advisable to get multiple perspectives vis-à-vis the immediate supervisor, the deputy manager, the manager, and the subsequent superior.

Data to be Gathered

■ ■ ■
The data to be gathered is dependent to a large extent on the use or purpose of the analysis.

The data to be gathered is dependent to a large extent on the use or purpose of the analysis. Information about training needs requires information about the transaction of the work so that the trainer can determine the critical skills and knowledge that must be improved. Selection decisions require the same information usually on a broader scale. A lot of information can be inferred from well-written task statements.

Examples of data that can be gathered include

- list of tasks
- list of decisions made
- indication of results if decisions are not made properly
- extent of supervision received
- supervision exercised
- kind of personnel supervised
- diversity of functions performed by supervised staff
- interactions with other staff (description of the staff interacted with)
- physical conditions
- physical requirements (For instance, how heavy are the objects that are lifted? How much stooping and bending is conducted and under what conditions?)
- software used
- programming language used
- computer platform used
- interpersonal contacts with outsiders (customers)

- interpersonal persuasive skills or sales skills
- amounts of mental or psychical stress
- necessity to work as a team member
- needed contributions to a work group
- authority or judgment exercised
- customer service skills

Note: It should be understood that collecting all information that will cater to all the uses job analysis can be put to is impossible with just one data gathering method. It is best to think of job analysis as a process of gathering information with various methods to use as tools to glean insights and information. This understanding is very important in organizations that have a strong developmental or training component. In this case, it is best to start out gathering the basic information and then to add other data in an effort to gradually put together a true picture.

Several methods exist that may be used individually or in combination. These include

- review of job classification systems
- incumbent interviews
- supervisor interviews
- expert panels
- structured questionnaires

- task inventories
- checklists
- open-ended questionnaires
- observation
- incumbent work logs

A typical method of job analysis would be to give the incumbent a simple questionnaire to identify job duties, responsibilities, equipment used, work relationships, and work environment. The completed questionnaire would then be used by the job analyst to conduct an interview of the incumbent(s). A draft of the identified job duties, responsibilities, equipment, relationships, and work environment would be reviewed with the supervisor for accuracy. The job analyst would then prepare a job description and/or job specification.

The method that you may use in job analysis will depend on practical concerns such as type of job, number of jobs, number of incumbents, and location of jobs. Table 5.1 provides Fine's functional job analysis (FJA) scale.

TABLE 5.1   Fine's functional job analysis (FJA) scale

Data	People	Things
Comparing	Taking instruction Handling	Serving Feeding/off-bearing Tending
Copying	Exchanging information	Manipulating Operating/controlling Driving/controlling
Computing Compiling	Coaching Persuading Diverting	Precision work Setting up
Analysing	Consulting Instructing Treating	
Innovating Coordinating	Supervising	

(Contd)

TABLE 5.1   (Contd)

Data	People	Things
Synthesizing	Negotiating	
Mentoring		

Various Aspects of Job Analysis

Job analysis should collect information on the following areas (Figure 5.2):

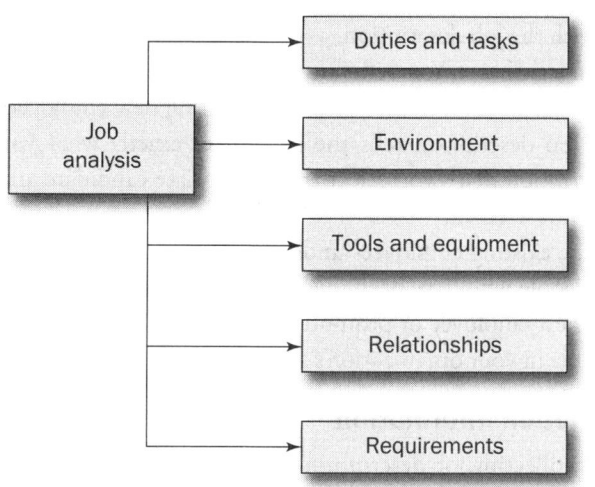

FIGURE 5.2   Various aspects of job analysis

- *Duties and tasks*: The basic unit of a job is the performance of specific tasks and duties. Information to be collected about these items may include frequency, duration, effort, skill, complexity, equipment, standards, etc.
- *Environment*: This may have a significant impact on the physical requirements to be able to perform a job. The work environment may include unpleasant conditions such as offensive odours and extreme temperatures. There may also be definite risks to the incumbent such as noxious fumes, radioactive substances, hostile and aggressive people, and dangerous explosives.
- *Tools and equipment*: Some duties and tasks are performed using specific equipment and tools. Equipment may include protective clothing. These items need to be specified in job analysis.
- *Relationships*: Supervision given and received, relationships with internal or external people, etc., have to be detailed in job analysis.
- *Requirements*: The knowledge, skills, and abilities (KSA) required to perform the job must be clearly defined. While an incumbent may have higher KSA than those required for the job, a job analysis typically only states the minimum requirements to perform the job.

JOB DESCRIPTION

A job description is a written statement of the duties, responsibilities, required qualifications, and reporting relationships of a particular job. The job description is based on objective information obtained through job analysis, an understanding of the competencies and skills required to accomplish needed tasks, and the needs of the organization to produce work. The job description clearly identifies and spells out the responsibilities of a specific job. The job description also includes information about working conditions, tools, equipment used, knowledge, and skills needed, and relationships with other positions.

■ ■ ■
A job description is a written statement of the duties, responsibilities, required qualifications, and reporting relationships of a particular job.

Job descriptions provide an opportunity to clearly communicate the vision and direction of the organization and where the employee fits in the

> ■ ■ ■
> Job descriptions provide an opportunity to clearly communicate the vision and direction of the organization and where the employee fits in the broad picture.

broad picture. Whether you are a small business or a large, multi-location organization, well-written job descriptions will help you align employee direction. Alignment of the people you employ with your goals, vision, and mission spells success for one's organization. As a leader, you assure the inter-functioning of all the different positions and roles needed to get the job done for the customer.

Job descriptions set clear expectations for what you expect from people. Ferdinand Fournies in *Why Employees don't do What They're Supposed to do and What to do About it* (1999) says you need to ensure that they clearly understand your expectations. This understanding starts with the job description.

Job descriptions help you clarify all your legal bases. You will want to ensure that the description of the physical requirements of the job is accurate. Whether you are recruiting new employees or posting jobs for internal applicants, job description tells the candidates exactly what you are looking for in them. A clear job description helps you select the appropriate candidate and respond to the queries of those who were not selected.

A well-written job description helps the existing employees understand the extent and limits of the new incumbent's responsibilities. People who have been involved in the hiring process are more likely to support the success of the new employee or promoted co-worker. Developing job descriptions is an easy way to involve people in your organization's success.

Methods of Collecting Job Description Information

This section discusses various methods of collecting job description information (Figure 5.3).

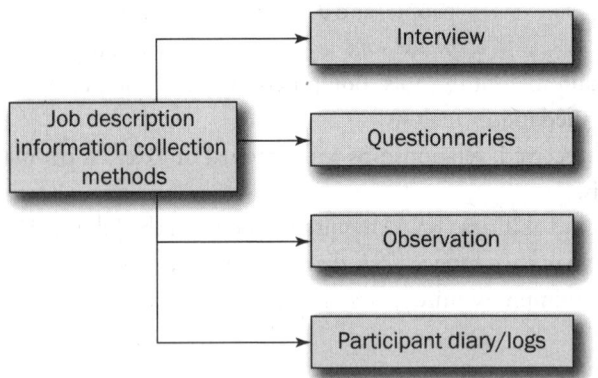

FIGURE 5.3   Methods of collecting job description information

Interview

Three types of interview can be used to acquire the job description information:

Interviewing the incumbent   In this method, the person holding the job is interviewed and the information is derived from the employee himself or herself. This is a very direct approach and is very useful when the employee understands the importance of the process of job analysis. Interviewing an individual employee is essential when there is no other job in the organization that matches the duties and responsibilities performed by the incumbent in that job.

There is also a possibility that in order to get ahead the employee would overstate his responsibilities.

Interviewing a group of employees   This method of interview is most useful when there is more than one employee performing a job with similar duties and responsibilities. Generally, inputs are taken from a group of employees having the same duties. This helps in saving valuable time and also gives a better job description due to the number of opinions that can be obtained from such an exercise.

Interviewing the supervisor   There are times when it is not possible to select a few employees among a group and question them regarding the job. This can result in a skewed response that cannot provide full information about the job. In such a case, the best method will be to take into consideration the opinion of the supervisor who is just above the incumbent. Generally it is observed that the supervisor has much more valuable information than the incumbent. This also helps in getting a complete picture of the job.

Questionnaires

■ ■ ■
There are two types of questionnaires —structured and unstructured.

Another good way of obtaining such information is asking the employee to fill in a questionnaire. There are two types of questionnaires:

- Structured
- Unstructured

Structured questionnaire   A structured questionnaire will have the same basic questions included in the questionnaire. These questions are applicable to all the jobs that are present in the organization.

However, there can be a few shortcomings in this process as describing each and every job through a set of few questions reduces the flexibility. Not all jobs can have the same functions, and thus the structured questionnaire highlights some duties while diminishing some other duties. In such a case, an unstructured questionnaire is more useful.

Unstructured questionnaire   This type of questionnaire can have a lot of open-ended questions asking the employee to describe the job. Such questions also have the potential to probe the employee in his efficiency and understanding of the job. Unstructured questionnaires are very useful in cases where the jobs are totally different from other jobs in the organization.

An optimum combination of structured as well as unstructured questions can lead to the best questionnaire. However, the time consumed in forming such a questionnaire and testing is very high, leading to costs that a company would like to avoid.

A questionnaire is the best alternative to interviewing a large number of employees. It is much more cost effective. Table 5.2 details the categories and respective elements of the position analysis questionnaire.

TABLE 5.2   Categories and the corresponding number of job elements of the position analysis questionnaire

Category	Number of job elements
Information input: Where and how does the worker get the information he or she uses on the job?	35
Mental processes: What reasoning, decision-making, planning, etc., are involved in the job?	14
Work output: What physical activities does the worker perform and what tools or devices are used?	49
Relationships with other people: What relationships with other people are required in the job?	36
Job context: In what physical and social contexts is the work performed?	19
Other job characteristics: What special attributes exist on this job? (E.g., schedule, responsibilities, pay, etc.)	41

Observation

> ■ ■ ■
> Observation cannot be considered appropriate for jobs that involve immeasurable mental activity.

When a job basically involves physical activity that is observable, the method of observation is very useful. Certain examples of observable jobs are that of a mechanic, a janitor, an assembly line worker, or an accounting clerk. Observation cannot be considered appropriate for jobs that involve a lot of immeasurable mental activity. Jobs such as that of a lawyer, design engineer, etc. cannot be described simply through the method of observation.

This method cannot be used in jobs where there are infrequent activities such as a nurse's job that might sometimes involve emergency cases. Waiting for such activities to occur can slow down the process of observation.

A major problem faced during the observation method might be a case of 'reactivity'. This is the case where workers tend to modify the way they work or perform more duties than they are allotted just because they are being observed.

Generally, observation is combined with interviewing in order to remove any discrepancies in the process. Any observation that was not understood by the observer is later clarified during the interview with the worker.

Participant Diary/Logs

Asking workers to keep a log of the activities they do in a diary can be extremely useful. This provides a complete picture of the job that is being performed, especially when the worker is later interviewed regarding the logs. One disadvantage of this method would be that the employee might forget to enter certain information due to time constraints. Some advances in technology have brought this method into higher usage by using recorders, dictating machines and pagers, wherein the worker does not have to remember to make his log. Instead, he is called over a pager to dictate the function he is performing.

Sometimes it is advisable to use more than one method or a combination of any of the discussed methods to get an accurate result. Exhibit 5.1 lists the guidelines for writing the job description. *Note*: There are websites now available that give an almost complete job description of a particular job title, for example, www.jobdescription.com.

EXHIBIT 5.1   Guidelines for writing the job description

Be clear: The job descriptions should be extremely clear. They should not contain references to other job descriptions. Any acronyms or abbreviations used in the job description should be clearly stated without causing any inconvenience to the reader.

Indicate scope of authority: When a position is being defined, the scope of authority should be indicated. The nature of work involved in a particular job also should be made clear. Phrases such as 'for the department' or 'as requested by the manager' can help in describing the job duties. Sometimes it is necessary to allow some additional duties into the job profile by mentioning that the job is not restricted to only the aforementioned duties but extends beyond them.

Be specific: It is easy for a person to get to immersed with the job description and state the events in detail. This should be avoided. Only the most specific words are to be selected. For example, the things that can be mentioned can include

(Contd)

EXHIBIT 5.1   (Contd)

- the kind of work
- the degree of complexity
- the degree of skill required
- the extent to which problems are standardized
- the extent of the worker's responsibility for each phase of the work
- the degree and type of accountability

To be able to convey all the responsibilities and duties of the job and being specific about the subject at the same time is a fairly difficult thing. This can easily be achieved using words known as 'action words'. Words such as analyse, gather, assemble, plan, devise, infer, deliver, maintain, supervise, and recommend are a few examples of action words.

Be brief: The use of short accurate terms and statements help in accomplishing the purpose in the best way.

Recheck: Once the job description is finished, it is essential to look at it from a newcomer's perspective. Further, if the job description was prepared through the interview of the candidate, it is useful if the employee himself reviews the job description. The following Table shows DOL'S Job analysis

Department of Labour's Job Analysis Process
Work functions

Data	People	Things
Synthesizing	Mentoring	Setting up
Coordinating	Negotiating	Precision working
Analysing	Instructing	Operating/controlling
Compiling	Supervision	Driving/operating
Computing	Diverting	Manipulating
Copying	Persuading	Tending
Comparing	Speaking/signalling	Feeding/off-bearing
	Serving	Handling
	Taking instructions, helping	

The following is an example of job description:

Job title: Benefits Manager   Occupational code: 166.167.018
Reports to: Director–Human Resources   Job No. 1207
Supervises: Staff of three   Date: February 2001
Environmental conditions: None
Functions: Manages the employee benefits programme for the organization
Duties and responsibilities:

- Plans and directs implementation and administration of benefits programmes designed to insure employees against loss of income due to illness, injury, layoff, or retirement
- Directs preparation and distribution of written and verbal information to inform employees of benefits programmes such as insurance and pension plans, paid time off, bonus pay, and special employer sponsored activities
- Analyses existing benefits policies of organization, and prevailing practices among similar organizations, to establish competitive benefits programmes
- Evaluates services, coverage, and options available through insurance and investment companies to determine programmes that best meet the needs of the organization

(Contd)

EXHIBIT 5.1 (Contd)

- Plans modification of existing benefits programmes utilizing knowledge of laws concerning employee insurance coverage, and agreements with labour unions, to ensure compliance with legal requirements
- Recommends benefits plan changes to the management, and notifies employees and labour union representatives of changes in the benefits programmes
- Directs performance of clerical functions such as updating records and processing insurance claims
- May interview, select, hire, and train employees

Job Characteristics

- A successful incumbent will have knowledge of policies and practices involved in personnel/human resource management function—recruitment, selection, training, and promotion regulations and procedures; compensation and benefits packages; labour relations and negotiations strategies; and human resource information systems.
- Excellent written and verbal communications skills as well as deductive and inductive reasoning skills are critical.

Source: Adapted from Bureau of Labour Statistics 2000, Occupational Outlook Handbook, 2000–01, Government Printing Office, Washington, DC, p. 58; and O*Net 2004, '*Human Resource Management*: Compensation and Benefits Managers', http://online.onetcenter.org/link/details/11-3041.00, accessed on 20 August 2004.

See annexure for job description samples at the end of this chapter.

JOB SPECIFICATIONS

Job specifications specify the minimum acceptable qualifications required by the individual to perform the task efficiently. Based on the information obtained from the job analysis procedures, job specification involves identification of the qualifications, appropriate skills, knowledge, abilities, and experience required to perform the job. It also specifies not only educational qualifications, but also certain personality characteristics that may be required specifically for a job. At times, certain temperamental qualities may also be specified in job specifications. In other words, this process identifies the particular qualities needed in an individual to perform the job. By reading them, the candidate should also get a fair idea as to the expectations of the organization. Another inherent factor is that the qualifications match with job requirements.

> ■ ■ ■
> Job specifications specify the minimum acceptable qualifications required by the individual to perform the task efficiently.

JOB EVALUATION

Job evaluation basically specifies the relative value of each job in an organization. It basically serves the purpose of compensation procedures. Job evaluation is a useful tool for making decisions about the compensation to be attached with a particular position. There are several systematic methods involved in the job evaluation process. These methods are discussed in the compensation chapter. What is clear is job evaluation is facilitated because of the data generated from job analysis. Exhibit 5.2 discusses cognitive work analysis and Cheshire Strategic Job Modelling.

> ■ ■ ■
> Job evaluation is a useful tool for making decisions about the compensation to be attached with a particular position.

EXHIBIT 5.2   Cognitive Work Analysis and Cheshire Strategic Job Modelling

Cognitive Work Analysis

Traditional approaches to work analysis tend to emphasize centralized work organizations, whereas turbulent or dynamic environments tend to require more distributed work organizations. Cognitive Engineering Laboratory (CEL) has adopted Rasmussen's (1986) framework for cognitive work analysis (CWA) as a basis for supporting worker adaptation (see also Vicente 1999). The focus of the CWA framework is on identifying the constraints that shape behaviour rather than on trying to predict behaviour itself. Rasmussen's framework provides separate descriptions of different classes of constraints such as the following:

Work domain: The functional structure of the work domain in which behaviour takes place.

Control tasks: The generic tasks that are to be accomplished.

Strategies: The set of strategies that can be used to carry out those tasks.

Social–organizational: The structure of the organization.

Worker competencies: The competencies required of operators to deal with these demands.

Therefore, CWA can be viewed as a complement to traditional task analysis in that it not only retains the benefits of these methods, but also adds the capability for designing for the unanticipated by describing the constraints on behaviour rather than behaviour per se.

CWA has been used extensively by CEL to design interfaces, experiments, and training as well as to analyse data and categorize performance measures and knowledge elicitation techniques. It has proven to be an invaluable research and design tool.

Cheshire Strategic Job Modelling

A recent proposal by Schippmann (1999) to align business strategy with human resources through 'strategic job modelling' presents an important evolutionary step for traditional forms of work analysis. Schippmann suggests that all HR interventions must directly contribute to realizing the vision, mission, and goals of the organization and identifies appropriate places for more traditional job analytic techniques (e.g., interviews, focus groups, surveys) to drive this alignment more fully. The Cheshire strategic job modelling process takes the perspective that organizations have a vision, called their end 'wow' state, a current or 'now' state, and a path directing them on how to achieve their end state. He proposes a set of steps that adjust the use of traditional job analytic techniques in a way that fully supports an organization's ability to transform themselves from 'now' to 'wow' with various integrated HR systems. Table 5.3 shows the sequence of steps taken in the Cheshire strategic job modelling process.

TABLE 5.3   Steps in Cheshire strategic job modelling process

Step no.	Questions	Parameters assessed	Examples of results
1	What are the organization's vision, competitive strategy, and associated strategic initiatives?	Desired organizational outcomes	• Market share targets • Customer delight goals
2	What HR applications are required to achieve desired outcomes?	The information gathering approach needed and the type/detail of information required	Plans to model for • selection • training • performance appraisal • compensation

(Contd)

TABLE 5.3 (Contd)

Step no.	Questions	Parameters assessed	Examples of results
3	Who is the target population?	Sources of existing information and information gathering methods	List of sources of job information for • executives • managers • engineers
4	What sorts of interview questions to ask? Where to get the information?	Interview/focus group protocol and sampling plan	• Questions • Sampling plan • Key SMEs
5	How is interview/focus group data collected and analysed?	Components of the rationally derived job model	• Content-valid model
6	What sorts of survey questions to ask? Where do data come from?	Composition of the survey and sampling plan	• Survey questions • Key SMEs
7	How are questionnaire data analysed and displayed?	Components of the empirically derived model	• Empirically derived strategic job model

Taking Schippman's lead, there are a number of professional developments from outside of the traditional industrial–organizational, psychological, and job analysis literature that can further contribute to HR's alignment with organizational goals. In particular, industrial engineering, Russian engineering, instructional design, and activity-based costing are key disciplines that offer new insights into strategic work modelling.

JOB DESIGN

This section discusses the various aspects of job design.

Definition

Job design has emerged as an important area of work analysis. It is based on growing conceptual and empirical base and has commanded research attention and is being widely applied to actual practice of management.

Job design concern and approaches are considered to have begun with the scientific management movement. Pioneering scientific managers such as Taylor and Gilbreth examined jobs with techniques such as time and motion analysis. Their goal was to maximize human efficiency on the job. Taylor suggested that task design might be the most important single element in scientific management.

> ■ ■ ■
> Job design concern and approaches are considered to have begun with the scientific management movement.

Job designing evolved into what is popularly known as job engineering. The industrial engineering approach is basically concerned with products, process, tool design, plant layout, operating procedures, work measurement, standards, and human–machine interactions. It has also been closely associated with sophisticated computer applications involving computer-aided design (CAD). These computer systems had a positive impact by reducing task and workflow uncertainty. Top management could readily perceive the immediate cost savings from job engineering, but certain behavioural aspevcts such as quality, absenteeism, and turnover were generally ignored.

> ■ ■ ■
> Job rotation programmes reduce boredom by switching people around to various jobs.

In the 1950s, different methods were being adopted by practicing managers. For example, IBM job rotation and job enlargement programmes

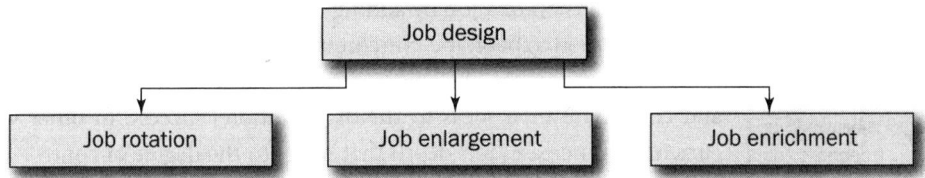

FIGURE 5.4   Approaches to job design

were introduced. Job enlargement programmes essentially loaded the jobs horizontally, and expanded the number of operations performed by the worker and made the job less specialized.

Job rotation programmes reduced boredom by switching people around to various jobs. Although boredom at work is still a significant problem in the last several years, attention has shifted to new demanding challenges facing employees on the job. For example, because of downsizing of organizations and increasingly advanced technology, jobs have suddenly become much more demanding and employees must differently adapt to unpredictable changes. For example, in manufacturing, assembly line methods are being replaced by flexible, customized production and computer-integrated manufacturing. This new manufacturing approach requires workers to deal with an ever-increasing line of products and sophisticated technology.

In this context, job design takes on special importance in today's HRM. It is essential to design jobs so that stress can be reduced, motivation can be enhanced, and satisfaction of employees and their performance can be improved so that organizations can effectively compete in the global market place. Figure 5.4 Illustrates the three job design approaches.

Job Rotation

An alternative to boredom in work place is job rotation. Job rotation implies moving of employees from one job to another without any fundamental change in the nature of the job. The employee may be performing different jobs that are of similar nature. The advantages of job rotation may be reduced boredom, broadening of employees' knowledge and skills, and making them competent in several jobs rather than only one. However, caution needs to be exercised while shifting people frequently from one job to another, as it may cause interruption or the employee may feel alienated in a new job. Another factor is job rotation does not provide the employee any challenge on the job and, hence, those employees who are seeking challenge may feel frustrated.

Job Enlargement

Job enlargement involves adding more tasks to a job. It is a horizontal expansion and increases job scope and gives a variety of tasks to the jobholder. It is essentially adding more tasks to a single job. It definitely reduces boredom and monotony by providing the employee more variety of tasks in the job. Thus, it helps to increase interest in work and efficiency. In one study, it was found that by expanding the scope of job, workers got more satisfaction, committed less errors, and customer service improved. However, research has provided contrary evidence also in that enlargement sometimes may not motivate an individual in the desired direction.

■ ■ ■
Job enlargement involves adding more tasks to a job.

Job Enrichment

Another approach to designing jobs is job enrichment. With the earlier two methods, human capabilities are not utilized fully and employees may feel frustrated. Job enrichment involves

> ■ ■ ■
> Job enrichment involves vertical expansion of a job by adding more responsibilities and freedom to it.

vertical expansion of a job by adding more responsibilities and freedom to it. According to Herzberg, job enrichment is the type of expansion of a job that gives employees more challenges, responsibilities, and opportunities to grow and contribute their ideas to the organization's success. In other words, job enrichment increases job-depth that refers to the degree of control employees have over their work.

Job enrichment basically provides autonomy, while retaining accountability. It generates feeling of personal responsibility and achievement. Job enrichment certainly improves the quality of work output, employee motivation, and satisfaction.

For example, in a private insurance company, the job of the receptionist was enriched to include the following:

- Communicating directly with clients
- Establishing a personal work schedule
- Checking on one's own quality performance
- Opportunity to correct his/her errors

The result was an increase in the quality output by 30%, reduction in errors by 5%, and decrease in absenteeism by 3%.

Every organization follows specific procedures for job designing. Each procedure may be different for different jobs. Certain aspects may be kept in mind while following the job enrichment procedure.

- Increasing the responsibilities of the employees by adding a variety of tasks
- Allowing employees to set their own standards of performance
- Providing autonomy for the employee to execute the job
- Encouraging the employees to innovate new techniques and review results
- Empowering the individual to make critical decisions in problem situations while on the job

SUMMARY

The chapter begins with a definition of job and job analysis. It examines the objectives, processes, and methods of job analysis. The various methods of job analysis elucidate clearly as to how the required information may be gathered about any job. Two important components of job analysis, that is, job specifications and job descriptions, have also been dealt with in detail. Further, job evaluation, an important outcome of job analysis, is also explained. The chapter ends with applications of job analysis in a job setting.

■ ■ ■ | EXERCISES

Multiple Choice Questions

1. Which of the following strategies is said to be most effective to motivate contingent workers?
   (a) Facilitate job security
   (b) Make jobs more appealing
   (c) Develop interest through job rotation
   (d) Provide challenging projects

2. The systematic exploration of activities within a job is called
   (a) job analysis
   (b) job design
   (c) job description
   (d) job specification

3. Achievable quality performance standards can be

set with the help of accurate
(a) job analysis
(b) job description
(c) job specification
(d) job evaluation

4. The document that provides information regarding the tasks, duties, and responsibilities of a job is called
(a) job identification
(b) job specification
(c) job description
(d) job evaluation

5. Job evaluation is based on the
(a) physical skills required for the job
(b) relative worth of each job in the organization
(c) complexity of the job to be performed
(d) conceptual skill required for the job

Fill in the Blanks

1. _____ involves moving employees to various positions in an organization in an effort to expand their skills, knowledge, and abilities.

2. _____ is used to identify what the job holder does, how it is done, and why it is done.

3. _____ is said to be an outcome of job analysis.

4. _____ can be used in compensation to identify or determine skill level.

5. According to _____, _____ is the type

of expansion of a job that gives employees more challenges, responsibilities, and opportunities to grow and contribute their ideas for the organization's success.

Concept Review Questions

1. Describe in brief the necessity for work analysis and design in organizations.

2. Critically analyse the role of job requirements database in work analysis and design.

3. Do you think work analysis and design would lead the present job match, if so please justify?

4. Explain the various methods of work analysis?

5. Describe in detail various aspects that are analysed in jobs.

6. Explain the role of job analysis in productivity and quality improvements.

7. Describe in brief the various steps to be initiated by the organization before work analysis and design.

Project Work

1. Prepare a brief report on the emerging trends of work analysis in the Indian context.

2. Analyse the need for work analysis and design in the IT industry.

3. Prepare a brief study report on the comparison of methodologies of work analysis in IT vs manufacturing sectors.

4. Based on the fieldwork, suggest better ways for implementation of results of work analysis.

■ ■ ■ | REFERENCES

American Psychological Association 1992, 'Joint APA, DOL report will investigate applications of cognitive task analysis', *Psychological Science Agenda*, September/October, 5(5): 12, APA, Science Directorate, Washington DC.

Arvey, R.D. and Murphy, K.R. 1998, 'Performance evaluation in work settings', *Annual Review of Psychology*, 49, pp. 141–68.

Blackhurst, J., Mitchell, J.L., Ruck, H.W., and Driskill, W.E. 1991, 'Integrating R&D results: A model for managing implementation of new MPT processes', *Proceedings of the 33rd Annual Conference of the Military Testing Association*, pp. 348–53.

Cascio, W.F. 1991, *Applied Psychology in Personnel Management*, 4th Edn, Prentice-Hall, Englewood Cliffs, pp. 331–60.

Cascio, W.F. 1995, 'Whither industrial and organizational psychology in a changing world of work?', *American Psychologist*, 50(11), pp. 928–39.

Deming, W.E. 1982, *Quality, Productivity, and Competitive Position*, Massachusetts Institute of Technology Press, Cambridge, pp. 185–232.

Driskill, W.E., Weissmuller, and Dittmar, M.J. 1992, 'Enlisted job classification technology: Initial development', *Presentation to the 34th Annual Conference of the Military Testing Association Conference*, San Diego, pp. 131–47.

Feigenbaum, Armand 1983, *Total Quality Control*, 3rd

Edn, Association for Quality and Participation, Cincinnati, pp. (4) 122–42.

Fleishman, E.W. and Quaintance, M.K. 1984, *Taxonomies of human performance: The Description of Human Tasks*, Academic Press Inc., Orlando, pp. 60–85.

Fleishman, E.W. and Reilly, M.E. 1992, *Handbook of Human Abilities*, Consulting Psychologists Press, Inc., Palo Alto, pp. 254–76.

Fournies, F. 1999, *Why Employees Don't Do What They're Supposed to Do and What to Do About It*, McGraw-Hill, New York.

Guion, R.M. 1998, *Assessment, Measurement, and Prediction for Personnel Decisions*, Lawrence Erlbaum Associates, Mahwah.

Jaccard, P. 1912, 'The distribution of flora in the alpine zone', *The New Phytologist*, 11(2), pp. 37–50.

Kirsch, M., Fisher, G., and Melkunas, C. 1991, 'Using CODAP as a quality improvement tool', *Proceedings of the 33rd Annual Conference of the Military Testing Association*, pp. 221–25.

Mitchell, J.L. and Driskill, W.E. 1986, 'Optimizing integrated personnel system training decisions and development', *Presentation in the Symposium, State-of-the-Art Applications of Job Analysis: Integrated Personnel Systems*, American Psychological Association Convention, August 25, Washington DC.

Peterson, N.G., Mumford, M.D., Borman, W.C., and Jeanneret, P.R. (Eds) 1999, *An Occupational Information System for the 21st century: The Development of O*NET*, American Psychological Association, Washington DC, pp. 231–53.

http://www.absolutehrsolutions.com/samplejobdescriptions.html, accessed on 23 April 2012.

http://www.archant.co.uk/assets/vacancies /1124_294 %20SALES%20MANAGER%20 Person%20 Spec%20Format%5B1%5D.pdf, accesed on 23 April 2012.

www.ashton-consulting.co.uk/uploads/ACPerson-specificationRC.doc, accessed on 23 April 2012.

CASE STUDY 1

Customer Concepts Pvt. Limited

Customer Concepts Pvt. Limited (CCPL) is a market research organization, specializing in providing market research data to organizations since the 1980s in India. Since liberalization in 1991, the marketing research scenario has witnessed transformation. Earlier, marketing was limited to advertising through print media and TV coupled with supply of goods. However, competition has transformed the scenario. Organizations now seek research-based evidence both in pre-decision and post-decision phases.

Initially, the company helped organizations in the areas of product positioning and branding. However, competition changed the dynamics and clients started moving towards global market research organizations or advertising agencies that have market research teams as well.

This necessitated CCPL to restructure its operations with the following departments:

- Customer relationship

- Branding and positioning
- Market research
- Analytics
- Experiential marketing

The chief executive officer (CEO) advised the HR head to conduct a job analysis for the roles in these departments to promote role clarity and create plans to develop and groom employees to provide value-added/comprehensive services to the customers. It was decided to provide job description for each of the roles based on the job analysis. As a logical progression, it was decided to conduct competency mapping for the existing manpower and talent acquisition to bridge the identified gaps.

Questions
1. Conduct the job analysis of these roles, based on market research or advertising agencies.
2. Prepare a job description for the head of each of these departments in consultation with your friends.

Applied Psychological Techniques Inc.

CASE STUDY 2

Overview

A top Fortune 100 aerospace company enlisted Applied Psychological Techniques Inc. (APT) consulting services to identify the critical knowledge, skills, abilities, and other characteristics, or competencies, required for successful job performance for their entire salaried, non-union classifications. This project demanded the creation of custom competencies for more than 3,000 individual positions. These competencies were integrated into the company's Internet-based hiring process to align its staffing strategies with its overall goals, strategies, and corporate mission.

Challenges

- Defining a 'best practice' competency development methodology that conformed with legal and professional standards, and yet was lean, efficient, and responsive to the organization's demands
- Training internal staff on the methodology for ongoing work
- Incorporating work into downstream processes, such as selection, performance management, and redeployment

Methodology

- Grouped positions based on the similarity of work behaviour to minimize the number of employees and required workshop sessions to expedite the completion of the competency development process
- Pilot tested the competency development workshop methodology to ensure its success
- Integrated the company's vision and values into the competency development process
- Defined a list of competencies, applicable across the positions within the company, which served as the foundation for beginning the competency development process. These initial competencies were then supplemented with job-specific competencies targeting the unique knowledge, skills, abilities, and other characteristics required to successfully perform the positions

- Equipped a team of internal employees with the requisite knowledge and skills to adeptly facilitate the competency development work-shop sessions using multiple coaching methods and techniques (e.g., train-the-trainer sessions, observation, role plays, question and answer sessions, completion of structured exercises, creation of training aides) to ensure their competence and expertise. This training minimized the company's reliance on APT consultants and resources to complete the statement of work
- Leveraged a computerized network to facilitate the sharing of the work products between sessions throughout the competency development process
- Reviewed and provided feedback on work products after specific milestones to ensure their quality, integrity, and consistency across teams
- Integrated web-based surveys into the methodology to expedite the collection of information, eased the demands associated with data collection, and minimized the company's reliance on APT consultants and resources to complete the statement of work
- Actively listened out for issues and/or short-comings related to the process and addressed them before they became problems

Results

- APT defined an efficient, job-related approach to identify critical knowledge, skills, abilities, and other competencies by training and developing the organization's internal employees. This minimized the client's reliance on APT consultants and resources to effectively complete the statement of work.
- APT identified the critical knowledge, skills, abilities, and other characteristics required for successful job performance for the company's entire salaried, non-union classifications.
- APT integrated the competencies into an Internet-based hiring process to align the company's staffing strategies with its overall goals, strategies, and mission.

- APT created over 2,600 unique job-related competencies.
- APT defined more than 3,500 major work behaviours describing the activities performed by more than 3,000 positions.
- The work products are currently being integrated into other HR processes (e.g., performance management, training and development, salary planning) to align the company's people resources with its overall goals, strategies, and corporate mission more effectively.

Questions

1. Critically analyse the work practices of Applied Psychological Techniques Inc.
2. Do you think the competency development in best practice organizations would help in work analysis and designing?
3. Critically analyse the methodology followed by the company for analysing best practices.
4. Are the results in correlation with that of the efforts of the company?

Job Analysis: The Kentucky State Police

CASE STUDY 3

The Southern Police Institute (SPI) was contracted by the Kentucky State Police to conduct a job analysis on the position of the Trooper. The desire of both parties was to develop an accurate understanding of the skills, knowledge, abilities, behaviours, and beliefs required to be a successful Kentucky State Police Trooper. Building on the data developed for the Trooper position, the Southern Police Institute was subsequently tasked with gaining an accurate understanding of the positions of Sergeant, Lieutenant, and Captain.

The process required the SPI to develop recommendations that would be used by the Kentucky State Police to accurately describe the positions of Trooper, Sergeant, Lieutenant, and Captain. The SPI provided recommendations to be used to develop those job descriptions, with additional recommendations appropriate to each position's job specification and job function. In following these recommendations, the Kentucky State Police was able to develop valid descriptions for positions and define standards for identifying the *best-qualified* individuals for positional placement at each level.

Unique to SPI's process was the development and implementation of a career ladder for non-ranked personnel, based on organizational needs, to continually enhance operational personnel, preparing them to become true law enforcement generalists. These officers can advance through their career in order from Cadet Trooper to Trooper, Senior Trooper, Trooper First Class, and eventually Master Trooper. This Trooper development programme includes assessing whether a Trooper is suitable to assume a particular classification by examining his or her achievements to identified 'suitability standards'. These 'suitability standards' are based on specific criteria, to include longevity, education, training, community involvement, conduct, driving record, attendance, and performance evaluation. Each Trooper classification includes monetary incentives. Non-ranked personnel can make the choice of becoming a qualified generalist and proceed through each level of trooper classification. An officer can take advantage of part, or all of this developmental opportunity. They may also elect to participate in the promotional process. These two processes, in combination, can lead to supervisors who are well-rounded, well-trained, and well-tested law enforcement officers.

The SPI and Kentucky State Police have jointly developed a valid promotional process, established yearly performance evaluations, and constructed an instrument to assess promotional potential to aid in career enhancement of individual personnel. The *promotability evaluation* has been designed to assist each qualified promotional candidate to prepare for the process designed to assess his or her skills, knowledge, and abilities. Each of these items are linked to specific job dimensions that have been validated throughout our developmental process.

Job Analysis or Job Task Analysis?

Working together, the SPI and Kentucky State Police determined that traditional job task analysis would not provide the comprehensive evaluation of positions that both parties desired. The job task analysis looks only at one dimension of the positions. The command staff of the Kentucky State Police quickly decided that they needed to develop measures that would allow them to gain an understanding of a Trooper in terms of values and beliefs, as well as what Troopers do and what they need to know. A job task analysis was out of the question because it would not provide the added data required to gain an insight into *who Troopers were and what they believed in*.

Clearly, they needed to develop measures to provide data sets that would allow them to understand Troopers on a personal and professional level. A full job analysis was required if they were to evaluate more than what Troopers do. They sought a multidimensional view of the positions being evaluated and that required a full job analysis and many months of effort. This approach was carried through to additional analysis of the ranks of Sergeant, Lieutenant, and Captain. These measures had to be custom-designed to this specific organization.

Primary Project Goals

The primary goals of this project required that the SPI assist the Kentucky State Police in defining best qualified for Trooper, Sergeant, Lieutenant, and Captain. The secondary goals required that the SPI recommend established measures and standards that would facilitate selection and recruitment, performance appraisal, career development, and an enhanced promotional process. This comprehensive approach, tailored to a specific law enforcement agency, allowed all involved to uniformly develop a job analysis process, and job performance enhancement process that is career long.

This comprehensive approach was taken to exceed and meet mandatory and non-mandtory standards for the Commission on Accreditation for Law Enforcement Agencies, Inc. (CALEA) accreditation. However, the Kentucky State Police also sought to significantly improve personnel development and career enhancement through effective personnel processes. This required the SPI to go beyond task and evaluate skills, knowledge, abilities, behaviours, and beliefs.

Job Descriptions, Specifications, and Functions

One of the objectives of SPI's research was to provide the Kentucky State Police a series of recommendations to be used to develop new positional job descriptions, job specifications, and job functions. These recommendations were to be used in part to define best qualified for initial selection and for future promotion. The only beginning assumption of the SPI was that every sworn position in the Kentucky State Police is first a Trooper. This assumption was based on organizational policy, behaviour, and philosophy. Therefore, future success was dependant on an individual's ability to master the position of Trooper.

The *job description* is essential to explain the basic elements of a job required for successful performance within a position. Through the job description, the reader learns what elements are essential to successfully fulfil the obligations of employment in a specific position. The job description must be clear, completely detailing a listing of responsibilities associated with a specific position.

The *job specifications* list the requirements that an applicant must possess for a specific position. It is through the job specifications that positional requirements are listed. These job specifications are mandatory for any person entering that position. The job specifications may range from educational requirements to a requirement to be within a pay grade or job classification for a specific period.

The *job functions* are a listing of tasks required of the position holder. These tasks may not be all-inclusive, but there are always some tasks that are essential to the position. Job functions detail the responsibilities associated with the position and may be used to define the training and evaluative requirements of the job.

Job Analysis Process

Focus groups The SPI employed focus groups to begin to understand the breadth of responsibilities associated with the position of Trooper. Twenty-seven Troopers participated in the focus group. These Troopers were brought together in three separate groups. They were selected by the command staff of the Kentucky State Police to represent road patrol, criminal investigators, support personnel, executive protection, crime lab, specialized units, and the northern, eastern, western, and central Kentucky assignment areas. The outcomes from these focus groups were used to assist in developing the survey developed to collect data for the job analysis.

Focus groups were also used as we began to narrow our potential questions to evaluate the functions and roles of the Sergeants, Lieutenants, and Captains. These groups were required to account for the wide varieties of specialized assignments, specific assigned areas of responsibilities, and types and degrees of accountability. These ranged from field assignment at individual posts to administrative assignments at headquarters. The SPI determined that in order to gain a complete understanding of positions, they would be required to have each position holder describe both the primary job function and the primary purpose of each assigned position.

The task of defining those specific job functions for which the current position holders were responsible was made somewhat easier since the SPI had used focus groups to assist in developing written promotional examinations in the recent past. In the spring of 2000, The SPI brought together two groups of nine Sergeants, one group of seven Lieutenants, and one group of seven Captains to assist them in understanding their job functions. The SPI also surveyed every sergeant in the Kentucky State Police to determine if the job junctions identified in the Sergeant's Focus Groups accurately described their roles and responsibilities before developing the written examinations. This information and data greatly enhanced their ability to develop a survey instrument for all supervisory and managerial ranks.

Command staff requirements The command staff desired to determine if there were regional differences among personnel. They were surprised to see that the data showed insignificant differences between regions. The expected differences were based on beliefs and data showing different types of activity throughout the Commonwealth. There were some differences in levels of activity, but there were insignificant differences in the criticality level of the same activities. Troopers from throughout Kentucky placed their priorities in very similar areas according to the analysis of the SPI.

The command staff also requested that the SPI survey to determine the basic physical requirements associated with the position of Trooper and to validate that the current physical standards of evaluation were appropriately job related. Their investigation determined that the current evaluation was job related and provides an assessment of overall physical fitness and abilities appropriate for entry into the Kentucky State Police as a Cadet Trooper.

Southern Police Institute requirements The SPI also sought to identify the human behaviours associated with sensing, communicating, writing, trusting, accountability, truthfulness, and decision-making. The SPI sought to develop a research instrument that evaluated the quantity, quality, and time required to perform job-related duties and tasks. The required job knowledge was verified as were the skills required and the personal attributes associated with each position. The context of the job was evaluated in terms of working conditions, work schedule, organizational controls and practices, and the social context of each position. The tools and equipment associated with the jobs were identified. Tools and equipment were evaluated and the associated degree of proficiency for the safe and proper utilization of these items was identified.

Survey instrument troopers The SPI developed a series of instruments to survey the personnel of the Kentucky State Police. Existing Troopers were given a comprehensive survey. The survey instrument used for the position of Trooper was by design a closed-end survey that offered only limited ability to add information. This survey was made up of six sections and had a total of 1,307 indicators.

Section 1: Background information This section sought information through 16 indicators. These areas dealt with the Troopers' work history and activities as well the specifics of each member with regard to his or her individual social, educational, and employment background. These 16 areas gave the evaluators demographic information on the target group, including specific information on time in grade, assigned region, assigned duties by type, assignment by title, educational level, and shift assignment. The SPI also included a specific request to identify their work activities to cover 25 working days. This was accomplished using 35 indicators and additional space was provided to write in non-specified work activities. Troopers identified their primary duties from a listing of 22 duties identified by the focus groups. Then information on the percentage of time the Troopers worked without close supervision, investigating crime, and alone on road patrol was gathered. They were asked about their prior police, military, and security job experience, if any. Finally, they were questioned about the appropriateness of Kentucky State Police Academy training.

Section 2: Response to calls for service This section sought information on three broad areas: motor vehicle-related duties, calls for police service, and criminal investigations. This section revealed information on the type of response the Kentucky State Police would make to each type of call. One hundred and twenty indicators were listed, and the Troopers could list up to nine more. Each call type was responded to by ranking the type of response the individual Trooper would make: zero indicated *no response would be made*; one indicated *a log entry would be made*; two indicated *a report would be taken*; and three indicated *a complete investigation would be made.*

Section 3: Small tools and equipment This section listed 160 indicators ranging from vehicles to specific computer software. It included items for fighting fire and giving first responder assistance to others. This listing also allowed Troopers to add up to eight additional items.

Section 4: Sources of research This section sought information on what Troopers used to keep themselves informed. The questions were asked for information through 67 source indicators. All the sources were printed material. They ranged from the Kentucky Conservation Game Code to specific newspapers.

Section 5: Behaviours and attitudes This section sought information on desirable behaviours by asking each Trooper to rank listed behaviour 1 = not desirable to 3 = very desirable. Behaviours questioned ranged from ethical behaviours to personal political involvement. Fifty-four indicators were developed for this section.

Section 6: Job tasks This section listed 920 job tasks. These tasks were grouped into 19 specific areas identified during our focus groups. We asked questions about 904 tasks and abilities. Troopers indicated the frequency associated with each task. Sergeants indicated the criticality of each task performed by the Troopers.

Survey Instrument for Sergeants, Lieutenants, and Captains

The survey for the positions of sergeant, lieutenant, and captain was designed as an open-ended survey. These positions were given the freedom to detail exactly what they do during the course of performance of their positional responsibilities. The SPI was able to collect data specific to each position within each rank.

We additionally sought information from the position holders through a series of structured questions beginning with identification of job duties. This section sought information on the position holders' top ten 'principle duties'. Additionally, they were also questioned about the degree of associated 'criticality' for each identified duty and sought information by questioning if the duty was below, at, or above the duty normally expected for the rank in question. A chart was given in the survey to act as a percentage guide—5%, for example, was presented as *30 minutes of a workday, 2 hours of a workweek, 1 day of a work month, or 2 and ½ weeks of a work year.* They were also asked to give specific data by rank based on individual opinion on minimum requirements in education, assignment, and work experience for each rank.

The skills section included 108 skills. The position holders were asked to rank the 'criticality' from 1 to 5 of each of the 108 identified skills. These skills were developed in part in the focus groups and in part by the researchers. Demonstrating 'readiness to make decisions, render judgments, take action, or commit oneself' was seen widely as one of the most critical skills.

The position holders were also asked to rank the following:

- Job-related knowledge and skills
- Impact of actions
- Complexity of position
- Decision-making
- Internal contacts
- External contacts
- ·Citizen relations

Seven levels were used to indicate the ranking of each of these. They ranged from *multifaceted* (7) to *standard* (1).

Finally, a series of environmental working conditions and safety factors were presented. The researchers largely developed these items. The Occupational Safety and Health Administration (OSHA) guidelines and requirements were reviewed and incorporated into this section. Factors that may affect the 'Americans With Disabilities Act' requirements, guidelines, and standards were used to construct examples of these associate work activities.

The final documents solicited data from the Sergeants, Lieutenants, and Captains that accurately depicted the duties and responsibilities associated with each rank. This approach also allowed the researchers to collect very specific information related to those within special assignment in each rank. The totality of the data allow them to understand each position and with absolute certainty develop reliable, effective, and efficient measures to identify the 'best qualified' individuals for assuming positional responsibility at each of the three levels.

The result

This effort gave us a comprehensive understanding of both the positions evaluated and the position holders. As a natural outcome, (a) the promotional processes became a better predictor of on-the-job success, and (b) performance appraisal became much more reflective of the position holder's actual job performance. The researchers saw other benefits from this project as the months unfolded. These included the ability of the Kentucky State Police to institute the 'Master Trooper Concept', jointly constructing the predictive tool that was used for *promotability evaluation*,

as well as for defining of positions and establishing job specifications.

(This case study is adapted from a case study submitted by Robert C. Crouse, Associate Director for Technical Assistance, The Southern Police Institute, USA. The Southern Police Institute is a division of the Department of Justice Administration, College of Arts and Sciences, University of Louisville.)

Source: http://www.calea.org/newweb/newsletter/No81/jobanalysis.htm, accessed on 20 August 2005.

Questions

1. Analyse the effort of the Kentucky State Police in doing a job analysis for defining the prerequisites of grooming a successful Kentucky State Police Trooper.
2. Are the processes in tune with the work requirements?
3. Critically analyse the methodology followed by the organization for preparing job descriptions for each position and its contribution in work analysis and design.
4. Compare and contrast the advantages and disadvantages of job analysis and task analysis in the organization.
5. Analyse the survey undertaken by the organization for job analysis.
6. Did the organization get the desired benefits through the exercises? If not, can you suggest changes in the project?

ANNEXURE: JOB DESCRIPTION SAMPLE

MANAGER OF FINANCE
Company: Kable Corp

Job description

Position: Manager of Finance	Incumbent:
Division: Human resources	Organization: Kable Corp
Location: Bangalore	Date: 20 July 2012

Approval signatures:

Incumbent   Director

Responsibilities

Responsible for providing efficient, timely, and accurate financial services for all Kable Corp departments. Supervises, directs, and audits the financial operations of the Accounting department in order to ensure information is efficiently and accurately processed. Ensures the department prepares timely and accurate financial and statistical information. Assists with annual strategic and business planning and business plan development.

Job Magnitude (annualized)

Total staff:	1,000
Total budget:	₹6 Crore
Department staff:	9
Department budget:	₹1 Crore

Organization Structure

The Manager of Finance reports to the Director of Finance.

There are nine positions reporting to the Manager of Finance:

Accounts payable accountant (1)

Prepares timely and accurate financial information by reconciling the general ledger and audits accounts payable documents.

Accounts receivable accountant (1)

Prepares timely and accurate financial information by reconciling the general ledger and audits accounts receivable documents.

Accounting clerks (7)

Performs accounts receivable and payable related functions, including maintaining sub-ledgers and general ledger accounts.

Nature of Work and Job Scale

The finance department provides services in a complex and multidisciplinary organization.

As the environment is constantly changing, the division is under considerable strain with regard to the consolidation of financial information and the financial accounting systems, policies, and procedures require additional standardization.

The Manager of Finance has a wide scope of authority and accountability. The broad scope of responsibility ranges from diverse external contacts to a direct working relationship with all levels of management within Kable Corp.

Major Functions

Plans, directs, and coordinates accounts payable and accounts receivable.

Evaluates the financial accounting processes in order to increase operational efficiency, enhance internal controls, and provide improved information to management.

Ensures that high standards of internal control are maintained through regular reconciliation of general ledger and bank accounts, journal entry reviews, and proper auditing of computer data.

Helps to design, implement, and maintain the financial reporting system, which includes accounts payable, accounts receivable, and cash management.

Helps the director to develop accounting policies and procedures in accordance with International Financial Reporting Standards (IFRS)

Accurately prepares various monthly financial reports for internal and external distribution. The incumbent collects, reviews, and analyzes financial and statistical information.

Develops and implements financial strategies and policies.

Prepares and documents the year-end audit and provides assistance to auditors.

Provides financial management skill development for all levels of staff in all departments.

Serves as the key resource for all levels of management regarding the department's revenues and expenditures.

Reviews internal controls, operating trends, business practices, and provides recommendations to departments in these areas.

Helps maintain a positive and efficient workplace by providing comprehensive financial services and information to all levels of the company.

Excellent communication skills are necessary to communicate and discuss changes to policies and procedures, the implications of such changes, and the resulting impact on workloads.

Selects, orientates, directs, evaluates, motivates, and disciplines staff. Determines schedules and deadlines.

Maintains working knowledge of all collective agreements and HR policies and procedures.

Coordinates the activities of finance staff for special projects.

Ensures supplier invoices are paid in a timely manner.

Directs and maintains a client and non-client billing process and an effective collection process.

Major Challenges

Must meet strict deadlines and respond to frequent requests for financial information in an extremely short time frame. Evaluating, planning, and prioritizing workloads with constant deadlines.

Must continually build, support, and meet the expectations of a diverse customer base including managers, staff, and suppliers.

Strategic and/or long-range planning is a major challenge given the rapid pace of change at Kable Corp, particularly during downsizing and restructuring.

Must adhere to sound and ethical business practices in an extremely political environment.

Many requests cannot be solved using a predetermined and/or structured process that is currently in place. The manager must evaluate the request and determine the appropriate course of action.

Develop and nurture a healthy cost-conscious attitude that would result in a more efficient and effective use of resources throughout the company.

Freedom to Act

The position has been delegated a wide latitude of responsibility.

The manager has the freedom to act and implement appropriate courses of action. All efforts are focused on achieving the overall goals and objectives of Kable Corp.

The manager has the freedom to plan, act, and make decisions within the job parameters.

This position operates under IFRS.

Contacts

The manager has frequent contacts with all levels of management and legal counsel.

The manager has frequent contacts with clients, insurance agencies, collection agencies, suppliers, external auditors, and financial institutions.

The manager works with external consultants on projects that are significant to the financial situation of Kable Corp. The manager has contact with the Internal Revenue Service (IRS) for rulings regarding the enter government legislation. The position has contact with state Kable Corp finance department for state tax rulings.

Specific Responsibilities

- Plans, coordinates, and directs accounts payable and accounts receivable.
- Ensures that Kable Corp assets are safeguarded by applying internal controls, reviewing accounting reports, identifying and reporting variances, and initiating corrective action.
- Ensures staff are fully trained and supervised.
- Contributes to a positive corporate image by conducting oneself in a professional manner with all levels of staff as well as external organizations and individuals.
- Improves Kable Corp's efficiency by reviewing financial procedures and work processes.
- Develops and improves financial policies that help to improve the timeliness and quality of information.
- Facilitates two-way communication among all managers regarding financial issues.
- Interprets and has Kable Corp follow all governmental laws/regulations with respect to taxes.

Working Conditions

Little physical exertion and involves a normal office environment.

Sitting for long periods of time in front of a computer is common. Results in repetitive strain on the neck and back. Travel requirements are low/infrequent.

Requires continual mental concentration and attention to details. Errors are difficult to detect and can have significant impacts on the optimal use of Kable Corp resources. Requires frequent extended periods of focus, attention, and computer use.

Strict deadlines must always be met and deadline induced mental stress is frequent. Frequent interruptions to workflow are common. The manager is required to adjust work hours and duties as required in order to meet deadlines.

The changing and complex environment and limited resources require leadership skills that alleviate employee distress and maintain quality of service. This contributes to the stress placed on the incumbent.

The manager is often required to make quick accurate day-to-day decisions based only on precedent and/or experience.

MANAGER OF INFORMATION SYSTEMS
Company: First One

Job description

Position: Manager of Information Systems	Incumbent:
Division: Information systems	Organization: First One
Location: Lucknow	Date: 22 August 2012

Approval signatures:

| Incumbent | Director |

Responsibilities

The manager is responsible for the supply and operations of the computer network infrastructure including all desktop computers, and networked peripherals.

Job Magnitude (Annualized)

Total staff:	1,000
Total budget:	₹60 Crore
Department staff:	10
Department budget:	₹1 Crore

Organization Structure

The Manager of Information Systems (IS) reports to the Director of Information Services.

Subordinate staff reporting to this position includes support desk operators, network technicians, and system analysts.

Nature of Work and Job Scale

IS operations provides office automation, computer communications, computer file and database management, and computer processing services.

The manager of IS operations plans, controls, and monitors the work of all subordinate staff. He/She has the authority to hire, fire, discipline, and organize the staff, receiving only general guidance from the director. He/She is responsible for achieving the service target levels set by the manager and director. The manager has the freedom to organize and manage the resources (people, assets, and money) within his/her budget in order to achieve these goals.

The largest challenge to this position is managing the expectations of large numbers of clients, and setting priorities that maximize the benefits to First One. This aspect of the job requires close and constant communication with all users of the service.

Specific Accountabilities

- Provide consistent and reliable office automation and database management services to all networked employees.
- Provide back up and recovery services during hardware/software failures.
- Provide support desk services for repairs, moves, installations, and added functionality.
- Provide on-call emergency services.
- Manage all software and hardware licensing and maintenance contracts.
- Monitor network traffic volumes and performance.
- Forecast additional system and network requirements.
- Forecast replacement demands.

Working Conditions

This position requires significant travel and communication within the organization. The work is typical office work with little or no physical effort.

Stresses involved in responding to numerous and varying levels of demand for services and repairs. Large number of interruptions.

Recruitment and Retention

Objectives

After studying this
chapter, you will be able to
understand
- the process of
  recruitment
- the constraints
  and challenges of
  recruitment
- the various methods and
  types of recruitment
- the significance of the
  process of recruitment
  for retaining people

INTRODUCTION

A growing body of research shows that progressive HRM practices can have a significant effect on corporate performance. Studies now document the relationship between specific HR practices and critical outcome measures, such as corporate financial performance, productivity, product and service quality, and cost control. Many of the methods characterizing these so-called high performance work systems have been researched and developed. Here is a summary of this research (Becker, B., et al. 2001):

- Large number of highly qualified applicants for each strategic position
- The use of validated selection and promotion models/procedures
- Extensive training and development of new employees
- The use of formal performance appraisal and management
- The use of multi-source (360 degree) performance appraisal and feedback
- Linkage of merit increases to formal appraisal processes
- Above-market compensation for key positions
- High percentage of entire workforce included in incentive systems
- High differential in pay between high and low performers
- High percentage of HR activities spent on outsourced activities (e.g., recruiting, payroll)
- High percentage of workforce working in self-managed, project-based work teams
- Low percentage of employees covered by union contract
- Relatively low number of employees per HR professional
- High percentage of jobs filled from within

Progressive HRM practices can have a significant effect on corporate performance.

Greater demands are now being made on HRM practitioners to respond to trends in the contemporary business environment. To break the competition, companies need to give more importance to human resources. It is the only source that gives increasing returns. It is both the means and the end of productivity. When properly trained and motivated, it can compensate

> **■ ■ ■**
> Recruitment, is defined as the art of discovering and procuring potential applicants for actual and anticipated organizational vacancies.

inadequacies and overcome any formidable obstacles. It has to be developed through a structured plan.

Recruitment forms the first stage in the process, which continues with selection and ends with the placement of the candidate. It follows the HR planning function. Recruiting makes it possible to acquire the number and type of people necessary to ensure the continued operation of an organization.

Recruitment then is the art of discovering and procuring potential applicants for actual and anticipated organizational vacancies. Accordingly, the purpose of recruitment is to locate sources of manpower to meet job requirements and job specifications.

Recruitment is considered as one of the most important functions in an organization. Unless the appropriate people are hired, even the best plans, organizational charts, and control systems would not yield good results. Decisions regarding employee testing, work policies, programmes, compensation, and corporate image all have an impact on recruiting.

FACTORS AFFECTING RECRUITMENT

All organizations, large or small, have to engage in recruitment. Some of them delegate the job to HR Managers, while others involve the HR Managers directly on the job. Some organizations continuously indulge in recruitment, while others may do it infrequently. Here, size may be an important factor. For example, an organization with hundred thousand employees will have to continually engage in recruiting. This practice is found in multinational corporations like fast food firms or service organizations.

The employment conditions in the community where the organization is located may be a factor for attracting potential job applicants. Here, certain geographic factors and location advantages play an important role.

The effect of past recruiting efforts, which show the organization's ability to locate and keep good people, is another criterion. For example, if an organization follows the promotional policy of recruiting from within, the employees will be motivated to continue in such an organization. Further, the compensation and benefits package offered by an organization also influence and attract the employees.

Organizations that are growing and expanding will always find it necessary to recruit and organizations that are not growing may not need any recruitment.

CONSTRAINTS AND CHALLENGES IN THE RECRUITMENT PROCESS

An ideal situation is where the number of applications received will significantly outnumber the number of posts to be filled. The recruiter then has a wide choice and makes best efforts to match job requirements with individual potentials. However, the realities are different. For example, the pool of qualified applicants may not include the best candidates or the best candidate may not want to be employed by the organization. If recruitment is considered as the art of attracting the best qualified people to the organization, what are the factors that might impinge on the process and act as constraints? Some such constraints are discussed here (Figure 6.1).

■ ■ ■
A negative image can affect an organization's ability to attract talent.

Image of the organization   It is a well-known fact that candidates will be attracted to a reputed organization only. This has been proved particularly in the younger age group and college students who are interested in building their careers. Further, employees who are already working in reputed firms would like to continue in such organizations. This scenario is perceived not only in India, but also universally. For example, in India, in 1970s the trend was towards getting employment in public sectors as the salaries were high and compensation packages attractive. With the new economic policy after 1990, people liked to associate themselves more with multinational corporations for salary and reputation of the companies. Likewise, there is a rise in the number of applications received in the IT sector companies such as Infosys and Wipro Technologies. These companies enjoy a positive image in the eyes of public at large. Microsoft too enjoys a positive image to the point where the company receives more than 12,000 resumes a month.

However, not all companies enjoy such reputation. The image of a company may be perceived as low because of its non-performance, low turnover, policies and practices that pollute the environment, poor quality products, unsafe or inadequate working conditions, etc. Such factors can and do reduce these organizations' ability to attract the best personnel available.

Attractiveness of the job   If the position to be filled is unattractive, recruiting a large and qualified pool of candidates will be difficult. In the recent past, it has been observed that employers find it difficult to get suitable candidates for jobs that are considered as routine, boring, physically hazardous, wrongly scheduled, anxiety creating, low paying, lacking in promotional potential, etc.

Organizational policies   Certain organizational policies like promotions from within may attract applicants at the initial level, but not at higher positions. Although this is promising, once one is hired, it may reduce the number of applications for higher positions.

Legislation   An organization has to comply with the existing rules governing the recruitment process and cannot make any discrimination on the basis of physical appearance, gender, religious background, etc. Further, in government offices, the reservation guidelines need to be followed wherever applicable.

Costs of recruitment   Recruiting efforts by an organization are always expensive. This continuing search for best applicants may be limited by budgetary constraints. Accordingly, an organization

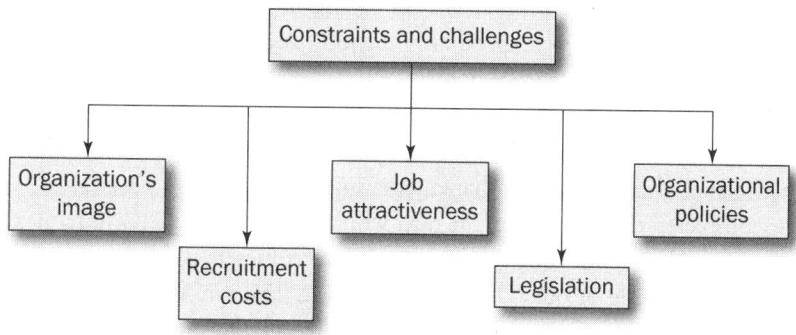

FIGURE 6.1   Challenges in the recruitment process

would like to maximize its recruiting travel budget by interviewing over the phone or through videoconference.

Keeping in view the above constraints and challenges, it would be better for an organization to have a recruitment policy of its own. Such a policy asserts the objectives of recruitment and provides a framework of procedures for implementation of the recruitment programme in the form of procedures. The policy may incorporate a commitment to broad principles such as filling vacancies with best qualified individuals, extent of promotion from within, and welfare measures for the employees. Therefore, a well-considered and pre-planned recruitment policy based on corporate goals, study of appointment, and corporate needs may avoid hasty or ill-considered decisions and may go a long way in procuring the right kind of personnel in the organization.

According to Yoder (1972), the recruitment policies involve the following:

- Carefully observing the letter and spirit of the relevant public policy on hiring and, on the whole, employment relationship.
- Providing individual employees with employment security, avoiding frequent lay-off.
- Providing each employee with an open road and encouragement in the continuing development of his talents and skills.
- Assuring each employee of the organization's interest in his personal goals and employment objectives.
- Assuring employees of fairness in all employment relationships, including promotions and transfers.
- Avoiding cliques, which may develop when several members of the same household or community are employed in the organization.
- Providing employment in jobs which are engineered to meet the qualifications of handicapped workers and minority sections.
- Encouraging one or more strong, effective, and responsible trade unions among the employees.

PROCESS OF RECRUITMENT

The process of recruitment is interdependent on and interlinked with other HR activities. Employee planning and work analysis precede the process of recruitment. Compensation packages and corporate image all have an impact on the recruitment process. At the outset, the objectives of the process of recruitment may be retention and satisfaction of the employee. Other aspects such as cost of filling jobs, speed of filling jobs, and total number of applications received would all contribute to the retention process.

The next step would be to design a strategy as to the number and type of people to be recruited and determine the source of recruitment. This also involves an important step, that is, how to communicate and advertise the fact that an opening exists.

Having completed the above step, the next would be to attain clarity in terms of both sources of recruitment and timeliness of recruitment. Here comes the role of recruiters. Positioning the recruiters by training or outsourcing is important. This will lead to the preliminary step of screening the applications. Obviously, when we receive a larger number of applications than the number of posts to be filled, it is a good sign that the organization can exercise a good choice.

However, care needs to be taken to verify the information provided in the application forms. In some instances, some amount of screening and filtering of the applications can also be done at this preliminary stage if a wide choice is available.

Each organization follows its own pattern of recruitment process. Broadly, the methods may be categorized into internal and external sources of recruitment. What is required is a comparison of objectives of recruitment with outcomes.

SOURCES OF RECRUITMENT

■ ■ ■
Internal source of recruitment refers to the source for identifying suitable candidates from among the current employees in an organization.

There are two general sources of recruiting—internal and external. Internal recruitment seeks candidates from among the ranks of those currently employed. With the exception of entry-level positions, most organizations try to fill positions with their current employees. Many large organizations will attempt to develop their own employees for positions higher than the entry level. According to Jack Stack (1998), the advantages of internal recruitment policy, by promoting from within wherever possible, are:

- It is good public relations.
- It builds employee morale.
- It encourages good individuals who are ambitious.
- It improves the probability of a good selection, since information on the individual's performance is readily available.
- It involves less cost than going outside to recruit.
- Those chosen internally already know the organization.
- When carefully planned, promoting from within can also act as a training device for developing middle- and top-level managers.

These variables have been shown to be correlated with low employee turnover rates and high productivity. These are also characteristics of a high-performing work system. Companies that practise internal recruitment are more likely to be successful financially than companies that rely on external recruitment for top positions. Internal recruitment policies of many companies seek to foster stability and continuity in the managerial ranks. Some companies have a policy in which newly hired college graduates receive a career-planning guide that describes the typical timetable for progression within the company for their best employees.

However, certain disadvantages also exist in the internal recruitment process. When the organization contemplates change, the existing employees may not act as change masters. A

■ ■ ■
Job posting is a process where announcements of positions are made available to all current employees through company newsletters, bulletin boards, etc.

monotonous kind of environment and familiar people may not be the right conditions for fostering creativity among employees. A third dimension is that more emphasis would have to be put on job specifications as, at times, internal candidates may make some irrational moves from one department to another for the simple reason that it would pay well. This is observed in the administrative staff.

In companies where internal recruitment is followed, there has to be in place a succession planning at the managerial level. This is possible in large organizations. However, in small and medium companies, job posting is a common practice. *Job posting* is a process where announcements of positions are made available to all current employees through company newsletters, bulletin boards, etc. When properly implemented, job-posting systems can substantially improve the quality of job placements that are made within an organization. They take advantage of a corporate intranet where employees can get information about job openings through connected computers.

Internal recruitment programmes must be carefully integrated with other HR functions. In succession planning, job analysis, personnel selection, and performance appraisal are all important for an effective system to fill the required positions with the most suitable people in the shortest time. One of the internal recruitment processes is employee referrals.

Employee Referrals

> ■ ■ ■
> Employee referrals are an excellent means of locating potential employees for hard-to-fill positions.

Employee referrals are an excellent means of locating potential employees for those hard-to-fill positions. A recommendation from a current employee regarding the job applicant is considered the best source because an employee will recommend someone only when he believes that the individual can perform efficiently. While recommending, the reputation of the person who recommends is at stake and, hence, a careful judgement is ensured.

The recommending employee often gives the applicant a more realistic view and information about the job than what is conveyed through advertisements. This information reduces realistic job anxieties and increases job survival. As a result, employee referrals tend to be more acceptable and once employed seem to have a high job survival rate. Moreover, employee referrals are an excellent means of locating potential employees in the hard-to-fill positions. Some organizations also reward an employee for recommending a candidate. In doing so, both the organization and the employee benefit—the employee receives monetary reward and the organization receives a qualified candidate without incurring major expenses in searching for candidates.

However, it has its own disadvantages. Employees may be tempted to recommend their friends and relatives to the organization with exaggerated potentials. This might develop unhealthy groupism, which may not be conducive for a healthy work environment. Another drawback is to recommend and include relatives into the organization. This might also lead to nepotism and may not exactly align with the objectives of the organization, even though employee loyalty and interest in the organization may be a long-term consideration. Finally, employee referrals may also minimize diversity in the workplace.

External Recruitment

External recruitment is concerned with recruitment from outside the organization. Researchers agree that this process facilitates entry of new people and ideas into the organization. However,

> ■ ■ ■
> External recruitment is concerned with recruitment from outside the organization.

the acceptance and reaction to a new entrant is sometimes sceptical and may have a negative impact on group cohesion and morale. Further, a new person may take longer time to learn the intricacies of the job. External recruitment is usually a costly process. Even if an organization outsources the process, the entire procedure involves lot of expenses.

An online portal's advertisement

The advent of Internet has proved to be of great advantage to the employers. Many big companies are posting their jobs on the Internet, which can be easily accessed by one and all and can attract the best applicants. However, in this process, very little information about the background of the employee is available for scrutiny. This has to be complemented with good assessment procedures rather than relying on performance data of the candidate. Good assessment procedures can be costly and at times deceptive also. Inflated letters of recommendation also may land both the employer and the employee in troublesome situations. Nevertheless, external source of recruitment is widely followed because of the variety of methods available for attracting the applicants.

Methods of External Recruitment

There are several methods available for external recruitment (Figure 6.2).

Walk-in/write-in The most common and least expensive approach to external recruitment is direct applications, which are submitted in the front office of a company unsolicited. Direct applications provide the company a pool of potential employees to meet its future needs. This method is best suited for filling in entry level and unskilled positions. There is a direct relationship between the reputation of the company and the number of applications it receives. For example, organizations such as Coca-Cola, IBM, Infosys, and Harvard University receive thousands of applications every year. There is a considerable reduction in the costs involved in hiring an employee as most of the information required is available in the applications. This also increases the probability of hiring the very best employees. Companies use software to match job specifications with resume information and the process takes very little time.

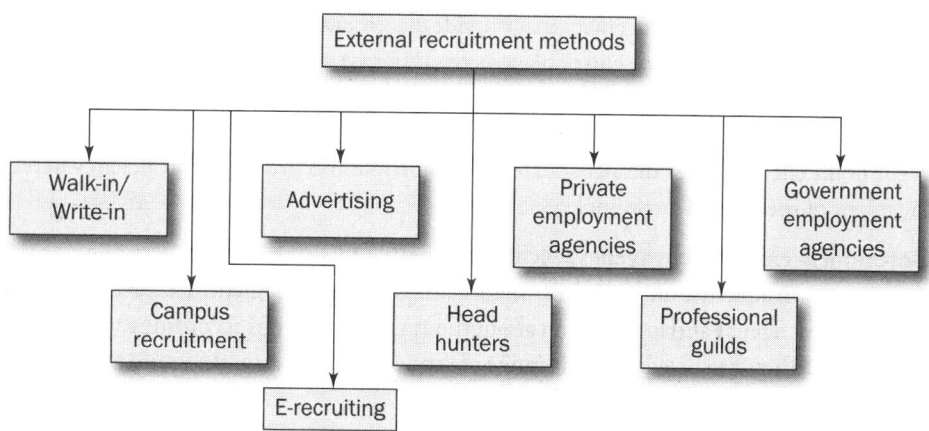

FIGURE 6.2 Methods of external recruitment

Advertising   Another common method of recruitment is advertising. Advertising can vary from a simple ad in a classified page to an elaborate media campaign through radio/television/Internet to attract applicants. While advertising in the newspapers, the geographical locations and availability of workforce in the local market need to be taken into consideration. Advertising in business-related journals/magazines is a common method. The higher the position in the organization and the more specialized the skills sought, the more widely dispersed the advertisement is likely to be. The size of the advertisement, position of the advertisement, colours used, choice of words, and information provided together attract the prospective employee. Today, almost all leading newspapers including *The Economic Times, The Hindu, The Times of India, The Indian Express*, and *Employment News* carry special supplements that advertise job vacancies.

First, a good advertisement will visualize the type of applicant one is trying to recruit. Second, the advantage and benefits that the employee would experience by joining the company needs to be highlighted. Third, the coverage area, whether local or national, has to be decided.

Some companies also give blind advertisements, that is, where there is no identification of the organization except a postbox number or the address of a consulting firm that acts as an intermediary between the applicant and the organization. Large organizations usually do not use blind advertisements.

Most experts agree that advertising through any media (including the Internet) should contain the following information:

- The job content (primary tasks and responsibilities)
- A realistic description of working conditions, particularly if they are unusual
- The location of the job
- The compensation, including the fringe benefits
- Job specifications (e.g., education, experience)
- Intended recipient of the application

Private employment agencies   Many companies use private employment agencies for identifying potential workers. These are agencies that provide placement services and charge either the employer or the candidate or both at the end of placement. These are most effective when the organization has difficulty in finding or searching for a potential candidate or when the particular skill or expertise is scarce in the market. The specializations of these agencies enhance their capacity to interpret the needs of the clients to seek out particular types of people and to develop proficiency in recognizing the talent of specialized personnel.

Government employment agency/exchange   Earlier this exchange was very popular as it was the main agency to advertise and have information on public employment. The prospective candidates register in this agency and information about the availability of jobs according to their qualifications is informed. They also provide a wide range of services such as counselling and assistance in getting information about labour markets and wage rates.

Campus recruitment   Campus recruitment offers an excellent source for professional and managerial positions. This method is very popular and successful. The candidates thus selected also proved to be quite successful in their careers and jobs. The philosophy in this procedure is catch them young. It is this scope to identify potential candidates and the adaptability of candidates to be moulded in the desired way that makes this method a highly successful one.

- The recruiting process should begin much before the academic year ends. A good presentation about the background of the company and profiles of the jobs need to be prepared by the recruiters. Most of the educational institutions, particularly professional colleges, have placement officers who coordinate with the recruiter and provide opportunity for pre-placement talks. This pre-placement talk usually attracts the candidate and encourages them to file in applications. Normally, this is followed by an interview in the organization before the job is offered.

- The method is undoubtedly popular and effective. There is a wide range and pool of applicants to choose from. Before making the presentation, the curriculum inputs/skills present in the candidates can be assessed and those that match the job requirements alone may be considered. Since the applicants are young, they can be moulded with the help of strong induction and training programmes.

Head hunters These are also professional agencies that maintain a database of executive positions. They are hired by the employers to find particular executive talent. These firms recommend persons of high calibre for almost all functional areas of management, engineering, and other skilled positions.

Military It is a good source of potential candidates in various fields. Candidates who retire early from the military service would like to be gainfully employed again and serve the society. In this sense, the military is a great source of potential.

Voluntary organizations Some voluntary organizations or clubs maintain some database about handicapped, widowed persons, old people, retired people, etc., which provides a pool of applicants at one source.

Professional organizations or guilds These organizations are more restricted to a single profession or a craft and association, or membership is restricted to people belonging to the same profession. A prospective employer may seek the help or guidance of these associations while looking for specific type of personnel.

Temporary help This trend is not yet popular in India, but the method involved is where few people belonging to diverse backgrounds and skills come together and form an association, and as and when a requirement arises in one or more organizations on a temporary basis, people go there, do the needful, and return.

Electronic recruiting This involves recruiting through the Internet.

Best Method of External Recruitment

It has been observed that companies use different methods or a combination of these methods and each one of them has been found to be varyingly successful. Various criteria have been used to assess the effectiveness of methods such as costs per hire, number of resumes, time lapse between recruitment and placement, interview ratio, applicant performance, and job tenure or turnover. Some companies found that informal methods such as walk-ins and employee referrals were successful, whereas some others had a history of recruiting from campuses. Some companies also excessively relied on the Internet. If a particular method is able to attract the largest pool of applicants, it is considered as the most effective one.

Much depends upon the recruiter's skills as well. The recruiter must possess strong interpersonal skills, knowledge of the organization, and enthusiasm and passion for the organization. However, the success of any recruiting agency is more dependent on the job characteristics themselves. College graduates do place importance on fringe benefits, pay, and the nature of the work. Recruiters need to consider these factors before adapting any methods.

Exhibit 6.1 discusses the global dimension of recruitment strategy.

EXHIBIT 6.1 Global dimension

There are a large number of companies that are multinational in nature and some portion of their business and profits is derived from overseas operations. Companies such as IBM, Exxon, Coca-cola, McDonald's, Infosys, and Wipro derive a substantial percentage of their revenue from overseas business. However, the recruiting strategy in these companies for global placement with few exceptions needs aligning between HR planning and strategic planning for international ventures. The competition for talent is global. The shifts in the economy have identified shortage of skilled workers around the world. All the fields including engineering, banks, consumer products, transport, etc., are experiencing shortage of skilled workers.

A few years back the search for employees meant looking at developing countries such as India, China, and Thailand. Now, developing nations are also concerned about brain drain and are making vigorous efforts to attract and retain local talent. For instance, job fairs are held in Ireland to attract the Irish diaspora in other countries, and Singapore offers a bonus for people who decide to return home from abroad. Such campaigns are evident around the world starting from Zurich, Paris, and Frankfurt to Hong Kong and Tokyo.

Being an American executive is not the first choice for people in every country. European companies prefer their top executives to be from Europe. According to Sharon Voros, author of Leadership Presence (Adams Media, 1999) and The Road to CEO (Adams Media, 2000), the most desirable of candidates are 'Americanized Europeans', that is, Europeans with MBAs from Wharton, Harvard, or some other prestigious US university and a stint with a firm such as McKinsey & Co. or Bain. Don Utroska, a partner with Chicago recruiter Dieckmann & Associates, says, 'Companies don't want to risk losing revenues and customers, and they feel Americans are less attuned to cultural issues and local customs.'

At the same time, Australian firms are doing their utmost to retain their employees. A study by Mercer Cullen Egan Dell found that 84% of organizations surveyed in 1999 offered some form of flexible work practice, up from 56% in 1998 and 32% in 1995 to increase their attractiveness as an 'employer of choice'. Mercer Cullen Egan Dell's HR information services team leader Merrilyn Earl said, 'Employers have to be able to tailor working arrangements to suit the needs of their key individuals—or risk losing them.'

Likewise, Asian companies are concerned about keeping their own employees while attracting talent from abroad.

We all agree that firms need to offer the kind of financial incentives comparable to that gained elsewhere, only then Global recruiters do their task of attracting and relocating the right people. People require not only the necessary skills, but also the capability of adapting to different cultures.

Certain conditions, such as volatile environment and political unrest in the host country, which affect overseas operations, make recruitment quite unpredictable. Almost all HRM functions such as staffing, performance management, reward systems, and employee development are more difficult and unpredictable in overseas operations because of the practice of differential methods in different places. For example, within the domain

(Contd)

EXHIBIT 6.1   (Contd)

of rewards and compensation, issues related to family, housing, insurance, and medical reimbursement tend to complicate the HRM function. One study identified the critical issues affecting the planning and recruitments aspects of international HRM (Dowling 1989). The major challenges were as follows:

- Identifying top managerial talent early in the process
- Identifying criteria for success in overseas assignments
- Motivating employees to take overseas assignments
- Establishing a stronger connection between strategic planning and HR planning

NIIT in India and many national and international companies have adopted online recruitment. Posting a resume and applying for a post to a prospective employer has become very easy with the help of new technology. Some companies may benefit from this process and may utilize this as an initial screening process.

Another related process of global recruitment is virtual interviews. Employers use video conferencing or telephones for the purpose of recruitment. Such use of technology makes applying for foreign firms financially viable for prospective employees, who might otherwise have to travel overseas for a job interview. The US has already begun to use this technology to put American employers in touch with candidates in London, Toronto, Vancouver, Mumbai, etc.

In the more industrial parts of the world, international recruitment companies such as Korn/Ferry and Heidrick & Struggles International Inc. can be found adopting this process.

RECRUITMENT PRACTICES IN INDIA

This section discusses recruitment practices in companies operating in India (Exhibits 6.2 and 6.3).

EXHIBIT 6.2   Recruitment practices at Google and Infosys

A recent survey by *Business Week* noted that Google was the number two choice among students as a place to begin their career. This is an incredible accomplishment for any firm, more significantly for a firm less than ten years old. All of the brand recognition around Google has been developed without employing any of the formal advertising approaches that many other firms rely upon. Google's recruitment process is based largely on a series of interviews with a series of different interviewers. The interview topics at Google cover a range of questions from programming and general logic puzzles to personality checks. Google is known for its intense interview process. While Google does have some outrageous benefits and management practices, what truly establishes their brand is their ability to get their management practices talked about in such a wide range of media outlets.

Infosys reportedly has one of the best recruitment practices. The company attracts the best talent from across the world, and has a selection process, considered to be one of the toughest in the industry. All the selected candidates are required to go through an intensive 14-week training programme. All the employees undergo training every year, and some select employees are trained at the Infosys Leadership Institute to take on higher responsibilities in the company. Infosys was one of the first companies to offer employee stock ownership plans (ESOPs) to its employees. The company follows a variable compensation structure, wherein an employee's compensation depends on the performance of the individual, the team, and the company.

Source: Best Recruitment Practices, http://toostep.com/insight/best-recruitment-practices, accessed on 21 September 2011.

EXHIBIT 6.3   Recruitment planning at ICICI

Recruitment Planning on the Basis of Budget

- The manpower planning process for the year would commence with the company's budgeting activity. The respective functional heads would submit the manpower requirements of their respective functions/ departments to the board of directors as part of the annual business plan. The requirement would be submitted after detailed discussions with the head of the HR function. The requirement would be supported with detailed notes on the projected figures on direct and indirect salary costs for each position.
- A copy of the duly approved manpower plan would be forwarded by the HR department to different divisions for further action during the course of the year. The annual budget would specify the manpower requirements of the entire organization, at different levels, for various functions/departments, at different geographical locations, and the timing of the individual requirements. It would also specify the requirement budget, that is, the cost allotted towards the recruitment of the budgeted staff and the replacement of the existing employees. The manpower plan would also clearly indicate the exact time at which the incumbent should be on board, so that the regional HR has adequate notice to minimize the time lapses involved.
- The regional HR departments would undertake the planning activity and necessary preparations in advance for the anticipated requirements, as monthly and quarterly activities on the basis of the approved budget and estimated separations and replacements.
- The vacancies sought to be filled or being filled would always be within the approved annual manpower budget. No recruitment process would be initiated without the formal concurrence of the regional HR head under any circumstance. The regional HR head would also have the responsibility to monitor the appointments being considered at any point of time with respect to the duly approved manpower budgets.

Review of Manpower Plans and Additional Manpower

- Review of manpower budgets would take place on a quarterly basis. In the event of any new position or any deviations to the original plan, details of the positions may be forwarded to the Vice-President–HR along with the adequate supporting information. The recommendations would normally require formal approval of the Managing Director (MD). Alternatively, Vice-President–HR may record the summary of his discussion with the MD, and the latter's approval on the recommendations, and take a final decision on the recommendations.

Sourcing of Suitable Candidates

The regional HR would tap various sources/channels for getting the right candidate. Depending on the nature of the position/grade, number of candidates required, and any other relevant factor, the regional HR would use any of the following sources:

- Existing database (active application data bank)
- Employee referral as per any company scheme that may be approved from time to time
- Advertisement in the print and electronic media, company's websites, and job sites
- Placement agencies (particularly for positions of managers and above)
- Headhunting firms, particularly for senior, specialist, and critical positions
- Direct recruitment from campuses/academic institutes
- Job websites
- Any other appropriate source

The norms for using any of the sources would not be rigid. Number, criticality, and urgency of the positions, confidentiality requirements, relative efficacy, and cost considerations would play a role in the choice of the appropriate sourcing mechanism.

(Contd)

EXHIBIT 6.3   (Contd)

Advertisements

- All recruitment advertisements (in any form and any medium) would always conform to the KLI compliance norms, and would not be released by any department or branch without the approval of the Vice-President–HR. Based on the specifics of each position, the regional HR may obtain assistance from the company's marketing department and/or any external advertising agencies for the preparation of the contents for recruitment advertisements. Key features of the positions as notified by the functional heads would normally form part of the advertisement text.
- The media for advertisement would depend on the level of the position being considered and the urgency of the requirement.
- The media for advertisement would be broadly specified as local/national newspapers, business magazines, and Internet sites.

Placement agencies/headhunting agencies

- Based on the vacancies, freshers suitable for different positions may be recruited from time to time from academic institutes of appropriate standard/reputation/grade, in requisite numbers and at the compensation/stipend amounts would be formally approved by the Vice-President–HR. Plans for such recruitment need specific special approval of Vice-President–HR. Norms regarding the identification of the appropriate institutes, constitution of the selection panels, timings of the recruitment, number of candidates to be recruited for different positions, choice of the appropriate selection process, and the tools thereof, would be decided by the regional HR head in consultation with the Vice-President–HR.

Source: http://www.oppapers.com/essays/Recruitment-In-Icici/503722, accessed on 21 September 2011.

RETENTION OF EMPLOYEES

After the process of recruitment, a major challenge being faced by managers is retaining the talent. In the last decade, job-hopping has become a common phenomenon. Several factors are enticing the employees and particularly when they possess rare skills or expertise, they are at an advantage. More than the costs involved in recruiting, employer loyalty is also an expectation from the employee. A demonstration of loyalty to current employees can prevent the loss of mobile employees during the tough times and their continued desire to stay even when they find opportunities to jump ship.

Companies should focus on the following aspects, while attempting to retain employees.

Plan ahead   Even though human resource planning identifies and anticipates future vacancies, at times some employees may try to leave the organization. The HR manager has to be sensitive to such moves and become conscious of the job requirement. The employee may be counselled not to leave or the search for a new candidate can start as soon as the company gets indication of somebody leaving. We may consider not only those who are looking for employment, but also those who are employed and fit our needs well could be counselled to make a job move.

Clarity in job requirements   Work analysis and design specify job descriptions and job specifications. Hence, searching for a fit candidate for an existing job will be an easy task and only clarity with regard to job descriptions need to be in place. If it is a new position, a draft job description has to be prepared fully describing all the tasks, responsibilities, and minimum necessary requirements in terms of education and experience.

> ■ ■ ■
> A big selection mistake is choosing a candidate who qualifies in several of the requirements, but is weak in essential responsibilities.

Identify a good source of recruitment In today's scenario, multiple sources of recruitment are available. Keeping in view the history of the organization and the earlier practices vis-à-vis recruitment, a particular method may be adopted. Whichever method has proved to be successful in the past may be followed or a new method such as employee referral may be introduced. One of the more novel approaches is to undertake a direct mail marketing campaign.

Screening and interviews By whichever method the candidates are identified, an initial screening would definitely prove to be fruitful. This eliminates not only undesirable candidates, but also reduces wastage of time. After the initial screening, prospective candidates may be called for an interview. While making the selection of a candidate, not only the qualifications, but also other behavioural aspects such as being a team player, willingness to work under pressure, flexibility, and communication skills may also be considered. A big selection mistake is choosing a candidate who qualifies in several of the requirements, but is weak in essential responsibilities.

Provide challenging work Research shows that individuals who successfully accomplish mentally challenging work are more satisfied and happy with their jobs. They are less likely to look for employment elsewhere. The manager may spend some time with the employees trying to identify what is motivating them and provide the necessary training and support system in executing the tasks. By keeping the promotional line clear, employees may also plan to reach them.

Focus on compensation and working conditions Salary should always be commensurate with the contribution of the individual and competitive in the existing labour market. Other perks and benefits offered along with salary also attract employees. Good infrastructure, support systems, etc., go a long way in attracting and retaining an employee.

In essence, recruitment is a very crucial process as an incompetent pool of employees will be detrimental to organization. Careful planning and judicious moves are required at every step in the process of recruitment.

SUMMARY

The recruitment scenario has undergone complete change in the wake of various factors affecting the organizations. From being a staff function, it has now become a strategic priority of organizations to attract and retain the best talent in the market. However, competition is having its toll on recruitment, as organizations are competing with each other to attract a tal-ented pool of professionals. The process of recruitment has become more time sensitive and e-recruitment has become a common phenomenon.

The chapter discussed the processes, methods, constraints, and challenges of recruitment, and various strategies for retaining the best employees.

■ ■ ■ EXERCISES

Multiple Choice Questions

1. Which of the following HR functions is the basic element of recruitment?

(a) Attract the applicants for the particular post.
(b) Select the best one among all applicants.
(c) Train the recruits as per organizational re-

quirements.

    (d) Fire the non-performing employees.

2. Which one of the following is not included in training and development?

    (a) Orientation

    (b) Career development

    (c) Employee education

    (d) Recruitment

3. What measure is required to ensure effective recruitment?

    (a) Keep a large pool of potential candidates to select the best out of them.

    (b) Address personal needs of applicants.

    (c) Meet economies of scale for an organization.

    (d) Clearly understand organizational goals.

4. The best hiring occurs when the goals of which of the following are consistent with each other?

    (a) HR managers, finance managers

    (b) Head office, branch

    (c) Organization, individual

    (d) Lower managers, top managers

5. After the recruitment process, a major challenge faced by managers is

    (a) to retain intellectual capital

    (b) to motivate employees to take overseas assignments

    (c) to attract more candidates

    (d) none of these

Fill in the Blanks

1. Organizations provide attractive salaries, fringe benefits, and career development opportunities to their employees in order to _____.

2. The basic goal of recruitment is _____.

3. _____ and _____ are successful informal methods of recruitment.

4. _____ refers to the source for identifying suitable candidates from among the current employees in an organization. Many large organizations attempt to develop their own employees for senior positions.

5. _____ and judicious moves are required at every step in the recruitment process.

Concept Review Questions

1. Identify the emerging trends in recruitment.

2. Analyse the recruitment challenges faced by recruitment managers in IT firms.

3. Discuss the role of recruitment in an integrative HR Strategy.

4. Discuss the role of e-recruitment in the overall recruitment strategy of organizations.

5. Discuss the role of competency planning and mapping with the recruitment.

Project Work

1. Perform a role-play based on one of the case studies discussed in this chapter.

2. Study the recruitment practices of a company and prepare a critical report.

3. Analyse the emerging trends in e-recruitment and prepare the report detailing the challenges and opportunities for the organization.

4. Conduct an interview of the recruitment manager of an IT firm on the recruitment practices in his/her firm and prepare a critical report.

■ ■ ■ | REFERENCES

Becker, B., Huselid, M., and Ulrich, D. 2001, *The HR Scorecard*, Harvard Business School Press, Boston.

Bernardin, H.J. 1989, 'Innovative approaches to personnel selection and performance appraisal', *Journal of Management Systems*, 1, pp. 25–36.

Fowler, E.M. 1989, 'Recruiters refocusing techniques', *New York Times*, November 18, p. 35; Savill, P.A. 1995, 'HR and Inova reengineer recruitment process', *Personnel Journal*, 75(6), June, pp. 109–14.

Golden, K.A. and Ramanujam, V. 1985, 'Between a dream and a nightmare: On the integration of human resource management and strategic business planning processes', *Human Resource Management*, 34, pp. 429–52.

Hanigan, M. 1987, 'Campus recruiters upgrade their pitch', *Personnel Administrator*, 32(56).

Heneman, H.G. and Sandver, M.G. 1977, 'Markov analysis in human resource administration: Applications and limitations', *Academy of Management Review*, 15, pp. 535–42.

Hooper, J.A. and Catelanello, R.E. 1981, 'Markov analysis applied to forecasting technical personnel', *Human Resource Planning*, 4, pp. 41–47.

Jordan, Ken 1997, 'Play Fair and Square When Hiring from Within', *HR Magazine*, January, pp. 49–51.

Mullins, T. 1994, 'How to Land a Job', *Psychology Today*, September–October, pp. 12–13.

Richey, B., Bernardin, H.J., Tyler, C., and McKinney, N. 2001, 'The effect of arbitration program characteristics on applicants' intentions toward potential employers', *Journal of Applied Psychology*, 86, pp. 1006–13.

Robert J. Grossman, 'HR in Asia', *HR Magazine*, July, p. 106.

Turban, D.B. and Greening, D.W. 1997, 'Corporate social performance and organizational atractiveness to prospective employers', *Academy of Management Journal*, 40(3), June, pp. 658–72.

Tyler, Kathryn 1996, 'Employees can help recruit new talent', *HR Magazine*, September, p. 60.

Wellner, P.F. and Maki, W.R. 1981, 'A case history of a manpower planning model', *Human Resource Planning*, 4, pp. 129–38.

Recruitment and Retention in Sitel India

CASE STUDY 1

Sitel India started its operations in India during the year 2000. The company was established as a joint venture between Sitel Corp., USA and the Tata Group. Sitel operates in over 20+ countries worldwide, with over 35,000 employees across various locations. The Indian operations of the organization began with one centre in Andheri East, Mumbai. Sitel is predominantly a voice-based international BPO that operates in the following verticals:

• Internet service provider (ISP)
• Telecom
• Information technology (IT)
• Financial needs analysis (FNA)

The year 2000 witnessed the entry of a number of BPOs in India, which included leading organizations such as Genpact, WNS, and IBM Daksh. The employees recruited by Sitel had to work 24x7 in various shifts. Initially, the company faced cultural resistance from employees, especially women coming from traditional families, on working in night shifts. The company faced the following HR issues:

• Issues in talent acquisition (recruitment)
– Recruiting employees who are willing to work in night shifts
– Identifying employees with neutral accent
– Recruiting employees with good English language communication skills, pronunciation skills, and fluency.
• Issues in employee retention

– Early attrition issues (0–6 months) due to various factors
– Employees leaving on health grounds due to work in night shifts
– Employees leaving for higher education
– Engineering graduates leaving for employment in IT sector
– Married women leaving for various reasons such as pressure/opposition from families

After stabilizing its operations, the company recruited Safir Adeni as its chief executive officer (CEO) for its Indian operations. Adeni had business foresight and could perceive that all other CEOs were aggressively expanding their footprint in various other Indian cities for two critical reasons: (a) Mumbai was getting saturated in terms of talent availability, (b) They wanted to project to the client a pan-India image, as that would help them attract larger contracts for multi-site operations, a growing trend. Therefore, the company started its operations in other Indian cities such as Hyderabad, Chennai, and Gurgaon in a span of one year.

During the India Leadership Summit in the year 2010, the top management wanted to venture into the domestic BPO space as the business was picking up and a number of players who were in international operations, especially the clients in the following verticals, started expanding their operations:

• Banking
• Insurance
• Telecom

The strategy behind expansion into the domestic space was two pronged: (a) To leverage the expertise gained by the organization in serving international clients, and offer same quality of service to domestic customers, (b) To optimally leverage office space on 24×7 basis, as the operations were predominantly in night shifts, that is, after 5.30 PM whereas the infrastructure remained idle during day time.

The BPO also witnessed several organizational level changes, as the Tata group offloaded the equity in Indian operations of Sitel to Sitel US under buyback arrangement for $100 million. A few months down the line, Client Logic, another US-based leading BPO had started sending feelers to Sitel US for a global merger, and after prolonged negotiations, the deal was concluded in early 2011. The merged entity has presence in over 35+ countries with a headcount of 65,000 employees.

Coming back to the HR scenario of Sitel India, the company witnessed a rise in recruitment and employee retention issues after the expansion of Indian operations. The CEO constituted an action group of site directors and site HR leaders to come out with an action plan to address the HR issues. After deliberation, the committee made the following recommendations to the CEO:

- Talent acquisition strategies
- Categorize the candidates coming into the recruitment funnel into three broad categories, that is, ready to recruit, trainable, and reject.
- Avoid recruitment of the BE/BTech candidates for non-IT/ISP processes, as the attrition levels of engineering graduates was high in other processes.
- Emphasize more on employee-referral driven recruitment as the attrition and hiring cost from this channel was the lowest.
- Leverage on trainable and reject list for hiring for domestic processes.

- Employee retention strategies
- Organizing Milap programme for employee interaction during training stage. The initiative consisted of departmental SPOCs (single point of contacts), that is, HR, training, process, administration, and information technology (IT) teams interfacing with the employees on a weekly basis, identifying the issues, and solving most of them on the spot.
- Coaching and mentoring for employees on on-the-job training (OJT) for a period of six months with tenured employees.
- Competency mapping for employees through the performance management systems, and learning initiatives to groom them according to their developmental aspirations.
- Management trainee programme, for internally grooming the front line managers, that is, the team leaders.
- Tie-up with universities such as ICFAI for MBA programmes, and provide for 50% course fee reimbursement as an employee growth and retention measure
- Cross-process training and job-rotation for tenured employees
- Online Milap, a virtual employee contact programme for resolution of employee issues within the turnaround time (TAT)

These strategies have not only reduced the issues in recruitment, but also improved the employee retention levels in the organization.

Questions
1. Analyse the employee recruitment issues and strategies of Sitel India
2. Discuss the employee attrition issues and the retention measures taken by Sitel.
3. Analyse the issues faced by Sitel vis-à-vis those faced by other BPOs in India.

Recruitment and Retention in a Medium-sized Company

CASE STUDY 2

A medium-sized company with a turnover of around ₹1,000 crore is into manufacture of semi-conductors and has a plant each in Pune and Goa, respectively. The corporate office is located at Mumbai. The company is a private limited company and the promoters hold the majority of the stake. The organization has recently recruited a new HR head, Stanley Joseph, to revamp the HR strategies.

After reviewing the existing status, he decided to focus on the recruitment policy, since he rightly identified that attracting the right manpower is the first step towards building competent human assets for the organization. The new HR policy is as follows:

- **Purpose:** The purpose is to ensure availability of adequate resources to attain better productivity and profitability.
- **Coverage:** It covers all levels in the organization for recruitment of permanent and temporary employees.
- **Policy:**
- Recruitment of permanent staff at XYZ shall be made as per the manpower budget prepared every year or employee requisition duly approved by the chief executive officer (CEO).
- An annual plan has to be prepared by all departments and units and sent to the HR department in the corporate office.
- The respective project leaders, in coordination with the HR department, would procure the resources required for various projects in accordance with the annual plan.
- For any requirement that is not a part of the formal plan, the concerned project leader has to forward the additional requirements to the HR head, who would then submit it with his inputs to the CEO for approval.
- As regards recruitment for any position, the order of priority would be as under:
  - Experienced people within the organization (internal resources)
  - Candidates referred by the employees or employee referrals (in case of recruitment, employees concerned would be given monetary rewards, after three months of joining of the new recruit, as motivation)
  - Open recruitment, that is, recruitment through advertisement, etc.
- The policy guidelines regarding recruitment of temporary staff are as under:
  - The CEO would authorize the recruitment of staff on temporary basis.
  - The period of recruitment of temporary staff cannot exceed six months or the duration of project, whichever is earlier. However, on a case-to-case basis.

- A committee consisting of the concerned departmental head or Project Leader, HR head, and Vice-President–Operations would conduct the selection process to carry on the recruitment.
- All employees with prior work experience will be on probation for a period of one year, while new recruits will be on probation for a period of one and half years. Probationary experience of employees will be considered for the purposes of performance appraisal and promotion. The probation period can be extended, based on the recommendations of the appraising and reviewing authorities. Employees would be confirmed in the service of the company after successful completion of the probation period.
- The company's recruitment policy aims at attracting and retaining the best available talent in the industry so that the appropriate quality and number of employees are available at the right time.
- **Objectives:** The objectives of the recruitment policy are as follows:
- To ensure that all positions identified in the organization are staffed by persons with the skills, knowledge, experience, and qualifications required to perform them effectively
- To provide career opportunities for deserving personnel in line with their skills and potential
- To infuse fresh talent, skills, and competencies in the organization to help enhance its capabilities
- **Manpower planning:** Manpower plans will be prepared annually for each department by respective department heads along with the annual budgeting process. The budget year for the purpose would be the company's financial year. The parameters to be considered for compilation of manpower include the following:
- Level of business operations
- Staffing requirements in terms of quality and numbers
- Existing staffing strength
- Planned promotions/transfers

The CEO will approve the final manpower plan, while the HR head will be responsible for monitoring and implementation of the approved plan.

- **Manpower sources:** For each of the positions identified and depending on the type of vacancy and skills required, the appropriate source of suitable personnel required for the position will be determined. The recruitment sources include:

– *Direct recruitment*
- Advertisement in newspapers, magazines, etc.
- Universities and educational institutions for entry-level professional positions where no experience is necessary
- Display on company notice board (if considered appropriate)

– *Placement consultants*
– *Employee gets employee scheme*: The existing employee can refer names of candidates for various positions being displayed on the notice board. If the candidate is selected, he or she will get rewarded with a one-time cash award of ₹2,500.

Questions

1. Critically analyse the recruitment policy of the company.
2. Is the organization tapping all the channels for recruitment?
3. What are the other channels of recruitment?
4. Suggest the required changes, if any, in the recruitment policy of the company.

Premier Chemicals

Premier Chemicals is a ₹2,000-crore company headquartered at Ahmedabad.

The company is into manufacturing of bulk drugs as well as formulations, and markets its products across the country as well as countries in Europe and South Asia.

The company is traditionally run and is fully controlled by the promoters. However, with the advent of a competitive environment, the company felt the need for revamping its operations and restructuring the organizational structure too.

The chief executive officer (CEO) in his meeting with the Vice-President–Operations, Vice-President–HR, and other departmental heads discussed and approved the revised organizational structure. The Vice-President–HR was given a period of three months for completing the revamping/recruitment process.

The Vice-President–HR engaged an HR consultant and assigned them the following tasks:

- Mapping the existing business profile and strategy of the organization
- Mapping the competencies of the existing manpower
- Reviewing the requirements of the existing manpower vis-à-vis the new organizational structure
- Identifying the competency and manpower gaps
- Retraining and redeploying of manpower
- Recruitment of additional manpower
- Preparing of a position-wise succession plan and a matching career plan for the employees

The company recorded an average performance of only 17% increase in sales and profit as against the envisaged target of 40%. The CEO in his annual review meeting with departmental heads reviewed the situation, and during the course of brainstorming, they identified the following:

- Some of the employees who did not possess the required level of competencies were recommended for promotion by the HR consultant and were promoted by the HR department with a view to complying with the recruitment and staffing target period.
- A few of the new recruits were found to be leaking confidential information to the competitors. A subsequent investigation revealed that some of them were actually implanted by the competitors.

Questions

1. What was wrong with the revamping strategy of the company?
2. What went wrong with the recruitment process?
3. Did the company take the right step by engaging the HR consultant?
4. Who should be held accountable for the organizational debacle?

Employee Selection

INTRODUCTION

After an organization identifies the vacancies to be filled, the process of recruitment begins and a pool of applications is obtained. Selection is the process of choosing the appropriate candidate from the obtained applications to match the requirements of the job. Hence, it is a process of matching the skills of the individual and the requirements of the job. The selection process plays a pivotal role in the functioning of the organization. Care has to be taken in hiring decisions, as these decisions affect not only the career of the individual, but also the future of the organization. The fluid nature of employment that Atkinson (1984) described as more evident in the 1980s implies that the selection process requires greater thought and emphasis because, although employees may work with the organizations for increasingly shorter periods of time, the quantity and quality of output required will only keep growing.

> ■ ■ ■
> Selection is the process of choosing the appropriate candidate from the obtained applications to match the requirements of the job.

STEPS IN SELECTION PROCESS

The selection of candidates typically follows a standardized process beginning with an initial screening interview and concluding with the final employment decision. A typical selection process (Figure 7.1) involves the following steps:

- Preliminary screening interview
- Completion of application form
- Employment tests, interview, or other methods of evaluation
- Medical examinations
- Background investigations, references, and medical check-up
- Final decision to employ or hire

> ■ ■ ■
> The selection of candidates typically follows a standardized process beginning with an initial screening interview and concluding with the final employment decision.

The purpose of the selection process is to select the most suitable candidate who would meet the requirements of the job. Such a person is selected after eliminating the unsuitable applicants through successive stages. Even though these steps are identified, the order and emphasis on each of these aspects may differ from company to company. Some give more importance to tests, some emphasize not just one but two or three rounds of interviews, some rely on background or reference checks, some others on graphology, etc. However, let us examine the process of selection with reference to the steps identified.

Step I: Preliminary Screening Interview

A large number of applications may be pooled by the organization at the end of the recruitment process. The larger the pool, the wider will be the choice for the organization. It is not essential for the organization to invite all the candidates for the interview or for group discussion or testing. A preliminary screening or an initial interview may be undertaken so that some of the candidates may be eliminated in the first step. The criteria for elimination may differ from job to job and from company to company. For example, only first class graduates will be called for interview or candidates with minimum three years of experience only will be considered, etc.

At times, companies conduct campus interviews and give a pre-placement presentation about the company. At the end of the process, interested students apply and a preliminary screening interview may be conducted then and there, and a short list of candidates may be prepared, to be considered for the final interview.

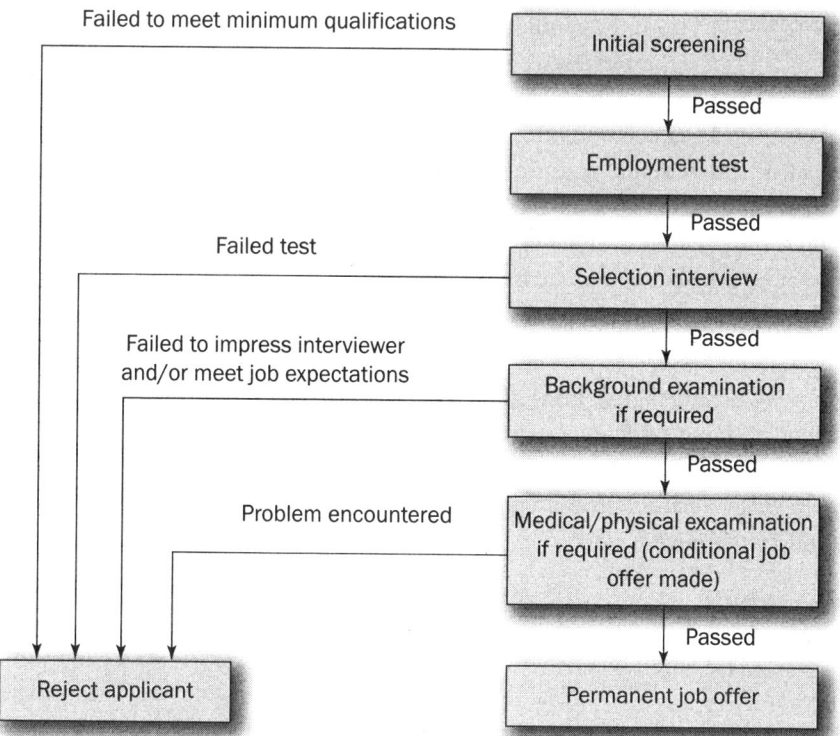

FIGURE 7.1 Selection process

Sometimes in an organization, a junior manager may be assigned the responsibility of conducting the preliminary interview. He/she may elicit information on some important aspects such as age, education, experience, pay, aptitude, location choice, etc. This usually helps the organization to screen out the misfits.

At the end of this step, a selection ratio may be worked out from the total number of applicants and the number of candidates to be considered for interview, with reference to the number of posts to be filled.

Selection ratio = Total number of applicants/Number of posts to be filled

Some of the criteria to be considered for screening of applications are as follows:

- Personality characteristics
- Language proficiency
- Experience

- Technical knowledge
- Aptitude
- Other factors

Since preliminary interview is the first point of contact for the candidate with the company, the interviewer must conduct the process very smoothly and courteously.

Those candidates who are chosen at the end of Step I may be required to fill an application form.

Step II: Application Blank or Form

An application blank is a comprehensive document that elicits information from the candidate in a systematic, codified manner. It is a useful device for an interview as it provides all the basic and necessary information including areas of interest, extracurricular activities, etc. It is also a convenient device for circulating information about the applicant to appropriate members of the management and is useful for storing information for later reference.

Most of the organizations have a standardized format, which elicits broadly the basic information about the candidate. Some of the formats may be too detailed or descriptive, while some others may be brief but comprehensive. Information is usually collected in the following lines.

- *Biographical data*: Name, father's name, place of birth, age, sex, identification marks, and marital status
- *Educational background*: Education completed, degrees awarded, grades obtained, year of passing, training undergone, awards, distinctions obtained, any other diploma or related course completed
- *Past experience data*: Previous employment, position held, salary drawn, nature of work, and reasons for shifting of work
    - *Other information*: Hobbies, interests, participation in sports, participation in NCC, NSS, or other voluntary services
    - *Reference checks*: Names of two or more people who can certify the suitability of the candidate

An application blank is a brief history sheet of an employee's background and can be used for future reference. The data submitted should help predict the candidate's chances of being successful in his/her job. The information sought should be relevant to the objective of selection. To ensure truthfulness, the application carries a threat of discharge at any time after employment if the information provided is false.

At the senior level, recruitment advertisements are released through various publications or alternatively, placement consultants hunt for suitable candidates. The shortlisted candidates have three levels of interviews, that is, at the first stage with the placement consultants, at the second stage with technical/project/regional heads, and finally with the HR functionaries to assess the suitability of compensation to the shortlisted candidate.

Weighted Application Blank (WAB)

■ ■ ■
WAB reduces employee turnover and helps the management to place an individual in the appropriate position.

Certain forms of application may be especially prepared by the companies to generate weighted scores. Any job would require a few skills or personal factors that directly influence the performance of the job. These are identified and candidates who have earlier experience in them are given extra points during the application screening. This process facilitates speeding up of the recruitment and selection processes. For example, the job of a sales representative would require good communication skills, young age and dynamic personality, and high levels of mobility and adjustment. Candidates who have undergone training in communication skills and are willing to travel would score higher than those who do not satisfy these criteria. It takes time to develop the necessary format for each job. However, it provides good data for scrutiny. It reduces employee turnover and helps the management to place an individual in the appropriate position.

In general, an application blank introduces the individual to the company and also provides a relative ranking of the candidate with respect to others.

Step III: Use of Selection Methods

Let us discuss use of selection methods in this section.

Employment Tests

As organizations become complex, the number and variety of jobs that employees have to perform also increase. To choose appropriate candidates from a pool of candidates, it is necessary to use tests, which are objective and multipurpose.

A standardized test usually satisfies the following criteria:

- *Standardization*: Standardization implies uniformity of procedure in administering and scoring the test. The test constructor provides detailed instructions regarding the exact materials employed, time limits, oral instruction, preliminary demonstrations, and any other detail about handling a testing situation. An important aspect of standardization is the inclusion of 'norms'. Norms refer to average or normal performance. The raw scores obtained from a test can be interpreted against the backdrop of norms and the performance of the candidate can be assessed. A psychological test should satisfy the criteria of standardization in terms of prescribing the conditions of administration and providing norms to interpret the raw scores.

■ ■ ■
As organizations become complex, the number and variety of jobs that employees have to perform also increase.

- *Reliability*: The second criterion for a good test is 'reliability', that is, how good is this test? Reliability refers to the consistency of scores obtained, irrespective of to whom or when the test is administered. This is inbuilt in the construction of statements in the test with a statistical procedure.

Reliability is usually stated in the form of an index in the manual. Reliability index is an indication of repeatability.

- *Validity*: Another criterion that has to be met is 'validity'. Validity refers to the degree to which the test actually measures what it purports to measure. It tells us what the test is actually measuring. A validity index for the text is developed before the test is published.

These three criteria are necessary for a test to be considered as standardized and ready to use. Over the years, there is an increase in the usage of tests in the industry. The various tests used may be briefly summarized as follows.

Intelligence tests   Intelligence tests are basic mental ability tests. Intelligence refers to the application of knowledge to a given situation leading to efficient resolution of a problem. Since intelligence does not refer to any single trait, the test also comprises a variety of aspects such as vocabulary, numerical ability, reasoning, spatial reasoning, and memory. Some of the popular intelligence tests are Weschler Adult Intelligence Scale, Stanford Binet Test, etc. Intelligence tests are frequently used in preliminary or screening tests, which are followed by tests of special aptitudes. Another general use of intelligence test in a clinical setting is the identification and classification of the mentally retarded. In almost all competitive examinations, these tests are used.

Aptitude tests   While intelligence tests may yield a score of IQ, the presence of job-specific skills does not get measured or identified through them. Aptitude tests are especially designed to assess the presence of such skills in an individual. The aptitudes assessed may vary such as clerical, numerical, mechanical, spatial, and verbal. Aptitude tests when used in combination with intelligence tests or personality tests give good results.

Personality tests   Personality refers to both intellectual and emotional traits of an individual. Since personality is popularly interpreted as a combination of traits, most of the tests try to identify the various dimensions that are included in personality. Some of the popular personality tests are the California Psychological Inventory (CPI) test, the Minnesota Multiphasic Personality Inventory (MMPI) test. These tests are very exhaustive and lengthy.

A psychological test is essentially an objective and standard measure of a sample of behaviour. Psychological tests are used for a variety of purposes, namely:

- Counselling students seeking admission to various courses
- Diagnostic purposes to assess personality for research on human behaviour
- Selection of candidates into organizations

There are also some specific dimensions of personality that may be assessed through some specific tests as follows:

Projective tests   Projective tests involve presentation of ambiguous pictures to the candidate and ask him or her to interpret the picture or write a story on it. Normally, when an individual interprets, his motives, attitudes, aspirations get projected onto the theme. By presenting these pictures, the projections and the underlying motives, frustrations or aspirations can be known. Some of the popular projective tests are thematic apperception test (TAT), inkblot test, etc.

> ■ ■ ■
> Tests usually identify the degree of absence or presence of a trait or ability, but these do not predict the success of the candidate.

Interest tests   The strength and direction of the individual's interests, attitudes, motives, and values represent an important aspect of personality. These characteristics materially affect educational and occupational adjustment, interpersonal relations, recreational pursuits, and other aspects of life. The basic idea behind the use of interest tests is that people are likely to be successful in jobs they like. In that case, they can be used as effective selection tools. Examples of interest tests are Strong's vocational interest blank (SVIB), Strong interest inventory (SII), etc. Interest is an indicator of aptitude, which predicts later achievement.

Achievement tests   Achievement tests measure the effects of learning. The emphasis is on what the individual can do at a given time. We may use these tests to study the effect of learning or training that an individual has undergone such as learning French language or computer programming. Some examples of achievement test are tests of achievement and proficiency (TAP), Stanford Test of Academic Skills (TASK), and California Achievement Tests (CAT).

Other tests   There are other tests that may be used singularly or in combination such as graphology tests, lie detector tests, and psychomotor tests.

In general, tests can be used as selection devices in that they elicit the latent or innate abilities that cannot be detected otherwise. The information thus obtained can also be objectively assessed. However, the information or data obtained from the tests need to be supplemented with group discussions, interviews, background checks, application blanks, etc. Tests usually identify the degree of absence or presence of a trait or ability, but these do not predict the success of the candidate. Nevertheless, these serve as effective selection devices.

Other Selection Methods

Let us discuss some other selection methods used by organizations.

Work simulations   A typical work simulation exercise is simulated so that a candidate's ability to do the job effectively can be assessed. For example, a managerial candidate may be asked to give solutions to a set of problems that are placed in the 'in-tray'. An accountant may be given some financial data and asked to prepare statements. The candidate then will be assessed on the relevance of content. The basic procedure involves choosing several scientific tasks that are crucial to performing the job for which a candidate is being recruited. The performance on the tasks is used as a predictor of later success.

> ■ ■ ■
> An assessment centre is a programme of tests, work simulations, exercises, and interviews designed to measure and assess a wide range of different abilities, skills, behavioural characteristics, and potential required for effective performance on the job.

It is a useful device for selection purposes as the actual work is being assessed. The fear of failing that might be present in case of employment tests has no scope here.

Assessment centres   An assessment centre has been described by Lewis (1985) as a selection procedure that uses multiple methods of selection. An assessment centre is a programme of tests, work simulations, exercises, and interviews designed to measure and assess a wide range of different abilities, skills, behavioural characteristics, and potential required for effective performance on the job. AT&T was the first company to use them in 1955. It is argued that setting up an assessment centre requires a database about all the skills required for all the jobs in an organization. Employees and candidates are subjected to periodic assessment of the skills and are provided feedback on the processes. It is not yet popular, but a useful selection device.

The following is a brief description of the various assessment centre exercises:

Customer situation   A large equipment user (a national customer) has been experiencing recent problems involving a particular piece of equipment, culminating in a systems down situation. The problem with the equipment could be faulty software or that parts received to fix the equipment were damaged. The participant will be required to review information about the problem for 30 minutes and generate a potential course of action. Participants will then meet in groups to devise a consensus strategy to deal with the problem. Assessors should expect a plan of action from the participants and may probe the participants for additional contingency plans. The participants will have 45 minutes to discuss the problem and develop a strategy.

Employee discussion   In this exercise, the participants must develop a strategy for counselling a subordinate (a senior customer service engineer) who has been experiencing recent performance problems. The participant will have 30 minutes to review information regarding the technician's declining performance over the last few months. The participant will then have 15 minutes to prepare a brief report on the individual with recommendations for submission to the general manager. The participant will then meet two assessors to discuss the strategy.

In-basket   In this exercise, the participant will assume the role of a newly transferred branch manager. The participant will have 90 minutes to review information related to various issues (technical developments, equipment maintenance specifications, customer information, etc.). The participant will be instructed to spend this time identifying priorities and grouping related issues as well as indicating courses of action to be taken. The participant will then take part in a 15 minute interview with an assessor to explain the actions taken and the logic behind the decisions made.

Problem analysis   In this exercise, the participant will be required to review information on three candidates and provide a recommendation on which of the three should be promoted to a branch manager position. The participant will have 90 minutes to review information and prepare a written recommendation.

The participants will then meet in groups to derive a consensus recommendation for the general manager.

Step IV: Interviewing the Candidate

Interview is the most popular method of selection. It is used along with employment tests and sometimes it is the only method used in the selection process. Its scope is quite comprehensive in that it integrates all the relevant characteristics about the applicant. It gives a great opportunity to assess the individual on a personal level. In organizations, interviewing is used for a variety of purposes such as selection, promotions, appraisals, counselling, and disciplinary actions. When used as a selection method, it provides an excellent assessment of the applicant's personality, including his or her intelligence, interests, general attitudes towards life, etc.

> ■ ■ ■
> Interviews are used by the employer to assess the applicant's personality as also intelligence, interests, general attitudes, etc.

An interview is an attempt to obtain the maximum amount of information from the candidate concerning his or her suitability for the job under consideration. Hence, an interview is the process wherein there is exchange of information between the interviewer and interviewee. To optimize this process and use it as an effective tool, both the interviewer and interviewee should do their homework properly and help to make it a success.

An interview may be conducted by one interviewer or a panel of interviewers. It may be conducted in one sitting or in a sequence of sittings. Interviews may be classified in many ways. The main differences arise from the way the interviewer communicates with the interviewee, responds to his answers, asks questions, and forms the structure of the interview. Generally, interviews fall into the various categories as discussed in the following sections. (Figure 7.2).

Structured Interview

This is the most common method of interview. Before the conduct of the interview, details of the information to be obtained are worked out and questions prepared accordingly. The questions include personal details, work experience, past life information, job shifts, future plans, family details, etc. The interviewer first establishes a rapport with the interview and starts asking the questions in the same order that is prepared. As far as possible, the interviewer prevents the dialogue form deviating from the planned structure and keeps the dialogue on track. While the process is on, the interviewer also observes the facial expressions and body language of the candidate to assess his or her emotional maturity, sincerity, and honesty in responses. Since the questions are all prepared beforehand, information can be recorded and verified later on. Comparison between candidates also becomes easy. The only disadvantage is that there is limited scope for the interviewer to give a detailed analysis.

Unstructured or Open-ended Interview

In an unstructured interview, essentially, there are no pre-planned questions. The interviewer first asks some leading questions, which elicit some detailed information about the candidate. The interviewee usually narrates his or her past and the interviewer records important information such as achievements, crisis management, and risk-taking behaviour. The interviewer looks for traits of character, nature of aspirations, and latent strengths and weaknesses in the interviewee. The purpose of such an interview is more to determine what kind of person the candidate really is.

Stress Interview

In a typical stress interview, the interviewer assumes a hostile role and asks questions rapidly, criticizes the interviewee, interrupts in between, makes derogatory remarks, floods the interviewee with a volley of questions, etc. The purpose is to find out how a candidate behaves in a stressful situation. This type of interview has to be handled carefully and the interviewer should be sufficiently trained and skilled to handle it.

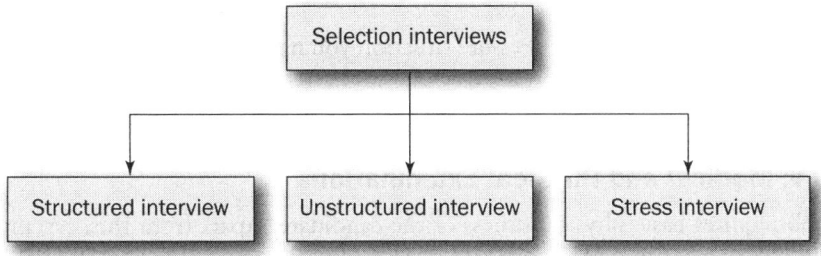

FIGURE 7.2   Selection Interviews

Errors in Interviewing

There are certain common errors in interviews, which need to be guarded against:

- *Halo effect*: Normally it is said that within 4–9 minutes of the start of the interview, the assessor arrives at a judgment about the candidate. The rest of the time is spent in justifying the impression. The impression may be positive or negative. Basing on one observed characteristic feature, a generalization about the candidate is made. This is referred to as the 'halo effect'. What is needed is a holistic assessment of the candidate at the end of the process.
- *Leniency*: A single assessor may at times be too lenient in rating the candidate. It signifies lack of interest, the attitude of playing safe, or lack of confidence on the part of the interviewer. On the contrary, a low rating may be due to high expectations, lack of understanding, and rigid personality of the interviewer.
- *Projection*: Errors of projection arise when an interviewer expects his or her own qualities, skills, and values in an applicant. Therefore, such selectors select candidates who resemble themselves.
- *Stereotyping*: General stereotypes exist in the minds of people about gender issues, certain communities or categories of people, etc. When such biases in the interviewer affect the rating of a candidate, it is considered as the influence of stereotyping.

Elements in an Interview Form

The following are the most common elements in an interview form:

- Name of the applicant
- Tell us about your most recent job. Why did you decide to change?
- As you look back on your recent job, what did you like most about it? What did you like least about it?
- What do you feel are your three most significant achievements in your last position?
- Could you tell us if you have any idea about what an effective manager should do?
- How do you feel your subordinates would describe you as a supervisor?
- Were you satisfied with the progress you made on your job? Why? Why not?
- What plans do you have for self-improvement during the next twelve months?
- What does success mean to you?
- What do people criticize about you the most?
- Many of us improve our ability to relate to people as we develop more maturity. In what way would you say you have improved over the last two years?
- What or who has contributed most to your self-development? Think about a difficult decision you have had to make recently regarding your work. Tell us how you went about making this decision.
- What has been the heaviest pressure situation you have had to face in the last year? Describe the circumstances.
- What goals you have set for the next three years?

Step V: Medical and Physical Examinations

Any job requires basic physical fitness of the candidate. Apart from this, certain jobs demand greater physical stamina, clear vision, etc. After the administration of tests and completion of

> Medical and physical examinations are conducted to test the general fitness and health of the candidate.

the interview process, the candidate is recommended for a thorough medical check-up. This is done primarily to establish the fact that the candidate has a sound physical system, does not suffer from disabilities, and is not carrying any contagious diseases. See Exhibit 7.1 for more details.

EXHIBIT 7.1   Specimen of a medical report

Name _____	Neck _____	Teeth _____
Age _____ Sex _____	Pulse _____	Blood pressure _____
Address _____	Lungs _____	Abdomen _____
General appearance _____	Spine _____	Blood group _____
Height _____ Weight _____	Identification mark _____	
Eyes (R) _____ Ears (R) _____	Past medical history _____	
(L) _____ (L) _____	Notes _____	
Nose _____ Throat _____	Place and date _____	

Signature of Doctor

Step VI: Background Information and Reference Check

The next step in the selection process is to check the background of the candidate (Exhibit 7.2). Normally, the candidate is expected to give two references at the end of the biodata or application blank. If the candidate is already employed, the previous employer's name is given. The personnel department contacts the referees and obtains the required information about the candidate. The following are the broad areas on which information is sought regularly at work—punctuality, character, progress in work, absenteeism, willingness of the previous employer to relieve the employee, etc. This step will also clarify whether any cases are pending against the employee. Once this procedure is completed satisfactorily, the hiring decision may be made.

EXHIBIT 7.2   Sample reference form for reference check

Mr .... has applied to us for the post of ....
He claims to have been in your employment from .... to .... Having had an opportunity to observe the aforementioned candidate as an employee, your frank answers to the questions below will be valuable to us, and would be greatly appreciated. We assure you that your replies will be kept strictly confidential.

1. When did the applicant serve your organization from .... to ....
2. Positions held ....
3. Attendance regular? Yes .... No .... If not, what was the cause of absence?
4. Liked by his co-workers (well-liked, acceptable, sometimes criticized)? ....
5. Rate of progress (slow, average, above average)? ....
6. Asked to resign or resigned voluntarily? ....
7. Would you re-employ him in a similar position? Yes.............................. No ....
8. What is your view of the applicant's character, ability, and dependability? ....

Step VII: Hiring Decision

After all the six steps are completed, the management makes the final decision as to hire the candidate. Each step has to be undertaken carefully and judgments have to be made about the candidate cautiously. A wrong judgement or choice will cost the organization dearly as it may lead to impairing the morale of the employees and loss of confidence in the selection process. Hence, suitable candidates are intimated about the hiring decision after careful assessment (Exhibit 7.3). Then the organization offers an appointment letter to the successful candidate, with which the selection process comes to an end.

EXHIBIT 7.3 ICICI Bank*

ICICI Bank is India's second largest bank with total assets of about ₹1,46,214 crore on 31 December 2004 and profit after tax of ₹1,391 crore in the nine months ended 31 December 2004 (₹1,637 crore in fiscal 2004). ICICI Bank has a network of about 530 branches/extension counters and over 1,880 ATMs. ICICI Bank offers a wide range of banking products and financial services to corporate and retail customers through a variety of delivery channels and through its specialized subsidiaries and affiliates in the areas of investment banking, life and non-life insurance, venture capital, and asset management. ICICI Bank set up its international banking group in fiscal 2002 to cater to the cross-border needs of clients and leverage on its domestic banking strengths to offer products internationally. It currently has subsidiaries in the United Kingdom and Canada, branches in Singapore and Bahrain, and representative offices in the United States, China, United Arab Emirates, Bangladesh, and South Africa.

ICICI Bank's equity shares are listed in India on the Stock Exchange Board of India, Mumbai, and the National Stock Exchange of India, and its American Depositary Receipts (ADRs) are listed on the New York Stock Exchange (NYSE).

On 4 April 2005, ICICI Bank, with free float market capitalization of about ₹308.00 billion (US$7.00 billion), ranked third amongst all the companies listed on the Indian stock exchanges.

ICICI Bank was originally promoted in 1994 by ICICI Limited, an Indian financial institution, and was its wholly owned subsidiary. ICICI's shareholding in ICICI Bank was reduced to 46% through a public offering of shares in India in fiscal 1998, an equity offering in the form of ADRs listed on the NYSE in fiscal 2000. ICICI Bank acquired Bank of Madura Limited in an all-stock amalgamation in fiscal 2001, and secondary market sales by ICICI to institutional investors in fiscal 2001 and fiscal 2002. ICICI was formed in 1955 at the initiative of the World Bank, the Government of India, and representatives of the Indian industry. The principal objective was to create a development financial institution for providing medium-term and long-term project financing to Indian businesses. In the 1990s, ICICI transformed its business from a development financial institution offering only project finance to a diversified financial services group offering a wide variety of products and services, both directly and through a number of subsidiaries and affiliates, such as ICICI Bank. In 1999, ICICI became the first Indian company and the first bank or financial institution from non-Japan Asia to be listed on the NYSE.

After considering various corporate structuring alternatives in the context of the emerging competitive scenario in the Indian banking industry, and the trend towards universal banking, the managements of ICICI and ICICI Bank formed the view that the merger would be the optimal strategic alternative for both entities, and would create the optimal legal structure for ICICI group's universal banking strategy. The merger would enhance value for ICICI shareholders through the merged entity's access to low cost deposits, greater opportunities for earning fee-based income, and the ability to participate in the payments system and provide transaction banking services. The merger would enhance value for ICICI Bank shareholders through a large capital base and scale of operations, seamless access to ICICI's strong corporate relationships built up over five decades, entry into new business segments, higher market share in various business segments, particularly fee-based services, and access to the vast talent pool of ICICI and its subsidiaries. In October 2001, the Boards of Directors of ICICI and ICICI Bank approved the merger of ICICI and two of its wholly-owned retail finance subsidiaries, ICICI Per-

*Based on data up to 2004.

sonal Financial Services Limited and ICICI Capital Services Limited, with ICICI Bank. The merger was approved by shareholders of ICICI and ICICI Bank in January 2002, by the High Court of Gujarat at Ahmedabad in March 2002, and by the High Court of Judicature at Mumbai and the Reserve Bank of India in April 2002. Consequent to the merger, ICICI group's financing and banking operations, both wholesale and retail, have been integrated into a single entity (Figure 7.3).

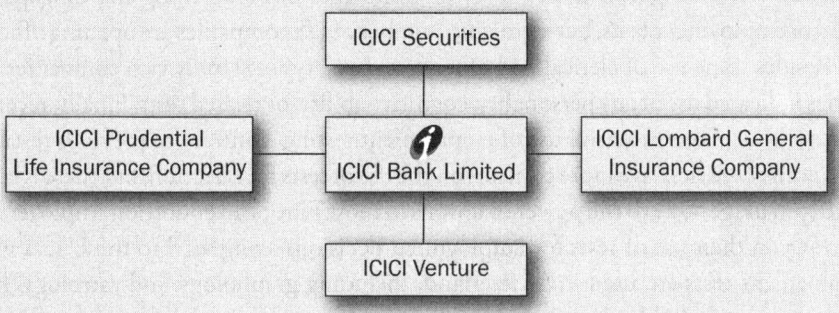

FIGURE 7.3   ICICI Bank Limited

Selection Process

The Bank continuously endeavours to improve the selection process for recruitment at all levels, and it has carried out an in-depth study of the competencies required to succeed in ICICI Bank. As per their research, the competencies that indicated success at the entry level in ICICI Bank are as follows:

- Drive for results
- Process orientation
- Interpersonal effectiveness
- Analytical thinking
- Innovation
- Team effectiveness

In order to assess these abilities, they use a set of three tools:

- Mental ability tests (for candidates with 0–2 years of work experience)
- Personality profiling system
- Personal interview

The mental ability test is designed to give a fair and objective assessment of candidates' skills in the areas of verbal reasoning, numerical reasoning, and diagrammatic reasoning. These are important skills for the role of an entry-level manager and people who do well in these tests tend to do well in their jobs at ICICI Bank. The total time taken in this exercise is two hours with each of the three sections lasting 40 minutes.

Candidates (at all levels regardless of the number of years of work experience) are also required to complete the occupational personality questionnaire (OPQ) before they appear for the interview, the results of which are integrated into their interview process.

Work Culture

It is a tech-savvy, non-hierarchical work environment, where early responsibility and independent decision-making enable each employee to reach his/her potential. Coupled with this is a strong performance management system that has built a system of meritocracy, where high performing, high potential individuals are duly rewarded.

SELECTION IN OTHER COUNTRIES

The use of employment tests in other countries of the world varies considerably as do the government regulations regarding the use of tests. According to a recent multinational comparison among other Asian countries, Korean employers use employment tests more extensively. These tests tend to be written examinations covering English language skills, common sense, and knowledge of specific disciplines. A smaller percentage of Japanese companies use employment tests. Some Japanese companies use the foreign assignment selection test (FAST) to identify Japanese who are more likely to be successful expatriates in the United States. The FAST assesses cultural flexibility, sociability conflict resolution style, and leadership style. Within Japan, however, most people are hired directly from the universities, and the reputation of the university attended is a major criterion for selection purposes. A survey of companies in Hong Kong and Singapore revealed little use of employment tests, but a growing number of US companies are opening offices in Hong Kong. Besides some use of clerical and office tests (e.g., typing), only two companies from these countries indicated use of any personality, cognitive ability, or related tests. Finally, recent evidence indicates China makes extensive use of employment testing, contrary to previous research.

European countries have more controls on the use of tests for selection, but there is considerable variability in usage. Due to the power of unions in most European countries, employers have more restrictions on their use of tests for employment decisions, compared to the US. A wide variety of employment tests are used in Switzerland, including graphology and astrology, but in Italy selection tests are forbidden by law. In Holland, Sweden, and Poland, job applicants have access to all psychological test results and can choose to not allow the results to be divulged to an employer.

Various surveys have given us some clues about the selection methods in England. One survey found that more than 80% of companies in England do some type of reference check, and another found almost 40% use personality tests and 25% use cognitive ability tests to assess managers. Interestingly, compared to the US, the use of graphology was relatively high in England, where 8% of the surveyed firms reported using this prcedure ocasionally.

SUMMARY

The chapter begins with an overview of selection, explaining its nature and steps involved in the selection process, such as preliminary screening interview, completion of application form, employment tests/other selection methods, interview, background and reference investigations, medical checkups, and the final employment decision to hire. The chapter also explains the various methods adopted in the selection process and addresses some of the issues involved in the selection process with the help of a case study.

■ ■ ■ | KEY TERMS

Application form   Company-specific employment forms used to generate specific information the company wants

Assessment centres   Using a more elaborate set of performance simulation tests to evaluate a candidate's managerial potential

Background investigation and reference checks   Any communication with an employee's current or former employer concerning the education, training, experience, qualifications, and job performance of the employee. It is used for the purpose of evaluating the applicant for employment

Comprehensive interviews   A selection device in which in-depth information about a candidate can be obtained

Graphology   The study of handwriting, especially when employed as a means of analysing character.

Personality characteristics   Complex inherent or perceived traits in an individual

Preliminary screening interview   This is an initial interview to identify the best applicants and is usually conducted by someone in the company's HR department. Many companies conduct phone interviews for this purpose

Realistic job preview   A selection device that allows job candidates to learn negative as well as positive information about the job and organization

Technical knowledge Knowledge of tools, languages, or software technologies that at least one group member will probably need to acquire or have in order to successfully complete the project

Weighted application form A special type of application form where relevant applicant information is used to determine the likelihood of success in the job

■ ■ ■ EXERCISES

Multiple Choice Questions

1. During which of the following interviews, does an interviewer questions the candidate about his/her work experience, job shifts, future plans, and observes the body language and facial expressions of the candidate?
   (a) Stress interview
   (b) Open-ended interview
   (c) Structured interview
   (d) Intelligence test

2. One well-known personality test is
   (a) thematic apperception test
   (b) Stanford–Binet test
   (c) California achievement test
   (d) California psychological inventory

3. The extent to which an employment selection test provides consistency of scores is known as
   (a) reliability (b) dependability
   (c) consistency (d) validity

4. Which of the following sources can be used to ensure the authentication of the information provided by the job applicant?
   (a) Reference check (b) Police verification
   (c) Bank statements (d) Social networking sites

5. Rating a candidate positive or negative on all items because of one characteristic during interview is known as
   (a) halo effect (b) biasness
   (c) stereotyping (d) leniency

6. Interviews are conducted for determining
   (a) the degree of fit between the applicant and the requirements of the job
   (b) the candidate's age
   (c) body language
   (d) physical attributes

Fill in the Blanks

1. The number of candidates to be considered for a particular job, compared to the number of individuals in the applicant pool is often expressed as _____.

2. Assigning weights to skills that directly influence the performance of a job is known as _____. This facilitates the recruitment and selection process.

3. The _____ problem occurs when the interviewer tends to rate all candidates consistently high or low. It signifies lack of interest or lack of understanding, and rigid personality of the interviewer.

4. During _____, candidates normally face derogatory remarks and criticism from the interviewer.

5. _____ tests evaluate the skills and knowledge that have been acquired, whereas _____ tests measure the effects of learning.

Concept Review Questions

1. Explain the importance of the selection process in the context of right recruitment.

2. Describe the various methods of selection.

3. Analyse the various issues involved in the process of selection.

4. Can selection process be a part of HR strategy? If yes, how?

5. Is there a correlation between selection process and the attrition rate in the organization?

6. What are the major problems of the interview as a selection device? What can HRM do to reduce some of these problems?

7. Why should a background investigation be done?

8. What do you think of realistic job previews? Would you be more likely to choose a position where recruiters emphasized only the positive aspects of the job?

Project Work

1. Study the selection process being followed in an organization of your choice and prepare a status report indicating the strengths and weaknesses and also suggest modifications, if necessary, to improve the process.

2. Critically analyse the selection processes vis-à-vis the HR strategy of an organization, that is, examine whether the selection process is facilitating the recruitment and retention of the manpower with the required skill sets and competencies.

3. Does the selection process contribute to organizational strategy realization? Substantiate your argument by analysing the selection process of an identified organization vis-à-vis its business strategy.

■ ■ ■ REFERENCES

Arthur, W., Doverspike, D., and Barrett, G. 1996, 'Development of a job analysis based procedure for weighting and combining content-related tests into a single testy battery score', *Personnel Psychology*, 49, pp. 971–85.

Atkinson, J. 1984, 'Manpower strategies for flexible organizations', *Personnel Management*, August, pp. 28–31.

Bernardin, H.J. and Bownas, D. 1985, *Personality Assessment in Organizations*, Praeger, New York.

Dipboye, R.C. 1992, *Selection Interviews: Process Perspectives*, Southwestern Publishing, Cincinnati, pp. 6–9.

Greenberg, Herbert M., and Sweeney, Patrick J. 1999, 'Hiring Expertise: How to Find the Right Fit', *HR Focus*, October, p. 6.

Huo, Y.P., Huan, H.J., and Napier, N.K. 2002, 'Divergence or convergence: A cross-national comparison of personnel selection practices', *Human Resource Management*, 41, pp. 31–44.

Latham, G.P. and Napier, N.K. 1990, 'Chinese human resource management practices in Hong Kong and Singapore: An exploratory study', in Nedd, A., Ferris, G.R., and Rowland, K.M. (Eds), *Research in Personnel and Human Resources Management: International Human Resources Management*, Suppl. l, Jai Press, Greenwich, pp. 173–99.

Levy-Leboyer, C. 1994, 'Selection and assessment in Europe', in Dunnette, M. and Hough, L. (Eds)., *Handbook of Industrial and Organizational Psychology*, Consulting Psychologists Press, Palo Alto, CA, pp. 173–90; Cascio, W.F. and Bailey, E. 1995, 'International HRM: The state of research and practice', In Shenkar, O. (Ed.), *Global Perspectives of Human Resources Management*, Prentice Hall, Englewood Cliffs, NJ, pp. 15–36.

Montgomery, C.E. 1996, 'Organizational fit is key to job success', *HR Magazine*, January, pp. 94–6; Fenn, Donna 1995, 'Promoting: Getting the right fit', *HR Magazine*, February, pp. 111.

Powell, Gary N. and Goulet, Laurel R. 1996, 'Recruiters' and 'applicants' reactions to campus interviews and employment decisions', *Academy of Management Journal*, 39(6), December, pp. 1619–40.

Schmidt, F.L. and Hunter, J.E. 1998, 'The validity and utility of selection methods in personnel psychology: Practical and theoretical implications of 85 years of research findings', *Psychological Bulletin*, 124, pp. 262–74.

Shimmin, S. 1989, 'Election in a European context', in Harriot, P. (Ed.), *Assessment and Selection in Organizations*, John Wiley and Sons, Chichester, pp. 109–18.

Tett, R.P., Jackson, D.N. and Rothstein, M. 1991, 'Personality measures as predictors of performance: A meta-analytic review', *Personnel Psychology*, 44, pp. 703–42.

Von Glinow, M.A. and Chung, B.J. 1990, 'Comparative human resource management practices in the United States, Japan, Korea, and the People's Republic of China', In Nedd, A., Ferris, G.R., and Rowland, K.M. (Eds), *Research in Personnel and Human Resources Management: International Human Resources Management*, Supplement l, Jai Press, Greenwich, pp. 153–71.

CASE STUDY 1 — Employee Selection Process in ITES Sector—HSBC GR

HSBC Global Resourcing (GR) is the captive BPO of the HSBC Bank Worldwide with operations in 16 sites over five geographies, that is, India, China, Malaysia, Philippines, and Sri Lanka. In India, it has eight sites with two each in Hyderabad, Bangalore, Kolkata, and one site each in Visakhapatnam and Gurgaon. GR supports the bank in all areas of business ranging from investment banking, financial analysis, mortgage, credit and risk management, payments and settlements, supply management operations, HR operations, etc. Figure 7.4 depicts the broad structure of GR.

HR Strategy

The HR strategy at GR has been to develop the organization with the philosophy of 'Best place to work'. As a part of the process, they have a whole range of HR initiatives such as the following:

- Rewards and recognition programmes
- Coaching and mentoring
- Growth and development opportunities
- Learning opportunities
- Structured employee feedback systems

Recruitment Process

The recruitment strategy at GR is a part of the overall resourcing strategy, and the organization looks at the cultural suitability of the individual as a part of the selection process. The recruitment team members present the broad overview of the organization and the career opportunities for prospective employees. The idea is to present a holistic view, rather than restrict the process to just a compensation-based hiring.

Table 7.1 describes the recruitment and selection process at GR.

TABLE 7.1 Recruitment and selection process at GR

Step	Process	Details
1	Manpower planning	Based on recruitment trends, general business scenario, and inputs from operations, the overall recruitment numbers (level-wise) are forecasted along with recruitment requirements on a quarterly basis.
2	Recruitment budgeting and sourcing channel strategy	The recruitment costs are estimated based on various channels: Vendors, job fairs, direct walk-ins, employee referrals, job sites, advertisements, etc. The cost per hire (CPH) and average cost of the CPH across all channels is estimated. Based on the corporate and HR strategy, the average CPH is set as a target, and accordingly the sourcing strategy is formulated.
3	Receiving monthly manpower requisitions	The operations team is required to estimate the manpower required for next month before 15th of the previous month, and there are agreed timelines for level-wise recruitment. No approval is required in case of requisition for replacement of an approved position. However, if the requisition is for a new position, the operations will have to submit an approval from the approving authority.
4	Sourcing through channel	Based on the sourcing strategy, the number of positions, and levels, the recruitment team will decide on the channels for sourcing.
5	Screening	Based on the advertised criteria and initial interaction (HR round), the profiles received are screened.
6	Technical round	In the technical round, the recruitment SPOC (single point of contact) will screen the profiles and interview the candidates. In the case of entry-level, the hiring process will comprise of group discussion, voice and accent round, aptitude test, HR round, and the operations round.
7	Background verification	As it is a financial BPO, it is mandatory to verify every short-listed candidate's background in terms of education, prior work experience, and criminal history.
8	Offer negotiation and roll-out	The HR will negotiate the offer based on the existing salary bands and criteria and the offer is rolled-out.
9	Post-offer follow-up	A recruitment team member will continue to be in touch with candidates till they join.
10	Joining and induction	A recruitment team member will coordinate for completing the joining formalities and the induction process.

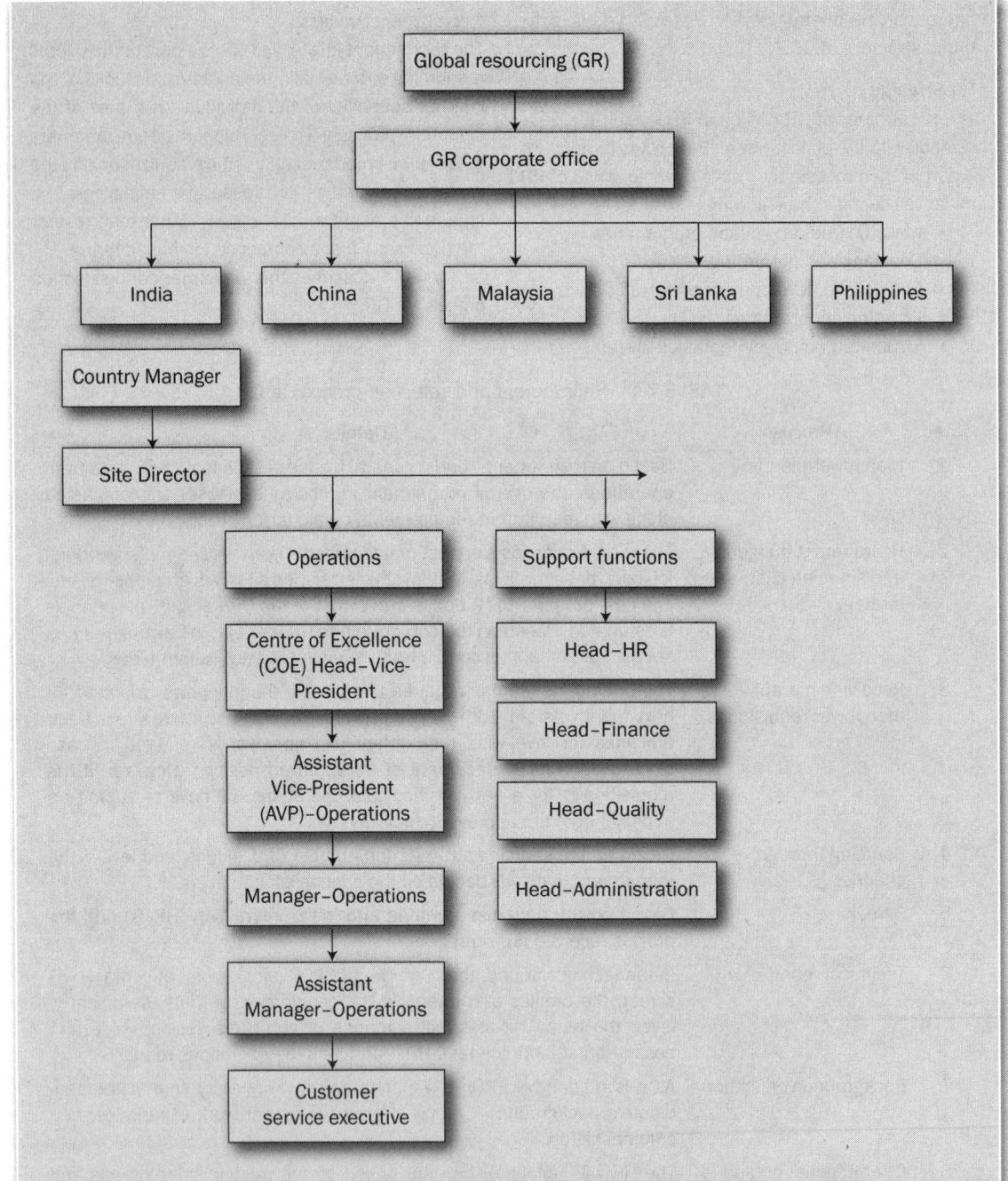

FIGURE 7.4 Structure of HSBC GR

Questions

1. Analyse the employee selection process at HSBC GR.

2. Evaluate the selection process at GR vis-à-vis recruitment practices of other ITES players in India.

Tata Consultancy Services*

Working with TCS

Beyond the obvious. For TCS, this is more than a mere signature line—it is a philosophy. It dictates their approach to all our business functions, be it consultancy or human resources.

What TCS Offers

TCS looks for talent and ambition to grow in its prospective employees. Their streams of competence embrace everything from technology and strategy to research and teaching. TCS also looks for versatility in its candidates, and it offers you a choice of three distinct career paths.

In the technology domain, it offers a choice of working in the following areas:

- Industry/service practice strategy/consultancy
- Technology specialisation
- System architecture/analyses
- Product specialisation
- Business/technical analysis
- Technology support
- Designing/developing

TCS Culture

TCS has an energetic and open workplace environment, and a collaborative culture that is based on teamwork. Pulling together is a central tenet of their work ethic.

Energetic and full of enthusiasm, TCS employees enjoy their day (and night) at work. Life at TCS is a stimulating and exciting experience. Not only do their offices have the best infrastructure and technology, they also have a knack of working hard and partying harder.

Diversity at Work

TCS is an equal opportunity employer and its employees come from many nationalities and speak many languages. Further, since they believe in celebrating everything under the sun, they sing carols at Christmas and do the dandiya dance at Navrathri with equal enthusiasm.

Employees at TCS also go on regular outings, be it with the project teams, with Maitree, or with just a bunch of other like-minded colleagues. They go on treks, nature camps, picnics, or just bus rides whenever they get the chance.

Doors are Always Open at TCS

The senior colleagues follow an open-door policy in which any associate can approach the chief executive officer (CEO) and senior management with work-related problems.

Communication is a big word at TCS and employees regularly take part in webcasts and chat sessions, through which important corporate issues or decisions are shared on real-time basis with associates worldwide.

They also have institutionalized open house sessions and engagement programmes in which associates at all levels meet and discuss various work issues. In addition, TCS employees can also take part in one-on-one sessions where they can interact privately with the senior management. These sessions are helpful in providing mentorship as well as understanding real-life issues that colleagues face at work. The queries and discussions are formally recorded and followed up.

The Better Half of TCS

Maitree, a fraternity comprising spouses of TCS employees, was formed with the objective of bringing the large and geographically widespread TCS community under a common umbrella.

Maitree has two distinct objectives. Primarily, it serves as an information-sharing body where useful titbits about living in a foreign country such as which are the good schools in Minneapolis and where does one get Indian spices in Stockholm, are shared by TCS employees and their families.

Maitree also functions as a forum where a wide range of socially relevant activities are conducted, be it improving the environment or taking care of the less privileged.

Challenges of Being With TCS

The professional challenges that come with working for TCS are many and varied. TCS has the organizational strength, infrastructure, reach, and, most importantly, people to master these challenges and deliver outstanding quality to its clients. Here is a primer on what enables TCS to do that.

*Based on data up to 2004.

Clients TCS has developed IT solutions for over 800 clients across the world. Its end-to-end solutions help its client organizations gain efficiency in their business processes. TCS has 95 branches all over the world, including 43 offices in the US. They believe that their global presence enables them to be close to their clients. At any given time, about 60% of their software professionals are working at client locations in different countries.

That their clients have high regard for their relationship with us is borne out by an impressive statistic: over 75% of their business comes from repeat clients.

Quality levels When it comes to quality levels, systems and processes have been placed at the top of the scale by various evaluating agencies:

- TCS has an organization-wide ISO 9001 certification.
- It has 14 'delivery centres' spread across India operating at 'Level 5', the highest point of SEI CMM certification.
- TCS has over 1,100 'certified quality assessors' (CQAs) among its people. This is the single largest number of CQA employees for any organization, and it constitutes over a third of the CQA fraternity in the world.
- TCS was the first organization in the world to be assessed at PCMM Level 4. It indicates that they have developed measurable people practices by empowering their workgroups, and by managing the capability and performance of their workforce. TCS currently has four centres functioning at PCMM Level 4.
- TCS has adopted 'Six Sigma' practices at two of its centres, and has 12 Six Sigma black belts in its fold.

This is the reason PCMM pioneer Dr Bill Curtis, of Tera Quest, said about TCS's people systems and processes: 'Absolutely impressive'.

Innovation TCS pioneered the offshore development methodology of software delivery in India by setting up its first client-dedicated 'offshore development centre' (ODC) for Compaq back in 1984.

The ODC model enables clients to get calculable business benefits such as reduced time to market and having a virtual extension of their IT department. TCS currently has over 20 client-dedicated ODCs across

India. This model has been replicated by various companies and has led to the development of the India Inc brand in software development.

TCS developed the world's first software factory in Pune in 1997. The Tata Research Development and Design Center (TRDDC) today produces industry-specific software products, applications, and products such as MasterCraft, which uses models to generate solutions for all layers of software architecture, and Adex, a modelling tool that offers a meta-modelling framework and is a repository for storing application models.

Global outlook From 1971, when TCS bagged its first international assignment to now, with 140 offices across 26 countries, TCS is truly global in its scope of operations.

The geographical proximity to its customers through its branches and 26 client-dedicated offsite centres helps it serve their needs faster and better. Add to this its rich experience in providing end-to-end InfoTech consultancy and services to over 800 customers spread across the world and you have a company that is a global powerhouse in its domain.

Training and Education

TCS sees the training and education of its people as a continuous value-adding process. This approach hones, improves, and enhances its skills, and makes the organization stronger.

TCS invests about 4% of its annual revenues in training, a shining example of which can be seen at the state-of-the-art training centre in Thiruvananthapuram in the south Indian state of Kerala.

Its training modules (Figure 7.5) have been developed to serve the specific needs of individual employees, and are based on their needs at various stages of development in the organization.

The 'induction training programme' (ITP), designed for all its recruits from engineering colleges, is a specially designed 77 day training course at the Thiruvananthapuram facility. The ITP is conducted with the objective of transforming engineers from diverse disciplines into software professionals.

Then there are the 'continuing education programs' (CEPs), which cover over 300 topics and can be delivered over a variety of channels: classrooms, computers, audio/video, contact sessions, seminars, conferences, and workshops.

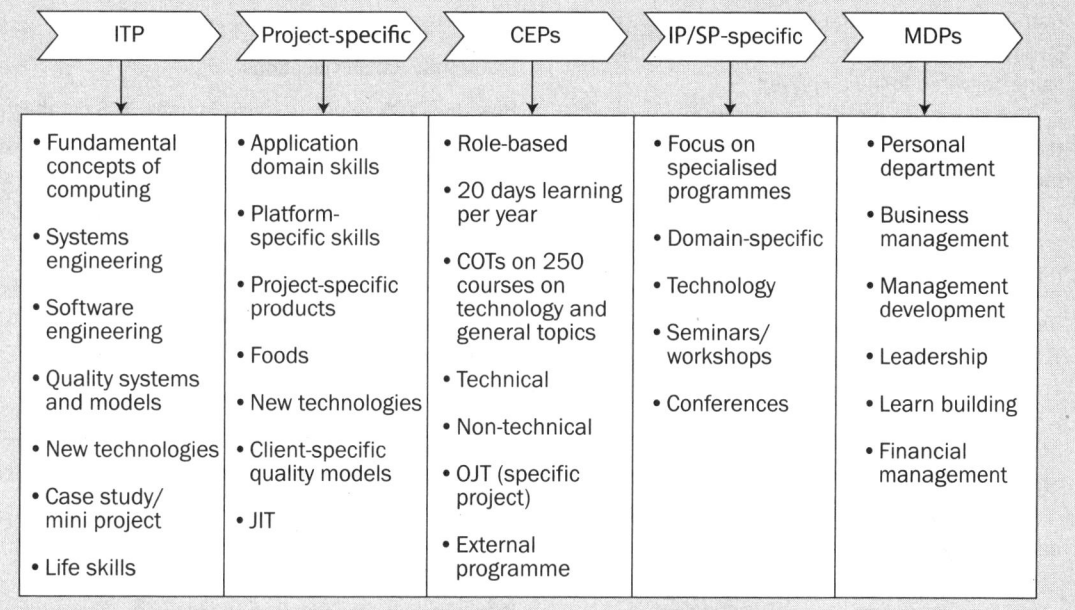

ITP	Project-specific	CEPs	IP/SP-specific	MDPs
• Fundamental concepts of computing • Systems engineering • Software engineering • Quality systems and models • New technologies • Case study/ mini project • Life skills	• Application domain skills • Platform-specific skills • Project-specific products • Foods • New technologies • Client-specific quality models • JIT	• Role-based • 20 days learning per year • COTs on 250 courses on technology and general topics • Technical • Non-technical • OJT (specific project) • External programme	• Focus on specialised programmes • Domain-specific • Technology • Seminars/ workshops • Conferences	• Personal department • Business management • Management development • Leadership • Learn building • Financial management

FIGURE 7.5 Training and education at TCS

Its dedicated training centre in Thiruvanantha-puram, established in 1998, sprawls over 58,000 square feet. The centre has 18 classrooms, a library, an auditorium, a conference hall, discussion rooms, and faculty and administrative areas. The facility has about 300 personal computers connected to servers.

TCS has 10 other centres in India fully equipped to conduct any type of training programme.

Other Benefits

TCS offers its employees a slew of benefits that go beyond the obvious. Important as it is, the end-of-the-month pay cheque is far from being the only measure of how valuable it thinks its employees are.

The employees are provided with loans for hous-ing, personal computers, high-investment household goods, automobiles, etc., and advance for housing accommodation rental loans.

As a part of counselling, employees are counselled on mentoring, career development, and stress reduc-tion.

Cultural

- Holiday homes across the country
- Picnics/get-togethers
- In-house gymnasiums and recreation facilities

Medical   Medical insurance for employees and family (including 50% for dependant parents).

Overseas

- Air fares for spouse and two children
- Competitive overseas allowances
- Medical insurance coverage
- Special language training for non-English speak-ing country assignments (Japanese/German)
- Assistance in accommodation and schooling

Others

- Bank extension counters at offices
- Assistance in school admissions (for transferred employees and those returning from overseas stints)
- Welfare trust facilitation for higher education
- Retirement benefits (provident fund, gratuity, superannuation)
- Membership in Tata Sons Welfare Trust, Consul-tancy Employees Welfare Trust, etc.

EVA Advantage

The 'economic value added' model that TCS follows ensures that the compensation packages of its employees are determined by the value they bring to the organization. The more they deliver, the more are their rewards.

Besides an extremely competitive compensation scale, TCS has adopted the highly effective 'economic value added' (EVA) model. They are the first organization in India to implement this competitive salary structure, which determines compensation based on value delivered to the employer.

EVA allows one's compensation to grow as fast as the results one produces. It is a basis for measuring performance and bonus, and is measured at the enterprise and department levels. The EVA system calculates profits after considering all costs, including that of capital.

Recognition

TCS guarantees high motivation levels of its employees through competitive compensation packages, stimulating job content, outstanding development opportunities, and, not the least, an innovative recognition mechanism.

The various ways in which TCS recognizes its people are as follows:

- Project milestone parties—to encourage efficient execution of projects
- Recognition of star performers/high fliers—to recognize outstanding talent
- Nomination to coveted training programmes—to encourage self-development
- Best project award—to promote a spirit of internal competition across work groups and to foster teamwork
- Best process improvement proposal (PIP) award—to encourage innovation and continuous improvement
- Best auditor award—to acknowledge participation in critical support roles
- Recommendations for new technology assignments/key positions—to ensure career progression and development of employees' full potential
- Spot awards—to ensure real-time recognition of employees
- Performance-based annual increments—to recognize high performers
- Early confirmations for new employees—to reward high-performing new employees
- Long-service awards—to build organizational loyalty
- EVA-based increments—to ensure performance-based salaries
- On-the-spot recognition—to guarantee immedi-

ate recognition of good performance

Frequently Asked Questions

How does TCS select its consultants? TCS carefully selects its consultants from top universities and from various professional backgrounds. Consultant selection is a planned operation involving aptitude tests, auditions, an interview process, and the recommendation of the institute concerned.

What is the need for service agreements? On joining TCS, entrants are required to sign service and confidentiality agreements, in which they accept to stay with TCS for the two years following their initial year of training. TCS invests a large portion of its resources in training and therefore requires such an agreement to be signed by permanent employees. The confidentiality agreement is aimed at providing protection to the intellectual property rights of TCS and its clients.

Why are entrants required to sign overseas agreements? The experience and skills acquired by consultants abroad are fruitfully used in enriching the knowledge of their counterparts in India, and are also applied in projects for Indian clients. TCS feels it is crucial to utilize this knowledge and experience. It is, therefore, in the interest of the country and of TCS that overseas deputation agreements are drawn up with its people.

How is location of work determined? The location of work is determined by the following considerations:

- Location of the client and the skills required by the client organization
- Redeployment of resources across branches to meet workload and skill requirements
- Location rotation of people to widen their horizons and professional outlook, and to provide opportunities to work as module leaders, project leaders, etc.

What are the features of the 'health insurance scheme'? All TCS employees and their families are covered under the New India Assurance health insurance scheme. The scheme provided for TCS employees is more extensive than any other health insurance scheme provided by New India. TCS has, from time to time, got New India to enlarge its scheme and enhance its benefits.

What are the allowances provided for membership of professional bodies? TCS provides an allowance of $70 (₹3,705) to its consultants to become members of reputed institutes and societies such as the Institute of Electrical and Electronics Engineering and ACM. This enables consultants to receive the literature of their use and interest and keep abreast of the latest in technology and science. TCS has well-equipped libraries at all of its branches, and has substantial facilities for providing material for consultants to meet their work and consulting needs.

Why does TCS make its recruits sign a bond? TCS does not make any recruits sign a bond per se. However, there is a standard service agreement that is more like a memorandum of understanding between the individual and the organization. As you are probably aware, TCS invests approximately 6% of its annual revenues in the training and development of its employees. In value terms, that works out to upwards of ₹200 crore a year. In addition to this formal training, there are a host of professional development and continuing education courses provided to employees to groom them into world-class professionals.

It is only fair that a service agreement is entered into to ensure that both TCS and the recruits optimally benefit from these inputs for at least two to three years. TCS would like its employees to be its partners in growth. TCS follows the '4E' approach for individual development—exposure, experience, expertise, and excellence. The agreement acts as a potent instrument in aligning the recruit's career with the 4E model.

What are the employee's chances of going abroad? For the first 18 months, TCS acclimatizes the new employees to the organization and to consulting as a profession through its domestic projects. After this, depending on project requirements, one gets a chance to prove one's mettle in overseas projects. It has generally been observed that a TCS employee gets to go abroad within 36 months of joining the organization.

Is there a practice of job rotation within projects? Yes, because TCS believes in shaping the employees' career, while ensuring that their skills are maximized. Consequently, they get exposed to different industry and service practices and software plat-forms. TCS follows a systematic job rotation process.

TCS salaries are considered to be low. Why? The salary levels on offer may appear to be low, if viewed strictly in terms of the take-home figure. However, compensation packages at TCS are designed scientifically, after taking into account current market trends. They are, in fact, enriched because they have short- and long-term components. The following elements are considered while designing a salary package:

- Long-term benefits such as provident fund and superannuation fund. These are given due importance and factored into the overall package.
- Being a good corporate citizen, TCS honours the tax liabilities of its employees. It does not disguise remuneration with clever tax evasion tactics.
- TCS follows the economic value added structure for remuneration. EVA is a performance-based incentive model that links remuneration directly with the value created by a TCS employee for the organization. So, EVA helps place an employee's remuneration literally in his or her own hands.
- Additionally, each compensation package has a number of welfare schemes that are not obvious in the initial offer.

Bearing the above factors in mind, it becomes clear that a TCS employee's salary, contingent to performance, is on par with the best in the industry.

Is it true that TCS offers only maintenance projects? It is not true. The TCS portfolio has a healthy distribution, from high-end consulting to maintenance projects. Employees get opportunities to work on a wide variety of jobs. Furthermore, the job rotation system ensures that employees do not get typecast or slotted into any kind of job permanently.

Does TCS allow its employees to take sabbaticals? Yes. Deserving employees are granted sabbaticals, with the understanding that their newly acquired knowledge will add value to the company.

Has the global slowdown affected TCS? In this day and age, when technology and networking have crunched distances and melted boundaries, no business entity can remain totally insulated from the global environment. However, due to its global presence, dynamic business strategies, wide assignment portfolio, longstanding client relationships, and credibility, TCS is confident of achieving significant business growth.

Issues

Of late, HR professionals at TCS have faced some major challenges, which are hindering the organization's performance. These challenges include the following

- The levels of attrition in the company are high, especially during the boom period.
- The high level of attrition at the middle and top management levels is leading to disruption of schedules of project execution and also complaints from the customers regarding the transfer of knowledge.
- Some customers have been complaining that quite often TCS recruits youngsters from campus interviews and posts them on assignments with the client without proper training, leading to inefficient and low quality delivery of service to the clients.
- Typically, the TCS strategy has been to recruit three times the manpower requirements, taking into consideration the employee attrition. In spite of this, the high level of attrition is leading to problems in quality service, customer satisfaction, etc.

Questions

1. Critically analyse the quality levels at TCS.
2. Analyse the support for innovation in the organization.
3. Explain the emphasis on training and education and its facilitation in building TCS as a brand that attracts the best talents in the market.
4. Analyse the perks/fringe benefits available to TCS employees and the contribution of these benefits to building TCS as an attractive brand.
5. Explain the reward mechanism in TCS that helps in retention of employees.
6. Critically analyse the recruitment/selection process at TCS.

Placement Procedures

INTRODUCTION

The step immediately succeeding the selection process is 'placement'. Placement refers to the procedure wherein an individual is assigned a job. It is the final decision taken by the management about the position that is to be occupied by the applicant. It also involves assigning a specific rank and responsibility to an employee. This decision is taken after matching the requirements of the job with the qualification of a candidate. Placement is an important HR activity. When handled carefully, it reduces absenteeism and employee turnover, prevents accidents, and classifies expectations. When the placement does not match with the skills of individuals, employees experience frustration, feelings of neglect, etc. To avoid this, organizations undertake the process of induction or orientation.

■ ■ ■
Placement refers to the procedure wherein an individual is assigned a job.

SOCIALIZATION AND INDUCTION

Socialization is the process by which an individual learns to appreciate the values, abilities, expected behaviours, and social knowledge essential for assuming an organizational role and for participating as a member of the organization. Therefore, socialization is commonly thought of as a learning process. Individuals learn how to operate within the explicitly (i.e., policies and procedures) and implicitly (i.e., cultural) expressed environments. Moreover, socialization takes place over time; it is not a discrete event. It may take months, even years, for employees to become fully adjusted to the organization's working environment.

Sears Roebuck and Company recently reduced the turnover rate by more than half, from approximately 17.5% to 7.5%. Mentoring was cited as the chief reason for that decline.

Induction is a process through which a new employee is introduced to the organization. It refers to the process of welcoming the individual into an organization. It is a process wherein an individual is made to feel comfortable and at home in the organization.

Induction is the process of integration attempted by the organization with the new employee.

Induction is the process of integration attempted by the organization with the new employee. The new employee can be handed over a rule book or documents of policy procedures, which are quite impersonal in nature. However, the employee feels a sense of belongingness when communicated to personally.

It is the responsibility of the HR department to execute the induction programme. It is either the HR manager or an HR representative who conducts this programme. Often it is an entire team, such as a group of management trainees or graduate engineer trainees, who are exposed to this programme. There is no model induction procedure. Each industry/sector develops its own procedure as per its needs.

The immediate supervisor or the plant manager might take the initiative to induct the new employee through the following steps:

- Welcomes the newcomer to the organization
- Explains the overall objectives of the company and the department
- Explains the employee's role in achieving the objectives
- Shows the location or place of work
- Hands over the rule book and job descriptions
- Gives details about training opportunities and promotional advancements
- Discusses working conditions
- Furnishes all details regarding salary and benefits
- Guides the employee through a tour of the entire organization

The topics covered in an employee induction programme may be as follows (Figure 8.1):

- *Organizational issues*
  - History of the company
  - Names and titles of key executives
  - Employee's title and department
  - Layout of physical facilities
  - Probationary period
  - Products/services offered
  - Overview of the company procedures
  - Disciplinary procedure
  - Employee handbook
  - Safety steps

- *Employee benefits*
  - Pay scales
  - Vacations, holidays
  - Rest pauses
  - Training avenues
  - Counselling
  - Insurance, medical, and retirement benefits

- *Introduction*
  - to supervisors
  - to co-workers
  - to trainers
  - to employee counsellors

- *Job duties*
  - Job location
  - Job tasks
  - Job safety needs
  - Job overview
  - Job objectives
  - Relationship with other jobs

An induction programme informs a new employee of the various organizational issues, employee benefits, and job duties.

The induction programme is usually completed in a single day. Some large organizations may show a video film about the company including the

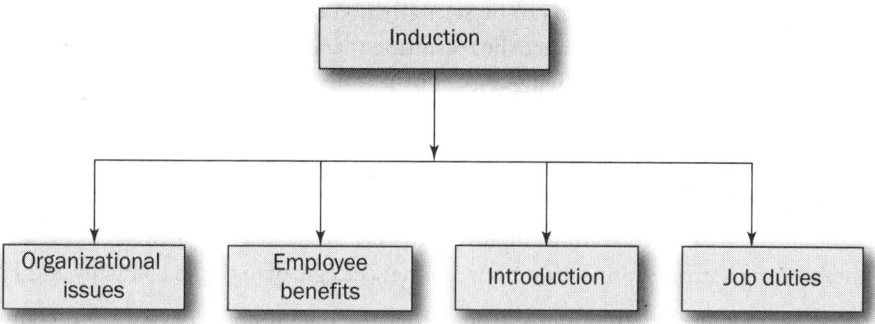

FIGURE 8.1   Elements of an induction programme

organization's past achievements. At times, personalities who have made significant contributions to the company and also serve as role models for others are also projected. At the end of the day, the new entrant is comfortable with the environment, understands his/her job responsibilities and duties clearly, identifies with his/her team members, and is clear about his/her career goal. A follow-up process follows the induction, usually after one week or so. This is just to obtain clarification as to whether the employee has understood the orientation programme and has adjusted to the company's processes. The immediate supervisor may initiate an interactive meeting with the new employees and find out whether clarification is required or the adjustment process is achieved.

One expert cautions against the following:

- Using too much of the valuable orientation time to complete paperwork
- Giving too much information too quickly
- Giving information that is irrelevant to adjusting to the position and the organization
- Scaring the employee by spending an inordinate amount of time discussing the negative aspects of the job
- Using lectures and videos rather than methods that allow for two-way communication
- Limiting orientation to the first day at work
- Selling the organization

Once an employee has completed the initial stages of socialization, he or she begins to perform the roles associated with the position he or she holds in the organizational structure.

GLOBAL PLACEMENT

Defined broadly, global placement is performance of the traditional HR functions of staffing, deciding compensation benefits, training and development, performance management, labour relations, and also being a strategic business partner within an organization that operates internationally. HR managers and professionals in multinational firms perform the following activities:

- Managing international relocation of expatriates and their families
- Providing a variety of services for relocating employees and their families
- Building close relationship with the other countries where the company operates

IBM, Exxon, McDonald, and Coca Cola derive close to 50% of revenue from their overseas operations. The relationship between HR planning and strategic planning for international ventures needs to be strengthened in many aspects. Various efforts are being made to enhance the recruitment and success of expatriates. One study identified the following critical issues affecting planning and recruitment aspects of international HRM:

- Identifying top managerial talent early in the process
- Identifying criteria for success in overseas assignments
- Motivating employees to take overseas assignments
- Establishing a strong connection between the strategic plan of the company and HR planning

Selecting people to make a move from either the parent country or a third country requires weighing a number of criteria:

- *Job-related skills*: Apart from the job skills, other related skills, such as motivating others and adapting to new surroundings, are also important.
- *Leadership skills*: Leadership skills also rank high on the criteria for placing expatriates. Leading people belonging to a totally different culture is a challenge by itself.
- *Cultural openness and adaptation*: This is a very important dimension, and is difficult to assess. Most of the time, people come back half way through their assignments because their families fail to withstand the cultural shock in the alien environment.
- *Language skills*: An expatriate is expected to have knowledge of the local language lest he or she would be at a disadvantage in government and local business negotiations and is almost bound to miss the nuances of employee issues.
- *Willingness to relocate*: Even though people see travelling abroad as glamorous, there are instances where employees express fears regarding spouses travelling along with them, family upheaval, etc.

With all these variables, it becomes the responsibility of the HR to maintain a database of potential candidates for worldwide positions, obtain work permits and entry visas, and provide relocation services ranging from travel to housing and schooling of children.

OUTPLACEMENT

Outplacement refers to the in-house help provided by organizations during the transition phase of downsizing to rehabilitation. Organizations can play an important role by providing the social safety net scheme. The services offered in this scheme include counselling, training, retraining, skill upgradation, and other types of help required by the employees. The services also include housing, reassignment, job placement, and other cash equivalents. The main objective is to reduce or prevent poverty in a specific group. After the introduction of voluntary retirement scheme (VRS) and large-scale downsizing, particularly in the public sector, the social safety net scheme has been introduced for the welfare of the employees.

PROMOTION, DEMOTION, AND TRANSFER

Employees in an organization change jobs frequently. Workforce mobility occurs in the form of promotions or transfers. From the individual's point of view, it may signify career development, but from the organization's point of view, these changes are necessitated by various factors. The mobility might take place between jobs in various departments or divisions.

Need for Internal Mobility

In response to external changes in the business environment, organizations may resort to restructuring, relocation, and reorganization of jobs. At times, the objectives of the organization, such as expansion and diversification, may necessitate promotions or transfers. Retirements and resignations may also lead to job changes.

Promotion

Promotions refer to upward movement of an employee from the present position to another one with increased responsibilities, pay, status, and prestige. Promotion may be defined as the advancement of an employee to a higher position with better pay, working conditions, facilities, challenges, etc.

Purpose of Promotions

Organizations promote employees for various reasons. Some of them are as follows:

- To increase organizational effectiveness
- To utilize employees' skills at various levels for employee satisfaction and organizational gain
- To elevate the employees to higher positions to encourage loyalty
- To reward employees for their meritorious performance
- To develop an internal structure of competent employees with high commitment towards organization
- To reduce discontent and unrest among employees
- To suggest logical training for advancement
- To provide an effective incentive for initiative, enterprise, and ambition among employees
- To enhance the self-esteem of the employees and encourage them to achieve higher goals

Bases of Promotion

> ■ ■ ■
> Promotions refer to upward movement of an employee from the present position to another one with increased responsibilities, pay, status, and prestige.

> ■ ■ ■
> Organizations need to strike a balance between a policy of promoting from within and external recruitment.

Organizations adopt different bases for promotions. Normally, the base of promotion is seniority or merit, or a combination of the two. The very purpose of promotion is to encourage employees and reward merit. Organizations that fail to reward excellence in service or rely too much on personal relationships or the length of service suffer in terms of both efficiency and morale. Organizations need to strike a balance between a policy of promoting from within and external recruitment. In large organizations, careful planning needs to be done as to how many positions may be filled from outside. While deciding on promotions, performance appraisals are taken into consideration vis-à-vis job postings. Career pathways usually signify the channel through which an employee moves. Promotions need to be synchronized with the jobs identified in the career pathways.

Promotion Policy

Usually every organization has its own promotion policy and it is based on its corporate policy. The basic characteristics of a systematic promotion policy may be summarized as follows:

- The policy should be applied uniformly to all employees irrespective of their backgrounds.
- The criteria for promotion should be specified clearly.
- There should be a systematic channel of promotion applicable to all employees.
- Appropriate authority should be appointed to make judgments about the eligible candidates.
- Avenues for career counselling have to be specified to the employees to facilitate promotions and also handle rejections.

Promotions vs Recruitments from Outside

Promotion is generally considered as a reward for excellent services rendered by the employees. Employees are encouraged to show initiative and assess their responsibilities in their jobs. At Ford, for example, employees complete the competencies-based job analysis by describing the knowledge and skills required for their present job and the knowledge or skills they would like to acquire. These responses are then linked to particular vacancies within the company for which the respective managers have already prepared descriptions. However, there are certain disadvantages of this method if followed singularly. For example, if the organization decides to change its business strategy, the existing managers may not properly fit into the new positions. Even though we do not have enough research evidence to support this statement, organizations usually believe in infusing new blood into the system to encourage divergent thinking.

Unless job descriptions and specifications clearly indicate the responsibilities of individuals, there is a possibility of mismatch between the individual and the job. However, decisions are made according to the need of the situation. Skilled and talented people are also available in the market and diversity at times proves to be an advantage.

Transfer

A transfer is a change in the job assignment. It may be linked with a promotion or there may not be any change at all in a status and responsibilities. We may interpret a transfer as a horizontal move of an employee requiring similar skills and at the same level of responsibility, status, and pay.

Purpose of Transfer

Organizations resort to transfer to attain the following objectives:

- Organizations may transfer employees when there is a change in technology, productivity, production schedule, product line, product quality, market conditions, or organizational structure to meet the new challenges, and match the right job with the right person.
- At times transfers are also administered on employees to meet their personal demands. Employees request transfers to work in their native place or where their family or spouse lives, or for any other personal reason.

- Transfers may be necessary for better utilization of employees' skills. In certain cases, employees may also be transferred to another place where their skills and capacities or expertise may be required.

- Sometimes employees may be transferred to different places or rotated in different jobs to expand their capabilities and provide them exposure to various situations and kinds of assignments.
- Transfers are also administered to provide relief and adjustment to employees who are engaged in overburdening or hazardous work for long periods.
- Transfers are also used as a disciplinary measure to desist employees from indulging in undesirable activities.

However, there are certain problems associated with transfers. At times, a transfer may be an unwelcome shift to an employee who would not like to move. There might be some adjustment problems also. There are also instances where productivity suffers because of transfer of an efficient employee. Hence, organizations need to clearly specify their transfer policy. The authority eligible to transfer issues the order for transfer specifying in unambiguous terms the time within which the transfer has to be effected and the pay and facilities attached with the transfer.

SEPARATION

A separation is a decision that the individual and the organization should part (Davis). The separation could be at the instance of the employer or the employee. Separations take several forms, some of which are as follows:

- *Long leave of absence:* Employees may apply for long leave from work on various grounds such as health, education, family, or work-related matters.
- *Resignation:* Employees may decide voluntarily to separate from the organization on grounds of health, marriage, better career prospects in other organizations, etc.
- *Retirement:* Retirement is a termination of services, which is termed as compulsory retirement, and normally employees retire between 58 and 60. The voluntary retirement scheme (VRS) is another retirement scheme, which has been introduced in various public and private sectors with a view to offload surplus staff and cutting down labour costs. In such instances, the management

■ ■ ■
A separation is a decision initiated by either the employee or the employer.

is also organizing counselling sessions to reduce anxiety in the minds of the employees about premature retirement and also offers financial advice to allow them to invest in a sound manner.

- *Death:* Separation in organization may also occur due to sudden death of an employee while in service. Some organizations offer employment to the spouse, child, or dependant of the deceased employee on compassionate grounds.

■ ■ ■
Downsizing, lay-off, and retrenchment are important separation procedures initiated by the employer.

These practices are commonly practised in almost all organizations. These are initiated by the employee, except retirement, which is as per the company policy, and not by the company. Lay-off and retrenchment are moves initiated by the employer.

DOWNSIZING, LAY-OFF, AND RETRENCHMENT

In some cases, downsizing is undertaken to reduce labour costs and streamline organizational operations. In other cases, downsizing results from mergers and acquisitions, in which the resulting

■ ■ ■
Dismissal of an
employee results in
termination of services
and is a punitive
measure for proven
misconduct.

company is plagued with redundant functions. Often, organizations often fail to realize the cost benefits they hoped to receive from downsizing because they must replace functions, either by hiring consultants or by training the existing employees. Moreover, productivity gains are short-lived; in fact, they are more a reflection of the reduction in operating expenses than of increase in output. Finally, motivation and morale are damaged, which can have indirect effects upon both the productivity and the economy of the organization.

Indeed downsizing can have devastating effects upon individual employees, both those who have lost their jobs and those who have not. Specifically, employees losing their jobs face many emotional problems. Their initial response may be one of shock, anger, or relief. Eventually, they need to confront the task of being re-employed without succumbing to frustration and self-doubt. The organization can help them avoid such emotions by preparing them for transition to a new job, a new organization, or a new career.

Even those employees who do not lose their jobs as a result of downsizing may face serious psychological consequences. Indeed, an analysis of the feelings of those who survive downsizing shows that they also feel anger, anxiety, cynicism, resentment against the upper management, and resignation mixed with some hope. There are also tangible consequences in the workplace that survivors must deal with. Many a time, organizations abolish staff positions that they need to devise a new 'leaner' strategy and vision, and thus benefits of downsizing are never realized. However, the energies and stress levels of survivors are stretched, given that the survivors are now expected to accomplish the additional work of those who have been released from the organization.

It should be noted that there are some instances of positive individual outcomes as a result of downsizing. Due to the relief from surviving the downsizing, and the heightened awareness of performance that downsizing brings, individual efforts after downsizing may actually increase. The degree to which overall outcomes are positive or negative, however, depends upon organizational measures taken to execute the downsizing efforts.

A lay-off is usually initiated by the employer because of inadequacies in organizational functioning such as breakdown of machinery or shortage of power, raw materials, and production delays. A lay-off can be temporary or permanent. It may be temporary if the lay-off is because of the business cycle or seasonal factors as is common in mines, sugar industry, etc. In such lay-offs, the employee has the opportunity of coming back to employment after a certain period. At times, factors such as downsizing, merger, and acquisition may also be responsible for lay-off. Such a lay-off often turns out to be a permanent one. When a lay-off becomes permanent, it is called retrenchment.

Retrenchment is generally on account of surplus staff, poor demand for products, economic slowdown, etc. It is obligatory on the part of the employer to pay compensation to employees who are retrenched. While laying off, the first-in-last-out principle is generally followed.

Suspension

Suspension means prohibiting an employee from attending work and performing normal duties assigned to him or her. It is a measure of punishment for an employee for a specific period. When an employee faces certain charges of misconduct or misdemeanour, an enquiry is made into it, and if the charges are serious, it might lead to suspension of the employee till he or she is either convicted or acquitted of the charges.

Dismissal

Dismissal of an employee results in termination of services and is a punitive measure for proven misconduct. The reasons for dismissal may be carelessness, insubordination, violation of rules, dishonesty, inefficiency, aggressive behaviour, unauthorized absence for a long time, etc. It is a serious measure that impairs the earning potential and the public image of the employee. It is usually used as a last resort; until all the necessary evidence is gathered, this step is avoided. The employee is also given an opportunity to defend his or her innocence before dismissal.

Resignation

It is a voluntary termination of service by an employee by serving a notice/resignation to the employer. Resignations can also happen involuntarily. Typically, involuntary resignations could occur for two main reasons. The first is when the company would like to terminate the services of an employee, which could happen on various counts such as dereliction of duty, misconduct, non-performance, and violation of regulations. The other type of involuntary resignation is on account of layoffs, which are determined by business reasons affecting the company and necessitating a reduction in the workforce. Involuntary resignations that arise due to an employee's fault are a strong recrimination against the employee. Such cases involving serious misconduct, harassment, or financial impropriety could result in legal action. This is a serious indictment of the employee, which could have a bearing on the employment record and future prospects.

Voluntary Retirement Scheme

Increased competition has prompted managements to take diverse steps including rightsizing of the workforce. Downsizing and rightsizing have become a common phenomenon in the post liberalized era. VRS is the most humane technique to provide overall reduction in the existing strength of the employees. It is a technique used for dispensing the excess workforce.

A business firm may introduce VRS (Exhibits 8.1 and 8.2) under the following circumstances:

- Recession in the business
- Intense competition due to which the establishment becomes unviable unless downsizing is resorted to
- Joint ventures with foreign collaborations
- Takeovers and mergers
- Obsolescence of product/technology

Companies can frame different schemes of voluntary retirement for different classes of their employees. The guidelines provide that the scheme of voluntary retirement framed by a company should meet the following requirements:

- The scheme applies to an employee of the company who has completed 10 years of service or 40 years of age.
- It applies to all employees, including workers and executives of the company, except the directors.

- It has been drawn to bring overall reduction in the existing strength of the employees of the company.
- The vacancy caused by voluntary retirement is not to be filled up, nor is the retiring employee to be employed in another company or concern belonging to the same management.
- The amount receivable on account of voluntary retirement of the employee does not exceed the amount equivalent to one and one-half months' salary for each completed year of service or monthly emoluments at the time of retirement multiplied by the balance months of service left before the date of his/her retirement on superannuation. In any case, the amount should not exceed rupees five lakhs in case of each employee.
- The employee has not availed in the past, any benefit from any other VRS.

However, implementation of VRS is not an easy task. Employees, trade unions, and other leaders within the organization oppose the scheme as it is usually sudden and hurts the individual. The objective of VRS is to offload those employees who cannot be retrained. However, things happen differently. When the company opts for downsizing and declares a VRS, there is a possibility of skilled employees leaving the organization. Hence, implementation of VRS requires proper HR planning, dialogue with trade unions, and effective communication with the affected employees.

EXHIBIT 8.1   Voluntary retirement scheme in National Carbon Company

National Carbon Company is a unit of Eveready Industries India Ltd, Kolkata, which was the first dry cell manufacturing plant in India. Over the years, technology was not upgraded and so the labour cost for this unit was quite high when compared to other modernized units. The management, in order to make the plant viable, took the drastic measure of downsizing its workforce through VRS.

It was found that downsizing alone cannot reduce labour cost for an industry. Technology upgradation along with downsizing can reduce labour cost. Repeated introduction of VRS time and again helped the organization to reduce the workforce from 3,500 to 414.

To conclude, VRS cannot be made successful if introduced unilaterally. A positive response in downsizing through VRS can be obtained provided the trade union extends wholehearted support for the same. The success story of VRS in the company is an eye-opener for research scholars, practising managers, trade union leaders, and management students.

Source: Basu, Soma and Datta, Saroj K. 2010, The success story of voluntary retirement scheme in National Carbon Company: A Unit of Eveready Industries India Ltd, *American Journal of Economics and Business Administration*, Science Publications, 2 (2), pp. 157–59.

EXHIBIT 8.2   Voluntary retirement scheme in Indian Oil Corporation

VRS was first introduced in Indian Oil Corporation (IOC) in June 1990. Since then, it has come into force for a specified duration, with/without modification, from time to time. The management has approved the following rules for proper administration of the scheme to provide for voluntary separation and payment of terminal benefits including ex-gratia payment to employees.

The modified scheme came into force with effect from July 2003. It shall remain in operation for such period/periods as may be notified from time to time.

(Contd)

EXHIBIT 8.2   (Contd)

Application

These rules shall apply to all regular employees of the IOC in the prescribed scales of pay, but shall not apply to the Chairman and directors, and

- those in casual/muster role employment or paid from contingencies;
- employees on deputation from other organizations;
- those appointed on contract basis;
- those deputed to other organizations and opting for permanent absorption in those organizations; and
- re-employed pensioners with less than 10 years service.

Eligibility

The scheme shall be applicable to only such employees who have attained the age of 45 years or have served the IOC for a minimum period of 20 years and to re-employed pensioners who have served the corporation for a minimum period of 10 years, in addition to meeting the age requirement.

Regulation of the Scheme

An employee who has attained the age of 45 years or has served the corporation for a minimum period of 20 years may seek voluntary retirement by a written request in prescribed form addressed through proper channel to the competent authority who may at his/her discretion, grant or not grant voluntary retirement for reasons to be recorded in writing.

An employee seeking voluntary retirement under the scheme must give one/three months notice as per the terms of his appointment. However, the management may decide to release the employee after approval of the application for voluntary retirement without any additional benefit.

The date of receipt of application by the controlling authority would determine the date from which the notice for voluntary retirement given by the employee should be considered.

Benefits

The following benefits shall be admissible to those permitted to separate under the scheme:

- Full provident fund (PF) contributions of the employer with accretions thereto in the account of the employee subject to the provisions of the PF rules applicable
- Gratuity for each completed year of service or part thereof as admissible under the gratuity rules applicable
- Encashment of leave available as credit on the day of separation, in accordance with the laid down rules
- Resettlement concession comprising benefits as admissible on transfer for self and family, provided the employee avails settlement concession within six months from the date of separation
- Ex-gratia payment equivalent to 60 days emoluments for each completed year of service or the monthly emoluments at the time of retirement multiplied by the balance months of service left before normal date of retirement on superannuation, whichever is less
- Superannuation benefit is admissible only to members who have served for the minimum qualifying period and it will be calculated as for deemed superannuation as on the date of separation, but payable from the notional date of superannuation.
- Post retirement medical attendance facility for employees seeking separation under the VRS and who have attained the age of 50 years on the date of such separation shall be covered by the provisions of the post retirement medical attendance facility, as amended from time to time. The aforesaid provisions will be applicable from the date of separation under the VRS.
- Medical insurance facility will be available to those who separate under the scheme before completing 50 years of age. On attaining the age of 50 years, they will be entitled for coverage under the provisions of the post retirement medical attendance facility.

Source: http://www.indianoilexpress.com/downloads/HRPolicies/vrs_07.pdf, accessed on 27 April 2012.

Superannuation

A superannuation scheme is introduced by a company to provide monthly pension benefits to its employees on retirement. Under the Income Tax Act, a company can contribute a maximum of 27% of the basic wage/salary to the employees benefit schemes such as provident fund/ superannuation scheme. One can invest a maximum of 12% in a PF scheme, which is contributory, and the remaining 15% in a superannuation scheme, which is non-contributory.

A superannuation scheme provides two methods of calculating benefits to the employees. One method, called benefit purchase scheme, involves fixing the amount of pension benefits in advance, whereas the other, called money purchase scheme, involves contribution at a fixed percentage periodically. The pension benefits are arrived at seeing the accumulated credit balance of the member at the time of superannuation (retirement).

The company can establish a trust to make investments as permissible under the law or the superannuation policy may be taken from the Life Insurance Corporation (LIC) of India. On the date of superannuation, the member is entitled to get one-third value of the benefits commuted tax free in cash (in case gratuity is also paid) and half value of the benefits commuted in cash (in case no gratuity is paid). A member gets the pension calculated according to the balance sum standing to his/her credit, after commutation through LIC of India only.

Superannuation Pension

A superannuation pension is a regulated payment method designed to provide a financially secure lifestyle after retirement. These pension amounts are actually superannuation funds, which are accumulated by voluntary and compulsory payments by employers and their employees. The amount is locked for a certain period of time till the retirement of the employee. Exceptions are pension release schemes.

Superannuation pensions are not heavily taxed with the intention of increasing contribution from the employee and employer. This helps in increasing the amount of the potential payout at the end of the term.

With rise in the average age expectancy and expanding workforce, superannuation pensions become essential for optimal financial planning and asset management. Superannuation pension policies are different in every country, but the objective of providing a steady income in life after employment remains the same.

Superannuation Pension in USA

In the US, the Social Security Administration (SSA) is by far the most prominent provider of superannuation pensions. The pensions here are funded by contributions from both employer and employees. The accumulated pension funds become prime investment capital for various financial instruments. The laws that regulate the tax liability of a superannuation pension fund have been reduced. Taxes on the interest are deferred till the withdrawal of the funds from the account upon retirement.

Superannuation Pension in Australia

Superannuation pensions in Australia are paid through employment-related contributions. The Australian superannuation scheme is employer funded and the deposits to the pension fund account are regulated by the government. Employers are entitled to pay up to 9% of the their earnings to the retirement fund.

Superannuation pension benefits are paid to persons over 60, tax free, provided he/she has been a citizen or resident of Australia for at least ten years.

Superannuation Scheme in India

In India, a superannuation scheme is a prerequisite facility given to employees in various organizations as part of their employee retention strategy. The superannuation scheme allows deduction up to 15% of the basic salary and in combination with the provident fund must not exceed 27% of the total compensation as per the existing income tax guidelines. Superannuation can be availed from different insurance providers, both government and private. Superannuation pension schemes are defined contributions in nature and an employee can withdraw from the scheme any time.

Exit Interviews

When employees leave, organizations often conduct exit interviews in order to assess the reasons for the employee's decision to part and to prevent it if necessary. Usually, this is conducted face-to-face by the HR Manager. Through this interview, the organization attempts to uncover the reasons of the employee's departure. The content and methodology of the exit interview varies from company to company. The aspects that are usually discussed in an exit interview are: reasons for leaving, satisfaction with the job, perception of the management, opportunities for advancement, adequacy of pay, training, and performance appraisal. In one sense, this information allows organizations to assess how well their retention strategies are working and update benefits and other programmes. The employees may also feel that their opinions are being valued by the organization. There are instances where the exit interview has been conducted by an external consulting firm. Assuring confidentiality by using such measures is likely to produce more candid responses. One study showed that employees are not truthful in exit interviews because of fear that they would be blamed and that their responses will not be held confidential. Some organizations do not conduct exit interviews. However, most organizations keep a record of the rate of turnover. Exhibit 8.3 lists some sample exit interview questions.

EXHIBIT 8.3   Exit interview questions—samples

The following are samples of the types of exit interview questions that employers commonly ask outgoing employees:

- What is your primary reason for leaving?
- Did anything trigger your decision to leave?
- What was most satisfying about your job?
- What was least satisfying about your job?
- What would you change about your job?
- Did your job duties turn out to be as you expected?
- Did you receive enough training to do your job effectively?
- Did you receive adequate support to do your job?

(Contd)

EXHIBIT 8.3 (Contd)

- Did you receive sufficient feedback about your performance between merit reviews?
- Were you satisfied with this company's merit review process?
- Did this company help you to fulfil your career goals?
- Do you have any tips to help us find your replacement?
- What would you suggest to make our workplace better?
- Were you happy with your pay, benefits, and other incentives?
- What was the quality of the supervision you received?
- What could your immediate supervisor do to improve his or her management style?
- Based on your experience with us, what do you think it takes to succeed at this company?
- Did any company policies or procedures (or any other obstacles) make your job difficult?
- Would you consider working again for this company in the future?
- Would you recommend this company to your family and friends?
- How do you generally feel about this company?
- What did you like most about this company?
- What did you like least about this company?
- What does your new company offer that this company doesn't?
- Can this company do anything to encourage you to stay?
- Before deciding to leave, did you investigate a transfer within the company?
- Did anyone in this company discriminate against you, harass you, or cause hostile working conditions?
- Do you have any other comments?

Source: http://jobsearchtech.about.com/cs/interviewtips/a/exit_interview_2.htm, accessed on 27 April 2012.

SUMMARY

The chapter begins with an overview of the concepts of placement and induction in an organization. It also explains in detail the organizational induction programme, including organizational issues, employee benefits, job duties, etc. The chapter also suggests some cautions against various issues, thereby supporting the organization to successfully complete the process of socialization. Further, the chapter covers the global placement procedure, the challenges involved in it, transfer of employees, criteria involved in selection of employees for relocation of services, etc. The chapter also explains in brief the promotion policy, purpose of transfer, separations, downsizing, layoff and retrenchment, suspension and dismissal of employees, etc. The various case studies attempt to familiarize the reader with the various internal mobility procedures. At the end, the chapter provides a brief discussion on exit interviews in order to assess the reasons for voluntary workforce turnover.

■ ■ ■ | KEY TERMS

Induction Introduction of a person to the job and the organization

Internal mobility The lateral or vertical movement of an employee within an organization

Lay-off The separation of the employee from the organization for economic or business reasons

Placement Actual posting of an employee to a specific job with rank and responsibilities

Promotion Employee movement from current job to another that is higher in pay, responsibility, and/or organization level

Retirement Termination of service on reaching the age of superannuation

Retrenchment A permanent layoff for reasons other than punishment, but not retirement or termination owing to ill health

Resignation A voluntary separation initiated by the employee himself

Separation A decision that the individual and the organization should part

Suspension Prohibiting an employee from attending work and performing normal duties asigned to him or her

Transfer Employee movement that occurs when an employee is moved from one job to another that is relatively equal in pay, responsibility, and/or organizational level

■ ■ ■ EXERCISES

Multiple Choice Questions

1. New employees are introduced to the organization's standards, goals, values, and culture through
   (a) promotion
   (b) global placement
   (c) induction
   (d) internal mobility

2. What is meant by the term appraisal?
   (a) A system used to improve the performance of workers
   (b) The main way in which an employee's wages are determined
   (c) The evaluation of an individual employee's performance
   (d) A system of reward points offered by retailers to attract customer loyalty

3. The practice of assigning a candidate to the right job is called
   (a) interview
   (b) promotion
   (c) placement
   (d) retrenchment

4. What is meant by the term retrenchment?
   (a) A process of giving employees greater autonomy and decision-making powers
   (b) A system that encourages workers to move more freely within the organization
   (c) Permanent lay-off of surplus staff due to economic slowdown
   (d) A formal system of leadership that relies greatly on control

5. How can an organization eliminate surplus workers?
   (a) By laying them off
   (b) By firing them
   (c) By offering them early retirement
   (d) All of these

6. Reasons for internal mobility are
   (a) restructuring, relocation, and reorganization of jobs
   (b) retirements and resignations
   (c) expansion and diversification
   (d) all of these

7. Which of the following is the best term to describe the process of maintaining a database of potential candidates for worldwide positions and obtaining work permits and entry visas?
   (a) Global placement
   (b) International HRM
   (c) Socialization
   (d) Separation

Fill in the Blanks

1. _____, _____, and retrenchment are important separation procedures initiated by the employer.

2. _____ data provides a useful steer as to where improvements need to be made.

3. The horizontal movement of an employee to a job requiring similar skills and at the same level of responsibilities is known as _____.

4. Dishonesty, inefficiency, violation of rules, absence for a long time, etc., are some fair reasons for _____ of an employee.

5. VRS has been introduced to offload surplus staff and cut down costs in both _____ and _____ sectors.

Concept Review Questions

1. Explain the term placement. Discuss its importance in the organization.

2. Define induction, discussing in detail the components of an employee induction programme.

3. What measures should be taken to make the induction programme a success in the organization?

4. What are the advantages and disadvantages of promoting employees from within the company?
5. Why do employers transfer employees?
6. What is the voluntary retirement scheme? Write a note on it.
7. Bring out the differences between lay-off and retrenchment.
8. Write a note on conditions that prompt the dimissal of an employee.

Project Work

1. Prepare a write-up on the placement process in an IT company and a non-IT company.
2. Critically evaluate the induction process of an IT company and suggest some improvements.
3. Conduct a role-play in the classroom on the placement process both for an IT and a non-IT company prepared by you.

■ ■ ■ | REFERENCES

Ashford, S.J. and Black, J.S. 1996, 'Proactivity during organizational entry: The role of desire for control', *Journal of Applied Psychology*, 81(2), pp. 199–214.

Baker, H.E. III and Daniel, C. Feldman 1991, 'Linking organizational socialization tactics with corporate human resource managementstrategies', *Human Resource Management Review*, 1(3), Fall, pp. 193–202.

Bauer, T.N. and Green, S.G. 1994, 'Effect of new comer involvement in work-related activities: A longitudinal study of socialization', *Journal of Applied Psychology*, April, pp. 211–23.

Blau, G. 1999, 'Early-career job factors influencing the professional commitment of medical technologies', *Academy of Management Journal*, December, pp. 687–99.

Cascio W.F. 1993, 'Downsizing: What do we know? What have we learned?' *Academy of Management Executive*, 7, pp. 95–104.

Dowling, P.J. 1989, 'Hot issues overseas', *Personnel Administrator*, 34, pp. 68–72.

Ferris, G.R. et al. 1992, 'Promotion systems in organization', *Human Resource Planning*, pp. 47–68.

Horowitz, A. 1999, 'Up to speed-fast', *Computerworld*, 33(7), p. 48.

Kanungo, R.N. and Conger, J.A. 1993, 'Promoting altruism as a corporate goal', *Executive*, August, pp. 37–48.

Levering, R. and Moskowitz, M. 2001, 'The 100 best companies to work for', *Fortune*, 143(1), pp. 148–168.

Lindo, D.K. 1993, 'Orientation express', *Office Systems*, 10(11), pp. 64–67.

Lublin, J.S. 1996, 'An overseas stint can be a ticket to the top', *The Wall Street Journal*, January 29, pp. B1–B5.

Maanen, J.V. and Edgar H. Schein 1979, 'Toward a theory of organizational socialization'. In Staw, B.M.

(Ed.), *Research in Organizational Behaviour*, Jai Press, Greenwich, pp 210.

Mendenhall, M.E. and Oddou, G. 1995, 'The overseas assignment: A practical look',. In Mendenhall, M.E. and Oddoe, G. (Eds.), *Readings and Cases in International Human Resource Management*, South-Western Publishing, Cincinnati, pp. 206–16.

Moran, R., Stahl, H., and Steel, R. 1989, 'Survey of personnel managers at 56 international companies', cited in O'Boyle, T. 1989, 'Grappling with the expatriate issue', The Wall Street Journal, December 11, pp. B1–B4.

O'Neill, H.M. and Lenn, D.J. 1995, 'Voices of survivors. Words that downsizing CEOs should hear', *Academy of Management Executive*, 9, pp. 23–34.

Rao, V.S.P. 2001, *Human Resource Management: Text and Cases*, Excel Books, New Delhi, pp. 172–86

Rogers, B. 1994, 'The making of a highly skilled worker', HR *Magazine*, July, p. 62.

Starcke, alice M. 1996, 'Building a better orientation programme', *HR Magazine*, November, pp. 107–13.

Wanous, J.P., Reichers, A.E., and Malik, S.D. 1992, 'Organizational socialization and group development', *Academy of Management Review*, 9, pp. 670–83.

Wooldridge, A. 2000, 'Come back, company man', *The New York Times*, March 5.

http://www.chrmglobal.com/articles/567/1/involuntary-resignations.html, accessed on 12 January 2012.

http://www.economywatch.com/investment/pensions/superannuation-pension.html, accessed on 12 January 2012.

http://www.gkcindia.com/Forms/1-SASCHEME.doc, accessed on 12 January 2012.

http://www.scipub.org/fulltext/ajeba/ajeba22157-159.pdf, accessed on 12 September 2011.

Induction Issues in an Indian BPO—Firstnet

Firstnet is a domestic BPO operating out of eight major cities in the country. They support customers in the telecom and insurance verticals. The total employees working across all the centres in the country is close to 10,000. The company has been recruiting close to 1,000 employees every month for expansion and replacement of outgoing employees.

The company has adopted the following steps (Table 8.1) in the recruitment process.

TABLE 8.1 Steps in the recruitment process

Step	Process
1.	Identification of manpower needs and manpower requirement forecasting
2.	Recruitment planning and channel mix decision
3.	Recruitment through various channels
4.	Induction and onboarding

During a monthly review meeting, the Chief People Officer (CPO) identified that early attrition (0–3 months) had spiked during the last three months. He advised the site HR managers to identify the causes and come out with possible solutions to the issue. The site HR managers held both formal and informal meetings with recent joinees and identified the following issues:

- The trainers conducting the induction and orientation programmes were not effective in terms of communication and imparting the skills required for performing on the job.
- The training content was quite contradictory to what the joinees were doing on the job.
- The training was too theoretical with very little hands-on training.
- There was very little support to get the queries addressed after hitting the floor.

After the review, the site HR managers made the following recommendations to the CPO:

- Train the trainers on communication and teaching methodologies.
- Review the training content along with the operations team and update accordingly.
- Have a weekly feedback session with training, operations, and HR head to understand the issues involved.

After the review, the CPO approved the implementation of the suggestions for the induction and training of new hires in the organization.

Questions
1. Analyse the placement issues in Firstnet.
2. Do you think the approach taken by them would address the issues? If yes, please explain why.

Induction in Industry

A global company with its headquarters in the United States and business divisions all over the world is very people oriented, and the parent company is keen to implement as many global processes as possible, with customization to meet country- and business-specific needs. There is, for example, a global performance and development planning scheme (appraisal) which occurs annually at the same time across the branches worldwide. Other processes have local (country and division) components. The aim is to make management processes as easy as possible; most of the support material and process tracking is available online. Across the board, the responsibility for managing and developing staff is very much vested in local managers: the HR departments do not have a 'policing' role. All activity is based on objectives (organizational and divisional objectives cascaded down the management to individuals). Individuals are also responsible for their own development as much as their managers are and there is a wide range of internal and external development opportunities for those who want them (where they are relevant to the job).

Levels of Induction

The company's induction practice in the UK is about to change, partly due to feedback from staff about induction and partly through a need to communicate coherently at the organizational (global) level following a merger. Induction has three tiers. There is a global, online, Web-based induction programme for all employees, which is just about to be released following a period of piloting. This has four elements: company strategies, structures and processes, values and behaviour, reward, and other 'individual' issues. At the country (UK) level, a new induction day has also started recently. This is particularly in response to staff feedback. Although new starters understood their role and place in the local organization, they were less clear about how the different UK businesses fitted together and how their role contributed to the UK-wide business as a whole. New induction day is observed every 2–3 months to bring together new recruits from across the country along with the UK Director and senior managers from the range of UK businesses. It is called a business and networking orientation event. An interesting component is the 'interview': New recruits divide into small groups, each of which interviews one of the senior managers and then provides feedback to the rest (in front of the managers) regarding what they have learned from the interview. There is also a quiz (unchecked) that aims to reinforce some of the learning from the day.

At the local level, each manager has a checklist (available through the company intranet) which they are prompted to use as soon as an appointment has been accepted. The recruitment and induction processes are therefore linked. The checklist highlights things to do before the new recruit arrives, such as ordering equipment, setting up voicemail, what to do on the first day and subsequently. This includes booking new staff on the local health and safety induction, which is the only part of the local induction not conducted by the managers. New starters are also sent an email confirming their automatic booking on the UK induction and highlighting things they must do as in the first few weeks. It is very much the manager's responsibility to make sure that induction is done effectively. There is no central policing of whether the checklist is being complied with. There is a very strong philosophy in the company that staff are managers' responsibility. HR will check attendance at the UK induction (but there is no check on effectiveness). This is expected to come through in performance monitoring processes (the performance planning process). Managers will set

objectives for new staff usually for a six month period, with regular reviews. Any issues arising from an ineffective induction should be highlighted as part of this. Any senior manager can see the performance plans and ratings of the managers and staff in their divisions.

Performance Planning Process (Appraisal)

There is no probation process as such, but.short-term objectives are set for the new staff, which are fed into regular reviews and the annual performance planning process at the same time across the entire organization. The scheme is objective-oriented and results in a 'rating' which indicates to managers what salary increase might be applicable for the staff. The system is automated, so that the previous year's objectives and development actions are brought forward for review. If no progress has been made, the manager has to explain this. Development actions in particular are the responsibility of both the manager and the employee. Training or development needs identified are taken forward within the context of company-wide training and development programmes.

There are core programmes, many of which are delivered over the Web, and specific business-related programmes, which are available for all staff and supported by the central budget. Any job-specific needs not covered by core programmes are met by courses or other activities paid for from the manager's budget. The company uses a system of 'job families' with a guide to the development needed for each: there is an expectation (but no compulsion) that employees will undertake the recommended training or development prior to moving up to a new level. Again, feedback and evaluation on the effectiveness of the performance planning process is left to individuals and managers rather than being part of any centrally driven activity. There is an employee comments section on each appraisal form, which is recorded. An open door policy is also followed, allowing any member of staff to refer to a senior manager if they are dissatisfied. Many of the Web-based programmes have been initiated by staff who have highlighted gaps in their own and their teams' knowledge or understanding.

Although a global company with global processes, the company's philosophy is very much one of management responsibility for people and people development. Supporting frameworks, materials, and processes are available, largely accessible via the company intranet, and are expected to be used. Trust must play a significant part. The online induction is interesting and it would be good to revisit this in a few months to see what, if any, feedback there has been on its success. Similarly, the 'interview' component of the UK-wide induction is worth noting, particularly the commitment that this requires from senior managers to attend and participate effectively. What is most interesting is that, whilst many apparently robust processes exist to support people management, it is the bottom line that is evaluated and measured (i.e., the success of the business and how well people meet their objectives and contribute to business success) rather than the processes themselves; implementation of processes may sometimes become an end in itself in other organisations. Finally, the company does not have any external accreditations for people management and does not follow any external quality frameworks such as Investors in People or EFQM excellence model, at least in the UK.

Questions
1. Critically examine the induction process and its role in placement of employees.
2. Do you think the three-tier induction would be enough for successful placement of employees?
3. Can the localization of placement be improved? If so, how?
4. Does the performance planning have a role in placement?
5. Critically examine the individualization of performance planning vis-à-vis centralization and its effectivenss in an organization.

LeasePlan Corporation

CASE STUDY 3

LeasePlan Corporation is the world's leading provider of vehicle fleet management solutions. Based in the Netherlands, LeasePlan Corporation is a global holding company which centralizes management and support functions for a group of operational subsidiaries in 27 countries across five continents. LeasePlan's broad product and service portfolio spreads across the entire automotive value chain from financing and insurance through to operational management, and ultimately to remarketing of vehicles. In order to maintain its dominant position as the driving force of innovation and development in its industry, LeasePlan Corporation is now positioning itself as the first truly global provider of integrated fleet management solutions with a globally harmonized product portfolio.

Problem

The existing organizational culture, traditionally characterized by strong local autonomy, does not fully support global objectives. A new, more networked, global way of thinking needs to be established at all levels of the organization without ignoring local differences and without creating unnecessary resistance to the change program. The central training function takes a key role in this endeavour. The Global Induction project is aimed at providing new employees with a wider, more global view of their organization right from the beginning. In order to streamline the way in which training is provided, the new Global Induction will have to follow a common overall process, while still taking care of the different culture, infrastructure, size, and maturity of the various local organizations (ranging from 15 to 1,000 employees).

Solutions

Eedo developed a roadmap to corporate induction. This is a flexible process model which provides the resources at subsidiaries (HR people, senior and line managers, 'buddies', etc.) with a range of training materials, tools, and checklists allowing them to customize each process step to best fit their specific conditions and requirements. Eedo's ForceTen Knowledge Platform was used for development and to support delivery of the program. ForceTen's browser-accessible authoring environment was used to develop the Web-based training components (pioneering the use of this medium in the organization), with subject matter experts and approvers dispersed throughout various countries and business units, all contributing in a collaborative online development process. Materials developed for the programme included a video component, supporting tutor guidance notes, as well as templates for PowerPoint presentations and Word documents.

Results

Feedback from trainees and local training staff has been universally positive. Having experienced the benefits of a highly accessible, useful, integrated package of 'how to' information and hands-on materials, personnel in the change programme have been won over and are fully supportive of the new training programme design. As a result, the global training function has won the credibility and authority to take further steps towards a more centralized steering of organization-wide training and knowledge transfer, thus, successfully implementing the key objective of enhanced organizational integration set by the management board.

Questions

1. Does the global perspective create a hindrance in localization of placement process?
2. Debate on the extent of global perspective vs location-related induction in placement of employees.
3. Examine the road map of corporate induction and its utility as a knowledge platform for self-development of employees.
4. Examine the role of a trainee in the overall context of induction and placement of employees.

Career Development

Objectives

After studying this
chapter, you will be able
to understand
- career, career planning,
  and career success
- career management
  from organizational and
  individual perspectives
- the distinction between
  a career and a job

INTRODUCTION

Today, the business environment is highly competitive and complex and there is a certain degree of ambiguity and uncertainty about career development. Consequently, employees are also confused about their career development. Earlier, employees enjoyed a sense of job security by taking up a position in an organization. It was a psychological bonding between the employer and the employee. The employees exhibited the characteristics of Protestant ethics, loyalty and devotion, principles that carried them to higher positions in an organization. In contrast, career planning for an employee is very difficult today. Career growth has crossed boundaries and has undergone great change. Switching organizations has become a common practice. The needs of the employees are also undergoing a sea change and trainers are experiencing difficult times in organizing and developing programmes to suit their needs. Moreover, restructuring, downsizing, right sizing, and lay-offs have all become common practices in organizations, and permanent jobs have given place to contractual employment.

> ■ ■ ■
> Today, the business environment is highly competitive and complex and there is a certain degree of ambiguity and uncertainty about career development.

Hence, the need of the hour is to increase the employability of individuals in an organization.

In this context, this chapter attempts to differentiate between career and job, identify steps in career planning, and analyse the steps required by an employee for success in his/her career.

Definition

In everyday parlance, the word 'career' is used in a number of different ways. People speak of 'pursuing a career', 'career planning', and attending 'career workshops'. Job fairs are held where information is available about different career options for college students. Career counsellors are also available on the spot or in colleges for advice and guidance. Webster's dictionary defines the term career as 'one's lifework or employment pursuing the stated occupation as a lifework'.

■ ■ ■

A career is a sequence of positions occupied by a person during the course of his or her life.

A career then is a sequence of positions occupied by a person during the course of his or her life. This may be considered as an objective perspective of career. In a subjective sense, it refers to where one is going in one's work life. The subjective viewpoint is more-or-less held together by a self-concept that consists of perceived inclinations and abilities, basic values, career motives, and needs. In both the perspectives, we assume that individuals control their destiny and that available opportunities need to be manipulated to maximize the success and satisfaction in their careers. Further assumption is that HR personnel should recognize career stages and assist employees with the development tasks they face at each stage. Career planning is important because the consequences of career success or failure are linked closely to each individual's self-concept, identity, and satisfaction with career and life. Despite downsizing and restructuring in organizations, career planning still plays a vital role in organizations for the following reasons:

- High educational levels and occupational aspirations
- Slow economic growth and fewer opportunities for advancement
- More concern for personal life planning and quality of work life

Hence, one should never leave one's career to chance. Moreover, it should be shaped and managed more by individuals than by the organization. A job is a position occupied by the individual, whereas a career is a series of progressive jobs that an individual does during his work life (Exhibits 9.1 and 9.2).

EXHIBIT 9.1   Ernst & Young: Building your professional career

At Ernst & Young, employees can look forward to enrich their knowledge and experience. It is natural and right that they should want to build their own market value as well as add value to their external or internal clients. Whilst the company excepts them to take a proactive approach to the management of their career, it also provides considerable support. It provides many opportunities for employees to specialize in an industry sector or in particular markets, and, in addition, excellent opportunities exist for the best people to develop experience through international assignments. To provide the in-depth learning required to support employee development, the company offers a comprehensive suite of high-quality training courses. Emphasis is also placed on developing expertise in individual counselling and coaching in order to encourage effective teamwork. Many courses are delivered by external specialists and there is a growing emphasis on the use of technology to provide direct training opportunities.

EXHIBIT 9.2   Microsoft India Development Center

The Microsoft India Development Center (IDC) is Microsoft's second product development centre outside USA. Through this team Microsoft develops end-to-end strategic products such as Windows Services for UNIX, Visual J#.NET, Outlook to Notes Connector, and Windows System Resource Manager. Its strategy is to align with the focus areas of Microsoft and for this purpose, it has recently created the Enterprise Storage Group, Windows Server Group, Windows Networking Group, Tablet PC Group, Business Solutions Group, Developer Tools Group, Messaging Group, and Subscription Group.

(Contd)

EXHIBIT 9.2   (Contd)

The IDC has three core functional units: development, testing, and program management. These units focus on product development starting from customer engagement, specification, architecture, design, development, and release management. Microsoft is always happy to meet computer science graduates having basic technical skills and excellent problem solving minds. If one is passionate about coding, testing, and creativity, there is no doubt he or she would enjoy the challenge of a career with IDC. Microsoft seeks those who thrive on team spirit and possess the confidence to conceptualize, architect, and develop new products that impact millions of people across the world.

■ ■ ■

> Career planning is a deliberate attempt by an individual to become more aware of his or her skills, interests, values, opportunities, choices, and consequences.

Career planning is a deliberate attempt by an individual to become more aware of his or her own skills, interests, values, opportunities, choices, and consequences. It involves identifying career-related goals and establishing plans for achieving those goals (Hall 1986). Career management (Exhibits 9.3 and 9.4) is considered to be an organizational process that implements and monitors career plans undertaken by individuals alone or within the organization's career systems (Hall 1986).

Application of studies, planning a career, and thinking about one's vocation during late childhood and early adolescence are important. Super, Ginzberg, Anne Roe, and Crites proposed theories emphasizing adolescent interests, careers, and occupations. It is vital at this stage to examine the theories in detail, since they speak about occupational values and interests that are closely related to work values.

EXHIBIT 9.3   Hongkong Shanghai Banking Corporation (HSBC)

The Executive Career Development Programme of HSBC in India spans over a four-and-half-year period during which a candidate gains both the knowledge and the experience to prepare for development into senior management. The training of candidates begins with a short period at one of the branches, where they are exposed to the various aspects of banking through a number of projects and attachments to different departments.

Then they attend the Executive Trainee Development Programme, which is an intensive seven-week training course held at the HSBC Group training facility in the UK. Alongside other HSBC trainees from around the world, the candidates gain an appreciation of the wider HSBC organization, its products and services, and the changing markets within which it operates. However, the course is not simply about studying. Just as important is the opportunity to work together with other trainees giving them an international perspective and enabling them to establish a network of contacts. The objective of the programme is to provide a perfect blend of formal training and informal activities to equip them with the skills and understanding to take on the management responsibilities they are going to assume.

On completion of the programme, the trainees return to India to undergo a three-week regional training, which is more specific to HSBC's business and products in India. At the end of this, they are ready to take up their first junior management position with independent responsibility for a small business unit. The Executive Career Development Programme then provides them with cross-functional exposure through postings to a variety of jobs in personal banking, credit, trade, finance, and support services, as well as exposure to areas such as private banking, factoring, custody, and cash management. During this period, there are likely to be other opportunities for training in India or overseas.

EXHIBIT 9.4   Motorola India

Believing in the mantra of talent acquisition, while keeping an eye on long-term prospects of an employee's career with the company, Motorola strives to be the number one employer by choice. One of its biggest initiatives in this regard is to consider potential employees from the existing employee base as a viable recruitment source, as it is committed to filling open positions, whenever possible, with qualified candidates from within the organization.

Motorola's philosophy of offering constant respect for people and the strategic initiative to create an empowered workforce of highly skilled, cross-trained employees is a key factor that makes people want to work with Motorola. The company requires critical talent at many positions and seeks to optimize the knowledge, skills, and abilities of its workforce. Motorola also provides the opportunity for career development by informing employees of career opportunities as they occur throughout the corporation, and by encouraging qualified employees to seek the coveted positions.

To be a part of Motorola and succeed, one has to have the 4E's + 1E (envision, energize, execute, edge + ethics), the Motorola criteria for success. This is a critical attribute that is evaluated in every potential employee. All Motorola employees are expected to be able to energize others with personal examples, trustworthiness, sensitivity, and providing help proactively. While individual brilliance is felicitated, Motorola believes that being effective in a team situation is equally important.

Return to India Programme

The return to India programme launched by Motorola India is a clear-cut initiative to tap the Indian talent pool in the US that wants to relocate to India. Motorola understands that India is a growing market and is clearly in the global employment map to attract excellent high-tech talent. The jobs could be based in any of their current locations such as Gurgaon, Bangalore, and Hyderabad.

Life of a Motorola Employee

Motorola strongly believes in the philosophy of work–life balance and envisages its work culture as a product of this philosophy.

Career Management

Careers in Motorola are based on performance and potential.

Rewards Philosophy

Motorola is committed to rewarding employees based on performance and providing opportunities for growth and development. With a strong belief that a balanced, equitable, and competitive compensation package is essential to attract, motivate, and retain high-calibre employees, Motorola makes sure that employees get more than they expect.

Performance Culture

Motorola's 'pay for performance' philosophy is based on a scheme of salary payment that recognizes and rewards individual performance, thus creating an environment with growth opportunities and satisfying job experience. Pay increases are therefore differentiated on the basis of performance, where the mechanism of 'pay for performance' drives the momentum—the better an employee performs, the more rapidly his or her salary will increase within the salary range.

Training and Development

Motorola's long standing commitment to training and development is clearly evident in its India operations. All Motorola employees in India receive extensive training in HR principles of participative management, empowerment, motivation, individual dignity, and ethics.

(Contd)

EXHIBIT 9.4 (Contd)

HR Policies
Health programmes

- Preventive health subsidy   • Wellness and health services   • Provident fund plan

Recognition programmes

- Lump sum award recognition   • Small wins

ROE'S THEORY OF CAREER CHOICE (1956)

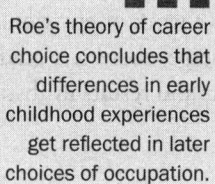

Roe's theory of career choice concludes that differences in early childhood experiences get reflected in later choices of occupation.

Anne Roe was among the first to use 'needs' explicitly and extensively in a theory of vocational development—taking Maslow's system as reference. Roe sought to find out what aspects of personality differentiated scientists in various fields. Roe concluded that differences in early childhood experiences were reflected in later choices of occupation. More specifically, she found that men from homes oriented to the needs of the children and those that put a premium on warm, satisfactory family relationships tended to enter occupations that provided more such warmth and support. Men whose occupations involved a minimum of contact with others on the job and for whom work was often a solitary activity come from homes in which the early relationships had not been close or rewarding.

These different types of parent–child relations were seen as producing a major orientation either towards or away from people. According to the theory, it is these orientations that lead to interest development and occupational choice. Roe further formalized her theory in a classification of all occupations on the two dimensions of field and level. The field dimension is based on interests and the primary focus of occupation, and the level dimension is defined in terms of responsibility, capacity, and skill in occupation.

Finally, according to Roe, the level of vocational activity is largely the product of genetic differences, which result in differences of interests and the way people attempt to manipulate various aspects of their environment. Therefore, careful appraisal of an individual's childhood and the individual's perception of his or her parents' attitudes along with an accurate assessment of the child's aptitudes should enable one to predict with accuracy the general occupational class to be pursued.

GINZBERG'S THEORY OF CAREER CHOICE (1951)

Ginzberg, Ginsburg, Axelrad, and Herma formulated a developmental theory of career choice that has been the prototype for subsequent thinking about how and why adolescents choose a career as they do.

Ginzberg's theory of career choice stressed that the choice of vocation is an irreversible process marked by three periods in early life.

The central proposition in this theory is that career choice is a process that extends from the age 10–21, encompassing the years of adolescence, principally through high school and also the upper elementary grades, five and six. Ginzberg states that the single most important factor in the process of determining a career is the series of interlocked decisions that adolescents make over time. The second proposition is that the process of career choice is largely irreversible—once launched, it becomes difficult to change directions.

Finally, Ginzberg proposes that the career choice process culminates in a compromise between needs and reality. This proposition rests upon the assumption that the ego mediates between what the individual wants (id impulses) and what reality allows (super ego, dictates) and environmental constraints.

Ginzberg and his associates constructed vocational choice as an irreversible process, occurring in reasonably clearly marked stages: fantasy, tentative, and realistic (Figure 9.1).

Fantasy Stage

The primary task the child accomplishes during the first stage of vocational development is part of the general maturation process of changing from a play orientation to a work orientation. As a child grows older and approaches the terminal point of the fantasy stage, there is a gradual reorientation towards vocational activity, which leads to accomplishments and results in abstract satisfaction such as pleasing a parent.

Tentative Stage

This occurs approximately between the ages 11 and 18 and is divided into three stages that differ in their vocational development tasks. The *interest stage* is the time, around the age 11 or 12, when the child begins to recognize the need to identify a career direction. The *capacity stage*, age 12–14, logically follows the interest stage. Here students introduce the notion of ability into their vocational considerations. In the *value stage*, that is, during the 15th and 16th years, students undergo a very marked change in their approach to vocational choice. The *transition stage* closes the tentative period around the age 17 or 18. This stage is characteristically calmer than the preceding stages of the tentative period.

Realistic Stage

It takes place approximately between 18 and 22 years of age or even as late as 24 years. The first stage is *exploration stage*. The principal task is simply the selection of a path to follow from among two or three strongly held interests. Next is the *crystallization stage*. By this time, students become more or less deeply involved in a specific field. They definitely have a clear idea of occupational tasks they wish to avoid. The final stage is the *specification stage*. It is the final point in career development. The individual acts upon his choice by selecting specific job or graduate school subspecialty.

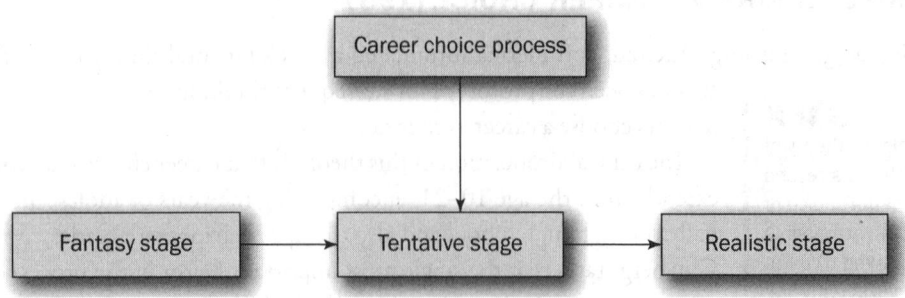

FIGURE 9.1 Stages in the career choice process

SUPER'S THEORY OF CAREER DEVELOPMENT (1957)

> ■ ■ ■
> Super's theory of career development stresses on the awareness of individuals to choose a career based on relevant information and planning about career.

While Ginzberg, et al. formulated their explanation of how career choices are made during adolescence primarily from an ego psychological point of view, Super (1957) adopted a largely phenomenological frame of references to conceptualize the process of career development. His basic tenet is that 'in choosing an occupation one is in effect choosing a means of implementing a self-concept'. Career development is also a continuous process and projects into adulthood as the individual continually adjusts to a career.

Super follows the tradition of Hall's theory of continuous development from childhood to adolescence with the self-concept being clarified and crystallized rather than conflicted. The implication is that Super considers synthesis rather than compromise as the outcome of adolescence career development. Super and Overstreet (1960) have hypothesized that there are three progressive trends in career development from early to late adolescence towards greater goal direction, independence, and realism. They do not identify periods or stages in the process, but Tiedeman and O'Hare (1963) also form a self-concept orientation and specify three criteria for delineating stages: discreteness, dominance, and irreversibility. The dimensions of career development cutting across these stages have been enumerated by Super as follows:

Awareness of the need to choose   It is a mark of career maturity, particularly in early adolescence, to recognize the societal expectation that all individuals declare a career of their choice.

Specificity of information and planning   By the time a young person reaches early adulthood, career choice should be based upon reliable and relevant information about the world of work and career plans should be feasible and easy to implement.

CRITES' MODEL OF CAREER MATURITY (1974)

Combining Ginzberg's focus on ego function in career decisions making with Super's emphasis on the dimensions of career maturity, and adding components from factorial analyses of ability, Crites (1974) has formulated a model of career maturity that encompasses both the content and the process of career decision-making. The model has been adopted from the research of British psychologists Vernon (1950) and Burt (1954) on the structures of abilities. They propose that abilities are organized in a hierarchical fashion. The lowest level of hierarchy includes specific factors such as knowledge of the world of work. The intermediate level comprises group factors of dimensions that converge upon the highest level of the hierarchical model—the general factor 'G'. This 'G' is the degree of career maturity. It can be defined in absolute terms as 'the place reached on the continuum of career development' (Super 1955) or in relative terms as the individual's standing in the appropriate age or grade reference group (Crites 1961).

> ■ ■ ■
> Erickson (1959) considered a career as an individual's course of development through chronologically successive life stages.

Erickson (1959) considered a career as an individual's course of development through successive life stages. This interpretation was later worked out in more detail by various researchers (Tiedman and O'Hara 1963; Havighurst 1952). A life or career stage is characterized, according to Erickson, by its limits or transition (career transition) from, respectively, the preceding stage to the present one and from the present stage to the next one. Such a transition takes place when a person is rather abruptly confronted with new circumstances or unfamiliar problems or tasks, or when he or she finds the ways of adjusting to the stage insufficient. In general, a process of reorientation, that is, adaptation or readjustment, will then be necessary to enable him or her to stand up to or feel at home in the new stage.

All the aforementioned theorists converge on three points. First, occupational and career thinking occurs during adolescence; second, values have their basis in abilities and attitudes; and third, vocational interests and work values seem to be closely related with each other.

Among the first to incorporate values into a theory of vocational development were Ginzberg, Eliginberg (1951), and a group of associates, who established three categories of sources of satisfaction from work:

- Intrinsic values are satisfactions derived from the activity itself.
- Extrinsic values are the returns that a job provides.
- Concomitant values are those aspects of work that are part of the task situation, although not necessarily part of the work itself, for example, in many tasks the appeal lies not in what one does, but in the interaction a person enjoys with others while working.

The common dimensions that have been identified most frequently (Van Geffon 1977; Hendrick and Super 1968; Crabel and Pruzek 1969; Rosenberg 1957) with respect to satisfaction are the following:

- *Security*: Desire to have a high income, economic security, good fringe benefits, etc.
- *Autonomy*: Desire to act independently or to exert influence
- *Affiliation*: Desire to maintain social contacts, either active or passive
- *Respect*: Wish to gain recognition, esteem, respect, and status
- *Self-expression*: Desire to express oneself in one's work to accomplish given tasks

The last four dimensions correspond to the 'higher needs' in Maslow's need theory (1953)—lower needs are not represented except for the security dimension. Whatever be the consensus of different authors regarding work values, the importance of work values has not been undermined. Further, almost all theorists agree that they have their basis in needs. The difference between an attitude and value is one of degree. Distaste for hard work itself reflects value, whereas unwillingness to do a particular task reflects attitude. In other words, values are holistic, conceptual, and broad oriented. Since they serve as criteria in judgment, they help an individual to choose the relevant aspects of work.

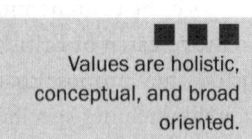

Values are holistic, conceptual, and broad oriented.

CAREER PLANNING—INDIVIDUAL'S PERSPECTIVE

It is becoming difficult for managers and employers to hold on to their employees as the latter are more concerned for their jobs than for the organization. Even in developing countries, a trend of migrating to greener pastures for availing good opportunities has been observed. What does an employee lack in such a situation? Is it occupational success, job satisfaction, or skill development? Traditionally, career development and success have been defined in terms of occupational advancement, which is clear and easy to measure. However, with the trend of downsizing, the threat of unemployment is forcing employees to consider other options. Multi-skilling and cross-

> Traditionally, career development and success have been defined in terms of occupational advancement.

functional experiences have become essential for career development and continued employability. When employees fail to meet these challenges, they experience stress and burnout. The present situation demands that an individual plans his career smoothly, calculatedly, and progressively.

The following guidelines may serve a purpose on this criterion.

Choosing a Field of Employment

The first step is to think in terms of where one wants to be ultimately in work life. Accordingly, career goals may be organized.

- Regard every position and job that is occupied with great value and potential. Ask yourself, 'How well will the present job help me in reaching the final goal?' For example, if you would like to occupy a senior position by 2020, consider the extent to which the present job facilitates training programmes, global orientations, leadership styles, etc., which will continue to be the key requirements for senior positions in the future also.
- Be prepared to make lateral moves or shift jobs for low pays if they are providing valuable opportunities for career growth.
- Carefully assess your current performance and get an idea as to how the top management is assessing your performance.
- Become sensitive to the stage of diminished utility, that is, where your contribution to the organization is not required.

Other Indicators

There are certain other indicators of job change—your advancement in the organization is blocked, the organization is poorly managed, the company is losing its market share, the reward structure is not suitable, or the present job does not fulfil your aspirations—that need to be cautiously handled.

Planning Your Exit

- Organize your exit so that you leave at your own convenience and not at the organization's convenience.
- Establish networking relationships while still on the job.
- Leave the organization on good terms and not under questionable circumstances.
- Do not leave a job until you find another one. It is easier to find a new job when you are currently employed.

CAREER PLANNING—ORGANIZATIONAL PERSPECTIVE

Organizations also need to plan for their employees' career development programmes. Companies are designing career programmes in an effort to decrease employee turnover, prevent job obsolescence, and improve the quality of employees' work lives (Montgomery 1996). In 1997, organizations such as Chevron, CIGNA, Sears Information Services, and Marriott International participated in a conference specifically to share their strategies for creating a career resilient work force (Callahan and Greenhaus 1999). A few recommendations for an employer are as follows:

- Provide employees with the tools and opportunities to enhance their skills
- Create an environment for continuous learning by supporting and rewarding employee development and learning
- Provide opportunities for self-assessment
- Provide opportunities for additional training, including orientation and training
- Have managers trained as coaches and mentors to assist employees
- Use reward systems that support the organization's career development strategy
- Make sure the career programmes are integrated with other HR programmes

Exhibit 9.5 provides insights on a carreer in company secretaryship in India

EXHIBIT 9.5   Institute of Company Secretaries of India

Q.1. What are the functions of the ICSI?

Ans. The Institute of Company Secretaries of India (ICSI) is a premier professional body constituted under the Company Secretaries Act, 1980, to develop and regulate the profession of company secretaries in India. The ICSI, besides conducting company secretaryship examinations and enrolling qualified students as members after practical training, supervises the members in matters pertaining to professional ethics and code of conduct. It also regularly organizes professional development and continuing education programmes and brings out research publications, guidance notes, secretarial standards, as well as a professional monthly journal *Chartered Secretary* for corporate executives and the *Student Company Secretary* and CS Foundation Course Bulletin for students.

The ICSI regularly interacts with government regulatory bodies, and chambers of commerce and industry on policy and professional matters. The institute has its headquarters at ICSI House, 22 Institutional Area, Lodi Road, New Delhi; regional offices at Mumbai, Calcutta, New Delhi, and Chennai; and 36 Chapters and 16 Satellite Chapters located in various cities all over India. The ICSI has on its rolls over 13,000 qualified members and nearly 2 lakh students are pursuing the course.

Q.2. What exactly is the role of a company secretary?

Ans. As the principal officer of the company, the company secretary (CS) is a vital link between the company, the board of directors, the shareholders, and the governmental and regulatory agencies. A CS is a business manager and an important adjunct in corporate management hierarchy, serving as the Registrar for the company. A CS acts as a confidante of the board of directors, takes part in the formulation of long-term and short-term corporate policies, maintains statutory books and records, and ensures compliances with legal and procedural require-ments under various enactments for effective corporate governance. A CS advises the board of directors on the ramifications of the proposals under the consideration of the board. As a corporate development planner, he/she identifies expansion opportunities, arranges collaborations, amalgamations, mergers, acquisitions, takeovers, divestments, and setting up of subsidiaries and joint ventures within and outside India. A CS looks after the entire secretarial functions such as preparing agenda, convening, conducting, and preparing minutes of meetings of the board of directors, shareholders' meetings, annual general meetings, inter-departmental meetings, and meetings with foreign delegations, financial institutions, and regulatory authorities.

A CS as a competent professional, comes into existence after extensive exposure provided by the Institute of Company Secretaries of India (ICSI), through comprehensive study material, compulsory coaching, highly exacting examinations, rigorous compulsory training, and continuing professional development programmes. Besides, render-ing statutory duties, as attending meetings, preparing minutes, maintaining register of members, ensuring timely transfer of shares, and ensuring compliances of various laws, a CS also assists the Board in various other aspects.

(Contd)

EXHIBIT 9.5 (Contd)

Q.3. What are the career prospects for company secretaries?

Ans. A qualified CS has access to openings in private and public sectors, financial institutions, stock exchanges, and even the Central/State Government. As per Section 383 A of the Companies Act 1956, companies with a paid up share capital of ₹50 lakh, or more must have a whole-time company secretary. In case of a company with a paid up capital of less than ₹50 lakh, a CS with an Intermediate pass is also eligible for appointment. All companies seeking a listing on stock exchanges are required to have a full time CS. The Department of Education, Ministry of Human Resources Development, has recognized membership of the ICSI for appointment to superior posts and services under the Central government. It is one of the essential qualifications for recruitment from Grade I to Grade IV in the accounts branch of the Central Company Law Service of the Department of Company Affairs. The Indian Banks Association has recommended to banks to consider appointment of company secretaries as specialists in the field of finance, accounts, law, and merchant banking.

Almost every kind of organization whose affairs are conducted by boards, councils, and other corporate structures, be it a company, cooperative society, trust, society, association, federation, authority, commission, board, or the like, finds it useful to appoint a person in a key administrative position who holds the qualification of company secretaryship. Members of the Institute may also go in for independent practice. Besides issuing statutory certifications and appearing before various quasi-judicial authorities as an authorized representative, a CS issues due diligence and comfort certificates and acts as a secretarial auditor and a finance and management advisor and consultant.

Q.4. What are the future plans of the ICSI for the new millennium?

Ans. In the early part of the new millennium, national boundaries will disappear for trade and commerce. There will be tremendous increase in international trade, with fierce competition increasing pressure for survival leading to leaner organizations with high efficiency and technological excellence. In such a scenario, a CS, being the principal coordinator, will be called upon to play a crucial role as an integrated business manager and as an in-house legal counsel. The CS provides support for the various economic activities and operations of the company, including finance and accounts, external audit, costing and budgeting, materials management, and commercial and general administration, besides legal and secretarial functions. He will have to act, advise, and guide on good corporate governance and assume a much wider role in ensuring compliances in an altogether new corporate set-up and legal procedural and disclosure requirements not necessarily originating from Company Law, but other laws which will be no less stringent and hitherto unknown to the corporate world in India.

Issues such as competition law, intellectual property, environment, mergers and acquisitions, information technology and cyber laws, corporate governance, focussed attention on investor relations, market exploration and sustaining investors confidence and interest in the company, and settlement of commercial disputes through alternative dispute resolution (ADR) methods will all engage the attention of company secretaries in the next millennium.

With a view to create professionals to meet the new challenges, the ICSI is shortly coming out with a new syllabus and is in the process of strengthening training of students in close coordination with trade and industry and practising members. For professional development of existing members, focussed attention is being directed by conducting professional development programmes as well as continuing education and participative certificate programmes.

CAREER DEVELOPMENT SYSTEM

An effective career development system attempts to integrate a series of individual career planning and organizational career management activities involving the employees, the management, and the

■ ■ ■

A career development system integrates individual career planning and organizational career management activities.

organization. For example, corporations such as Wal-Mart, IBM, Bell Atlantic, and Xerox involve career assessment by the employee with the manager serving as a facilitator and the organization providing a supportive environment. Research on the effectiveness of career development programmes (Exhibit 9.6) is sparse and yet promising. One study found that 44% of administrators of career development programmes for Fortune 500 companies regarded them as very helpful (Keller 1987). IBM evaluated the effectiveness of its career development workshop and found improvements in the participants' abilities and responsibilities for their own career planning (Bardsley 1987). Peatt and Whitney reported that its turnover rate for new engineers had decreased by 25% after instituting a career development programme.

Besides organizing these programmes, the management focuses on individuals at various levels.

Entry Level

Once an individual enters the organization (Exhibit 9.7), the next step is to settle down and start building a career in the organization. This requires greater involvement with the organization.

EXHIBIT 9.6 Working at KONE

KONE is a global, forward thinking company. It seeks talented people who are ready and willing to learn. KONE takes care of its employees and actively encourages their career development. An international business environment in over 60 countries provides excellent career and learning opportunities.

Clear Vision

KONE wants to be recognized as the company that sets the standards in the industry. The company is proud of its R&D specialists whose product innovations continue to change the way the world thinks about elevators and escalators. Acquisitions around the world increase company size and bring in new talent as well as new and challenging market areas. At the same time, the company is fine-tuning its methods to become even more efficient. KONE is focused on long-term decision-making. However, it follows the markets closely and is capable of acting flexibly and quickly. KONE's vision and quick response time have kept it at the head of development.

Continuous Learning

KONE may be recognized for its breakthrough product innovations, but to achieve business targets it must also be innovative in managing its business and people. At the moment, it emphasizes customer focus in addition to technical expertise. Assignments that call for the application of a worker's competence are motivating. It can compete both locally and internationally. KONE supports personnel development in many ways. In performance development process discussions, an employee's personal targets are identified and integrated with company targets. Managers coach and encourage their people towards agreed targets.

KONE's international operational environment offers excellent possibilities for job rotation and career advancement. Local and international learning programmes are available to support competence development. Parts of these programmes are executed in cooperation with leading universities. Several web-learning tools are also being used. KONE's working environment is supportive and positive.

KONE's Strengths

The latest job satisfaction research indicates that KONE employees are strongly committed to company targets. The average KONE employee can look forward to a long career. All employees are respected and listened to regardless of gender, age, and ethnic background. Personnel have a strong sense of togetherness. People at KONE are proud of their place of employment; they believe that the company will continue to be successful in the future.

■ ■ ■
Once an individual enters the organization, the next step is to settle down and start building a career in the organization.

This process begins with the socialization and induction programs. Knowledge about the organization and peer group facilitates an individual to exercise greater control. One of the successful procedures being followed to reduce employee turnover is 'mentoring'.

A 'mentor' is a teacher, advisor, sponsor, and confidant. A mentor is also one who has understood the dynamics of power and politics in the organization. At times, the mentoring process may take place in groups, that is, a set of new entrants may be attached to one mentor. The process is satisfying both ways—the mentor experiences a sense of satisfaction and a boost in self-esteem while the protégés derive comfort in the association. The mentor's role is to be a culture carrier, to teach new hires, to provide feedback on how they are being perceived by others, and to act confidentially in all work-related problems. Certain behavioural modifications may also be suggested by the mentor to reduce employee stress and turnover in an organization.

■ ■ ■
The mentor's role is to be a culture carrier.

EXHIBIT 9.7   Lowe Lintas

Sujaya Banerjee was the Vice President–HRD and Personnel at Lowe Lintas India. She shared her views on a range of HR issues pertaining to the company during her tennure.

Q.1. Describe the current job prospects with Lintas India Group companies.

Ans. Recruitment is an ongoing activity and we regularly hire experienced professionals from the industry. We are always open to talented and creative individuals with experience on large brands in leading advertising agencies. Currently, we are looking at hiring graduate trainees as interns for Lowe. These would be graduates from different streams, passionate about making a career in advertising. Our Integrated Marketing Action Group (IMAG) is also constantly looking at hiring talented public relations (PR) and event management professionals (for Linopinon and Advent), persons with knowledge of relationship marketing and CRM (for Lowe Personal), and those interested in making a career in rural communications (for Linterland).

Q.2. What are Lintas' recruitment policies?

Ans. Client servicing personnel for Lowe, IMAG, and Initiative Media are primarily management postgraduates from leading business schools. The entry point is as management trainee and those selected after a rigorous procedure for selection are put through a robust cross-functional induction programme that includes on-the-job training on active power brands.

Recruitment at other levels requires candidates to have sound academic credentials coupled with relevant work experience on leading brands at other agencies or marketing organizations. For the creative stream at entry point, we look for candidates from leading schools of art or design or simply those who display great writing potential and have a passion about the communications business.

Q.3. What do you look for in aspirants?

Ans. While hiring, we typically look for people who have a strong grasp of the fundamentals, good communication skills, a well-rounded personality, the ability to think problems through and generate solutions, a keen sense of attention to detail and persistence, an attitude to get along with people and be team players, a keen interest in learning, and have passion for making a career in advertising.

Q.4. Lowe Lintas was recently awarded for its innovative HR practices. Enumerate some.

Ans. The HR practices at Lowe Lintas won the award for HR excellence due to the way they reached out to and reassured their employees that the HR was a friend. While the transactional work continued, they worked on some

(Contd)

EXHIBIT 9.7 (Contd)

transformational HR initiatives (360 degree feedback, performance review system, Lintas Career Development Programme, etc.). Other initiatives attempted to add a smile to the function and create a sense of belongingness for the organization among the employees by creating an environment of fun and togetherness.

These initiatives were: Lintas Talkies (Lintas film club), Lintas Box office (taking the employees out to watch a blockbuster with family and friends), Luncheon Series (inviting celebrities and achievers from different walks of life to share lunch with employees), Lingainz (employee engagement programme that provides discounts and special offers on products and services to employees often included with their payslips, in-house bazaars, etc), Afterhours (Lintas Hobby club), Ce'Lowe' Brations (celebrating India Day, Diwali, Christmas, New Year, and some other occasions).

Q.5. Why choose Lintas?

Ans. The advantages of working with Lintas are: it is a great learning platform that develops well-rounded communications professionals in different disciplines, it provides an opportunity to work on power brands, it invests huge resources in training and development of managers, and it offers a merit-oriented culture that rewards excellence and helps internalize process-oriented working using best practises in various areas of operations, thus ensuring a systematic working style that does not leave brilliance to chance.

Lintas has always been a trendsetter—an organization committed to not only building brands, but also building people.

Source: Adapted from an interview published in *Times Ascent*.

Impact of First Job and Career Success

■ ■ ■
The initial experience of satisfaction on the first job is responsible for laying down the foundation for later success in career.

Several studies have focused on the relationship between satisfaction on the first job and later career success. The positive impact of an initial job challenge upon career success and retention has been found on various occasions. For example, among engineers, it was observed that challenging early work assignments were related to strong initial performance as well as to maintain competence and performance throughout their career. It also prevents career obsolescence. Further, the role of the supervisor is also critical. Besides playing the role of an ideal mentor, the supervisor must be willing to share information and knowledge and train subordinates in a secure fashion. The mentor has to act like a role model. Initial experience of satisfaction on the first job is responsible for laying down the foundation for later success in career. Career aspirations such as achievements and significant contribution to the field take shape during the early stages of career.

Managing Employees in Mid-career

To a large extent, the middle stage of one's career is the least understood in terms of career success. Physiologically speaking, the middle career spans between 35 and 55 years of age. The impact of early success or struggle in career is quite obvious in the mind of the employee. Responsibilities both in personal and work life increase. There is a sense of maturity and an increase in the competencies and skills. If an employee has been continuing in the same job for over 10 years then job promotions and mobility become the prime concerns. With increase in age, mobility decreases and family responsibilities increase. Employees need to accept that a career plan is a part of life and they have to meet such challenges by making lateral moves or job shifts.

■ ■ ■
Organizations can encourage their employees to become multi-skilled by making lateral moves and providing opportunities for training and retraining.

Today, organizations frequently indulge in expansion and restructuring. Hence, the middle-level managers need to be carefully handled by the management (Exhibit 9.8). Career counselling becomes necessary for the senior and middle-level employees to meet the future requirements of the organization and the emerging market trends. Organizations can encourage their employees to become multi-skilled by making lateral moves and providing opportunities for training and retraining. Certain behavioural modifications such as fostering intellectual abilities, sustaining high levels of motivation, and developing personal flexibility may also be contemplated.

In the recent years, another trend that has been observed is the rise of 'outsourcing managers' who after gaining considerable experience in an organization start small ventures of their own and supply materials to the organization they used to work with.

The aforementioned are some of the moves that can be made both by the individual and the organization. At times, there may be a total re-evaluation of a career goal or the original career plan may be persuaded. Some employees experience a career plateau and some of them make a smooth progression into the future.

Managing VRS—Its Impact

In the last decade, the central and state-level public sectors, government offices, and certain nationalized banks have offered the voluntary retirement scheme (VRS) to employees for various reasons. When the management offers the VRS, employees get the option of premature retirement from

EXHIBIT 9.8   SAS

Competency Development Programme

SAS' Competency Development Programme provides employees with opportunities to enhance their technical and professional skills.

Competency development programmes vary depending on the specific needs of the work streams such as sales and marketing, professional services, industry intelligence solutions, research and development, and advisory services.

Together with their managers, SAS employees engage in a structured process that examines in detail their strengths, development needs, job requirements, and personal values. They then prepare for a development discussion with their manager focusing on aligning their values with growth opportunities in their current jobs for increased job satisfaction and productivity.

Management Development Programmes

SAS offers workshops to managers to help them acquire the skills and knowledge required to elicit peak performance from their teams. The workshops cover key management principles of goal setting, delegation, coaching and developing employees, decision-making, handling conflict, managing change, and rewarding and recognizing employees.

The company's expenditure on competency development is almost 10% of its total employee compensation, which has been the highest amongst 27 countries in Europe, Middle East, and Africa for the year 2003.

Source: http://www.sas.com/offices/asiapacific/india/jobs/competencydevelopment.htm, accessed on 6 September 2005.

employment. When the management offers this option in the name of downsizing, it may lose skilled or good performers in the process. The skill gap that is created in the process is something that the organization should be ready to cope with. Alternative arrangements in terms of retraining other employees or succession planning are some of the steps that may be considered.

Managing Dual Career Couples

One of the most challenging career management problems organizations face today is that of dual career couples. Dual career couples face the problem of balancing work and family responsibilities. Many a times, there is interference or overlapping of roles. All this leads to stress. The issue is further compounded by spouse's, career plans or motives. Planning for an individual's career development may be meaningless unless the spouse's options are also considered.

As of now, in India, the civil services do take this point into consideration. However, there are certain sectors such as banking and insurance where a large proportion of employees are women and are subjected to frequent transfers involving relocation and separation from family. Both the organization and the employees are helpless in such cases. Since transfers are policy matters, few options are available, particularly for women employees.

Organizations can play their part effectively by providing day care centres, introducing flexible timing work schedules, etc. Even though the law stipulates that all organizations with more than 50 women must provide crèche/day care facilities, except for certain government institutions, there is no crèche facility in many offices. There are also several instances where women deprive themselves of a promotion for fear of job relocation. Further, when the banking sector introduced the VRS scheme, a large number of middle-level women employees opted for it.

What does this indicate? This indicates that the problem is a serious one and needs to be handled carefully. Protecting the employee's family interest definitely helps in gaining loyalty and commitment. Many companies in India have not yet introduced flexi timings and hence employees are forced to work in a full-time traditional manner.

Another dimension of this issue is the attention to be focused on children and related aspects. Normally, organizations grant maternity leave according to norms, which may not be adequate for the mother. Therefore, this may be supplemented by paternity leave.

Nevertheless, the problem is a serious and sensitive one and will continue as long as organizations continue to exist.

CAREER SUCCESS

How do we define career success? Career success for an individual means being able to apply one's individual capabilities, moving up the career ladder, and experiencing satisfaction. Career development programmes must be integrated with and supported by the existing HR programmes in

> ■ ■ ■
> Career success for an individual means being able to apply one's individual capabilities, moving up the career ladder, and experiencing satisfaction.

the organization if they are to be successful. Career programmes and HR programmes are linked to the degree they help meet the individual's growth needs and the organization's staffing needs. 3M has established a career resources department to better integrate its career programmes, performance appraisal process, and HR planning systems. Similarly, Boeing developed a programme called Careers, which is linked with the HR programmes (Green Laus 1994).

Exhibit 9.9 discusses career development at Renishaw.

EXHIBIT 9.9   Career development at Renishaw

Opportunities for career development are available in line with the changing needs of the business. Renishaw's policy is to encourage and recognize the career goals and aspirations of everybody, that is, 'careers not jobs'.

Renishaw's comprehensive appraisal programme is designed to allow all employees to discuss and identify their training needs, concerns, and career ambitions.

Career development may include the opportunity to work overseas, either on visits or with one of the subsidiaries. This may be on a temporary or permanent basis. Some employees have become true 'world travellers' working for the Renishaw Group.

Let us check out the career paths of some of its employees.

Mike Brown

General Manager, Renishaw Oceania Pt Ltd, Australia

- October 1984—joined as a sponsored student
- September 1988—graduated from the University of Manchester Institute of Science and Technology (UMIST) in Mechanical Engineering
- July 1990—appointed Product Support Engineer, Renishaw Sales Division
- April 1992—seconded to Renishaw SpA, Torino, Italy as a Product Marketing Executive (At the time of joining, he didn't speak Italian and didn't like pizza—now he is fluent in Italian and knows his pizzas!)
- February 1996—formally transferred to Reni-shaw SpA as a permanent employee of the Italian subsidiary with the title of Sales Manager, Renishaw SpA
- February 1998—appointed General Manager of Renishaw's new liaison office, located in Bangalore, India
- July 1999—appointed General Manager of Renishaw's new liaison office in Australia, which was converted to full subsidiary status in 2001

Louise Callanan

Mechanical and Manufacturing Engineering, Trinity College, Dublin, Corporate Staff

- 1995-96—summer placements in Dublin factory
- August 1997—graduated from Trinity College, Dublin, with a BAI Hons degree in Mechanical and Manufacturing Engineering
- September 1997—joined Renishaw as a Graduate Engineer in Laser and Calibration Products Division (Design)
- July 1998—promoted as a Design Engineer
- April 1999—transferred as a Design Engineer to Coordinate Measuring Machine Products Division
- July 2000—joined Group Marketing Services working on e-business and other group projects

Gareth Hankins

Manufacturing Systems and Manufacturing Management, Cardiff, Production Manager

- August 1988—joined Renishaw as a Mechanical Technician Apprentice from school
- October 1990—completed apprenticeship and became a Renishaw-sponsored student
- August 1993—graduated in Manufacturing Systems and Manufacturing Management from Cardiff University
- January 1996—became a Cell Leader in Assembly at New Mills
- November 1996—became a Product Group Leader in Electronic Assembly, New Mills
- December 1997—appointed a Trustee of the Renishaw Pension Fund
- November 1998—seconded to Renishaw Ireland's new factory in Dublin as the new Production Manager
- January 2001—returned to the UK to manage the transfer of manufacturing to the newly acquired Woodchester site

Source: http://www.renishaw.com/client/category/UKEnglish/CAT-217.shtml, accessed on 6 September 2005.

CAREER DEVELOPMENT IN DOWNSIZED ORGANIZATIONS

Downsizing and right sizing have become a routine affair in organizations. Is the career growth of an employee blocked once the organization resorts to downsizing? It is no doubt that traditional vertical progressive layers are less available. An increasing percentage of people are working in small and micro organizations. Employees are entering work life at an early age and consequently career planning is also setting in at an early stage. An ideal step to be followed is retraining and counselling the employees who would be displaced. Training in alternative skills or in self-employment is a better option.

All said and done, career is the responsibility of the individual and he has to create his or her own career opportunities. One has to recognize that power flows from expertise and not from position. Careers are made not in hierarchies, but in markets. Further, career success is determined more in terms of becoming a generalist or specialist rather than in terms of moving from one company to another.

SUMMARY

This chapter defines in detail the meaning of career, career planning, and career success. It also helps in understanding career management from the organization and individual perspectives. This chapter also attempts to bring out the differences between career and job, identifies the steps in career planning, and analyses the steps that need to be taken from the individual and employee's point of view for career success.

■ ■ ■ | KEY TERMS

Adulthood The state (and responsibilities) of a person who has attained maturity

Career The general progression of an individual's working or professional life

Career choice Implementing a self-concept

Continuum A continuous non-spatial whole or extent or succession in which no part or portion is distinct or distinguishable from adjacent parts

Cross-functional People from various parts of the process working together to define and implement changes and improvements

Crystallization To take on a definite, precise, and usually permanent form

Downsizing Becoming smaller in size by reducing the number of existing personel in an organization

Intellectual abilities General adaptability to new problems in life; ability to engage in abstract thinking, capacity for knowledge and knowledge possessed, the ability to judge, understand, and reason

Multi-skilling Acquiring knowledge and skills in a number of different disciplines

Occupation An activity that serves as one's regular source of livelihood

Orientation The direction followed in the course of a trend, movement, or development

Performance Process or manner of functioning or operating

Proposition A plan suggested for acceptance or a proposal

Psychological bond An individual's beliefs regarding the terms and conditions of a reciprocal exchange agreement between that person and another party

Reward system All the monetary, non-monetary, and psychological payments that an organization provides in exchange for the work performed

■ ■ ■ EXERCISES

Multiple Choice Questions

1. Despite downsizing and restructuring in organizations, career planning still plays a vital role for one the following reasons:
   (a) Increased concern for personal life planning and quality of work life
   (b) Small wins
   (c) Desire to express oneself in one's work
   (d) Decreasing occupational aspirations

2. Reluctance to do a particular task reflects
   (a) values
   (b) satisfaction
   (c) attitude
   (d) respect

3. Which of the following guidelines must one consider in planning a career?
   (a) Shifting jobs for higher pays even if they are providing fewer opportunities for career growth
   (b) Do not leave a job until you find another one. It is easier to find a new job when you are currently employed.
   (c) Leave the organization on good terms.
   (d) Both (b) and (c)

4. The process through which someone becomes aware of personal skills, interests, knowledge, and motivations; acquires information about opportunities; identifies career goals; and establishes action plans to attain those goals is called
   (a) organizational development
   (b) career management
   (c) career development
   (d) career planning

5. A mentor's role does not include
   (a) teaching new hires to act confidentially in all work-related problems
   (b) suggesting behavioural modifications to reduce employee stress and turnover in an organization.
   (c) being a culture carrier
   (d) interviewing the candidates

Fill in the Blanks

1. According to _____, differences in early childhood experiences were reflected in later choices of _____.

2. Ginzber constructed vocational choice as an irreversible process, occurring in reasonably clearly marked periods: fantasy, _____, and _____.

3. Career aspirations such as _____ and significant contribution to the field take shape during the early stages of career.

4. Protecting the employee's family interest gains _____ and commitment.

5. In India, flexi timings in the organizations have not yet been introduced and hence employees are forced to work in a _____.

Concept Review Questions

1. Define career development and its importance in the contemporary context.

2. Explain the various stages of career development.

3. What is the importance of career development from an individual's perspective?

4. Explain the pitfalls and challenges for a budding youngster.

5. Do organizations have a role in the employees' career development in the context of high rates of attrition.

6. Will the career development paradigm totally shift to individual perspective in future?

Project Work

1. Identify an organization and study the career development policies and practices.

2. Compare and contrast the career development in IT vs traditional manufacturing companies.

3. Prepare a career plan for yourself over the next five years.

4. Prepare a brief write-up on mid-career crisis and the need for multi-skilling to avoid it.

■ ■ ■ REFERENCES

Allen, T.D., Poteet, M.L., and Burroughs, S.M. 1997, 'The mentor's perspective: A qualitative inquiry and future research agenda', *Journal of Vocational Behav-* *ior*, 51(1), pp. 70–89; Allen, T.D., Poteet, M.L., Russell, J.E.A., and Dobbins, G.H. 1997, 'Factors related to supervisors' willingness to mentor others', *Journal of Vocational Behavior*, 50, pp. 1–22.

Callanan, G.A. and Greenhaus, J.H. 1999, 'Personal and career development: The best and worst of times'. In Kraut, A. and Korman, A. (Eds), *Evolving Practices in Human Resource Management: Responses to a Changing World of Work*, pp.146–71, Jossey-Bass, San Francisco; Sullivan, S.E., Carden, W.A., and Martin, D.F. 1998, 'Careers in the next millennium: Directions for future research', *Human Resource Management Review*, 8(2), pp. 165–85.

Hall, D.T. 1996, 'Protean careers of the 21st century', *Academy of Management Executive*, 10 (4), pp. 8–16;

Alfred, B.B., Snow, C.C., and Miles, R.F. 1996, 'Characteristics of managerial careers in the 21st century', *Academy of Management Executive*, 10(4), pp. 17–27.

Hall, D.T., et al. 1986, *Career Development in Organizations*, Jossey-Bass, San Francisco.

Hall, D.T., et al. (Eds) 1996, *The Career is Dead—Long Live the Career*, Jossey-Bass, San Francisco, CA.

Pfeiffer, J. 1994, *Competitive Advantage Through People*, Harvard Business School Press, Boston.

Realin, J.A. 1997, 'Internal career development in the age of insecurity', *Business Forum*.

CASE STUDY 1

Career Development Issues in XYZ Bank

XYZ Bank is a scheduled private sector bank headquartered in Bangalore. The bank was started in 1930 by a promoter and it grew over a period of time to assume national presence. The advent of liberalization resulted in the inflow of equity and subsequent control by a major European bank.

The bank currently has over 700 branches with employee strength of over 10,000. The average age of employees in the bank is 37 years and the average tenure of employees is 12 years. Most of the employees who joined the bank as non-officers were promoted as Scale-I Junior Officers.

The bank serves customers from the middle class and trading communities. The foreign partner in the bank has undertaken a massive exercise for rebranding and reengineering the work processes before implementation of IT.

The tenured employees felt that they were no longer relevant in the revised scheme of things as none of them were promoted during the last three years. This had an impact on the employee morale and motivation as well as on the growth of the business. .

During the annual business review conference, the chief executive officer (CEO) of the bank questioned the regional managers (RMs) on the drop in growth and missing of targets by some critical regions. The RMs cited the lack of growth opportunities for the tenured employees as the cause.

The CEO advised the Vice-President–HR, to do a comprehensive study of the situation and submit a report on the necessary steps to address the situation. The latter called for a meeting of the regional HR managers (RHRMs) and asked them to prepare an action plan on the entire aspect within a month's time. The RHRMs after detailed deliberation submitted the following action plan:

- Design a questionnaire for employee feedback with emphasis on career development opportunities
- Conduct group discussions and meetings with tenured employees across all the regions
- Develop an action plan based on the insights received through meetings

In the follow-up meeting, the Vice-President–HR approved the action plan after discussions with the RHRMs and advised them to revert in a month's time. The RHRMs went ahead with the action plan and obtained the feedback through both the questionnaires and group discussions with tenured employees. After analysing the feedback, they identified the following:

- The tenured employees sought training in core banking software, customer relationship management (CRM), best practices for service excellence, and communication skills.
- They felt that this would enable them to re-establish their relevance in the context of changing work processes and a rebranded identity of the bank.
- They opined that training and a renewed sense of relevance to the bank would improve the prospects of career progression.

Questions
1. Analyse the action plan and feedback from employees.

2. Do you think that the feedback, if implemented, would help improve the situation?

Work Culture: HCL Perot Systems

CASE STUDY 2

HCL Perot Systems (HPS) is a joint venture between HCL Technologies and Perot Systems Corporation. The company's emphasis on HR gets reflected in the infrastructure, work culture, and even the method of communication with employees as well as customers. Established in 1996, HPS provides IT application services in verticals such as finance, travel, telecom, healthcare, and insurance. Rajnish Kohli, head of corporate communications for HPS, says that the organization has focused upon HR since its inception. The company wanted to do away with all those HR policies that most of the time create conflicts within the organization. This meant transforming into a flat organization, having no titles to define people (everyone being called 'associates'), and working as a team. Taking this into consideration, HPS has evolved over the years as one of the most employee-friendly companies. The company was among the first to introduce the concept of spouse working in the same organization and at the same location. Everyone (including the head of the company) travels by economy class. Interestingly, lifts are not used in the building. According to Kohli, this is a conscious health-related effort to make employees get a break from their sedentary positions and do some exercise.

Matter of Freedom

At HPS, one mantra that overrules all is 'having fun at the workplace'. Firmly believing that a good atmosphere can help increase productivity, HPS has invested a lot in making its workplace a lively and fun place. Unlike many companies, HPS believes in celebrating space and that is what gets depicted as soon as one enters its campus in Noida. Right from the sprawling campus to the huge hanging sculptures from the ceilings of the four-storied building, the purpose is to offer a sense of freedom to the employees. The sculpture (which is a major attraction for people visiting the facility) depicts 'free spirits in free space'. 'The design stems from the concept of the "Tree of Life". The stem of this tree is based strongly on the ground with all free sprits flying high in space,' says Kohli.

The company is also very conscious of its employees' preferences and most of the changes within the organization are made keeping their suggestions in mind. This even gets reflected in different colours such as orange, ochre, yellow, blue, and green (a different colour at each floor) that have been chosen keeping in mind the average age of the employees of the group. In addition, the company also has 4,500 blow-ups of movie stars, cinema hoardings, sports celebrities, national festivals, and latest gizmos, which have been extensively used to decorate different spaces. Each wing on the four floors, which house different divisions of the company, has a chosen theme and posters to match.

Recruitment Process

Entry into HPS is not an easy task. The basic characteristics required to get a placement in the company are an individual's technical and behavioural strengths, along with domain knowledge and leadership skills. In addition, the company emphasises entrepreneurial spirit and an individual's enthusiasm to make things happen. HPS generally recruits graduate engineers, MCAs, and MBAs for all technical positions, with domain expertise. Besides the screening of resumes, there are several rounds of interviews to judge the competency of an individual. HPS currently employs approximately 2,100 people across the globe and is looking at recruiting close to 500 people by this year-end.

Continuous Training

Training is an ongoing process at HPS. Apart from induction training, the company also has monthly and quarterly training. Besides, the company also has competency development centres (CDCs) and centres of excellence (CoEs), which help in improving its manpower capabilities. The CDCs take care of the continuous enhancement of organizational and associate level capabilities. They also analyse trends and develop programmes to equip the associates with expertise in new technology areas. CoEs, on the other hand, focus on developing emerging technology and product competencies.

In addition, the company also has a specialized programme for their top performers. Titled RACE (renewed adaptability in a changing environment) Training, the programme helps participants to understand and apply newfound knowledge, skills, and perspectives within a single learning initiative. It is a combination of various forms of learning such as classroom, psychometric-tool-based, outbound, and one-on-one coaching.

HR Policies

The company has been very innovative in its HR policies and has introduced concepts such as 3Ts, 3Cs, and 3As, which has helped HPS improve its communication, synchronization within teams and achieve sustained growth even during tough times. While 3T stands for 'Triumph Through Teamwork', 3C is for 'Contact, Connect, and Communicate' and 3A stands for 'Access, Assist, and Advice'. The 3T programme seeks to foster teamwork through various types of team-building programmes, including outbound, adventure sports-based training sessions, while 3C is aimed at discovering latent talents. The 3A programme is especially targeted at employees spread across the globe. It is a mail- or intranet-based system providing employees at all locations a single window through which they can get information, voice concerns and can also get their grievances addressed. The company also follows a 'project-based hierarchy', with no designations to differentiate associates from one project to another. 'In such a system, there is no room for resentment. The purpose is to offer an open-ended environment and level playing field within the organization,' he says. While constituting a new team, people at a higher level in the previous team can be placed below those at a lower level in the new team. Firmly believing that employee development results in the overall growth of the organization, the company pays a lot of emphasis on career development activities of its employees. There is a wide scope for lateral movement and also an emphasis on the rotation plan to utilize the latent potential of professionals.

Appraisal System

For appraisal of personnel, HPS does not follow a formal structure. After the end of every project, HPS conducts project reviews. According to Kohli, this also helps them in assessing an individual's true competence, which can be later used for his career development. To identify underperformers, HPS has a robust management system called 'performance improvement plan'. This system is also linked to their future training needs for identifying and plugging skill gaps. While HR policies at HPS are linked to performance and contemporary framework, compensation is linked to role, responsibility, qualification, experience, and skill level of each associate, assessed at the time of joining. There are also schemes to identify and recognize 'star performers' and 'star teams'. The performance and potential of an associate plays a crucial role in his growth and progression. The company's reward management plan incorporates rewards such as associate of the year, exceptional contributor, quality champion, and competency development. To retain its workforce, last year the company had started a new programme for the top management. Under this, the senior managers and top management would be offered dynamic profiles as rewards.

Commitment to Quality

HPS got ISO 9001 certification just after one year of getting established and is now planning for the next level of PCMM level certification, that is, PCMM Level 5. According to Rakesh Soni, the head of quality group for HPS, the focus on quality has been there since the beginning of the company's operations. The latest Capability Maturity Model Integration Certification (CMMI Level 5 of version 1.1) certification makes it the youngest company to reach this level according to the company officials (the company started its operations in 1996). Hence, there have been many changes in terms of people development, role progression, and maintaining transparency within the organization. Besides, the company is also involved in social welfare activities under its social welfare foundation. The priority areas for the foundation are education to the economically disadvantaged, public health, gender justice, woman empowerment, and creating equal opportunities for people with disabilities.

Questions

1. Critically analyse the work culture in HCL Perot Systems.
2. Does the training system support the career development plans of an employee?
3. Do you think that the HR policies are geared to promote career development of employees?
4. What changes do you suggest in the HR policies for supporting the career development initiatives?

Training and Development

Objectives

After studying this chapter, you will be able to understand

- the nature and concept of training
- the difference between training and other related concepts
- the importance of training in organizations
- the various methods of training in organizations
- the new training techniques such as outward bound training and fishbowl technique
- how training is evaluated

INTRODUCTION

In the present competitive and dynamic environment, it has become essential for organizations to build and sustain competencies that would provide them sustainable competitive advantage. During the industrial and manufacturing era, organizations and managers adopted an *ad hoc* and paternalistic approach to this concern. However, in this knowledge era, where human assets are valued more than physical assets, it is but natural that organizations adopt a strategic and planned approach towards the maintenance of human resources. In this context, training has assumed more importance than ever before.

Dynamic and growth-oriented organizations recognize training as an important aspect of the managerial function in a rapidly changing economic and social environment. Training is a continuous and incessant learning process in human resource development. It helps to develop one's personality, sharpen his/her managerial and interpersonal skills, increase motivation, and improve effectiveness in an organization. It also helps to achieve congruence between corporate and personal goals. As the strength of any organization lies in the strength of its people, training is undoubtedly the most important part of organizational renewal as an ongoing process.

Training is a process through which a person enhances and develops his/her efficiency, capacity, and effectiveness at work by improving and updating his/her knowledge and understanding the skills relevant to his or her job. Training also helps a person cultivate appropriate and desired behaviours and attitudes towards work and people.

▪ ▪ ▪
Training is a continuous process of learning in human resource development.

Training and development in public and private enterprises is a big business. It encompasses various players, that is, trainees, instructors, support personnel, and managers and supervisors. Keeping in view the number and variety of training programmes, resources required, and objectives/goals sought, training may be a Herculean task.

No enterprise can last long in a highly competitive society unless it keeps pace with the emerging market trends and technological changes. If an enterprise has to compete successfully, its products or services must excel. In addition to an aggressive and imaginative research and engineering effort, it also requires a sustained and forward-looking training effort.

Sweeping technological changes are affecting the labour market and are changing the whole mix of jobs and skills needed to perform them. While some occupations are dying, others are emerging and each new technological breakthrough speeds up the process. This has a great impact on the people in organizations. Unless training is provided, the jobs of employees in organizations are at stake.

Training Programme

A training programme can be defined as a planned process through which an organization seeks to attain the objectives of performance enhancement by developing the skills of a set of learners or by fulfilling the learning requirements of an identified group of employees. The planning process identifies the group of learners, the trainers, the venue, and the required resources (financial and physical). Hence, the main functions of a training programme may be summarized as follows:

- It helps the trainees acquire knowledge of the subject matter. For instance, the banks in the country conduct exclusive training programmes for different departments, such as credit, marketing, and treasury.
- It brings about a change in attitudes, understanding, and behaviour among the trainees with respect to particular objects, programmes, and policies. The public sector enterprises such as Bharat Dynamics Limited (BDL), apart from conducting technical training programmes, also conduct behavioural training programmes for employees to develop their personality. Bharat Heavy Electricals Limited (BHEL) conducts an exclusive training programme when its blast furnace division embarks upon a new project for overseas clients, to sensitize its employees to the specific requirements of the client.
- It helps in putting the theories into practice and bringing out general guidelines from various hypotheses. New recruits in banks, after training in theoretical aspects, are exposed to practical aspects through mock banking exercises in the staff training colleges.

> ■ ■ ■
> A training programme is a planned process by which an organization seeks to attain performance enhancement.

- It helps evaluate the abilities, competencies, and potentials of the trainees for a particular job or work skills. The assessment centre concept, which is widely adopted by organizations, is aimed to assess the skills/competencies/potentials of employees and thereby plan for a career path for them.
- It induces zeal and enthusiasm for self-learning and development among the trainees. The induction training typically encompasses group and self-learning exercises, mainly to induce the self- and shared learning among the trainees.

> ■ ■ ■
> In-basket exercises, such as role-plays, used in off-the-job training are aimed at improving the decision-making skills of trainees.

- It enhances the problem-solving and decision-making capabilities of the trainees. The in-basket exercises, such as role-plays, used in off-the-job training are aimed at improving the decision-making skills of trainees.
- It helps in narrowing down the gap between the expected level of performance and the actual level of performance among the trainees. The training agenda is prepared by the reporting officers, who specify performance gaps,

and the training system designs the programme accordingly. However, the real efficacy of a training programme is judged by the improvement in performance, as perceived by the reporting officers after the training.

- It provides new recruits or trainees a scientific pace for imbibing the knowledge and skills required to discharge their duties and responsibilities meaningfully and purposefully.

According to Flippo, training is the act of increasing the knowledge and skills of an employee for doing a particular job. The major outcome of training is learning, that is, transformation in the behavioural process in the form of increased performance, technical know-how, performing the job more effectively, and also preparing the individual for higher-level jobs.

We may then define training as a planned, sequential process aiming at bringing about a significant change in knowledge, skills, attitudes, and social behaviour of employees. The outcomes of the training programme may be summarized as (a) increased knowledge and skills for doing a job, (b) bridging the gap between job needs and employee skills, knowledge, and behaviour, and (c) enhancement of operative skills.

Training vs Development

Training is often referred to as imparting specific skills and behaviour. The specificity is in terms of learning a specific course content or skill such as a computer language, machine operations, and playing tennis. The focus is on improvement in performance after training along with a perceptible behavioural change. In that sense, they differ slightly from conceptual or intellectual ones.

Training often caters to organizational needs. The training programme may be prompted because of certain changes present or anticipated in the structure and processes of organizations. Hence, the impact of training may be experienced and assessed by the organization immediately. Usually, administrative, supervisory, and technical workforce may be exposed to training programmes.

The banks in the country in the early nineties had implemented advanced ledger posting machines (ALMS) and, for this purpose, they undertook extensive training of their operational and systems people. Similarly, now most of the public sector banks are implementing core banking solution (CBS) and for this purpose they are training their systems, networking, and operations personnel.

Development on the other hand is holistic, often aiming at overall personality development. The content of a development programme includes conceptual or theoretical inputs, perspective strategic thinking or focusing on behavioural aspects such as leadership skills and managing teams and groups. The intent is to provide training in non-technical aspects so that individuals may discharge organizational functions more effectively in the areas of problem solving, decision-making, people skills, etc.

> ■ ■ ■
> Training is often referred to as imparting specific skills and behaviour.

Thus, we may say that training is imparted to operatives, whereas development is a process of grooming mainly used for executives or managers. The impact of a training programme ends with learning the skill, while that of a developmental programme is a continuous and ongoing process.

> ■ □ ■
> Training focuses on improved performance, skills, and behaviour.

The need for training the employees stems mostly from organizational requirements, whereas the need to undergo a developmental programme is internal, that is, prompted by employees themselves. Nevertheless, in both

EXHIBIT 10.1 Vysya Bank

The Vysya Bank (now ING Vysya Bank), realizing the importance of infusing young blood into the officer ranks, had recruited young MBAs as management trainees during the mid-1990s and they were given extensive training for a period of one year. In this period, along with banking/technical skills, they were imparted training in behavioural aspects. This is an instance of developmental approach, where the organization takes a long-term view of grooming future leaders with well-groomed personalities.

instances, organizations gain in terms of increased or effective performance. Yet another distinction that may be brought about is that training serves immediate organizational requirements, while development is futuristic and aims at growth of both the individual and the organization (Exhibit 10.1).

Training vs Education

■ ■ ■
Education aims at identifying the potentials; training improves upon them.

Education refers to the process of imparting knowledge and building the character of individuals in a formal setting. It is a process aimed at overall development and enabling the individuals for developing right perspectives and channels of thinking. The term *educated* implies a certain level of transformation, which has already taken place as a result of the learning process. It is more experienced in the approach and attitude towards things.

Training is specific-content based, job oriented, context based, and vocation oriented. Education is imparted in formal institutions such as schools and colleges, whereas training is usually company specific and practice based. Education aims at identifying the potentials; training improves upon them. However, we may perceive them as complementary and mutually supportive.

Purposes of Training

Training per se can be used by organizations for multiple purposes, and a variety of factors can influence the organizations' approach towards training. The objectives of training can be multifarious and some of them are as follows (Figure 10.1):

- *Induction*: Training can be used by organizations for inducting new recruits into the organization. The initial period plays a predominant role in the assimilation/association of the organization. The induction training is used by organizations for acclimatizing and also introducing to policies/procedures of the organization. Realizing its importance, in organizations such as Wipro Corporation, the Chairman, Azim Premji, makes it a point to spend an entire day with the new recruits to communicate his/her ideals and build a rapport with them.
- *Updating*: Training can also be used for periodical updating of skills of the employees. This may become essential because of new policies and launch of new products. The refresher courses conducted by banks for their employees are an example.
- *Preparing for future assignments*: The organizations also use training as a tool to prepare employees for higher responsibilities in future. Organizations also conduct training in order to build loyalty among the employees. The public sector organizations, especially the banks, conduct an exclusive training programme for promotee clerks/officers.

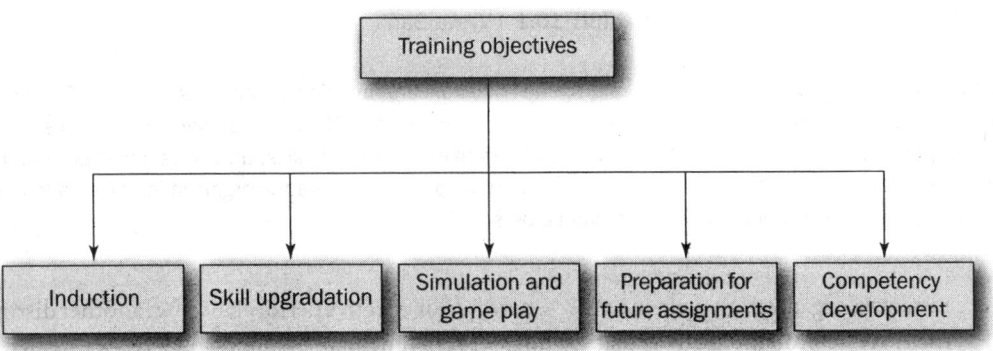

FIGURE 10.1 Objectives of training

- *Competency development and identification of training needs*: It is a known fact that identification of training needs and competency development are increasingly recognized as imperative to stay alive in competition. The Vysya Bank during late nineties had adopted a core competencies programme. The bank had identified five areas—marketing, credit, cash management services, treasury, and HRM. The employees were selected through a written examination and an interview and the selected candidates were given extensive training in the training college and also the work places.

- *Simulation and game play*: In case of technical subjects and complicated projects, it would not be feasible for the employees to be trained on the job, and, in such cases, organizations create simulated work conditions to train the employees. In the aviation industry, pilots are trained in a simulated environment. In the armed forces, the recruitment is done through game-plays and the new recruits are also placed through game-plays to improve their decision-making skills. Private sector organizations take their employees on trekking trips and expeditions to build rapport among them and also to improve their ability to adapt to new challenges or situations.

The other innovative purposes for which training is being deployed by the organizations are organizational analysis, task analysis, man and equipment analysis, HR clinics, incubators, etc.

Training for Different Levels

The training system has to adapt itself to the needs of employees at various levels. Typically, training programmes in manufacturing organizations can be categorized broadly into four levels, that is, induction, supervisory, technical, and management development. The purpose of induction training has been explained earlier. Supervisory training is aimed at improving the supervisory skills of the supervisors. Technical training focuses on improving the technical skills or knowledge of the employee.

> ■ ■ ■
> The training system has to adapt itself to the needs of employees at various levels.

In the case of BDL, the employees working in various missile divisions are trained about technical nuances. Depending on the requirements/exigencies, two types of training can be clubbed together. The supervisors can also be trained in supervisory and technical skills simultaneously. The training needs of the managers are addressed through management development programmes.

NEED AND IMPORTANCE OF TRAINING

■ ■ ■
Training is job-oriented and aims at maintaining and improving the current level of job performance.

Training is mainly job-oriented; it aims at maintaining and improving current job performance. The need for a training programme may arise due to the following.

- *Entry of new recruits*: New entrants need training to attain clarity in job responsibility, nature of the job, and other organizational matters so that person-hours are not wasted.
- *Promotions*: Preparation of employees for higher level jobs such as promotions requires skill upgradation or competency building.
- *To prevent skill obsolescence*: Training and development programmes foster the initiative and creativity of employees and help to prevent obsolescence of skills, which may be due to an employee's age, temperament, motivation level, or inability to adapt to technological changes.
- *To increase productivity*: Instruction can help employees increase their level of performance on their present assignment. Increased human performance often leads to increased operational productivity and increased company profit.
- *To improve quality*: With globalization, increased competitiveness has resulted in greater emphasis on producing or delivering quality goods and services. Hence, training in quality maintenance and quality management becomes essential.
- *To meet organizational objectives*: Future organizational goals and plans dictate training of its existing workforce, particularly, where there is a dearth of skills to match the needs of organizational plans.
- *To improve organizational climate*: Organizational climate refers to the overall relations and effective orientations of the employees towards the organization. These orientations may be positive or negative. Positive orientations will result in increased productivity and employee morale. Training is essential to maintain and sustain positive orientations of its employees.
- *To prevent accidents*: Training can create awareness about safety hazards and accident proneness and may equip the individuals with better orientations to handle crises.
- *To avoid boredom, monotony, and fatigue*: Refresher courses may be organized intermittently for all employees in the rank and file category to relieve job fatigue and monotony of everyday work-life.
- *To support personal growth and development*: Employees gain a lot by training and developmental programmes. Management development programmes seem to give participants a wider awareness, improved skills, and enlightened artistic philosophy and make enhanced personal growth possible.

It may be observed that the need for training may arise because of one or more of the aforementioned factors.

Scott and Cloutier observes that 'training is the outcome of sound management, for it makes employees more effective and productive. It is actively and intimately connected with all the personnel or managerial activities. The training experts are increasingly attempting to justify the time and money on the training systems through the transfer of learning. In order to ensure maximization of transfer of learning, scientific methods are essential for training needs identification (TNI). Training proves to be highly beneficial to both the individual and the organization.

Benefits for individuals

- It enhances their skills/knowledge, which increases their personal worth and employability.
- It makes employees effective and efficient and as a result there is a reduction in wastage of resources and time.
- Employees can realize their career goals easily.
- Career moves and job-hopping, which happen to be the order of the day, can be made in a flexible manner.
- There will be greater awareness, fewer errors, increased productivity, and boost in the morale of the employees.

Benefits for the organization

- Increasing the intellectual capital of the organization
- Achieving higher standards of quality, building up a satisfactory organizational structure, delegating authority, and motivating employees to perform better
- Reducing employee turnover and absenteeism
- Minimizing waste
- Implementing job enlargement and job enrichment programmes
- Strengthening employee loyalty through continuous training

CONCEPT OF TRAINING

■ ■ ■

A successful training programme will begin with successful identification of training needs and creation of the right kind of environment for conducting the same.

The entire philosophy of training rests on the principles of learning. Since any training programme involves investment in time and effort, care has to be taken in the design of it. It should be such that it serves both the organizational requirements and individual needs. The trainer has to take care and guard against over-training, use of poor instructions, imitation of programmes that may not be relevant in the present organization, misuse of tests, inadequate tools and equipment, or over-reliance on one singular technique.

A successful training programme will begin with successful identification of training needs and creation of the right kind of environment for conducting the same (Figure 10.2). The trainer should have the requisite skills and expertise, choose appropriate methods, have a pleasing personality, and also be able to relate the value of training to an enterprise. To this end, training

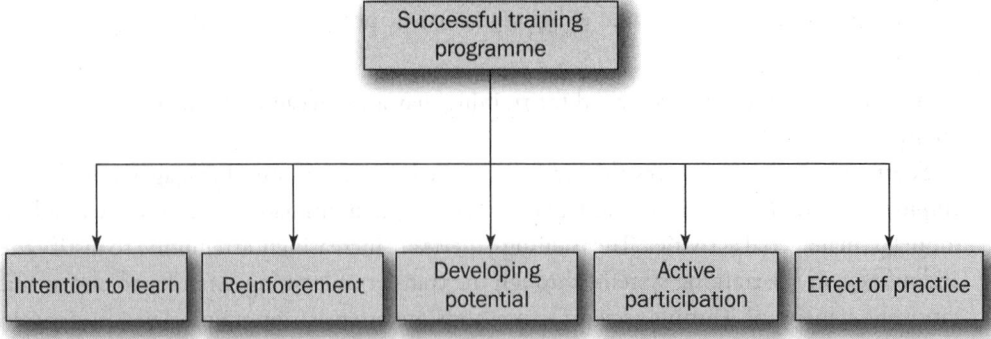

FIGURE 10.2   Guidelines for a successful training programme

efforts must invariably follow certain learning-oriented guidelines, which may be summarized as follows:

Intention to learn   Intention to learn or motivation to learn is a basic requirement in the training/learning process. The objectiveness, intentions, and changes that are anticipated by way of training may be spelt out clearly before the onset of the programme. Motivation to learn is influenced by these aspects. Individuals learn quickly when the material is relevant and important to them. Further, active participation accelerates learning and memory is long lasting. ICICI Bank has tied up with management institutions to enable its employees to register and pursue various courses for improvement of qualifications.

Reinforcement   Learning is more effective where there is reinforcement in the form of rewards and punishments. In the process of training, we aim at changing the process of thinking, attitudes, or some other specific aspect. During the process of training, while there is a perceptible change in the positive direction, positive reinforcement in the form of rewards or recognitions go a long way in internalizing the learning. The public sector banks award to their employees one increment after completion of CAIIB—Part I and two increments after completion of CAIIB from the Indian Institute of Bankers (IIB).

Developing potential   Every human being has some latent potential or capacities, and every individual is capable of learning from training. Training aims at developing their potentials and latent abilities.

Active participation   Effective learning results when there is active involvement of its participant. Research has confirmed that people remember 10% of what they had read, 20% of what they hear, 30% of what they see, 50% of what they see and hear, 70% of what they say, and 90% of what they say while also performing the task. Learning and memory retention are high when there is active involvement of the participant.

Different training methods are used for different types of learning. For example, cognitive learning stresses visual and audio experience to gain understanding. It may involve reading, lectures, audiovisual presentations, case problems, etc. Affective learning (attitudes, values, and interest acquisition) may best be learned through field trips, role-plays, open-ended discussion, counselling, or reflection. Psychomotor skills (eye–hand coordination, finger dexterity, etc) are best acquired through practice. Therefore, the value of multi-sensory learning exercises should be emphasized

Effect of practice   Training is most effective when it is supplemented or followed by practice. It is said that practice makes a man perfect. Whatever material or skill is acquired when it is either memorized or practised, the process of internalization takes place quickly. The approach becomes mature, the number of errors gets reduced, and the time taken to complete the tasks also becomes less.

Transfer of learning   Training should be as real as possible so that the trainees can successfully implement the knowledge acquired in their jobs. The components or the issues dealt with in the training process should be such that they can be successfully applied in their jobs. Once a broad concept or principle is understood, it could be generalized to other situations. For example, a manager who has understood the technique of contingency leadership theory may be capable of analysing a wide variety of motivational problems and developing solutions to them on the basis of a few principles.

Transfer of training can be successfully accomplished by (a) maximizing the similarity between the training situation and work situation, (b) providing adequate experience with tasks during training, (c) providing a variety of examples when teaching concepts or skills, (d) identifying important features of the task, and (e) making sure that the trainee understands general principles.

Learning Curve

Psychologists have analysed the relationship between amount of learning and the time taken to learn. This is presented in the form of a curve, which is popularly known as the learning curve.

Learning does not take place at a constant speed. It varies according to the difficulty of the task and the ability of the individual. By using suitable measures of learning, such as errors made in each trial, time taken per trial, and the right responses learnt per trial, the progress of learning any skill can be obtained and plotted in the form of a learning curve. The curves for individuals will differ widely because of the individual differences in learning. However, certain commonalities also occur.

When we observe the curve carefully, we notice that there is rapid rise in the rate of learning initially. The second characteristic feature is that the rate of learning slows down as we move towards the middle of the curve. The third distinct feature, which may be observed in most of the curves, is a 'plateau' in the learning curve.

The 'plateau' in the curve is significant in many ways. It basically means no change in learning. Plateaus also occur when the task is complex, when crucial stages in learning are reached, when learners have to make extra effort, and the trainer has to provide additional incentives to the learner, etc. Other reasons that may cause plateaus are distractions during learning, lack of motivation, inefficient performance method, or, very often, ineffective teaching or training.

Another characteristic feature of the learning curve is after the plateau stage, there is a sudden increase in the rate of learning, which is termed as 'end spurt'. This sudden rise could be because of the awareness that the learning process is coming to an end or because of the changes introduced by the trainer in the process during the plateau stage.

Learning curve has many practical applications, such as the following:

- It provides for a method whereby goals can be established and performance towards these goals can be established.
- Scheduling of production improvement can be made if performance levels are known.

> ■ ■ ■
> The relationship between the amount of learning and the time taken to learn is represented as a curve, known as the learning curve.

To address the plateau in learning curve, organizations are tuning their learning systems towards adult learning with more components of hands-on experience and practical experience. Training institutions are incorporating project work in the theoretical modules to sustain the interests of the learners. The IT training institutions have incorporated a project work module in industry to improve the learning and also build the confidence of the learners.

Areas of Training

The broad areas in which training is usually imparted in organizations may be classified under the following headings:

Enhancing knowledge/building concepts   Basic principles or advanced inputs with regard to specific concepts or sometimes knowledge about company, culture, etc., form the major themes in the training programme. For example, in ICICI Bank, the training programmes for the branch managers on sales and marketing impart knowledge on neurolinguistics and consumer psychology to improve their marketing skills.

Technical skills   Often training programmes impart specific skills in the areas of computers or operating machines. This is usually provided with the help of experts and on the job. For instance, in the area of networking and security, the trainers are trained on aspects such as network configuration, network security, intrusion detection system, and ethical hacking.

Interpersonal/behavioural skills   Here, individuals are exposed to self-awareness programmes to develop the right mental attitude towards their job, colleagues, and the company. The main focus is on teaching the employee as to how to become a good team member and lead the company. The T group training/sensitivity training is an excellent programme for the purpose. The management trainees in the public sector banks are trained on behavioural aspects such as FIRO-B.

Trainer

The function of imparting training is by and large the responsibility of the HR department. The director/general manager/vice-president oversees the training calendar, and identifies appropriate people, and allocates various training programmes to them. In organizations where the infrastructure is well developed, the HR managers may conduct the training programme by themselves or by inviting other resource people. A large group may then get trained at a time in such instances. In other occasions, employees are sent off the job to some specific programme organized by independent training agencies at a central location. Any organization can nominate its employees for the same. In this type, only a few people can get trained at a time, as many people cannot be off the job at the same time.

A comprehensive and holistic training system would typically follow the following steps in devising and implementing a training plan:

- A training plan is jointly prepared by the HR department and the training head taking into account various parameters such as the corporate goals/objectives, perspectives of the top management, and training needs identified by the branch/regional heads.
- After preparation of a tentative training plan, it is placed for the consideration of the top management for approval.

■ ■ ■
The function of imparting training is by and large the responsibility of the HR department.

- On approval by the top management, a training calendar is prepared and widely circulated among the branches/regions for information dissemination.
- The branch/regional heads nominate employees for the training, depending upon their training needs and the job requirements.

- The training programmes are designed optimally to supplement theory with hands-on experience and also to ensure maximization of learning among the participants.
- The transfer of learning is assessed through performance measurement in the annual performance appraisal, which ultimately leads to feedback for the training system.

In most of the central public sectors and some of the state-level public enterprises, the personnel department has identified a manager (training) whose specific responsibility is to manage the training needs of the employees of the organization. The manager and his/her team members organize the programmes in such a manner that they don't affect the daily routine work of the organization.

TRAINING PROGRAMME

> Training is most effective when it is planned, implemented, and evaluated in a systematic way.

Training is most effective when it is planned, implemented, and evaluated in a systematic way. Unplanned, uncoordinated, and haphazard training efforts greatly reduce the learning that can be expected. Hence, training efforts must aim at meeting the short-term (individual) and long-term (organizational) goals. This involves conducting a preliminary assessment of training needs at various levels in the organization. A specific training programme may be a result of organizational, group, or individual requirements. A preliminary identification of the needs would help the organization to act in a proactive manner and realize its objectives. Therefore, we may consider identification of training needs at the following levels:

- Organizational
- Group
- Individual

Training Needs at the Organizational Level

Some basic assumptions regarding the training needs of an organization are as follows:

- The organization has objectives to achieve for the benefit of stakeholders, employees, customers, suppliers, and neighbours.
- These objectives can be achieved only by harnessing the abilities of its employees and providing them opportunities to realize their full potential.
- Therefore, people must know what they need to learn in order to achieve organizational goals.

Training needs at the organizational level involve a study of the entire organization in terms of its objectives and resources, utilization of various resources, interaction patterns in the environment, etc. Most of the time, training needs address-specific problems in operation, and through a training programme, solutions are obtained.

Such problems are related to productivity, high costs, poor material control, poor quality, excessive scrap, grievances, high employee turnover, absenteeism, fatigue, failure to meet standards and targets, etc.

> Training needs at the organizational level involves a study of the entire organization.

Often, anticipating impending and future problems, such as expansion of business and introduction of new products, new services, new plants, and organizational changes concerned with manpower inventory for the present and future needs, may also necessitate a training programme. The business environment and the political, socio-cultural, and technological factors and their influences in effective management might also prompt a training programme.

Information about organizational needs can be obtained from organizational policies and discussions with the top management, and gaps in the realization of objectives can be determined by getting feedback from employees and conducting a survey.

Training Needs at the Group Level

An organization functions in a nature of high task interdependence and role relationships. Organizational structure determines the positions that the individual will occupy and the role relationships that are attached with it. While there is emphasis on individual effectiveness, group processes and dynamics go a long way in bringing cohesiveness among the employees. Hence, managing subordinates, art of delegation, handling superiors, bringing about inter-group process dependency, providing feedback, counselling, mentoring, and meeting the performance standards are some of the aspects that might prompt a training programme.

Information in these areas may be obtained by interacting with heads of the departments, conducting performance appraisals, and conducting specific interviews with customers, suppliers, etc.

Training Needs at the Individual Level

Training at the individual level may be required to improve performance, modify deviant or undesirable performance or behaviour, or equip the individual with additional skills, which will result in capacity building and utilization. This step is closely related to manpower analysis, wherein the organization makes an assessment of present and future skill requirements for the organization. Personal observation, performance reviews, supervisory reports, diagnostic tests, and self-evaluation help in collecting the required information and selecting particular training options that would improve the performance of employees.

If there is a match between individual needs and organizational requirements and the employees are trained accordingly, it would result in enhanced performance, increased job satisfaction, and employee loyalty.

In general, any training programme will aim at the following:

- Implementing (doing things well); for example, meeting current organizational objectives
- Improving (doing things better); for example, setting higher objectives and trying to reach them
- Innovating (doing new and better things); for example, changing objectives and strategies

It is then obvious that identification of training needs may be prompted by one or a combination of these aspects: internal or external factors, the processes or relationships, the functional heads or HR managers, external influences such as major technological or environmental changes, and budgetary and time constraints (Figure 10.3).

> ■ ■ ■
> Training at the individual level may be required to either improve performance, modify deviant performance, or equip an individual with additional skills.

It is interesting to note that 'the determination of training needs in American industry ranges from subjective beliefs about the value of training and education to a systematic identification of problems requiring solutions. The latter seems to be the wisest course in order to ensure that training contributes to the goals of an enterprise' (French 1970). In a survey of 150 firms, it

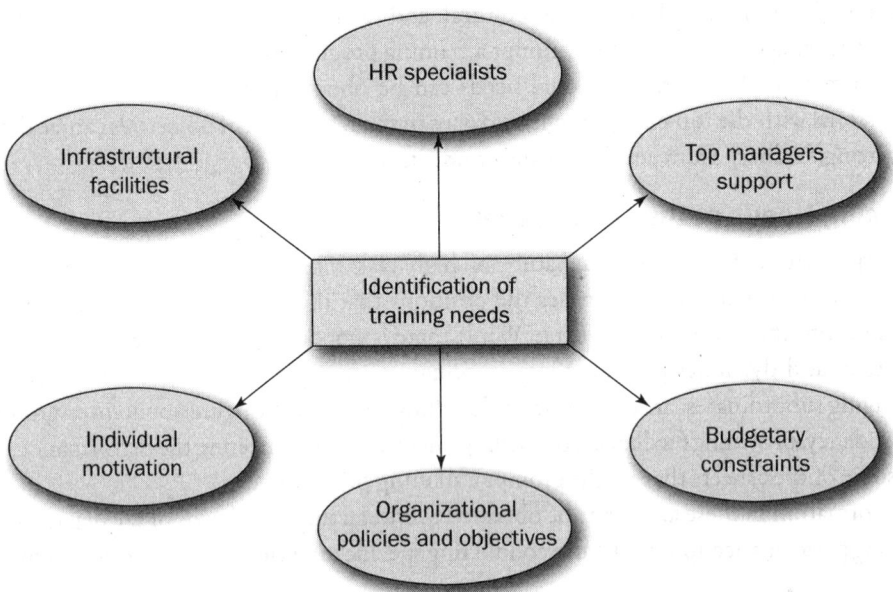

FIGURE 10.3 Dynamics of organizational learning

was found that the training needs of an organization were determined generally by requests from the top management (Mahler, et al. 1952). Presumably, perception, judgment, intuition, the expressed needs of the first level and middle managers, and a desire to follow the practices of other firms were the determining factors in these requests.

The other methods that were often used were informal observations, talks with supervisors, and group discussions and conferences; methods used less often were analysis of various reports (such as cost, turnover, grievances, and suggestions), formal training advisory committees, employee questionnaires, and merit or performance rating (Dudley, Waite). In another enquiry, it was found that the development of training needs was based on supervisory recommendations in 73% of the firms, on the analysis of job requirements in 58%, and on an analysis of job performance in 32%. Suggestions by employees were a factor in 66% of the firms. Organizations have several sources of information which assist them in determining their training needs; and in this determination of needs, supervisors play a major role.

The next step after identification of training needs is formulating training objectives. Objectives form an important part in the design of the programme, as they convey the intention and direction of the learning process. The programme may be based on any one or more of the needs and the objectives are determined thereof. Some examples of training objectives may be as follows:

- To enable participants to conduct effective appraisals
  - To introduce the new report writing standards
  - To identify participant's strengths and development needs in the project manager's role
  - To increase participants effectiveness and confidence as team leaders
  - To improve levels of customer service

> The next step after identification of training needs is formulating training objectives.

TRAINING METHODS

The next step in the process of formulating a training programme is choosing an appropriate method of training. The training methods may be broadly classified as on-the-job and off-the-job methods. The programme may also be in-house or outsourced. According to the theme, number of participants, and time available, a suitable method may be chosen.

The various methods of training the employees are interrelated and each method suits for a given situation. One type of training may not serve the purpose of a situation, and these techniques are usually multifaceted in their dimension and scope. Hence, the choice must be made very carefully based on the learner and the job he/she is involved. The following objectives are necessary for an effective training method:

- Motivate the trainees.
- Improve their job performance.
- Develop a willingness to change.
- Involve trainees' participation.
- Provide feedback and permit practice.

Some of the training methods are as follows:

On-the-job Training Methods

In the on-the-job training (OJT) methods, skilled co-workers or supervisors instruct employees and they learn the job by personal observation and practice. Sometimes they even handle the job by themselves and thus this method is also known as 'learning by doing'. 'Coaching, apprenticeship, job rotation, and special assignments' are some of the types of on-the-job training.

Public sector organizations such as Hindustan Aeronautics Limited (HAL) and Bharat Heavy Electricals Limited (BHEL), and private organizations such as Tata Steel (TISCO) recruit apprentice trainees in technical areas from technical institutes and train the young individuals for a period ranging from six months to one year and also pay stipend during the period. During the apprenticeship period, the trainees/apprentices are exposed to different sections of the department and thereby gain practical experience and exposure to the industry, which ultimately helps them in getting the job on completion of their courses.

Merits

- The trainee will know the actual production conditions and requirements, since he/she works in the real environment with actual equipment.
- This type of training is very economical as there are no additional personnel or facilities.
- The trainee acquires full knowledge of the rules, regulations, and procedures by watching and doing.
- Companies with adequate jobs and employees can easily adopt this type of training.
- This type of training is very convenient where the jobs are difficult to simulate or the skills can be learned quickly.

Demerits

- Instructions may not be properly comprehended at times in this type of training.

- Learners are often distracted by the noise at the office or workplace.
- This may cause low productivity if the employee fails to develop adequate skills during the training.

Job Instruction Training (JIT)

This method is also known as 'training through step-by-step learning' as it involves all necessary steps in the job, each in proper sequence, which are as follows:

- Preparation of the trainees for instruction
- Presentation of trainees for instruction
- Performance of the job by the trainee
- Motivating the trainee to follow up the job regularly

This method provides immediate feedback on results, quick correction of errors, and opportunity for additional practice when required. New recruits in banks are provided with job cards, which provide step-by-step instructions to perform various tasks in various departments such as general banking, clearing, and credit.

Vestibule Training (Training Centre)

In this method, the trainee is exposed to an artificial working environment wherein on-the-job situations are duplicated in a company classroom. Equipment and machines, which are identical with those in use in the place of work, are utilized to impart the training.

Here, theoretical training is given in the classroom, while the practical work is conducted on the production line. It is very useful to train semi-skilled personnel, particularly when many employees have to be trained for the same kind of work at the same time. Lectures, conferences, case studies, role-plays, and discussions are some forms of vestibule training.

Merits

- Trainees are less distracted as the training is imparted in a separate room.
- Effective utilization of a trained instructor is possible.
- Learners can learn correct methods that will not interrupt the production.
- Trainees are given ample freedom to practice what they have learnt, since there is no constant supervision of the supervisors.

Demerits

- Since the responsibilities are distributed, it may lead to organizational problems.
- It is not so economical, as an additional investment in equipment is necessary.
- This method is of limited value for the jobs that utilize non-duplicable equipment.
- The training environment is mostly artificial.

Training by Experienced Workers

In this method, experienced workers impart training to the trainees, especially when they need helpers. This type of training is more useful for departments in which workmen advance through successive jobs to perform a series of operations. The apprentices during the period of apprenticeship are assigned to one of the senior workmen, who are assigned with the responsibility of training and coaching them.

Training by Supervisors

In this type of training, the training is imparted on the job by the worker's immediate supervisors. Thus, it provides opportunities to the trainees to develop good rapport with their superiors and also by which the supervisors can assess the abilities of the trainees based on their performance. The supervisors guide the trainees on the skills required for the job and the skills include technical and behavioural skills, etc.

Demonstrations and Examples (Learning by Seeing)

As the name implies, in this method the trainer uses several examples and demonstrates the job to the trainee by performing it himself or herself. These are often used with lectures, pictures, text materials, discussions, etc. However, their usefulness is limited when it comes to training management personnel.

Simulation

It is the technique wherein the actual conditions are duplicated in a specific job. The vestibule training method is a good example of simulation. This type of training is mostly used in the aeronautical industry.

Merits

- It creates interest in the trainees and motivates them.
- This type of training is very useful to avoid any costly errors or the destruction of valuable materials or resources.

■ ■ ■
The vestibule training method is a good example of simulation.

Demerits

- This type of training usually involves huge costs.

Apprenticeship

This is the oldest and most common method of training, wherein most of the training time is spent on on-the-job productive work. In this method, each apprentice or trainee is given a programme of assignments according to a pre-determined schedule, which enhances the quality of training for improving the skills of the trainees.

Merits

- This type of training brings out a skilled workforce.
- Training gives immediate returns.
- It provides for an efficient workmanship.
- Lower production costs and a reduced turnover make this training less expensive.
- Employees develop loyalty towards the job and thereby the growth prospects are high.

Classroom or Off-the-job Training Methods

The various off-the-job training methods are discussed here (Figure 10.4).

Lectures

When it comes to the teaching of facts, concepts, principles, attitudes, theories, and problem-solving skills, lectures are considered to be the most useful method of imparting training. Lectures impart knowledge in the form of organized formal talks. Induction training usually begins with lecture sessions, the aim being to impart theoretical knowledge on relevant subjects/aspects to the trainees.

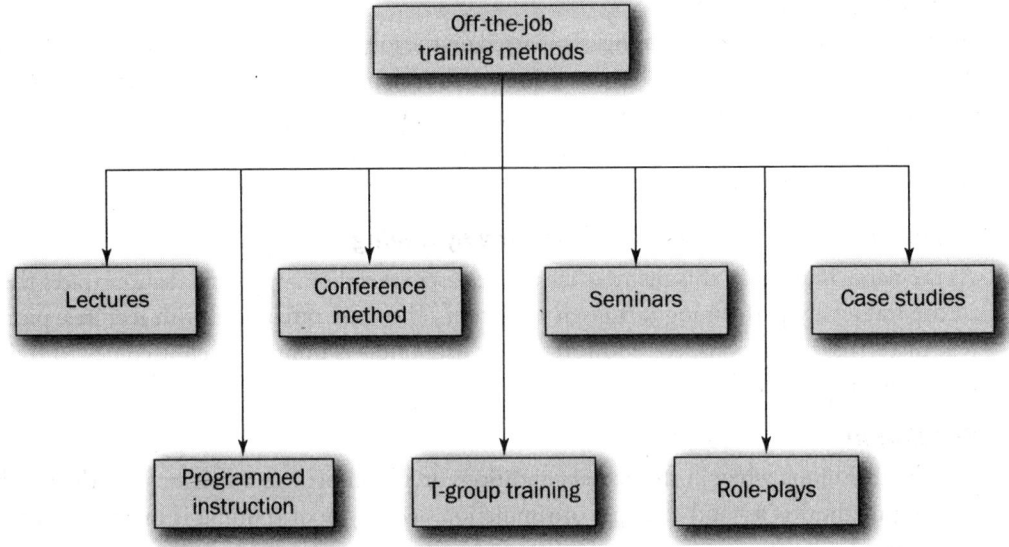

FIGURE 10.4   Off-the-job training methods

Merits

- This method reduces the cost per trainee when large groups are to be trained in a short span of time. As this method clearly explains the purpose, the trainees feel less anxious about the forthcoming events or organizational changes.
- This method is simple and effective.
- This method presents more material within a given time compared to any other method.
- It gives clear idea of applying the rules, principles, of a subject providing a review, clarification, and summarization of the subject introduced.

Demerits

- In this method, we can find only passive participants as it only provides for learning and not doing.
- There is no feedback from the audience due to one-way communication.
- Sometimes it becomes less effective, since the management personnel or the trainers often lack the time for preparation.
- Normally, a listener can pay attention only for 15–20 minutes and later gets distracted.
- Whenever a listener is uninformed, it becomes difficult to stimulate a discussion following a lecture.
- The listeners may get confused when an untrained lecturer lacks information or provides more information than required.
- Common listeners may not understand an extremely professional presentation and therefore, it must be prepared in such a way that it is easily understood.
- Sometimes the lecture may concentrate more on the facts and figures and ignore the actual application of the knowledge.
- The same material may not be applicable to individuals at times, while it may be applicable to a group.

Conference Method

It is a kind of interactive session in a formal meeting where the trainees are encouraged by the trainer to participate actively, thus developing their knowledge and understanding. There are three types of conferences, namely the *directed discussion*, which explains the facts and concepts, the *training conference*, where the knowledge of the trainees is pooled based on their past experiences, and finally the *seminar conference*, where a problem is defined by the trainer and the solution is sought by encouraging full participation of trainees in the discussion.

Merits

- This method is very useful in analysing the problems and issues and examining them from different viewpoints.
- It is very helpful in developing the conceptual knowledge in the trainees.
- Since the trainees are actively involved in this method, dogmatism is reduced, attitudes are modified, and solutions are easily sought.

Demerits

- This method is limited only to small groups.
- It is a long process and hence the progress also gets delayed.
- Irrelevant issues may creep in sometimes as part of discussions.

Seminar or Team Discussion

It is considered as an established method of training and is conducted in many ways. The trainees may prepare a paper on a selected subject after consulting the person in charge of the seminar, the person in charge may distribute the material to be analysed in advance, or, sometimes, valuable working material from actual files may be provided to the trainees for discussion.

Case Studies (Learning by Doing)

Under this method, the trainees are presented with a case and they are allowed to master the facts by acquainting themselves with the contents of the case. They are expected to identify the problems in the case and discover the probable causes, develop alternative courses of action, examine the alternatives using the objectives, select the best alternative, define the controls needed to bring that chosen alternative into action, and finally to role-play the action to test its effectiveness and find conditions that may limit it.

Merits

- Since the trainees are encouraged to think and act, their analytical skills and problem-solving abilities are improved.
- It enhances an open-minded approach and thus, serves as a means of integrating the knowledge obtained from different basic disciplines.
- Since the cases provided to the trainees are real incidents, the trainees develop more interest in that.
- This method is acceptable by everyone as it is based on the real life situations.
- As the trainees learn about the problems faced by their managers or superiors, they prepare themselves and learn to handle similar situations with possible remedies.

Demerits

- If the trainees are taught purely from books, it may become difficult for them to cope with future uncertainties.
- Instruction in the methods of analysis may not be given due importance.
- The cases analysed by trainees may become permanent in their minds and may be used by them at times indiscriminately.
- This method demands more time and money and does not promise the desired outcome, which may not be worth the expenditure incurred.

Role-playing

It has been defined as 'a method of human interaction which involves realistic behaviour in the imaginary situations'. In this method, the trainees enact a given role, while others observe their projections. This method of training primarily involves employee–employer relationships.

Merits

- The trainees learn more effectively by doing.
- Human sensitivity and interactions are stressed.
- Immediate results are known.
- A high involvement of trainees is seen.
- The trainees develop the necessary skills and ability to apply knowledge, particularly in areas such as human relations.
- This method is successful in bringing a desired change in the trainee's behaviour and attitudes.

Demerits

- Role-playing may not adhere to the objectives of the training programme, unless the trainer engages in coaching.
- Reinforcement of the desired behaviour may be sometimes lacking when the trainer fails to state the criteria for behaviour.

Programmed Instruction (Machine Method)

A programmed instruction involves breaking information down into meaningful units and then arranging these in a proper way to form a logical and sequential learning programme or package. In this method, the trainees learn with the use of a textbook or a teaching machine. The programme involves presenting questions, facts, or problems to the trainees to utilize the information given; and the trainees instantly receive feedback on the basis of the accuracy of their answers. The job card example from the banking industry is relevant to the programmed instruction tool.

> ■ ■ ■
> A programmed instruction involves breaking information down into meaningful units and then arranging these in a proper way to form a logical and sequential learning programme.

Merits

- Trainees learn from their own efforts and are free from the supervision of instructors.
- The material to be learnt is broken down into parts or small units, which provides for easier and quick learning.
- Feedback is available immediately.

- Learners take an active part at each step in the programme.
- Individual differences can be taken into account.
- Training can be imparted at any time and at anyplace.
- High level of learners' motivation is possible.

Demerits

- The setting of instructions is impersonal.
- Further study is not possible until the preliminary information is acquired.
- Only factual subjects can be programmed.
- This method is of little use to in teaching philosophical or attitudinal concepts and motor skills.
- Creating such programmes is expensive.

T-group Training

In this type of training, members belonging to a professional association receive training in new techniques and ideas pertaining to their own vocations. They are kept informed of the latest developments in their particular field through a regular supply of professional journals and informal social contacts or gatherings. This method usually comprises association, audio-visual aids, and planned reading programmes. The management trainees and probationary officers trainees in public sectors, are provided T-Group training with a view to sensitizing them to their weaknesses and developing their strengths.

> ■ ■ ■
> T-group training comprises association, audio-visual aids, and planned reading progammes.

Retraining

As the term indicates, this involves training again employees who have long been in the service of an organization. This method of training is employed when

- the employees are confined to one specific task and lose their all-round skills,
- they are called back after prolonged lay-offs,
- the employee is expected to adopt new technical skills in the job,
- an employee falls sick for a long period, or
- there is an urgent need for versatile workforce during economic depressions or cyclical variations in production.

NEW TRAINING TECHNIQUES

In the following sections, we discuss many new training techniques used in organizations such as outward bound training (OBT), fishbowl technique, videoconferencing, and online training.

Outward Bound Training

The new training techniques that have gained importance in recent times in developing leadership traits and team building are mostly outbound and involve various activities. These outbound concepts are known by different terms such as OBT, outward bound learning, and on-board training. The programme involves a cross section of employees from the organization, and the duration depends on the needs of the group. Essentially, the programme, is outbound in a totally different, attractive, and inspiring environment. The process in the programme involves a transformation from a situation of 'can't do' to 'can do'. The facilitator manipulates the environment to simulate experiences and assesses the consequences. Every activity is designed to embrace the primary need for team-building, leadership development, and personal growth, by teaching through experience. A process review follows every activity, the participants analyse their performances and reactions, and are guided as to how best to overcome weaknesses.

Fishbowl Technique

The fishbowl exercise is a technique for discussing difficult and controversial issues between two groups of people who may be in disagreement. It overcomes barriers to communication such as pressure to conform from peers, 'professional detachment', and intimidation.

The fishbowl is useful for all levels of employees and is particularly successful where two groups differ. In this exercise, the facilitator splits the group into two teams and allows one team to sit in the middle, while the other team encircles the former. Only the inner team is allowed to discuss the issue and the other members act as observers. Later, the teams are interchanged and the process goes on until the points for discussion are exhausted between the teams.

The fishbowl technique works well to accomplish the following objectives:

- Determine the areas of common belief.
- Determine the areas of major controversy.
- Identify the range of informational sources exerting influence in a marketplace.
- Explore the fundamental beliefs or attitudes driving a variance of perception or opinion.
- Identify *disconnects*—variances in expectations and sources of dissatisfaction and disappointment related to a product or service.
- Assess reactions to various concepts, messages, programmes, or services in order to determine what might work for all employees.
- Assess reactions to various concepts, messages, programmes, or services in order to determine how to customize things to best serve each distinct audience.

Videoconferencing

With the advent of IT, many firms are using videoconferencing and satellite classrooms for delivering training and development programmes. The approach is interactive and offers flexibility and spontaneity like a traditional classroom. A lot of thought goes on in preparing the content, choosing trainees, and in scheduling the programmes. Multinational companies benefit by this method as it reduces travel, time, and cost. The method also increases access to training, ensures consistency of instruction, and reduces the cost of delivering the training programmes.

Online Training

Online training may be used for learning a particular skill, a module, or an entire course. Here, the instruction is in an environment where teacher and student are separated by time and space. The teacher provides course content through multimedia resources and the Internet. The Internet provides a wide variety of opportunities to deliver training programmes to employees. Online training takes advantage of the speed, memory, and data manipulation capabilities of the computer to gain greater flexibility in providing instructions. Many virtual study programmes are text-based, using HTML, PowerPoint, or PDF documents. The student and teacher can communicate by using voice text-chats and emoticons. The courses usually meet a standard 50-minute schedule. A basic benefit of online training is that it is self-paced and work can be done at convenience. General Motors allows its employees to earn an MBA through an Internet-based school of the New York institute of Technology and Cardean University. Indiana University and Arizona State University have also entered the online MBA market (Crawford 2005).

EVALUATION OF TRAINING

Training, like any other organizational endeavour, requires time, energy, and money. Therefore, the organization needs to know whether their investment is being spent effectively and if it is worth the effort.

The top management may be primarily concerned with evaluation as a process by which the effectiveness of the organization's programs and operation procedures may be demonstrated. Supervisors may be more concerned with evaluating the specific 'results' of training as measured by improvement in the worker's on-the-job performance. The training institute and staff may wish to evaluate the training process itself, the degree to which current spending priorities in the training budget are justified, or the performance of the instructional staff.

What is Evaluation?

> ■ ■ ■
> Evaluation is the systematic appraisal by which an organization determines the worth, value, or meaning of something to someone.

Generally speaking, evaluation is the systematic appraisal by which an organization determines the worth, value, or meaning of something to someone. In the case of training, the HR is concerned with providing information on the effectiveness of the training activity to decision-makers who will initate measures.

- to increase effectiveness of the current training programme,
- to increase the effectiveness of the programmes to be held next time, and
- to help participants get feedback for their improvement and efficiency.

In evaluating the effectiveness of any training programme, whatever be the method used, the following criteria should always be kept in mind:

- Objective
- Cost–benefit analysis
- Flexibility
- Results obtained
- Staff required
- Improvement possible

Process of Evaluation

Evaluation of training means assessment of the impact and effects of training on trainee performance and behaviour. A training programme is devised for an employee with some specific objectives in view. These learning objectives can serve as the evaluation criteria for evaluating a training programme, and also to find out whether the training has helped in improving performance.

> ■ ■ ■
> The process of evaluation involves devising evaluation criteria and pre-test to know the level of the worker before training.

Comparison of one's performance before and after the training is necessary. Evaluation of training requires setting of evaluation criteria. The learning objectives of training serve as the criteria. These should be determined before the training begins. Thus, the process of evaluation involves the following steps:

- Devising evaluation criteria before training begins
- Conducting pre-test to know the skill level of the worker before training

Methods of Evaluation

Let us discuss the various methods of evaluation in this section.

- *Questionnaires* (feedback forms) or 'happiness sheets' are a common way of eliciting trainee responses to courses and programmes.
- *Tests or examinations* are common in formal courses, which provide a certificate, for example, diploma in Word processing skills, although end-of-course tests can be provided after short courses to check the progress of trainees.
- *Projects* are initially seen as learning methods, but they can also provide valuable information to instructors.
- *Structured exercises and case studies* are opportunities to apply learned skills and techniques under the observation of tutors and evaluators.
- The *opinions of those who deliver the training* are important. Tutor reports give a valuable assessment from a different perspective.
- *Interviews* of trainees are conducted after the course or instruction period to assess its effectiveness. These can be informal or formal, individual or group, and direct or telephonic.
- *Observation* of courses and training by those devising strategies in the training department is very useful and information from these observations can be compared with trainee responses.
- *Participation and discussion* during training requires people who are adept at interpreting responses, as this can be highly subjective.

For complicated training evaluations, it is recommended that a combination of these approaches be used. It is necessary to elicit the responses from the trainees and the tutors or trainers, and others involved in the assessment process, and then compare and contrast the responses for correlation.

What is Evaluated?

Donald Kirkpatrick developed a conceptual framework to assist evaluators in determining what kind of data is to be collected. His concept calls for four levels of evaluation—*reaction, learning, behaviour*, and *results*.

- *Reaction*: Reaction is defined as what the trainees thought of the particular programmes. It is an indication of how well the trainees liked a particular programme including materials, instructors, facilities, methodology, content, etc.
- *Learning*: Here, the trainer is concerned with measuring the learning of principles, facts, techniques, and attitudes that were specified as training objectives. The measures must be objective and quantifiable indicators of learning that has taken place in the training programme
- *Behaviour*: The term 'behaviour' is used in reference to the measurement of job performance. Just as favourable reaction does not necessarily mean that learning will occur in the training

programme, superior training performance does not always result in similar behaviour in actual working conditions.

- *Results*: Evaluations in this level are used to relate the results of the training programme to *organizational objectives*. Some of the results that could be examined include costs, turnover, absenteeism, grievances, and morale.

Why does a Training Programme Fail?

■ ■ ■
A training programme does not always result in a positive change.

A training programme does not always result in a positive change. There are many factors, operating at the individual and the programme level, that affect the success of a training programme. The main aspect could be individuals' resistance to learn. If this resistance is not combated, definitely no learning will take place.

Further, the entire attitude towards the programme, the instructor, and the content influences the learning process. A questioning and suspicious approach will not help the learner to progress further.

According to Burcak and Smith, the following factors have been regarded as responsible for the failure of training programmes:

- The benefits of training are not clear to the top management.
- The top management hardly rewards supervisors for carrying out effective training.
- The top management rarely plans and budgets systematically for training.

Reasons for Resistance to Training

The reasons for resistance to training could be the perceptions of an individual. At times, the objectives of the training may not be clear or may not fit with the individual work; outcomes may not appear profitable, there may be a feeling of insecurity or perceived exposure of incompetency, etc. (Lippitt 1983). The reasons are best summarized as follows:

- When the purpose of the training is not clear
- When the training does not involve the persons affected by it
- When an appeal for training is based on personal reasons
- When the habit patterns of the individual are ignored
- When there is poor communication regarding the training
- When there is fear of failure
- When there is excessive pressure
- When the cost is too high or the reward is inadequate
- When anxiety over personal security is not relieved
- When there is satisfaction with the status quo

Limitations of Training

The following are some limitations of training:

- Training is a costly affair. The costs involved in training include the travel and halting expenses of the participants in the programme, cost of displacement, or absence of participants, etc.
- Training may result in dislocation of work and loss of output because regular office work is likely to be interrupted or delayed because of the time spent in training.
- Sometimes it is difficult to obtain good trainers and instructors.

NEW PERSPECTIVES ON TRAINING

As we enter the twenty-first century, the use of e-learning is revolutionizing how people obtain training. Multimedia training programs are now available on CD-ROMs or through the Internet or intranets. A major advantage of information and communications technology is the ability to provide training faster, at all places at the same time, and potentially at a lower costs compared to class-room based instruction. Of course, the value of e-learning is enhanced when it is designed for maximum interactivity. Moreover, e-learning basically provides an active learning experience.

As opposed to the computer-based training of the 1990s, the term e-learning is used to refer to training imparted through computers involving technologies that support interactivity beyond the scope of a single computer. E-learning is a method of learning through the use of devices based on computer and communications technology. Such devices include personal computers, CD-ROMs, digital television, and mobile phones. Communications technology enables the use of Internet, e-mail, virtual discussion forums, collaborative software, and team learning systems. E-learning may also be used to support distance learning through the use of wide area networks (WAN).

E-learning provides an excellent platform for organizations to maximize their productivity and human resource potential. It provides good opportunities for content and course providers. The process has an embedded learning management system that enables learners to perform a variety of activities including content creation, tracking, reporting, and management of the learning function. The system is designed for every learner's learning ability by refreshing their memories with summary and points to remember.

E-learning derives its value also from the fact that certain skills, such as IT skills, product knowledge, and knowledge of company processes, can be taught in an automated way. Thus, knowledge can be disseminated and all employees can benefit from it at the same time. E-learning can be combined with any training process. The archives of the training processes may be put on line to avail them to the employees any time. E-training has a definite advantage over real-time training. It is possible to reach out at the same time to many people who are geographically dispersed.

One major reason for companies to adopt e-learning is the savings on costs and traveling time. The course content used once can always be saved and retrieved. Further, the material used in one part of the world can also be used in other parts.

There are four types of e-learning:

- *Informal learning*: In this type, a learner accesses a website or focused online community and finds pertinent information. This type of e-learning is not training because it does not include a formal instructional strategy consisting of presentation of materials, application exercises, and feedback.

> ■ ■ ■
> E-learning provides an excellent platform for organizations to maximize their productivity and human resource potential.

- *Self-paced learning*: It refers to the process whereby learners access computer-based training (CBT) or Web-based training (WBT) materials at their own pace, normally on a CD-ROM for CBT or over a network or the Internet for WBT. Learners select what they wish to learn, decide when they will learn it, and set the pace of their learning.
- *Leader-led learning*: Unlike self-paced learning, this type of e-learning always involves an instructor, coach, or facilitator. There are two basic

forms: (a) learners access real-time (synchronous) materials via videoconferencing or an audio or text messaging service such as Internet chat, or (b) learners access delayed materials (asynchronous) through threaded discussions or streamed audio or video.

- *Performance support tools*: This is an umbrella term for online materials that learners access for help in performing a task, especially related to software. Performance support tools normally lead the user through the steps required to perform a task.

According to Brooke Broadbent, the benefits of e-learning for learners are as follows:

- Creates interactions that stimulate understanding and the recall of information when learners exchange questions during online discussions
- Accommodates different types of learners and fosters learning through a variety of activities that apply different learning styles
- Fosters self-paced learning so learners can learn at the rate they prefer
- Provides convenient access to learning material any time, anyplace
- Reduces travel time and travel costs
- Encourages learners to browse for information through hyperlinks to sites on the World Wide Web
- Allows learners to select targeted and appropriate material on the Web
- Provides context-sensitive help through performance support tools
- Develops technical abilities required to use the Internet
- Encourages learners to take responsibility for their learning and builds self-confidence

According to Brooke Broadbent, the benefits of e-learning for instructors are as follows:

- Provides convenient access for instructors any time, anyplace
- Allows pre-packaging of essential information for all students to access and frees instructors to concentrate on high-level activities in the delivery phase
- Retains records of discussion and allows for later reference through the use of a threaded discussion or streaming video
- Generates more personal gratification for instructors through quality e-learner participation
- Reduces travel and accommodation costs associated with training programs
- Encourages instructors to access up-to-date resources on the Web
- Allows instructors to communicate information in a more engaging fashion than possible in text-based distance education programs

According to Brooke Broadbent, the benefits of e-learning for managers are as follows:

- Provides automated, continuous assessment and reporting of employee participation and progress
- Reduces capital costs associated with traditional bricks-and-mortar schools and training facilities
- Reduces costs of learning materials, mailing, and telephones associated with distance learning programs
- Allows access to the same materials through a variety of platforms, such as Windows, UNIX, and Mac, through the use of html files in a browser
- Creates more consistency in the training programme through a template approach

- Creates a one-stop shopping centre through training coordination software to offer courses from across the organization
- provides access to leading instructors worldwide

Every e-learning process, usage, or method is not necessarily 'exclusively e-learning'. Sometimes, a hybrid learning system is also used, combining the following:

- Remote e-learning with direct contact through close-at-hand human educational resources
- Software-driven resources with human intervention, whether remote or local, computer mediated (email or chat) or non-computer mediated (face-to-face or telephone)
- Software-driven resources with any other educational resource (television, radio, books, tape, etc.

Advances in technology have allowed for the growth of collaborative Web-based learning opportunities. Asynchronous activities use technologies such as blogs, wikis, and discussion boards, and allow participants to contribute when time allows. Synchronous activities occur with all participants joining in at once, as with a changed session or a virtual classroom or meeting such as those offered by Web Ex.

Debate still continues on the effectiveness of educational technology in general and the Internet in particular. Many authors have stressed that education at all levels will increasingly employ the Internet (Peha 1995, Owens 1999). Increasing connectivity and capabilities through broadband technology coupled with continued resources funneled into the educational system from various governmental and corporate agencies promise to further this trend.

However, research results regarding its benefits are are mixed. Fleming and Raptis (2000) conducted a topographical analysis of the literature concerning educational technology and found that the effectiveness is largely unproven. Fabos and Young (1999) concur and label much of the literature 'contradictory, inconclusive, and possibly misleading'. Lawson and Comber (2000) note that researchers are divided into two schools of thought as to the role that technology will have in education: an increment list role and a transformation role. Their own research was somewhat mixed, with technology and Internet connectivity transforming certain aspects of education, but merely increasing efficiency of other aspects.

Golian (2000) summarizes the strengths and weaknesses of the Internet as an educational tool. The benefits of the learning through the Internet are (a) learning at one's own pace, (b) accessibility, (c) active learning, (d) cost-effectiveness for certain activities, (e) collaborative learning, (f) personalized learning environment, and (g) non-linear learning. The weaknesses include (a) shift of the searching responsibility to the learner, (b) data overload, (c) data unreliability, (d) network/hardware unreliability, (e) access control, and (f) teaching of application rather than theory.

Barriers to utilizing networked e-learning technology have been categorized into four areas: institutional, instructional, technical, and personal (Piotrowski and Vodanovich 2000). Institutional constraints include issues such as financial support and incentive systems. Instructional issues involve time commitments and interpersonal interaction. Equipment reliability and software adequacy fall into the realm of technical barriers. Finally, personal barriers include technological competence and attitudes towards acceptance of the learner and the instructor. However, Piotrowski and Vodanovich (2000) found research results in these areas to be equivocal. Several studies have attempted to gauge educator attitudes regarding the use of technology and the Internet. Teachers have typically expressed a conservative view of the effectiveness of computers in education (Vermette, et al. 1986). Research has indicated that utilization of the Internet by teachers is related to personal experience with the Internet in particular and computers in general, and institutional support and training (Honey and McMillen 1996; Pugalee and Robinson 1998; Takacs, et al. 1999, Becker and Ravitz 1999).

EMERGING ISSUES IN TRAINING

Some of the emerging issues in the field of employee training are as follows:

- There is a lack of corporate commitment, as usually only the managers are nominated for training programmes and the non-executive staff are by and large ignored.
- The aggregate organizational expenditure on training is inadequate.
- There is a growing concern in the corporate world that the training provided by the universities and business schools does not exactly match the business requirements.
- Training has to be perceived as an investment for the betterment of the employees in an organization. On the contrary, it is perceived as an expense, as the outcomes are not highlighted or there are no immediate benefits for the organization.
- In today's economy, organizations are unable to allocate enough resources to reempoy the lad-off employees.

IDENTIFICATION OF TRAINING NEEDS—OTHER METHODS

The following sections discuss the use of task analysis and performance analysis to identify training needs.

Task Analysis

It is a detailed study of a job to identify the skills required so that an appropriate training programme may be planned. This method is also known as skills gapping process. Employers determine the skills that each job requires and match them with the skills of the current or prospective employees. Then they design a training programme to eliminate the skills gap (Jones 2000). For example, task analysis for an accountant's post may help identify the specific skill that the job requires, such as knowledge of the Tally software. One may obtain further information from job specifications and descriptions. The gaps might further reveal the areas of training.

Performance Analysis

Performance analysis identifies the gap between the expected and the actual performance of the individual. The performance gap forms the basis for training and enables the management to make a choice between imparting training or relocating the individual.

Whatever be the method adopted for identification of training needs, both the trainer and the participants may set concrete and measurable training objectives after discussion. Here, the participants get to know the outcomes of training and begin to value the effort and the time to be invested. Motivation and desire to learn should be an innate phenomenon rather than externally induced. Therefore, facilitating active learning process, providing positive feedback, and highlighting the negative consequences, enhance the motivation of the learner (Jones 2000).

SUMMARY

The chapter begins with an introduction to the contemporary competitive scenario and explains the importance of training. It explains the differences between training and development and between training and education, and defines the utility and purposes of training, the levels of training, the need and importance of training, and the benefits of training to the individual and the organization.

It expounds on the philosophy of training, learning curve and plateaus, approaches to training programme, identification of training needs in an organization at group and individual levels, dynamics of organizational learning, methods and processes of training, evaluation of training, purposes or objectives of training, etc. It explains the reasons for the failure of a training programme and its limitations. It also presents emerging techniques in identification of training needs and discusses issues in training.

■ ■ ■ KEY TERMS

Development Future-oriented training, focusing on the personal growth of the employee

Education The process of the imparting skills and character building in a formal setting

Evaluation training A process initiated to study the effectiveness of the programme and the extent to which the training meets job requirements

Learning An active process which results in a more or less permanent behavioural changes that mani-

fest in the form of habits

Methods of evaluation Methods used to evaluate the effectiveness of training

Training A learning experience that seeks a relatively permanent change in an individual that will improve his/her ability to perform on the job

Training methods The active methods utilized by the trainer to facilitate desired change in the trainee

■ ■ ■ EXERCISES

Multiple Choice Questions

1. An HR manager conducts new employee orientation for a large organization. His/her work is within which basic HRM function?
   (a) Management
   (b) Motivation
   (c) Career planning
   (d) Training and development

2. Employee involvement requires extensive additional HRM activity in which of these areas?
   (a) Training
   (b) Benefits
   (c) Labour negotiation
   (d) Marketing

3. The cost associated with employee separations and turnover includes
   (a) recruitment and selection costs
   (b) training cost
   (c) separation costs
   (d) all of these

4. Training instruction for a small group, which employs techniques such as role-playing or simulation and involves give-and-take sessions and problem-solving techniques, is called
   (a) career counselling
   (b) workshop
   (c) development plan
   (d) on-the-job training

5. Which of the following measures is taken to assess employees' satisfaction and their attitude towards the training programme?
   (a) Continuous feedback
   (b) Profitability rate
   (c) Market share
   (d) Productivity levels

6. Evaluation of training programmes is conducted

(a) at the initial stage while designing the training programmes

(b) prior to the need assessment phase

(c) parallel to designing the training content

(d) at the last stage of training

Fill in the Blanks

1. _____ employment testing approach requires individuals to perform activities similar to those they might encounter in an actual job.

2. Career counselling is part of _____ functions of HRM.

3. The relationship between critical incident method and BARS (behaviourally anchored rating scale) is that _____.

4. A training programme is a planned process by which an organization seeks to attain _____.

5. The term _____ implies a certain level of transformation, which has already taken place as a result of the learning process.

Concept Review Questions

1. Explain the philosophy of training and the need of training for contemporary organizations.

2. Distinguish between training and development, and between training and education.

3. Explain the purposes of training with examples from your real-life experiences.

4. Analyse the importance of training at various levels in the organization.

5. Explain the methods and approaches to training.

6. How can objectivity be ensured in the evaluation of training?

7. Explain the new trends and perspectives in training.

■ ■ ■ | REFERENCES

Bernardin, J.H., *Human Resource Management: An Experimental Approach*, Tata McGraw Hill, New Delhi, pp. 48–50.

Crawford, Krysten 2005, 'A degree of respect for online MBAs', *Business 2.06*, December, pp. 102–4.

Dudley, W.W., 'Using performance reports for identifying foreman training needs', *Journal of American Society of Training Direction*, pp. 25–27.

Fleming, Thomas and Raptis, Helen 2000, 'A topographical analysis of research, 1990–99', *Teacher Librarian*, 27(5), June, pp. 9–15.

French, W. 1970, *The Personnel Management Process: Human Resources Administration*, Houghton Mifflin Company, Boston, p. 484.

Golian, Linda Marie 2000, 'Utilizing Internet resources by education professionals in the new millennium', *Information Technology and Libraries*, 19(3), September, pp. 136–43.

Honey, M. and McMillen, K. 1996, 'Case studies of K-12 educators', *Use of the Internet: Exploring the Relationship Between Metaphor and Practice*, Centre for Children and Technology, New York.

Jones, Marica 2000, 'Use your head when identifying skills gaps', *Workforce*, March, p. 118

Jyothi, P., *Training of Trainers: Material Composed for Training Programme*, Institute of Public Enterprise, Hyderabad, pp. 48–50.

Lawson, Tony and Comber, Chris 2000, 'Introducing information and communication technologies into schools: The blurring boundaries', *British Journal of Sociology of Education*, 21(3), pp. 419–33.

Lippitt, Gordon 1983, *A Handbook for Visual Problem Solving: A Resource Guide for Creating Change Models*, Development Publications, Bethesda.

Mahler, W.R. and Monroe, W.H., 1952, *How Industry Determines Need For and Effectiveness of Training*, pp. 24–28.

Owens, W.T. 1999, 'Preservice teachers' feedback about the Internet and the implications for social studies educators', *The Social Studies*, 90(3), May/June, pp. 133–40.

Peha, J.M. 1995, 'How K-12 teachers are using computer networks', *Educational Leadership*, 53(2), October, pp. 18–25.

Pepper, A., *Managing the Training and Development Function*, Gower Publishing, Aldershott, pp. 48–50.

Poitrowski, C. and Vodanovich, S.J. 2000, 'Are the reported barriers to Internet based instruction warranted? A synthesis of recent research', *Education*, 121(1), Fall, pp. 48–53.

Rao, V.S.P. 2001, *Human Resource Management: Text and Cases*, Excel Books, New Delhi, pp. 193–212.

Rudrabasavaraj, N.M. 1969, *Personnel Administration Practice in India*, Vaikunthalal Mehta Institute of Cooperative Management, Pune, pp. 321–23.

Vermette, S.M., Orr, R.R. and Hall, M.H. 1986 'Attitudes of elementary school students and teachers toward computers in education', *Educational Technology*, 26(1), January, pp. 41–46.

http://handbooks.homeless.org.uk/hostels/environment/participation/fishbowl, accessed on 7 May 2012.

http://www.adventurezone.8k.com/custom2.html, accessed on 7 May 2012.

http://www.bsr.org/consulting/Facilitator_RECIPE_guide.pdf, accessed on 9 January 2012.

http://www.mbaknol.com/management-concepts/causes-of-resistance-to-organizational-change/, accessed on 7 May 2012.

http://www.schulersolutions.com/resistance_to_change.html, accessed on 7 May 2012.

Training and Development in Aegis BPO Ltd

CASE STUDY 1

Aegis BPO is a subsidiary of Essar Group, a multi-billion dollar group with interests in steel, oil, telecom, and shipping across several countries in the world. Aegis is listed in the US and operates in India, US, and Philippines. Though Aegis started as an international BPO, considering the emerging opportunities in the domestic BPO space, it has ventured into telecom, banking, and insurance verticals by entering into service contracts with leading players such as Airtel, Idea, HDFC Insurance, and ICICI bank. The organization has now grown to 17 centres in India with over 20,000 employees. It has another 15,000 employees across US and Philippines.

The company, which has been recruiting close to 4,000 employees across its sites for replacement, has drawn a comprehensive training and development strategy to train and develop its employees:

- **Training for new hires:** For the new hires, the company has the following two kinds of training:
- *Voice and accent training*: The company trains the new hires on the voice, accent, and culture of the regions to which they would be providing contact services.
- *Technical/product training*: After the new hires clear the voice and accent training, the company trains them in the product/service to ensure that they are empowered with required product knowledge.

- **Training for tenured employees:** In order to address the developmental aspirations, the organization has drawn a detailed plan as follows:
- Training for next-generation team leaders
- Training on communication and interpersonal skills
- Yellow and green belt certification to train them in problem-solving and quality improvement aspects
- Training for first-time managers
- Training for process trainers and quality analysts
- Training calendar for training needs identification (TNI) of employees.
- On-the-job training on management information (MI) reporting and people management for tenured customer service executives (CSEs)
- Coaching and mentoring skills for tenured CSEs to train new hires

These training initiatives have not only helped Aegis to reduce early attrition, but also address the developmental aspirations of the tenured employees.

Questions
1. Briefly analyse the training strategies of Aegis BPO.
2. Compare the training and developmental initiatives at other BPOs in the country.
3. Suggest changes (if any) to the training strategy of the organization.

Hindustan Aeronautics Limited (HAL)

Vision

'To make HAL a dynamic, vibrant, value-based learning organization with human resources exceptionally skilled, highly motivated and committed to meet the current and future challenges. This will be driven by core values of the company fully embedded in the culture of the organization.'

Training and Development

Training is one of the most important interventions for developing human resource. Hence, identification of training competency profile in terms of the vision and mission of the company would help in formulating a training and development strategy for the company. The following objectives have been set in this regard:

- to provide training to all employees at regular interval in a plan period of 5 years
- to make training an integral component of individual professional evolution by
- updating knowledge to avoid obsolescence
- enhancing professional creativity
- enabling employees to shoulder higher responsibility
- to create a business bias and strategic thinking
- to take up new business challenges (creation of a centre of excellence, etc.)

The goals of training will be to progressively achieve seven days training per employee per year with a budget of 2% of annual wage bill. Keeping in view the organizational requirements and the goals and objectives of training, the following have been identified as the key focus areas of training:

- Technology
- Tooling
- Quality
- Information technology

Further, to facilitate development of soft skills (change of mindset, managerial development) training would be imparted on a continuous basis. Tie-ups with centres of excellence, such as IITs, NDC, and FIAS, France, for training would be given prime importance.

Scheme for Learning and Certification of Executives

An organization has to be a 'learning organization' for survival in the present era of liberalization, privatization, and globalization. Therefore, 'knowledge' is the only core competence of organizations for coping with changes. Since individual knowledge is the starting point for organizational knowledge, only the employees can convert knowledge into efficient actions. In line with the above philosophy, among other initiatives like institutionalizing learning centres in divisions, etc., HAL has also introduced the Scheme for Learning and Certi-fication for executives as a starting point for building individual knowledge. The scheme inter alia provides opportunity for the junior and middle management cadre executives to broaden their perspectives by learning not only about all functions and procedures in their respective disciplines, but also about related areas, the overall organization, and its environment. So far, approximately 45% (both for 'O' and 'A' level) of executives have been certified. It is proposed to expand the coverage of this scheme further, if required, by linking it to some kind of reward mechanism. Lastly, the HRD plan will also include time-to-time OD interventions to address specific requirements of the company.

Question

Examine the HR strategies of HAL and the training approaches adopted by it to address the problems.

Coal India Limited

Human Resource Development in Coal India Limited (CIL)

The human resource development function in Coal India has been set up to deal with the development of existing human resources as well as to look ahead with a clear perspective on techno-logical advances and growth of manpower to fulfil the demands of production.

Technical Training

Technical training is conducted to provide knowledge regarding the technology being used in each subsidiary and any other technology being conceived at the corporate level to meet the current shortage of skilled manpower and also preparing statutory personnel for meeting statutory obligations through training. For this purpose, workers are exposed to the following:

- *Basic course*: This is appropriate to technology, equipment, and system.
- *Refresher course*: This is taught once in three years to those who have already gone through the basic course or are already working in a specific skill area.
- *Specialized course*: In case of change of technology, in equipment configuration and capacity and improvement in the system of production, suitable inputs are given to all the new entrants in the critical-skill areas.

Management Training

A need-based training is imparted to executives at each level and at the time of assuming the charge at the new position, that is, entry to the higher level, at the Management Training Center of each subsidiary companies for the level from E1 to E5 and at the Apex Training Center, Indian Institute of Coal Management, Ranchi, for higher level executives, that is, from M1 to M3 level.

Transformation Training

This is a planned attempt to help those who join CIL as part of the management policy and for the workmen who are required to acquire skills to move from conventional to semi-mechanized mines with intermediate technology or at the instance of closure of mines and surplus manpower. These trainees are used as a source of supply of manpower in critical and non-critical areas of skills for the technology specific to the subsidiary company.

General Development Training

When there is a change in the scenario with reference to the status of a mine, specifically in Eastern Coalfields Ltd (ECL), Bharat Coking Coal Ltd (BCCL) and, to an extent, Central Coalfields Ltd (CCL), and separate focus for Mahanadi Coalfields Ltd (MCL), Northern Coalfields Ltd (NCL), South Eastern Coalfields Ltd (SECL), and Western Coalfields Ltd (WCL), knowledge about the vision of the company, the financial status of the organization, the criteria for raising productivity, cost parameters, criteria for excellence in performance, etc. is imparted through intra-organizational communication as well as face-to-face interaction with workers and supervisors in a planned way. This is called general development training, Table 10.1 highlights the performance of HRD in CIL.

TABLE 10.1 HRD performance at a Glance—Coal India Limited and its subsidiaries

In company

Category \ Year	2011–10	2010–09	2009–08	2008–07	2007–06
Executives	6,101	6,397	7,135	7,418	5,913
Supervisors	9,251	6,927	7,515	8,315	10,414
Workers	17,478	18,406	16,743	19,270	17,648
Total	32,830	31,730	31,393	35,003	33,975

Out of company

Category \ Year	2011–10	2010–09	2009–08	2008–07	2007–06
Executives	1,991	1,826	2,198	1,927	2,075
Supervisors	400	383	509	197	299
Workers	620	496	703	585	637
Total	3,011	2,705	3,410	2,709	3,011

Training abroad

Year \ Category	2011–10	2010–09	2009–08	2008–07	2007–06
Executives	13	18	18	25	52
Supervisors	5	0	9	6	7
Workers	0	0	0	11	20
Total	18	18	27	42	79

Workers training at vocational training centre

Year \ Category	2011–10	2010–09	2009–08	2008–07	2007–06
Executives	4,350	6,331	6,385	4,826	9,494
Supervisors	48,364	49,969	55,130	50,395	57,749
Workers	17,613	17,883	18,707	19,759	32,813
Total	70,327	74,183	80,222	74,980	1,00,056

Note: The figures in these tables have been changed for the purpose of the case study, and do not reflect Coal India's actual figures.

Questions

1. Can training be a solution for larger organizational issues? Examine it in the context of the case study.

2. What steps has Coal India Limited taken to develop existing human resources and balance the need for technology with manpower growth?

SchoolNet India Ltd

SchoolNet India Ltd is an initiative of Infrastructure Leasing and Financial Services (IL&FS), recognized for its infrastructure and development activities. With a turnover of ₹2,000 crores, SchoolNet, which was founded in March 1999, is committed to bring about positive changes in the way the lessons are delivered to school children by integrating technology, content, and training. The activities include teacher training, content development (syllabus-based lessons), web-based learning, implementation of a programme at schools, etc. The cornerstone of SchoolNet's K-10 programme is the concept of networked learning. It creates networks of like-minded schools, students, and teachers who exchange ideas, views, and learning resources. Networked learning is founded on three major com-ponents, namely technology, content, and training.

The impact of in-service training on school teachers' performance has been identified based on a survey, pursued through primary data collection pertaining to the variables in the training of teachers. The survey was carried out through a questionnaire, clearly focusing on the current situation of training among school teachers and the present pitfalls in the existing training courses. The questionnaire also surveys the need for additional training for school teachers and other related determinants for school teacher training. Apart from the questionnaire, general counselling and interviewing also helped to deduce the determining forces for the in-service teacher training. The schools covered were within the scope of Hyderabad.

Findings

- The attitudes of many respondents towards the design of the training programme were based on the prescribed syllabus.
- Modern sources of knowledge upgradation were not within the reach of school teachers.
- Many of the respondents put forth that there were hindrances from the management for making it convenient for the school teachers to attend the training programmes.
- Most of the school teachers showed deep interest in envisaging a system that would assist in the implementation of new teaching skills.
- The existing training programmes only aim at horizontal coordination among school teachers.
- A careful study of the syllabi, text, and examination papers at the school reveal that very little concentric development in the subject matter is made by a student.
- There were very few organizations that dealt with coordination among different schools for proper integration of educational pursuits and goals.
- Student's calibre and efficiency is assessed by promotional examination, which makes learning monotonous.
- Advanced technology usage is still stagnant. There is misutilization of advanced educational resources.
- Student's performance is directly linked with the length and coverage of the syllabus. An unnecessarily bulky syllabus retards skills and creativity, both in the student and in the school teacher.
- Classroom teaching is generally based on the concept of passive learning.

Suggestions

- The standard facts elucidated in the textbook need to be supplemented with adequate references.
- A more comprehensive and integrated study of teaching area should be adopted by the in-service teacher training centres.
- Efforts should be channelized within the training centres to make the syllabus of the subject amenable to the future inclusions apart form being precise, brief, and informative. It is also a prerequisite, which fashions the syllabus that much of practical work should be attached for each topic.
- The process of learning should be activity based, including experience, experiments, and teamwork.
- Orientation learning with audiovisual aids can uplift the student's performance. So, the teacher may be trained to use these aids.
- Within a training team, coordination among teachers should be given due importance. Primary-level teachers can coordinate with the middle-school teachers and, thereafter, senior-secondary-level teachers for building up a common goal and purpose.
- Organizations such as SchoolNet can help in organizing inter-school cooperation among teachers. Additional material can be circulated among teachers. Quality circles of teachers may be organized to help the less talented teachers.
- Critical teaching and creative teaching should be the basic cornerstones for the application an realization of knowledge.

Question

Critically examine the impact of SchoolNet India on improving the reach of infrastructure and financial services to classrooms.

CASE STUDY 5

India Movie Corp Limited

India Movie Corp Limited (IMCL) is an entertainment company set up in 1995 by Manoj Mehta, one of the top movie stars of Bollywood. As an attempt towards establishing a full-fledged infrastructure, he has recruited a Vice-President–HR. He has designed a full-fledged HR policy for recruitment, promotion, training, etc. The company has the following four divisions:

- Movie production
- Movie distribution
- TV software production
- Space selling

Each of the divisions is headed by a Vice-President and supported by a team of 50 experienced people from the areas. Being a start-up company, it was essential for the organization to recruit experienced people along with youngsters from respective fields. Mehta believes in sincerity and dedication and he envisions that all employees of the organization also cherish these values and try to uphold them. In the initial two years, the movie production company produced around two big-budget movies and two small-budget ones. The two big-budget movies, where Mr Mehta himself was the lead star, bombed at the box office. One of the small-budget movies was an average money-earner, while the other was a moderate hit. As regards the movie distribution, the movies purchased by the company for distribution did not do well at the box office. The morale of the employees was severely affected. The initial public offering (IPO), was oversubscribed, but as the company did not do well, the stocks soon lost their sheen in the stock market. Mehta at this juncture felt it necessary to revive the state of affairs of the organization and engaged the services of a HR consultant and financial expert to review the matters and suggest remedies for a turnaround of the company.

The financial expert, after examining the financial matters, suggested the following remedies:

- Restructure debt by reducing the high-interest borrowing from banks and financial institutions and replacing them with lower interest advances.
- Co-produce the movies with renowned producers who are willing to take the financial burden.
- Reduce the exposure of the company to production and distribution of movies and increase the focus on production and marketing of TV content, which is a low-risk area.

The HR expert, after examining the organizational structure and profile of all the employees vis-à-vis the pay scales, felt that the organization has not recruited the right personnel for the right job. In its anxiety to create the hype about the organization, the company went about recruiting high-profile executives with astronomical salaries from the FMCG sector, who were not aware of the nuances of the business of the company. The HR expert suggested the following steps for organizational restructuring:

- Replace the key functionaries in the movie production and distribution divisions with personnel with exposure from respective areas.
- Recruit employees for the TV content business from other leading channels in the field.
- Create a full-fledged marketing department to aggressively market the TV software/content to various TV channels and ensure steady revenue streams of the company.
- Train the employees in movie production areas by making provisions for them to be associated with the leading directors.
- Train the financial team who can keep an eye on the financial health and suggest suitable steps from time to time.
- Train the employees in the movie production and distribution divisions in creativity and innovative thinking.

Question

Do a role-play with your co-learners and prepare a turnaround strategy for IMCL (Case Study 5).

Developing Managers

INTRODUCTION

Contemporary organizations have realized the importance of the human capital and are increasingly finding it necessary to continuously train and develop human resources. The quality of leadership determines the quality of the organization and it is in this context that training of the management consisting of the top, middle, and junior levels becomes imperative. The managers form the core and the fulcrum and catalyse the pace of activities in the organizations. The reasons for undertaking executive development in organizations may be summarized as follows:

- Change and competition are continuous features that require continuous adaptation by the organizations. Therefore, continuous upgradation of skills and competencies at all levels, specifically at the management levels, is necessary.
- There is a need to hone the leadership skills of managers. Today's organizations need leaders, not managers. The executive development programme (EDP) aims to address this particular need.
- Continuous learning and knowledge development inform and mould managers, which also helps them gain the respect of their subordinates. Motivating the management towards learning executive development is a systematized approach.
- Information technology (IT) has become an all-pervasive phenomenon and a majority of the present-day organizational processes are seamlessly integrated with IT. The decision-making process has also been made easy with the help of IT support. It is thus necessary for the managers to become IT savvy to use IT for enhancing the performance of their departments.
- People management skills, along with technical skills, play a crucial role in the growth and evolution of managers. The EDP addresses the need for developing the human competencies of managers.

> ■ ■ ■
> The quality of leadership determines the quality of the organization.

EXECUTIVE DEVELOPMENT PROGRAMME: THE PROCESS

> ■ ■ ■
> Individual training needs should be considered in the larger organizational context.

The training and development needs of an employee cannot be looked at in isolation; any proactive organization has to view the individual training needs in the overall organizational context. The training and development processes are no longer adjunct to other departments, but have become a part of organizational strategy and one of the key corporate objectives. The process of arriving at the developmental needs of the managers can be comprehensively viewed through the process discussed in Figure 11.1.

Stage I

At the macro level, that is, stage I, the three key parameters to be considered are the competitive environment, organizational strategy, and organizational objectives. The analysis of the competitive environment helps the organization to decide on its competitive positioning in the marketplace, based on which the organizational strategy is drawn out in an attempt to transform or reposition the organization. The macro view is broken down into specific organizational objectives for further dissemination to functional/departmental, group, and individual levels.

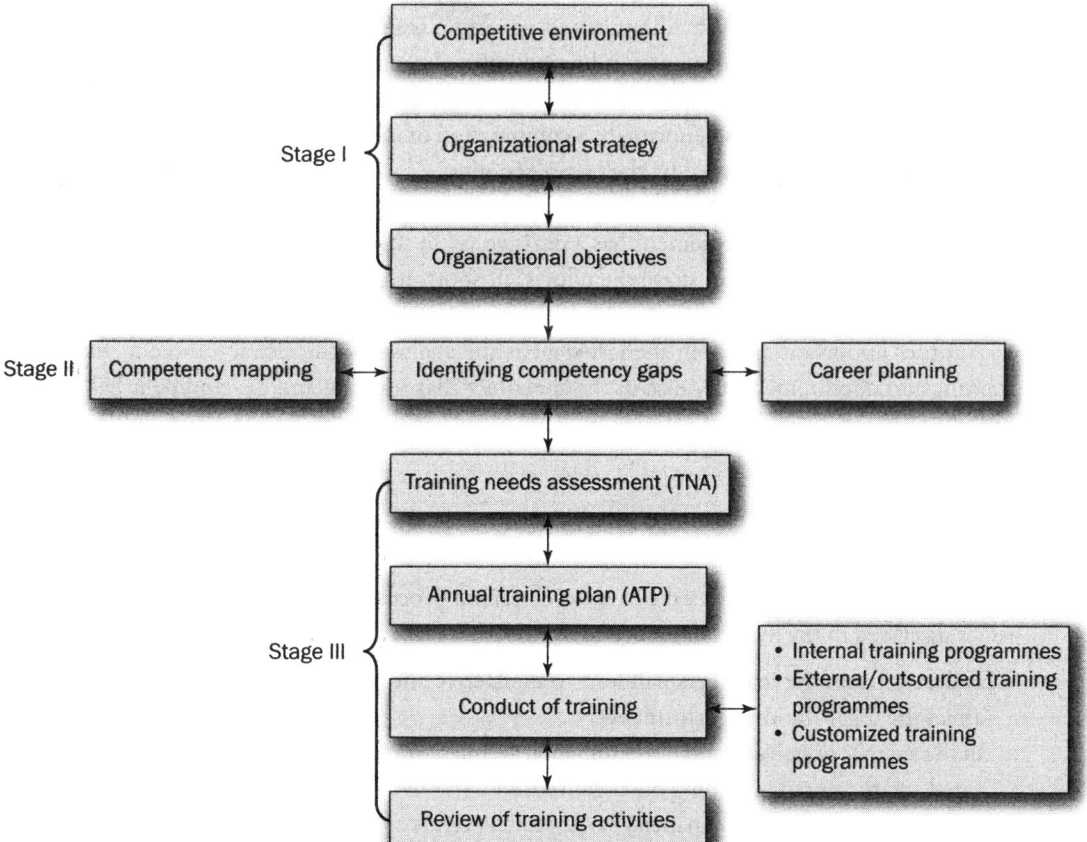

FIGURE 11.1 Process of executive development

Stage II

The second stage is the most critical aspect in the process of analysis where three key parameters, competency mapping, identification of competency gaps, and career planning, are to be analysed. The first step in stage II, that is, competency mapping tries to capture the competencies of all the human resources in the organization, including that of the management while, the second step analyses the competency gaps, that is, the organizational requirements vis-à-vis the available competency baskets. The third step, that is, career planning, examines the organizational needs vis-à-vis the individual growth needs and provides information regarding the developmental needs of the managers. Each of these three parameters is mutually interactive and integrated.

Stage III

Any strategy/action plan is of little relevance if it is not translated into action or implemented effectively. The third stage, the implementation stage, is three-tiered. The first tier involves the assessment of the training needs, collectively and individually, of all the employees, based on which the annual training plan (ATP) is drawn out. Based on the ATP, the employees are either brought into the corporate training system, in case of internal training programmes, or nominated to external organizations. While deciding on the location and nature of training programmes, the HR departments and the learning facilitators look at various issues such as the number of managers to be trained, cost factors involved in conducting internal programmes vis-à-vis outsourcing, availability of technical/required expertise in the organizations, etc. Further, in case of organizational development-related exercises, normally, a combination of initial external facilitation followed by internal programmes is planned by the organizations.

One of the important aspects is the ownership of the executive development initiatives in the organizations. The top management has a decisive say in the entire process, and the HR department and the training system share the efforts. In short, it is more of a collective phenomenon, that is primarily led by the motives and initiatives of the top management.

Another important aspect in the last stage is the analysis of the efficacy and effectiveness of training and development, because of the sheer fact that training and development has become prohibitively expensive and it is imperative for organizations to assess the return on investment (RoI).

FACTORS INFLUENCING EXECUTIVE DEVELOPMENT

A host of factors influence the executive development processes in organizations. Apart from the issues discussed in the model in Figure 11.1, the other factors are as follows:

- Failure to train the managers will lead to ineffective and inefficient managers who negatively affect the organization's performance.
- In the absence of training and developmental avenues, the performing managers may get demotivated and frustrated in leading the organizations. This would lead to severe losses for the organization in financial parameters, in terms of the cost of recruiting and training the new incumbent.

■ ■ ■
A host of factors influence the executive development processes in organizations.

- The organizational performance may be affected by the loss of market shares, lower sales, reduced profitability, etc.
- The absence/shortage of trained and skilled managers makes it important

for the organizations to have appropriate retention strategies. Training and development is being used by organizations as a part of their retention strategy.

- The competitive pressures make it necessary for organizations to continuously roll out new products and services, and also maintain the quality of the existing ones. The training and development of managers would help them in developing the competencies in these areas.
- The competitive environment makes it imperative for the organizations to continuously restructure and reengineer, and to embark upon these processes, it is essential for the organizations to train the managers for the new scenarios.

Executive Development and E-learning

The IT environment has, in a way, created challenges and also opportunities for organizations. The challenges include the rapid pace of changes, and on the opportunities front, it has provided the following advantages:

- Knowledge management has become easy for implementation. In the traditional environment, sharing of intellectual resources and knowledge was a Herculean task. Organizations had to prepare, print, and mail the circulars across the organization for the dissemination of information, which frequently led to the obsoleteness of information because of the time gap, by the time the employees, received it. Further, it was tough for the organizations to come up with strategies to continuously collect, update, and disseminate the information.
- Knowledge management has provided various forums such as intranets, online discussion forums, and expert panels.
- E-learning has made learning easy, irrespective of the time and distance factors. It has led to the empowerment of employees, since the employers are now able to decide upon the pace and content of learning, depending on their requirements.

These developments have affected the executive development process in a significant way and have helped in transforming the brick-and-mortar learning scenario to an e-learning scenario.

EXECUTIVE DEVELOPMENT—METHODS AND TECHNIQUES

Broadly, the types of executive development programmes are categorized into on-the-job and off-the-job methods. The *on-the-job methods* include job rotation, coaching/under-study, and action learning. Job rotation involves movement of the management trainees/managers from one department to another, in order to familiarize them with various facets/functions/departments of the organization. It also helps to develop an in-depth knowledge about the various businesses and processes of the organization. In coaching/under-study, the junior manager is placed under the guidance of a senior manager who continuously coaches and provides counseling for developing the junior executives for assuming higher responsibilities. Action learning involves the full-time involvement of managers who are assigned to work on specific projects or problems. This helps the managers develop the capability of undertaking and completing a project and also solving the problems, which enhances their managerial and leadership capabilities.

> Executive development programmes are categorized into on-the-job and off-the-job methods.

The *off-the-job methods* include management games, which hone the problem-solving and analytical capabilities, outside seminars in technical as well as interpersonal areas, role playing to expose the managers to realistic

TABLE 11.1   Methods of executive development

S. no.	Competency development area	Methods
1.	Decision-making skills	• In-basket • Business game • Case study
2.	Interpersonal skills	• Role play • Sensitivity training
3.	Job knowledge	• On-the-job experience • Coaching • Understudy
4.	Organizational knowledge	• Job rotation • Multiple management
5.	General knowledge	• Special courses • Special meetings • Specific readings
6.	Specific individual needs	• Special projects • Committee assignments

situations and develop their skills, behaviour modeling for exposing the managers to the right way of doing things, letting them practice those methods, and more importantly, giving feedback on their performance during the practice.

The other ways of categorizing the methods of executive development is given in Table 11.1.

FACTORS IN DESIGNING AN EXECUTIVE DEVELOPMENT PROGRAMME

It is often said that a well-drafted plan is half the job done, and it is in this context that the careful designing of the EDP assumes importance. The key factors influencing the designing of an EDP are as follows:

- Learning characteristics and its applicability to design
- Knowledge of results
- Reward mechanism
- Scale of learning
- Individual differences of the learners
- Periodicity of the learners
- Applicability to the work environment
- Meeting of learning objectives through the content design
  Exhibit 11.1 discusses the strategic role of executive development.

EXHIBIT 11.1   Strategic role of executive development

Organizations are increasingly sending their top management personnel to business schools (or, in many cases, are having select business school faculties come to them) for customized programmes tailored specifically to their

(Contd)

EXHIBIT 11.1 (Contd)

organization. Such programmes place less emphasis on courses such as 'finance and accounting for non-financial managers', instead, they focus on helping the organizations to meet high-level strategic challenges. 'We help organizations through some of their most pressing strategic issues,' said Gale Bitter, Associate Dean of Executive. Education at Stanford. 'We work closely with senior management and help devise plans to execute their strategy, and in some cases provide frameworks to help them create and refine new strategies.'

Role in Strategic Planning and Execution

The strategic planning process, formulating the organization's high-level goals and execution plans, is an especially compelling area of focus for executive development and education. Why? Strategy formulation is the process of choosing the best path for an organization, based on customer needs, competitive realities, and internal capabilities. Organizations that can integrate all three effectively into strategic planning are more likely to have robust strategies and will perform better. When managed proactively, executive development improves not only the delivery of strategic plans, but also the design of the strategy itself. This article will present a list of recommendations to help Chief Learning Officers (CLOs) integrate executive development into the strategic planning process, not only to provide excellent developmental experiences for senior management, but also to bring about change within the organization.

What is Typical?

Many CLOs argue that executive development can have a direct role in contributing to both the execution and creation of strategy for organizations. However, does this contribution occur in practice for most organizations? While some organizations may actively link executive development to strategic planning, few may actually be considering executive development when it comes to crafting a strategy in the first place.

Why the Disconnect?

Why don't organizations integrate executive development with strategic planning? According to Bernard Jaworski, President of Monitor Executive Development, a specialty management development consultancy, there are three key reasons. First, executive managers are not motivated to integrate executive development and strategic planning. They simply haven't seen good examples of how the integration can be done, either for the benefit of the executive going through the training or the planning process itself. Second, there is no ability to integrate the two processes. Doing it well involves both art and science. The organization needs individuals who understand the development processes and have expertise in management evaluation and development, balanced with long-term strategic planning and insight into the operational realities of the organization. Most often, these developmental professionals are not 'at the table' for executive management meetings (since they are probably the Vice-President of HR), nor are they involved with corporate planning. Third, there are no great opportunities to integrate the processes. The planning process can happen relatively quickly, usually with a small group of insiders, and, at times, must be done beyond the regular schedule of corporate planning, which does not afford ample opportunity for management development discussions. According to John Beck of North Star Leadership Group, since corporate strategy is usually something that only the true insiders of the organization (i.e., the top 10–20 executives) are involved in, the reality is that the head of training will often not be included.

Three Types of Integration

One may categorize organizations into three types—those that treat executive development as a discrete process, others that partially integrate it with strategic planning, and a third set that have fully integrated it as a driver of strategic planning (Table 11.2).

(Contd)

EXHIBIT 11.1 (Contd)

TABLE 11.2 Integrating executive development with strategic planning

	Level of integration		
	Discrete process	Partial integration	Integrated and drives strategy
Goal of executive development process	Build general skills for key managers so they can handle 'typical' management situations	Help management execute strategy once it is completed	Help management craft and implement corporate strategy
Number of organizations	50% or more	35–45%	5–10%
Common characteristics	• Developmental plans do not take current business imperatives into account • Training executive likely not at table of senior management	• Developmental plans are formed as a result of current business imperatives • Training executive likely to be present at table of senior management	• Developmental plans result from current business imperatives and provide input for strategic direction • Training executive proactive in strategic planning
View towards executive development activities	Often cynician of developmental 'spending'	Worthwhile 'activity'	Critical 'investment'

Source: Saslow (2004)

Significant differences are likely to exist across industries. In many modern service industries, where the service delivered is based on knowledge and the people delivering it (e.g., management consulting or other service industries), one would expect to see a better approach to the integration of strategic planning and executive development. In such situations, people are absolutely essential, as they are both inputs and outputs of the business. Of course, in traditional industries such as manufacturing, there are plenty of examples of companies that have sophisticated approaches.

Ramifications

What are the ramifications for the majority of organizations that fail to completely integrate strategy formulation and execution with executive development? The biggest problem is the creation of strategies that simply don't work, since they are not grounded in reality. Sometimes, executives assume that any strategic plan, however radical it may be for the existing organization, is achievable, and with the right development activities, management will 'grow' into new roles. However, the fact is that management talent, like any corporate resource, can only change to a limit, especially within the tight timelines that are often presented. Some organizations find themselves with great plans, but no one is capable of leading the execution. In other situations, the planning process gets too far ahead of the management development process, and the talent pipeline does not deliver the quantity or quality of senior managers that the organization needs. The result is that the organization must go to external sources to get its talent. While hiring outsiders has proven value in bringing fresh perspectives, it can be costly, especially at senior levels. 'When organizations have to consistently bring in outside talent to fill new management roles, that is an indication of a failed internal development process,' said Steve Burnett, Associate Dean at the Kellogg School of Management at Northwestern University. This poses serious problems, since outsiders in management roles have mixed track records. Often, there is difficulty integrating new senior management into an organization.

Solution

What must a CLO do? For those organizations that already understand the role that executive development plays in driving change and improving corporate performance (Burnett estimates this at only 50% of the S&P 500 com-

(Contd)

EXHIBIT 11.1   (Contd)

panies), as well as for those who are new to this concept, there are some key principles that a CLO can adopt.

Acquaint himself/herself with the current strategy-formulation process   The last thing a CLO wants is to be left out of the loop, but this often happens. 'Transformations are sought by the board, C-level executives, and we typically don't interface with training and HR,' Burnett said. David Sachs, Harvard Business School's Executive Director of Executive Education agreed, 'We often are hired by and work hand-in-hand with the CEO.' In these scenarios, it seems that executive management acknowledges the importance of executive development, but turns neither to the CLO nor to the Vice-President of HR to manage the interface with outside specialists. Does the organization currently work with business schools to drive programmes? Has the organization retained a strategy consulting firm to help craft a new set of organizational plans? Which executives are charged with driving new strategies? CLOs need to have the answers to these questions since, once the strategy is agreed upon, the executive team starts to think about execution, and that is where the CLO comes in. If a CEO picks up a new strategic plan and his first move is to call the head of a business school to discuss how to achieve the strategy, it is possible that the CLO has not instilled visibility or credibility for the organization's capabilities. How can one get that call?

Insist on senior-level involvement   CLOs need to ensure that the top management, starting with the CEO, is not only aware of executive development programmes, but also has bought into the process. In a recent study by Exec-Sight, which provides executive development consulting services, it was found that the biggest factor affecting the success of executive development programmes was the CEO's involvement (way beyond simple awareness of such programmes). CEOs can and should help in designing programmes via active feedback, provide their own time as instructors and moderators of specific training sessions, and act as advocates for executive development to the rest of the organization. A few years ago, 3M brought in a new CEO, Jim McNerney, who had come from General Electric after years of positive experiences with executive development as a strategic tool. According to Al Vicere, a Penn State Professor and leadership specialist who worked with 3M at the time, 'They had Jim as the CEO who saw the value of linking the processes, and that can make all the difference. He set the tone for the entire organization.'

Integrate business plans and executive development plans   CLOs need to be careful not to allow the separation of business plans and people-plans, which occurs in many organizations. CLOs need to make a strong case for their involvement in the strategic planning process, based, in part, on their unique perspective on matters such as succession planning, as well as a reality check on the assumptions that determine which managers are ready for new roles. Other management insiders may see aspects of the organization that the CLO has not experienced, but the CLO is often best suited to determine how much development activity is needed. CLOs should try to get ahead of the curve and know what a given open management position calls for in terms of skills and capabilities, and know who is best suited for that role. According to Mark Nevins, a leadership development expert who previously ran Booz Allen Hamilton's and Korn/Ferry's global EDPs, 'CLOs need to ensure they not only have both a mastery of learning and developmental frameworks, but increasingly critical is to have a general manager's perspective on this business. The CLO, or any executive development professional in the company, needs to understand (and be perceived as understanding) the business, goals, and challenges of the organization, so they can advise on the talent needs, help translate plans into action, and create development programmes that will really help the business achieve its objectives.'

Inject objectivity and facts   There needs to be a ruthless pursuit for having the right leaders in the right roles at the right time for the organization, which means casting aside politics as much as possible—something that is sometimes easier for a CLO who is removed from the business units. CLOs also need to bring the facts to the table in the same way that other functional areas in the business do. The head of marketing brings market facts, the head of production brings manufacturing data, and so on. As the head of talent, CLOs need to bring information on the current level of senior management in the organization and who is in the pipeline in the context of strategic plans and organizational needs. Consider using a succession database to track management assets, based on in-depth discussions with the business unit senior management and executive management to investigate their

(Contd)

EXHIBIT 11.1 (Contd)

needs and talent supply. CLOs must have the facts 'in their back pocket' about what it takes (time, money, etc.) to develop executives versus hiring outsiders.

Balance with intuition They must know their limitations as a CLO. They may not have had the same chances to observe management candidates in situations of character and personality that other senior management may have. The people process is both a science and an art of intuition. Recognize that others will bring valuable perspectives such as finding the best candidate for a role in terms of chemistry—not something that a competency model can capture. It takes real skill to balance hard facts (market share, competitive realities, etc.) and the 'soft issues' around management development, and sometimes intuition and instinct can aid the process. David Dotlich, CEO and Managing Partner at leadership development firm CDR International, a Mercer Delta company, has worked with companies such as Johnson & Johnson (J&J), whose executive management is able to maintain this balance. 'At J&J, known for its stellar management, their executive team was capable of blending the art and science, but it takes talented executives who understand the need for both, which is rare in most organizations,' said Dotlich.

Do not forget the day job As plans get communicated throughout the organization and responsibilities cascade to all levels of employees, specific goals and objectives become a defined part of top management responsibilities. At this point, there is typically another process of awakening to the skill deficiencies, given the new plans and roles in which the management must operate. CLOs should proactively see that these gaps are addressed, monitor the progress of top executives, and be able to address potential derailment early on. While planning happens periodically, great execution on the part of the CLO, which earns the required visibility and credibility to become further entrenched in the next cycle of strategic planning, happens every day.

Summary
Executive development is playing a very different role in the organization than in the past, and this role will continue to evolve. CLOs can manage executive development in a more strategic fashion than just building competencies in the upper ranks. Executive development's potential to both craft and execute strategy is waiting to be unleashed.

Source: Adapted from Saslow, Scott 2004, 'The strategic role of executive development', http://www.clomedia.com/content/templates/clo-feature-hc.asp?articleid=655&zoneid=56, accessed on 5 September 2005.

RELATIONSHIP WITH ORGANIZATIONAL DEVELOPMENT

The success of the existence of any organization is closely linked to the quality of human resources and the organizational development (OD) efforts. OD is the planned process of change, aimed at building internal competencies of individual employee needs and groups. The history of OD in India can be traced back to as early as 1960, and some of the successful organizations that have implemented OD are Larsen & Toubro, State Bank of India, etc. The characteristics of OD are as follows:

- It is based on behavioural science and plans for an organized way of changing the behaviour of the people in the organization.
- It adopts a normative process based on the existing organizational values vis-à-vis the present value framework to which the organization would like to migrate.
- It is a deliberate process, initiated at the instance of the top management for the overall growth and development of the organization.

- It has an educative element since the process involves the development of employees through a behavioural approach.
- The approach has legitimacy since it is initiated officially and is system-driven.
- It is action-driven since the managers especially are involved in identifying the change areas, action plan for the change, and more importantly, implementing the plan with consultative support from the external consultant.

The core process of OD has its focus on the education and development of the executives, who are expected to lead the organization into the growth mode.

EVALUATION OF EXECUTIVE DEVELOPMENT

In the prevailing competitive scenario, where the focus is on efficiency, profitability, and the return on investment (RoI) on all the activities of the organization, executive development cannot be an exception. The evaluation of the process assumes importance from the following perspectives:

- Improving the quality of the training and development process
- Improving the efficiency and competency of the trainers
- Making improvements in the system to make it more responsive and realistic
- Aligning the training activities to the organizational objectives
- Building the cost implications of the training into the organizational budget
- Evaluating the RoI on account of training and development to justify further investment
- Changing the perception of the management on training as an expenditure to more as an investment for the future growth of the organization

The levels of evaluation include the reaction level, immediate level, intermediate level, and ultimate level. For the purpose of evaluation, it is essential to collect the data for which there should be appropriate measures, both during the course of the training programme and after the training programme. Some of the methods being used by experts are self-complete questionnaires, interviews, observations, and desk research. The desk research involves analysis of the existing data to view the trends and also the expectations. It is used extensively since it depends on the existing data and involves low cost and less amout time.

SUMMARY

Executive development plays a crucial role since it is the managers/executives who can determine the destiny of the organization by strategizing, implementing the strategies, and more importantly, leading the employees to higher levels of efficiency and performance. The chapter begins with an introduction to the emerging scenario, explains the process of the executive development programme (EDP) in the overall organizational context and also the various stages involved. It explains the factors influencing executive development. Executive development, its interrelationship with e-learning, and the methods and techniques involved have been discussed. The factors involved in the design and development of EDP have been discussed in brief and the EDP has been viewed in the context of organization development. It also discusses the parameters for evaluation of executive development.

■ ■ ■ KEY TERMS

Annual training plan The plan which specifies the types of training and also the categories of employees to whom the training is to be imparted

Career planning The process of planning for the career of the employee from the time of joining to the time of retirement

Competency mapping The process of listing out the competencies of all the employees in the organization

Continuous learning The process of improving one's skills and competence to keep pace with the organizational changes

Executive development The process of developing the executives and managers in the organization

Human capital The collective potential of all the employees in the organization

Off-the-job methods The methods which require employees to be away from the workplace during the course of learning

On-the-job methods The methods in which the employee continues on-the-job and learns new skills

Organization development The planned process of facilitating change in the organzation

Sensitivity training The process of sensitizing employees to their personality traits and also improving their responsiveness to other employees

Systematized approach The approach that is drawn out on the basis of systems and procedures

Training needs assessment The process of identifying the training requirements of the employees in the organization

■ ■ ■ EXERCISES

Multiple Choice Questions

1. The quality of leadership determines the quality of
   (a) the industry
   (b) a manager
   (c) the organization
   (d) IT systems

2. Which of the following is not considered in the process of analysis?
   (a) Competency mapping
   (b) Identification of competency gaps
   (c) Organization strategy
   (d) Career planning

3. On-the-job training does not include
   (a) job rotation
   (b) coaching
   (c) job enlargement
   (d) action learning

4. Role plays and management games are techniques used in
   (a) on-the-job training
   (b) off-the-job training
   (c) induction programmes
   (d) orientation

5. Success of any organization is linked to
   (a) the quality of HR
   (b) organizational development efforts

   (c) education and executive development
   (d) all of these

Fill in the Blanks

1. Continuous learning and _____ inform and mould managers, and also help them gain the respect of their subordinates.

2. The analysis of the _____ helps the organization to decide on its competitive positioning in the marketplace.

3. Failure to train the managers can lead to_____ and inefficient managers who negatively affect the organization's performance.

4. _____ has led to the empowerment of employees, as the employees are now able to decide upon the pace and content of learning, depending on their requirements.

5. _____ of the executive development programmes is half the job done.

Concept Review Questions

1. Briefly explain the importance of executive development.

2. Analyse the process involved in the design and development of executive development programmes.

3. Do you think that the factors influencing executive

cuss.

4. Indicate the methods in which the e-learning and technology enablers can be leveraged by organizations to facilitate executive development.

5. Discuss and debate the interdependency of executive development with organization development.

6. Explain the methodologies of making the evaluation process more objective.

Project Work

1. Study the executive development programmes in an organization of your choice.

2. Analyse the importance of executive development for that organization's strategy.

3. Prepare an alternative training plan for executive development in that organization.

4. Prepare a brief report on executive development and its importance to manufacturing organizations.

5. Compare and analyse the differences in the approaches in designing executive development programmes for organizations from the manufacturing and services sectors.

■ ■ ■| REFERENCES

Bee, F. and Bee, R. 1994, *Training Needs Analysis and Evaluation*, Chartered Institute of Personnel, pp. 173–88.

Dessler, G. 2000, *Human Resource Management*, Prentice Hall, New York, pp. 204–14.

Grundy, T. and Brown, L. 2003, *Value-based Human Resource Strategy*, Elsevier, Boston, pp. 27–45.

Mabey, C. and Salaman, G. (Eds) 2000, *Strategically Managing Human Resources*, Infinity Books, New Delhi, pp. 154–56.

Rao, V. S. P. 2001, *Managing Human Resources—Text and Cases*, Excel Books, New Delhi, pp. 213–36.

Saslow, S. 2004, The strategic role of executive development, *Transforming Corporate Leadership: Best Practices in Executive Education*, Exec Sight.

Thite, M. 2004, *Managing People in the New Economy*, Sage Publications, New Delhi, pp. 1–45.

CASE STUDY 1 Talent Assessment Framework in HSBC Global Resourcing

HSBC Global Resourcing (GR) is a captive subsidiary of HSBC Bank PLC, UK, with operations spread over five geographies. The organization supports the bank in all business areas. During the recent restructuring exercise, the bank created HSBC Technology and Services (HTS) units across the 85 countries that HSBC PLC operates in. The idea is to ensure consistency in service delivery for the customers of the bank across the world. The restructured HTS unit integrates all the three critical components, that is, service units of bank in the branch, the technology division, and the BPO division.

One of the critical factors for success is to create next generation leadership that seamlessly operates across HTS units worldwide. For this purpose, the GR team has come out with a talent assessment framework (TAF). To groom global leaders at level M6 (manager) and above in the hierarchy, the identification criteria is as follows:

- Rating of 1 and 2 in one of the two preceding years and rating of minimum 3 in other years (the performance rating scale being 1–excellent, 2–very good, 3–good, 4–ok, and 5–need to improve)
- Recommendation by the concerned business unit head
- Based on these two criteria, the company identifies the eligible employees across the levels
- After identification, GR advises the shortlisted employees to undertake the following steps:
- Take an analytical test of English, reasoning, data interpretation, and analytical abilities.
- Take feedback from reporting manager on their strengths and weaknesses.
- Get rating of SFG (scope for growth) assigned for each employee in a meeting of all business unit heads facilitated by the HR. The definitions of each SFG rating (a 3-point rating ranging from 1–3) is as follows:

- *SFG 1*: Ready for the next level and can undertake additional responsibilities immediately
- *SFG 2*: Needs training for 6–12 months before undertaking higher level responsibilities
- *SFG 3*: Needs to go through a learning curve for sometime before undertaking higher responsibilities
- The respective centre manager signs off the ratings assigned by business unit heads.
- After sign off by the respective center manager, these ratings are forwarded to the executive committee of the respective geography or business area.
- After sign off by the executive committee, the company announces the list of employees who have been identified as 'high potential employees' for that year.
- The exercise is annual and the list is valid for a period of one year.
- During the course of one year, the employees listed in the 'high pot' pool get several learning/developmental opportunities as follows:
- To identify the process/business improvements projects in their business units and work on them under the guidance of senior executives
- To mentor in functional/business areas of their choice, based on their career aspirations
- To interact with group executives during their visits to their business areas
- To be part of a shared learning community in the high pot pool that facilitates collective learning through sharing of learnings
- To receive monthly newsletter on thought-provoking articles and activities lined up for them
- To champion corporate social responsibility (CSR) activities to develop their leadership skills
- To be a part of virtual projects (teaming up with high pot employees from other geographies), gain cross-cultural exposure, and prepare to become global leaders

Questions
1. Briefly analyse the TAF at HSBC.
2. Do you think that TAF will help in grooming global leaders in the organization?
3. Suggest improvements, if any, after analysis.
4. Compare the leadership development initiative at HSBC with similar initiatives in other organizations.

Executive Development and the Fates

CASE STUDY 2

It Starts with Frustration

I have used 360 degree feedback with our executives. They don't like it. I have sat them down and delivered performance feedback. They resent it.

I have scheduled coaching sessions to remedy long-standing developmental problems. They undermine it.

Through a stroke of luck, I have discovered a more viable alternative: I now read them their horoscopes.

I know it is not professional. Peter Senge would surely deride me. Yet, I don't have statistical data to document it as a 'best practice'. However, it seems to work and I may be in good company: Nancy Reagan used it to help run the White House when things were dismal for Ron.

So why not for executives with a somewhat smaller span of control than the entire USA?

Tragedy Tomorrow; Comedy Tonight

As with most of the business breakthroughs that I have stumbled upon, it all started quite by accident. My astrologer friend gave me a copy of *The Secret Language of Birthdays* by Goldschneider and Elffers as a gift. I read my profile (May 21st) and reeled back in shock. It was uncomfortably, and hysterically, accurate. There in public view were my strengths and weaknesses, my intentions as well as my outcomes.

I wondered: if this were true for me, might it be true for others? What better place to test it out than with executives. So at my next meeting with a long-standing cantankerous officer, I brought the book along. As he discussed his ongoing antagonistic relationship with a higher-ranking executive, I burst out: 'But of course you can't stand her. She's a Leo and you are an Aries!'.

He looked at me with disdain, but some interest. 'What are you talking about?' I went on to read him his horoscope describing his requisite strengths (powerful; inspirational; humorous) and his weaknesses (contentious; emotionally unstable; repressed).

Then I read him the profile of his corporate nemesis. They were exact opposites and on a collision course to destruction.

Like me, he was both shocked and surprised by the horoscope's accuracy. I told him about the long-standing conflict between these rival Rams and Lions and painted in graphic detail its harrowing dynamic. He roared with laughter, informing me that it depicted exactly the tenor of his everyday interaction with this adversary.

As the fates would have it, at that very instant, his archrival walked past the office. 'Hey, Carole. Come in here for a minute. I want you to hear this!' and he asked me to read his horoscope to her. 'Sound familiar?'

Carole said: 'Read my horoscope.' It was both damning and inspiring at the same time. They both laughed uproariously together over this twist of fate that had them working together in the same company.

These two serious executives spent considerable time giggling, bantering, and initiating the beginning of what turned out to be an improved, albeit, imperfect, business relationship.

Not Everything is Solveable

So what happened here? I am not sure. I think part of what transpired was that we got to discuss some harsh business realities without placing blame on anyone or having to chart a developmental plan. It was almost like the conflict was preordained and caused by the hand of destiny. They were both just two hapless mortals unwittingly cooperating with the gods in fulfilling their corporate responsibilities.

Another odd thing was present that made this conversation different: humour. This is not a traditional characteristic accompanying our business discussions, but something George Bernard Shaw must have seen when he quipped, 'If you are going to tell people the truth, you would better make them laugh. Otherwise, they will kill you.'

I think we may have lost the ancient art of the human touch in our serious work of executive development. Somehow forgetting that, ultimately, people change when they want to. Quantifiable data be damned if the timing isn't right. Maybe there are parts of people's lives that are simply not going to change. A disturbing thought to some.

Companies might need to just learn to live with the imperfection of the human condition as they strive for business success.

Another ancient piece to this puzzle of development is the aspect of mystery in the human journey. Some things just cannot be defined, chartered, or proscribed. The unfolding of the human spirit is sacred. It is a process we seldom fully know, are often unable to quantify, and are rarely in a position to manage. We are well served to recall the advice of the Zen masters for the requisite decorum when confronting the sacred: awe, reverence, surprise.

What to Do

Even though I have gone on to use horoscopes in my regular conversations with leaders, does this mean we abandon all the tools and trappings of our trade? Not necessarily, although on a bad day that is exactly where I tend to wind up. As with the example of President Reagan, there remains a great work to be done and we are best served by moving forward—with or without the counsel of an astrologer.

Nevertheless, in that journey, having a conversation about destiny helps. Recognizing that we live and work with ambiguity helps. Knowing that people change only when they are good and ready helps.

Further, acknowledging that star-crossed mortals will always populate our business plans with both tragic and humorous outcomes greatly helps.

Source: Adapted from Moore, Kenny 2002, 'Executive Development and the Fates: A Case Study', http://www.itstime.com/jul2002.htm, accessed on 5 September 2005.

Questions

1. Do you think the 360 degree feedback will help in executive development?
2. Critically examine the limitations in implementing the 360 degree feedback.
3. How could an organization maintain the interpersonal balance while designing the 360 degree feedback system?

Role of the Manager in IBM—By Drew Morton

IBM Learning believes that management development is a transformational and extended process, rather than a classroom event. The global, technology-enhanced marketplace is transforming the manager's role. Managers require more skills: accommodating an ever-changing matrix environment of shared leadership and report-to roles; leading teams that are geographically dispersed and mobile; creating an environment that encourages continual innovation vis-à-vis rapid market changes, and more. Managers at IBM are no different. So, how could we get managers the skills they needed?

At IBM, managers work 10 to 12 hours per day, sometimes longer. The option to increase the two-day off-site class time for skill building and networking was not feasible. IBM needed a new approach to create dialogue, collaboration, individual development, and action plans. IBM Learning responded by creating the Role of the Manager@IBM (RM@IBM) programme. RM@IBM is guided by the following four main objectives:

- Use the learning process to address business-unit priorities and define action plans
- Create new e-approaches to align teams on key business objectives
- Target the managers' individual development needs in leading performance through people
- Provide a learning and communications initiative that would support peer learning and shared objectives.

Enter Blended Learning

Enhancing leadership and management skills in a time-efficient way is of critical importance to managers. Moreover, being able to fulfill the managers' individual performance–support needs in a just-in-time manner is equally compelling. The task was to create an instructional model that uses our network infrastructure to allow managers to make best use of resources, both collaborative and online, to fulfill their organizational unit's learning needs and the skill-building needs of our individual managers.

RM@IBM blends four tiers of delivery in the tradition of a learning hierarchy. Each tier builds upon the learning developed at the previous tier, beginning with information transfer and progressing on to skills

development and collaborative person-to-person interaction. The tiers together comprise a system of tools and applications that constitute a continuing process of learning instead of events such as one-time classes or workshops.

Tier 1: Online information transfer and performance support

Online resources are available to the manager via the company intranet anytime, anywhere—before, during, and after the two-day RM Learning Lab. The primary purpose is to prepare managers for the Learning Lab. Best thinking on over 150 leadership and people management topics are available, including customized materials from Harvard Business School Publishing. Printable worksheets and checklists for specific action issues and links to important external websites are highlighted. As we team globally, managers need access to policies and practices in different countries. Tier 1 allows managers fast access to all global HR material.

Tier 2: Interactive online skill building and simulations

Managers enhance their knowledge and skill development by engaging in immersive simulations of issues presented in tier 1. The online Coaching Simulator comprises eight different scenarios with more than 5,000 screens of actions, decision points, and branching results. More than 30 other simulations and quick cases cover other people management skills such as the following:

- Motivating employees
- Entertaining employees
- Enabling high performance
- Creating an environment for innovation
- Team leadership
- Multicultural issues
- Work–life issues
- Employee business commitments

Tier 3: Online collaboration

Tier 3 features ManagerJam and Manager ActionNet, which has managers participate in organizational groupware spaces to discuss and solve critical leadership issues with peer managers and their executive teams. Collaborative spaces using same-place, different-time communication enable a global learning environment, eliminating problems of time zones and travel, and creating networks that live beyond the RM@ IBM initiative.

Tier 4: Face-to-face, classroom learning lab

Face-to-face human interaction is arguably the most powerful learning intervention for developing manager skills. Workshops of management teams create and commit to shared learning action plans to drive change. The two-day classroom-based experience requires the learner to master the material contained in tiers 1, 2, and 3 so that the precious time spent in learning labs can target deeper and richer skills development.

Managers learn in phases

The four tiers—online information, online skills practice, online collaboration, and face-to-face action learning and skill building—are delivered over four phases. Phase I starts with ManagerJam, which is an enterprise-wide online conversation hosted by our chief executive officer (CEO). In short, it's a massive company-wide dialogue for all 30,000 managers worldwide. Company managers discuss six key management issues, each with its own discussion forum. The objective of this dialogue is to begin non-hierarchical conversation among managers and improve manager behaviour change in collaboration, networking, and open sharing of ideas. In addition, we want to start building a sense of community among managers, as well as create a knowledge library based on manager insights. The launch in 2002 was the largest conversation on management topics in our company's history, with more than 7,002,000 total page reads and 4,554 responses within the six discussion forums. The solutions, ideas, and success stories rated by participating peers as having the most potential have been made available permanently to the global management team on our KM website. In Phase II, employees interact with Edvisor, a patent-pending online tool that creates a guided path for each of our managers, including those working remotely. Edvisor prepares the manager for the RM Learning Lab through the use of several tools as follows:

- A blend of e-learning (online performance support, online simulations, and virtual collaboration) to enhance the Learning Lab classroom experience

- A personally-customized career-learning path for each individual manager
- Customized reports based on business-unit and individual manager survey data.

After some face-to-face instructions in the learning labs, employees were able to access Manager Action-Net, which is a web-based community that enables focused and organization-wide discussion, work, and knowledge sharing.

Partnerships Inside and Outside the Organization

All instructional materials comprising the RM@IBM intervention have been designed and developed in concert with other organizations, within and outside the company. For example, the online Coaching Simulator was co-designed with our executive development division; the simulator contains four manager scenarios and four executive scenarios. Both groups together benchmarked the coaching field and, for the purpose of alignment up and down the company, agreed to adopt the same coaching model. The role of the Manager Simulator was developed with the cooperation of Harvard Business School Publishing (HBSP). For the first time in its history, HBSP permitted a client to customize its flagship product—Harvard Business Review (HBR) articles. Our company revised the HBR articles for our audience, repurposing seven selected HBR articles to serve as the instructional content for the RM online simulator. We licensed an HBSP book (Winning Through Innovation) for use in our Learning Lab, and it forms the basis of the in-class case study. The Manager Quickviews was co-developed by HBSP and us. As HBSP was building its Harvard ManageMentor and we were building our Manager QuickViews, we mutually shared our design ideas, feedback from users, and interface insights. Thus, the two tools work in a similar fashion, and the HBSP content fits perfectly within our interface, allowing us the advantage of easily adding HBSP content appropriate to our needs. Meanwhile, our company's focus team, charged with identifying critical line issues, was accorded the role of decision maker on what QuickView topics would be written and incorporated, in order to align these performance-support tools with real business issues and concerns of managers. Finally, our Multicultural QuickView and website were co-designed with the Intercultural Business Institute of the University of North Carolina, Charlotte. The cross-cultural model and all 300 interactive cross-cultural scenarios were co-developed with the director of the Institute. Other QuickViews are written by subject matter experts from across the HR and policy functions. We participate in professional endeavours to share knowledge with thought leaders in the field, co-sponsoring benchmarking studies on e-learning with Brandon Hall and other professional associations.

Evaluating Success

To ensure objectivity, an outside intervention analysis firm was hired to define and implement an independent third-party evaluation of the programme's effectiveness and business impact. This firm conducted a two-phase evaluation strategy over nine months.

Various data collection and analysis procedures were used, including the following:

- Observation of Learning Lab sessions and reviews of programme components to assess programme readiness
- Surveys immediately following Learning Lab sessions to assess participant satisfaction and achievement of learning objectives
- Surveys of participants 45 and 90 days following learning sessions through Manager ActionNet and e-mail to assess behavioural changes and application of action plans
- Interviews with participants to assess the business impact of the programme
- Reviews and analyses of the Global Pulse Survey (GPS) results to assess the impact of the programme on employee attitudes
- Targeted interviews with selected executives to assess their perception of the programme and its impact

During both phases, various procedures were used to collect data at the following four levels:

- Level 1: Participants' perceived value of the programme
- Level 2: Participants' self-assessment of how well they achieved the learning objectives
- Level 3: Actions taken by participants to implement action plans defined in the Learning Lab portion of the programme, and barriers to implementation in the work environment

- Level 4: Business impact of actions taken during the implementation of action plans

To date, the programme has been delivered to nearly 29,000 executives, managers, and leaders worldwide. Here are the measurement findings in the following areas: participant satisfaction, achievement of learning objectives, actions taken, business impact of those actions, impact on employee attitudes, and executive perspective.

Satisfaction with 'Role of the Manager@IBM'

Surveys conducted with all participants immediately after the Learning Lab showed that 92% of participants were satisfied with the programme. Since the programme's inception, the rating of overall satisfaction has averaged above 90% for all business groups and geographies.

In addition, follow-up interviews were conducted with random samples of participants several months after attending the Learning Lab. When managers were asked whether the investment in RM@IBM should continue, given the cost constraints that IBM is facing, over 90% believed that the programme should continue.

Achieving learning objectives

Surveys conducted with all the participants immediately after the Learning Lab showed that an average of 87% of participants indicated that they had achieved the learning objectives of the Learning Lab. The following list shows participants' ratings for each of the five learning modules in the programme:

- Apply motivation theories to improve individual employee motivation: 91%
- Take greater accountability for their actions and describe the benefits of this behaviour: 91%
- Apply conflict resolution and negotiation principles to effectively collaborate with individuals in their network: 83%
- Use boundary management to foster innovation and change in their team: 77%
- Provide clear direction and support to their team on their business and customers in order to achieve business results: 87%
- Use the GROW model to coach others on improving their performance: 96%

In the follow-up interviews conducted with random

samples of participants several months after attending the Learning Lab, a majority of the participants (ranging from 61% to 80%) perceived the programme to be a valuable learning experience.

Behavioural change on the job

In surveys conducted with all the participants immediately after the Learning Lab, 97% indicated that they intended to take action based on their participation in the programme. Intention to take action has remained high for all geographies (ranging from 96% to 99%) and all business groups (ranging from 94% to 99%) throughout programme deployment.

A follow-up survey conducted with a sample of probable leaders, however, showed that only 64% of participants have taken action. A number of factors contribute to this drop. Some action plans are too ambitious and require action by other teams and organizations. Some action plans fail to address the fundamental needs, and thus do not garner the needed support. Some participants mentioned barriers within their own teams, including a lack of discipline, competing demands and priorities, and a lack of resources, not to mention time constraints. Many of these factors are also connected to the last group of barriers—a need for stronger executive support and sponsorship, and existing metrics and measurement and reward structures, which do not provide sufficient motivation.

Business impact

Follow-up interviews with random samples of participants from various business groups and geographies showed that the implementation of team or individual action plans has had a considerable impact in a wide range of areas. Benefits have included improved communication among extended team members and increased employee motivation, engagement, morale, and empowerment. Employees have also demonstrated an increased awareness of business strategies and imperatives.

The implementation of some action plans has resulted in more effective use of employees and other resources, as well as greater accountability. Implementation of other action plans has resulted in increased collaboration among various brands and groups, operational efficiencies, such as cycle time reduction and process improvement, and improved productivity.

The implementation has also resulted in improved relationships with customers and business partners, and increased customer satisfaction. The cumulative effect has been the achievement of IBM's strategic objectives, including the selling of solutions rather than point products and an emphasis on on-demand business, with associated cost saving, cost avoidance, and revenue enhancement.

Based on interviews with random samples of imperative leaders, 111 individual cases have been identified that demonstrate the impact achieved by participants who have implemented their action plans. In addition to the impact on operations and the work environment, these cases show that significant revenue enhancement has resulted from the implementation of a relatively few action plans. According to imperative leaders of these cases, RM@IBM has been a 'contributing factor' in helping them achieve an estimated US $335 million in new revenue and $1.5 million in cost savings and avoidance. These estimates are very conservative and are based on a small number of action plans identified in random samples.

Analysis of GPS results

GPS data was used to assess the impact of RM@IBM training on employee attitudes. The results showed that business groups with more participants in RM@IBM have had more improvement in employee satisfaction, clarity, and leadership ratings than units with fewer or no participants in RM@IBM. Although causal relationships cannot be proven from this research, the data does provide strong support for a relationship between the programme and improvements in workplace climate, leadership, and manager behaviour.

Executive perspective

A select number of executives were interviewed to gain insight into their experiences with RM@IBM and their perception of its impact. These executives praised the programme for its ability to engage managers in a process of learning and action planning that has enabled IBM to achieve strategic business priorities. They appreciated the fact that RM was not just a training event, but that it engaged the managers in their organization in a number of learning, communication, and collaboration activities over a period of time. They felt RM@IBM created an environment for managers to spend time with their colleagues away from everyday work to plan and work on business- and people-related issues in the context of IBM's and their group's business imperatives. Finally, they cited a number of benefits that the organization has achieved through the implementation of action plans initiated in the programme.

Source: *Adapted from* Morton, Drew 2004, 'A Case Study: Role of the Manager @ IBM', http://www.learningcircuits.org/2004/nov2004/morton.htm, accessed on 5 September 2005.

Questions

1. Do you think that the objectives of management development at IBM are well-balanced? Explain.
2. Critically analyse the extent of blending of learning into the work environment at IBM.
3. Do you think the approach adopted by IBM to facilitate the learning of managers will be appealing to them? State reasons.
4. Is the evaluation process of the RM@IBM comprehensive? If not, suggest modifications.

Need and Importance of Performance Appraisal

Objectives

After studying this chapter, you will be able to understand
- the concept and importance of performance appraisal
- the methods of performance appraisal
- the concept of potential appraisal
- the process of designing an appraisal system
- the relationship among performance appraisal, performance planning, and performance improvement

INTRODUCTION

The advent of the 21st century has marked the importance of performance in the organizational context, more than ever before. Researchers from various fields, such as organizational strategy, organizational design, organizational culture, organizational behaviour, and human resource management (HRM), have carried out extensive research, both normative and descriptive, on performance management through the control approach, manipulative approach, and, of late, the facilitative approach. The emphasis on performance began with Henry Fayol, who proposed the scientific principles of management for organizational performance improvement, where the underlying assumption was the manipulation of human resources. The Hawthorne experiments, which were based on concern for human values, can be truly considered as the begining of the scientific approach towards understanding the factors affecting the performance of employees.

At the end of every year, most organizations conduct the performance evaluation of their employees. This may be done in a formal way by using questionnaires, inventories, or outsourcing the entire process. Whatever be the method adopted, the objective is to assess the performance of the employees, which would lead to performance improvement. Despite the importance of performance appraisal, few organizations clearly define what it is that they are trying to measure. The parameters for evaluation differ, depending on the nature of the job, and several factors need to be taken into consideration before drawing an inference. However, clarity regarding what they are evaluating—the end-performance or the process—does not exist. Another envisaged difficulty is that each organization specifies its own standards of performance and tries to evaluate it against that background. Performance appraisal is linked to promotions, satisfaction, and career planning from the individual point of view and from the organization's perspective. It is also related to output, productivity, and profits.

> ■ ■ ■
> At the end of every year, most organizations conduct performance evaluation of their employees.

Individual performance is a highly varying factor. A lot of subjective and work-related aspects contribute to the effectiveness of the performance of an individual. Even though an organization specifies the standards and clarifies the job descriptions, performance levels fluctuate between employees, and also for the same employee, from time to time.

The important issues the management should focus on are as follows:

- How do we maintain optimum performance levels in the employee?
- How can we constructively utilize the feedback for performance improvement?

PERFORMANCE APPRAISAL

Performance appraisal can be described as the process of reviewing employee performance, documenting the review, and delivering it to the employee in the form of feedback. It is one of the phases of the performance management cycle.

'It is at this juncture that we have the presence of performance management systems. We may begin with a definition of performance. Performance is defined as the record of outcomes produced on specified job functions or activities during a specified time period.' (Bernardin 1984)

Objectives of Performance Appraisal

The information collected from performance measures is used for compensation packages, employee development, identification of training needs, providing feedback, and personal development of the employee.

Performance Management and Compensation

Supervisors may use performance appraisal information to manage the performance of their employees. Appraisal data will reveal the employee's weaknesses, and the managers can easily identify them, while setting standards and advise the employee accordingly. Besides, the managers can also programme incentives in such a manner that the employee is motivated and his performance is enhanced (e.g., pay for performance, incentives, bonus, rewards, commissions, etc.).

Performance Appraisal and Promotions

The information obtained from appraisals is also used for internal staffing or promoting the individual. Most organizations do believe in the policy of promotions from within. For this, the data obtained from the performance appraisal is highly beneficial. The only difficulty faced here is that performance appraisal is done for the current job. However, when offered a promotion, the vertical movement might involve different kinds of skill sets, which the employee may or may not possess.

Training Needs Analysis

Most organizations use the data obtained from performance appraisal to determine employees' needs for training or development. Companies such as Microsoft, IBM, and Honeywell use this data to train their employees.

Performance Appraisal and Personal Development

Information obtained from the appraisal is usually conveyed to the employees in the form of feedback and counseling is offered to the employees about their performance levels. This process is usually beneficial to the employees in identifying their performance weaknesses and modifying them, thereby resulting in personal development.

What is to be Appraised?

The content of the appraisal process usually comprises contributions to organizational objectives, productivity, savings in terms of costs, return on capital, etc. The appraisal process may also include certain behavioural measures such as punctuality, relationships, movements, and physical actions.

Measures of Performance

Performance measures seek to quantify the effectiveness, quality, and efficiency of services in terms of the goals these services aim to fulfil.

Quantification of Performance Measures

Performance measures are usually first quantified and then interpreted.

Quantification   A measure is more easily acquired, interpreted, and compared if it is directly quantified. Some measures, such as those of user satisfaction, are qualitative in nature. Of these, many can be expressed in or converted to a quantitative form such as a scale of satisfaction. However, some relevant measures may not be amenable to quantification and must remain in a qualitative form.

> ■ ■ ■
> Performance measures seek to quantify the effectiveness, quality, and efficiency of services in terms of the goals these services aim to fulfil.

Interpretation   Any performance measure, whether quantitative or qualitative, should be regarded as only one of the components to be taken into account when assessing the performance of an employee or deciding on an action. No performance measure or set of measures should be regarded as conclusive in itself or as justifying any particular action on its own. The overall context and factors other than those chosen for measurement should always be considered.

Levels of Measure

Atomistic   The building blocks of performance measures are elements, which can be directly measured. Examples are the number of full-time equivalent (FTE) students or the number of workstations available to students. Such atomistic measures are often not directly meaningful.

Compound   Meaningful performance measures are usually derived from a number of atomistic measures. A simple example is the number of workstations per FTE student.

Classes of Measure

> ■ ■ ■
> Output measures are measures of effectiveness.

It is important to distinguish the class of the thing being measured. In particular, measures of resources input should be distinguished from measures of results achieved. The following simple classification is intended to support the most important distinctions and takes account of earlier work.

Input   Input measures are measures of resources input (including capital) and contextual factors. They are outside the direct control of the unit (department, institutional service area, or institution), which is the subject of the performance measurement exercise. Input measures are often atomistic. Input measures do not measure what a service is delivering.

Output   Output measures are those of what is achieved. They are measures of effectiveness. They must be substantially influenceable by the unit which is the subject of the performance measurement exercise. They may be atomistic or compound. They measure what a service is delivering, but without taking into account the level of resourcing, needs, or constraints.

Efficiency   Efficiency measures are measures of output in the light of input. They are necessarily compound. Efficiency measures relate what a service is delivering to the resources used and other constraining factors.

Method   Method measures address the process, procedure, or structure used to deliver a service. They are usually qualitative, at least in origin. Method measures normally imply a prior judgement about the desirability of certain methods of operation internal to the the unit which is the subject of the performance-measurement exercise. They should be used with extreme caution.

Process of Appraisal

Comprehensive and effective participation within the performance appraisal process consists of (a) developing performance standards, (b) setting job expectations, (c) designing, (d) employee self-appraisal, and (e) appraisee participation in the interview.

Developing Performance Standards

Clear and specific standards of performance are major elements of a valid and reliable performance appraisal system. The key is to develop standards that measure the essential job duties and responsibilities utilizing a balance of process, outcome, and individual and group-based performance standards. The development of reliable, valid, fair, and useful performance standards is enhanced by employee participation, as workers possess the requisite unique and essential information necessary for developing realistic standards.

> Clear and specific standards of performance are major elements of a valid and reliable performance appraisal system.

Setting Job Expectations

The performance of an employee is primarily dependent on the fact that he/she should have a clear idea of the performance-related expectations. For this purpose, the appraisal has a major role in explaining the employer's expectations to the employee in terms of work output, which can become the basis for assessing his/her performance. Therefore, organizations need to design a performance management system and develop a manual explaining the role of appraiser and the appraisee.

Designing

Employee participation in developing the rating form and appraisal procedures is the logical extension of the development of performance standards. The rating form summarizes the formal operational definition of what the organization considers worthy of formal appraisal. As such, it is important to gather employee input on the aspects of performance formally appraised as well as the measurement scales provided. For example, employees may prefer a pass/fail system if the focus is on global feedback, rather than versus more detailed individualized assessments.

> ■ ■ ■
> Employee participation in developing the rating form and appraisal procedures is the logical extension of the development of performance standards.

Self-evaluation

Self-appraisals provide employees with the opportunity to systematically assess their performance. Studies indicate that self-appraisal increases employee preparation and readiness for the appraisal interview, enhances overall satisfaction, increases perceived appraisal fairness, and can reduce defensive behaviour if used for developmental purposes. Employees can self-evaluate by completing their own appraisal and presenting the draft for discussion with the manager or can review a draft of the manager's appraisal. Managerial and employee ratings frequently do not agree, but in a participatory system the goal is not absolute agreement, but a process directed towards achieving consensus over time. The self-appraisal process is improved significantly if clear performance standards are used, the employees are experienced, and trust levels are high.

Performance Appraisal Interview

Most of the appraisal research focuses on the influence of participation in the appraisal interview. There is a large body of research stretching from the 1960s to the '90s indicating that employee participation in the interview is associated with a variety of desirable appraisal-related outcomes, including appraisal system fairness, appraisal satisfaction, supervisory support, satisfaction with supervisors, appraisal system acceptance, and greater employee acceptance of negative feedback.

Use of Appraisal Data

> ■ ■ ■
> The use of appraisal data depends on the perspective with which the appraisal management system is designed and implemented in organizations.

The use of appraisal data depends on the perspective with which the appraisal management system is designed and implemented in organizations. Quite often, organizations use the data from the appraisal process for determining the rewards and also decisions regarding career progression. Proactive organizations use the appraisal data for a variety of purposes such as competency building, training, needs, identification, and assessment (TNI&A), culture building, and organizational building.

It is essential that HR functionaries, while designing and developing the appraisal system, be clear about the end-use of appraisal data. Further, it is equally essential that the users/participants of the appraisal system—appraisers, appraisees, reviewers, reporting authorities, etc.,—should be conscious and aware of the end-use of the system, such as competency development, culture building, and career progression.

Who will Appraise?

In most organizations, self-appraisals are commonly used. Apart from this, the appraisal process may also be done by supervisors, peers, HR managers, consultants, etc. Usually, the appraisal process is carried out once a year, but there are instances where the appraisal is also done half-yearly or quarterly.

Appraisal Process

The steps usually involved in the appraisal process are as follows:

- Establishing standards of performance
- Communicating the performance
- Measuring the actual performance
- Comparing the actual performance with the established standards and discussing the appraisal process
- Taking corrective actions wherever necessary

METHODS OF PERFORMANCE APPRAISAL

In this section, we will look into the various methods involved in performance appraisal. Some methods measure absolute standards, some measure relative standards, and others measure standards in relation to objectives. Further, in the last 30 years, the appraisal process has undergone a lot of changes, and in line with its importance, new methods have also emerged. Hence, we examine the methods under two headings: traditional methods and modern methods. These methods have been listed in Figure 12.1.

Traditional Methods

The traditional methods of performance appraisal have been briefly discussed as follows:

Graphic Rating Scales

This is the oldest and most commonly used method. It is also known as the linear rating scale or simple rating scale. In this method, a printed form is used to evaluate the performance of each employee. A variety of traits such as employee initiative, leadership, attitude, loyalty, creativity, coop-

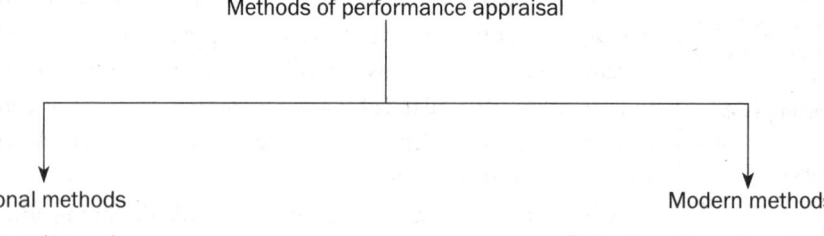

Methods of performance appraisal

Traditional methods

- Graphic rating scales
- Ranking method
- Paired comparison method
- Forced distribution method
- Checklist methods
  - Simple checklist
  - Weighted checklist
  - Critical incident method
- Essay form appraisal
- Group appraisal
- Confidential reports

Modern methods

- Behaviourally anchored rating scales
- Assessment centres
- Human-asset-accounting method
- Management by objectives
- 360° performance appraisal

FIGURE 12.1 Traditional and modern methods of performance appraisal

eration, quality and quantity of work done, goals achieved, and coordination towards co-workers and supervisors, are included. These traits are then evaluated on a rating scale by the rater according to the employee performance. The advantage of this method is that it is easy to use, easy to understand, and many employees can be evaluated quickly. The drawback is its low reliability, subjectivity, and the descriptive words used in such scales, which may have different meaning to different raters.

Ranking Method

This is a relatively easy method. In this method, each person in the group is assigned a rank in comparison with others in the group. Normally, the ranking is done based on the performance of the employees. The top performer is usually assigned rank 1 and the ranks decline as the performance levels decrease. Even though ranking is done, it is difficult to evaluate and assign ranks to average employees. The method also has its limitations. Only a relative ranking of the employee is obtained, but not the degree of difference in proficiency. Another limitation is that only the work-related aspects are compared and not other behavioural aspects. This method is not practicable for a large group.

Paired Comparison Method

Paired comparison method is a systematic method where each employee is compared with all other employees in the group, for each trait, one at a time.

Forced Distribution Method

In this, the system rater appraises the employee on two dimensions: job performance and other factors of promotability. A five-point performance scale is used to describe and classify the employees. The extreme ends denote good and bad performances. For example, employees with outstanding performance may be placed among the top 10% of the scale. An advantage of this method is that it brings about uniformity among the rates. Since performance depends on many factors, employees who have been classified as low performers may experience low morale.

Checklist Methods

It is a simple rating method in which the rater is given a list of statements and is asked to check the statements representing the characteristics and performance of each employee. There are three types of checklist methods—simple checklist, weighted checklist, and forced-choice method.

Simple checklist method   It consists of a large number of statements concerning employee behaviour. The rater's task is simply to check if the behaviour of an employee is positive or negative to each statement. Employee performance is rated on the basis of the number of positive checks, negative checks are not considered.

Weighted checklist method   The weighted checklist method involves weighting the different statements about an individual to indicate that some are more important than others. The rater is expected to look into the questions, which relate to the employee's behaviour, and tick such statements that closely describe his/her behaviour. In the weighted method, the performance ratings of the employee are multiplied by the weights of the statements and the coefficients are added up. This cumulative coefficient is the weighted performance score of the employee, which, in turn, is compared with the overall assessment standards in order to find out the overall performance of the employee. However, this method is expensive to design and time consuming in nature.

Critical incident method In the critical incident method, the rater or manager prepares a list of statements on the basis of the effective and ineffective behaviour of an employee. These incidents represent the behaviour of employees on their job. The rater periodically records the critical incidents and maintains it. At the end of the rating period, these critical incidents are used to evaluate the overall employee performance.

Essay-form Appraisal

In an essay-form appraisal, the manager writes a short essay describing the employee's performance.

In an essay-form appraisal, the manager writes a short essay describing the employee's performance. This form, prepared during the rating period, emphasizes the evaluation of the overall performance on the basis of their strengths/weaknesses. A major limitation of this method is that the quality of ratings depends on the writing skills of the manager, rather than the performance of an employee.

Group Appraisal

In this method, an employee is appraised by a group of appraisers. The group consists of the immediate supervisor of the employee, manager or head of the department, and consultants. The group may use one or multiple methods. The group first appraises the performance of the employee, compares the actual performance with the standards, finds out the deviations, and discusses the reasons for it in order to suggest ways for improving the performance of the employee. The group also prepares a plan of action, studies the need for change in job analysis and standards, and recommends change. This method is used for the purpose of promotion, demotion, and retrenchment.

Confidential Reports

Under this method, the supervisor appraises the performance of his subordinates on the basis of his observations, judgement, and intuitions. This method is usually used in government organizations and is prepared at the end of every year. The report states the strengths, weaknesses, sincerity, punctuality, attitude, knowledge, skills, conduct, and character of the employees.

Modern Methods

The modern methods of performance appraisal are as follows:

Behaviourally Anchored Rating Scales (BARS)

Behaviourally anchored rating scale (BARS) is a combination of the rating scale and critical incident method.

This is a recently developed appraisal method. It is a combination of the rating scale and critical incident method. We will now discuss the five-step procedure for BARS.

Step I: Collect critical incidents People with knowledge of the job to be appraised are asked to describe specific illustrations of effective and ineffective performance behaviour.

Step II: Identify performance dimensions   These people then cluster the incidents into a smaller set (of say, 5–10) of performance dimensions. Each cluster (dimension) is then defined.

Step III: Reclassify the incidents   Another group of people who have knowledge about the job, reclassify the critical incidents. They are given the cluster definitions and critical incidents, and asked to redesign each incident to the dimension it best describes. Typically, a critical incident is retained if some percentage (usually 50% to 80%) of this group assigns it to the same cluster as the previous group did.

Step IV: Rate the incidents   This second group is generally asked to rate (7 or 9-point scales are typical) the behaviour described in the incident in terms of how effectively or ineffectively it represents performance on the appropriate dimension.

Step V: Develop the final instrument   A subset of incidents (usually six or seven per cluster) is used as 'behaviour anchors' for the performance dimensions.

Assessment Centre

This method is used to test candidates in a social situation, using a variety of procedures and a number of assessors. The most important feature of the assessment centre is job-related simulations. These simulations involve characteristics that managers feel are important to job success. The evaluators observe and evaluate participants (in several situations) as they perform activities commonly found in these higher-level jobs. Assessments are made to determine employee potential for the purpose of promotions.

> ■ ■ ■
> The most important feature of the assessment centre is job-related simulations.

Assessment centres are used for the following purposes:

- Measure the potential for first-level supervision, sales, and upper management positions, and also for higher levels of management for development purposes.
- Determine the individual training and development needs of employees.
- Select recent college students for entry-level positions.
- Provide more accurate human resource planning information.
- Make an early determination of potential.
- Assist in implementing affirmative action goals.

Human Asset Accounting

> ■ ■ ■
> Human asset accounting deals with the cost and contribution of human resources to the organization.

Human asset accounting is a sophisticated method, which deals with the cost and contribution of human resources to the organization. Cost of employee includes cost of manpower planning, recruitment, selection, induction, placement, training, development and benefits, etc. Employee contribution is the employee's service towards the organization. Employee performance is positive if the employee contribution is more than his/her cost to the company.

Management by Objectives

Management by objectives (MBO) is described as 'a process whereby the superior and subordinate managers of an organization jointly identify its common goals, define each individual's major areas of responsibility in terms of results expected of him and use these measures as guides for operating the unit and assessing the contributions of each of its members'. Management by objectives is a modern method of evaluating the performance of employees—it measures each employee's contribution to the success of the organization.

To establish objectives, the key people involved should engage in the following three activities:

- Meet to achieve the objectives within a given period of time.
- Develop plans to accomplish the objectives.
- Agree on the yardsticks for determining whether the objectives have been met.

So, MBO is a complete system of planning, control, and philosophy of management.

360 Degree Performance Appraisal

The appraiser can be any person who has knowledge about the job done, the contents to be appraised, the standards of contents, and observes the employee while performing a job. The comprehensive appraisals from the supervisors, peers, subordinates, and the employee himself/herself are called 360 degree appraisal. The appraiser should assess the performance without bias and must also be capable of determining what is more important and what is less important.

POTENTIAL APPRAISAL

Potential appraisal is a process to identify unrevealed skills and abilities in a person. It is a future-oriented appraisal, which aims to track the potential of the employee to rise in his career. It is an important tool in making decisions about career advancements.

Potential appraisal serves the following purposes:

- Advises employees about their overall career development and future prospects
- Helps the organization to chalk out succession plans
- Motivates the employees to further develop their skills and competencies
- Identifies the training needs and update training efforts from time to time

Organizations use various techniques for potential appraisal, such as self-rating, peer appraisal, superior rating, performance appraisal, and psychological and psychometric tests.

However, organizations must use potential appraisal with caution. They cannot use this appraisal for all employees at all levels. Some employees may be bright, but may not deliver results when given additional responsibilities. On the other hand, a highly capable individual may be difficult to retain. Usually, organizations conduct performance appraisal annually, but there is no fixed time schedule for potential appraisal. As and when the requirements arise, organizations may conduct potential appraisal.

Potential appraisal helps organizations to identify future requirements so that they can guide and direct their efforts to achieve individual growth and organizational goals. Therefore, organizations must include potential appraisal as a part of the performance appraisal.

POSSIBLE ERRORS IN THE APPRAISAL PROCESS

The performance appraisal process and techniques that have been suggested make an assumption that the rater is free from all biases and is very objective in his assessment. There are a few common errors, which might accidentally occur in the rating process. Some of them are as follows:

Leniency Error

Every rater has his or her own way of evaluating individuals against or irrespective of a standard of performance. Sometimes, this might result in a high marking or a low marking. This is referred to as the leniency error. When raters are positively lenient in their appraisal, an individual performance becomes overstated, resulting in a positive leniency error. Similarly, a negative leniency error understates the performance, giving the individual a lower appraisal.

Halo Error

■ ■ ■
The halo effect is a tendency to rate high or low on all factors due to the impression created by a high or low rating on some specific factor.

The halo effect is a tendency to rate high or low on all factors due to the impression created by a high or low rating on some specific factor. For example, if an employee is found to be dependable and sincere, there will be a tendency to rate the individual high on other positive personal attributes. One way to avoid this error is to rate the individual on all dimensions before the final rating. This procedure can be practised by involving many raters.

Similarity Error

Usually, people tend to perceive and interpret behaviour by projecting their own perceptions on others. When evaluators do so, it is called a similarity error. For example, the rater who perceives himself/herself as honest may evaluate others by looking for honesty.

Error of Central Tendency

It is possible that the general findings of the appraisal results might fall in the average category. Very few people might fall in the extremes. Here, the rater shows reluctance to give absolute markings either on the positive or on the negative side. This is referred to as the error of central tendency. Failure to rate the employees in the extreme categories, even when they deserve it, might create some problems for the employees.

■ ■ ■
Data from appraisal may be utilized for performance planning and improvement.

Despite the aforementioned errors, the appraisal process is a powerful tool to enhance and motivate an employee's performance. The data from the appraisal may be utilized effectively for performance planning and improvement.

PLANNING FOR PERFORMANCE IMPROVEMENT

The importance of planning the organizational strategy for performance improvement (PI) has been discussed in the following section.

Organizational Strategy and Performance

In the organization per se, the focus has to begin at the strategy level, and hence, in his/her path of discovering the performance improvement (PI), one would briefly make an attempt to understand the various theories propounded by strategists. The word 'strategy' as a term was coined in Athens, around 508–7 BC, where the Athenian war council, comprising ten strategoi, wielded military and political power. Parallely, in the Asian region, the Chinese warrior Sun Tzu had authored *The Art of War*, a masterpiece on strategy planning in the military context. In the corporate context, the executives, such as Chester Bernard of AT&T (1938) and Alfred Sloan of General Motors (1963), have emphasized on a strategic approach for performance management and profitability improvement. Peter Drucker (1954) advocates an active approach rather than passive reaction for organizations. Alfred Chandler of Harvard Business School, in his classic *Strategy and Structure* (1962), had explored the adaptation of administrative structures to accommodate strategies of growth. Ignor Ansoff, in his *Corporate Strategy* (1965), through his product/mission matrix, has provided a 'common thread' for five interrelated issues, that is, (a) product market scope, (b) growth vector, (c) competitive advantage, (d) internally generated synergy, and (e) make or buy decisions, and has stressed on mutual reinforcement.

Boston Consulting Group has pioneered influential concepts such as the 'experience curve' and 'growth share matrix'. Michael Porter gave the concept of 'five forces framework' for industry analysis, which helps in positioning for performance enhancement.

Organizational paradigms, with assumptions of entities of the social world, have viewed several paradigms with component parameters, such as strategic choice by dominant coalition and realized strategy and performance, in the context of environmental developments.

The researchers in the areas of strategic thinking and planning have examined the learning perspective, with the help of single-loop and double-loop learning for improving performance. Argyris (1977) focused on the distinction between single- and double-loop learning. Single-loop learning relates the organizational action design and outcome, or correction through suitable action, but without a critical examination of the governing variables for action, while double-loop learning looks precisely at this area.

Researchers in the area of *leadership* have examined the qualities of leadership and its interrelationship with organizational performance. The various approaches used by them include the trait approach, which focuses on the traits of a leader. Ohio State University, in its studies on leadership styles, has examined it on two dimensions. These are—(a) 'consideration', that is, concern and support of the leader to the subordinates, and (b) 'initiating structure', which indicates the extent to which the leader defines his own role and that of the subordinates towards the accomplishment of goals and objectives.

The research studies at the University of Michigan identified three types of leadership behaviours to distinguish between effective and ineffective leaders, through 'task-oriented behaviour', 'relationship-oriented behaviour', and lastly, 'participative leadership'. Blake and Mouton (1964) have identified various types of leadership on similar lines.

Researchers in *organizational change* have emphasized the need for change from the perspectives of survival requirements and also performance improvement. However, the failures in the process have lead to cynicism on account of various factors such as lack of communication, and opportunity of meaningful participation leading to lower commitment, lower job satisfaction and motivation, ultimately leading to lower performance of the employees.

Dru and Lumberg (1977) have proposed successful strategic re-positioning of organizations, to facilitate higher levels of organizational performance in relation to their competitors. The approaches to strategy implementation have also examined the role of the chief executive officer (CEO) as a commander, architect, co-coordinator, coach, and premise setter, which plays a role in the improvement of organizational performance.

■ ■ ■
Organizational culture
has a profound impact
on performance and
survival.

Organizational culture has a profound impact on performance and survival. Barney (1986), Deal and Kennedy (1982), and Peters and Waterman (1982) are a few of the researchers who have studied the effects of organizational culture. Johnson (1987, 1988), through the 'cultural web', has examined the components and behavioural manifestations of organizational culture. According to him, the culture paradigm can be perceived through the following:

- Communications
- Control systems
- Incentives
- Organizational structures

- Power structures
- Symbols
- Stories/myths
- Rites/routines

Heracleous and Devoge (1998), in their research, have focused on the strategic change process as an organization development (OD) approach. The practitioners have examined the action research in the OD area in the context of descriptive relevance, goal relevance, operational validity, non-obviousness, and more importantly, timeliness. In the integrated organizational model (Heracleous 2003), it is proposed to integrate the leadership with the six key factors—management processes and systems, organization team and job design, work processes and business systems, values and culture, individual and team competence, and finally, reward and recognition. In the entire process, it is obvious that the emphasis is more on bringing in the desired performance level by correlating the competence with rewards to ensure sustained motivation, with the assumption of other four factors as prerequisites.

In the early 1980s, USA, under the leadership of President Ronald Reagan, and the UK, with Prime Minister Margaret Thatcher at the helm of affairs, gave an impetus to the privatization process in the respective economies, and also to the world. The underlying assumption was that private ownership would contribute to performance improvement. The other factors that led to the privatization process are as follows:

- Shift in ideology
- Pressure from the donors
- Regional bandwagoning
- Fiscal imperatives

- Globalization of finance
- Institutional capacity
- Growth of the middle class
- Technological advancement

The studies (Galal, et al. 1994, Megginson, et al. 1994) covering 61 privatized enterprises in 32 industries of eighteen countries found that the profitability, sales, operating efficiency, and capital investment increased significantly after privatization.

Another issue of debate has been–does corporate governance make a difference to the organizational performance? The agency theory (Eisenhardt 1989) suggested that the separation of the roles of the Chairman from that of the CEO can lead to a conflict of interests on account of self-interested actions of the managers, vis-à-vis the ideals of the owners. Similarly, there has been research on the composition of insiders vs. outsiders on the board. However, the conclusion of several rigorous studies on CEO duality and composition of the board is that these factors do not make a significant difference to the organizational performance.

■ ■ ■
The shaping up of current
and future organizations
is essentially based on
two factors—globalization
and technological
advancement.

The shaping up of current and future organizations is essentially based on two factors—globalization and technological advancement (Hirt 2000, Hitt, et al. 1980).

The other forces that affect the future of organizations are as follows:

- Leadership, which is bound to play a key role in developing a strategic vision to inspire and motivate employees
- Employee empowerment in a culture, which is based on trust, as against control
- Developing the learning capacity of organizations for the effective management of internal and external knowledge
- The increasing focus of organizations on performance improvement
- Evolution of flat or delayered, project-based organizations
- Decentralization of operational as well as strategic decision-making aspects.
- Outsourcing, which has just begun, will pick up momentum and become the order of the day.

HRM and Strategic Management

The HRM function, in the Indian corporate context, has evolved from being a mere administrative function to being a part of the team involved in the strategy planning process. The HR experts, in their evolutionary process, taking cue from the organizational behaviour (OB) experts, have accepted the paradigm change that performance effectiveness is not incidental, but requires sustained effort, coupled with organizational support in terms of values and culture, systems and processes, reward and recognition mechanisms, and performance incentives—both monetary and non-monetary.

Change and Learning

The concepts of learning organization and organizational learning have made it imperative for organizations to understand the correlation between the learning environment and its resultant impact on the level of performance of employees. 'In times of change', said Eric Hoffer, 'the learners inherit the world, and the learned will remain beautifully equipped to deal with a world that no longer exists'. This quote aptly sums up the absolute importance for everyone to continuously learn and update himself/herself in a continuously changing world.

Though it's fashionable in corporate circles to believe that 'change is the only permanent thing in the ever changing world', rarely do we see concrete action for adaptation to change. Most leaders continue to be perched in the prison of previous success, and in the process, they fail to perceive the emerging changes in the environment. All changes, per se, occur on account of the learning of individuals and groups. The definition of learning, as indicated by psychologists, elucidates the link between the leaning and change. Learning has been defined as 'relatively permanent change in the behaviour of an individual or group'. The key element in the definition is 'permanency', due to the spontaneity of new behaviour, similar to a reflex action. Another key element is 'relativity' of permanency, since the learning should provide for any future changes in the behaviour. The change induced by the key elements is in the 'behaviour' of the individuals/groups.

In the backdrop of the aforementioned definitions, researchers have identified two categories of learning—'single-loop learning' and 'double-loop learning'. In single-loop learning, the emphasis is on the individuals' to identify a

> Learning has been defined as 'relatively permanent change in the behaviour of an individual or group'.

solution to an existing problem. In double-loop learning, on the contrary, the focus is on searching a solution to an existing problem, along with reflection and reinterpretation of the situation, and change in mental models underlying those decisions/actions, which ultimately lead to paradigm shifts.

The transactional analysis (TA) school of psychology specifies that human beings have three psychological needs, in the sense that they are not negotiable or postponable. The three types of hunger are (a) stimulus hunger, referring to one's need to interact with the external environment, (b) structure hunger, which refers to one's need to make sense of one's experiences, and (c) recognition hunger.

In the context of the term 'learning organization', certain amount of distinction has been made between 'learners' and 'non-learners', based on the extent of affinity of individuals towards learning. In a survey of one of the organizations, it was found that employees could be classified into three categories—(a) natural learners (20%), (b) neutral learners (60%), and (c) negative learners (20%), and accordingly, it has been termed the '3-N Model', which is fairly stable across the organizations.

The performance focus of the organizations is to convert the 'neutral' into 'natural' learners. 'Negative' learners who are negative from the perspective of the current work assignment, can be transformed into 'natural' learners by job rotation into assignments which hold their interest. By doing so, the organizations can raise the learning tempo across the organization, in all the categories of employees, and thus 'transform' it into a learning organization.

Change and Performance Management

A study by Manimala (2000) involving the case studies of turnaround organizations postulates that there are four stages in the change process of organizations. These are—(a) arresting sickness (through cost cutting and liquidation of unused assets), (b) focusing on 'core business' by hiving off/outsourcing of non-core businesses, (c) expanding of core businesses through diversification into related businesses, and more importantly, (d) the institution-building process, simultaneous to the other three processes, through the enculturation process for changing the collective mindset of all the employees. The study revealed that while the Indian organizations in the study would stagnate at the first stage, and in western cases, they would progress only up to the second, or, at the most, third stage, whereas Japanese organizations would undertake the enculturation process parallel to the other three processes.

In order to inculcate the learning attitude among the employees, organizations need to undertake the following four steps:

- Create an intrinsic interest in the work among the employees, by instilling in them a sense of 'self-worth' and 'satisfaction' by correlating the rewards with their performance.
- Break down the organizational goals into strategic business unit (SBU)/group targets and make the linkage transparent.
- Institutionalize and manage change through empowerment and autonomy to employees who share the vision, goals, and ideology of the organization.
- Last but not the least, an organization has to create opportunities for employees for formal and informal interaction, through discussion groups, seminars, celebration of achievements/events, etc.

Knowledge, Learning, and Performance

■ ■ ■
Organizational knowledge
is what an organization
knows, how it uses what
it knows, and how fast it
can know something new.

The learning concept has made it necessary for organizations to understand the knowledge, capture it, and facilitate its dissemination to achieve the organizational learning objectives. The knowledge, by definition, resides in people, for people have to identify, interpret, and internalize it. In the organizational context, it can be represented in various ways—mechanical, visual, and digital. The organization, in order to derive competitive advantage out of individual knowledge, has to harness it through its systems and procedures and transform it into organizational knowledge in order to add value to its businesses.

The key concepts as identified by Archana and Srinivasan (2000) are as follows:

- *Organizational knowledge*: what an organization knows, how it uses what it knows, and how fast it can know something new (Prusak 1997)
- *Organizational memory*: An explicit, disembodied, persistent representation of knowledge and information in the organization (Liebowitz and Beckman 1998)
- *Knowledge management*: A systematic and organized attempt to generate knowledge within an organization, in order to transform its ability to store and use knowledge for improving performance

Nonaka and Takeuchi (1995) have identified four modes for conversion of knowledge within the organizations. These modes have been shown in Table 12.1.

TABLE 12.1 Modes of conversion of knowledge within an organization

	Tacit knowledge	Explicit knowledge
Tacit knowledge	Socialization	Externalization
Explicit knowledge	Internalization	Combination

Source: Nonaka and Takeuchi (1965)

The sharing of tacit knowledge across individuals and organizations happens through the socialization process, where employees learn from peers through an implicit knowledge-sharing process. Externalization is the process by which experienced employees share their knowledge through concepts and theories. Internalization is related to organizational learning, and is a critical mode for knowledge conversion from individual learning and memory to organizational learning and memory. Combination, on the other hand, is a process of sharing of explicit knowledge in the organization through formal meetings, documents, etc.

The specific steps involved in the knowledge management programme, as identified by Archana and Srinivasan (2000), are as follows:

■ ■ ■
Externalization is the
process by which
experienced employees
share their knowledge
through concepts and
theories.

- Specifying the goals of knowledge
- Identifying the knowledge being sought
- Collecting the required knowledge along with the sources
- Processing and developing the acquired knowledge for presentation purposes
- Transfer of knowledge across the individuals and groups in the organization

- Application of knowledge for value addition
- Storage of knowledge for ensuring timely availability
- Assessment of transferred and disseminated knowledge with the help of feedback, for modifications and changes

The entire process of managing the knowledge within the organization and deploying it across the learning infrastructure would facilitate learning, in order to provide impetus to the organizational focus of performance improvement.

Organizational Culture and Performance

■ ■ ■

Organizational culture is defined as the commonly shared beliefs, values, and characteristic patterns of behaviour that exist within an organization.

The effectiveness of the organization is dependent on the organization culture. Though there have been numerous studies on organization culture, there has been no agreement. Culture is assessed on several components such as climate, environment, and ethos. Organizational culture has been defined by Taguiri and Litwin (1968) as a 'relatively enduring quality of the internal environment of an organization that is (a) experienced by its members (b) influences their behaviour and (c) can be described in terms of the value of a particular set of characteristics, and (or attributes) of the organization'. Margulies and Raja (1978) have simply defined it as 'the commonly shared beliefs, values and characteristics, and patterns of behaviour that exist within an organization'.

The functions of organizational culture, as summarized by Ott (1989), are to provide knowledge about the following:

- Shared patterns of cognitive interpretations or perceptions, thus communicating the expected thought processes and behaviour to employees
- Shared patterns of feelings to ensure that employees know what they are expected to value and how they are expected to feel
- Role modeling, teaching, and coaching by leaders
- Explicit rewards, status system, and promotion criteria
- Stories, legends, myths, and parables about key people and events
- What leaders pay attention to, measure, and control
- How organization is designed and structured
- Organizational systems and procedures
- Criteria used for selection, promotion, and retirement of people

The organizational culture implicitly conveys to individual employees or groups, the acceptable level of efforts or commitment that would provide them the higher levels of rewards, thus driving them to higher levels of performance.

HR Strategy and Performance Planning

The changing business requirements have made it necessary for organizations to change the corporate strategy, and along with it, the HR strategy. The focus of HR strategy has moved into new areas:

- Identifying and integrating the business opportunities
- Motivating the employees

■ ■ ■
HR strategy is defined as the long-term direction to the HR function.

- Developing the employee competencies
- Creating coherent functional/project teams
- Setting the performance goals in conjunction with the project/functional head
- Facilitating the performance planning and achievement of employees

HR strategy, by definition, is the long-term direction to HR function and it describes the options suitable to the organization, in consonance with the existing systems and processes, resources, and, more importantly, the environment. It facilitates the effective functioning of the organization and effective management of the employees, in relation with the business environment.

Strategic gurus, such as Michael Porter and C.K. Prahlad, have defined the specific business capabilities required by the organization as core competencies. In order to achieve the required core competence for the business, the HR function has the role of identifying the people capabilities, since, essentially, it is these that constitute the business capabilities of the organization.

The next step for the organization would be to identify the strategic intent (SI). Strategic intent, as defined by C.K. Prahlad, indicates the goals/objectives of the organization, slightly higher than the existing level of core competencies. In the processes, the organization would be training its employees to higher levels of 'stretch performance', and thus, would be able increase the performance capability across the organization.

These processes emphasize the need for HR functionaries to set performance targets. They, in the process of defining the HR strategy, need to gel with the organization, map the competencies, coordinate the process of identifying the SI, and more importantly, facilitate the performance of employees across the organization. This aspect would be the value addition by the HR function to the business goals of the organization.

Organizational Learning and Performance Feedback

In the competitive landscape, the organizations are becoming increasingly obsessed with the identification of low-performance areas and deciding the response pattern, to address the issue of concern. To do so, the organization should be able to trace the feedback from performance across the infrastructure, in order to achieve higher levels of performance.

Managers set their own performance standards, based on their aspiration levels, in the context of organizational requirements. The focus is the adjustment of the aspiration levels, based on the performance feedback in organizations. Researchers have provided ample evidence to prove the phenomenon of organizational inertia for change, even in the face of low performance. Part of the failure can be attributed to the lack of mechanisms to provide performance feedback that can lead to learning and spirited performance. Part of it can be due to the dilemma faced by the managers on account of problems in decision-making because of future uncertainties.

The precursors of performance feedback theory can be found amply in organizational and psychological literature. Behavioural theorists (March 1963, March and Simon 1958, Cyert and March 1992, Schultz 2001) have suggested that goal setting should be based on the aspiration levels of the individuals, as performance feedback affects organizational learning.

The key concept to be understood in the entire process is 'bounded rationality'. It implies that decision makers have limited information, attention, and processing ability that enable them to perform tasks aimed at profit maximization. One of the definitions views it as a loosely specified statement of limits to knowledge that leads to minor adjustments in behaviour.

■ ■ ■
The goal setting process of individuals is aimed at fulfilling individual goals.

The goal setting process of individuals is aimed at fulfilling individual goals (Locke and Latham 1990), and though this behaviour can be strengthened by linkage with rewards, the linkage is not direct.

The experiments related to risk theory (Staw 1976, 1981, and Ross 1987) have probed the behaviour of managers in the event of receiving negative performance feedback and found that the risk-taking ability of managers rises in a situation perceived to be leading to loss.

■ ■ ■
The goal selection process is a complex phenomenon and is influenced by precedence, politics, payoffs, and proselytizing.

Another aspect of study is that groups rather than individuals make decisions in the organizational context. These decisions are made on the basis of the feedback received from other groups and experts. The differences in individual aspiration levels can lead to lower levels of performance of groups.

Search is another concept in behaviour theory, and includes activities such as varying work procedures for improving effectiveness in performance, and also for relieving boredom. Search is an everyday phenomenon in organizations and multiple processes drive it (March 1981). It has been categorized into slack search, institutionalized search, and problemistic search.

The research on the determinants of response to performance feedback (Greve 2003) indicates that two critical factors are inertia and risk-seeking behaviour below the aspiration. The three processes of organizational search are as follows:

- Increased problem availability in decision-making processes
- Increased risk tolerance in low-performance context, to increase probabilities for change
- Organizational inertia, pulling back the propensity for change

Research relating to the process of selection of goal variables by managers in relation to performance indicates that the goal variables should be dependent on the individual aspirations, and need not always be in accordance with the performance goals of the top management. The goal selection process is a complex phenomenon and is influenced by precedence, politics, payoffs, and proselytizing.

Another influencing variable in the goal setting process is the risk-taking level in the organization. The performance feedback behaviour of managers is largely dependent on the organizational factors.

Technology-based Learning and Performance

The advent of information technology on the organizational horizon has made the entire process of learning much simpler. The traditional model of learning was an extensive, cost-prohibitive, and more importantly, time-consuming affair. In the era of speed, where organizations are grappling with continuous change, there is a felt need for increasing the frequency of learning. The influx of technology has made the entire process quite simple, on account of various technology tools such as the following:

■ ■ ■
The advent of information technology on the organizational horizon has made the entire process of learning much simpler.

- Networked organization
- E-mails
- Intranet
- Bulletin boards
- Discussion rooms and chats

- Electronic performance support systems
- E-learning and web-based learning

The physical learning infrastructure can effectively leverage the technology platforms for facilitating organizational learning. Organizations have adopted several models such as complete in-house efforts on e-learning, outsourcing, and some have followed the hybrid model by keeping the critical personnel internally, and outsourcing the rest.

Each of these models has its own advantages and disadvantages. The complete in-house approach would give a complete control on the process. However, it is time consuming and in an era of rapid technological advances, it may not be prudent to invest huge amounts and time on a process where the results are not explicit and immediate.

The complete outsourcing model will give flexibility and maneuverability, but may at times become cost-prohibitive, if the organization does not have internal capabilities to identify the exact requirements and solutions. In most cases, the organizations end up having vendor-driven solutions, not those that would meet its requirements.

The hybrid model would provide the advantages of both the models, and in addition, would keep the costs under control and would provide flexibility to adopt the e-learning infrastructure to meet the changing organizational requirements.

This discussion may at times appear to be disjunctive, in the context of discussion on performance improvement. However, the extensive literature in psychology, starting from Pavlov's theory period, suggest that any behaviour is influenced by training, and in the organizational context, learning. As such, the performance of the individual employee is an outcome of the learning imparted to the employees. The discussion is more appropriate in the era of networked and virtual organizations, more than ever before.

The challenge before the HR professionals is to leverage the technology infrastructure to facilitate learning at individual, group, and organization levels.

Transition from Performance Appraisal to Performance Improvement

Performance appraisal had a different connotation in the industrial era, when there was hardly any difference between machines and men. In terms of OB experts, the focus was on controlling human beings, since the perception was through the theory 'X' perspective that inherently, employees try to avoid work and that they have to be continuously controlled and monitored if work is to be extracted from them. Subsequently, during the early twentieth century, the focus was shifted to theory 'Y'—a theory of self-initiated employees, who have to be guided to higher levels of performance.

In the IT era, where the employees, specially in IT firms, belong to the age group of mid-twenties, and are usually self-motivated, the organizational perceptions have undergone a considerable change as compared to the traditional era. In the restructured organizations, traditional concepts, such as respect to hierarchy, seniority preceding over merit, and life-long careers, are no longer relevant.

> Today, employees are professionals who are journeying through organizations in search of their professional goals.

Today, the employees are more of professionals who are journeying through organizations in search of their professional goals. The loyalty, per se, is more towards the profession rather than the organization. Even during the short stint in the organization, the employees transit through various teams, since the contemporary organizations are structured into project teams. The leader of the team is more of a facilitator than a formal controller. Increasingly, the employees are assuming the project leader position by the age of early thirties. The membership of the teams is based on the competencies and skill sets that each member is expected to contribute.

The traditional appraisal approach is flawed, on account of the following reasons:

- It is incongruent with the value-based, vision-driven, and participative modern organizations.
- It promotes the legacy of the top-down and bureaucratic approach, which is out of sync with the current requirements.
- The traditional appraisal has a subjective element, and most often, is influenced by the recent events rather than the performance of the employee during the entire appraising period.
- The modus operandi of appraisal systems has more to do with being judgmental and finding faults, with little focus on performance improvement.
- The aforementioned nature of appraisals perpetuates the distance and differences between the appraiser and appraisee, rather than providing the forum or opportunity for a healthy discussion.
- The employees as well as the reporting authority are more inclined towards defending their own viewpoints, rather than arriving at any common platform, which is acceptable to both.
- In case of majority of the organizations, the appraisal process is more of a ritual being practiced to avoid getting into trouble with the HR departments.
- Theoretically speaking, the appraisal process is a way of safeguarding the position-power of the reporting authority.
- Quite often, the appraisal formats are poorly designed, or once designed, they become so sanctimonious that organizations refuse to acknowledge the need to change the structure, to stay in tune with the changed requirements.

Performance appraisal has thus defeated the very purpose of its existence, which is to holistically view the performance of the appraisee during the review period and align the individual goals/objectives with that of the SBU/organization. It is envisaged that the work would become more meaningful to the employee, since he would be able to perceive the relationship between his individual goals and the organizational objectives. The ultimate objective is to facilitate the organization to achieve higher levels of growth and performance. In contrast, performance appraisal has become more of a tool for politicking, and has become a pawn in the coroprate power games.

SUMMARY

In this chapter, an important function of HR—performance appraisal—has been discussed. An employee's growth, personal development, and job satisfaction are all dependent on his/her performance. Similarly, an organization's growth, future planning, and employee development are all contingent upon employee performance. Further, an employee's performance is also used as an indicator for compensation packages, career counseling, and identifying training needs. This chapter discusses both traditional and modern methods of performance appraisal. It also relates performance to aspects such as strategy, change management, and learning. The process of appraisal usually involves comparing the performance with a standard. An employee's performance against these standards is judged by using different methods. There are a few raters' biases, which might interfere in the rating process. This can be overcome effectively. Further, the data obtained from the appraisal process may be utilized effectively for performance planning and improvement, thereby establishing a performance management system in the organization.

▪ ▪ ▪ | KEY TERMS

Behaviourally anchored rating scales A technique that generates critical incidents and develops behavioural dimensions

Checklist appraisal A performance appraisal method in which the rater checks the qualities that are applicable

Critical incident appraisal A method that focuses on key behaviours that make the difference between doing a job effectively and doing it ineffectively

Essay appraisal A method where the narrator writes an essay about the employee

Forced choice appraisal A method in which a rater chooses between two specific statements about an employee's work behaviour

Management by objectives A method that includes mutual objective setting by managers and subordinates and evaluation based on the attainment of specific objectives

Performance Record of outcomes on specified job functions during a specific time period

Performance appraisal Process of evaluating an individual's work or performance

▪ ▪ ▪ | EXERCISES

Multiple Choice Questions

1. Common uses of information generated through performance appraisal include all of the following except
   (a) administrative/personal decisions
   (b) organizational training and development programme
   (c) inputs for job content evaluation
   (d) feedback on an individual's performance

2. Which performance appraisal technique lists traits and a range of performance?
   (a) Alternation ranking
   (b) Graphic rating scale
   (c) Management by objectives
   (d) Paired comparison

3. The continuous process of evaluating and managing both the behaviour and outcomes in the workplace is known as
   (a) training and development
   (b) performance appraisal
   (c) compensation management
   (d) job analysis

4. Organizations put maximum effort in measuring the performance of employees because
   (a) it is cost effective
   (b) it helps in detecting the problems
   (c) it leads to product innovation
   (d) it assists in implementing new technology

5. Which of the following performance appraisal methods is usually adopted for evaluating performance in managerial positions?
   (a) Management by objectives
   (b) Critical incident
   (c) Paired comparison
   (d) Essay method

Fill in the Blanks

1. Rating a person high or low on all items because of one characteristic during performance appraisal is known as _____.

2. When supervisors identify performance deficiencies of the subordinates and provide suggestions for improvement, the process is called _____.

3. Assigning scale points with specific examples of good or poor performance refers to _____ appraisal method.

4. The evaluator uses a list of behavioural descriptions and checks off those behaviours that apply to the employee. This method of appraisal is called _____.

5. Learning is defined as a _____ in the behaviour of an individual or group.

Concept Review Questions

1. Discuss the importance of the appraisal process.

2. Contrast the traditional methods of appraisal with the modern methods.

3. Write a note on assessment centres.

4. What steps can be taken to reduce rater biases in the appraisal process?

5. Suggest linkages between performance appraisal and performance management.

6. Identify the role of organizational culture in performance planning.

7. What, in your opinion, is an effective performance management system? Discuss.

Project Work

1. Study the performance appraisal system in a manufacturing company and IT company and evaluate the reasons for success/failures in the respective organizations.

2. Prepare a brief support document on organizational culture and performance management.

3. Prepare a write-up explaining the need for adapting the international systems to the Indian context, with reasons.

4. Survey the performance appraisal system in an IT company by covering all the tiers in the organization and prepare an action plan for its improvement.

5. Write an analytical report defending or opposing modern appraisal systems such as the feedback in a public sector organization.

6. Prepare a model which can reduce, if not eliminate, the errors in perfomance assessment.

■ ■ ■ | **REFERENCES** _____

Axline, L.L. 1994, 'Ethical considerations of performance appraisals', *Management Review*, March, p. 62.

Bernardin, H.J. and Beatty, R.W. 1984, *Performance Appraisal: Assessing Human Behaviour at Work*, Kent Publishing, Boston, p. 86.

Bernardin, H.J., Hagan, C., Kane, J.S., and Villanova, P. 1998, 'Effective performance management: A focus on precision, customers, and situational constraints'. In J. Smither (Ed.), *Performance Appraisal: The State of the Art in Practice*, Jossey-Bass, San Francisco, pp. 3–45.

Church, A.H., Rogelberg, S.G., and Waclawski, J. 2000, 'Since when is no news good news? The relationship between performance and response rates in multi-rater feedback', *Personnel Psychology*, Summer, pp. 435–51.

Coleman, D. and Borman, W.C. 2000, 'Investigating the underlying structure of the citizenship performance domain', *Human Resource Management Review*, 10, pp. 25–44.

Findley, H.M., Mossholder, K.W., and Giles, W.F. 2000, 'Performance appraisal process and system facets', *Applied Psychology*, August, pp. 634–40.

Henderson, R. 1994, *Compensation Management: Rewarding Performance*, 6th Edn, Prentice Hall, Englewood Cliffs, p. 433.

Park, J. and Chong, K.S. 2000, 'A comparison of absolute and relative performance appraisal system', *International Journal of Management*, September, pp. 423–29.

Sahl, R.J. 1990, PhD, 'Design effective performance appraisals', *Personnel Journal*, October, pp. 56–57.

Segal, J.A. 1999, 'Performance management for Jekyll and Hyde', HR Magazine, February, pp. 102–35.

http://info.shine.com/career-advice-articles/appraisal/potential-appraisal/1582/cid776.aspx, accessed on 19 March 2012.

CASE STUDY 1

Performance Appraisal in an Indian BPO

FirstIndia BPO was started in the year 2000 by Chandran, a first generation entrepreneur and the chief executive officer (CEO) of the company. Initially, the company provided non-voice based services to its clients in Australia. However, the real breakthrough came when the company bagged a 300 FTE (full-time equivalent employees) voice-based call support contract for an Australian health care business solution provider.

The employees were supposed to answer the incoming calls and address the customers' queries on insurance coverage, claims status, and also sell the insurance products in case the customers evinced interest to take an enhanced coverage.

The company was able to manage the performance in the non-voice based business as the employees were only required to fill in the customer insurance application forms on the system, based on the scanned filled-in forms received. However, the company found tracking and appraising the performance of employees in the voice-based business, a different ball game altogether.

Chandran called his HR manager and advised him to develop an appraisal framework to manage and review the performance of the employees. The HR manager arrived at the following framework for performance appraisal after conducting job analysis and holding a series of discussions with the operations manager:

- Employees would state the generic goals and objectives at the beginning of the year.
- Employees would record their daily performance on the following metrics:
- Average hold time for the customer
- Revenue per hour (RPH)
- Number of calls per hour
- Average handle time (AHT)
- Customer satisfaction rating
- Employees would capture the aforementioned details on a daily basis. The team leaders (the first line managers of employees) would randomly audit these details to check their authenticity.
- Managers would appraise the employees on a monthly basis through one-to-one meetings.
- Managers would evaluate the employees on all the aforementioned parameters.
- The company would coach and counsel employees on career development aspects.
- The company would rate employees on a perfor-

mance scale of 1–5 as follows:
- Rating 1: Excellent
- Rating 2: Very good
- Rating 3: Good
- Rating 4: Satisfactory
- Rating 5: Needs improvement
- The company would place the employees with ratings of 4 and 5 on a performance improvement plan (PIP) of one month to coach and mentor them for better performance.
- At the end of one month, if the performance improved on all parameters, the company would pull out employees from the PIP.
- If the employee's performance does not improve at the end of one month, the company would extend the PIP by another one month.
- If the performance improves by the end of the extended month, the company would pull out employees from the PIP. If there is no improvement, they would be put on a disciplinary action process. At the end of enquiry process, if it is established that in spite of all the required support, there is no improvement, the company would give the employees an option to resign or it would terminate them.

Questions
1. Briefly analyse the performance appraisal process at FirstIndia BPO.
2. Do you think the performance appraisal process is employee friendly? Please comment.
3. Can you suggest any improvement in the cited process?

CASE STUDY 2

Executive Development and Performance

A leading commercial bank, with its headquarters in a capital city of southern India, has branches across the country. The bank has a history of more than seven decades, and was initially owned by Indians, but with the recent trends in liberalization, one of the leading foreign banks has taken over a majority equity in the bank. One of the significant effects of this transformation has been the reduction of the headcount, multi-skilling of the employees, and more importantly, devising and implementation of an effective performance and development system (PDS).

The philosophy of the bank has been: 'It is imperative to have a tool to manage performance in an objective, transparent, and consistent manner.'

Managing Performance
Managing performance helps to manage individual and team performance, and ultimately, the performance of the whole company. The main objective is to provide a framework for the Manager to be neutral in the assessment, which should be transparent to provide a clearly defined set of performance evaluation criteria, and consistent to make performance comparable across business areas and regions.

The performance and development system is designed to deploy goals and encourage desired behaviour. Table 12.2 shows how a list of goals and

TABLE 12.2 Goals of an organization and desirable behaviour

Goals	Desirable behaviour
• Financial	• Personal values
• Customer-related	• Capacity to think
• Internal process-related	• Capacity to act
• Employee-related	• Capacity to relate
	• Capacity to learn

desired behaviour can be laid down in an organization. The process of performance management is represented in Figure 12.2.

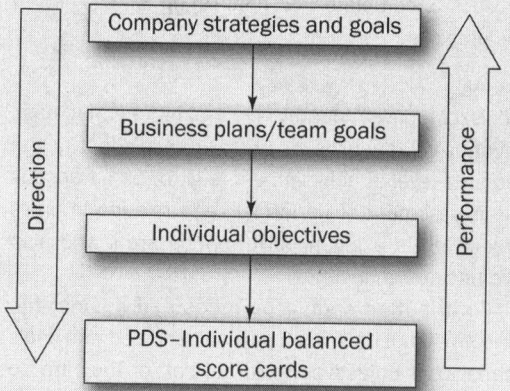

FIGURE 12.2 The performance and development system

PDS is linked to, and supports, the strategic goals of the company. It encompasses everybody in the business and links the everyday actions to the business strategy. In particular, it supports the delivery of high-quality customer service across the company by

- establishing a framework, which breaks down the company's strategic goals and business plans into individually set and agreed objectives;
- providing a mechanism to measure each per-son's achievements against their objectives, on a consistent basis; and
- focusing the individual talents to achieve the strategic goals to enhance the company's com-petitive position.

Balanced Scorecards

A balanced scorecard (BSC) covers four critical aspects of performance related to the following:

- Shareholder (financial objectives)
- Customer (expectations from internal and ex-ternal customers)
- Internal processes and systems (developing and adhering to key internal business processes)
- Employee and learning (expectations from subor-dinates on development, etc.)

Why the balanced scorecard?

- The traditional measurement systems for business performance have been financial.
- The balanced scorecard helps the organization to focus on the drivers of future performance, in terms of customers, processes, and employees.

Understanding the scorecard   The various elements of the balanced scorecard listed in Table 12.3 are briefly explained as follows:

- *Shareholder:* Financial goals generating or saving money through operational efficiency and innovation.
- *Customer:* Building and maintaining customer relationships. Meeting the needs and expectations of internal and external customers.
- *Internal processes/systems:* Developing and adhering to internal processes and systems to achieve and maintain competitive advantage.
- *Employee:* Attracting, retaining, and developing high-calibre people. Meeting expectations of subordinates. Focus on self-development.

How to measure performance   Contribution identifies what one has achieved, measured against the objectives. A rating against goals should be given in each of the four performance areas. All staff will have something to contribute/achieve in all of the areas. For example, an assistant can make an economic contribution by a cost-effective use of company resources. If objectives were not set, or they are no longer relevant, then results can be compared against one's expectations of the role, or the team's objectives, if available.

Assigning weightages

- Weightages help to study the relative importance of a parameter for a particular job/function.

TABLE 12.3 The balanced scorecard

Dimension	Measure of performance	Target	Result	Variance
Shareholder/financial weightage =				
Customer weightage =				
Internal process/system weightage =				
Employee/learning and growth weightage =				

- The four parameters of the scorecard together have a maximum weightage of 10, which gets distributed across the four parameters, depend-ing on the importance of the parameter to the job role/function. An example has been shown in Table 12.4.

TABLE 12.4 Example of the weightages for the balanced scorecard

Parameters	Branch manager	Customer support officer–SME
Shareholder		
Customer		
Internal processes and systems		
Employee and learning		

Performance evaluation

The performance rating scale criteria for 2011–12 have been listed in Table 12.5.

There shall be no change in the process that has been followed for the performance review cycle of 2011–12, however, the ratings will be communicated to the appraisee only after the moderation/review process is complete and final rating is assigned to the employee.

Rating

Goals/objectives identify one's aims (e.g., increase revenue). *Measures of performance* identify the required level of achievement (e.g., by 5%). *Rating* is the assessment of performance in relation to one's objectives in a given performance area, and also overall performance.

Contribution should be measured against the objectives that have been previously agreed with one's manager. If objectives were not set, or they are no longer relevant, then contribution should be measured according to one's expectations of the role, or the team's objectives, if available. A rating of 3 indicates a good and acceptable level of performance.

TABLE 12.5 Performance rating scales (2011–12)

Rating	Quantitative goals	Qualitiative goals and competencies
4	Target achievement ≥ 125% of goal set	Achievement substantially surpasses expectations
3	Target achievement ≥ 100%, but less than 125% of goal set	Achievement meets or marginally exceeds
2	Target achievement ≥ 75% of goal set, but less than 100% of goal set	Achievement is marginally less than expected goals
1	Target achievement < 75% of goal set	Achievement is substantially lower than expected goals

One's role in the performance and development process The roles of the various individuals involved in the rating process have been shown in Figure 12.3. These are as follows:

Appraisee Every staff member is expected to complete his/her self-evaluation/appraisal process and indicate the objectives for the following year.

Primary appraiser Where an individual has people management responsibilities and is the direct supervisor, he/she may be expected to perform the following tasks:

- Provide inputs on the performance of the employee after going through his/her self-appraisal.

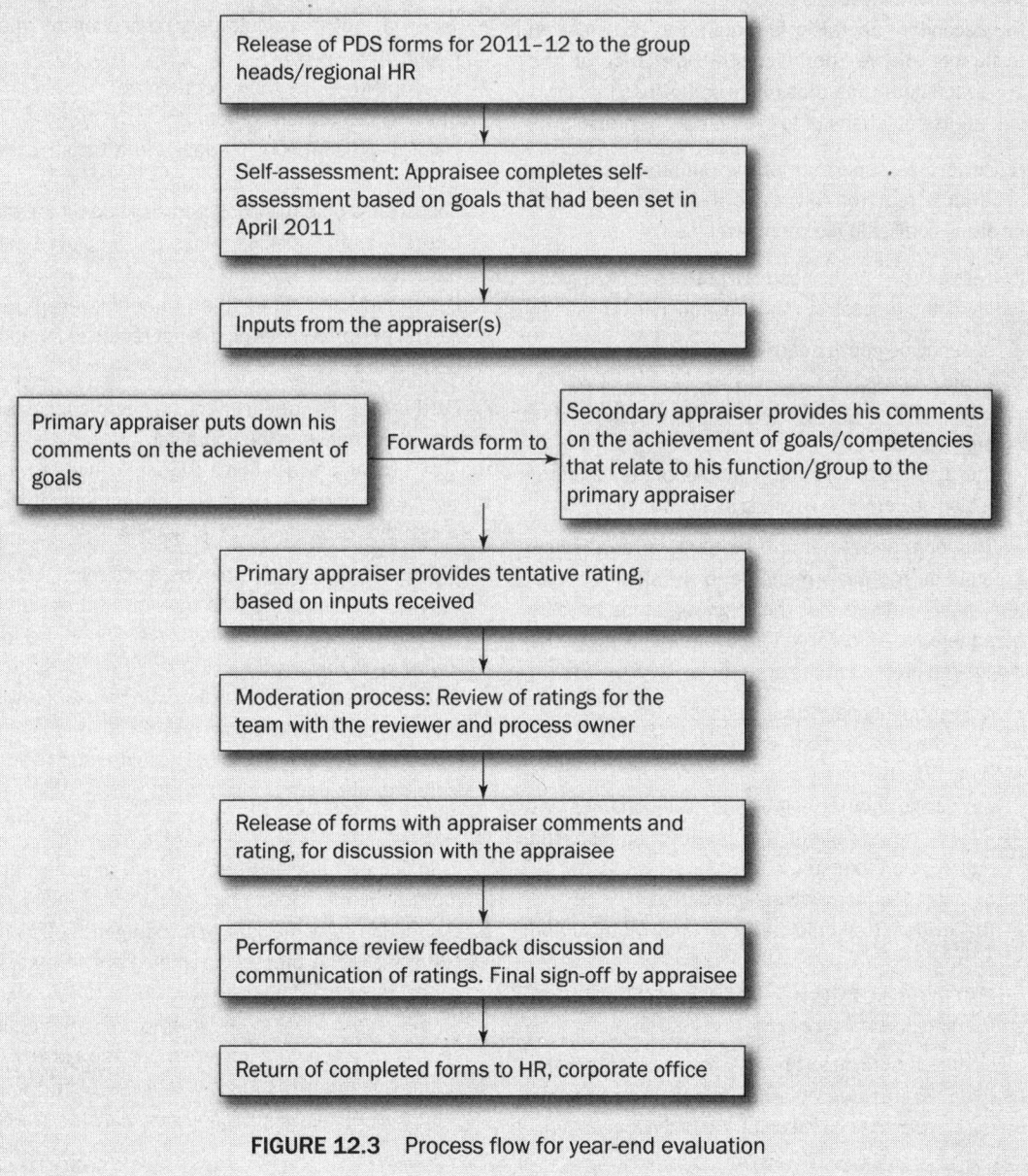

FIGURE 12.3 Process flow for year-end evaluation

- Take inputs from the functional reporting officer wherever the employee has a dual reporting relationship.
- Provide feedback on performance and agree upon objectives with the appraisee.
- Communicate the final rating to the employee.

Secondary appraiser This role will only occur in cases where the employee has a dual reporting relationship; the secondary appraiser is required to complete an evaluation of the appraisee's performance on the goals/competencies that relate to his/her function/sub-areas and submit it to the primary appraiser.

Reviewer As supervisor of the primary appraiser a reviewer is required to provide inputs only in cases involving conflict in the rating assigned.

Process owner As the head of a business unit/region/function, the process owner is responsible for

- ensuring objectivity, consistency, and transparency of the process,
- ensuring timely and effective completion of the process, and
- the distribution of ratings across one's function/region as per the guidelines indicated.

The top management of the bank, after a review meeting on the performance and development system, has identified that the following steps need to be adhered to, in order to improve the efficacy of the evaluation process in the system.

- Gather quality performance data.
- Rate the detailed competencies.
- Write effective comments:
- be specific about strengths and development areas
- include details about the situation or task, the action, and the result
- highlight the most valuable evidence
- the evidence should be objective, factual, and accurate
- provide more evidence for particularly high/low ratings

Further, the HR department, in consultation with the heads of various departments, has identified certain steps/measures to be taken by the individual employees to improve the efficiency of the system, and also to facilitate the contribution of the system to employee development. Some of the measures suggested by the HR department are as follows:

- Prompt, rather than delayed
- Focused on important issues rather than trivial ones—things that would really improve the employee's performance
- Two way—get the employee's perception of what needs improvement
- Descriptive, rather than judgmental
- Specific, rather than general
- Helpful—present your feedback in a constructive way
- Focus on problem-solving and developing for the future—identify specific things the employee can do differently
- Developmental, rather than remedial—every job can be performed better; it is not reserved for poor performers

Further, the HR department has also suggested that relations between the appraisee and appraiser in the goal setting process has a major role in improving the efficiency of the system. For this purpose, it has prepared the following set of guidelines:

- Clarify the expectations of a person's role
- Provide the benchmark to monitor and evaluate performance on an ongoing basis, and in the following year's evaluation
- Provide a clear direction in line with the company's strategy and business plans
- Help in addressing individual development needs
- Help improve performance

Questions
1. Critically evaluate the performance and development system in the bank.
2. Do you think that the bank has undergone sufficient cultural-change process to implement the latest concepts such as balanced scorecards? If yes, why? If no, suggest some steps which you feel the bank should initiate before implementing the system.
3. Comment upon the review process of the system, and also the guidelines issued by the top

management as well as the HR to the employee for improving the efficiency of the system.

4. Do you think that the bank should initiate the culture-building exercise, particularly to implement the performance and development system (PDS)? Dscuss your views.

Aditya Communications

CASE STUDY 3

Aditya Communications is a media company promoted by some of the leading entrepreneurs in southern India. The company has floated vernacular news channels in two major South Indian states—Andhra Pradesh and Karnataka. The media and entertainment industry is mainly constrained in either Mumbai or Delhi, and because of the size of the market, the news channels in the country have been either in English or in Hindi—the national language. However, over a period of time, the media industry has discovered that there is immense scope for launching news channels in vernacular languages because, in India, people have a strong language and regional affinity.

Keeping in view the various factors, such as time constraints, and balancing of interests and aspirations of people from different regions, the promoters of Aditya Communications decided to launch the new vernacular channel in Telugu in Andhra Pradesh. However, the challenge before the company was to identify and recruit the suitable personnel, in all areas, who could lead the channel directly into the homes of the people in the state. However, the company discovered that there was very little ready-made native talent available in a vernacular language, and because of this, the company had to initially look over existing general languages and had to take up the news team from those channels. In terms of human resource management, the company management found it necessary to identify, design, and implement a suitable performance management system (PMS) which was in sync with the market realities. It also had to be able to meet the hopes and aspirations of the young employee team, and at the same time, facilitate compensation structuring which was in sync with market requirements, and also provide career development avenues to the performers. The HR department, while designing the PMS, identified the need for an effective PMS in the following way:

An effective PMS is a key ingredient for the success of any organization, especially in these challenging times. And it is crucial in the product development space, especially in smaller teams. An 'up or out' culture is what enables the teams to be on their toes and raise the performance bar constantly. It has been the company's endeavour to build a high performance and high productivity culture which is just and fair to all associates at the company.

The annual appraisal workflow of the company for the year 2011–12 is shown in Figure 12.4.

Performance Review Procedure

The performance review procedure of Aditya Communications is as follows:

- The appraiser as well as the appraisee would use the annual appraisal module with built-in e-tools to complete this year's annual appraisal exercise.
- The two core areas that will be assessed as part of the company's appraisal system are as follows:
- What has been achieved in the review period, and
- How have these been achieved?
- HR will share specific deadlines via e-mail to all associates for the completion of the performance review process for this year. The appraisal tool would remind the appraiser as well as the appraisee regularly, to ensure that these deadlines are adhered to.
- The annual performance review would be conducted for all associates who have completed at least three month's confirmed service with the company as on 31 March.
- Appraisers will be able to view appraisal templates for their team members who are eligible for this year's annual performance appraisal, with their review period start and end date.

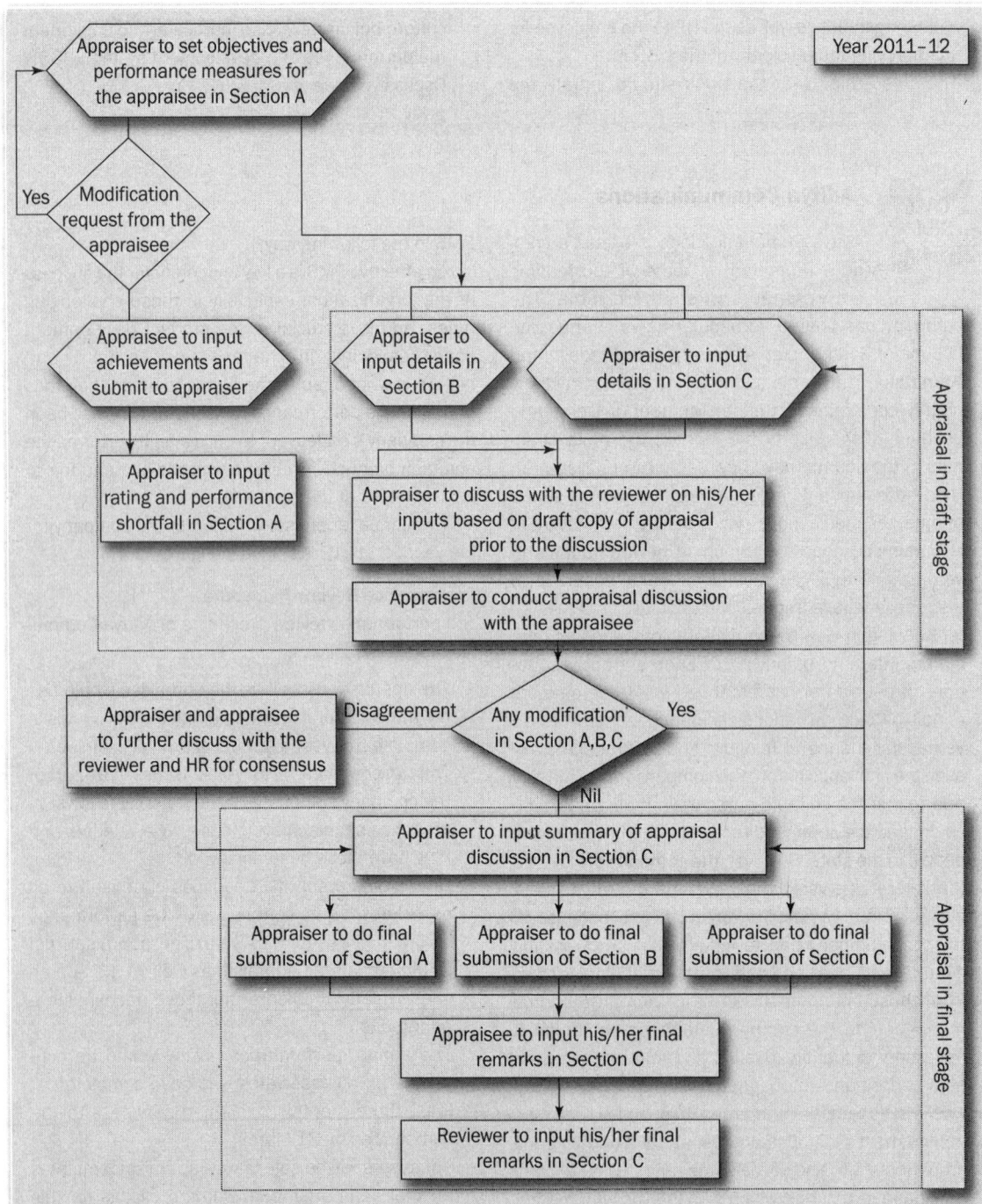

FIGURE 12.4 Annual workflow of the company (2011–12)

- First, the appraiser should complete the performance objectives and measures for the performance section in the objective setting part and submit it to the associate. The appraisee is required to fill in his/her achievements against the objectives.

- Once the associate submits his/her achievements, the appraiser would complete section A in full, and highlight reasons for performance shortfall and corrective action to be initiated by the appraisee.
- The appraiser needs to fill in the competency, summary, and the values and ethics section of the appraisal form in details, sharing relevant data in the required field.
- The appraiser can share a draft copy of the appraisal form with the appraisee via the tool either prior to the appraisal discussion, or at the time of the review discussion.
- The appraiser has to fix a date for the performance review meeting with the associate.
- If an associate has not been a part of a project/team for the entire review period, the appraiser needs to conduct the review jointly with his/her previous Manager/Project Leader. Alternatively, the appraiser should collect feedback/review from the Manager or Project leader on the associate's performance while he/she was in his/her project.
- The appraiser may modify his/her evaluation, if required, based on the appraisal discussion.
- The appraiser should complete the total performance review form in full after the appraisal discussion with the associate. Further, he/she should allow the associate to read the final form, get his/her consent via the tool, and record any comments connected with the review.
- The associate will also be able to view the final copy of his/her entire performance appraisal form via their login id.
- Any associate in the company in the job grade of associate consultant/project leader (equivalent designations) and above will be eligible to carry out the annual performance assessment. Due care should be taken to ensure that every appraiser is directly responsible for, in direct contact with, and aware of the work performed by the appraisee. Business unit heads would play the role of reviewers for appraisals completed by their direct subordinates.
- In cases where more than one assessor is required to assess the associate's work (transfer/different projects, etc.), it will be the responsibility of the current supervisor to contact the previous superior and to ensure that the overall evaluation takes into consideration all other assessments for the current performance year.
- The associate will be informed of his/her final rating in the revision letter.
- HR will maintain the performance review data in e-tools for future reference.

Questions

1. Critically evaluate the organizational culture vis-à-vis the performance management culture at Aditya Communications.
2. Critically examine the relative advantages vs. disadvantages of the performance management system at the company. Do you suggest any changes in the processes or procedures in the company?

Performance Appraisal System in the Cyprus Civil Service

CASE STUDY 4

Problems

The aims of the performance appraisal system currently being used in the civil service, as provided in the relevant regulations are as follows:

- to decide whether employees on probation should be permanent,
- to identify employees' readiness to be promoted to higher posts,
- to help employees develop their abilities, and
- to promote a better functioning and management of the civil service.

Unfortunately, there are no signs that the system is being used for the latter two [(c) and (d)] purposes, and if it is used, it is done very rarely and not systematically. Since, also, without exception, all the employees on probation are considered fit to become permanent, the system is, in practice, used for promotion purposes only. However, ironically, even for promotion purposes, the system is not effective at all, because of the widespread overestimation prevailing—97% of employees are appraised as having outstanding performance. As a result, outstanding and bad performers are equalized, and therefore, promotion is basically based on seniority alone, despite the fact that it should officially (according to public service law) be based on merit, qualification, and seniority.

The Public Administration and Personnel Department, which is the central government agency responsible for all HR matters in the whole public service, is, since a long time, examining ways to overcome or minimize this problem, and ultimately, boost the morale of the employees and the productivity of the public service.

This case study describes the problems of the appraisal system currently being used in the civil service, their significance to the performance of the public service, and possible ways to address the problem in the most efficient manner.

The problem described in the earlier paragraph and other problems of the system can be attributed to two main categories of reasons—those arising from the system itself, and those arising from the way it is implemented.

Problems arising from the system are as follows:

- Only one appraisal form is used for all civil servants, without taking into consideration the duties and responsibilities of each post.
- The evaluation scale of four ratings (outstanding, very satisfactory, satisfactory, and non-satisfactory) is inadequate to accurately measure employees' performance. These ratings have a reflection on 'personality' rather than performance—something which should be avoided.
- The description of duties on the appraisal form is completely inadequate.
- The criteria contained in the appraisal form are subject to different interpretation by appraisers.
- No common standards of appraising exist throughout the whole civil service.
- No appeal mechanism exists in case of disagreement between the appraiser and the appraisee.
- No provision for appraisal interviews exists for setting common targets to be attained by the employee during the next year.

Problems related to its implementation are as follows:

- Performance appraisal system is not considered as an ongoing yearly cycle process, but as a mecha-

nistic, once a year obligation (filling of a form).
- There is a lack of dialogue between the appraiser and the appraisee.
- Criteria are not used as they were supposed to be used, and there is a lack of specific objectives and agreed targets to be achieved, either at the departmental or the individual level.
- There is a lack of commitment from civil service managers and no initiative from the top to make the system work.
- The appraisers seem reluctant to fairly evaluate employees, so as to avoid negative reactions and conflicts.
- Employees themselves are not willing to accept 'criticism' and comparison with their colleagues.
- There is a perception, among some employees, that appraisers are unable to appraise in a fair manner.
- Both appraisers and appraisees are not trained to a satisfactory extent.
- External interference and influences exist in the system.
- The system is quite vulnerable to problems related to human nature, such as subjectivity, and to pressures related to family and other relationships.
- There is a tendency for appraisers to appraise in a more lenient manner, in cases where promotions are imminent.

Cyprus Public Service

It would be impossible for a performance appraisal system to operate in isolation. In order for such a system to serve its purpose, and to be an effective management tool, it must be designed bearing in mind the environment in which it operates, and in correlation with the organization's missions and strategies. It must also be closely linked to all other human resource management policies.

Some negative situational factors are as follows:

- The structure of the public service is basically bureaucratic, with a high degree of centralization, and inflexible organizational structures and procedures.
- Objectives and targets, both at the departmental and individual level, are either absent or vague.
- The current payment system in the civil service is a very competitive one and a vast difference exists

between the level of public service pay and that of private sector pay, especially with regard to the entry-level posts (pay in the private sector is lower than that in government). In addition, it does not contain any incentive elements; on the contrary, the majority of civil servants are entitled to uninterrupted salary acceleration irrespective of actual performance.

- The civil service is highly unionized, with one powerful union—Pancyprian Public Servants Trade Union (PASYDY).
- Cyprus is a small country; its citizens are inevitably close to each other and this may lead, to some extent, to a culture of favouritism.

Some promising changes in the recent years are as follows:

- Some years ago, the Council of Ministers approved a 'comprehensive plan for reforming the entire civil service', most of the provisions of which are at the implementation stage. The plan includes measures for controlling the size of the public service and improving its productivity. Among others, it provides for
- reforming the existing payment system, in order to make it more realistic, fair, and flexible,
- improving the public service performance appraisal system,
- restructuring departments and moving towards decentralization,
- improving the schemes of service (job descriptions) with a view to re-designing and enriching jobs and adhering to European Union requirements,
- enhancing mobility of staff within the civil service,
- improving the selection and recruitment procedures,
- simplifying procedures, and
- introducing new technology.
- The House of Parliament, political parties and the new government, elected in 2003, support the plan for reforming the civil service, and, especially, the introduction of a new performance appraisal system.
- The civil service trade union, PASYDY, seems to agree with the public service plan to improve the appraisal system.

Addressing the Problem

Early in the previous decade, it was made clear that the performance appraisal system was not succeeding in its goals; therefore, a decision had to be made to either partly change the current system, or introduce a new one. Because of the complexity of the subject and its importance with regards to the productivity of the civil service, it was decided to design and implement a new appraisal system.

To achieve that, first, it should be made clear what went wrong with the current system and how the mistakes of the past could be avoided. The meth-odology of redesigning a new system should involve

- collection of data from all interested parties (e.g., top-level management, PASYDY, political parties, etc.) via personal interviews and questionnaires, and
- careful examination of appraisal systems used in other countries, with a view to incorporating any useful elements into the new system, always taking into consideration the Cypriot civil service culture.

After a comprehensive evaluation of the data collected a suggestion should be prepared for a new appraisal system and presented to the decision makers to approve its implementation. Decision makers are— (a) the Minister of Finance who is responsible for the civil service HR matters, (b) the Council of Ministers, and (c) the House of Representatives. Top civil service managers (permanent secretaries of ministries and heads of departments) and PASYDY, the public service trade union, should be consulted, and they should agree on all the provisions of the proposed system.

The Public Administration and Personnel Department, in cooperation with a private consulting firm, conducted a survey and came up with a preliminary suggestion that includes, among others, the following:

- Separation of the appraisal process conducted for promotion purposes, from that conducted for development purposes, in an effort to eliminate the pressure, on behalf of appraisers, to overrate employees so that they will be promoted to the next level.
- Introduction of quota system in an effort to minimize the risk of appraising all employees as 'outstanding performers'.

- At this stage, the 'criteria' for appraisal should include competencies (performance indicators). Assessment on the basis of targets / objectives may be incorporated into the system at a later stage, when the necessary culture prevails.
- Detailed definitions of criteria for appraisal, taking into account the duties and responsibilities of each post, and setting up of departmental committees that will ensure homogeneous evaluation.
- Training of appraisers to equip them with the skills, knowledge, and especially, attitudes needed for effectively appraising employees.
- Incorporation of the 'appraisal interviews' into the system, so as to enhance communication between the appraiser and the appraisee.
- Introduction of the 'self-appraisal process' in an effort to foster critical self-examination of one's performance and areas that one needs to develop.

The next step/challenge is to finalize the suggestion for a new performance appraisal system. It should be done by taking into account the views of the Attorney General of the Republic regarding the legality of certain provisions, presenting it to the Council of Ministers and the rest of the decision makers, gaining the support of all influenced parties including trade unions, and then proceeding with its implementation.

Questions
1. Critically analyse the performance appraisal system of the civil service system in Cyprus.
2. Suggest methods for improving the use of the performance appraisal system for the two key factors—employee development and improving the functional efficiency of civil services in Cyprus.
3. Analyse the problems arising out of the implementation of the performance appraisal system and suggest methods to overcome them.
4. Do you think that designing a performance appraisal system in isolation, without addressing the negative situational factors, would lead to the desired results in this case? If not, suggest an action plan.

E-HRM

Objectives

After studying this chapter, you will be able to understand
- the current state of HRM in the information technology era
- the needs and various benefits of e-HRM practices
- the way organizations can manage employee details and assign jobs or assignments using e-HRM functions
- the e-HRM process levels

INTRODUCTION

The rapid developments in information and communication technology (ICT) have resulted in changes in the working pattern and processes in companies. This has led to greater adoption of Internet-based working processes and advanced versions of electronic technologies for generating fast and efficient outputs. Organizations are progressively incorporating new technologies such as web-based processes and information systems in their various functions. As human resources are one of the major assets of an organization, they need to be effectively managed. The human resource management (HRM) practices adopted by a firm play a vital role in acquiring sustainable competitive advantage and achieving success. HRM works as a catalyst that enhances and bridges the policies and practices of the company with its people. In today's competitive and dynamic environment, it is crucial for every organization to transform HRM practices into electronic HRM (e-HRM) for effective management of its people. This chapter aims to describe the new approaches of HRM in the ICT era and provide insights on the adoption of effective e-HRM and human resource information systems (HRIS).

DEFINITION

The term e-HRM refers to conducting HR activities using the Internet or the intranet. The origin of the term can be traced back to the mid-1990s. Initially, e-HRM was considered to be a sub-function of the overall computerized management information system (MIS). MIS was introduced in the 1980s when some HR functions were incorporated in HRIS. These functions were intended to support the planning, maintenance, administration, and control of HRM. The term e-HRM is also known with different names, such as web-based HRM, online HRM, digital HRM, computer-based HRIS, HR portals, and virtual HRM, according to the purpose.

■ ■ ■

E-HRM can be defined as the application of information technology for networking and supporting at least two individual or collective actors in their shared performing of HRM activities.

With increased use of information technology and systems, there is more pressure on organizations to enhance the productivity of each employee to ensure overall superior business performance. It is evident that HR functions are the main drivers for any change in the organization. Therefore, organizations have started use of integrated systems such as computer hardware and applications that can be used to gather, store, and analyse information regarding their human resources. The information may comprise the people, policies, procedures, and data required to manage the various HR functions aligned with the business strategy. This ICT-based HRM is termed as e-HRM, which is a more dynamic version of HRM. The functions of e-HRM, such as e-training and e-recruitment, are relatively similar to traditional HRM functions.

E-HRM is a web-based tool to automate and support HR processes. It can be defined as the application of information technology for networking and supporting at least two individual or collective actors in their shared performing of HRM activities (Strohmeier 2007). E-HRM can also be explained as a technology that serves both as a medium for connecting spatially segregated actors and as a tool for completing tasks. It supports actors by substituting for them in executing HRM activities to facilitate smooth decision-making. Thus, e-HRM results in administrative and operational efficiency, though this is not its primary purpose. E-HRM provides the way to implement HR strategies, policies, and practices in organizations through a conscious and directed support of and/or with the full use of web technology-based channels (Ruel, et al. 2004). Therefore, e-HRM is a platform that organizations use to represent and implement various HR functions with the use of desktop architecture, corporate intranet, and the Internet.

The purpose of adopting or implementing e-HRM differs according to the demands of the organization. Largely, four types of goals were identified for implementation of e-HRM technologies in organizations (Ruel, et al. 2004). These e-HRM goals are as follows:

- Reducing cost/improving efficiency
- Improving client service or facilitating management and employees
- Improving strategic orientation of HRM
- Allowing integration of HR functions (of different organizational units or an entire organization)

This overall process of e-HRM is described as 'an umbrella covering all possible integration mechanisms and contents between HRM and IT that aim at creating value within and across organizations for targeted employees and management' thereby suggesting the integration of the following four aspects (Bondarouk and Ruel 2009):

- *Content of e-HRM*: This focuses on the type of HR practices and IT used, and the best match between them.
- *Implementation of e-HRM*: This focuses on the process of adoption and appropriation of e-HRM by organizational members.
- *Targeted employees and managers*: This focuses on the specific stakeholder groups. As the modern HR function goes way beyond both the HR department and even the whole organization, any new approach needs to focus on the line management and employees actively involved in using e-HRM applications.

- *E-HRM consequence*: This focuses on a multilevel perspective that views e-HRM value creation, as subjectively realized by a target user who is the focus of value creation.

Advantages of E-HRM

Adoption and implementation of e-HRM systems provides several advantages such as the following:

- Organizations achieve better synergies such as faster results by integration of all the HRM functions under one software suite.
- Users get more independence in terms of accessing information and making modifications to their own data without the assistance of either the IT or HR professionals.
- Organizations are more administratively efficient in terms of maintaining employees' basic information, payroll and attendance management, and updating company related information such as disciplinary rules, health/safety guidelines, and welfare facilities. This efficiency helps organizations in controlling HR operational costs such as administrative and tangential costs.
- Allows organizations to align the HR processes to organizational goals, and retrieve the right information at the right time to facilitate strategic HR decisions. Having access to data of a large number of individuals at one place also enables HR planning and managerial decision-making to be based on factual information, rather than managerial perceptions or intuition.
- Ensures HR data transparency and visibility, which further promotes employee empowerment, improves employee satisfaction, and facilitates decisions on employability, retention, and employee work–life balance.
- The fast response time for processing each function facilitates better time management, improves employee communication, provides more accurate information, and ensures faster processing of information.
- Enhances organizational learning by providing a better platform for knowledge sharing. For example, if an employee received training from outside, then the knowledge acquired by the individual can be stored and transferred to others in the organization.
- Allows organizations to use spreadsheets to export compensation and benefit details for comparison with external survey figures. It also helps in managing the entire recruitment cycle.

■ ■ ■
Adoption and implementation of e-HRM systems provides several advantages to organizations.

- Enables an organization to perform position management by defining and recording the required skills, competencies, experience, and qualifications for various positions and jobs.
- Enables organizations to undertake career management functions relating to the competencies, assessments, suitability matching, graphical ranking, and succession planning

Functions of E-HRM

According to the primary focus of e-HRM, three distinct functions have been suggested: publishing of information, automation of transactions, and transformation of the HR function (Lengnick-Hall and Moritz 2003).

- *Publishing of information*: It involves one-way communication from the company to the employees or managers. In this form of e-HRM, the company uses the intranet as the primary information delivery medium.

- *Automation of transactions with integration of workflow*: In e-HRM, paperwork is replaced by electronic input. Intranets and extranets are used frequently with several different application programs.
- *Transformation of the HRM function*: E-HRM liberates the HR function from its operational focus and redirects it towards a strategic one. HRM takes up tasks such as partnering with the line, creating centres of expertise, service center administration, and aligning every function of HRM to the common goal.

COMPONENTS OF E-HRM

■ ■ ■
Early human resource information approaches in many organizations were limited to the basic functions of communication and static information retrieval.

In general, e-HRM is an extended form of HRIS. Basically, HRIS is a specialized HR software deployed for collecting, compiling, recording, maintaining, storing, analysing, retrieving, and disseminating HR-related information needed by the organization. HRIS is usually a part of the organization's larger MIS that integrates a variety of activities in a logical and meaningful way to accomplish the given objectives.

As discussed earlier, e-HRM is a way of implementing HR strategies, policies, and practices in organizations through a conscious and directed support of and/or with the full use of web-based channels (Ruel, et al. 2004). The systems identified in this definition of e-HRM rely on advances enabled by HRIS. Early human resource information approaches in many organizations were limited to the basic functions of communication and static information retrieval. With the development of e-HRM, organizations have incorporated more strategic and long-term HR planning issues, and integrated related information into transactional and management information decision-making processes.

Broadly, basic components of e-HRM and traditional HRM are relatively similar. In e-HRM, the basic functions of HRM are linked with web-based technology and terminology such as e-recruitment, e-career management, e-training and e-development, e-performance management, and e-compensation. The advanced tools used for e-HRM differentiate it from the traditional HRM, and can be explained through three generations of e-HRM (Evans, Pucik, and Barsoux 2002). Major components of the e-HRM system can be better understood through these generations, which are discussed as follows:

First Generation of E-HRM

It involves initial attempts to exploit e-HRM. These attempts are predominantly transactional, using intranet or electronic means to speed up service delivery or to reduce costs. Examples include payroll processing and providing training-related information so that people can satisfy their skill development needs on a real-time basis. The first generation of e-HRM covers the following aspects:

Self-service human resources (SSHR) The SSHR system allows employees to input and update personal data, manage benefit packages, view compensation information, sign up for training programmes, and review internal job postings. This function explains how to organize employees while describing how employer can manage employment information, assignments, employee details, employee development, and track employees' roles and activities. This application includes fundamental information such as: (a) Operation basics—payrolls with calendars, pay periods, currencies, and methods of payment; (b) Organizational structure—internal organizations such as companies, divisions, departments, work groups, production team and hierarchies, grade and grade scale structure; (c) Employees' essential personal information, their current work status (actively assigned, on maternity leave, terminated, assigned to an internal organization, etc.), grade, job and position, and pay details.

E-recruitment The e-recruitment system is a subset of e-HRM, designed to automate the recruitment process. This system comprises several sequential activities of recruitment such as posting jobs on the intranet or the Internet, providing the facility to applicants to give their own details and apply for a job, processing the application pool, maintaining the online CV database, sending invitation for interviews, and making the final selection.

E-recruitment originated in the form of independent job sites called bulletin board systems in the 1980s. Organizations are now aggressively seeking the best talent worldwide. E-recruiting enables organizations to discover talent beyond their own national boundaries. E-recruitment systems broadly cover two functions, namely, applicant tracking and hiring management. The applicant tracking system tracks the demographics of applicants and selects potential recruits according to a predefined criterion of skills and qualifications, whereas hiring management systems use job boards and corporate websites to select the most compatible recruit for a specified job.

Technological advances and the rise in e-recruitment activities have also affected the ease with which applicants can acquire information about an organization through websites, weblogs, and other news media to make proper judgments about an organization before even having direct contact with an organizational representative. Advancements in technology have also enabled employers to utilize computers to administer online employee selection tests, which result in lower costs, increased efficiency, and fewer transcription errors.

The e-recruitment system provides several advantages to organizations such as quick response time, faster communication, wide range of applicants, worldwide accessibility, and lower cost per hire. For example, Nike was able to reduce the average time to fill job positions from 62 to 42 days and the recruitment costs by 54% through e-recruitment. E-recruitment allows applicants the luxury of accessing jobs online, at their own convenience, 24 hours 7 days a week. It provides the comfort of scrutinizing jobs without physically going through the stress of an interview. Finally, it allows applicants to gain an understanding of the organization and its culture before joining.

> ■ ■ ■
> E-recruitment originated in the form of independent job sites called bulletin board systems in the 1980s.

Second Generation of E-HRM

It involves qualitative changes and improvements in the way HRM services are offered. For example, when 360 degree feedback is performed online, new possibilities for multiple appraisals open up. Such tools allow one to undertake functions such as benchmarking the functional competencies of the firm that were not feasible previously.

E-performance management Performance appraisals have become an integral part of organizations' HRM approaches. They provide managers with a process for evaluating, motivating, and managing performance outcomes at one or multiple levels (individual, group, and organizational). The evolution of this approach has been driven by developments within organizations to use performance management to accomplish goals and the adoption of new technologies, which provide additional capability to monitor and track performance at all levels.

> Electronic performance monitoring (EPM) refers to the monitoring of employees in the workplace using technologically mediated systems and devices.

Electronic performance monitoring (EPM) refers to the monitoring of employees in the workplace using technologically mediated systems and devices, and involves the tracking of many aspects of an employee's job through telephone calls, performance metrics, screen sharing capability and navigation, video camera observation, and data entry components. The introduction of EPM has resulted in the shift from occasional to constant monitoring. Prior to EPM, employees were usually monitored through document review and observation. These methods provided employees with some type of control over the monitoring process. The development of web-based technologies has enabled organizations to have an always-on approach to monitoring with access to information in real-time or through electronic retrieval through EPM. These electronic sources provide vast amounts of information to review employees in areas such as attendance, work time, accuracy, quality, interactions with customers, and so on.

E-compensation and reward management   Traditionally, organizations of any size or activity focused only on automation of payroll and benefits administration and these IT managed services were not meant for overall compensation and reward management.

Compensation systems are integrated with some other HR or non-HR systems within the organization. For example, a compensation professional needs to track up-to-date employee attendance information or performance review to make corresponding changes in the compensation. The web-based software helps in streamlining all aspects of compensation planning and implementation such as online job analysis to identify pay differences, job evaluation, salary budgets, compare budgeted against actual spends, review and approve, data export to payroll, and communicate flexible benefits and health policies. For example, PeopleSoft ERP package supports budgeting and salary planning by groups and allows multiple budgets. The system includes employee review functions to accommodate the needs of employee participation in the planning process. In addition, its stock administration module allows employees to view their personal stock option information online, model future stock earnings, check vesting periods, and exercise options. Similarly, compensation applications in My SAP HR allows managers to design and implement innovative reward plans including performance-based pay, competency-based pay, and various short-term and long-term incentives.

E-training and e-learning   Effective training is one of the crucial functions of HRM in the present fast-paced business era. Since the 1990s, corporate learning has moved online. This has resulted in flexibility, just-in-time learning, and cost savings in delivering training. Online instruction and corporate training for employees is more convenient and facilitates training anywhere, any time. Due to this, e-learning has reached a high level of (technical) sophistication, both in terms of instructional development and the effective management of resources in companies with high performance learning function (ASTD 2006).

The growth of the Internet, company-wide intranet through the world wide web (WWW), and technological advancements have increased the demand for virtual connectedness to make the most of the intellectual capital of the organization and to provide online instructions to the employees. This has provided further impetus to the concepts of e-training and e-learning, which are more cost effective. The integrated approach of e-learning is aimed at incorporating all

> ■ ■ ■
> The integrated approach of e-learning is aimed at incorporating all learning activities and deliver training through web-based course material.

learning activities and deliver training through web-based course materials or activities to engage learners either alone or in groups. These learning groups/individuals could be geographically dispersed, while engaging or participating in such a kind of system.

An e-learning system has two-fold approach. First, organizations are able to create manageable learning programmes to introduce new employees to the business environment and augment learning based on their performance. Secondly, this system helps in synthesizing the employee's performance electronically to identify and isolate training needs. Further, e-learning modules are automatically forwarded to the employee to receive additional training in the area to assist with on-the-job performance development. In this way, if it is applied in the right circumstances, such as self-paced competency development, e-learning can serve as an effective element of the training programme.

Third Generation of E-HRM

It involves the use of technology to do things that could not be done before. An example would be the possibility to measure, on a regular basis, the energy that people put into their work.

E-coaching   Effective managers tend to have good coaching and mentoring skills as they try to bring out the best from their employees. Through coaching and mentoring, managers educate, guide, counsel, and train their subordinates to enable them to perform effectively and groom them for future growth as well. Similar to the traditional mentoring system, e-coaching is the mentoring and supervision of employees by managers or supervisors with the use of web-enabled programmes and devices. Web-enabled systems facilitate easier access to employee information enabling supervisors to provide instant feedback to employees. This ability to provide feedback at the time of the action or behaviour enables the development of employees within the role. E-coaching is primarily focused on the performance management metrics for individual, group, and organizational levels. For example, a supervisor can use various types of web-enabled applications to set thresholds and triggers to highlight abnormalities in employee performance. The supervisor can create automatic responses to employees' signalling the required change or congratulatory message, or engage in online chat to fully explore the issue and work with the employee. Similarly, employees in some operations may have the ability to click a button to connect with a supervisor directly to work through an issue or emergency.

E-competency management   E-competency management is one of the greatest challenges in an Internet economy in terms of retaining and developing valuable assets of the organization with the use of advanced technology. Consequently, competency management (CM) automation practices is becoming the most valuable approach within the e-HRM domain to manage this new business scenario, in which a very high percentage of the total workforce is comprised of indispensible talent and knowledge workers. Organizations gain real advantages by using the Internet for the measurement and management of their talent needs and the human capital. According to recent studies, a comprehensive competency management software product incorporates functionality to address four macro phases. The first phase involves competency mapping aimed at defining required competencies to satisfy the objectives. The second phase focuses on competency diagnosis to obtain the current status and assesses gap analysis between the current and required levels of competencies. The third phase deals with competency development through e-learning initiatives and finally, the fourth phase focuses on continuous monitoring of competencies. Thus, competency management can be defined as a comprehensive HR management process that starts by defining the required organizational competencies, assigns them to employees, observes them through behaviour, assesses them according to the organization's defined values, and causes improvement. Oracle HRMS application provides the feature for *Competence Validation and Driving Alerts*, where Oracle Alert's automatic mail notification keeps an employer informed about when an employee's competencies need certification and renewal. It compares the renewal period date with the date on the person's competence profile, or the last training class.

SUMMARY

Technology and innovation are increasingly becoming critical for success of organizations. The benefits of IT extend far beyond productivity; the emergence of tools based on the new information and communication technologies (ICTs) also affects the working methods of businesses. As a consequence, numerous changes are taking place within the organizational context. This chapter discusses the basics of e-HRM and highlights its benefits. E-HRM involves use of web-based technology to manage people, perform HR functions (e.g., e-recruitment, e-selection, etc.), and deliver e-services to employees (e.g., employee self-service, e-learning, etc.).

The view of e-HRM outlined in this chapter provides a foundation for understanding the needs and importance of e-HRM in the present era. This chapter describes the functions and generations of e-HRM. The various generations define the level of implementation of e-HRM processes in organizations, and provide a description of HR functions through the use of web-based technology. The chapter explains some of the key ways in which HRM can enhance the development, implementation, and success of new technologies. It also discusses the ways in which HRM can enhance its own value through the use of new technologies.

KEY TERMS

Competency management A comprehensive HR management process that starts by defining the required organizational competencies, assigns them to employees, observes them through behaviour, assesses them according to the organization's defined values, and causes improvement. In other words, competency management is a set of competencies to manage HR in a way that performance contributes effectively and efficiently to organizational results.

Employee self-service Enables employees to view the company and personal information. They can change individual information, put in employment-related enquiries, manage benefit packages, view compensation information, apply for new jobs internally, or apply certain requests online for manager approval (e.g., holidays)

E-coaching The mentoring and supervision of employees by supervisors with the use of web-enabled programs and devices

E-HRM Application of the Internet and intranet along with other technologies for implementing HR strategies, policies, and practices, and supporting at least two individual or collective actors in their shared performing of HR activities

E-learning The use of web-enabled programs/devices to deliver training programmes and modules to employees

E-recruitment The complete automation of the recruitment process that consists of applications for employee selection, recruitment, and hiring functions. E-recruitment systems can be two-fold, namely, applicant tracking and hiring management.

E-training Training delivered through the electronic means in the form of web-based training programmes and activities

Functions of e-HRM Publishing of information, automation of transactions, and transformation of the HRM function

Generations of e-HRM The first involves speeding up and reducing costs of traditional HRM functions, the second involves qualitative changes and improvements, and the third allows one to do things that could not be done before

■ ■ ■ | EXERCISES

Multiple Choice Questions

1. Monitoring employees in the workplace using technologically mediated systems refers to
   - (a) e-recruitment
   - (b) electronic performance monitoring
   - (c) HRM
   - (d) MBO
2. Basic components of e-HRM and traditional HRM are relatively
   - (a) different
   - (b) uncorrelated
   - (c) similar
   - (d) none of these
3. Which of the following is not a part of comprehensive competency management software product?
   - (a) Competency mapping
   - (b) Competency diagnosis
   - (c) Competency development
   - (d) Competency matching
4. E-learning has reached a high level of technical sophistication, in terms of effective management and
   - (a) performance appraisal
   - (b) faster communication
   - (c) instructional development
   - (d) electronic performance monitoring
5. Applicants enjoy the luxury of accessing jobs online at their own convenience through
   - (a) online recruitment
   - (b) e-HRM
   - (c) a visit to a company
   - (d) e-coaching

Fill in the Blanks

1. The e-recruitment system is designed to _____ the recruitment process.
2. E-coaching is focused on the _____ for individual, group, and organizational levels.
3. E-learning is an effective element of a _____ programme.
4. E-HRM provides intangible benefits because of HR data _____ and visibility.
5. _____ automation practices have become the most valuable approach within the e-HRM domain to manage new business scenario

Concept Review Questions

1. Explain the benefits of the e-HRM system with appropriate examples.
2. Explain the term e-HRM. What are the major goals of e-HRM?
3. Describe the four integrated goals of e-HRM.
4. What are major functions of e-HRM?
5. Explain the first generation e-HRM practices.
6. What are the second generation e-HRM practices?
7. Explain the significance of the first, second, and third generations of e-HRM.
8. Distinguish between second and third generations of e-HRM practices.
9. Explain the extent to which planned use of web-tools for HRM functions enable organizations by using information collected through the Internet.

Project Work

Working individually or in groups, compare the features of e-HR practices of 2–3 organizations by using information collected through the Internet. Analyse to what extent web-based HR practices help organizations to achieve competitive advantage.

■ ■ ■ | REFERENCES

Bondarouk, T.V. and Ruel, H.J.M. 2009, 'Electronic HRM: Challenges in the digital era', *The International Journal of HRM*, 20(3), pp. 505–14.

Galanaki, E. and Panayotopoulu, L. 2009, 'Adoption and success of e-HRM in European firm'. In Teresa Torres-Coronas and Mario Arias-Oliva (Eds), *Encyclopedia of HRIS: Challenges in e-HRM*. Information Science Reference, New York.

Lengnick-Hall, M.L., and S. Moritz (2003), The impact of e-HR on the human resource management function, *Journal of Labour Research*, 24 (3), pp. 365–379.

Rivera, R.J., and Paradise, A. (2006), *State of the Industry in Leading Enterprises*, American Society for Training and Development (ASTD).

Ruel, H., Bondarouk, T., and Looise, J. 2004, 'E-HRM innovation or irritation: An explorative empirical study in five large companies on web-based HRM', *Management Review*, 15, pp. 364–80.

Strohmeier, S. 2007, 'Research in e-HRM: Review and implication'. *Human Resource Management Review*, 17, pp. 19–37.

http://my.safaribooksonline.com/book/hr-organizational-management/9781599048833/a-research-classification-for-hr-intranets/193#X2ludGVybmFsX0ZsYXNoUmVhZGVyP3htbGlkPTk3ODE1OTkwNDg4MzMvMTkz, accessed on 2 March 2012.

HRIS in Mobitel Pvt. Ltd

CASE STUDY

Mobitel Pvt. Limited was started by a first generation entrepreneur for developing Mobiphone (landline phones) in competition to the public sector enterprises. However, the real leap in business came with the roll-out of cellular phone licenses by the Government of India. With the vision to be the leader in cellular business, the organization launched 'Mobitel' across the country. The company soon captured the leadership position in all 21 circles, where it was conducting operations.

The employee headcount grew from the initial 1,000 employees to 25,000 employees across the circles. It consisted of both the employees on the rolls of Mobitel and those outsourced from its vendors.

During the years 2004–06, the company witnessed a decline in the growth rates. During a business review meeting, the chief executive officer (CEO) queried the regional circle heads on the reasons for the slowdown. They indicated the following reasons:

- The performance of individual employees could not be captured accurately and reviewed periodically
- They faced challenges in employee development and job-rotation as timely HR information was not available to them
- The outsourced employees are unable to connect with the company, and the organization is witnessing attrition among the outsourced employees leading the sales effort.
- The incentive and rewards could not be designed and administered due to lack of people and performance information flow

The CEO constituted an HR review committee under the chairmanship of Senior Vice-President–HR to look in to all the issues and find solutions.

The committee, after detailed deliberations, identified that HRIS is the crux of the issue and came out with an action plan.

The company decided to roll out an integrated HRIS system to attain the following objectives:

- To have integrated database
- To provide accurate and real-time information
- To support the management information (MI) querying capability
- To integrate the performance capturing and review module built into it
- To capture the training and developmental aspects in it
- To support in administering and reviewing the rewards and incentive programmes
- To create a subsidiary (Mobi Comtel) to employ all the outsourced employees

The CEO reviewed the recommendations and approved them. The company decided to go ahead with Oracle HRMS, also used for other functional requirements (e.g., finance, supply chain management, etc.), as the vendor agreed to customize the system for all company requirements.

Questions

1. Do you think that the committee was correct in its recommendations?
2. Do you foresee any problems in the implementation of the recommendations?
3. Justify if the recommended solution will help the company overcome the business challenges.

Employee Motivation, Incentive Plans, and Fringe Benefits

INTRODUCTION

Why does a scientist spend long hours at work in the laboratory, foregoing other activities and pleasures? Why does an athlete endure months of painful training in preparation for the Olympics? Why does one person devote all efforts to amassing a fortune, and another to working with impoverished people in a remote area? The answer is simple. In all these examples, individuals are motivated by an inner urge or desire to perform and excel. The external behaviour is only a manifestation of deep inner desires. Often, these desires do not have a biological basis, but are psychological in origin. Since individuals differ in their inner desires, there is a difference not only in the nature and variety of the tasks they undertake, but also in their levels of performance.

Performance, output, and productivity form the backbone of organizations. High performance, high commitment, and loyalty are the primary expectations of organizations. Individuals enter organization with some needs, aspirations, and expectations about work life. Organizations, on the other hand, focus on productivity, commitment, and loyalty.

Individual performance is a function of the product of ability and motivation, which may be presented as

Performance = f(ability × motivation)

Ability here may be interpreted as competence, skill, or knowledge. The interaction of the basic abilities with motivation leads to performance. If that is so, why does the same individual have fluctuations in his or her performance graph? Why do, employees with the same competencies or abilities, other factors being constant, differ remarkably in their performance levels. One of the fundamental challenges being faced by today's organizations is to sustain the motivational levels of their employees. There is a paradigm shift in the nature of

High performance, high commitment, and loyalty are the primary expectations of organizations.

> ■ ■ ■
> Individual performance is a function of the product of ability and motivation.

functioning of today's organizations with delayering, downsizing, cultural diversity, job hopping, and increased focus on individual competencies. However, the bottom line, that is, employee performance, still remains. Hence, in this chapter, we will make an attempt to understand the basic nature of the motivational process and its implications in an organizational setting.

Motivation in an individual may be considered to be the result of an intrinsic or extrinsic factor. When individuals are self-motivated, the rewards that they may experience are also more or less personal and abstract in nature. It may take the form of satisfaction, commitment, enthusiasm, or loyalty in different degrees. In the absence of this, organizations may resort to various techniques to create or sustain the motivation of the employees. It is here that the role of management in extrinsic rewards comes into play, and the rewards system becomes critical to employee performance and organizational success. The organizations may have the latest technology, well thought-out strategic plans, detailed job descriptions, and comprehensive training programmes, but unless the staff are rewarded for their performance-related behaviours, the entire effort may be meaningless. The challenge for the management is to understand the behavioural reality, eliminate the undesirable influences, and reward the desirable behaviour more effectively. Thus, the organizational reward system becomes the key, often overlooked factor in bringing about improved performance and success.

As organizations are becoming leaner and attaining a global status, money is definitely playing an important role. However, non-financial rewards are playing an even more important role in motivating employees. According to recent surveys, employees placed far more value on non-financial rewards than on financial ones. In a study of 1,500 employees, it was found that instant recognition from managers was the most valued reward. In another study, the major reason cited for leaving the organization was the lack of praise and recognition from managers. In other words, there is little doubt that non-financial factors can be very powerful, but as a reward technique to manage behaviour and improve performance, these are often overlooked.

In this background, we will analyse the basic motivational processes that form the backbone of performance, and also the operation of various needs responsible for performance. Hence, we first examine the theories that explain the motivational processes, and later see their applications in the organizational setting. When we talk about the applications of motivational theories in an organizational setting, we refer to the efforts made by the management to motivate the employees by structuring and designing the nature of the work. This involves goal setting, management by objectives, etc. Apart from this, efforts made by organizations by providing various types of incentives are also discussed in this chapter.

BASIC MOTIVATIONAL PROCESS

Motivation is a basic psychological process. Few would deny that it is the most important factor in the context of organizational behaviour. It is one of those aspects which gives us more insights into the 'why' of behaviour. It is also closely related to other cognitive aspects, such as perception, learning, and attitudes. Nevertheless, like other aspects of personality, motivation is an inferred hypothetical process. The word 'process' implies that it is based on experience. It is personal and subjective. The impact of motivation on the workforce can be observed only from their

> Motivation is defined as an innate need or desire with a physiological or psychological basis that propels an individual to undertake an activity to satisfy the need or desire.

performance or behaviour. In fact, while recognizing the central role of motivation, many of today's organizational behaviour theorists think it is important for the field to re-emphasize behaviour.

The word motivation is derived from the Latin word *mover*, which means 'to move'. That which propels the organism to undertake an activity is motivation. It is normally experienced in the form of a wish, want, desire, need, or motive. Hence, motivation may be defined as an innate need or desire with a physiological or psychological basis that propels the organism to undertake an activity to realize the goal and satisfy the need. There are three steps involved in the motivational process (Figure 14.1).

Step 1   The first step is an awareness on the part of the individual that a need is operating, or the deficiency of which is being experienced. For example, a need that has a physiological basis may be identified as hunger or thirst. Similarly, a psychological desire may be identified when the individual is striving hard to acquire wealth. Here, we may make a distinction between need and motive. If we relate need to a deficiency which has a physiological basis and other desires stemming from mental processes to motives, things may become clearer. In that sense, hunger and thirst are considered as needs, and other desires such as achievement, power, and affiliation are considered as motives.

Step 2   Once the organism is aware of the deficiencies, be they physiological or mental in origin, the next step involves searching for or identifying mechanisms to satisfy the need. A hungry person going towards the refrigerator in search of food or a thirsty person moving towards a water dispenser are examples of drive. Similarly, another individual who has set his eyes on a promotion and is working hard and trying to meet the targets on time is again an example of drive. Hence, drive may be interpreted as an action-related sequence of behaviours undertaken by the organism to satisfy a need. We may also observe a linear relationship between need and drive. Greater the intensity or strength of the need, the more purposeful and goal-directed the actions become. This aspect is important as it helps us to understand the work-related behaviours of employees in organizations.

Step 3   The drive mechanism (Figure 14.1) undertaken by the organism results in goal attainment or need satisfaction. In other words, the action sequences undertaken by the individual have proved to be successful. Continuing with the previous example, the individual found food in the refrigerator and the employee who worked hard got a promotion.

It may also be said that complex physiological systems determine the conditions under which a need for food or water exists, resulting in the organisms becoming predisposed to eat or drink, or to engage in behaviours that have, in the past, led them to food or water. When sufficient food and water have been ingested, the system detects this fact and the organism is no longer predisposed to eat or drink.

Basically, these physiological systems are designed to maintain a steady state in one's body. As such, they are said to act according to the principle of homeostasis.

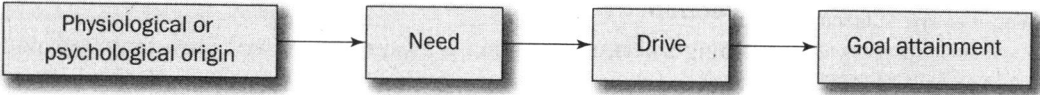

FIGURE 14.1   Drive mechanism

The physiological systems underlying our biological needs appear to operate in a similar fashion. We have sensors that detect when we need food and water. When the need reaches a critical level, we become motivated to act in ways designed to obtain and ingest food and water. When we eat or drink, the system senses that the need is reduced, and modifies our behaviour so that we stop eating or drinking at the appropriate time. Besides these, other social and cultural influences also determine how we eat and how much we consume, and also the appropriate time of eating or drinking.

However, not in all instances will the drive mechanisms result in goal attainment. In the previous example, for instance, the individual may not find food in the refrigerator and the employee may not get a promotion. In such a case, it would naturally result in some frustration in the individual. There would be some amount of tension and anxiety as a result of disappointment. How does an individual cope with such anxieties or frustrations? Freud (1958) explained how individuals resort to various coping mechanisms while dealing with frustrations. People use defence mechanisms to reduce their anxiety and guilt. According to Freud, the basic needs are instinctual in nature, and the persistence of unsatisfied demands results in a state of anxiety, to cope with which a person builds up defences. Freud described several defence mechanisms by which the ego disguises, redirects, hides, and otherwise copes with basic demands.

Even though opinions differ among theorists regarding the origin of these feelings and anxieties, many do agree that these mechanisms account for some of the ways in which people cope with their problems. Thus, defence mechanisms are generally accepted as a useful way of looking at how people handle stressful situations and conflicts. The following are some of the defence mechanisms.

Repression

In Freud's theory, repression is the fundamental technique people use to reduce anxiety. Repression is a mental process by which a person pushes down the information of the anxiety-arousing situation into the unconscious mind or simply tries to forget it. For instance, a student insulted by his/her teacher may deliberately and consciously try not to think about it, may not discuss it with his/her friends, and also avoid any thoughts about the incident. However, the memories are still alive and strong and seek expression, and sometimes emerge in the form of slips of the tongue or neurotic symptoms.

Reaction Formation

Reversal of motives is another method by which people attempt to cope with conflict. A motive that would arouse unbearable anxiety if it were recognized is converted into its opposite. A boy who has been conditioned to believe that smoking or alcoholism is a taboo might join a camp against alcoholism or smoking to ward off the urge to smoke or drink. The implicit principle seems to be that the best defence is a good offence. Thus disguised, the unwanted motives can be controlled.

■ ■ ■
Repression is a mental process by which a person pushes down the information of the anxiety-arousing situation into the unconscious mind or simply tries to forget it.

Projection

Blaming others, or projection, is a way of coping with one's unwanted motives by shifting them onto someone else. The anxiety arising from this may be lessened and the problem dealt with as though it were in the external world.

People with this tendency may project their own unacceptable hostile feelings about others onto a whole system of thinking in which they feel that others are out to get them. For example, an insecure student may have a strong desire to cheat in an examination, but his conscience will not allow him even to consider such a thing. He may begin to suspect that other students are cheating, while in reality they are not.

Rationalization

This defence mechanism substitutes an acceptable conscious motive for an unacceptable, unconscious one. Aesop's fable of the fox and the sour grapes is another example of rationalization. Something we cannot get becomes something we did not want any way. It is a common mechanism we use to boost our self-esteem.

Intellectualization

Closely related to rationalization, intellectualization involves reasoning. Here, however, the intensity of the anxiety is reduced by addressing or sharing the experience from a third-person perspective. For example, a nurse may describe in an intellectual fashion an encounter with a dying or injured patient.

Displacement

In displacement, the motive remains unaltered, but the person substitutes a different goal object for the original one. For example, a person who is angry with his boss, but cannot show it for fear of being fired may go home and scold the children or the watchman. Thus, by displacing aggression, the individual finds a substitute outlet.

Regression

In the face of a threat, one may retreat to an earlier pattern of adaptation, possibly a childish or primitive one. This is called regression. During stress-producing situations, an adult may revert to childish episodes of exaggerated dependency. Such behaviour may ward off anxiety by focusing attention on earlier ways of achieving tranquility.

Most of us will recognize in ourselves a few of the aforementioned coping patterns. We use them from time to time and when they are used sparingly and without harming others, they are nothing to worry about. However, if a person comes to depend on them excessively, then the patterns may be harmful. We must remember that they do not solve problems, but only relieve anxiety. The more conscious we are of our use of these mechanisms, the more rationally we can come to terms with our behaviour.

■ ■ ■
During stress-producing situations, an adult may revert to childish episodes of exaggerated dependency.

Nature of Work and Work Motivation

It is an accepted fact that human beings spend two-thirds of their lives doing some work or the other. To work is an innate need, an inborn propensity, or characteristic of human beings. Apparently, activity is carried out for achieving satisfaction. Human beings invest large portions of their energies to alter the existing state or add an extra dimension to their personalities. When viewed form this perspective, work has different meanings at different age levels. During infancy, work is understood as play. During childhood and adolescence, work may be interpreted as orientation

> **■ ■ ■**
> Human beings invest large portions of their energies to alter the existing state or add an extra dimension to their personalities.

to studies, planning, and thinking of a career or vocation, etc. During young adulthood and adulthood stages, work means the job that an individual does.

Activity begins very early, even before birth, and continues until one's death. (Activity is not only an important aspect of life, but it is essential for growth and health.) There is a fundamental need for activity—it is through activity that every form of life adjusts itself to its environment. Sometimes, activity is engaged in for its own sake, sometimes it is reflexive, and often it is purposive in that it is engaged in with an end, object, or purpose in view. Purposive activities are termed as work.

To describe work in terms of the science of man, the elements of responsiveness, purpose, adjustment, habit, interest, motive, drive, intelligence, aptitude, self-direction, and adaptive behaviour along with minor complexities must be introduced (Cleeton 1949).

The economic purposes of work are obvious and require little comment. Work is the means by which we provide the goods and services needed and desired by ourselves and our society. Work also serves a number of other social purposes. The workplace has always been a place to meet people, converse, and form friendships. The type of work has always conferred a social status on the worker and the worker's family. However, far less attention has been paid to the personal meaning of work, in spite of the fact that research has indicated that work plays a crucial and perhaps unparalleled psychological role in the formation of self-esteem, identity, and a sense of order (Organ 1978).

The various functions served by work have been summarized by Sofer (1970) as follows:

- Work is instrumental for survival.
- Work roles contribute to personal identity.
- Work roles provide opportunities for interaction with others.
- Having a work role enables an individual to sustain status and self-respect.
- Work roles provide scope for personal achievement, meeting, and surpassing objectives recognized by others as valuable or praiseworthy.
- Work provides for assuring oneself of one's capacity to deal effectively with one's environment and developing that capacity.
- Work provides the individual with opportunities to relate himself to society, and to contribute to society by providing needed goods and services.

It is then obvious that work serves many purposes. When the scientist asks why a phenomenon occurs, he typically means, under what conditions it occurs. Similarly, when we ask why people work, we mean under what conditions they work. There are two types of conditions that affect the likelihood that people will work. One is economic in nature. In order for people to work there must be an opportunity to work. There must be a demand on the part of the members of a society for goods and services and one on the part of the employers for people to produce these goods and

> **■ ■ ■**
> There are two types of conditions that affect the likelihood that people will work: economic and motivational.

perform these services. The second type of condition is motivational. People must prefer working to not working. We may say that people prefer to work when the outcomes they expect to attain from working are more positive than that they expect to attain from not working.

These two types of conditions—economic and motivational—may vary independently from one another. There may be a larger number of job vacancies than there are people seeking work, or there may be a larger number of people who prefer to work than there are job vacancies. Both sets of conditions must exist to the same degree in order that there can be full employment.

It is the motivational aspect of this problem that is of interest here. Work has been the chief means through which human beings have conquered an indifferent and inimical environment, but it has always had its dark sides as well. Various theorists have given their comments about the pervasive nature of work.

Freud's (1956) remarks on work are scattered very sparsely through his writings. On the one hand, he argues that work is one of the two great spheres of human activity, without which human society cannot be understood. For Freud, work involves a renunciation of instincts, entails giving up the pleasures of childhood, and means a life ruled by the reality principle rather than the pleasure principle.

The emphasis many neo-Freudians place on ego development and the process of adaptation has turned the attention to somewhat different problems than those which preoccupied the classical Freudians. Erikson (1959), for example, holds that later important stages of development are crucial for personality development. It is of particular interest to note here that, according to Erikson, one of the crucial later stages is the industry stage, in which the young person first begins to develop his or her attitude towards work and achievement. Freud seems to imply that attitudes towards work and important persons encountered while working are substantially determined by the events of early childhood. The manner in which the person works out his or her relationship with the nuclear parents during the early childhood stages is necessary, but not sufficient to account for adaptation to the demands of work.

Lantos (1943) has written two papers specifically on work. In the earliest paper, she begins her observations on the dynamics of work by commenting on the play of children. She speculates that children's play involves two distinct kinds of pleasure: (a) pleasure in the function itself and (b) pleasure in achievement. Like Erikson, Lantos feels that the transition from pleasure in activity to pleasure in achievement takes place during the latency period. Finally, Lantos asks why feelings of independence, freedom, and security are pleasurable, and points to their connection, in most people, with the ability to guarantee one's existence by one's own achievements.

By and large, the earlier psychological studies of human work have tended to take for granted that human beings can work, and have focused their attention on the detection, measurement, and description of individual differences in occupational behaviour. However, the later psychologists have considered the environment as an important dimension in the development of work motivation. The environment is interpreted in terms of opportunities, encouragement, peer relationships, etc.

> ■ ■ ■
> Later psychologists have considered the environment as an important dimension in the development of work motivation.

The psychological theorists have made another interesting point. Since each individual varies in his/her aptitude, skill, and interests, he or she responds differently to the environment. In other words, the work environment has considerable influence on the work motivation of the individual. Beginning with the classical principle, later, the neo-classical and, at present, the modern organizational theorists have always tried to study the discrepancies between work and personality.

Interest in people at work was awakened by F.W. Taylor in 1900. He was the first to call attention to people in the work situation as important factors in the quest for efficiency in production. He is often called the father of scientific management. In the 1920s and 1930s, the famous Hawthorne experiments conducted by Mayo and Roethlisberger demonstrated the influence of and role played by the work environment and informal groups in determining productivity and performance in the organization.

Following the Hawthorne experiments, McGregor propounded his theory X and theory Y. Theory X assumes that work is inherently distasteful to most people. People have to be directed and coerced to achieve organizational objectives. They have little creativity and lack responsibility. On the other hand, theory Y states that work is as natural as play, and self-control is indispensable in achieving organizational goals. People can be self-directed and creative at work, if properly motivated. Today, we emphasize management by objectives, management by integration and self-control, supportive management, decentralization, job enrichment, etc. The techniques are applicable in organizations where self-motivated, self-contented, mature, and responsible people work. McGregor believes that research in the behavioural sciences have shown that the assumptions of what he calls theory Y may be more valid than the precepts of theory X.

Chris Argyris' Immaturity—Maturity Theory

Chris Argyris (1962) has examined industrial organizations to determine what effect management practices have on individual behaviour and personal growth within the environment. Argyris proposed two different value systems: (a) bureaucratic or pyramidal value systems and (b) humanistic or democratic value systems. According to Argyris, following bureaucratic values leads to poor, shallow, and mistrustful relationships. Such values do not permit the natural and free expression of feelings, and reduce interpersonal competence. They lead to intergroup conflict and a decrease in organizational success. If humanistic values are adhered to, authentic relationships develop among people as also increased interpersonal competence, intergroup cooperation, and flexibility. In a democratic environment, people are treated as human beings; organizational members as well as the organization itself are given an opportunity to develop to the fullest potential.

Argyris further examined the impact of managerial practices and concluded that the concepts of formal organization lead to assumptions about human nature that are incompatible with the proper development of maturity in human personality. He sees a definite incongruity between the needs of a mature personality and the formal organization. He also challenges the management to provide a work climate in which everyone has a chance to grow and mature as individuals, as members of a group by satisfying their own needs, while working for the success of the organization. Argyris also proposes changes in the personality characteristics of the individual when they have to move from immaturity to a maturity dimension. The directions of the change may be summarized as shown in Table 14.1.

The implication of the theory is that there is a tendency on the part of the individuals to move towards maturity with age. However, the role of culture, individual personality, and management practices do play a significant role. Argyris views that immaturity tends to exist not because of their nature of

> ■ ■ ■
> Argyris proposes a programme of gradually replacing the existing pyramidal organization structure with a humanistic structure and the existing management system with a more flexible and participative management system.

TABLE 14.1   Change from immaturity to maturity

Immaturity characteristics	Maturity characteristics
Passivity	Active
Dependence	Independence
Capable of behaving in a few ways	Capable of behaving in many ways
Shallow interest	Deep interest
Short-term perspective	Long-term perspective
Subordinate position	Superordinate position
Lack of self-awareness	Self-awareness and control

laziness, but because of organizational setting and management practices. When an individual joins the organization, he or she is given little opportunity to control the environment and is encouraged to be passive, dependent, and subordinate, and hence behave immaturely.

Argyris has suggested that a healthy organization is one which is realistic about itself and its situations, flexible, and is able to summon its resources to meet whatever challenges it may encounter. He proposes a programme of gradual phasing out of the existing pyramidal organizational structure to create a humanistic system, and replacing the existing management system with a more flexible and participative management system. The latter would definitely provide individuals the opportunity to grow mature and keep them psychologically healthy.

As the number of human problems facing the management started to mount, the limitations of the traditional human-relations approach to motivation began to surface. Starting around the early 1960s, those concerned with work motivation began to search earnestly for a new theoretical foundation and to attempt to devise new techniques for application. In particular, humanistic psychologist Abraham Maslow's hierarchy of needs was adapted to work motivation. Next came the two-factor theory of Herzberg. Later Alderfer recognized the Maslow hierarchy as three groups of core needs—existence, relatedness, and growth (ERG).

Because of the lack of research for content approaches, Vroom presented an alternative theory of work motivation based on the expectancy model explained later in the chapter. Recently, there has been a focus on the potential contribution that the attribution theory, locus of control, and equity theory can make to work motivation. At present, the content and process theories have become established explanations for work motivation, and there is continued research interest on attribution theories. However, there is no agreement over all theories. We will now examine the content and process theories in detail.

> ■ ■ ■
> Content theories of work motivation attempt to determine what motivates people at work and are concerned with identifying the needs or drives that motivate people and how those are prioritized.

CONTENT THEORIES OF WORK MOTIVATION

These theories attempt to determine what it is that motivates people at work. Motivation for content theorists arises from the operation of needs. The theorists are concerned with identifying the needs or drives that people have and how these are prioritized. They are also concerned with the type of goals and incentives that people strive for in order to satisfy their needs.

Maslow's Need-hierarchy Theory

The need-hierarchy model of motivation as espoused by Abraham Maslow (1951) is one of the classical and original theories. Originally, Maslow stated his need theory in the context of describing the nature of the human personality. In his famous book *Motivation and Personality*, Maslow further elaborated his need-hierarchy model. The theory may be summarized as follows:

G needs
• Self-actualization
• Esteem
• Belongingness

B needs
• Safety
• Physiological

FIGURE 14.2 Maslow's need hierarchy

- The functional disposition of human beings is their needs. Needs determine their behaviour.
- Human being is a composition of needs.
- Accordingly, human beings prioritize their needs, which they operate in a hierarchy. Hence, the name of the theory is 'hierarchy theory'.
- A person advances to the next level of hierarchy only when the lower-level need is satisfied.

It may be observed that basic or physiological needs and safety or security needs together may be considered as basic needs or B needs and the other needs, that is, belongingness, esteem, and self-actualization needs as growth needs or G needs (Figure 14.2). Each of the needs is now briefly discussed.

Physiological Needs

The most basic needs required for the survival of the organism are hunger, thirst, sleep, protection from extreme temperature, and sensory stimulation. They are responsible for the biological maintenance of the organism and are universal in the sense that they are common to all species in the universe. Another characteristic feature is that they are instinctual in nature, implying that they are involuntary, personal, and universal. Physiological needs are crucial to the understanding of human behaviour. For example, in moments of crisis such as war, it is the physiological needs that are of prime importance to the homeless refugees, and they would, in all probability, not be overly concerned about higher-order needs.

Physiological needs are instinctual in nature, implying that they are involuntary, personal, and universal and are crucial to the understanding human behaviour. Safety needs also have an instinctual basis, and, according to Maslow, once the safety needs are satisfied, they no longer act as motivators.

Safety Needs

Once the physiological needs are satisfied, the next level in the hierarchy, that is, safety needs get activated. Just like physiological needs, safety needs also have an instinctual base. Protecting oneself from the environment and other extreme dangers is a common phenomenon observed in all species. Safety or security may have as well as physical emotional connotations. An infant feels secure in the company of its mother and research conducted on other species, such as chickens, ducklings, and monkeys, further reiterates this fact. It is also observed that human beings continually indulge in behaviours which are safety-seeking mechanisms. According to Maslow, once the safety needs are satisfied, they no longer act as motivators.

Belonging Needs

Once the basic physiological needs are satisfied, human beings turn their attention to the group, community, or society to which they belong. Man is a social animal. This statement is true in the sense that human beings would like to be loved, share their feelings, affiliate with a group, and establish an identity with the group. These feelings usually begin with the family and extend towards the peer group and into other social situations of life. One may conclude that these may form a link between basic needs and other growth needs.

Esteem Needs

The esteem needs represent the higher needs of human beings. Esteem may be interpreted here as the desire to achieve competence, confidence, and also experience feelings of 'worth' about one's self. It means not only the desire to achieve, but also to get it reinforced by the group to which one belongs. In other words, there is a desire for recognition.

Need for Self-actualization

This is the highest level in the hierarchy. It is the ultimate need that people seek in their lives. According to Maslow, people who have attained self-actualization are self-fulfilled and have realized their potential. Rogers (1961) believes that the basic force motivating the human organism is self-actualization—'a tendency towards fulfillment, towards actualization, towards maintenance and enhancement of the organism'. The characteristics of self-actualized individuals have been studied by Maslow. Maslow began his investigation in an unusual manner by selecting eminent historical figures and included in the list were Abraham Lincoln, Thomas Jefferson, Eleanor Roosevelt, Madam Curie, and Bernard Shaw. After studying their lives, Maslow arrived at a competitive picture of a self-actualizer. Later, Maslow extended his study to a population of college students. He selected the students who fitted into his description and found them to be in the healthiest 1% of the population and were making effective use of their talents and capabilities. The following are the personal qualities of self-actualizers and the behaviours he considered important to the development of self-actualization (Maslow 1967).

Characteristics of self-actualizers   Perceive reality efficiently and are able to tolerate uncertainty, accept themselves and others for what they are, spontaneous in thought and behaviour, problem-centred rather than self-centred, have a good sense of humour, highly creative, concerned for the welfare of humanity, capable of deep appreciation of the basic experience of life, inclined to establish deep interpersonal relationships with a few, and are able to look at life from an objective viewpoint.

Behaviours leading to self-actualization

> ■ ■ ■
> The need for self-actualization is the highest level in the hierarchy of needs, and, according to Maslow, people who have attained self-actualization are self-fulfilled and have realized their potential.

- Experience life as a child does with full absorption.
- Try something new.
- Listen to your own feelings rather than the voice of tradition and authority, or the majority.
- Be honest and avoid pretence or game playing.
- Assume responsibility.
- Be prepared to be unpopular with your views.
- Work hard at whatever you do.
- Try to identify your defences and have courage to give them up.

The need for self-actualization is distinctive and elusive. The more satisfaction of it a person obtains, the more important the need for it becomes. Though all human beings have a natural desire to realize their potentials, usually only about 1% of the population fulfils their need for self-actualization.

Maslow did not intend that his need hierarchy be directly applied to work motivation. It was Douglas McGregor, in his widely read book *The Human Side of Enterprise*, who popularized Maslow's theory in management literature. The need hierarchy had a tremendous impact on the modern management approach to motivation. In one sense, Maslow's need hierarchy theory can be converted into the content model of work motivation as shown in the Figure 14.3.

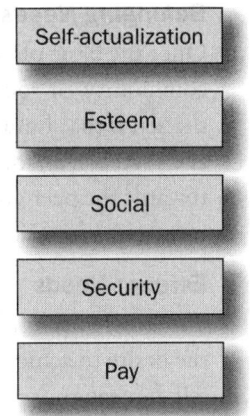

FIGURE 14.3 Maslow's model in a work situation

At the initial level, basic needs may be interpreted as pay and safety needs as related to job security matters such as seniority plans, insurance, and pension plans. Social needs may be satisfied by associating with formal and informal groups, work teams, committees, and so on. Satisfaction of esteem needs is usually experienced as in receiving awards, titles, status symbols, promotions, and so on. When individuals strive towards personal growth and make attempts to realize their potential, then it may be interpreted as striving towards self-actualization.

Evaluation of the Theory

Maslow's theory is the most popular and widely appreciated. Even though later research did not provide much insight into it or support it, it is still acclaimed as one of the classical theories. No doubt, we depart from Maslow's viewpoint that needs operate in a hierarchy and that a satisfied need no longer acts as a motivator. A decade later, Maslow himself clarified that gratification increases the need rather than reducing it. He also recognized that human behaviour is determined and motivated by multiple factors.

Herzberg's Two-factor Theory

Focusing on needs as activators of behaviour, Herzberg presented his theory on work motivation. His theory originally was stated as the job satisfaction theory, and since it dealt with two sets of factors which act as motivators, his theory is also popularly known as the two-factor theory.

Like Maslow, Herzberg also directed his research on the on-the-job factors as well as the contextual factors that lead to motivation of the individual. Herzberg, Mausner, and Snyderman (1955) conducted a study on 200 accountants and engineers employed in Pennsylvania. They used the critical-incident method of obtaining data. The subjects of the study were asked essentially two questions: (a) When did they feel particularly good about their job (b) When did they feel exceptionally bad about their job?

Responses obtained from this method were interesting and fairly consistent. It was observed that good feelings were generally associated with job experiences and job content. For example, when an employee was associated with a challenging project, he took pride in his work and was gratified when it led to successful results. Reported bad feelings were associated with work environment or context factors.

Herzberg concluded that job satisfiers are related to the job and job dissatisfiers to the job context. The former were labeled as 'motivators' and the latter as 'hygiene' factors. 'Hygiene' factors are those that prevent dissatisfaction, but do not motivate per se. However, their absence leads to dissatisfaction.

There are a lot of similarities between Maslow and Herzberg. Both of them focus on needs and their operation in motivating the organism. Upon close examination, one can find that Maslow's basic needs are somewhat related to hygiene factors and the growth needs to motivators. While Maslow speaks with reference to a hierarchy, Herzberg's model does not have a hierarchy. Probably one may also classify individuals as motivation seekers and maintenance seekers. Those who are concerned about hygiene factors are maintenance seekers and those who are achievement oriented are motivation seekers (Figure 14.4).

Hygiene factors	Motivators
Company policy and administration	Achievement
Supervision, technical	Recognition
Salary	Work itself
Interpersonal relations, Supervision	Responsibility
Short-term perspective	
Working conditions	
Advancement	

FIGURE 14.4   Herzberg's two factors

Evaluation of the Theory

Herzberg's main contribution is identifying the motivators. The aspects which if present in the nature of the task would certainly motivate the individual. Later, organizations did take the cue from here and designed their jobs to include at least some aspects of this theory.

Closer examination reveals that motivators as well as hygiene factors contribute to satisfaction and dissatisfaction. The theory does not focus on situational variables. It is more a description of job satisfaction rather than motivation.

Alderfer's ERG Theory

Alderfer's is yet another content theory, where ERG stands for existence, relatedness, and growth. These are again needs in operation, which motivate the individual. The departure from Maslow's dimension is that while Maslow arranged the needs in a hierarchy, Alderfer placed them in a continuum.

At the beginning of the continuum, we have existence needs, which when satisfied lead to relatedness needs, followed by growth needs.

Comparison of Maslow's and Alderfer's Theories

The similarity of Alderfer's theory to Maslow's theory (Table 14.2) can be drawn from the fact that the existence needs are the same as the basic or physiological needs and the relatedness needs as the social needs, and the growth needs have the same meaning in both the theories.

TABLE 14.2 Comparison of Maslow's and Alderfer's theories

Maslow's theory	Alderfer's theory
Self-actualization needs	Growth
Esteem needs	Relatedness
Belongingness needs	Existence
Safety needs	
Basic/physiological needs	

Theoretically, one set of needs may lead to another, but in reality the striving of individuals might differ.

Evaluation of the Theory

When compared to Maslow's theory, Alderfer's theory appears to be more practical as it explains individual differences in pursuit of development regardless of whether or not other needs are satisfied. However, it is a little difficult to predict human behaviour on the basis of this theory as we are not sure as to what motivates individuals.

McClelland's Achievement Motive Theory

David C. McClelland (1961) and his associates conducted research in the area of motivation in Harvard University. He identified three fundamental needs—the needs for achievement, power, and affiliation as existing in all individuals and acting as prime motivators of behaviour. All three needs are present in all human beings, but differ in degree and intensity. The result is that some people are success or result oriented, some are people oriented, and others are power oriented. This explains individual differences in work settings.

A brief description of these three needs follows.

Need for Achievement

Individuals with a high achievement motive are success oriented and would like to excel in a competitive situation. They have a strong, innate urge to excel and be successful. The characteristics of high-achievement-oriented individuals may be summarized as follows:

- Predisposition to challenging tasks with moderate difficulty level
- Love for autonomy and independence while executing a task
- Goal-directed action and perceiving each success as a stepping stone to higher goals
- Interest in getting immediate feedback of their performance so that they are aware of their drawbacks

McClelland postulated that even though achievement motive is a need, it can also be developed through the process of learning and training. All the background and environmental factors, such as family, peer group, school and college education, socio-economic aspects, and cultural background, play a decisive role in the development of this need. Research studies have shown a high positive correlation of 60% between mother and son on the dimension of the achievement motive. Further, in economically backward societies, if the need to achieve is cultivated, it would result in a large group of people aiming to be success oriented. Thus, a high-achieving society may be developed, which would contribute to the overall development of the state at large.

In a work setting, we have some individuals who are high in their achievement motive, strive for their personal satisfaction, and thereby contribute to organizational growth. It is desirable that most employees possess this need to some degree.

Need for Power

Persons who are high on the need for power derive satisfaction from the ability to control others. They also seek positions where they can exercise and wield authority. They would like to influence and control not only people, but also decisions. People high on this need generally opt for positions in the military or politics.

Need for Affiliation

Individuals who are high on this need seek people-oriented tasks or situations. Their actions always take them towards people and they experience a high sense of belongingness in a group. Given a choice or opportunity, they prefer to work or move in situations involving others.

Evaluation of the Theory

We may say that it is a different kind of need theory since it focuses on three major ones. The interpretation of this theory in relation to the work setting may be tough in that employees with different motives choose their professions accordingly. Hence, we see a close relation between motivation and satisfaction in this theory.

Nevertheless, the theory is criticized—how can motives be trained or learned? Secondly, the permanence need is also questioned. Lastly, in a typical socially backward society, how much of an achievement motive can be expected to be there among the members of the community?

PROCESS THEORIES OF WORK MOTIVATION

Content theorists by and large focused their attention on innate needs and their operation in motivating individuals. However, they did not take into consideration the contextual or situational factors. Work in the organizations takes place in relation to the environmental aspects. These aspects wield a powerful influence in motivating the individual. The process theories, of which we will discuss the following, made their contribution in this regard.

- Vroom's expectancy model
- Adam's equity theory
- Porter–Lawler's performance–satisfaction model

Vroom's Expectancy Model

■ ■ ■
Content theorists by and large focused their attention on innate needs and their operation in motivating individuals, but they did not take into consideration the contextual or situational factors. The process theorists—Vroom, Adam, and Porter-Lawler—made their contribution in this regard.

The expectancy theory is one of the most popular and accepted theories of work motivation. It has its base in cognitive psychology and in the works of Lewin and Tolman. Cognitive psychology places emphasis on awareness, action sequences, and expectations. The understanding of a situation leads to certain expectations and when those expectations are reinforced, individuals tend to repeat the behaviour.

The three constructs of Vroom's theory are (a) valence, (b) instrumentality, and (c) expectancy.

Valence

Valence refers to the degree of desirability of outcomes as perceived by the individual. In other words, it refers to the strength of an individual preference for a particular outcome. A valence of 0 indicates neutrality or indifference to the outcome.

Instrumentality

■ ■ ■
Vroom's theory has highlighted the process involved in understanding the nature of work behaviour. The outcomes influence the work values of employees depending upon what is important to them and the way in which each individual sequences his or her work-life activities.

Instrumentality refers to the awareness of the individual as to what behavioural sequences need to be undertaken in order to realize the goal. The action sequences leading to expectations are manifest and may be observed by one and all. For example, an employee may be working hard. He/She has set his eyes on promotion. The fact that he or she is working hard is being observed and the employee also understands that the organization values hard work. Working hard is the first-level outcome and getting a promotion is the second-level outcome.

Expectancy

Expectancy refers to the belief that the action sequences will lead to the desired second-level outcome. The individual would make an estimate as to the probability of the outcome based on the effort involved. Hence, it differs from instrumentality in that while expectancy refers to the belief system, instrumentality refers to the action sequences. The individual will not contemplate undertaking an activity, if his expectancy level is low.

In essence, we may say that the probability that an individual will undertake certain actions depends upon not only the strength of the motive, but also on the estimate of the individual about the occurrence of the outcome.

Evaluation of the Theory

Vroom's theory has highlighted the process involved in understanding the nature of work behaviour.

■ ■ ■
Adam's equity theory focuses on rewards as managed by an organization. As an individual moves towards equity, it results in job satisfaction and better performance.

The outcomes influence the work values of the employees depending upon what is important to them and the way in which each individual sequences his work-life activities. However, the generalization of the theory in all contexts is questioned. Often, employees may not have a clear idea about organizational values and support systems. Further, even though we assume that instrumentality leads to expected behaviours, there are numerous instances when the contrary has taken place. Nevertheless, the theory has found application in organizations, such as in management by objectives and goal setting.

Adam's Equity Theory

The equity theory has its origin in Stacey Adam's theory in the field of economics. The world 'equity' denotes balance, fairness, etc. The theory advocates that individuals expect to be treated equitably in their work relationships. Fairness in treatment is meted out in terms of wages and other fringe benefits. Employees make constant comparisons with other's inputs and other's rewards and efforts are made to restore balance in the same direction.

Evaluation of the Theory

The theory focuses more on rewards as managed by the organization. As the individual moves towards equity, it results in job satisfaction and better performance. The theory also has a cognitive base and puts emphasis on an employee's ability to understand and evaluate the situation accurately. There has been lot of research on this theory, and the findings have supported it.

Porter–Lawler's Performance–Satisfaction Model

The entire work-motivation theory hinges on the fact that motivation leads to high performance, thereby resulting in satisfaction on the job. Porter and Lawler, in their classic theory, for the first time treated them as separate variables and relate them in ways different from what has traditionally been assumed. The theory has some similarities to Vroom's theory. At the first step, we have effort as invested by the individual. Effort is again mediated by abilities and results in performance. Performance on the job would naturally be reinforced by the organization in the form of rewards. Rewards again may be experienced by the individual as extrinsic rewards in the form of pay or other benefits or as intrinsic satisfaction, etc. Here, we have a similarity to Vroom's theory in the sense that the value an individual attaches to the rewards would again influence the effort invested by the individual. At times, there may be high performance, but the employee may or may not experience satisfaction.

> ■ ■ ■
> Porter and Lawler in their classic theory separated the variables of motivation—performance and satisfaction—for the first time and related them in ways different from what was traditionally assumed.

Evaluation of the Theory

The theory for the first time separated the variables of motivation—performance and satisfaction. It generated considerable research and raised further questions as to how satisfaction may be related to commitment and employee morale, etc.

GENERAL EVALUATION OF THE THEORIES

All the theories need to be appreciated in the context and time in which they were stated. The content theorists, in general, focused on the individual, the operation, and prioritization of needs and the factors that need to be present on the job to create motivation. McClelland's theory is unique in the sense that he postulates that motivation can be developed from the early stage of one's life through conditioning and socialization practices. The process theorists, on the other hand, focused on the mechanisms that operate on the job. Hence, there was a shift from individual needs to job content and work environmental aspects.

Hence, we see that in the implication of motivation theories, all these aspects are taken into consideration. Specific applications are found in job designing and job enrichment programmes, which have a direct relation to Herzberg's theory.

APPLICATIONS OF MOTIVATIONAL CONCEPTS

The theoretical base provided earlier in this chapter is no doubt supported by research findings. Further, conventional wisdom also exists that work experience enhances performance. However, the issue still remains as to what motivates the individual at any point of time. Since it is difficult to predict the nature of needs, probably the organization would like to focus on job-related matters as stated by the theorists to sustain the motivation in the individual. It is here that the applications of motivational concepts and theories become significant. The specific forms in which theories and concepts are applied may be considered under the headings of job designing, goal setting, and management by objectives. Let us examine them briefly.

Job Designing

Job design has emerged as an important application area for work motivation. Job design concerns and approaches are usually considered to have begun with scientific management. The goal of such management was to maximize human efficiency in job performance. The scientific-management approach resulted in 'job engineering', which focused on product and process, plant layout, human–machine interactions, etc.

Advances in technology, computer systems, etc., have resulted in job specialization. Even though specialization resulted in better control and efficiency, other aspects such as motivation and satisfaction were neglected. Consequently, over a period of time, efficiency decreased and dissatisfaction prevailed among the work force. The problems today are compounded with downsizing and increased use of technology. For academicians as well as practitioners, job design takes on special importance as it reduces stress, enhances motivation, and results in satisfaction.

> ■ ■ ■
> Some important application areas of work motivational concepts are job designing, job enlargement, goal setting, and management by objectives.

While focusing attention on job design, one may identify the organizational factors or perspectives as related to job design, that is, whether the task is done by one person or by a team, the relevance of qualifications, knowledge of the job-related aspects, and so on. Further, the organization also places importance on the location of job in the plant facilities, the easy availability of tools, etc. Attempts are also made to match the abilities of the person with the requirements on the job and the amount of 'autonomy' that may be permitted on the job. Autonomy here is interpreted in terms of decision-making, freedom in exercise of choice, and so on. When organizations put these aspects in practice it results in job enrichment and job enlargement programmes.

> ■ ■ ■
> Job designing approaches are usually considered to have begun with scientific management, and its goal is to maximize human efficiency in job performance. Job enlargement refers to the horizontal expansion of the scope of the job.

Job Enlargement

Some amount of boredom may be relieved by this approach. Job enlargement refers to expansion of the scope of the job horizontally. In simple terms, it means increasing the number of tasks that need to be executed. For example, if an assembly-line worker was inserting 100 nuts in a day, he would perhaps increase it by another 50. The variety that is experienced by the individual is only in terms of the number of tasks.

Job Enrichment

Job enrichment represents an extension of job enlargement. It is a direct outgrowth of Herzberg's theory of motivation. The proposition of Herzberg that motivators when present enhance the motivational aspects of the individual finds its direct application in a job enrichment programme. In 'enrichment', the job is enlarged vertically so that there is greater variety of work content, it requires a high level of knowledge and skill, gives workers more autonomy and responsibility in terms of planning, directing, and controlling their own performance, and provides opportunities for personal growth and a meaningful work experience.

Research has supported us with evidence that there is more employee satisfaction, better customer service, less employee overload, and fewer employee errors in case of job enrichment. Another study also found that employees were more creative when they worked in an enriching context of complex, challenging jobs, and a supportive, non-controlling supervisory climate.

Although, there are several benefits of job enlargement, certain disadvantages cannot be ignored. First, the workers need to be trained or multiskilled in order to handle the variety of jobs. Maybe it requires a new way of functioning in an already existing system. Moreover, it may not be possible to introduce job enlargement programmes for all the jobs in the organization.

Goal Setting

Goal setting has become an effective tool for the practice of human resource management and an overall performance–system approach. The goal setting theory stems from the original concept of 'intentions' as stated by Locke, who was inspired by Ryan. 'Intentions' may also be interpreted as motives and when motives become strong, they translate into a value or valence, and the individual undertakes certain actions which result in consequences. We may then say that intentions also result in purposivism of behaviour. Thus, we see that the goal-setting theory is not exactly new, and similarities may be found in Taylor's, Herzberg's, and Tolman's cognitive theory.

Incentives

The operation of non-financial rewards take different forms in the organization. Even though they are considered as non-financial, they prove to be costly to the organization. For example, some organizations in the public sector provide subsidized lunch, tea, coffee, clothing, shoes, and gifts to their employees. These are considered as consumables, which cost money to the organization.

In certain levels, either in the private or in the public sector, certain manipulatives are also involved, such as club memberships, usage of company facilities, accessories, or furnishings, etc. Recognition, attention, and praise tend to be very powerful social rewards. Normally, social rewards cost nothing to the organization. However, the employees experience satisfaction as their ideas get accepted or implemented. In most organizations, employees are encouraged to form teams and suggest mechanisms for cost cutting. The most viable suggestion gets accepted and the employee who has suggested it derives the maximum satisfaction.

> ■ ■ ■
> Incentives or non-financial rewards and ownership plans help organizations in gaining the commitment of the employees and create greater job satisfaction. These include provision for food, club memberships, bonus, etc.

Besides these types of non-financial operations of rewards, organizations also gain the commitment of the employees through various ownership plans. Some of them are as follows:

- Minimum wages are guaranteed to all workers.
- Incentives by way of bonus, etc., are offered to efficient workers for time saved.

- A standard time is fixed and the worker is expected to perform the given work within this standard time. The standard time is set after making time studies for the performance of a specific job.

Taylor's Differential Piece-rate System

This system was formulated by F.W. Taylor, the father of scientific management. The main features of this plan are as follows:

- There will be two piece work rates, one lower and another higher.
- The standard of efficiency is determined either in terms of time or output based on a time and motion study.
- If a worker finishes the work within the standard time (or produces more than the standard output within the stipulated time), he will be given a high piece rate.

The system penalizes the slow worker by paying a low rate because of low production, and rewards an efficient worker by giving a high rate because of higher production.

Merrick's Differential Piece-rate System

In Taylor's method, the effect on the wages is quite severe in the marginal cases. To remove this defect, Merrick came up with a multiple piece-rate system. There are three piece rates under this scheme instead of two, and workers producing below the standard output are not penalized by the low piece rate. Since the earnings increase with increased efficiency, performance above the standard is rewarded by more than one higher differential piece rate. The basic features of this scheme are (a) workers producing upto 83% of they standard output are paid at the ordinary piece rate, (b) those producing 83% to 100% are paid 110% of the ordinary piece rate, and (c) those producing above 100% are paid at 120% of the ordinary piece rate.

Halsey Plan

F.A. Halsey (an American engineer) came up with a plan that recognizes individual efficiency and pays bonus on the basis of time saved. The main features of this plan are as follows:

- A standard time is fixed for each job or operation.
- Time rate is guaranteed and the worker receives the guaranteed wages irrespective of whether he or she completes the work in the time allowed or takes more time to do the same.
- If the job is completed in less than the standard time, the worker is paid a bonus of 50% ($33\frac{1}{3}$% under the Halsey–Weir plan) of the time saved at the time rate in addition to his or her normal time wages.

$$\text{Total earnings} = (\text{time taken} \times \text{hourly rate}) + \text{bonus}$$
$$\text{Bonus} = 50\% \text{ of time saved}$$

Merits

- It is easy to follow and relatively simple to operate.
- It guarantees minimum wage and thus provides security to the employees.
- It provides increasing benefits and incentives to efficient workmen.
- The benefit from time saved is shared equally between the employer and the workman.
- It emphasizes the saving of time rather than larger output, and hence the workers do not resist its adoption.

- The system is based on time saved and not on output, thus preventing overproduction.
- The saving in time reduces both labour cost and overhead expenses.

Demerits

- The worker may be encouraged to rush through work and thus neglect the quality of production to save more time and earn a higher bonus.
- It does not provide adequate incentive to highly efficient workmen as it involves the sharing of benefit with employers.
- The fixation of a standard is not easy.
- The earnings are reduced at a high level of efficiency. Therefore, it does not act as a sufficient incentive.

Rowan Plan

This plan was introduced by D. Rowan in 1901. As in the Halsey plan, the bonus is paid on the basis of time saved. However, unlike a fixed percentage, this takes into account a proportion as follows:

$$\frac{\text{Time saved}}{\text{Time allowed}}$$

Thus, under this plan, bonus is that proportion of the wages of time taken which the time saved bears to the time allowed or standard time.

$$\text{Bonus} = \frac{\text{time saved}}{\text{standard time or time allowed}} \times \text{time taken} \times \text{hourly rate}$$

$$\text{Total earnings} = \text{time taken} \times \text{hourly rate} + \text{bonus}$$

Merits

- It assures minimum time wages. It is more liberal than the Halsey plan in that it provides incentive to work and earn extra remuneration.
- As the increase in effort is much less rewarded after a certain stage, an automatic check for limiting production of inferior quality of goods is ensured.
- This automatic check enables the worker to earn a fair wage, because there is less chance of rate cutting by the employer, as the employer is not paying extraordinary wages.

Demerits

- The ordinary worker may find the bonus calculation a bit difficult to understand.
- Like the Halsey plan, this plan does not encourage extraordinary efficiency. For example, if the time saved is more than half the total, earnings begin to decrease.

Gantt Task and Bonus Plan

This plan combines time, piece, and bonus systems. The main features of this plan are as follows:

- Day wages are guaranteed.
- A standard time for the task is fixed and time wages as well as a high rate per piece are determined.
- A worker who cannot finish the work within the standard time is paid on a time basis.
- If a worker reaches the standard, he or she is paid a time wage plus a bonus at a fixed percentage (20%) of the normal time wage.
- If the worker exceeds the standards, he or she is paid a higher piece rate.

Merits

- This plan is not as harsh as Taylor's differential piece-rate system. Hence, it is more acceptable to the workers.
- Workers can easily understand its working.
- It ensures guaranteed time wages to inefficient workers also.
- It makes a distinction between efficient and inefficient workers because the system ensures time wages for inefficient workers and piece wages plus a 20% bonus for efficient workers.
- Labour cost per unit decreases with increase in production due to the incentive for efficiency given under this plan.

Demerits

- It classifies workers into two competing categories (efficient and inefficient), and this may bring disunity among workers.
- When this method is used, labour cost will be high for low production.
- Extreme care is to be exercised in fixing the guaranteed time rate and determining the standard output. Any error due to lack of experience will lead to unfavorable consequences.

Group Bonus Plans

A system of wage payment under which incentive is provided to a group of workers engaged in a particular task is known as a group bonus plan. The bonus or incentive premium is fixed for the group as a whole. It may be computed for the group as a whole on the same basis as in the Halsey or Rowan plan or Gantt Plan. The amount of bonus is divided among the workers in the group in proportion to the wages that would have been payable to individual workers on a time (hourly) basis. Thus, the workers receive a share of the bonus according to their relative skill. A minimum time wage is generally guaranteed to each member of the group.

The various schemes which may be introduced for this purpose may include (a) Priestman's production bonus, (b) the Rucker or 'share of production' plan, (c) Scanlon plan, and (d) the Towne's gain sharing scheme.

■ ■ ■
Group bonus plan is a system of wage payment under which an incentive is provided to a group of workers engaged in a particular task and individuals receive a share of the bonus according to their relative skill.

Priestman's production bonus   Under this system, a standard is fixed in terms of units or points. If actual output, measured similarly, exceeds the standard, the workers receive a bonus in proportion to the increase. Therefore, this system can operate in a factory where there is mass production of a standard product with little or no bottleneck.

■ ■ ■
Major types of group bonus plans include Priestman product bonus plan, Rucker or share of production plan, Scanlon plan, and Towne's plan.

Rucker plan or share of production plan   In this plan, employees receive a constant proportion of the 'added value'. The term 'added value' means the change in market value resulting from an alteration in the form, location, or availability of a product or service, excluding the cost of bought-out materials or services.

In this plan, the ratio between earnings and added value is ascertained and any reduction of the ratio of earnings to added value will result in proportionate bonus payment. This plan presupposes a great deal of consultation between management and workers to help workers make more effective efforts.

Scanlon plan   Under this plan, a constant proportion (i.e., the ratio of wages to the sales value) of the added value of the output is paid to the workers who are responsible for the addition of the value. The added value is the change in market value (including profit) resulting from an alteration in the form, location or availability of product service, excluding the cost of purchased materials or services used in production.

Towne's plan   The main objective of this plan is to bring about cost reduction by foremen and workers. However, bonus is paid upon a reduction in labour cost alone. A standard labour cost per unit for a particular period is determined and if labour cost per unit is less than the standard labour cost, 50% of the saving in labour cost is distributed among workers and foremen in proportion to their wages.

Profit-sharing or Stock-option Plans

Profit-sharing plans are incentive programmes wherein employees get a share of the organization's net profits in a specified period on compliance with certain conditions and qualifications. Such incentives strengthen the loyalty of the employees. The firm, under this incentive, offers its employees an annual bonus, which is over and above the normal wages. The annual bonuses are provided to the employees who have been with the organization for a definite period. The annual bonus may be in the form of a cash reward or company shares (also known as bonus shares).

In addition to profit-sharing plans, gain-sharing plans are also being undertaken. They are rewards to the employees for bringing about improvements in the organizational productivity. Through employee suggestion and participation, gain-sharing plans focus on reducing labour costs. They have their merits and demerits.

Merits
- They ensure that employees remain sincere and loyal to the organization.
- They supplement the remuneration of workers.
- They help motivate the workers and other staff, and ensure better and quicker work. This increases the profits of the company and the employees' share is increased. This is a cyclic process.
- They help attract talented people who join the firm keeping in view the high salary offered.
- They reduce the burden of close supervision of the employees as they are self-motivated and work to their full capacity, in order to increase the profits of the firm.

Demerits
- Workers may gain if the firm is successful. On the other hand, if the firm does not succeed then the employees do not gain anything.
- The management can report false profits, which are less than the actual profit. In doing so, the management deprives the employees of their share in the profits.
- They impair the unity and oneness of trade unions as the workers develop a loyalty to the organization.
- Fixing the workers' share of profits is risky. The organization may or may not reach the stipulated profits.

> ■ ■ ■
> Profit-sharing or stock option plans are incentive programmes that provide employees a share of the organization's net profits in a specified period in compliance with certain conditions.

Spot Bonus

It is usually awarded to a single employee though it may be awarded to a team as well. It is not measured according to any standards. It may be awarded to an employee who has worked for a longer time or in recognition of excellent customer service offered. It is over and above the individual's salary.

It is also awarded to teams or groups. In such cases, each member of a group gets a reward over and above his or her salary. The group is rewarded if it collectively reaches a specified standard for performance, productivity, or other work-related behaviour.

Exhibit 14.1 discusses employee motivation principles.

EXHIBIT 14.1   Employee motivation principles

When Michael started his own consultancy, he employed top people—people he had worked with in the past who had shown commitment, flair, and loyalty, and who seemed to share his values. However, a few months down the line, one of his team members started to struggle. Jo was putting in the hours, but without enthusiasm. Her confidence was dropping, she was unfocussed and not bringing in enough new business. Michael explained to Jo the seriousness of the situation. Without new business, he would lose the company and that would mean her job. He showed her the books to illustrate his point. He again ran through her job description and the procedures she was expected to follow. He told her that he was sure she was up to the job, but he really needed her to bring in the new business or they would all be out on their ear. Jo told Michael that she understood. She was doing her best, but she would try harder. Yet, a month later nothing had changed. After an initial burst of energy, Jo was back to her old ways.

No matter how experienced a leader you are, chances are at times you have struggled to motivate certain individuals. You have tried every trick in the book. You have sat down one-to-one with the individual concerned and explained the situation. You have outlined the big vision again in the hope of inspiring them. You have given them the bottom line: 'Either you pull your finger out or your job is on the line'. You have dangled a carrot in front of them: 'If you make your targets you'll get a great bonus'. Sometimes it works, but not every time. Sometimes, there have been casualties. Ultimately if someone cannot get the job done they have to go.

The pioneer of motivation theory, Frederick Herzberg, called traditional motivation strategies as 'KITA' (something similar to 'kick in the pants'). He used the analogy of a dog. When the master wants his dog to move, he either gives it a nudge from behind, in which case the dog moves because it does not have much choice, or he offers it a treat as an inducement, in which case it is not so much motivated by wanting to move as by wanting choc drops! KITA does the job (though arguably not sustainably), but it requires hard work. It means every time you want the dog to move you have to kick it (metaphorically). Wouldn't it be better if the dog wanted to move by itself? Transferring this principle back to the workplace, most motivation strategies are 'push' or 'pull' based. They are about keeping people moving either with a kick from behind (threats, fear, tough targets, complicated systems to check if people follow a procedure) or by offering choc drops (bonuses, grand presentations of the vision, conferences, campaigns, initiatives, etc).

Source: 'Employee motivation principles—a short case study sounds familiar?; http://www.businessballs.com/employeemotivation.htm,accessed on 24 August 2005.

Employee Stock Ownership Plan (ESOP)

Employee stock ownership plans originated in the USA in the early 1990s. Such plans did not gain popularity in India initially, due to the absence of legal provisions in the Companies Act covering stock options. However, in 1988, the government allowed stock options to software professionals, recognizing the importance of retaining talent within the country.

Under this plan, the eligible employees are allotted company's shares below the market price. The term 'stock option' implies the right of an eligible employee to purchase a certain amount of stock in the future at an agreed price. The eligibility criteria may include length of service, contribution to the department or division where the employee works, and so on. The company may even permit employees to pay the price of the stock allotted to them in instalments or even provide them advance money, to be recovered from their salary every month. The allotted shares are generally held in trust and transferred to the name of the employee whenever he or she decides to exercise the option. The stock option empowers the employee to participate in the growth of the company as a part owner. It also helps the company to retain talented employees and make them more committed to the job.

Merits of ESOP

The following are the merits of such a plan.

For the employer

- Employees remain loyal and committed to the company.
- It motivates them to do well and share the fruits of progress.
- Better industrial relations, reduced employee turnover, and less supervision are other incidental benefits.

For the employee

- He or she becomes a part owner, sharing dividends, bonuses, and other benefits like any other shareholder.
- If the stock appreciates, he or she gains substantially.

Benefits

Benefits are indirect financial and non-financial payments an employee receives. They include health and life insurance, vacations, pension, education plans, and child care facilities. They represent an important part of every employee's pay. Offering these benefits is becoming increasingly difficult as the workers are more sophisticated and demanding, and also because some benefits need to comply with laws.

Fringe Benefits

These are extra benefits provided to workers other than the usual compensation paid in the form of wage or salary. These benefits are referred to as 'fringe benefits' because many years ago, they were small, relatively inconspicuous, or fringe components of compensation. However, over the years, they have also grown. They now form part of the comprehensive compensation package offered by the employer to the employees.

Payment for time not worked   This is a type of fringe benefit. This category includes hours of work and paid holidays.

- Hours of work: Section 51 of the Factories Act, 1948 specifies that no adult worker shall be required to work in a factory for more than 48 hours in any week. Section 54 of the Act restricts the working hours to a maximum of nine on any day. In some organizations, the number of working hours is less than the legal requirement.

- Paid holidays: According to the Factories Act, 1948, an adult worker shall have weekly paid holidays, preferably Sunday. When a worker is deprived of weekly holidays, he is eligible for compensatory holidays of the same number in the same month. Some organizations allow the workers to have two holidays in a week.

Health benefits   Today, various medical services such as hospital, clinical, and dispensary facilities are provided by organizations not only to employees, but also to their family members.

Sickness benefit   Insured employees are entitled to a cash benefit for a maximum of 56 days in a year under this benefit.

Maternity benefit   Insured women employees are entitled to maternity leave for 12 weeks (six weeks before the delivery and six weeks after the delivery) in addition to a cash benefit of 75 paisa per day or twice the sickness benefit, whichever is higher.

Disablement benefit   Insured employees, who are disabled temporarily or permanently (partial or total) due to employment injury, occupational diseases, or both, are entitled to a cash benefit under this head. A disability plan provides income replacement for the employee who cannot work due to illness or accident. These plans are either short-term or long-term. They can be distinct from workers' compensation because they provide benefits for non-work-related illness or injury.

- Short-term disability: A short-term disability is usually defined as an employee's inability to perform the duties of his or her normal occupation. Benefits may begin on the first or the eighth day of disability and are usually paid for a maximum of 26 weeks.
- Long-term disability: Long-term disability (LTD) benefits usually begin after short-term benefits conclude. LTD benefits continue for the length of the disability or until normal retirement.

Dependant's benefit   If an insured person dies as a result of an employment injury sustained as an employee, his dependants, who are entitled to compensation under the Act, shall be entitled to periodical payments referred to as dependant's benefit.

Life insurance   Traditionally, life insurance pays death benefits to beneficiaries of employees who die during their working years. There are two main types of life insurance.

- Survivor income plans, which make regular payments to survivors.
- Group life insurance plans, which normally make lumpsum payments to specified beneficiaries.

Protection provided by one-year, renewable, group-term life insurance, with no cash surrender value or paid-up insurance benefit, is very popular. Frequently, health insurance programmes offer this coverage.

Medical benefit   A serious illness or injury can be devastating to an employee and his or her family. It can threaten their emotional and economic well-being. Thus, adequate health insurance is important to employees and is part of a solid group plan.

Group health plans help attract and keep employees who can make the business a success. They relieve the employees of the anxiety of health care costs by providing the care they need before illness becomes disabling, thus helping the employer avoid costly employee sick days.

Group health plans usually cost less than purchasing several individual policies with comparable coverage. Moreover, there are tax advantages on offering health care benefits: the employer's contribution may be deductible and the insurance is not taxable income to the employees.

This benefit is provided to an insured employee or to a member of his or her family where the benefit is extended to his or her family.

Accommodation   Generally, where any employee, whether higher-paid or not, is provided with accommodation either rent-free or for a very low rent, the difference between the rent paid, if any, and the annual value of the property is taxable.

Hotels and temporary accommodation   The cost of hotels and temporary accommodation while travelling for business purposes is not taxed. However, if an employee is given an overall cash allowance to cover these costs, this will be taxed, but anything spent on accommodation for the purpose of his/her job can be deducted from the taxable income as a tax relief.

Car fringe benefits   A car fringe benefit generally arises when a car owned or leased by the organization is either used privately by or made available for the private use of an employee. If the employer's car is garaged at an employee's house, then it is treated as having been made available for private use.

Property fringe benefits   A property fringe benefit may arise if the organization provides an employee with property either free or at a discount. Property includes

- all goods, for example, items of clothing or uniforms or a musical instrument;
- real property, for example, land, buildings; and
- other property, for example, shares.

Other fringe benefits   In addition to the fringe benefits we have discussed, there are certain others, which are listed here.

- The organization may provide an employee with entertainment fringe benefit by way of food, drink, or recreation. Accommodation or travel provided in connection with such entertainment is also deemed to be entertainment.
- If the organization pays an allowance to an employee to cover additional expenses incurred because the employee is temporarily required to live away from his or her usual place of residence in order to perform duties of employment, a living-away-from-home allowance fringe benefit may arise.

- The organization may give a loan or advance to an employee interest free or at an interest rate that is less than the statutory interest rate.
- If an employee owes a debt to the organization, the organization may release the employee from the obligation to repay the debt.
- The company may provide personal attendants such as a sweeper, gardener, and watchman to the employee.

- It is increasingly common for employees and their family members to be provided with vacation and holiday facilities.
- The perquisite of free meals varies widely from uniform canteen food, coupons, etc., to lavish hotel meals. Such free or subsidized meals should, however, be provided at the office premises or through non-transferable vouchers for only meals during working hours.
- It is customary in India as it is in other parts of the world to provide presents directly or indirectly in the form of vouchers or tokens to employees on social and religious occasions such as Diwali, Christmas, and New Year. Such gifts of up to ₹5,000 in the aggregate per annum are one type of fringe benefit.

Fringe Benefits and Motivation

All these fringe benefits are aimed at addressing the different levels of motivational needs as defined in Maslow's hierarchy, such as physiological, safety, love, and esteem. For instance, the provision of free or subsidized meals is aimed at satisfying the physiological needs, that is, the hunger of the employees. The gift voucher is aimed at the esteem needs of the employee; since the employee feels proud to receive the gift voucher, he or she can use it during special events along with his or her family members.

The various categories of fringe benefits and the levels of motivational needs they address are briefly mentioned in Table 14.3.

TABLE 14.3 Fringe benefits and the motivational needs they satisfy

S. no.	Motivational need	Fringe benefit
1.	Physiological	• Subsidized canteen facilities • Recreation facilities • Uniform, etc.
2.	Safety	• Life insurance • Medical benefits
3.	Love	• Vacation with family • LFC • Furniture grant, etc.
4.	Esteem	• Car facility • Furnished accommodation • Servants • Holidays abroad, etc.
5.	Self-actualization	• Membership of quality circles • Holding offices of clubs, associations • Performance rewards/awards, etc.

SUMMARY

This chapter begins with an introduction to the concept of motivation. It also discusses the processes and steps involved in motivation, the various theories of motivation, and their applications in the organizational context while designing incentives and fringe benefits, and various HR processes such as job enlargement and job enrichment.

It briefly deals with the conceptual background behind incentives, their features, types of incentive systems, and their merits and demerits.

■ ■ ■ KEY TERMS

Actualization To realize in action or make real

Amassing To accumulate or assemble a large quantity

Bureaucratic Relating to or resembling a bureaucrat or bureaucracy

Discrepancy Divergence or disagreement, as between facts or claims

Displacement Removal from the normal location or position

Entail To have, impose, or require as a necessary accompaniment or consequence

Extrinsic Not forming an essential or inherent part of a thing

Humanistic Concerned with the interests and welfare of human beings

Hypothetical Conditional; contingent

Incentive An additional payment (or other remuneration) to employees as a means of increasing output

Motive An emotion, desire, physiological need, or similar impulse that acts as an incitement to action.

Neo-classical A revival of classical aesthetics and forms

Passivity The condition or quality of being passive, inactivity, quiescence, or submissiveness

Psychological Influencing or intended to influence the mind or emotions

Renunciation Rejecting or disowning or disclaiming as invalid

■ ■ ■ EXERCISES

Multiple Choice Questions

1. Not giving a compliment for a job done very well can cause
   (a) punishment
   (b) extinction
   (c) negative reinforcement
   (d) demotivation

2. Who distinguished between hygiene factors and motivators?
   (a) Frederick Taylor
   (b) Frederick Herzberg
   (c) David McClelland
   (d) Edward Deci

3. The inner drive that directs a person's behaviour towards goal attainment is known as
   (a) performance
   (b) motivation
   (c) need
   (d) attitude

4. The extra benefits provided to workers other than usual compensation are categorized as
   (a) salary
   (b) fringe benefits
   (c) wage
   (d) commission

5. Why do organizations lay emphasis on attractive salaries, fringe benefits, and career development opportunities to their employees?
   (a) To retain valuable human resource
   (b) To be a market leader in the future
   (c) To attract more people
   (d) To enforce government regulations

Fill in the Blanks

1. A horizontal expansion of the scope of the job to increase task variety is called _____.

2. Expectancy theory focuses on the relationships between three factors _____, _____, and _____.

3. McClelland believes that the need for _____, _____, and _____ are most important.

4. Under the _____, employees are allotted company's shares below the market price and empowered to participate in the growth of the company as a part-owner.

5. According to this chapter, the major reason cited for leaving the organization in a study was _____ and _____ from managers.

Concept Review Questions

1. Describe the nature and concept of motivation.
2. Briefly explain the defence mechanisms.
3. Explain Maslow's theory of motivation and relate it to Herzberg's and Alderfer's model.

4. How do performance and satisfaction relate to each other? Analyse with the help of Porter and Lawler's theory.

5. Explain what you understand by pay for performance.

6. How do you structure a gain-sharing programme?

7. Differentiate between competence-related pay and pay for performance.

8. Enumerate the various benefits provided under the Factories Act.

9. In compliance with good governance, what are the recommendations for boardroom directors?

10. Do incentives motivate an individual in the long term? Discuss.

Project Work

1. Compare and contrast the applicability of motivation and its parameters in small organizations as against large organizations.

2. Critically analyse the incentives and fringe benefits provided in manufacturing organizations.

3. Prepare a write-up on specific characteristics of incentives for knowledge workers.

4. Prepare a brief incentive system prevailing in the IT services industry.

5. Critically analyse the correlation between employee motivation and incentive plans in an organization of your choice.

■ ■ ■ | REFERENCES

Bretz, R.D., Jr. and Thomas, S.L. 1993, 'Perceived equity, motivation, and final-offer arbitration in major league baseball', *Journal of Applied Psychology*, June, pp. 280–87.

Evans, M.G. 1980, 'Organizational behaviour—the central role of motivation', *Journal of Management*, vol. 12(2), p. 203.

Feather, N.T. 1993, 'Authoritarianism and attitudes toward high achievers', *Journal of Personality and Social Psychology*, July, pp. 152–64.

Gibson, V.M. 1995, 'The new employee reward system', *Management Review*, February, p. 18.

Hackman, J.R. and Oldham, G.R.1976, 'Motivation through the design of work: Test of a theory', *Organizational Behaviour and Human Performance*, vol. 16, pp. 250–79.

Hackman, J.R. 1977, 'Work Design', In J.R. Hackman and J.L. Suttle (eds), *Improving Life at Work*, Goodyear, Santa Monica, California, p. 129.

Locke, E.A., 1975, 'Personal attitudes and motivation', *Annual Review of Psychology*, vol. 26, pp. 457–80, 596–98.

Malow, A.H. 1943, 'A theory of human motivation', *Psychological Review*, July, pp. 370–96.

Matthes, K. 1993, 'Giving employees the benefit of time', *HR Focus*, August, p. 3.

McFillen, J.M. and Podsakoff, P.M. 1983, 'A coordinated approach to motivation can increase productivity', *Personnel Administrator*, July, p. 46.

Mitchell, T.R. 1982, 'Motivation: New Directions for Theory, Research, and Practice', *Academy of Management Review*, January, p. 86.

Nelson, B. 1996, 'Secrets of successful employee recognition', *Quality Digest*, August, p. 26.

Quinones, M., Ford, J.K., and Teachout, M.S. 1995, 'The relationship between work experience and job performance: A conceptual and meta-analytic review', *Personnel Psychology*, vol. 48, p. 887.

Rao, V.S.P. 2001, *Human Resource Management*: Text and Cases, 2nd Edn, Excel Books, New Delhi, pp. 374–75.

Rathus, S.A. 1990, *Psychology*, 4th Edn, Holt, Rinehart and Winston, Fort Worth, Texas, p. 312.

Tubbs, M.E., Boehne, D.M., and J.G. Dahl 1993, 'Expectancy, valence, and motivational force functions in goal-setting research: An empirical test', *Journal of Applied Psychology*, June, pp. 361–73.

Employee Motivation in Indian Chemical Industries Limited

CASE STUDY 1

Indian Chemical Industries Limited was founded during the year 1985 in Hyder-

abad. The company manufactured domestic paints and marketed them under the brand 'Index Paints' in the country. Within a decade, the company surged into the top five players in the country through focused advertising/branding and distribution strategies.

During a corporate review meeting held in 2005, the top management, after detailed deliberations, established the target of being among the top three paint players in the country by 2015. Apart from the need to retain its forte in production quality, the management also realized the need to develop motivational plans to differentiate and incentivize its marketing and distribution staff to achieve the set target.

The chief executive officer (CEO) constituted a core group consisting of the Vice-President–HR, Vice-President–Marketing, and Vice-President–Finance to discuss and develop incentive plans. The core group arrived at the following recommendations after holding a series of discussions and reviewing the plans of the competitors:

- Set the base/fixed salary at 60% of the cost to the company (CTC).
- Set the variable salary component at 40% of the CTC.
- Offer sales incentives to the top three salespersons in each region under the 'Hum Honge Kamyab Top 3' marketing contest for the next two years for monthly and quarterly durations. Adjudge the salesperson who continuously wins the best salesperson for the month and the quarter consistently for two quarters as best salesperson of the year. To

be eligible, a salesperson must do the following:
- Achieve minimum 15% additional sales.
- Add at least three new distributors during the month/quarter.
- Pay 15% additional bonus on the awarded bonus and 10% additional increment to the best salesperson of the year.
- Organize an all-India salespersons' convention to launch the marketing contest and conduct a training programme to instill the achievement spirit and leadership capabilities in the salespersons.
- Increase the sales expenses reimbursement to ₹1,500 per month to motivate all salespersons.
- Offer concessional loans to the salespersons to purchase a two-wheeler to facilitate mobility and help them achieve additional sales.

Questions
1. Briefly analyse the employee motivational incentives/benefits at Indian Chemical Industries Limited.
2. Do you think the incentives will help the salespersons achieve their targets?
3. Study the sales incentives of a field sales force organization and compare them with the incentive plan designed by the core group.
4. How would you introduce the return on investment perspective in the incentive plan designed by the core group?

Best Practices—SmithKline Beecham Pharmaceuticals

In today's marketplace, retaining and recruiting top-notch employees is one of the biggest headaches for human resource professionals. Competitive salaries are simply not enough, and once revolutionary perks, such as stock options and casual Fridays, are now virtually industry standards. What lengths do companies need to go to recruit workers? What new benefits must be added to packages to satisfy and maintain current employees? Tom Johnson, company spokesperson for SmithKline Beecham (SKB), shares the company's recipe for HR relief. Johnson had difficulty singling out a single perk or benefit that is a sure-fire hit with SKB recruits and employees. Individuals maintain very different lifestyles, so packages may appeal—or not—for very

different reasons. For example, a recent BA graduate may prioritize profit sharing, while the experienced MBA might be looking for a job with flex time, in order to spend more time with family. SKB does surveys of its current workers in order to gauge their satisfaction with current benefits, and learn what new perks they need to implement to keep folks happy. They also do substantial research on innovative trends being tried out in other companies across the country. Their mission, according to Johnson, is to 'give support to our employees [in order to help them] successfully integrate their personal and professional lives'. The idea being, of course, that satisfied workers are productive workers, and that dissatisfied workers tend to be productive too—at finding other jobs. After further consideration, Johnson did list some perks in the SKB benefits package that are sure-fire crowd pleasers. One of these is free financial planning seminars. The seminars cover topics from successful investment strategies and managing kids' college tuition to estate planning. Another perk offered is additional insurance. Over and above the complete medical, dental, and life plans that SKB already provides, supplementary life and home-owners' insurance is offered to employees at discounted prices. One very special benefit Johnson mentioned was SKB's elder care referral service. We are in an era of ever-increasing life expectancies. The responsibility for caring physically, as well as financially, for elderly loved ones has never been as great. As the baby-boom generation's offsprings enter the workforce, with fears of depleted social security benefits and parents who will most likely live into their eighties (if not nineties!), affordable elder care is of paramount importance. SKB employees who are presented with the misfortune of not being able to care for their elderly parents can consult an elder care referral service at no cost. Not only does the service provide lists of care options and aid with financial planning, it also provides support services designed to help families cope with the stress of such an emotionally trying situation.

Source: Trip, T. 2005, 'Best practices case study—SmithKline Beecham Pharmaceuticals, benefits, best practices', http://www.vault.com/nr_newsmain.jsp?nr_page=3&ch_id=401&article_id=19266&cat_id=1089, accessed on 24 August 2005.

Questions
1. Briefly analyse the role of fringe benefits in employee motivation.
2. Critically analyse fringe benefits to employees and their impact on motivation in SmithKline Beecham Pharmaceuticals.
3. Suggest a revised/additional fringe benefit to make a job more attractive.

Compensation Packages and the Wages and Bonus Act

Objectives

After studying this chapter, you will be able to understand

- the goal of compensation management
- the factors influencing the various compensation structures
- competence-based compensation programmes
- why executives are paid differently
- different methods of working out compensation packages

INTRODUCTION

Compensation is what employees receive in exchange for the services rendered in an organization. The term 'compensation' refers to all forms of financial returns and tangible benefits that employees receive as part of the employment relationship. In the era of globalization, where the business environment has become increasingly complex and challenging, structuring an effective compensation package to attract and retain talent is an important function of organizational effectiveness. Designing an effective compensation programme, given cost constraints, greater demands, and greater professional expertise, requires more creativity and vision than ever before.

In the recent past, several changes have taken place in compensation packages. There has been a tremendous increase in the diversity of pay packages being offered by organizations. There was a time when employers in public sector organizations were the most highly paid in terms of scales of pay and benefits offered. The state-level public sectors had their own pay structures, and the private sector had its own strategy in this respect.

The important issue is 'does money matter?' The answer is yes. Money definitely provides a means for having a more affluent lifestyle—better clothes, vacations, better education, and so on. How much we earn often determines how we view ourselves, and our social status. In job situations, money motivates behaviour when it rewards people in relation to their performance or contributions, that is, when the employer or management is perceived as fair and equitable and provides rewards in recognition of the employee's true value. It is also interesting to note that particular components of pay have different values for different people. For example, research indicates that younger people tend to focus on cash compensation, whereas as people age, their preferences shift to benefits and workplace flexibility. Hence, at different stages in one's life and career, pay and compensation are perceived differently.

■ ■ ■
Compensation plays a key role in recruitment, job performance, and job satisfaction.

Employees' satisfaction with pay is an important criterion. Research also indicates that individuals differ in the way in which they conceptualize pay satisfaction. Pay satisfaction is a result of input–outcome ratio. Here inputs refer to effort, skill, education, previous work experience, special interest, and so on. Outcomes are what people get out of their jobs, such as pay, promotions, recognition, and so forth. Besides this, employees also tend to compare themselves with others in terms of their inputs and outcomes. When the employee perceives that there is some amount of fairness in the compensation they receive, the likelihood of experiencing satisfaction is more. Research also indicates that employee satisfaction with pay is directly proportional to commitment to the organization and trust in the management, while it is inversely related to absenteeism and lateness, seeking alternative employment opportunities, terminating employment with the organization, and incidence of theft.

OBJECTIVES OF COMPENSATION PLANNING

■ ■ ■
The most important objective of any pay system is fairness or equity.

The most important objective of any pay system is fairness or equity. The term equity has three dimensions.

- *Internal equity* ensures that more difficult jobs are paid more.
- *External equity* ensures that jobs are fairly compensated in comparison to similar jobs in the labour market.
- *Individual equity* ensures equal pay for equal work, that is, each individual's pay is fair in comparison to that of another person doing the same or a similar job.

In addition, there are other objectives of compensation planning, and an effective compensation system typically has the following characteristics.

- It enables an organization to attract and retain qualified, competent individuals.
- It motivates employee performance, fosters a feeling of equity, and provides direction to their efforts.
- It supports, communicates, and reinforces an organization's culture, values, and competitive strategy.
- Its cost structure reflects the organization's ability to pay.

Pay is the dominant organizational reward. Organizations provide rewards to their personnel to motivate their performance and encourage their loyalty and retention. These organizational rewards take a number of different forms including money salary, bonuses, incentive pay, recognition, and benefits. Reward management is about development, implementation, maintenance, communication, and evaluation of reward processes. These processes deal with the assessment of relative job values, the design and the management of pay structures, performance management, paying for performance, competence or skill (contingent pay), the provision of employee benefits and pensions, and the management of reward procedures. Reward management is also concerned

■ ■ ■
Reward management processes cover financial as well as non-financial rewards.

with the development of appropriate organizational cultures, underpinning core values, as well as increasing the motivation and commitment of employees. Reward management processes cover financial as well as non-financial rewards. In any organization, the motivating factor for the employees to increase productivity is compensation and other benefits attached to it.

Compensation Management Defined

Compensation management is a systematic approach to providing monetary value to employees in exchange for work performed. It may help to achieve several purposes, such as recruitment, job performance, and job satisfaction.

HOW IS COMPENSATION USED?

Compensation is a tool used by the management for a variety of purposes to further the existence of the company. It may be adjusted according to business needs, goals, and available resources. Compensation can be used to

- recruit and retain qualified employees,
- increase or maintain morale/satisfaction,
- reward and encourage peak performance,
- achieve internal and external equity,
- reduce turnover and encourage company loyalty, and
- modify (through negotiations) practices of unions.

Compensation may also be used as a reward for exceptional job performance. Examples of such plans include bonuses, commissions, ESOPS, profit sharing, and gain sharing.

■ ■ ■
Profit sharing is an incentive-based compensation programme to award employees a percentage of the company's profits.

An ESOP is a defined contribution employee benefit plan that allows employees to become owners of stock in the company they work for. It is an equity-based deferred compensation plan.

Profit sharing is an incentive-based compensation programme to award employees a percentage of the company's profits. Gain sharing compensates workers based on improvements in the company's productivity.

PSYCHOLOGICAL CONTRACT

When an employee enters an organization, it is obviously to fulfil certain expectations. Similarly, the employer's expectations about the employee's performance and productivity need to be managed and rewarded. Thus, both of them enter into a psychological contract. Expectations are built into the employment relationship, the starting point of which from the reward point of view is an undertaking by an employee to provide effort and skill to the employer in return for which the employer provides the employee with a salary or a wage. A contract, as defined by the Oxford English Dictionary, is a written or spoken arrangement or agreement made between two or more persons, usually enforceable by law. The word psychological means that the arrangement is only in the minds of those concerned, it is only a tacit agreement. Even though the concept is contradictory in nature, it has entered the domain of HR terminology and is used while referring to all aspects of employment relationships. Schein (1965) defined a psychological contract as follows: 'The notion of a psychological contract employee is that there is an unwritten set of expectations operating at all times between every member of an organization and various other managers.' Sims (1994) defines a psychological contract as the set of

■ ■ ■
A psychological contract is a system of beliefs that includes an employee's expectations on the one hand and the employer's trust on the other.

expectations held by the employee that specifies what the individual and the organization expect to give and receive from one another in the course of their working relationships.

A psychological contract then is a system of beliefs which includes on the one hand an employee's expectations and on the other the employer's trust. It is implicit. The aspects that might be covered in the contract may be

- how the employee is treated in fairness, equity, and consistency, and
- security of employment, career expectations, involvement in decision-making, trust in the organization, etc.

From the employers' point of view, the contract covers such aspects as

- competence,
- effort,
- compliance,
- commitment, and
- loyalty.

The importance of the psychological contract was emphasized by Schein who suggested that the extent to which people work effectively and are committed to the organization depends on the following factors:

- The degree to which their own expectations of what the organization will provide to them and what they owe to the organization in return matches the organization's expectations regarding what it will give and get in return, and
- The nature of what is actually to be exchanged (assuming there is some agreement)—money in exchange of time at work, social-need satisfaction and security in exchange of hard work and loyalty, opportunities for self-actualization and challenging work in exchange of high productivity, high-quality work, and creative effort in the service of organizational goals, or various combinations of these and other things.

Even though the contract is unarticulated, employees expect their competencies and effort to be rewarded suitably and to be provided opportunities for career advancement. It is for the management to manage its rewards in such a way that the employee's expectations are fulfilled. Otherwise, employees are likely to be disappointed and frustrated, and this may manifest itself in poor performance, low productivity, and behavioural aberrations. The basis of these expectations lies in the needs of the individuals. Needs are better understood in the backdrop of motivational theories and concepts. Exhibit 15.1 discusses the guidance on executive compensation and benefits by the US Treasury Department.

EXHIBIT 15.1   Executive compensation and benefits

Treasury Department Issues Guidance under IRC Section 409A in Notice 2005-1

11 January 2005

On 22 October 2004, President Bush signed into law the American Jobs Creation Act (the 'Act'). The Act created Section 409A of the Internal Revenue Code (IRC) of 1986 (the 'Code') that provides material changes to the tax treatment of nonqualified deferred compensation plans and arrangements. On 20 December 2004, the United States Treasury Department issued guidance on Section 409A in the form of Notice 2005-1 (the 'Notice').

(Contd)

EXHIBIT 15.1   (Contd)

The key areas in which the Notice provided guidance are outlined here.

Definitions

Section 409A of the Code provides that deferrals of compensation under a nonqualified deferred compensation plan for all taxable years are currently includible in gross income to the extent not subject to a substantial risk of forfeiture and not previously included in gross income, unless certain requirements are met.

A *deferral of compensation* occurs when an individual has a legally binding right during a taxable year to compensation that (a) has not been actually or constructively received and included in the individual's gross income and (b) is payable to such an individual in a later taxable year.

A *nonqualified deferred compensation plan* is any agreement, method or arrangement that provides for the deferral of compensation. The definition includes arrangements that apply to one or more individuals and is not limited to arrangements between an employer and an employee. As noted in the following paragraphs, this definition includes discount stock options and discount stock appreciation rights.

Compensation is subject to a *substantial risk of forfeiture* if entitlement to the amount is conditioned on the performance of substantial future services or the occurrence of a condition related to a purpose of the compensation, and the possibility of forfeiture is substantial. This is similar to (but broader) than the rule that applies under Section 83 of the Code. A forfeiture which would be triggered by the violation of a non-complete agreement is not a substantial risk of forfeiture.

Treatment of Stock Options and Stock Appreciation Rights

Options   Incentive stock options (ISOs) and nonqualified stock options (NSOs) issued with an exercise price of not less than fair market value (FMV) on the date of grant are not considered a deferral of compensation and therefore are not subject to Section 409A. However, NSOs that have an exercise price that is less than the FMV of the stock on the grant date will be subject to Section 409A. For companies that do not have publicly traded stock any *reasonable valuation method* may be used for purposes of determining the FMV of the stock at the date of grant. (This needs further definition and should be expanded to have at a minimum a 'good faith' standard similar to the valuation standard used for ISOs.) In addition, if an arrangement that allows the recipient to defer compensation beyond the later of exercise or disposition of the option, such as arrangements involving options and stock appreciation rights, even an ISO or an NSO with an exercise price that is at fair market value on the date of grant, will be subject to Section 409A. An option that has a feature such as an exercise price that was below FMV on the date of grant or other provision that would otherwise be subject it to Section 409A, will not be subject to Section 409A if it is exercised within 2½ months of the of the end of the option recipient's tax year or the option issuer's tax year in which the option becomes vested.

Stock appreciation rights   Stock appreciation rights (SARs) will not be subject to Section 409A provided: (a) the SAR exercise price is not less than the FMV of the underlying stock on the date the SAR is granted and cannot become less than such amount, (b) the stock of the service recipient subject to the SAR is traded on an established securities market, (c) only such traded stock of the service recipient may be delivered in settlement of the SAR upon exercise, and (d) the SAR does not include any feature for the deferral of compensation other than the deferral of recognition of income until the exercise of the SAR. However, if either: (a) under the terms of the SAR, the exercise price is less than the FMV of the stock on the date of grant, (b) the SAR may be settled upon exercise in a medium other than the traded stock of the service recipient, or (c) there is an agreement or arrangement under which the service recipient will purchase the stock delivered in settlement of the SAR upon exercise, then the grant of the SAR will be subject to Section 409A. (Until further guidance is issued, a payment of cash pursuant to the exercise of an SAR, or the cancellation of such right for consideration, where such right is granted pursuant to a programme in effect on or before 3 October 2004, will not be subject to Section 409A if: (a) the SAR exercise price may never be less than the FMV of the underlying stock on the date the right is granted and (b) the SAR does not include any feature for the deferral of compensation other than the

(Contd)

EXHIBIT 15.1 (Contd)

deferral of recognition of income until it is exercised.) An SAR that has a feature such as an exercise price that was below FMV on the date of grant or other provision that would otherwise be subject to Section 409A, will not be subject to Section 409A if it is exercised within 2½ months of the end of the SAR recipient's tax year or the option issuer's tax year in which the SAR becomes vested.

Corporate transactions In the event of a corporate transaction the substitution of a new option for an outstanding option, or the assumption of an outstanding option, will not cause the substituted or assumed option to be subject to Section 409A, provided the number of shares subject to the new option corresponds directly to the number of shares subject to the original option and the ratio of the option price to the FMV of the shares subject to the option immediately after the substitution or assumption is not greater than the ratio of the option price to the FMV of the shares subject to the option immediately before the substitution or assumption (as in the manner described in the Treasury regulations for substitution or assumption of ISOs in a merger). A corporate transaction is defined in the Notice as either: (a) a change in ownership of the corporation, (b) a change in effective control of the corporation, or (c) a change in the ownership of a substantial portion of the assets of the corporation, each of which is further defined in the Notice. In addition, a corporate transaction is a permissible distribution event under Section 409A (note—certain key employees may be required to wait for six months to receive a distribution, after a corporate transaction.

Replacement options and SARs Options and SARs that contain features that would cause them to be subject to Section 409A can be replaced with options and SARs respectively that do not contain such provisions. The replacement options or SARs will not be subject to Section 409A provided that (a) the cancellation and reissuance occurs on or before 31 December 2005, (b) the replacement option or SAR if it had been granted upon the original date of grant of the replaced stock option or SAR would not be subject to Section 409A, (c) the number of shares which form the basis of the new option or new SAR corresponds directly to the number of shares subject to the original option or SAR (as in the manner described in the Treasury Regulations for substitution or assumption of ISOs in a merger), and (d) the new option or new SAR does not provide any additional benefit to the service recipient (other than the benefit directly due to a change in form of the award to a form not subject to Section 409A). Further, the conversion of an SAR into an option would not cause the option to be subject to Section 409A provided the aforementioned requirements were satisfied.

Restricted stock Restricted stock that does not contain an additional deferral feature is not deferred compensation within the meaning of Section 409A.

Restricted stock units Restricted stock units (RSUs) are subject to Section 409A, but because RSUs are typically payable at a specific date, they generally do not present the type of problems that result in adverse tax consequences to the recipient under Section 409A.

Severance plans Severance plans that are either collectively bargained for or cover no key employees are not required to meet the requirements of Section 409A during 2005 provided the plan is amended by 31 December 2005 to comply with the provisions of Section 409A. Further guidance will be necessary to determine if severance payable to key employees will be outside the scope of Section 409A provided the amount is payable within a specified period of time following termination of employment.

Traditional Deferred Compensation Plans

The Notice provides several points of guidance on the transitioning of traditional deferred compensation plans to comply with Section 409A.

Freezing or terminating a plan Amending a plan in effect as of October 3, to stop future deferrals on or before 31 December 2005, will not cause payments under the plan to be subject to Section 409A. Also, terminating a plan and distributing the amounts of deferred compensation thereunder on or before 31 December 2005 will not

EXHIBIT 15.1 (Contd)

cause the plan or amounts distributed to be subject to Section 409A, provided that all amounts deferred under the plan are included in income in the taxable year in which the termination occurs.

Amending a plan to comply with section 409A Plans adopted before 31 December 2005 will be treated as complying with the requirements of Section 409A during 2005 only if (a) the plan is operated in good faith compliance with the provisions of Section 409A and the Notice during the calendar year 2005, (b) the plan is amended on or before 31 December 2005 to conform to the provisions of Section 409A with respect to amounts subject to Section 409A.

Elections to defer 2005 compensation An election made on or before 15 March 2005 to defer compensation that relates all or in part to services performed on or before 31 December 2005 will comply with timing requirements of Section 409A, provided that (a) the individual deferring the compensation does not have a right to receive the compensation at the time of election, (b) the plan under which the deferral election is or was made was in existence on or before 31 December 2004, (c) the elections to defer compensation are made in accordance with the terms of the plan in effect on or before 31 December 2005 (other than a requirement to make a deferral election after 15 March 2005), (d) the plan is otherwise operated in accordance with Section 409A with respect to deferrals subject to Section 409A and (e) the plan is timely amended to comply with the requirements of Section 409A.

Subsequent Steps

Option and SAR awards Employers who have issued NSOs or SARs that will vest after 31 December 2004 should review those awards to ensure that they do not contain provisions that would require treatment of such awards as a deferral of compensation (such as an exercise price less than FMV at the date of grant, or an additional deferral feature subsequent to exercise). Further, companies that are not publicly traded should refrain from issuing SARs until additional guidance is provided with respect to their treatment under Section 409A.

Option plans Employers should review the provisions of their option plans that govern the treatment of awards in a corporate transaction to ensure that the treatment will comply with the requirements of Section 409A. If options are being substituted or assumed in a corporate transaction, care should be taken to ensure that the assumption or substitution will not result in a material modification that would make the option subject to the provisions of Section 409A.

Freeze vested plans If a plan only contains deferrals that will be vested prior to 31 December 2004 and were not materially modified after 3 October 2004, it should be frozen immediately to prohibit additional deferrals under the plan and a new plan adopted that conforms to the requirements of Section 409A.

Termination and amendment of plans with unvested deferrals If a plan contains deferrals that will not be vested as of 31 December 2004 it should either be (a) terminated with all deferrals under the plan distributed by 31 December 2005 or (b) the plan provisions applicable to all deferrals that are not fully vested as of 31 December 2004 should be amended to comply with the requirements of Section 409A by 31 December 2005.

If a plan is terminated, any new plan that is adopted should contain all the necessary provisions in order to comply with Section 409A.

Deferred compensation If an employee wishes to defer compensation that relates to services performed in 2005, the employee must make an election on or before 15 March 2005 with respect to such compensation. The employee may not have a right to the compensation to be deferred at the time of the election and the election must be made pursuant to a plan that was in existence as of 31 December 2004. The plan must be operated in accordance with the requirements of Section 409A during 2005 and be amended to comply with requirements of Section 409A by 31 December 2005.

(Contd)

EXHIBIT 15.1 (Contd)

Grandfathered provisions and material modifications   If an award under a plan was earned and vested as of 31 December 2004 and there has not been a material modification to that award after 3 October 2004 then the award and all subsequent earnings attributable to that award will be 'grandfathered' and therefore not subject to Section 409A. In the event a material modification is made to an award after 3 October 2004 such award will lose its grandfathered status and will be subject to Section 409A even if the terms of the material modification do not violate Section 409A. Generally any addition or enhancement of a benefit to an award such as adding provisions that allow early distribution with a penalty or accelerating vesting of an award will qualify as a material modification. Amending a plan to bring it into compliance with Section 409A will not qualify as a material modification.

Participant termination or deferral cancellation   A plan amendment allowing plan participants to terminate their participation in the plan or cancel a deferral election any time on or prior to 31 December 2005, with respect to amounts subject to Section 409A will not cause such amounts or the plan to be subject to Section 409A provided (a) the amendment is enacted and effective on or before 31 December 2005, and (b) the amounts subject to the termination or cancellation are includible in income of the participant in the taxable year in which the amounts are earned and vested.

This summary highlights certain key aspects of the Notice. The Notice contains several other points of guidance not mentioned here and is only the first of many publications issued by the Treasury Department on Section 409A.

THEORIES UNDERLYING MOTIVATION AND REMUNERATION

Discussed here are the major theories underlying the relation of motivation and remuneration.

- Maslow's need-hierarchy theory
- Herzberg's two-factor theory
- Porter and Lawler's model
- Adam's equity theory

Maslow's Need-hierarchy Theory

Abraham Maslow propounded a theory of human nature that proposed that everyone is motivated to satisfy a series of needs. According to Maslow, needs in a human being are arranged in hierarchy, beginning with physiological or basic needs, which are essential for survival. These include the need for food, water, shelter, rest, sleep, and so on. The next in the hierarchy are safety and security needs, which include the needs for protection from physical and psychological threats in the environment. Next in the order are social and belongingness needs, which include the needs for love, affection, social interaction, and acceptance of others. Self-esteem needs come next, which include the needs for recognition, respect from others, status, power, and competence. Self-actualization needs form the apex in the hierarchy, which include the needs for self-fulfilment, achievement, growth, and realization of one's potential.

■ ■ ■
Maslow believed that needs are arranged in a hierarchy, and a need that is satisfied will no longer motivate an individual.

Maslow believed that needs are arranged in a hierarchy, and a need that is satisfied will no longer motivate an individual. If we were to interpret Maslow's hierarchy in the context of an organization, basic needs would be interpreted as those relating to pay, safety as job security, social needs as the needs for belongingness or affiliation to formal and informal groups, esteem needs as the desire for recognition, status, awards, and so on, and self-actualization as the need to maximize one's potential for the maximum benefit of the organization and society at large.

Here, we may observe that the growth needs, which comprise esteem needs and self-actualization, are the ones that are relevant to compensation packages. The differential in expectations among the employees is responsible for the differential in performances. This theory also helps in understanding human behaviour and designing compensation packages that benefit both the organization and the employees.

Herzberg's Two-factor Theory of Motivation

■ ■ ■
Motivators include interesting and meaningful work achievement, recognition, responsibility, personal growth, and advancement.

Herzberg propounded his theory by identifying two sets of factors that operate in a work environment—hygiene factors and motivators. Hygiene factors include pay, working conditions, supervision, company policy, administration, and interpersonal relationships. According to Herzberg, hygiene factors are basic and do not motivate an individual. However, their absence causes dissatisfaction. Motivators include interesting and meaningful work achievement, recognition, responsibility, personal growth, and advancement. The absence of these factors would simply mean lack of motivation among employees. Hence, an organization must ensure that hygiene factors as well as motivators are present in the work environment.

The implication for compensation management is that when employees expect motivators to be present and are willing to expend effort for the benefit of the organization, they would also expect to be suitably rewarded.

Porter and Lawler's Model

Porter and Lawler's model of motivation, contrary to other popular models, treats performance, motivation, and satisfaction as three distinctly different variables. Though it is rather similar to Vroom's theory, since both postulate that the efforts put in by the individual are commensurate with the rewards received by him/her, good performances may not always indicate job satisfaction. Porter and Lawler's model helps to comprehend better, the key variables in employee effort and performance.

The theory has generated considerable research and raised questions as to how satisfaction may be related to compensation, employee morale, etc. Porter and Lawler have also opined that the reward policies of organizations should be re-evaluated in the light of factors such as employee satisfaction and performance.

Adam's Equity Theory

The equity theory has its origin in Stacey Adam's theory in the field of economics. The word equity denotes balance and fairness. The theory advocates that individuals expect to be treated equitably in their work relationship. A fair treatment is ensured in terms of wages and other fringe benefits. Employees constantly compare their rewards and inputs with those of other employees, and make efforts to restore the balance in this respect. This may be diagrammatically presented as shown in Figure 15.1.

■ ■ ■
The implication of Adam's equity theory is that employees compare their rewards and inputs with those of other employees and make efforts to restore balance in this regard.

The motivational implications are that employees strive to attain equity and restore balance in comparison with others. The theory focusses more on rewards as manipulated by the organization. As the individual moves towards equity, it results in job satisfaction and better performance. The theory again has a cognitive base, and under emphasis is the employees' ability to understand

and evaluate the situation accurately. The motivation theory has certain implications so far as financial and non-financial rewards are concerned. First, there are no simple methods to increase motivation. Motivation is a complex process and depends on individual needs and aspirations,

Individual rewards	Other's rewards
Individual inputs	Other's inputs

FIGURE 15.1   Adam's equity theory

which are variable, intrinsic and extrinsic, and the perceived equity of the individuals regarding their performance or contribution. Reactions to reward policy and practices depend largely on the values and needs of the individuals and on their employment conditions. Pay certainly motivates. Pay also delivers messages about what the organization believes to be important. However, research by Porter and Lawler, and others, has also shown that higher paid employees are likely to be more satisfied with their rewards, but the satisfaction resulting from a large pay increase may be short-lived. Other factors such as perceived equity and other work-related aspects are also responsible for satisfaction or dissatisfaction.

Adams (1966) suggests that individuals can

- change inputs, that is, can reduce effort, if underpaid,
- try to change their outcomes, that is, ask for a pay rise or promotion, and
- psychologically distort their own ratios or those of others by rationalizing differences in inputs and outcomes, and
- change the reference group to which they compare themselves in order to restore equity.

FACTORS AFFECTING PAY LEVELS

Pay structures are designed in accordance with judgements about job values in comparison with other jobs, and market rates of pay for comparable jobs. These judgements are made against the background of the factors, which influence job values. Job values may be established by using some form of job evaluation. Among others, the following factors determine pay levels:

- Belief about the worth of the job, which includes influence of the position, responsibility, skill requirements, and other duties;
- Individual characteristics such as age, experience, seniority, qualifications, special skills, contribution, and performance; and
- Demand and supply—the compensation package is also influenced by labour supply and demand in general or at the local labour market.

Apart from this, organizations also use several methods to formulate a competitive pay rate, such as the use of job-market surveys, an exchange of information between organizations, and paying more for a scarce skill.

- Each company formulates its own compensation policy and strategy, which are reviewed from time to time and are influenced by central and state laws.

■ ■ ■
Job values may be established by using some form of job evaluation.

- Depending on their bargaining power, trade unions attempt to pressurize managements into increasing pay at least at the time of inflation. Unions press for higher rates on the grounds of the organization's ability to pay, the trends in the market, and the going rate for specific jobs, and may attempt to restore lost differentials.

- The government may intervene in the employment relationship by attempting to influence wage inflation through initiatives introduced in the public sector and by encouraging certain types of compensation such as profit sharing or share-options schemes.

The pay levels of individual jobholders are influenced by three factors in addition to the rate for their jobs.

- Their market worth
- Their levels of skill or the competence they possess—their inputs
- Their level of performance in the job—their outputs and the overall contribution they make to organizational success

The amount of influence these factors exert will depend on the job and the internal environment of the organization. In a non-bureaucratic and flexible firm, where the level of technology is high and a large proportion of the staff comprises knowledge workers, individual worth will be more important than position in a job hierarchy. As Kanter has stated, 'Major employing organizations are rethinking the meaning of worth itself. And as they are doing this, they are gradually changing the basis for determining pay from position to performance, from status to contribution.'

ASSESSING JOB WORTH

Assessing job worth is an important step in designing a compensation package. Such assessment includes job analysis and job evaluation.

Job analysis is a process of collecting, analysing, and setting out information about jobs in order to provide a basis for job description. It provides data for job evaluation and performance management, and has been dealt with in Chapter 5.

In this chapter, we will consider job evaluation in the context of compensation management. Job evaluation is a process of assessing the relative importance of jobs within an organization. It involves using the information obtained through job analysis to systematically determine the value of each job in relation to all jobs within an organization. In other words, job evaluation seeks to rank all the jobs in the organization and place them in a hierarchy that reflects the relative worth of each. Job evaluation assumes normal performance of the job, and the process ignores individual abilities or the performance of the jobholder. The ranking that results from the evaluation is a means to an end and is used normally to determine pay structures. Even though other influencing factors operate for determining the pay structure, job evaluation methods provide an objective standard in relation to which modifications can be made. Three basic job evaluation approaches are most common:

> ■ ■ ■
> Job evaluation is a process of assessing the relative importance of jobs within an organization.

- Job ranking
- Job classification
- Point-factor method

Job Ranking

> ■ ■ ■
> Job ranking compares the whole jobs and does not take into account the different aspects of each job.

It is the simplest, fastest, and oldest method of job evaluation. It compares the whole job and does not take into account the different aspects of each job. It determines the positions of jobs in a hierarchy by placing them in a rank according to perceptions of relative importance. It involves the placing of jobs in an order from the most important or difficult to the least important or the least difficult, using a single factor such as job complexity or the importance of the job to the firm's, competitive advantage. Even though it is the simplest method, it has its own demerits. There is no rationale to defend rank order. It becomes difficult to attain clarity as to the criterion used in ranking. When jobs have many dimensions, placing them in an order becomes difficult. Different evaluators may give a different weightage to the same aspect. Ranking dissimilar jobs is also difficult. The discrepancies between the ranks, particularly in the middle, may not be pronounced. Finally, the ranking approach provides no information concerning how much more valuable one job is in relation to another, or how the knowledge, abilities, and skills of one job relate to those of another. This could be a key drawback for an organization that is committed to employee development, internal mobility, cross-training programmes, and career ladders.

Job Classification

A method involving job classification compares job descriptions to pre-established grade descriptors. It is based on an initial decision regarding the number and characteristics of the grade into which the jobs will be placed. The grade definitions attempt to take differences in skill, responsibility, and also some specific criteria, such as knowledge, education, and training, to do the work. Jobs are allotted to grades by comparing the whole job descriptions with the grade definition. The classification system is relatively inexpensive and easy to administer. It is simple, quick, and easily implemented. It attempts to provide some standards for judgement in the form of grade definitions. However, when specific level descriptions do not exist, the method becomes unclear and difficult. At times, the descriptions can become very generalized. This method also tends to be inflexible in that it is not sensitive to changes in the nature and content of jobs.

> ■ ■ ■
> Job classification compares job descriptions to pre-established grade descriptors and is based on an initial decision regarding the number and characteristics of the grade, in which jobs are placed.

Point-factor Method

The third method used in job evaluation is the point-factor method. In this method, jobs are classified on the basis of certain criteria, and the extent to which each of these jobs fulfils the criteria allows for classification in a particular way. Some of the identifiable criteria are skill, effort, and responsibility. In choosing factors, the organization also raises fundamental questions such as: What particular job components are valued? What job characteristics should we pay? Besides mental effort, decision-making responsibility, complexity of work, consequence of error, physical demands, skills required, and working conditions are the most common factors. Depending upon the importance of each criterion to performing the job, appropriate weights are given, points are summed, and jobs with similar point totals are placed in similar grades. A job's relative worth is the sum of the numerical values for each degree within each factor. A job hierarchy is derived by ranking jobs by their total point score. Jobs may change over time, but the weighting scales established may stay in time. The fact that jobs are broken down into parts and evaluated using the same criteria over and over again limits the possibility of rater bias. On the other hand, factor plans are complex, costly, and time consuming to develop. The key criteria must be carefully and clearly identified. Degrees of factors have to be agreed upon and point values

> ■ ■ ■
> The point-factor method classifies jobs on the basis of characteristics such as skill, effort, and responsibility.

TABLE 15.1   Example of a point-factor method

Job class: Clerk

Factor	1st degree	2nd degree	3rd degree	4th degree	5th degree
Skill					
• Education	22	44	66	88	110
• Problem solving	14	28	42	56	70
Responsibility					
• Safety of others	5	10	15	20	25
• Work of others	7	14	21	28	35

Problem solving

This factor examines the types of problems dealt with in your job. Indicate the one level that is most representative of the majority of your job responsibilities.

Degree 1: Actions are performed in a set order according to written or verbal instructions. Problems are referred to the supervisor.

Degree 2: Solves routine problems and makes various choices regarding the order in which the work is performed within standard practices. May obtain information from varied sources.

Degree 3: Solves varied problems that require general knowledge of company policies and procedures applicable within area of responsibility. Decisions made are based on a choice from established alternatives. Expected to act within standards and established procedures.

Degree 4: Requires analytical judgement, initiative, or innovation in dealing with complex problems or situations. Evaluation not easy because there is little precedent or information may be incomplete.

Degree 5: Plans, delegates, coordinates, and/or implements complex tasks involving new or constantly changing problems or situations. Involves the origination of new technologies or policies for programmes or projects. Actions are limited only by company policies and budgets.

must be assigned to these degrees. However, it is one of the widely used methods. This method offers greater stability when compared to the other methods (Table 15.1).

DEVELOPING PAY STRUCTURES

Once the job evaluation is complete, the data generated become the basis for the development of the organization's pay structure. It means that pay rates will be established that are compatible with the ranks, classifications, or points arrived at through job evaluation. The way an organization structures its compensation packages is primarily a matter of organizational philosophy though market trends play an important role. An organization can choose from several options available. It can use a single-rate structure in which all employees performing the same work receive the same pay. The second method is tenure based, that is, based on the time for which an individual has been associated with the organization. There can be a combination of seniority and tenure-based plans also. At times, pay can be linked to performance or productivity. The job evaluation methods provide necessary inputs for developing an organization's overall pay structure. Besides these methods, other sources exist to procure information about wages, such as

> ■ ■ ■
> The way an organization structures its compensation packages is primarily a matter of organizational philosophy.

- surveys,
- reports published by the Ministry of Labour,

- pay commission reports,
- reports of Wage Boards appointed by the government,
- reports of employees' and employers' organizations,
- trade journals of specific industry groups, etc.

At times, these sources may not include information about the actual type of job, which may be specific to a particular organization. In such instances, other survey methods are generally used to collect relevant wage-related information.

- *Key job matching*: Under this method, similar key jobs are identified in other organizations and the relevant wage particulars about those comparable jobs are collected.
- *Key class matching*: Similar classes of jobs are identified and the necessary data about those classes are collected.
- *Occupational method*: Certain basic occupational groups, such as clerks, officers, and managers, are identified and the necessary data are collected.
- *Job-evaluation method*: All the parties participating in the survey method use the same method and the same mechanism for evaluating similar jobs.
- *Broad classification method*: Under this method, broad groups of relatively homogeneous jobs, that is, according to industry, profession, or geographical area, are formed and the relevant information about these jobs is collected.

Grouping Similar Jobs into Pay Grades

A pay grade consists of jobs of approximately equal difficulty or importance as determined by job evaluation.

In this step, similar jobs (in terms of their ranking or number of points ascertained by the job evaluation committee) are grouped into grades for pay purposes. The organization can now focus on, say 10 to 12 pay grades, instead of hundreds of pay rates. A pay grade consists of jobs of approximately equal difficulty or importance as determined by job evaluation. If the point-factor method is used, the pay grade consists of jobs falling within a range of points. Ten to sixteen grades per job cluster (factory jobs, clerical jobs) is common.

Fine-tuning Pay Rates and Determining the Wage Structure

Here the employers fix a pay range for each grade (Officer Grade I, II and III, for example, in the banking industry). The wage structure of a company is nothing, but a pay scale showing ranges of pay within each grade. However, the pay structure depends on several other factors, such as the organization's ability to pay, supply and demand of labour, the prevailing market rate, cost of living, productivity, the trade union's bargaining power, job requirements, and so on.

PRINCIPLES OF WAGE AND SALARY ADMINISTRATION

According to Webster's dictionary, wage is a 'payment for service rendered, especially such payment calculated by the hour, day, or week, or for a certain amount of work'.

The generally accepted principles governing the fixation of wages and salary are as follows:

- The organization should have a definite plan to ensure differences in pay as per job requirements.
- The general level of wage or salary should be in line with the prevailing market rate.

- There should be equal pay for equal work.
- Special abilities and skills should be rewarded suitably.
- The wage structure should be flexible and adoptable according to changing economic conditions.
- A wage should be such that it fulfils an individual's basic needs.

Wages and Payment of Wages Act

> ■ ■ ■
> The basic wage is the remuneration by way of basic salary paid to the employee.

The term 'wages' in the broad sense means any economic compensation paid by the employer under some contract to his employees for the services rendered by them. The basic wage is the remuneration by way of basic salary paid to the employee. Allowances on the other hand are paid in addition to the basic wage to maintain the value of the basic wage over a period of time. Such allowances include holiday pay, overtime pay, bonus, and social security benefits. Under the Payment of Wages Act, 1936, Section 2 (vi), 'any award of settlement and production bonus, if paid, constitutes wages.'

The following types of remuneration, if paid, do not amount to wages under any of the Acts:

- Bonus or other payments under a profit-sharing scheme, which do not form a part of the contract of employment
- Value of any house accommodation, supply of electricity, water, medical attendance, travelling allowance, or payment in lieu thereof or any other concession
- Any sum paid to defray special expenses entailed by the nature of the employment of a workman
- Any contribution to pension, provident fund, or a scheme of social security and social insurance benefits
- Any other amenity or service excluded from the computation of wages by a general or special order of an appropriate governmental authority

Theories of Wages

Several theories of wages have been propounded by various thinkers in the last three centuries.

Adam Smith's Wage Fund Theory

Adam Smith (1723–90) assumed that the employer has a reservoir of funds and utilized them for paying the wages of employees. If the fund was large enough, correspondingly the payment of wages was high. If the fund was small, the wages were low. The demand for labour and the wages that could be paid were determined by the size of the fund.

Subsistence Theory

This is also known as the Iron Law of Wages as stated by David Ricardo (1772–1823). It states that labourers should be paid to enable them to subsist without increase or diminution in their numbers. It assumes that when they were paid more than the subsistence level, they might indulge in enjoyment and consequently their numbers would increase, and this would result in a low rate of wages. If the wages fell below the subsistence level, the number of workers would decrease as many would suffer from malnutrition and disease. Then the wage rate would increase as the number of labourers would decrease.

Karl Marx's Theory

According to Marx, labour is an article or commodity that can be purchased on payment of a price. The price of any product is determined by the time and effort needed to produce it. The labourer is not paid in proportion to the time spent and the surplus goes to the management to meet other expenses.

Residual Claimant theory

Francis Walker (1840–97) stated that there were four factors involved in production—land, labour, capital, and entrepreneurship. Wages represent the amount of value created in production, which remains after payments have been made for all other factors of production.

Marginal Productivity Theory

This theory was developed by Philips, Henry, and Clark. It assumes that wages depend on the demand for, and supply of, labour. Hence, labour is paid for according to its worth. As long as each worker contributes more to the total value created than his or her cost in wages, it is viable for the employer to continue, and when this becomes uneconomical, the employer may resort to other measures.

Minimum Wage, Living Wage, and Fair Wage

Money is often looked upon as a means of fulfilling the basic needs of man. Food, clothing, transportation, education, and security are possible because of money. Promotions, monetary benefits, and other allowances act as motivators. In India in 1948, the Committee on Fair Wages was set up to bring out a report on minimum wage, fair wage, and living wage.

Minimum Wage

A minimum wage is defined by the Committee as the wage that must provide not only for the bare sustenance of life, but also preserve the efficiency of the worker. Hence, the minimum wage must also meet the requirements of the worker's family's education and health.

The 15th Indian Labour Conference (1957) formally qualified the term 'minimum wage' thus:

- In calculating the minimum wage, the standard working class family should be taken to comprise three consumption units for one earner, the earnings of women, children, and adolescents being disregarded.
- Minimum food requirements should be calculated on the basis of a set intake of calories as recommended by Dr Aykroyd for an average Indian adult of moderate activity.
- Clothing requirements should be estimated on the basis of a per capita consumption of 18 yards per annum, which would give for the average worker's family of four a total of 72 yards.

> ■ ■ ■
> Minimum wage in India is defined as the wage that must not only provide for the bare sustenance of life, but also preserve the efficiency of the worker.

- In respect of housing, the rent corresponding to the minimum area provided for under the Government Industrial Housing Scheme should be taken into consideration in fixing the minimum wage.
- Fuel, lighting, and other miscellaneous items of expenditure should constitute 20% of the total minimum wage.

Living Wage

The living wage as defined by the committee is one which should enable the earner to provide for himself and his family food, clothing, shelter, and also education and medical needs, social

■ ■ ■
The living wage should enable the earner to provide for himself/herself, the food, clothing, and shelter required for his/her family, and also his/her education and medical needs.

needs, and a measure of insurance. Such a wage was determined keeping in view the national income and the capacity to pay. The living wage may be somewhere between the lowest level of the minimum wage and the highest limit of the living wage, depending upon the bargaining power of labour, the capacity of the industry to pay, the level of the national income, the general effect of the wage rise on neighbouring industries, the productivity of labour, the place of industry in the economy of the country, and the prevailing rates of wages in the same or similar occupations in neighbouring localities.

Fair Wage

According to the Committee on Fair Wages, it is a wage that is above the minimum wage, but below the living wage. The lower limit of fair wage is the minimum wage and the upper limit is the capacity of the industry to pay. Hence, a fair wage may depend upon such factors as productivity of labour, prevailing rates of wages, level of national income, the place of the industry in the economy, and so on.

Payment of Bonus Act, 1965

The word 'bonus' implies something paid as a gesture of goodwill. It is a payment made to the employee out of the profits earned by the employer, over and above the remuneration that the employee gets. It is not an exgratia payment, but the statutory right of the employee. The Bonus Act is the outcome of the recommendation made by the Tripartite Commission, set up by the Government of India way back in 1961. On 2 September 1964, the government implemented the recommendation of the commission with certain changes. Accordingly, the Payment of Bonus Ordinance, 1965 was promulgated on 26 May 1965. Subsequently, it was accepted by the parliament and accordingly, in the year 1965, the Payment of Bonus Act was enacted. The Act was amended in 1968, 1969, 1975, 1976, 1977, 1978, 1980, 1985, and 1995.

The main objectives of the act are as follows:

- To impose a statutory obligation on the employer of every establishment defined in the Act to pay a bonus to all eligible employees working in establishments
- To outline the principles of payment of bonus according to a prescribed formula
- To provide for payment of minimum and maximum bonus and link the payment of bonus with the scheme of 'set off' and 'set on'
- To provide a machinery for the enforcement of bonus

Scope and Application

The Act extends to the whole of India. The Act is applicable to those establishments employing 20 or more workers employed on any day during a working year. Subsequent reduction in the strength will not make the Act inapplicable to an establishment. The Act does not apply to any public enterprises, except those in competition with similar private undertakings. It is also inapplicable to non-profit organizations such as the RBI and LIC, and departmentally managed undertakings. However, all banks are covered under this Act. The appropriate government by notification in the official gazette can make the provisions of the Act (applicable to any class of establishment's specified theories,) in-

■ ■ ■
The Payment of Bonus Act, 1965, is applicable to the whole of India and applies to establishments employing 20 or more workers on any day during a working year.

cluding factories. However, if the number of employees falls below 10, then the Act cannot be enforced.

Important Definitions

Certain terms have been defined in Section 2 of the Act, such as

- accounting year,
- allocable surplus,
- available surplus,
- appropriate government,
- award,
- employee,
- employer, and
- wage or salary.

The Act also provides the appropriate proforma in which gross profits and available surplus are to be calculated.

Eligibility for Bonus

Every employee shall be entitled to receive any bonus in a given accounting year according to the provisions of the Act, provided he or she has worked in the establishment for not less than thirty days in that year notwithstanding anything contained in the Act. An employee shall not be entitled to any bonus if his or her services are terminated on account of

- fraud,
- riotous or violent behaviour within the establishment, or
- theft, misappropriation, etc.

There is a provision of minimum and maximum limit of bonus in the Act. (minimum 8.33% of wages and salary, and not exceeding 20%). The amount of bonus is required to be paid to any employee within a period of 8 months from the close of the accounting year. Any dispute between an employer and an employee regarding bonus will be deemed an industrial dispute under the purview of the Industrial Dispute Act. Penalty for offences are imprisonment for a term, which may extend to six months or a fine, which may extend to ₹1,000, or both.

It is the statutory obligation on the part of the employees to maintain a register in the prescribed format showing all the details. (computation of allocable surplus, disbursement of bonus, etc.).

REGULATION OF WAGES

The Government of India has adopted various methods to regulate wages in India, such as prescribing minimum rates of wages, regulating payment of wages, settlement of wage-related disputes, setting up wage boards, and so on. The Minimum Wages Act provides for prescribing minimum wages that can be fixed on hourly, daily, or monthly basis. The Act also provides for the setting up of tripartite bodies consisting of government employees and trade unions to provide guidelines in fixing and revising minimum wage rates. The rates may be subjected to a revision periodically—the period between subsequent revisions should not exceed five years. The main objective of the Act is to regulate payment to the worker without any deductions. The Act prescribes the following permissible deductions to be made from the employee's salary: fines, deductions for (a) absence, (b) loss of goods entrusted to the worker, (c) house provided by the employer, (d) services provided by the employee, (e) advances given to the worker, (f) tax payable by the employer, and (g) deductions under court orders, cooperative society, provident fund (PF), insurance premium, etc.

Any dispute regarding wages is normally settled through the collective bargaining process in which various employee problems are settled through the mechanism of joint consultation. If problems do not get settled in this fashion, they may be settled through voluntary arbitration or adjudication. The Government of India also appoints wage boards, separately for each industry, for the fixation and revision of wages. Each wage board consists of one neutral chairman, two independent members, and representatives of workers and the management. The wage board considers the following factors for fixing or revising the wages in various industries: (a) job evaluation, (b) wage rates for similar jobs in comparable industries, (c) the employees' productivity, (d) the firms' ability to pay, (e) various wage legislations, (f) the existing level of wage differentials and their desirability, (g) the government's objectives regarding social justice, social equality, economic justice, and economic equality, (h) the place of the industry in the economy and the society of the country, and the region, and (i) the need for incentives, improvement in productivity, etc.,

The wage boards fix and revise various components of wages such as basic pay, dearness allowance, incentive earnings, overtime pay, house rent allowance, and all other allowances.

Wages and allowances of Central and State Government employees are determined through pay commissions appointed by the government. We have had the reports of five pay commissions. The disputes arising out of the pay commission's recommendations and their implementation are decided by commissions of enquiry, the adjudication machinery, and the joint consultative machinery.

EXECUTIVE REMUNERATION

Executive remuneration basically centres around factors such as job complexity, the company's ability to pay, and executive human capital. Organizations decide executive compensation packages consisting of basic pay allowances, perquisites, and stock options, based on a number of factors. The Phoenix plan uses 28 compensable factors. The Hay group uses three compensable factors—accountability, problem solving, and know-how. The compensation survey report of Business International, Asia-Pacific Limited, Hong Kong, considered the following factors to determine the executive compensation: education, experience, scope of activities, need to negotiate, types of problems handled, decision-making authority, size of the unit managed, influence on results, number of people supervised, and number of reporting steps to the head of the unit. Indian companies usually structure executive compensation based on the following factors: salary, bonus, commission, PF, family pension, medical reimbursement, pension funds, leave travel assistance, house rent allowance, and other perquisites. In recent years, other types of allowances including stock options and developmental initiatives have also been included.

CURRENT TRENDS IN SALARY ADMINISTRATION

In recent years, salary administration and wage calculations have undergone changes. Three major approaches have resulted—broadbanding, pay for competence or knowledge, and team pay.

Broadbanding

Broadbanding is an approach to base pay that is receiving considerable attention in the business press. It is the compression of a hierarchy of pay grades or salary ranges into a smaller number of wide bands. The 1996 survey by Hay management consultants produced the following list of the most common reasons given for introducing broadbanding:

- It allows more flexibility in making and administering pay decisions.
- It recognizes that careers are more likely to develop within homogeneous levels of responsibility, rather than by progressing up a number of steps in a hierarchy.
- It reduces the problem of a grade drift, common in conventionally graded structures.
- It reduces the preoccupation with grade status, which can be a feature of more narrowly banded structures.
- More responsibility can be developed among line managers to manage pay within their own departments.
- It provides opportunity to simplify benefits and make the provision of these more flexible.
- It focusses on the value-adding tiers within an organization.

Broadbanding is more applicable to flat and lean organizations. In simple terms, it means consolidating the existing pay grades into fewer grades in a meaningful manner. The width of the pay is larger, and the difference between the minimum and maximum may be more than 200%. For example, if the traditional pay grade ranged between ₹10,000 and ₹18,000, in the newer approach it would range between ₹10,000 and ₹40,000. It basically creates more flexibility, enabling a firm to shift people within the organization in the name of job rotation. This facilitates employee empowerment and team-building processes. General Electric collapsed 30 pay grades covering administrative, executive, and professional employees into five broad bands. Hewitt Associates studied the experience of 106 organizations that replaced traditional pay grades with broad bands by conducting focus groups that included affected employees, the managers responsible for administering the new plans, and top organizational executives. An American Compensation Association study of broadband organizations found that 78% considered the approach to be effective. Broadbanding has the following advantages:

- It enhances flexibility in pay delivery, managing the reward system and adjusting pay in response to market-rate variations—there is more scope for varying the rates of pay offered to new employees on the basis of their market worth, and new or wider responsibilities can be allocated to people or assumed by them (and in either case rewarded appropriately) without going through an appeals procedure.
- It can reflect and support the operation of a process-based organization with fewer levels of management and supervision.
- It supports teamwork by encouraging the development of multifocus roles and a 'boundary-less organization'.
- It enables organizations to provide rewards for lateral career development, continuous learning, and the achievement of high levels of competence and contribution.
- It provides a means of integrating reward and employee-development strategies.

Broadbanding creates more flexibility in the organization and facilitates employee empowerment and team-building.

- It addresses the personal-growth needs of people by offering pay opportunities for mastering new competencies within the band—pay progression is not restricted by narrow and rigidly enforced salary ranges.
- It enhances the ability of the organization to reward people for what they bring to the business beyond their job descriptions.
- It directs employee attention toward career growth, indicating through the wider spread of pay opportunities that only significantly larger job responsibilities merit moving to a higher pay band.
- It reduces the time spent in analysing and evaluating jobs because there are fewer levels between which distinctions need to be made.
- It reduces the pressure for upgrading and, therefore, grade drift, which is often present in multigraded structures, while still presenting ample pay opportunities.
- It can allow the devolution of more responsibility and accountability to line managers to make pay decisions.

The advantages of broadbanding may seem to be considerable, but there are some important disadvantages.

- Broadbranding appears to restrict the number of promotional opportunities. Lateral career development pay may alleviate the problem, but employees may still look elsewhere to further their careers (although it could be said that this problem is a function of delayering rather than broadbanding, which often simply mirrors a flattened organization).
- It may meet with strong resistance from employees and their trade unions, if any—the benefits of broadbanding may be obvious to the management, but may not necessarily be equally compelling for employees.
- Employees formerly in higher grades may feel that their jobs have been devalued when they are placed in the same band as those previously in a lower grade—team leaders and their staff could be in the same band.
- It may result in employees being concerned by the apparent lack of structure and precision— they may miss the 'career signposts' previously defined by an extended hierarchy of grades through which they could progress.
- It may mean a return to the bad old days of management favouritism, subjective judgments, and inequalities because of the increased freedom for line managers to make their own pay decisions.
- It can make heavy demands on the interest and skills of line managers.
- It takes much time and effort to establish and maintain broadbanding.
- It requires significant commitment of training and communication resources.
- It can build up employee expectations of significant pay opportunities, which may not be met in many cases if proper control of the system is maintained. It should be made clear to the employees how the system will operate. While it should be indicated that there will be opportunity and reward for career development, it should be emphasized that these rewards will have to be earned.
- It may lead to escalating payroll costs unless very careful control is exercised over the operation of the system. However, there is a delicate balance to be achieved between allowing for sufficient flexibility and simultaneously maintaining the right amount of control.

- It may conflict with the culture of traditional hierarchical organizations where status is defined by job grading and progress is measured by the speed and extent to which people move up the grade hierarchy.
- It may lead to difficulties in ensuring that equal pay for work of equal value imperatives are dealt with where analytical job evaluation is not done extensively.

These disadvantages can be alleviated by such means as extensive consultation, communication, participation, and training. In addition, even when the policy is to devolve responsibility to line managers, the HR function has a key role in providing guidance, help, training, and information to managers. Monitoring and budgeting procedures can be used to ensure consistency, equity, and control. However, the disadvantages could outweigh the advantages, and this is why it is important to weigh carefully the extent to which the organization is ready for broadbanding and the amount of work required before committing resources to developing it.

In essence, broadbanding will be successful when organizations are willing to create a flexible structure, when status consciousness is not a matter of concern, and when they are willing to create more scope for employee reward.

Pay for Competence or Skill

The transaction between an employer and an employee is that of knowledge, competence, or skill. The application of skill or competence is what leads to performance, and performance is the criterion for evaluating effectiveness. Hence, it becomes obligatory on the part of the employer to foster, nurture, and reward competence or skill. How do we define competence? According to Webster's dictionary competence is defined as 'the state of being sufficiently able or qualified'.

Thomas Cook views competence as the knowledge, experience, and skills required to meet the demands of a role and the aptitudes required to perform the role to the required standard.

According to Boots, competence is 'any personal trait, characteristic, or skill which can be shown to be directly linked to effective or outstanding role performance'. The concept is further complicated as some view it as a combination of knowledge, skills, and behaviour, while others contend that it is the effective use of these traits or abilities.

Theorists in favour of pay for competence advocate that such a programme increases productivity and product quality and also reduces absenteeism, turnover, and accident rates. In the USA, more than 40% of the large organizations use this approach. In India differential payment is practised in the private sector. In certain professional areas, for example, technical and scientific disciplines, pay for knowledge is a common practice to motivate and retain expertise. It is common to observe that with increased education and experience, pay also rises. Such plans are based on the assumption that professional competence increases with training and experience.

> ■ ■ ■
> A pay-for-competence programme enhances productivity and product quality and reduces absenteeism, turnover, and accident rates.

Recently, the approach has been to pay for skill at the entry level itself. Scientists engaged in different sectors such as pharmaceuticals, space research, and biotechnology are paid a high premium at the entry level. Besides, at various levels, the incentives that are offered for expertise clearly indicate the firm's attitude. In this process, skill development can take place laterally and deeply. When employees are able to handle different tasks or jobs, their skill breadth improves. Further, when employees learn about specialized areas, it enhances their ability to solve difficult problems.

The advantages of this scheme may be summarized as follows.

- It creates an empowered workforce in a flat structure.
- It require few supervisors.
- It provides the employee an opportunity for charting out the course of his or her own career.

> ■ ■ ■
> The effectiveness of competence-related pay depends on the fair and consistent measurement of competence levels.

The maintenance costs of skill-based employees are high and unless they are compensated by high productivity, it becomes uneconomical to employ them. Do organizations at all times utilize the specialized skills? If they are not, they become rusty.

An important dimension to be considered is whether organizations should pay for skill or for performance. Since performance is an outcome, should not organizations reward its employees for performance? Does possession of skill ensure performance?

The following are the advantages of competence-related pay:

- It focusses attention on the need for higher levels of competence.
- It encourages competence development.
- It fits delayered organizations by facilitating lateral career moves.
- It encourages staff to take responsibility for their development.
- It helps to integrate role and generic competencies with organizational core competencies.

The disadvantages of competence-related pay are as follows:

- Unless careful control is exercised, costs may escalate if employees are paid for competencies they rarely, if ever, use.
- Assessment and documentation of competence levels can be time-consuming and expensive.
- The effectiveness of competence-related pay depends on the fair and consistent measurement of competence levels, and this may be difficult.
- Implementing such a system requires considerable resources in terms of training and support.
- There is a possibility of gender bias.
- Implementing such a system makes considerable demands on the commitment and skills of line managers.

Team Rewards

Another new method of compensation that is gaining popularity is rewarding a group or team members. A team is a small number of people with complementary skills who are committed to a common mission, performance goals, and approach for which they hold themselves mutually accountable. Groups emphasise individual leadership, individual accountability, and individual work products. Teams emphasize shared leadership, mutual accountability, and collective work products.

The following are the characteristics of a well-functioning, effective team.

> ■ ■ ■
> Teams emphasize shared leadership, mutual accountability, and collective work products.

- The atmosphere tends to be relaxed, comfortable, and informal.
- The team's task is well understood and accepted by its members.
- The members listen well to one another; most members participate in a good deal of task-relevant discussion.

- People express their feelings as well as ideas.
- Conflict and disagreement are related to ideas or methods, not people.
- The team is conscious of its own operation and function.
- Decisions are usually based on consensus, not majority vote.
- When actions are decided, clear assignments are made and accepted by members of the term.

Teams make important contributions to organizations in work areas that lend themselves to teamwork. Complex, interdependent work tasks and activities that require collaboration particularly lend themselves to teamwork. Teams are appropriate where knowledge, talent, skills, and abilities are dispersed across organizational members and require integrated effort for task accomplishment.

The recent emphasis on team-oriented work environments is based on empowerment with collaboration, not on power and competition. That teams are necessary is a driving principle of total quality efforts in organizations. Total quality efforts often require the formation of teams—especially cross-functional teams composed of people from different functions, such as manufacturing and design, who are responsible for specific organizational processes. Participation and cooperation are foundations for teamwork and a total quality programme. In a study of 40 machine crews in a northeastern US paper mill, it was found that specifically helpful behaviour and sportsmanship contributed significantly to the quantity and quality of team performance.

In a 1995 study of 230 large organizations, Hay Associates reported that 80% were satisfied with the use of teams, but only 40% with the related pay programme. Rewards are the mode of payment for teams usually according to a performance-related criterion, or related to an overall criterion. At times, bonus is also related to the achievement of predetermined organizational or team objectives.

Team pay can

- encourage teamwork and cooperation,
- clarify team goals and priorities, and provide for integration of organizational and team objectives,

> **■ ■ ■**
> Teams are appropriate where knowledge, talent, skills, and abilities are dispersed across organizational members and require an integrated effort for task accomplishment.

- reinforce organizational change in the direction of an increased emphasis on teams in flat and process-based organizations,
- act as a lever for cultural change in the direction of, for example, quality and customer focus,
- enhance flexible working within teams and encourage multiskilling,
- provide an incentive for the group to work collectively to improve performance,
- encourage less effective performers to improve in order to meet team standards, and
- serve as a means of developing self-managed or directed teams.

> **■ ■ ■**
> Rewards are the mode of payment for teams usually according to a performance-related criterion, or related to an overall criterion.

The disadvantages of team pay are as follows:

- Its effectiveness depends upon the existence of well-defined and mature teams—but they may be difficult to identify, and even if they can be, they may not be motivated by a purely financial reward.

> ■ ■ ■
> Peer pressure which compels individuals to conform to group norms could be undesirable.

- Team pay may seem inappropriate to individuals whose feelings of self-worth canot not be diminished. It is not always easy to get people to think of their performance in terms of how it impacts other people.
- Singling out the individual team members who contribute could be a problem. This may not be regarded as a disadvantage by a fervent believer in teams, but individual contributors who have to operate inside as well as outside a team setting may be demotivated.

- Peer pressure which compels individuals to conform to group norms could be undesirable. Insistence on conformity can be oppressive and the way in which team leaders manage their performance needs to be monitored.
- Pressure to conform, which has accentuated team pay, could result in the team maintaining its output at the lowest common denominator levels—sufficient to gain what is thought collectively to be a reasonable reward, but no more.
- It can be difficult to develop performance measures and methods of rating team performance, which are seen to be fair—team pay formulae could be based on arbitrary assumptions about the correct relationship between effort and reward.
- The entire team may have to pay for individuals.
- Organizational flexibility may be prejudiced—people in cohesive, high-performing, and well-rewarded teams might be unwilling to move even to help overall organizational performance, and it could be difficult to reassign work between teams, or to break up teams altogether in response to product market, process development, or competitive pressures.
- High performers in low-performing teams may be dissatisfied and press for a transfer, especially if they believe they are being penalized on the reward front.

Exhibit 15.2 discusses the effect of recession on compensation.

EXHIBIT 15.2   Effect of recession on compensation

Employees at every level on the corporate ladder are feeling the heat of the ongoing recession. While there is much discussion about the compensation packages of executives and whether or not they are being affected by the recession, things are difficult from the top to lower levels. The recent cuts in both salary and bonus compensation of executives in many of the nation's top firms reflects this phenomenon.

One of the reasons why this is the case has to do with the stock market and the fact that many executive bonuses are tied to the success of a company's stock. For example, in 2008, the total compensation package of Anish Phookan, an executive who was previously earning over ₹1 crore, fell by more than 50%. Though the majority of the executives are still managing to meet both ends meet, the percentage declines are enough to scare many people.

The scariest thing about the current recession and trends in executive compensation is that a number of industries that are otherwise stable are also witnessing their chief executive officers (CEOs) and associates take dramatic pay cuts. For example, some law firms have done away with the old lockstep form of compensation. Instead of paying members of the firm on the basis of their experience, these firms are now paying associates on the basis of their performance. Consequently, many individuals are receiving less pay than they were under the old system, thereby causing reduction in the overall compensation in this field.

For the majority of CEOs, this problem is compounded by the fact that they have retirement funds and

(Contd)

EXHIBIT 15.2 (Contd)

pensions that are filled with the company's stock. This might have been a good thing a few years ago, when a great deal of the company's interest was tied up in the ownership of those shares. However, with the fall in the prices of these stocks, the CEOs are now left with much less receipts overall from their compensation package. The bigger question then becomes, 'Are CEOs and the like in for more cuts in the near future?'

This depends upon just how bad the economy gets and whether the current recession runs its course in terms of reduced compensation. The majority of CEOs are still doing well, but reports of them still raking in huge bonuses are mostly overblown. They are struggling right along with their company, at least in relative terms. However, the salaries are still comfortable; it is just that the majority of big dollar bonuses have taken a hard hit over the last few years.

Source: http://www.articlesbase.com/finance-articles/executive-compensation-and-the-current-recession-1888416. html#ixzz1F3TJfcv7, accessed on 22 February 2010.

INTERNATIONAL COMPENSATION

In recent years, globalization, the rapid growth of emerging markets, and the need to develop employees for management in global organizations have necessitated the movement of managers from one continent to the other. This may take different shapes such as a short-term assignment or a long-term one. An overseas training programme, for example, might extend for a period of one year, whereas taking up assignments or projects might involve a long-term assignment. Decisions have to be made as to how much an expatriate has to be paid to be retained and sufficiently motivated. Managing an increasing number of people from developed as well as developing countries at different stages of their careers makes it difficult to have a single remuneration system. It is well known that the cost of sending an employee abroad far exceeds the salary outlay. In addition, the company must also consider air fares for the employee as well as his or her family apart from the accommodation costs, relocation expenses, language training, school fees, and so on.

There are instances when expatriates have failed in their assignments. The failures may mainly be attributed to adjustment or relocation problems faced by the employee or his or her spouse. Adapting to a different culture is time consuming and often leads to failures. Such failures prove costly to the management. A pre-assignment trip to the host location to allow the expatriate and any accompanying family members is desirable. They can then decide whether they can live in the host location and adjust to the cultural patterns. Usually, language tuitions and independent financial counselling are also arranged for the expatriates.

The salary of an expatriate usually begins at the home-based one. Another criterion is to take the local market rate into consideration. Apart from this, several other factors also operate, such as

- reason for the assignment (managerial, developmental, or skill based),
- nationality of expatriates and countries to which they are sent, and
  - duration of the assignment.

> Adapting to a different culture is time consuming and often leads to failures.

Apart from salary, special allowances are also paid to cover the cost of living, relocation, and so on. In some instances, a hardship allowance is also paid in recognition of potential discomfort and difficulty in the host country, such as extremes of climate, health hazards, poor communications, and so on. This allowance is usually built into the salary itself so that the package is made attractive.

Benefits

There are a number of allowances which are offered in the name of benefits. Housing allowances are sometimes built into the package or are paid separately. Some employers provide free accommodation, while others provide an allowance. Allowances on certain utilities, such as electricity, water, gas, etc., are also provided in some countries. However, there is a ceiling in terms of their usage to prevent extravagance. A car allowance is yet another common benefit which is provided to expatriates. Such an allowance may be provided in terms of money, or, alternatively, a car belonging to the company may be provided. The usage and practice varies from city to city and from continent to continent. Most companies usually pay for the children of expatriates to be educated in the host country. Club membership fees and subscriptions are usually paid for by an expatriate's employer if there is a good business case. The social environment is seen as an important part of the settling in process as well as a useful source of business contacts, particularly in developing countries. In some cases, companies pay for the expatriate and his family to visit their home country once in a year or once in two years. There are variations in this practice. Apart from this, pensions and health insuranes of exptriates are also taken care of.

> ■ ■ ■
> The social environment is seen as an important part of the settling in process.

SUMMARY

This chapter begins with an outline of compensation and its theoretical background. It explains the objectives of compensation planning, definition of compensation, types of compensation, factors influencing the compensation structure, and theories defining the compensation pattern. It also discusses the techniques involved in deciding compensation, the process of developing pay structures and its implementation, the system of balancing the pay structures to make them acceptable, the process of wage administration and the statutory issues, theories connected to wage determination, statutory requirements regarding the Payment of Bonus Act, and so on. It provides an introduction to executive remuneration and current trends. It also briefly discusses the concept of broadbranding and its advantages and disadvantages, balancing the compensation with competencies and skills, linking individual performance with team performance and rewards, and trends in international compensation.

■ ■ ■ KEY TERMS

Bonus   A payment made to the employee out of the profits earned by the employer, over and above the remuneration that the employee gets

Broadbanding   The compression of a hierarchy of pay grades or salary ranges into a smaller number of wide bands

Compensation management   A systematic approach to provide monetary value to employees in exchange for the work performed

Executive remuneration   Compensation paid to the higher-level employees

International compensation   Financial returns and tangible benefits that employees receive for overseas assignments

Job evaluation   A process of assessing the relative importance of jobs within an organization

Wage structure   A pay scale showing ranges of pay within each grade

■ ■ ■ | EXERCISES

Multiple Choice Questions

1. The following are all examples of direct compensation except
   (a) pension
   (b) salary
   (c) bonus
   (d) income

2. Cost of human resources refers to
   (a) company profits
   (b) employee shares
   (c) salary packages
   (d) earned revenues

3. The relative position of an organization's pay incentives compared to other companies in the same industry is known as
   (a) pay structure
   (b) pay appraisal
   (c) pay level
   (d) pay feedback

4. An employee's compensation usually comprises
   (a) high monetary rewards
   (b) quality rewards requested by employees
   (c) benefits such as medical and transport allowances
   (d) financial and non-financial rewards

5. Which of the following is a part of non-financial compensation?
   (a) Monthly commission
   (b) Employee autonomy
   (c) Stock option
   (d) Medical allowance

Fill in the Blanks

1. _____ exists when individuals performing similar jobs for the same firm are paid according to factors unique to the employee.

2. Under _____, similar classes of jobs are identified and the necessary data about those classes are collected.

3. The thorough and detailed study regarding jobs within an organization is termed as _____ .

4. Jobs are compensated on the basis of _____, which is also an important step in designing a compensation package.

5. _____ compares job description to pre-established grade descriptors and is based on an initial decision regarding the number and characteristics of the grade in which jobs are placed.

Concept Review Questions

1. Define compensation. Differentiate between compensation, salary, and wage.

2. Discuss the role of direct and indirect compensation programmes in an organization.

3. Review the different methods of job evaluation and bring out their effectiveness in usage.

4. Explain broadbanding with examples.

5. Experts are of the opinion that we must pay the individual and not the job. Comment.

6. Discuss the various changes that are taking place in executive remuneration.

7. Discuss some of the aspects to be considered while designing international compensation.

8. With a few examples, show how we can structure a team-based pay.

9. How are wages determined according to the Wage Act? Should we raise the minimum wage?

10. Explain the main features of the Bonus Act.

Project Work

1. Study the compensation pattern at the worker level in a manufacturing organization.

2. Critically analyse the compensation structure for executives in an organization.

3. Critically relate the various theories with the compensation structure prevalent in an organization.

4. Prepare a write-up on the trends in compensations in the IT Industry.

5. Write a theoretical paper justifying that compensation is a motivator and not just a satisfying factor.

■ ■ ■ | REFERENCES

Adams, J.S. 1966, 'Inequity in social exchange', *Advances in Experimental Social Psychology*, 2, pp. 267–99.

Compensation in Chennai Plastics Ltd

Chennai Plastics Ltd (CPL) was founded during the year 1992 in the outskirts of Chennai to manufacture and market domestic and industrial plastics. The company had employees at two different levels, that is, worker level and management level.

These categories were further subdivided into the following categories (Table 15.2):

In addition to salary and bonus, the company also decided to offer the following benefits to its employees, as a part of the compensation package:

- Mediclaim insurance coverage for the employees and their dependents
- Group personal accident coverage for employees
- Employees state insurance (ESI) coverage for employees drawing salary of less than ₹10,000 per month
- Provident fund (PF) contribution at 12% of basic pay
- Accommodation in the housing complex adjacent to the factory
- Concessional educational loans to support educational requirements of employees' kids

TABLE 15.2 Employee classification and compensation at Chennai Plastics Ltd

Employee level	Employee categories	Prerequisites	Salary range	Bonus
Workers	Grade I	ITI with 0–5 years experience	₹6,500 –₹10,000	8.33%
	Grade II	ITI with 5–10 years experience	₹7,500 –₹12,000	8.33%
	Grade III	ITI with 10–15 years experience	₹8,500 –₹14,000	8.33%
	Grade IV	ITI with 15–20 years experience	₹10,000 –₹15,000	10%
	Grade V	Diploma with 0–5 years experience	₹8,000 –₹10,000	10%
	Grade VI	Diploma with 5–10 years experience	₹10,000 –₹15,000	10%
Management	Grade I	BE/B Tech/MBA with 0–5 years experience	₹12,000 –₹18,000	Performance-linked incentive
	Grade II	BE/B Tech/MBA with 5–10 years experience	₹15,000 –₹20,000	Performance-linked incentive
	Grade III	BE/B Tech/MBA with 5–10 years experience	₹20,000 –₹25,000	Performance-linked incentive
	Grade IV	BE/B Tech/MBA with 10–20 years experience	₹25,000 –₹50,000	Performance-linked incentive

Further, the company decided to support the employees in forming an Employees Cooperative Credit Society to promote the savings habit and provide access to credit for various personal requirements such as marriage of self/children, construction of house, and other ceremonies in accordance with the framed rules/guidelines. The chief executive officer (CEO) of the company would be the chairman of the proposed society. The other members of the society's board would include representatives of workers and management-level employees.

The society would continue to extend it services to retired employees and their dependents such as spouse and children.

Questions

1. Briefly comment on the compensation packages at Chennai Plastics.
2. Study the compensation package of a manufacturing plant and compare them with the components of CPL.
3. Do you think CPL can be viewed as an employee-centric organization? If yes, explain why.
4. Do you think that the compensation and facilities will motivate the employees, and CPL can aim to become the preferred place to work?

The Search that Went Wrong

Today's economy is demanding more from business executives than ever before: creativity, judgment, motivational skills, and sometimes sheer courage. In these trying times, many chief executive officers (CEOs) are rediscovering the truth in their bland annual mantra that 'people are our most important asset'. However, if having the right people is all-important, how do you get them in the first place? The answer is long, and you have probably heard it all before. So let us make it more interesting by taking a look at an executive search that failed. This case study is based on a real incident. Only the identifying details have been changed. The client company was involved in processing agricultural products in western Canada. It was just becoming aware of a potential new market for one of its product lines, so it asked a consulting firm to help find a new sales executive who could exploit the market. The consultants tried to help, but the organization made almost every mistake in the book.

As soon as the consultants sat down to discuss the job, they could see they might have trouble. The compensation package, the company envisioned for its new sales executive was liberal by its own internal standards. However, for a position that required pioneering and personal risk, the outside marketplace paid more. The client, Harry, said increasing the compensation for this new person would disrupt his firm's entire salary structure—a decision with huge implications for attracting a top candidate. Further, the consultants quickly determined that the combination of seniority and experience their client was looking for was extremely rare in Canada. 'So look in the States,' said Harry. The consultants warned him it was not usually quite that easy.

First, the compensation gap would be an even bigger problem for US executives. The consultants determined few potential candidates there who were interested in coming to Canada. One researcher compared it to someone in Toronto or Calgary being offered a job in Gander. For most of these executives, Canada was not even on their radar. Casting around again for possible Canadians, the consultants finally found one in Quebec. One problem: she did not want to move her children outside the province. The consultants played up the concept of French immersion schools and asked Harry to call and use all his persuasion skills to tell her about the job's present and future rewards. Harry refused. 'I won't try to sell her on this job,' he said, not realizing that is exactly what many organizations are doing these days to attract top talent.

The consultants found another candidate, who was introduced to Harry and his team. Unfortunately, he bonded only with Brad, Harry's youngest executive. Everyone else, he told the consultants later, seemed old enough to be his father. Worse, by the time the consultants could arrange another meeting, Brad had left the firm. Now, there was no one in the top management close to the candidate's age. The consultants tried to get Harry to bring another young manager to the meeting, to give the candidate someone to identify with, but it did not happen. The meeting went badly. Perhaps the search was doomed from the start. Perhaps the consultants should have done more. For whatever reason, the consultants never filled the position. There were too many problems standing in the way. The client did not take his search seriously; he never made it a priority. He failed to offer sufficient incentive, taking into account the shortage of qualified candidates and the need to motivate them to make a gutsy move. He was unwilling to look at more junior candidates who might be attracted by the salary and see the opportunity as a step up. Further, it never occurred to him that there might be people who did not want to move to his province, let alone Canada.

Finally, despite prompting, Harry never tried to understand what was going on in the candidates' minds. What would influence their decisions? Harry paid no attention. Further, if you do not know what your best candidates want, you are unlikely to satisfy them when it comes to balancing opportunity versus risk. Many business people are afraid to admit they made a mistake. However, we learn more from failure than from success.

Questions

1. Analyse the client's constraint in not accommodat-

ing the compensation demands of the would be recruits.

2. Critically analyse the parameters influencing compensation in the client company.

3. Analyse the cross-cultural and inter-country compensation-related problems in shifting from the USA to Canada in the context of the case.

4. Analyse the recruitment practices vis-à-vis compensation practices in the company.

Source: Stern, M. 2003, 'The search that went wrong', *Naional Post*, 28 April.

CASE STUDY 3 — Innovating Consulting Limited

Innovating Consulting Limited is a leading organization providing consulting services to the banking and financial sector in the country. The company was established by a team of six principal consultants who were working in various reputed consulting organizations and had a minimum experience of 20 years. Initially, the company obtained business because of the contacts of the principal consultants. During a brainstorming discussion, the six consultants decided to increase the scope of activities and cover other emerging sectors such as telecom, retailing, etc. Further, they also thought of increasing the headcount of the organization and decided to design the organizational structure as shown in Figure 15.2.

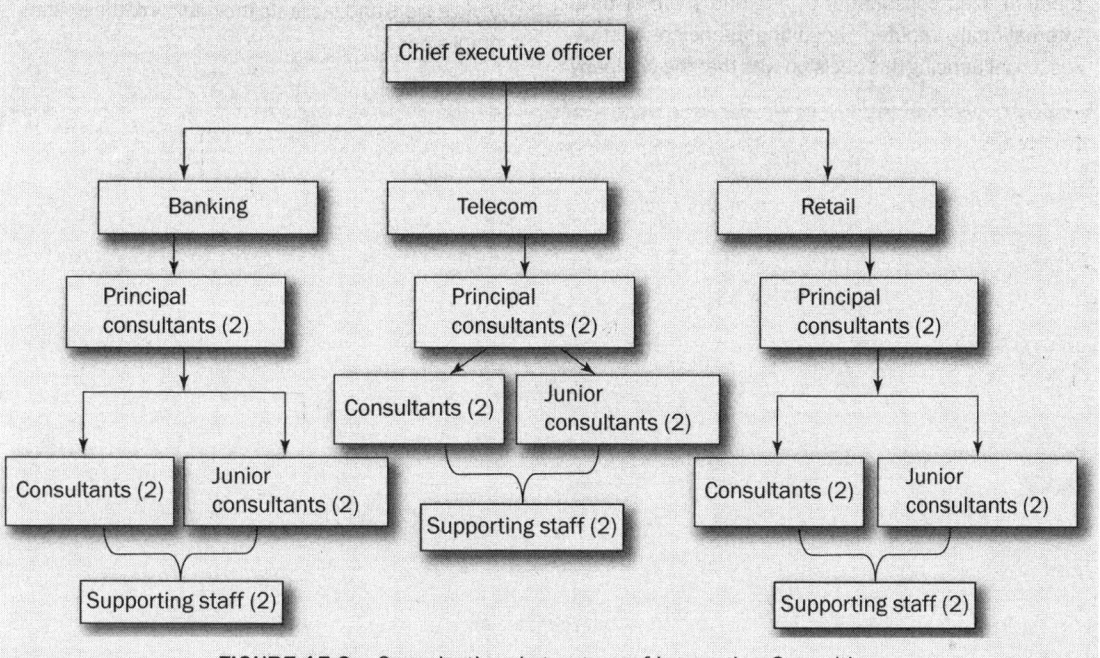

FIGURE 15.2 Organizational structure of Innovating Consulting

After deciding on the organizational structure, the next issue was structuring the compensation package. After detailed deliberations, the following compensation packages were agreed upon (Table 15.3).

Table 15.3 Compensation package

S. no.	Designation	Pay scale (per annum)
1.	Chief executive officer	₹18,00,000 – ₹22,00,000
2.	Principal consultants	₹5,00,000 – ₹8,00,000
3.	Junior consultants	₹3,00,000 – ₹5,00,000
4.	Supporting staff	₹1,50,000 – ₹2,00,000

The next challenge faced while deciding the compensation structure was to provide the total figure to the concerned candidate and give the option to him or her to fix the break-up of the components or alternatively to fix the break-up of the remuneration. The company initially decided to save expenditure on compensation by recruiting consultants and other staff from medium-sized consultants or beginners rather than internationally reputed consulting agencies. Another reason influencing this decision was that the company felt that high-fliers would not have any organizational loyalty, but would try to execute their personal agendas. Accordingly, the company advertised for and recruited the required personnel. After functioning for over two years, it discovered that its revenue had become stagnant and, in fact, observed that apart from the banking and finance group, which included the founders and principal consultants, the other two areas, that is, the telecom and retailing group, were not growing at all. After reviewing the situation, the company decided to recruit high-fliers in these two areas, who could bring in more business through their contacts. Thus, the company was forced to offer higher compensation packages to the new employees. This led to discontent, and the existing employees began to deliberately delay the pace of work.

Questions
1. If you were the CEO, how would you manage the existing employees vis-à-vis the high-fliers?
2. Critically analyse the compensation structure vis-à-vis the organizational structure.
3. Can you suggest a better compensation structure for the organization?
4. Should the organization attract a greater number of high-fliers and facilitate the outflow of the existing employees?

Industrial Relations and Issues

Objectives

After studying this chapter, you will be able to understand
- the conceptual background of employer–employee relations
- industrial relations and HR strategies
- industrial relations in the international and the Indian context
- the role and importance of trade unions
- dispute resolution mechanisms and best practices in industrial relations
- industrial legislation in India

INTRODUCTION

The history of employer–employee relations can be traced back to the struggle for independence, which dates back to the early eighteenth century. The workers of the textile industry took the support of the leaders of the independence movement to revolt against the oppressive practices of the British, whose sole aim was to totally destroy the textile industry in the country and reduce it to a mere supplier of raw material to the textile industry in Britain.

When Mahatma Gandhi joined the independence movement, he changed the scenario of industrial relations in India. The workers closely participated in the struggle for independence and used methods such as *satyagraha*, with support from leaders of the freedom movement.

This in a way marked the beginning of the growing nexus between the fledgling trade union movement and political parties such as the Indian National Congress, communist parties, etc. The trade union movement grew parallel to the freedom movement and by the time India had gained its independence, the trade union movement had graduated from infancy to the early adult stage.

The industrial policies conceived and implemented by the Government of India, under the leadership of Jawaharlal Nehru, towards the establishment of a massive and large-scale infrastructure in the steel, cement, textile, hydroelectrical, and thermal power areas contributed to the strengthening of trade unions in the organized sector.

Another macro development was the growing influence of the socialist philosophy of the Soviet Union on the economists and planners in the Government of India, which laid emphasis on the rights of the workers and the equitable distribution of wealth. This philosophy naturally crept into the perspective of trade union leaders, who happened to be politicians.

> ■ ■ ■
> A major factor impacting the growth and evolution of the trade union movement was the influence of politicians.

A major factor impacting the growth and evolution of the trade union movement was the influence of politicians. Blue-collar workers and their families were viewed as a means to developing the stature of union leaders in their respective parties, opening up an avenue to corridors of power.

The socialist perspectives of the government have led it to devise a number of regulative, legislative, and legal support mechanisms for the rights of workers, and to guide their movement for self-protection.

The passing of the Industrial Disputes Act, 1947 by the Parliament is a major step in this direction. Some of the critical clauses of the Act are as follows.

- Section 3 of the Act stipulates that it is mandatory for industrial establishments, which employ 100 or more workers to set up a Worker Committee, with equal composition of employer and employee representatives. The employee representatives must be chosen in consultation with trade unions.
- Section 9 C of the Act stipulates that industrial establishments with 50 or more workers must provide for a Grievance Settlement Authority including representatives from employees and employers for settling disputes with individual employees. The establishment or the trade unions cannot make any references to Boards of Conciliation, Labour Courts, or Industrial Tribunals, unless any dispute has been first referred to a Grievance Settlement Authority.
- To safeguard the interests of women workers, a women's wing of the Standing Committee of Public Enterprises (SCOPE), an apex organization of public sector enterprises, looks into the following aspects:
  - Development of a database and information network
  - Training and development, including entrepreneurial training
  - Counselling services
  - Day care centres, etc.

The present era of competition has made it imperative for organizations to define and sustain performance parameters at all levels (organization, group, and individual). In view of this, it is absolutely necessary for them to involve employees in the developmental process as partners.

Another significant development is the advent of the digital era, where information and communication technology (ICT) and knowledge workers have become the key factors for organizational growth and development. It is now recognized that employees or human resources can make or mar the development of the organization.

This has led to a paradigm shift in the mindset of employers as well as employees. The ICT organizations are largely non-unionized and the characteristics of the industry are now such that the traditional labour law framework is archaic and totally unsuitable. The dominant relationship between the employer and employee is not that of master and servant, but that of partners working for a common cause. The HR managers have challenges such as skills shortage, competency building, balancing work and family life, and gender issues.

> ■ ■ ■
> The present era of competition has made it imperative for organizations to define and sustain performance parameters at all levels.

> ■ ■ ■
> The ICT organizations are largely non-unionized.

Globalization along with ICT has created global citizens, rather 'netizens', and employees whose mobility across organizations, countries, and time zones is fluid and dynamic and is dictated by market dynamics, and resultant career opportunities. The policies and practices in ICT organizations are based on four key features:

TABLE 16.1 How focus has shifted in work

Aspect	Traditional agriculture	Early/traditional industry	Post-industrial service/ high-tech
Wealth	Land	Money	Mind/information
Skill/effort	Brawn/muscle	Machine-tending	Brain/mind, attitude and ability matter, not just skill
Management philosophy	Unilateral	Pluralistic	Egalitarian
Management style	Autocratic	Paternalistic	Collegial
Employment context	Master–servant	Employer–employee	Partners
Relationship	One-sided dependence	Interdependence	Mutuality and independence
Communication	Top-down	Two-way	Transparent
Motivation	Fear	Favour	Fairness
Performance appraisal	Information confidential, boss	Formal, one way	Formal, open, participative appraisals
Control	Direction and control	Inducement	Consensus/commitment

Source: Venkata Ratnam (2001).

- Virtual reality and organizations
- Flexible and adaptive work environment
- Performance-based and variable compensation structures
- Democratic governance with provision for employee participation

The shifting focus in the realm of work is captured in Table 16.1.

THEORIES OF INDUSTRIAL RELATIONS

Theories of industrial relations may be categorized as political and apolitical. The political theories consider various macro-social aspects and politico-economic factors. The apolitical theories are based on micro and organizational issues such as strategic, functional, and operational aspects. Some of the theories of industrial relations are briefly cited here.

Miller and Form's Model

■ ■ ■
The Dunlop model views industrial relations as a system involving workers, organizations, managers, and government agencies.

This theory provides an overview of the structure pertinent to industrial relations along with its complexity arising out of the interaction between the formal and informal systems. It explores the relations between the various players—management, workers, trade unions, and so on. The model visualizes the organization as a cultural pattern in which collective bargaining incorporates a range of activities including collective action, grievance redressal, bargaining, etc.

Dunlop's Model

This model views industrial relations as a system involving workers, organizations, managers, governmental agencies, and so on. The interaction of these components creates a set of rules in the form of agreements, orders, regulations, policies, etc., which facilitate the smooth functioning of the organization.

Effect of Globalization in India

The effect of globalization in India has had its impact on the labour market and some of the paradigm shifts involved include the following:

- Drift towards market economy
- Changing composition of workforce
- Transformation in the role of trade unions
- Fluctuating market conditions and flexible labour market

APPROACHES TO INDUSTRIAL RELATIONS

We can view industrial relations from different perspectives such as psychological, sociological, Marxist, and Gandhian. Each perspective provides an understanding of the basis of its own ideology or theory. A psychologist interprets the dynamics in work place as different transactions between the employer and the employee, with level and attitude differences. The typical sociological perspective highlights the role of the group/organization as a figure of authority and the consequences of associating in it. The Gandhian and the human relations perspectives focus on the workers as individuals with a lot of potential. Hence, it is clear that no single approach is complete and satisfying, but a holistic perspective would deepen our understanding of industrial relations. The problems in the field of industrial relations cannot be solved within the limits of a single discipline, and hence, it is bound to be interdisciplinary in approach. A few approaches are discussed here.

Psychological Approach

Psychologists explain behaviour in relation to certain personality aspects such as perceptions and attitudes. Certain groups of people have a stereotyped way of thinking. For example, they project union–management relationships with a bias. The results of a study about the behaviour of union leaders and executives through a test led Mason Harie to reach the following conclusions:

- The general impression about a person is radically different when he/she is seen as a representative of the management than as a representative of the labour.
- The management and labour consider each other as less dependable.
- The management and labour consider each other as deficient in thinking regarding emotional characteristics and interpersonal relations.

Bias in perceptions and insufficient information cloud the transactions between the labour and the management. Attitude towards the labour is negatively stereotyped and further strains the relationship.

Sociological Approach

Industry is a part of the larger social system and reflects the societal culture. Societal norms, values, and culture all reflect in an organization. Workers' behaviour influences the goals of the management—productivity and efficiency. Factors such as work stress, mobility, health, wages, migration, and compensation packages influence the productivity of the work groups. Because of social changes, workers are now more intelligent and aware than in the past. Thus, managements are also promoting welfare concepts.

Human Relations Approach

With the advent of human relations approach, the entire gamut of industrial relations is undergoing a change. This approach believes that labour has certain needs, goals, and aspirations. The labour groups share similar emotions and sentiments that operate within people of other levels of the organization. Further, the styles of leadership also affect the workers. Research indicates that the democratic and participatory style of leadership is more welcome than autocratic style. The human relations approach deals with issues in an objective manner and resolves conflicts satisfactorily through a win–win approach.

Gandhian Approach

Gandhism stands for truth, non-violence, and sathyagraha. This approach highlights Gandhi's views on workers, management, customers, and all other groups involved in an industry. It advocates equality of all groups. It lays emphasis on the need for management and labour to work in unity to achieve the objectives of the company. It urges the management to be humane, while dealing with the labour. The Gandhian approach emphasizes a socialistic pattern with equal distribution of wealth among the owners and the labour. It advocates Gandhi's proposition that requires labour to become more aware of their role, rights and obligations, and perform their work diligently. It advocates resolution of conflicts through the collective bargaining approach. It urges labour to avoid going on strike, resort to strike as a last step, and even during strike, remain peaceful and non-violent.

Marxist Approach

This approach views industrial relations in the context of a capitalist society, where there is a natural division between capital and labour. This creates a divide between labour and management and results in inequalities in power and wealth. Therefore, conflict is inevitable and trade unions act as vehicles to ventilate feelings of exploitation by the management. While there may be periods of acquiescence, the Marxist approach opines that institutions of joint regulation enhance rather than limit the position of managements, as they presume the continuation of capitalism rather than challenging it.

INTERNATIONAL LABOUR ORGANIZATION

The International Labour Organization (ILO) promotes social justice and internationally recognized human and labour rights, and pursues its founding mission that labour peace is essential to prosperity. Today, the ILO helps advance the creation of the economic and working conditions that provide working and business people, a stake in lasting peace, prosperity, and progress. Its tripartite structure provides a unique platform for promoting decent work for all women and men.

The following are the four strategic objectives of the ILO:

- Promote and realize standards, fundamental principles, and rights at work.
- Create greater opportunities for women and men to gain decent employment and income.
- Enhance the coverage and effectiveness of social protection for all.
- Strengthen tripartism and social dialogue.

Exhibit 16.1 discusses the impact of ILO on labour laws in India.

EXHIBIT 16.1　Impact of the International Labour Organization on labour laws in India

The ILO was set up in the year 1919 with an aim to improve the conditions of labour around the world. Through its conventions and recommendations, the ILO helps nations to draw their own set of labour laws for the better treatment of the working class and the preservation of their rights. Creation of the international labour standards through conventions and recommendations serves as the principle means of action by the ILO.

Labour law regulates matters such as labour employment, remunerations, work conditions, trade unions, and labour–management relations. The approach of India towards international labour standards is positive. The country uses ILO conventions as a standard for reference, rather than as a legally binding norm for labour legislation and practices. India is cautious in ratifying conventions, as ratification of a convention imposes legally binding obligations on the country concerned.

Core Conventions of the ILO

ILO has eight core conventions, also called fundamental/human rights conventions (convention numbers are given in brackets).

- Conventions ratified by India
  - Forced Labour Convention (29)
  - Abolition of Forced Labour Convention (105)
  - Equal Remuneration Convention (100)
  - Discrimination (Employment Occupation) Convention (111)
- Conventions yet to be ratified by India
  - Freedom of Association and Protection of Right to Organized Convention (87)
  - Right to Organize and Collective Bargaining Convention (98)
  - Minimum Age Convention (138)
  - Worst forms of Child Labour Convention (182)

Consequent to the World Summit for Social Development in 1995, the ILO categorized the first seven of the aforementioned conventions as the fundamental human rights conventions or core conventions. Later on, the body added Convention 182 to the list.

The reporting procedure of the ILO requires member states that have ratified the priority and core conventions, to submit detailed reports every two years.

ILO is playing a vital role in two projects—Child Labour Action and Support Programme (CLASP) and International Programme on Elimination of Child Labour (IPEC).

Effect of ILO on Labour Legislation in India

The Factories Act 1881 is the basis for all labour and industrial laws of the country. It also prohibits child labour.

(Contd)

EXHIBIT 16.1   (Contd)

The Government of India set up an enquiry committee in 1926 to ascertain the loopholes in labour laws that allow irregular payment of wages to industrial workers. Most of the labour legislations in India are pre-constitutional. However, the country enacted many new laws to incorporate the guidelines of the conventions of the ILO ratified by it. The success of these labour legislations must be attributed to the ILO, as the guidelines issued by the ILO formed the basis for these legislations. By observing the passage of labour legislations in India, through the various amendments and enactments, it is evident that the ILO has had a great impact on the labour laws in India.

Source: Karmakar (2009), http://jurisonline.in/2009/05/impact-of-ilo-on-labor-laws-in-india/, accessed on 15 September 2011.

ROLE OF GOVERNMENT IN INDUSTRIAL RELATIONS

The government is one of the key players in significantly influencing industrial relations in the country and some of the roles played by it are paternalistic, interventionist, and, more importantly, that of an employer. Sometimes it plays the role of the adopter and protector of the policy of Laissez Faire. The directive principles of state policy are among the core guiding factors influencing the labour policy, supported by the various plan documents. Articles 39, 41, 42, 43, and 43A pertain to labour. Article 39 emphasizes that the policies of the government should be aimed at providing equal pay for equal work for men as well as women. Further, it states that the state should ensure the well-being of the workers and also prevent the economic exploitation of children and other employees. Article 41 stipulates that the government should take steps in the direction of capacity building and economic development to ensure the implementation of the right to work and education, and also provide public assistance, in the event of unemployment, old age, sickness, etc. Article 42 stipulates that the government should provide secure and humane conditions at the workplace. Article 43 stipulates that the government should endeavour to legislate policies which are aimed at providing a decent standard of living and also enabling people to social and cultural events. Article 43 A indicates that the government shall take steps, by suitable legislation or in any other way, to secure the participation of workers in the management of undertakings, establishments, or other organizations engaged in any industry.

The Government of India has been making conscious attempts to improve industrial relations right from the first five-year plan. The key actions taken during various five-year plans are as follows.

■ ■ ■
In India, the directive principles of state policy are among the core guiding factors influencing the labour policy.

■ ■ ■
The Government of India has been making conscious attempts to improve economic and social conditions right from the First Five-Year Plan.

- *First Five-year Plan (1951–56)*: For addressing disputes relating to wages and working conditions, the plan envisages the formulation of tripartite wage boards and also protection of the rights of workers of associations, organizations, and collective bargaining. It also envisaged the creation of a legal framework for determining an appropriate bargaining mechanism, and also the fixing of responsibilities for the enforcement of collective agreements.
- *Second Five-year Plan (1956–61)*: The stress was on socialist ideals as borne out by the constitution of joint management councils apart from statutory provisions, which provided for the recognition of unions. Further, the plan

document emphasized the need for limiting the number of outsiders as union office bearers, providing additional protection to union office bearers from victimization, strengthening the trade union finances, etc.

- *Third Five-year Plan (1961–66)*: The plan took into account various aspects such as the structuring of industrial relations for ensuring peace in the industry, a code that facilitated a grievance redressal mechanism, the need for controlling inter-union rivalry for protecting the interests of the industry and the workers, and, more importantly, the failure to implement awards and agreements by the managements as well as unions.
- *Fourth (1969–74) and Fifth (1974–79) Five-year Plans*: The fourth plan emphasized the need for according priority to the healthy growth of the trade-union movement, promoting collective bargaining, and, more importantly, increasing the industrial activity through labour–management cooperation. The coverage of Employee State Insurance Corporation was expanded for providing medical care to even the workers employed in shops and other commercial establishments in selected centres. Workers and their dependants in non-power units where 10 or more workers were employed were also covered. The fifth plan laid stress on greater involvement of labour and vertical mobility. It stressed the need for strengthening the industrial relations mechanism through conciliation apart from a better enforcement of labour legislation.
- *Sixth Five-year Plan (1980–85)*: It made a comprehensive policy statement on labour and the objectives of the plan were effective implementation of welfare measures, programmes for improving worker education, and protection of the interests of female workers. In the case of workers in organized sectors, the focus was on improving the services of ESI, EPF, and FPS apart from promoting cooperation between workers and employers. Further, the plan document identified the disparity between the small, organized, and the unorganized sectors. The plan emphasized the need for reducing the wage inequity between these sectors.
- *Seventh Five-year Plan (1985–90)*: The plan emphasized the need for improving capacity utilization, efficiency, and productivity. It stated that the success of any labour policy could be viewed in the context of productivity standards. It laid stress on the need to improve labour productivity by adopting modern technology in production processes apart from taking measures to address industrial sickness.
- *Eighth Five-year Plan (1992–97)*: The objectives stated in this plan document were to improve the quality of labour, productivity, competence, welfare, and security measures, and provide better working conditions, especially for those working in the unorganized sector. The thrust was on improving employment opportunities.
- *Ninth Five-year Plan (1997–2002)*: The plan envisaged industrial development and for the purpose, suggested various measures including the delicencing of coal, lignite, and petroleum products (other than crude oil), amalgamation of mines and minerals, and liberalization of technology imports. Some of the other impacting measures included the restructuring and revival of potentially viable PSUs, bringing down the government equity in non-strategic PSUs to 26% or lower, and protecting workers from the effect of industrial unrest. The plan focussed upon improving the quality of employment and, for the purpose, it emphasized the need for improving productivity. Further, it laid stress upon the skill development of the workers, apart from free and compulsory education. In addition, special programmes were also proposed

to develop skills, enhance technology levels, and provide marketing opportunities to people engaged in traditional occupations.

- *Tenth Five-year Plan (2002–07)*: The tenth plan also emphasizes the need for improving the productivity of labour. Further, it acknowledges that attitude towards work and the value placed by society on dignity of labour are important factors that can help increase productivity of labour. The plan lays stress on the need for the development of vocational training programmes and also reducing occupational hazards. In addition, it endeavours to ensure reasonable returns on labour through legislation.

BEST EMPLOYER PRACTICES

The best employers consistently outperform others in all aspects. In a study by Hewitt, it was found that best-employer organizations surpass others not only in terms of the number of initiatives they have in place, but also in delivery and execution. They have a clear vision, and they know how to communicate and achieve it.

The purpose of the study (Misra and Misra 2002) was to find

- what distinguished the best employers from the others,
- how best employers aligned their people strategy with business drivers,
- effective HR systems, practices, and philosophies, and
- emerging workplace trends for future vital statistics.

The study covered 204 companies and the data was collected from more than 52,000 employees. A total of 15 industry groups had participated, of which the maximum participation was from the IT and consumer goods (FMCG and consumer durables) industries. About 40% and 60% were multinational and Indian companies, respectively, 70% were publicly owned, and 30% were privately owned. The total number of employees covered was 91,950.

Based on the survey response, 65 companies were short-listed for on-site audit in respect of the following aspects:

- Core values
- Involvement of line and top management in HR initiatives
- HR measurement and success criteria
- Empowerment
- Involvement of employees in organizational change
- Openness
- Employee orientation (for example, human attitude towards exceptional situations)
- Constant innovation in people programmes
- Efficacy in delivery of HR services, including usage of technology
- Work environment

A total of 25 best employers were identified through the rigorous exercise and it was observed that they had striking similarities in the following aspects.

- High degree of employee satisfaction, commitment, and morale
- A sense of ownership and belonging—a collective relationship fostered by the organization
- Opportunities for accelerated growth and development

The best employers gauge the level of morale of the people, incorporate their feedback, and provide them the opportunities, systems, and practices they need.

- Depth, breadth, and consistency in application of HR practices
- Unique HR practices—many of which were home-grown and developed by the employees
- Sensitivity towards a balance between work and personal life
- Effectiveness of HR practices in meeting employee needs
- Alignment of HR practices to business context
- Stature of organization in the business community as evidenced by employees

The best employers in India have highly committed people. On an average, the satisfaction score of the employers working for them was as much as 20 points higher than that of those working in other companies. The best employers tended to go out of their way to gauge the level of morale of their people, incorporate their feedback, and give back to them the opportunities, systems, and practices they needed. The core beliefs that underlie the actions of best employers are as follows:

- *Best employers never underestimate the power of dreams*: They realize that talent provides them a wealth of ideas, creativity, and innovation. This input is used to enhance business performance and make improvements in products and processes. According to the study, it was observed that 18% of the employees formally made suggestions and as many as 37% were implemented by the organization in one year. Cross-functional movement and teams were encouraged to inculcate fresh thought.
- *Best employers understand the influence of human relations*: They leverage strong employee relationships for success in business. Bonding programmes for senior executives, employee referrals, adventure sports for new recruits, regular core-value-building exercises, and involvement of families are examples of programmes aimed at building a sense of cooperation and common purpose. The employees laid more emphasis on team orientation and the support of colleagues than employees of other organizations.
- *Best employers know that everybody has a potential for greatness*: They lay emphasis on a variety of programmes such as leadership and management development programmes and fast-track development practices, and focus attention on good performers. They also lay stress on potential assessment for identifying employees for strategic positions, building organization structures, and performance management built around competency maps.

Role of the CEO in Building a Best-employer Organization

The chief executive officer (CEO) plays a major role in defining an organization's culture and practices. Often the CEO in an organization tends to perceive that having excellent policies drafted is a sure way of building a best-employer organization. However, what is more important for the leader in the organization is to ensure that the personnel down the line in the hierarchy understand the philosophy behind the designed policies and then implement the policies.

The chief executive officer has an important role in creating and nurturing attributes that create a good organization.

Many leaders of Indian organizations have transformed their companies into best-employer organizations. For instance, N.R. Narayana Murthy of Infosys is a living legend who has done the Indian software industry proud even

TABLE 16.2 Responsibilities of CEOs

Most important things personally done by a CEO to contribute to an organization being a best employer	Most significant people issues faced by CEOs of best-employer organizations
Regular listening, communication and sharing, and being in touch with employees	Changing attitudes and mindsets; helping people adapt to new realties
Leading by example, inspiring, motivating, and bringing out the best in people	Focussing on common goals and objectives
Building culture and pride	Managing career aspirations and challenges
Being a coach, mentoring, and supporting people in times of crisis	Constantly motivating and keeping people charged
Promoting empowerment, involvement, and accountability	High performance orientation

among the developed nations. He sincerely believes that the real potential of Infosys is its employees. Similarly, Azim Premji of Wipro lays stress on training and development. The CEO has an important role in creating and nurturing attributes that create a good organization. The dual responsibilities of CEO are as follows (Table 16.2).

TRADE UNIONS

Webbs has defined a trade union as a continuous association of wage earners formed with the objective of maintaining and improving the conditions of working. As per the Trade Unions Act, 1926, a trade union has been defined as 'any combination be that temporary or otherwise permanent formed with the sole objective of regulating the relationship between the employees and employers or otherwise for imposing of restrictive conditions on conduct of any kind of trade/business'. The definitions refer to the following aspects:

- Association of employees or employers or otherwise of independent workers
- Relative permanent formation of workers
- Association formed for securing economic benefits such as better wages and better working/living conditions and social benefits such as educational, recreational, and medical benefits for the members. The collectiveness of the employees offers strength against any kind of irrational, arbitrary, and illegal action of the employers.

The objective of the trade union was to primarily provide solutions to any problems the worker encountered while discharging his responsibilities, both personal and organizational. In other words, the primary objective of the trade union was to protect the interests of the workers and the employers in the organization. The areas of focus for the trade union include the following:

■ ■ ■
The primary objective of the trade union is to protect the interests of the workers and employers in the organization.

- Providing satisfactory wages and salaries to each member and worker
- Improving the working conditions of workers and providing better health and safety provisions
- Inculcating a sense of discipline among themselves, which would facilitate smooth conduct of negotiation between the employees and the employers

- Facilitating the fight of the workers against any irrational policies of the management
- Striving for the welfare of the members through guidance and counselling.

There are currently more than 9,000 trade unions in our country (inclusive of unregistered trade unions), and 70 federations/confederations registered under the Trade Unions Act, 1926. The spread of trade unions is significant in the organized industrial sector, while it is negligible in the agricultural/unorganized sectors. There are currently 11 central trade union organizations in the country. The major ones are the All India Trade Union Congress (AITUC), Indian National Trade Union Congress (INTUC), Hindustan Mazdoor Sang (HMS), United Trade Unions Congress (UTC) Lenin Group, and Centre of Indian Trade Unions (CITU). Approximately 10% of the workforce in the country is unionized.

Trade Unions Act, 1926 and the Legal Framework

According to the Trade Unions Act, 1926, a minimum of seven persons have the right to form a trade union, which can be registered under the Act, subject to their abiding by the provisions of the Act and provided that a copy of the rules has been submitted to the Registrar of Trade Unions. In case of unions which have been in existence for more than a year, the application to form the union needs to be supported with the statement of the assets and liabilities of the union and should also contain the name of the union, the address of its head office, and the details of its office bearers and members.

Recognition of Trade Unions

In order to ensure the smooth functioning of collective bargaining, various Acts have been promulgated, which include the Bombay Industrial Act, 1946, the Madhya Pradesh Industrial Relations Act, 1946, and the Industrial Dispute (Rajasthan amendment) Act. Some of the provisions defining the registered unions are as follows:

- The members of the representative union should comprise at least 25% of the total number of employees in the industry.
- Qualified unions should have at least 5% of the membership in the industry.
- Primary unions should have at least 15% employees in the undertaking.

The representative union, under the act, will have the first right to appear in any proceedings, the right to submit a dispute for arbitration, and, more importantly, their office bearers cannot be dismissed or discharged.

EMPLOYERS' ASSOCIATIONS

■ ■ ■
The employers' associations have come into existence due to the formation of the International Labour Organization (ILO) and the growing influence of trade unions.

The employers' associations have come into existence due to the formation of the International Labour Organization (ILO) and the growing influence of trade unions. The reasons for the evolution of employers' associations include the needs for promoting healthy and stable industrial relations, facilitating the collective bargaining process, and, more importantly, bringing out a unified view of the employers on issues pertinent to industrial relations. Such associations in the country include the Associated Chambers of Commerce and

Industry of India (ASSOCHAM) and Federation of Indian Chambers of Commerce and Industry (FICCI). Employers' organizations are mainly structured at three levels—local, regional, and central [All India Organization of Employers' (AIOE), Employers' Federation of India (EFI), and the International Organization of Employers (IOE)].

GRIEVANCE

Organizations often face situations, where certain actions of either the employees or the employers may result in grievances. Grievances may prove to be detrimental for the organization. Therefore, the nature, purview, as well as redressal mechanisms of grievances from the perspective of industrial relations should be understood. The term 'grievance' refers to any action or situation concerned with the relations between the employer and the workers that affects or may affect the conditions of employment of one or more than one worker, if the action or situation appears contrary to the provisions of an applicable collective agreement or individual contract of employment, rules of work, laws and regulations, custom of wage or that of the occupation, or any type of economic or national activity, the only stipulation being that it should be based on good faith.

Usually, grievance encompasses the claims by employees or trade unions relating to the individual or collective rights under the purview of some applicable collective or individual agreement, laws and regulations, customs, and usages. However, in other cases, grievances may even refer to the disputes arising over rights or legal aspects.

Typically, grievances arise out of the day-to-day functioning of organizations concerning incidents such as dismissals and disciplinary issues, payment of wages and other benefits, promotions and transfers, overtime, seniority issues, job classification problems, etc. In the industrial context, it is expressed by the workers or trade unions protesting against an action, incident, or violation of workers' rights. Thus, grievances should be handled carefully and a feasible solution, acceptable to the parties involved, should be found.

GRIEVANCE SETTLEMENT MACHINERY

In India, the Industrial Disputes Act, 1947 provides for the settlement of industrial disputes through conciliation and adjudication. The Act makes a distinction between disputes arising in public utility services and those in other industries. The procedure and machinery provided under the Industrial Disputes Act have been modified periodically based on the effectiveness of the provisions, decisions of the judiciary, and influence of various bipartite and tripartite settlements.

Industrial Relations Machinery

The machinery for the settlement of industrial disputes comprises

- conciliation,
- arbitration, and
- adjudication.

The salient features of this arrangement may be divided in the following manner for the purpose of our discussion:

- Collective agreement
- Voluntary arbitration
- Conciliation
- Adjudication

Collective agreement Since independence, the trade unions have been growing and agreements between the employer and employees have become common. The changing attitude of employers and employees has also helped in arriving at collective agreements. The collective agreements in the Indian context may be classified into the following categories:

- Agreements that have been drawn up after direct negotiations between the parties, and are purely voluntary in character for the purpose of their implementation
- Agreements that combine the elements of voluntaries and compulsion, that is, those negotiated by the parties, but registered before a conciliator
- Agreements that require legal status when the matter is sub judice

Conciliation Statutory provisions for the conciliation machinery were made for the first time in the Trade Disputes Act, 1929, which provided for the setting up of a Board of Conciliation by the government to settle industrial disputes. The Trade Dispute Act was amended in 1938 to provide for the appointment of conciliation officers. The Industrial Disputes Act, 1947 and other state enactments authorize the government to appoint conciliation officers with the duty of mediating in and holding conciliation proceedings for the settlement of industrial disputes.

The Government may also appoint a Board of Conciliation consisting of one chairman and four members. Conciliation is necessary in all disputes in public utility services and optional in other industrial establishments. To expedite conciliation proceedings, a time limit has been prescribed: (a) fourteen days for conciliation officers, and (b) two months for the Board of Conciliation. An agreement arrived at in the presence of a conciliation officer is binding on the involved parties.

However, both workers and employers have expressed dissatisfaction over certain specific areas of functioning of the conciliation machinery such as

- the delays involved,
- casual attitude of one or the other party, and
- conciliation officer's lack of adequate knowledge and understanding of the major issues.

In case the conciliation fails, the parties may opt for voluntary arbitration or compulsory adjudication.

Voluntary arbitration In India, voluntary arbitration was introduced for the first time in the textile industry in Ahmedabad as early as in 1920 under the guidance of Mahatma Gandhi who said 'we should not resort to law courts but should have dispute settled by private arbitration.' It was followed in other industries also.

Voluntary arbitration as a method of resolving industrial conflicts was recommended in the plans. The Industrial Disputes Act was amended to make a provision (Section 10A) for joint reference of industrial disputes to voluntary arbitration.

To make voluntary arbitration acceptable to the parties and to coordinate efforts for its promotion, the government established a National Arbitration Promotion Board (NAPB) with a tripartite composition. Its main task was to evolve principles, norms, and procedures for guidance to arbitrators and parties. It was expected that the formation of NAPB would achieve its objectives, but the progress made by NAPB was slow and can be attributed to the following factors:

- Easy availability of adjudication in case of failure of negotiations
- Shortage of suitable arbitrators who command the confidence of both the parties
- Absence of recognized unions, which could bind the workers to common agreements
- Legal obstacles
- No provision for appeal against an arbitrator's award
- Absence of simplified procedures
- Expensive, particularly to the workers

Adjudication   Adjudication means a mandatory settlement of industrial disputes by labour courts or industrial tribunals under the provisions of the Industrial Disputes Act, 1947 or any other corresponding state statutes. This is the ultimate remedy for settlement of unresolved disputes. Labour ourts, constituted under Section 7 of the Act, have jurisdiction over the following matters:

- The propriety or legality of any order passed by an employer under the standing order
- The application and interpretation of standing orders
- Discharge or dismissal of workmen including reinstatement of, or ground of relief to, wrongfully dismissed
- Withdrawal of any customary concession or privilege
- Illegality or otherwise of strikes or lock-out
- All matters other than those specified in the third schedule of the Industrial Disputes Act, 1947

Any matter listed in the second and third schedule of the Act could be referred to the Industrial Tribunal/National Industrial Tribunal. The central government has the authority to constitute the National Industrial Tribunal. These tribunals have the authority to entertain appeals against the decision of the registrar/labour Commissioner/labour court/wage board constituted under the respective Acts.

The adjudication machinery has exercised considerable influence on several aspects of work conditions and labour management relations, but it has also faced criticism on the following grounds:

- Considerable delays
- Sometimes discriminatory as the powers rest with the government
- Quite expensive because in case of failure, the employee may prefer a writ petition in a high court/or the Supreme Court
- Prohibits collective agreement
- Failure to achieve industrial peace

HRM PRACTICES—CHANGE IN PERSPECTIVE

There is a growing debate among human resource management (HRM) practitioners and students as to what constitute good practices. Essentially they can be defined as those practices that

■ ■ ■
Good practices are defined as those that nurture the three Cs—competency, commitment, and culture—for effective organizational functioning.

nurture the three Cs—competency, commitment, and culture—for effective organizational functioning. Each of these factors has its own importance.

Organizations should have the right mix of competencies among the employees and departments for sustaining and improving organizational performance. There is an ancient saying, 'One can take a horse to water but cannot make it drink.' Similarly, it is not sufficient for organizations to have merely competent people. What is more important is to ensure that they have commitment to the organizational goals and objectives. This is dependent upon the third and most important C, that is, the culture of the organization, which can be understood through the written and informal policies and practices. Researchers have found the following HR practices to be effective:

- Provision of financial incentives for better performers
- Practices that motivate employees to contribute by optimally using their knowledge and skills on the job
- Effective recruitment policies
- Satisfactory, that is, more than industry average, compensation structures
- Information dissemination to make the employees comprehend the organizational plans and promote their involvement
- Employee empowerment
- Training and development, which ensures assured minimum training to each employee
- Career progression possibilities
- Periodic assessment and evaluation of HR practices

Good HRM practices can be defined as those that facilitate the following aspects:

- Aligning the HR strategy with the corporate strategy
- Nurturing a positive work culture among the employees
- Recruitment and retention practices which ensure that the organization has the best talent
- Performance management systems which nurture employee development and improvement of performance through counselling and guidance.

Individual Pay Determination

HR departments in many organizations have introduced the system of individual pay determination (IPD) and individual performance related pay (IPRP). Mihal (1983) suggested the following three relevant premises:

- Individual differences in performance can be accurately measured and communicated,
- Pay differences can be related to performance differences, and will be perceived as being related, and
- Individuals will increase their effort to gain more rewards, resulting in improved performance.

These premises are based on the expectancy theory proposed by Vroom (1964), and Porter and Lawler (1968). Thompson (1992) indicated that 'The growth of HR as a managerial strategy does appear to be correlated (in intuitive terms) with a wider uptake of individualized payment systems.'

Surveys undertaken by the Thompson Institute of Manpower Studies during 1992 and 1993 covering 20 organizations in the UK in the public as well as the private sector examined the employer experience (1992) and employee experience (1993) of IPRP. The conclusions of the survey are discussed here.

Employer survey

- In terms of context issues, the report finds that organizational restructuring (in terms of relationship to produce markets and levels of decision-making) can often be seen as an important, but not necessarily planned pre-requisite for the introduction of IPRP. A coherent and communicated pay philosophy also appeared to be an important context for the successful introduction of IPRP, but few employers appeared to have one.
- Coverage of IPRP varied, with some employers limiting it to professional and managerial staff and others extending it to lower-level employees.
- Although most schemes were introduced in unionized environments, the scale and nature of union involvement differed widely. At one extreme was the use of IPRP as part of a derecognition process, whilst at the other, unions were involved at the outset in design and implementation of the scheme.
- IPRP schemes require devolution of responsibility to line managers. This may create problems similar to those consequent upon the introduction of devolved collective pay determination.
- Some organizations experienced problems of integrating IPRP with HRM policies and existing payment systems. For example, IPRP created tensions between the short-term and bottom-line needs of the organization and the long-term development needs of the individual.

Employee survey

- IPRP does not serve to motivate (even those with high performance ratings) and may do more to demotivate employees.
- There was little evidence to suggest that IPRP could help retain high performers and no evidence to suggest that poor performers were seeking to leave the organizations.
- Employees are negative or broadly neutral on its impact on organizational culture even in schemes that have been in operation for three or more years.
- Employees are unclear as to whether IPRP rewards are fair, although high performers are more likely to perceive it to be fair than low-rated employees.
- There is a risk that IPRP may contribute to a downward spiral of demotivation for the bulk of employees and this draws into question the real costs and benefits of such pay systems.
- The poor skills of line managers may, in the short term, contribute to staff turnover and lower morale. In the long run, IPRP may serve to highlight to an even greater extent, the failures of the UK management and prompt employers and policy makers to invest in management, training, and development. Such action, rather than the introduction of IPRP, is more likely to yield productivity growth in the future. Paradoxically, the failure of IPRP may serve to hasten this investment.

Human Resource Policies and Practices—Impact on Trade Unions

At the outset, it is difficult to separately analyse the impact of HRM on trade unions and collective bargaining, as a whole gamut of changes in the political and economic spheres weakened

■ ■ ■
HR practices have helped in building a direct rapport between management and employees, making trade unions totally or partially irrelevant.

the position of trade unions. However, a few HR practices, such as selection processes, appraisal, direct communication, task-level participation, training, performance-oriented pay, cultural change, and organizational initiatives, have helped in building a direct rapport between managements and employees, making the trade unions totally or partially irrelevant. The suspicious attitude of the trade unions towards the HR initiatives was in a way predicted by the managers, and this caused the trade unions to take a subversive and anti-employer stance. If the trade unions do not change with the times, they run the risk of becoming defunct.

■ ■ ■
Industrial relations is the outcome of HRM and employment relations.

However, one noticeable phenomenon is that trade unions continued to be important during wage negotiation and there are cases of industrial conflict in various global companies such as Ford, British Rail, and Lucas. This substantiates the view that initiatives, such as direct communication and job-level involvement, would not translate into conflict dissipation over pay revision.

The temptation to use HR techniques as a 'softening up' measure prior to annual negotiations was usually countered by the realization that such measures would prove counterproductive in the long run. In most progressive companies, HR functionaries look after the requirements of managers and higher categories of employees, and personnel specialists look after the interests of the other employees. The elitist image of the HR professionals, with their easy access to power centres, has led to their lack of credibility on shop floors.

In multinational companies (MNCs) such as ICI and Eaton, the unions faced problems of a different kind. The mainstream organizations adopted a 'cool' instead of a hostile approach towards the unions. However, this was not a direct result of HR initiatives. The marginalization of unions appears to be a symptomatic characteristic of the commitment to the HRM paradigm.

The term 'industrial relations' (IR) refers to the relationship between the employees and the management in the context of the day-to-day working environment. However, when looked at in the wider sense, the concept refers to the functional interdependence among the economic, social, technological, and legal variables, and the very fact that a relationship exists is because of the necessity of collaboration between both the players.

As per the definition of the International Labour Organization (ILO), industrial relations deals with the relationships among the state, the employer, and workers' organizations, or the relationship between the organizations themselves. Industrial relations involves the individual relations between employers and employees at their place of work, joint consultants, collective relations between the employers and their organizations as well as the trade unions, and also the role of the state or government in the regulation of these relations.

Industrial relations refers to the relations mainly between the employer and the employee and is the outcome of the HRM and employment relations. These relations emphasize the accommodation of the interests, values, and needs of both the parties through cooperation. They are governed by the rules and regulations framed by the government, with the main objective of maintaining harmonious relations between employers and employees, which provide for grievance redressal procedures and collective bargaining processes (Exhibit 16.2).

EXHIBIT 16.2   Flexibility deals in Komatsu and Hitachi

In Komatsu, there is complete flexibility and mobility of employees; changes in processes and practices will be introduced to increase competitiveness and...these will improve productivity and affect manning levels. To achieve such change, employees will work as required by the company and participate in the training of themselves or other employees as required. Manning levels will be determined by the company using appropriate industrial engineering and manpower planning techniques. In Hitachi, all company members will agree to the complete flexibility of jobs and duties. ...When necessary to fit the needs of the business, all company members may be required to perform whatever jobs and duties, within their capability. The company accepts its responsibility to train, retrain, and develop company members to broaden their skills, develop their potential, and meet the needs of rapid technological change. The company also accepts that in instances where more competitive manning levels can be achieved by agreed flexibility...manning levels will be achieved without compulsory redundancy. (Oliver and Wilkinson 1992).

TRADE UNIONS AND INDUSTRIAL RELATIONS IN FUTURE

Given the growing number of white-collared workers, the increased awareness of the blue-collared workers, and the general growth of individualism among the employees, four major scenarios could emerge.

- The unions and negotiated procedures for union–management relations could be done away with, leaving scope for the emergence of new approaches.
- The unions per se could be ignored—this would be equivalent to their derecognition.
- The new systems and relationship methodologies could run in parallel to the existing methods.
- The existing arrangements could be integrated into the new approach that evolves over a period of time.

The crucial distinction between 'individualistic' and 'collectivistic' was made by Purcell (1987), which was subsequently modified by Marchington and Parker (1990). Marsden and Thompson (1990), in their study on the impact of flexibility agreements on British manufacturing productivity, found that changes in 'working methods' were a precursor to those in 'working practices', which ultimately led to changes in levels of periodicity. The change dynamics were found to have the following factors:

- Market changes
- Technical redesign
- Collective renegotiation
- Cultural preparation of human resources

In the context of these developments, the managements have to change their perspective towards the role of trade unions by responding to the following questions.

- What stance had the management taken with regard to trade unions (i.e., in terms of the grade of recognition or moves to derecognition, and what action had been taken in relation to shop stewards)?
- Irrespective of the institutional security of trade unions and their representatives, what stance had the managers adopted concerning collective bargaining?

- To what extent were trade unions treated as partners in the process of managing change?
- What impact did the new management initiatives on direct employee communications, task-level involvement, and the like have on the trade unions and industrial relations?

Exhibit 16.3 provides insights on employee relations management at Rover.

EXHIBIT 16.3 Deal at Rover

Rover has adopted a distinctive approach to employee relations (ER) management with the following principles:
- strategic interventions designed to elicit commitment and to develop 'resourceful' employees,
- strategic interventions designed to secure full utilization of labour resources, and
- both the aforementioned interventions to be integrated with the business strategy.

The outcome of this strategic approach to HRM was the 'new deal' that is summarized here:

- Rover will be a single-status company. All are employees and the only distinction is the contribution they make. All distinctions between 'staff' and 'hourly-paid' status will be ended.
- Continuous improvement will be a requirement for everyone—the company must continually improve its performance and competitive position through the elimination of waste, increased levels of efficiency, and reduced levels of power—'working smarter rather than harder'.
- Employees will be expected to be flexible subject to their ability to do do the job, after training if necessary, and subject to safe working practices being observed.
- There will be maximum devolution of authority and accountability to the employees actually doing the job. Teams will be responsible for quality of work, routine maintenance, process improvements, cost reduction, work allocation, job rotation, training of each other, and material control.
- It is our intention to establish a single-grade structure for all our people.
- Productivity bonus schemes will be progressively phased out.
- Employees who want to work for Rover will be able to stay with Rover.
- Constant open and honest two-way communications with employees throughout the company will be the norm. The process of daily, weekly, monthly, and annual employee briefings will be strengthened.
- All employees will be expected to participate in discussion groups, quality action teams, suggestion schemes and other activities to continuously improve processes and company performance.
- Employees will continue to have the opportunity to be represented by the recognized trade unions.
- Consultation with representatives of recognized trade unions will be enhanced to ensure maximum understanding of company performance, competitive practices and standards, product and company plans, and all areas of activity affecting the company and its employees.

Source: Rover document

CHANGE IN PERSPECTIVE—INSTITUTIONAL INTEGRITY OF TRADE UNIONS

The advent of the liberalized environment has led to the growing importance of the adoption of proactive HR policies by organizations. Organizations in the contemporary context perceive employees more as assets and collaborators facilitating the realization of organizational objectives. Therefore, HR departments are adopting an employee-friendly approach as against the confrontationist approach adopted by the erstwhile industrial departments. This has led to a debate regarding whether trade unions have any relevance.

The integrity of trade unions has also been questioned quite often since the unions in India are highly politicized, meaning that the political leaders dictate terms to the management based on their personal agendas, and the innocent employees are misled by the directives of these political leaders. Further, the trade union leaders play a subversive role, influenced by the politicians. Such irresponsible behaviour made all concerned question the institutional integrity of the trade unions. People also doubted whether they were committed to the welfare of the employees and that of the organizations.

These developments led to an attack on trade unions through several methods. Some organizations have shifted to individual contracts for certain grades of employees along with withdrawal from collective negotiations by these groups of employees. These developments have taken place notwithstanding the fact that large established organizations make reassuring noises with regard to their official policies towards trade unions. Memos have been issued to trade unions indicating a rigid managerial stance. The managements consciously allowed their industrial relations officers to continue with their rigid posture towards trade unions to weaken the base and credibility of the unions among the employees (Exhibit 16.4).

In contrast, certain progressive companies, such as Ford in Britain, have adopted innovative policies including employee involvement (EI) without any attempts at undermining the role of trade unions. However, organizations with progressive HR departments and policies have adopted the method of direct communication with the concerned aggrieved employee, bypassing the block and joint consultative committees, which were so far used for conflict resolution.

EXHIBIT 16.4   Trade unions in Sri Lanka: Workwear Lanka Pvt. Ltd

The factory, located in the Biyagama Free Trade Zone (opened in 1995) produces various types of rubber-coated gloves. Approximately 700 workers are employed in the factory; 60% of the workers are women. Workwear Lanka Pvt. Ltd produces gloves for IAB Industries Lindarbeitsschu (Germany), Midas Safety Inc. (Canada), Shelby Group (US), Main Glove (US), Fitzner (Germany), Interbar Gloves (Spain), BM Polyco (UK), Mitane Textile (Japan), Cutters Gloves (US), and Entrix Sports (Canada).

The company has five directors: one director from Tanzania, and three from Pakistan. The managing director is Mustafa Mussa Kassam Somji (Tanzanian), who is also a major shareholder in the company.

Anti-union Campaign: Chronology of Events

Approximately 263 Workwear Lanka workers joined the FTZGSEU union and formed a branch union at the factory in December 2003. Almost immediately management launched an anti-union campaign.

The workers formed their union on 28 December 2003. When they came to work the following day management representatives asked about the union, and requested that they resign from the union. On 30th and 31st December, the management questioned each worker about his or her affiliation to the union and asked that he or she resign. Management threatened the workers with dismissal and possible closure of the factory unless they resigned from the union.

On 31 December, the management sent letters to seven workers, including the vice president, treasurer and committee member of the union, and the other activists, charging them with instigating a strike and causing losses to the company in relation to a work stoppage that took place on 27 December when work stopped from 9:30 a.m. until 1:30 p.m. in protest of the verbal abuse of an employee who had inquired about management's failure to pay workers their monthly salary.

On 1 January, the union officially informed the company of the formation of the branch union and the names of the office bearers and committee members. The next day management continued harassment and intimidation of the union members. When the branch union president and four committee members reported for work, they were denied entry to the factory and not permitted to work

(Contd)

EXHIBIT 16.4 (Contd)

On 4 January, the union requested a meeting with management to discuss the anti-union harassment and intimidation and also filed a complaint with the minister of employment and labour and the commissioner general of labour requesting their intervention in this matter. The next day the commissioner general of labour requested that union and management representatives meet him on 12 January to discuss the situation.

On 8 January, the company issued a charge sheet to the branch union secretary stating that she had instigated the 27 December work stoppage and had caused the company to lose money. [Note: A charge sheet is a written statement from management detailing charges against the workers; workers are supposed to provide reasons why they are not guilty of the charges. This is different from a warning letter, which is issued after workers are found guilty of those charges.] That same day several union members were demoted because they refused to resign from the union. An additional 15 workers (not union members) were dismissed. The management justified the layoffs by saying that the workers were casual workers and no longer needed.

On 11 January, the union filed a second complaint with the Commissioner General of Labour regarding the ongoing harassment of union members and unfair labour practices, requesting that these issues be discussed at the 12 January meeting. However, management did not show up for the meeting on the 12th. Instead, management informed the union officials that those facing various charges should plead guilty, apologize in writing, and be prepared to face punishment should they commit similar offences in the future. The workers who received the letters wrote to management saying that they would not plead guilty because they had not committed any acts of misconduct.

On 14 January, the union filed another complaint with the Commissioner General of Labour regarding the ongoing anti-union campaign and the dismissal of another 47 workers (not union members) under the pretext that they were casual workers and they were no longer needed.

On 26 January, the Commissioner General of Labour informed the union and the management that they should participate in a meeting on February 9 to discuss the union victimization complaints. Meanwhile, management maintained that there was no union and demanded that they be provided with a list of members with their signatures. The union contacted the Commissioner General of Labour to contest management's failure to recognize the union (copy to the management), but offered to provide a list of members with signatures if management would reinstate the terminated workers and stop their anti-union campaign.

On 3 February, the management suspended the union's officer bearers, committee members, and the activists who have been issued charge sheets, claiming that they were unwilling to accept the charges levelled against them.

On 9 February, Workwear Lanka management again failed to attend the meeting called by the Commissioner General of Labour. The union president was demoted to floor sweeper and eventually resigned.

As of 10 February, approximately 100 workers were dismissed from Workwear Lanka on the grounds that they were casual workers and their services were no longer needed. However this is clearly an attempt by the management to break the union. The workers, recruited as contract/casual workers, had worked from one month to one year, and were sympathetic to the union because the union position was that they should be made permanent. Though the management maintains that these workers are no longer needed, it is currently recruiting new workers through a manpower agency. Recently, the management has tried to use religious difference to create anti-union sentiment among the workers.

According to the union, the management's actions qualify as unfair labour practices under the provisions of Sri Lanka's Industrial Dispute (Amendment) Act No. 56 of 1999. These anti-union activities also violate ILO Conventions 87 and 98.

Union Demands

The union is demanding that Workwear Lanka Pvt. Ltd management immediately stop all anti-union activities, specifically

- management must reinstate all the workers whose services have been terminated;

(Contd)

EXHIBIT 16.4   (Contd)

- withdraw the suspension of union branch office bearers, committee members, and activists and call them back to work;
- cancel all transfers and demotion of the union members and restore them to their earlier positions; and
- respect workers' right to organize by preventing interference in the conduct of the trade union's activities.

Source: www.cleanclothes.org/urgent/04-03-29.php, accessed on 28 August 2005.

STRATEGIC MANAGEMENT OF INDUSTRIAL RELATIONS

The central assumption of HRM is that it takes strategic orientation to the employee management in relation to the traditional personnel management or industrial relations model. Two sets of models are commonly identified—'best practice' and 'contingency'.

Best Practice Model

Human resource management policy is decided by the choices exercised by the stakeholders and situational factors, and the decisions made on the basis of such policy result in beneficial HR outcomes. Industrial relations practices and outcomes are the result of environmental forces and their interaction with the strategic choices and values of managers, union leaders, employees, etc. Strategic choice determines the type of industrial relations system that emerges at three main levels—strategic decision making, collective bargaining, and day-to-day workplace activities. These decisions emerge from decisions regarding new investment, new technology, workforce adjustment strategies, and new forms of work organizations.

Contingency Model

This model assumes that there is variation in policy in accordance with changing business conditions. Further, it argues that the type of industrial relations strategies and organizational priorities are contingent upon the life cycle of the organization. The contingency model is concerned with identifying a specific strategy and structure and linking it with the industrial relations policy and choices as well as the HR policy and choices. The strategic choices are driven by three strategic options—innovation, quality enhancement, and cost reduction.

> ■ ■ ■
> The contingency model assumes that there is variation in policy in accordance with the changing business conditions.

In effect, there is single effective model of industrial relations and the kind of model suitable for an organization depends on the specific characteristics of that organization.

HISTORY OF INDUSTRIAL LEGISLATION IN INDIA

Let us begin with a brief review of industrial legislation during the British rule in India.

Legislative History

The history of labour legislation in India is naturally interwoven with that of British colonialism. Considerations of British political economy were naturally paramount in shaping some of the early laws. In the beginning, it was difficult to get enough regular Indian workers to run British establishments and hence, laws for indenturing workers became necessary. There was obviously labour legislation in order to protect the interests of British employers.

Then came the Factories Act. It is well known that Indian textile goods offered stiff competition to British textiles in the export market. Therefore, in order to make Indian labour costlier, the Factories Act was introduced in 1883 because of the pressure exercised on the British parliament by the textile magnates of Manchester and Lancashire. Thus, we received the first stipulation of eight hours of work, the abolition of child labour, the restriction of women in night employment, and the introduction of overtime wages for work beyond eight hours. While the impact of this measure was clearly welfarist, the real motivation was undoubtedly protectionist!

To date, India has ratified 39 ILO conventions, of which 37 are in force. Of the ILO's eight fundamental conventions, India has ratified four—Forced Labour, 1930, Abolition of Forced Labour, 1957, Equal Remuneration, 1951, and Discrimination (employment and occupation), 1958.

Trade Unionism and the Trade Unions Act, 1926

There are almost ten major central union organizations of workers based on different political ideologies. Almost every union is affiliated to one of the political parties. These central organizations have state branches, committees, and councils, from where they work down to the local level.

The first central trade union organization in India was the All India Trade Union Congress (AITUC), which was formed in 1920—almost three decades before India won independence. At about the same time, workers at the Buckingham and Carnatic Mills, Madras, went on strike, led by B.P. Wadia. The management brought a civil suit against the workers in the Madras High Court and not only obtained an injunction order against the strike, but also succeeded in obtaining damages against the leader for 'inducing a breach of contract'. This was followed by widespread protests that finally led to the Trade Unions Act, 1926, giving immunity to the trade unions against certain forms of civil and criminal action. Apart from this, the Trade Unions Act also facilitated registration, internal democracy, a role for outsiders, and granted a trade union permission for raising a political fund subject to separate accounting requirements.

The Trade Unions Act facilitates unionization both in the organized and the unorganized sectors. It is through this law that the freedom of association that is a fundamental right under the Constitution of India is realized.

> ■ ■ ■
> The first central trade union organization in India was the All India Trade Union Congress (AITUC), formed in 1920.

The right to register a trade union, however, does not mean that the employer must recognize the union—there is in fact no law which provides for recognition of trade unions and, consequently, no legal compulsion for employers, even in the organized sector, to enter into collective bargaining. Yet, in reality, because of the strength of particular trade unions, there is fairly widespread collective bargaining, especially in the organized sector.

Colonial Dispute Settlement Machinery

The Industrial Disputes Act, 1947, provides for the dispute settlement machinery. The framework of this legislation, which is the principle dealing with core labour issues, is of colonial origin.

This law has its origins first in the Trade Disputes Act, 1929, introduced by the British when there was a spate of strikes and huge loss of person days, and secondly in Rule 81A of the Defence of India Rules, 1942, introduced because the British wanted to maintain wartime supplies to the allied forces. Interestingly, the interim government on the eve of formal independence retained this framework by enacting the Industrial Disputes Act.

Developments after Independence

Even though the Industrial Disputes Act was primarily meant for industry in the organized sector, its present application now extends well into the unorganized sector, through court rulings. Its pro-worker protection clauses and safeguards against arbitrary job losses have evolved over a period of time through the process of sustained legislative amendments and that of judicial activism spread over more than five decades.

The original colonial legislation underwent substantial modification in the post-colonial era because independent India called for a clear partnership between labour and capital. The content of this partnership was unanimously approved in a tripartite conference in December 1947, in which it was agreed that labour would be given a fair wage and fair working conditions and in return capital would receive the fullest cooperation of labour for uninterrupted production and higher productivity as part of the strategy for national economic development, and that all concerned would observe a truce period of three years free from strikes and lockouts.

Regulation of Job Losses

Space does not allow a detailed discussion of the transformation in labour policy and consequent amendments to labour law, but provisions that deal with job losses must be noted. Under the present law, any industrial establishment employing more than 100 workers must make an application to the government seeking permission before resorting to lay-off, retrenchment, or closure; employers resorting to any of the said forms of creating job losses are acting illegally and workers are entitled to receive wages for the period of illegality. The Reserve Bank of India commissioned a study into the causes of sickness in the Indian industry and reported cryptically, 'sickness in India is a profitable business'. This chapter in the Industrial Disputes Act, which has been identified to be highly rigid in the area of labour redundancy, has been targeted for change in the present era of globalization and liberalization.

> ■ ■ ■
> Industrial Disputes Act, which has been identified to be highly rigid in the area of labour redundancy, has been targetted for change in the present era of globalization and liberalization.

Protection of Service Conditions

A feature of the Industrial Disputes Act, is the stipulation that existing service conditions cannot be unilaterally altered without giving a notice of 21 days to the workers and the union. Further, if an industrial dispute is pending before an authority under the Industrial Disputes Act, then the previous service conditions with respect to that dispute cannot be altered to the disadvantage of the workers without prior permission of the authority concerned. This has been identified as a form of rigidity that hampers competition in the era of the World Trade Organization.

> ■ ■ ■
> A feature of the Industrial Disputes Act, is the stipulation that existing service conditions cannot be unilaterally altered without giving a notice of 21 days to the worker and the union.

Removal From Service

A permanent worker can be removed from service only for proven misconduct or for habitual absence—due to ill health, alcoholism, and the like, or on attaining retirement age. In other words, the doctrine of 'hire and fire' is not approved within the existing legal framework. In cases of misconduct the worker is entitled to the protection of standing orders to be framed by a certifying officer of the labour department after hearing both the sides, the management and the trade union. Employers must follow the principles of 'natural justice', which again is an area that is governed by court rulings. An order of dismissal can be challenged in the labour court and if it is found to be flawed, the court has the power to order reinstatement with continuity of service, wages, and consequential benefits. This again has been identified as an area where greater flexibility is considered desirable for organizations to be competitive.

Return to Colonial Days

Almost all pro-worker developments that have occurred since independence are now identified as areas of rigidity and in the name of flexibility there is pressure on the Government of India to repeal or amend all pro-worker laws. Interestingly, if such a proposal is fully implemented, labour law, especially for the organized sector, will become the same as in colonial times, when state intervention was meant primarily to discipline labour, not to give it protection.

Disputes and Resolving Mechanisms

The various types of disputes between the management and the workers, and the resolving mechanisms have been discussed here.

Strikes and Lockouts

■ ■ ■
Workers have a right to strike, even without notice, unless they are employed in a public utility service. Disputes may be settled by collective bargaining, conciliation, or compulsory adjudication.

Workers have the right to strike, even without notice, unless they are employed in a public utility service; employers have the right to lockout, subject to the same conditions as those for a strike. The parties may sort out their differences either bilaterally or through a conciliation officer who can facilitate, but not compel a settlement, which is legally binding on the parties, even when a strike or a lockout is in progress. But, if these methods do not resolve a dispute, the government may refer the dispute to compulsory adjudication and stop the strike or lockout.

Conciliation, Arbitration, and Adjudication

When the parties engaging in collective bargaining are unable to arrive at a settlement, either party or the government may commence conciliation proceedings before a government-appointed conciliation officer whose intervention may produce a settlement, which is then registered in the labour department and becomes binding on all parties. If conciliation fails, it is open for the parties to invoke arbitration or for the appropriate government to refer the dispute to adjudication before a labour court or a tribunal whose decision may then be notified as binding on the parties. Disputes may be settled by collective bargaining, conciliation, or compulsory adjudication.

Globalization and its Impact on Industrial Relations

The most perceptible change arising from globalization is the increasing trend of offloading or subcontracting. Generally this is done through the use of cheaper forms of contract labour, where there is no unionization, no welfare benefits, and often not even statutorily fixed minimum wages. Occasionally, labourers are hired on contract in the primary plant itself. This is often preceded by downsizing, and since there is a statutory regulation of job losses, the system of voluntary retirement with a 'golden handshake' is widely prevalent, in the public as well as the private sector.

Regulation of Contract Labour

■ ■ ■

The most perceptible change arising from globalization is the increasing trend of outsourcing.

The Contract Labour (Prohibition and Regulation) Act 1970 provides a mechanism for the registration of contractors (if more than 20 workers are engaged) and for the appointment of a Tripartite Advisory Board that investigates particular forms of contract labour. If found to be engaged in areas requiring perennial work connected with the production process, then the Board could recommend the 'abolition' of the form of contract labour. A tricky legal question arises as to whether the contract workers should be automatically absorbed or not after the contract labour system is abolished. Recently, a Constitutional Bench of the Supreme Court held that there need not be such automatic absorption—in effect, this 'abolished' the contract labourer, and gave rise to a serious anomaly.

We are already witnessing a reduction in the organized labour force and an increase in the ranks of the unorganized. The Act is a kind of interface in the process of regulating the transition from regular to irregular employment. If contract labour is seen as introducing a form of flexibility, a strict enforcement of this Act could have had a salutary effect on the transition process. Instead, the enforceability of the Act has now been diluted and consequently even the minimum protection envisaged under this law to contract labourers is in jeopardy. Dominant thinking in relation to globalization has had its effect on the judicial process also, ignoring the Directive Principles of State Policy.

FUTURE OF INDUSTRIAL RELATIONS

The future of industrial relations is going to be totally different from what it has been due to various factors such as the increasing number of knowledge workers, the higher education level of the workers, and so on. These developments indicate the growing maturity level of workers, which increases their capability to resolve their individual grievances and reduces their dependence on union leaders.

Another factor that would have a significant impact is that political parties, over time, will no longer play a significant role in trade unions in the country. The experience of the last five decades has led to attitudinal changes among employees, since it is obvious to them that they have been exploited for the selfish ends of politicians. Another thing they have learnt is that prolonged industrial disputes jeopardize the existence of organizations.

Another important factor is that many people in our country are employed in the services sector, followed by the IT sector. Both these sectors mainly employ knowledge workers. By virtue of their job profiles, the employees in these sectors have little time for union activities.

The reduced importance of public sector enterprises and manufacturing sectors in the economy would lead to a changed and reduced role of trade unions. In future, trade unions would adopt a cooperative attitude towards the employers or management in contrast to the previous, confrontationist attitude.

SUMMARY

This chapter begins with an overview of employer–employee relations in our country in the context of the struggle for independence. It covers the industrial policies of the government, the socialistic philosophy, the various Acts, the emerging organizational scenario in the context of ICT, and the paradigm shift from industrial relations to HR. It covers various theories of industrial relations in brief, the role of the government in industrial relations through initiatives such as five-year plans, the best-employer practices and their impact on the industrial relations scenario, the role of the CEO in industrial organizations, the evaluation of trade unions, the legal framework, the changing paradigm of HR practices and its impact on trade unions, and the emerging scenario of trade unions. It discusses the institutional integrity of trade unions, and the strategic aspect of trade unions with various models. It also discusses in detail the history of industrial legislation in India.

■ ■ ■ | KEY TERMS

Adjudication   The act of pronouncing judgment based on the evidence presented

Arbitration   The process by which the parties to a dispute submit their differences to the judgment of an impartial person or group appointed by mutual consent or statutory provision

Blue-collared worker   Someone who does physical work, often in a factory

Collectivistic   The principles of ownership and control of the means of production and distribution by the people collectively

Conciliation   The act of placating and overcoming distrust and animosity

Dissipate   To gradually disappear or waste away

Empower   To invest with power, especially legal power or official authority

Globalization   To make global or worldwide in scope or application

Individualistic   One that asserts individuality by independence of thought and action

Performance orientation   Perceiving learning as a means for external purposes such as outperforming peers

Politicize   To engage in or discuss politics

Prerogative   An exclusive right or privilege held by a person or group

Promulgate   To make known by public declaration

Satyagraha   Method of resisting injustice, the pursuit of truth; *satya* means truth or love and *agraha* means force

Tripartite   Involving three people or organizations

White-collared worker   Someone who works in an office, doing mental rather than physical work

■ ■ ■ | EXERCISES

Multiple Choice Questions

1. White-collared worker is someone who
   (a) does mental work rather than physical work
   (b) does physical work
   (c) is a union leader
   (d) none of these
2. To safeguard the interests of women workers, a women's wing of the Standing Committee of Public Enterprises (SCOPE) looks into the following aspects, except
   (a) development of a database and information network

   (b) fringe benefits
   (c) counseling services
   (d) day care centres
3. The major factor impacting the growth and evolution of the trade union movement was
   (a) the influence of politicians
   (b) the white-collared workers
   (c) the economy
   (d) the company policies
4. The objective of trade union is to
   (a) provide solutions to problems encountered by the workers

(b) protect the interests of the workers and the employers in the organization

(c) ensure welfare of the members

(d) all of these

5. The culture of an organization can be understood through

(a) the written and informal policies and practices

(b) pay levels

(c) trade unions

(d) none of these

Fill in the Blanks

(a) The _____ has an important role in creating and nurturing attributes that create a good organization.

(b) The Government of India has been making conscious attempts to improve _____ and social conditions right from the first five-year plan.

(c) _____ and knowledge workers have become the key contributors to organizational growth and development.

(d) Good practices are defined as those that nurture the three C's— _____, _____, and _____ for effective functioning of organizations.

(e) The poor skills of line managers may contribute to _____ and lower morale.

Concept Review Questions

1. Explain the importance of the employer–employee relationship.

2. Analyse the trade union movement in the context of employer–employee relations.

3. What is the influence of HRM policies on industrial relations practices?

4. What are the socio-political factors influencing the growth of trade unions?

5. Analyse the strategic options that a management has for aligning industrial relations and HR practices.

6. Compare and contrast the international and domestic industrial relations scenarios.

7. Describe the change in perspective of trade unions.

8. Discuss the institutional integrity of trade unions and their relevance.

9. Explain the nature, importance, and role of trade unions in the present industrial environment.

10. Describe the characteristics of trade unions in India.

11. Distinguish between the dilemmas and challenges of trade unions.

12. Explain the methods and mechanisms to resolve industrial disputes.

13. Describe the role of trade unions in the liberalized era.

Project Work

1. Prepare a write-up on the emerging trends in industrial relations.

2. Write a brief essay on industrial relations in the globalized era.

3. Study a manufacturing company, and prepare a brief report on its industrial relations scenario.

4. Prepare a report on the influence of politics and politicians on trade unions.

5. Prepare a case study based on an industrial dispute in a manufacturing organization.

6. Prepare a case study substantiating the need and relevance of trade unions in the globalized scenario.

■ ■ ■ | REFERENCES

Dwivedi, R.S. 2000, *Managing Human Resources—Industrial Relations in Indian Enterprises*, Galgotia Publishing Company, New Delhi, pp. 2–35.

Marsh, D. 1992, *The New Politics of British Trade Unionism: Union Power and Thatcher Legacy*, Macmillan, London.

Misra, M. and Misra, P. 2002, 'Best employer's in India 2002', Hewitt Associates, LLC, Mumbai.

Oliver, N. and Wilkinson, B. 1992, *The Japanization of British Industry*, Blackwell Business, Oxford, pp. 293–4.

Salaman, G. 1992, *Human Resource Strategies*, Sage, London.

Thompson, M. 1992, 'Pay and performance: The employer experience', *IMS Report*, 218, IMS, Sussex, p. 3.

Venkata Ratnam, C.S. 2001, *Globalization and Labour Management Relations*, Sage Publications, New Delhi, p. 303.

Karmakar, Apurv, 21 May 2009, http://jurisonline.
in/2009/05/impact-of-ilo-on-labor-laws-in-india/,
accessed on 15 September 2011.
http://www.ilo.org/, accessed on 15 September 2011.
http://www.ilo.org/global/about-the-ilo/mission-
and-objectives/lang--en/index.htm, accessed on 15
September 2011.
http://studentbuzz.hpage.com/get_file.php?id=676
431 &vnr=244152, accessed on 19 June 2012.

Industrial Relations and Mumbai Textiles Pvt. Limited

CASE STUDY 1

Mumbai Textiles was founded by Naroji Baba during the 1850s. He was patriotic and wanted to stop the export of raw cotton to England and develop the textile manufacturing capability of India. He also actively supported the independence movement through financial contributions to the freedom fighters.

After his death in the 1940s, the responsibility was passed on to his son, Karoji Baba. Unlike his father, Karoji was aligned to the capitalist views of US/UK and dissociated from freedom fighting.

The unions, who until then had peaceful relations with the management, comprehended the changed approach of the management and became more aggressive to realize their rights. In 1945, one of the shop floor workers was slapped by a production incharge for negligence in the job. The employee suffered serious injuries and was hospitalized. The labour welfare officer refused to get involved in the incident and aggravated the situation by commenting that the erring employee was solely responsible for the situation. He even informed to union members that the company would not bear any cost beyond the primary medical treatment expenses.

The incident led to serious friction between the union and the management, and the union members called for a strike in the factory. Karoji responded that as daily wage earners, the employees would not survive if they did not get their salaries, and it was to their own peril, if they wanted to go ahead with the strike.

The strike went on for about two months and the company suffered severe losses. The company declared lockout, and the management filed an application for closure of the unit.

Questions
1. Analyse the industrial relations scenario in Mumbai Textiles.
2. Where do you think things went wrong?
3. What could have been a better way to handle the situation?

Vysya Bank

CASE STUDY 2

Vysya Bank is a traditional bank with many branches across India. The majority of these branches are located in the southern region and the rest are distributed over the rest of the country. Established in 1930, the bank has gradually grown over a period of more than seven decades. The trade union movement in the bank is as old as the bank itself and the characteristics of the trade unions have been changing along with the trade union movement in the country. Traditionally, the banking sector in the country has had very strong trade unions for officers as well as other staff. Wage negotiations and pay settlements are based on collective bargaining at the industry and national level, with the Indian Banks Association (IBA) on one side and the unions and associations of officers on the other. The national level agreement is a binding agreement. Any additional pay revision is made according to the bargaining capacity of the bank vis-à-vis the unions. The bank has four unions, two each for the officers and the other staff. The officers' associations have been traditionally liberal with the management, while the other associations have been aggressive with the management and have protected the interests of the employees.

During the early 1980s, when the bank started computerization, the officers' as well as the workers' associations opposed the move. They agreed to computerization only as per the guidelines of the national level agreement. However, since the early 1990s, the competition in the banking sector intensified with the arrival of a number of private sector banks. The officers' and the workers' associations could sense the changed scenario, and agreed with the management that it was necessary to increase the levels of computerization in order to make the bank competitive and provide better services to customers.
The management has been following the guidelines of national level agreements regarding pay scale. However, perks and various benefits are being determined based on collective bargaining and bank-level negotiations between the officers' and workers' associations and the management of the bank.

During the late 1990s, an MNC bank picked up a minority stake in Vysa. By 2003, it hiked up its holding to significant levels. The new management brought in new HR policies such as signing a memorandum of understanding (MoU) with the top management, that is, the assistant vice-president and those above him or her in the management, and also placed the officers in these cadres on contract basis based on a cost to the company (CTC) approach. As far as the officers in the lower cadre and the workers were concerned, the bank adopted a cost to the company approach in a phased manner and simultaneously rolled out a VRS policy for the workers in order to reduce their numbers over a period of time. The officers' and employees' associations, were initially non-supportive of the management initiatives, but when they found that the industry trends were similar, they had little choice.

Questions
1. Analyse the trade union movement in the bank vis-à-vis the concept discussed in the chapter.
2. Conduct a role play with the Presidents of the officers' and the workers' associations along with the CEO, Vice-President–HR, and Vice-President–Industrial Relations to find a better solution or approach.
3. Do you think that the strategy adopted by the bank is correct? if yes, give reasons.

Amazon Textiles

CASE STUDY 3

Amazon Textiles is a textile industry located in the old industrial district of Mumbai. The company was established in 1870 and has seen several ups and downs. It suffered extensively on account of the export and import policy of the British regime, whose main aim was to discourage the growth of the textile industry in India and use the country as a supplier of material for the textile industry in Manchester, UK. The promoter of the company, Manoj Birla, was a patriot and was closely associated with the independence movement. He was a liberal man and had a paternalistic approach towards the employees. The growth of trade unions during his period (1870–1930) was minimal, since the trade union leaders were also co-leaders in the independence movement.

After the demise of Manoj Birla, Sanjay Birla took over as chairman of the company. He shifted the focus of the company from pure silk to other categories of textile goods such as cotton and polyester. During the process, he modernized the looms and the machinery. In order to increase productivity, he did not increase the wages of the employees over a period of one decade, during which the productivity of the company rose by 20%. However, the trade union leaders could see through the ploy of the chairman and became vociferous and demanding. There were two violent agitations and strikes by the two trade unions, who were also supported by the leaders of the independence movement. In order to improve his business prospects, Sanjay Birla sided with the Britishers, much to the annoyance of the leaders of the independence movement. The trade union leaders, now wise about the changed loyalties of the management, started agitating on the smallest issues. However, Sanjay

Birla died in an air crash in 1946. At this juncture, his younger brother Yash Birla took over as Chairman of the company. He was the true son of his father and a loyal patriot who strongly supported the independence movement. His style of management was paternalistic and caring, and he was proactive in wage revision of the employees. The situation was peaceful till the 1970s until Mohan Samant, a powerful trade union leader in Mumbai industrial circles arrived on the scene. The latter believed in adopting a confrontationist attitude towards the management, irrespective of whether or not it was just. He tried to influence the trade union leaders in the company, but with little success. During the mid 1980s, there was a serious crisis in the textile industry and Amazon Textiles was not an exception. There was a sharp decline in exports as well as in domestic sales, which led to a sharp drop in profits, and, ultimately, losses over a continuous period of four years. The banks and financial institutions refused to refinance the sick company and Yash Birla began to scout for an opportunity to turn around its fortunes. At this juncture, he could foresee that the denim market would expand in a big way over the next 10 years and immediately set up modern textile mills in Ahmedabad to exclusively manufacture branded and generic denim.

The modern units in Ahmedabad flourished while the sick units in Mumbai could not be turned around since the cost of modernizing them was prohibitive. After detailed discussions with the trade unions, Mr Yash Birla convinced them that it was best to close down the sick mills in Mumbai. Those desirous were relocated to the new units in Ahmedabad and the option of VRS was given to the other workers.

Questions

1. Examine the socio-political influence of the growth and development of trade unions on the company.
2. Analyse the interrelationship between the approach of the management and trade union activism.
3. Do a role-play based on the case study.

CASE STUDY 4 — Super Spinning Mills

Super Spinning Mills Limited was established in 1920 in Coimbatore for manufacturing yarn and supplying it to the cotton mills in and around the city. The company was initially founded with limited capacity and over a period of one decade, it grew to become one of the largest yarn mills in Coimbatore. The founder of the company, Murali Iyengar, was a follower of Gandhian philosophy and believed in a paternalistic approach towards the employees, because of which there was little scope for grievance. However, after some time, owing to the influence of politicians and freedom fighters, the trade union movement picked up in Coimbatore. Due to pressure from the workers of other units, two trade unions were formed in Super Spinning mills, one with the support of the communists and the other with the support of the Indian National Congress. The leaders of these unions were very keen to increase the membership. To do so, they began to rouse the anger of the employees against the 'injustice' being done to them. Iyengar, in spite of his best efforts, could not convince the unions to maintain harmonious industrial relations. The union leaders, to meet their own selfish ends, started to create industrial unrest on even minor issues, leading to loss of production. There were strikes lasting from five days to one month over a span of two years. On each of these occasions, the management took the help of leading freedom fighters for conciliation and arbitration, and were able to reduce industrial unrest.

Questions

1. Critically analyse this case and identify the problems faced by the management.
2. Do you think that the management was right in redressing the grievances of the employees?
3. What could have been the best approach of the management towards proactively addressing the industrial unrest?
4. Would you suggest any other approaches for resolving the problems?

Andhra Pradesh State Road Transport Corporation

Andhra Pradesh State Road Transport Corporation (APSRTC), the autonomous body providing public transport services in the state of Andhra Pradesh, was established in the early nineteenth century as a part of the erstwhile United Railways and Road Transport Corporation. The company was started by the then Nizam of Hyderabad, with a fleet of around 10 buses in the twin cities of Hyderabad and Secunderabad. In the early 1950s, after independence and the formation of the state of Andhra Pradesh, an independent road transport organization (APSRTC) was set up. The Corporation is one of the largest road transport undertakings in the country with a fleet of over 20,000 buses and an employee strength of more than one and half lakh. It has two major trade unions, namely Employees Union (EU) and Bharatiya Mazdoor Sangh (BMS). It has a record of peaceful industrial relations and the elections to the unions lead to one of the them coming to power alternately. Liberalization and privatization meant that private road transporters were allowed to operate, leading to severe competition. The Corporaion, which has a record of employee welfare, has to compete with the private players, who do not adhere to statutory obligations. It also suffers on account of certain welfare policy measures, which have been announced by the state government, such as concessional and free bus passes to a certain segment of citizens. In addition, it has to pay Motor Vehicle Tax to the state government at a high rate, leading to severe losses. Further, there have also been rumours that the Corporation would soon be privatized on account of the accumulated losses. The trade unions felt it was their responsibility to safeguard the existence of the corporation. For this purpose, they placed the following demands before the management as well as the state government:

- Waive Motor Vehicle Tax.
- Provide budgetary support to offset the losses on account of concessions being announced by the state government.
- Stop privatization/outsourcing of private buses,

improve maintenance operations, and purchase more buses.
- Reduce the administrative staff and streamline the purchase procedures.

Based on these demands, the unions had prolonged discussions with the management. However, the management could not respond to the major demands and referred the matter to the state government. The state government, on account of the severe financial crunch, refused to accept the major demands of the unions, following which the unions went on a strike for 20 days. This led to severe losses to the Corporation and the government encouraged the private players to run additional services in order to weaken the position of the unions. Further, the state government also persuaded one of the unions to withdraw from the strike, which led to the partial restoration of bus services. The employees of the other union put pressure on the union leaders to stop the strike. The other union leaders had negotiations with the state government and agreed to stop the strike on the following conditions:

- The management would not initiate any disciplinary action against the employees.
- Participation in the strike would not be a ground for disqualification from the timely release of increments.
- The state government would consider the waiver of the Motor Vehicle Tax and also provide partial budgetary support to the Corporation.

Questions
1. Critically analyse this case study.
2. Do you think that the unions were right in going on a strike?
3. What could have been a better strategy adopted by the unions to protect the interests of the Corporation?
4. Do you think the management had any role in preventing the industrial unrest.

Collective Bargaining and Workers' Participation in Management

Objectives

After studying this chapter, you will be able to understand
- the nature, scope, and process of collective bargaining
- the comparison of collective bargaining in developed and developing countries
- the role of collective bargaining in wage negotiation and employee welfare
- the significance of workers' participation
- the forms of workers' participation in management
- the Indian schemes of workers' participation
- the function of quality circles

INTRODUCTION

The history of collective bargaining is as old as the history of trade unions in the country. The growth and development of the process of collective bargaining has progressed along with the four phases of trade union development:

- First phase (1950s–60s)—period of substitution
- Second phase (mid 1960s–79)—period of economic stagnation and political instability
- Third phase (1980–91)—period of uneven economic development
- Fourth phase (1991 onwards)—post-economic reforms and structural adjustment

The phrase 'collective bargaining' was coined by Sydney and Beatrice Webb, and according to their definition, it is a method by which the trade unions strive to protect and improve the working conditions of the workers. In the initial industrialization era, the workers had to fight with the management for their rights. In the globalized scenario, the companies are increasingly realizing the need for shedding the anti-labour attitude and working towards building a cooperative and cordial relationship with the trade unions and workers.

Collective bargaining per se has been defined by *Encyclopaedia Britannica* as 'the ongoing process of negotiation between representatives of workers and employers to establish the conditions of employment. The collectively determined agreement may cover not only wages, but also hiring practices, layoffs, promotions, job functions, working conditions and hours, worker discipline and termination, and benefit programs'.

It has been defined by the *Encyclopaedia of Social Sciences* as 'a process of discussion and negotiation between two parties, one or both of whom is a

> Collective bargaining is defined as the ongoing process of negotiation between representatives of workers and employers to establish the conditions of employment.

group of persons acting in consent. The resulting bargain is an understanding as to the terms and conditions under which a service is to be performed... . More specifically, collective bargaining is a procedure by which employers and a group of employees agree upon the conditions of work.'

The International Labour Organization (ILO) has defined it as 'Negotiations about working conditions and terms of employment between an employer, a group of employers, or one or more employers' organizations, on the one hand, and one or more representative workers' organizations on the other hand, with a view to reaching an agreement'. It also says that the terms serve as a code of defining the rights and obligations of each party in their employment and fix a large number of detailed conditions of employment. According to ILO, during its validity, none of the matters it deals with can in normal circumstances be given as a ground for a dispute concerning an individual worker.

From the time of industrial revolution, the managements have the single point agenda of improving the productivity and functional efficiency. Initially, experiments had been carried out by Frederick Taylor and other management theorists, who believed in scientific management. The approach of scientifically measuring time, work, etc., had only resulted in marginal improvement and over a period of time it got negated. These developments were increasingly perceived as another method of exploitation by the union leaders and employees.

Exhibit 17.1 discusses some examples of industrial unrest.

The advent of the human relations concept has led to the basic thought that employees are human beings and they deserve to be treated properly and not like machines. It is here that the human approach has assumed significance in union–management relations. The organizations after a lot of exploration and experimentation have come to a consensus that the only way to improve productivity and maintain cordial industrial climate is to engender a sense of commitment and involvement among the employees. However, to inculcate commitment, it is essential that the employees are involved in the day-to-day management of affairs for bringing in the feeling of being a stakeholder in the organization. The organizations have for this purpose decided to democratize and decentralize the decision-making process and thus, pave the way for the process of participation of workers in the management.

EXHIBIT 17.1   Workers shot dead by company thugs

Five estate workers died when thugs working for the Assam Tea Protection Security Force shot at a crowd of 1,000 peaceful protestors on 29 September 2003. Nine people were injured in the shooting. Demonstrators were demanding an increased bonus for an upcoming festival at the Khobong tea estate in Tinsuka district of Assam. The Khobong tea estate produces over half of the tea produced in India and the tea prices in 2003 were lower than the 2000 levels. In protest, the workers were on a strike for 12 hours on 1 October 2003 when the murdered workers were buried. In another case, about 300 tea plantations were closed by a strike on 11 August in 2003 in north Bengal organized by the Joint Coordination Committee for Plantation Workers. Strikers demanded improvements in basic facilities. They also protested the closure of around 32 plantations. Poor or non-existent basic amenities such as access to decent health services and housing, result in many plantation deaths.

Source: World Socialist Web Site 2003, www.wsws.org, accessed on 4 October 2003.

The advent of democratic governments has raised the hopes and aspirations among the employees for industrial democracy. Thus, workers' participation in management (WPM) has assumed more significance. It implies that the organizations follow participative and consultative decision-making processes, especially in matters pertinent to wages, working conditions, and jobs of workers. It is an indication of mental and emotional involvement of an employee or groups of employees, which would ultimately encourage their contribution to the goals and objectives of the organization.

> ■ ■ ■
> Workers' participation in management tries to reduce the dichotomy created by industrial revolutions.

Workers' participation in management tries to reduce the dichotomy created by industrial revolution, which led to watertight compartments called management and operational workers or personnel. It tries to bring in synergy by addressing the hopes and aspirations of the workers of being involved in the decision-making processes relating to wages and conditions. The participation enhances the employee's ability to influence decision makers and the decision-making process at different levels of hierarchy and also motivates the employee to assume responsibility for his or her action. The participation can mainly occur at three levels, that is, shop-floor level, departmental level, and board level.

Freedom of Association

The Committee on Monitoring International Labour Standards, the National Research Council of USA has created a template for evaluating a country's compliance with freedom of association and effective recognition of the right to collective bargaining from three perspectives:

- Legal framework (at all levels of government)
- The government's performance in implementation
- The overall outcome

Some of the criteria for assessment are as follows:

- Presence of a legal provision that entitles workers or employers to establish organizations of their choice without prior authorization
- Extent of legal restrictions on the ability to organize certain categories such as civil servants, teachers, and workers without contracts
- Presence of certain sectors where there is no right to organize
- Presence of various forms of distinction and discrimination in the right to organize based on factors such as nationality, sex, and political affiliation
- Legal provisions that permit government's interference in the freedom of association of workers or employers
- Legal restrictions on political activities of unions or employees' associations
- Legal provisions for protecting workers from discrimination on their joining the union or related activities
- Protection for collective bargaining by a law
- Presence of legal restrictions on the process of collective bargaining
- Extent to which certain categories of workers are not permitted to negotiate for collective bargaining agreements such as civil servants and teachers
- Presence of legal regulations that ban employer lockouts

- Presence of legal regulations that permit employers to dismiss or replace striking workers

The overall outcome is assessed based on various factors, such as union density, frequency and length of strike, and percentage of workers covered by collective bargaining.

Exhibit 17.2 provides insights on a legal decision on the 'right to strike' by the Supreme Court of India.

EXHIBIT 17.2 In defence of the Supreme Court ruling on strikes

The Supreme Court judgement on the right to strike is only a reiteration of its earlier decision in 1962. In the All-India Bank Employees' Association versus National Industrial Tribunal (AIR 1962 SC 171), the Supreme Court observed: 'A right to form union guaranteed by Article 19 (1) (c) does not carry with it a fundamental right in the union so formed to achieve every objective for which it was formed. Even a very liberal interpretation of this Article cannot lead to the conclusion that the trade unions have a guaranteed right to an effective collective bargaining or to strike, either as part of collective bargaining or otherwise. The right to strike or the right to declare a lockout may be controlled or restricted by appropriate industrial legislation...'.

In the subsequent year, in O.K. Ghosh versus E.X. Joseph (AIR 1963 SC 812), the Supreme Court observed: 'Rule 4A, Central Civil Services (Conduct) Rule, 1955, in the form in which it now stands prohibiting any form of demonstration is violative of government servants' rights under Article 19 (1) (a) (Right of speech and expression) and (b) (Right to assemble peaceably and without arms) and should, therefore, be struck down. But in so far as the said rule prohibits a strike, it cannot be struck down for the reason that there is no fundamental right to resort to strike'.

Again, in Radhey Shyam versus Post Master General, Nagpur (AIR 1965 SC 311), the Supreme Court observed: 'A perusal of Article 19 (1) shows that there is no fundamental right to strike.' In this case there was a violation of orders, which were issued under the Essential Services Maintenance Ordinance, 1960, prohibiting strikes in any postal telegraph or telephone service, by the employees of the Post and Telegraph Department by resorting to strike.

Clearly, strike cannot be the fundamental right of an employee. It can be held as a valid restriction as is permissible by the application of Article 19 (2) to 19(6). However, any such restriction must satisfy the following three board tests as has been held by the court in various judgements: A restriction may be imposed only by or under the authority of a law made by appropriate legislature, there must be a nexus between the restriction imposed and the objects enshrined in the respective clause, and the restriction must be reasonable. When the entire administrative machinery in the state comes to a standstill due to a strike, instead of crying hoarse, the trade unions must emulate the European and Western trade unions who protest silently without halting their duties. The Supreme Court has taken the right initiative and, as responsible citizens, it is our duty to honour the judgement in letter and spirit.

Source: Bhalla, R., *The Tribune*, 20 August 2003, Chandigarh.

Features of Collective Bargaining

The main features of collective bargaining are as follows:

- It is essentially a group action and is initiated by the representatives of workers.
- The process is flexible as it provides for both parties a scope for compromise and facilitates a mutual give and take environment for final agreement or settlement. According to Bakke and Kerr, 'Essentially, a successful collective bargaining is an exercise in graceful retreat—without seeming to retreat.'
- It is a two-party process, where both strive to arrive at an agreement for settling a dispute, devoid of animosity, and mutual hatred.
- It is a continuous process, which provides for building and sustaining relationships between the

management and trade unions with the common objective of resolving employee grievances and plant problems.

- It reflects implementation of industrial democracy. The workers are provided with an opportunity for self-governance and a powerful tool which holds a check for arbitrariness and unilateralism.

Why Collective Bargaining?

■ ■ ■
The advantages of collective bargaining include prompt and fair redressal of workers' grievances and regulation of the terms and conditions of employment.

The growth and development of industrialization in the West has been more stable and orderly on account of sound wage structures, which is the result of a successful collective bargaining process. The maturity of the industry is related to the maturity of the collective bargaining process. It plays a vital role for settling and more importantly preventing industrial disputes. The advantages of the process of collective bargaining are as follows:

- Improving the economic strength of the union as well as the management
- Facilitating uniform working conditions
- Prompt and fair redressal of workers' grievances
- Improving operational efficiency
- Promoting industrial harmony
- Regulating the terms and conditions of employment
- Providing flexibility for adjustment of terms and conditions of employment in relation to the changes in the industry
- Building industrial jurisprudence by introducing civil rights

Principles of Collective Bargaining

The principles for efficient functioning of the collective bargaining process for unions as well as management are as follows:

- The process should provide scope for union leaders to educate the management about the desires and grievances of employees, and in contrast it should also provide a scope for the management to explain the economic constraints in not accepting the proposals of unions.
- Both union leaders as well as the management should approach collective bargaining with a view to find the best possible solutions and not with a concessional approach.
- Both parties should have respect for each other and should also have the power to enforce the terms of agreement mutually agreed upon.
- Both parties should have the spirit to abide by the laws applicable for collective bargaining at the state and national levels.

Types of Collective Bargaining

The following are some of the types of collective bargaining:

- *Single plant bargaining*—the bargaining between a single trade union and management at the plant level, which is currently prevalent in the USA and India
- *Multiple plant bargaining*—the bargaining between the management having multiple manufacturing plants and the workers employed in these plants

EXHIBIT 17.3   Court ruling outlaws strikes

In an unprecedented legal decision in India on 6 August 2003, the Supreme Court (SC) ruled that public workers no longer have a legal or moral right to strike. The decision was a direct result of the strike by the government staff and teachers in Tamil Nadu. In a so-called 'concession', it ruled that a total of 1,56,106 of the sacked Tamil Nadu workers may be re-hired provided they apologize and sign a no-strike agreement. Tapan Sen, secretary of the Centre of Indian Trade Unions (CITU) said, 'The working class must assert its hard-earned right to strike through a countrywide united struggle.' Attorney General Soli Sorabjee rejected the SC ruling on the right to strike saying the court's opinion that workers have 'no moral or equitable right to go on strike' was 'uncalled for and beyond comprehension... The right to collective bargaining and ancillary right to strike was an invaluable right of government employees. It has been secured after years of toil and effort.'

The ILO, made aware of the court ruling in a letter from M.K. Pandhey, General Secretary of the CITU, wrote to the national government asking it to renew commitment to workers' rights at national and state levels and to reinstate collective bargaining in Tamil Nadu state. Gurudas Dasgupta, head of the Communist Party of India (CPI) union that represents some of the Tamil Nadu strikers, said that the right to strike is not an issue for the courts and is not open to judicial reinterpretation. Six days after the SC ruling, Chief Minister Jayalalithaa took official measures to deregister twenty six key trade unions and 200 affiliate unions, as well as remove recognition of the Joint Action Committee of Teacher's Organizations (JACTO) and Confederation of Teacher's Association (COTA) union confederations. Over 6,000 sacked strikers were not reinstated, instead they were charged with violence and inciting to strike and would be judged by a panel of three retired judges.

Sources: International Metalworkers' Federation, India, 6 August 2003; Yahoo, India News, 7 August 2003; *The Indian Express*, 11 August 2003; *The Hindu*, 25 August 2003.

- *Multiple employer bargaining*—the bargaining between unions of workers and managements. For instance, the bargaining between the bank employees' union and the Indian Banks Association in the banking industry

Exhibit 17.3 provides insights on a legal decision in India outlawing strikes.

Stages of Collective Bargaining

The collective bargaining process has three main stages, that is, the identification stage, the negotiation stage, and the stage of contract administration. In the process of identifying the problem, both parties have to decide if the problem needs to be addressed immediately or alternatively can be deferred for some time. The influencing factors in the problem identification stage are selection and size of representatives, negotiation period, agreement duration, etc.

While negotiating for the agreement, the chief negotiator from the management side presides the process and presents the problem, its scope, and invites views from both parties. After listening to the arguments and counter arguments, he or she facilitates a solution, which is acceptable to both parties. The essentials to be included in the collective agreement are the purpose of the agreement, rights and responsibilities of the management and the trade union, terms and conditions of employment, procedures of grievance redressal, dispute settlement methodology, and termination clause for ending the agreement.

■ ■ ■
The collective bargaining process has three main stages:
• Identification
• Negotiation
• Contract administration

Exhibit 17.4 discusses the role played by the International Union of Food, Agricultural, Hotel, Restaurant, Catering, Tobacco and Allied Workers' Association (IUF) in building coordination and cooperation among tea unions.

EXHIBIT 17.4   IUF tea unions build coordination and cooperation

Following the decisions of the First Agricultural Workers' Trade Group Conference, the IUF is building solidarity and cooperation among unions in the industry by bringing together tea workers' unions from the world's principal tea-producing regions. The conference designated tea together with coffee, sugar, cocoa, and bananas as target sectors for international organizing geared to sharing information and resources and coordinating collective bargaining and the defence of trade union and human rights. Initial meetings were held in Africa and India and a global meeting bringing together plantation and processing workers was planned.

Africa

Poor pay, bad housing, and poor health and safety standards were among the issues identified by tea unions as the major problems and organizing priorities facing tea workers at the IUF's first African regional tea meeting, held in Arusha, Tanzania, from 16 to 20 October 1995. Participants were present from IUF-affiliated unions in Kenya, Uganda, Tanzania, Zimbabwe, and Zambia plus observers from Malawi and South Africa. Opening the meeting on behalf of the Friedrich Ebert Foundation, Claire Lwehabura welcomed the decision to hold the event in Tanzania as 'a move to support the ongoing transition in the trade union system of the host country', as the development of independent trade union structures was, she added, 'not quite over yet'. The meeting focused on identifying the main problems faced by workers and their unions, sharing experiences and information on the tea sector in Africa, and exploring the possibility of a code of conduct for tea plantations. Unions felt strongly that any such code should not substitute collective bargaining, but should give unions the space to organize and to strengthen their collective bargaining capacity.

Basic pay rates varied from $10 per month in Uganda to $30 per month in Zimbabwe, Kenya, and South Africa. The meeting identified the main pesticides used routinely in tea plantations, some of which were on the 'dirty dozen' list of the most toxic pesticides. The situation of seasonal and casual workers was another key discussion item with unions agreeing in principle that these workers had to be organized, to win for them equal rights like those of full-timers. This could discourage employers from trying to further increase casualization in the industry. The possibility of linking with organizations promoting fair trade was also debated. So far, many fair trade organizations have concentrated on guaranteeing fair prices for small farmers producing plantation crops such as cocoa and coffee. Recently, there has also been some work done on establishing criteria for fair trade of tea from plantations employing workers. Unions felt that the emphasis here should be on fair trade groups working with unions, to strengthen freedom of association and collective bargaining agreements.

South Asia

Unions organizing tea plantation workers, tea estate staff workers, and tea processing workers in Bangladesh, India, Nepal, and Sri Lanka met in Calcutta from 6 to 10 November. The meeting brought together unions from the full spectrum of South Asia's politically divided labour movement, including tea unions affiliated to the national centres such as the All India Trade Union Congress (AITUC), Centre of Indian Trade Unions (CITU), Hindustan Mazdoor Sangh (HMS), Indian National Trade Union Congress (INTUC) and National Labour Organization (NLO) in India and Nepal Trade Union Congress (NTUC) and General Federation of Nepalese Trade Unions (GEFONT) in Nepal. Tea plantation workers in South Asia constitute, for the most part, a captive migrant workforce whose desperate situation is exacerbated by the geographical and social isolation maintained by the employers. Poverty wages make it necessary for two or three family members to work in the plantations to achieve a subsistence minimum. Reports to the meeting noted the presence of an estimated 75,000 child labourers in the Indian tea industry (with the highest number in Assam) and a substantial number in Nepal. Protective legislation was either inadequate (India's Plantation Labour Act authorizes the employment of children 12 years or older) or not enforced. Protection against agri-chemicals and pesticides was likewise inadequate or non-existent, with workers suffering the effects of widespread water and ground water contamination. In India, political fragmentation had seriously weakened the unions'

(Contd)

EXHIBIT 17.4   (Contd)

bargaining strength despite the relatively high level of unionization. To build greater unity, the unions present agreed to oppose the presence of multiple unions in tea gardens and packing units and to work together around the following key points:

- Low wages
- Rising casualization
- Increasing womens' representation in trade union structures
- Child labour
- Establishing a network of health and safety officials to deal with the problem of pesticides
- Developing the exchange of information pertaining to the living and working conditions of plantation and processing workers and collective bargaining

At a special session of the meeting, Martin Kunz of Transfair International, a European-based fair trade organization, and Annie Van Wezel from the Dutch union center, FNV introduced a discussion on fair trade issues and consumer action and their potential links to plantation workers' unions. The possibility of unions organizing processing workers to meet the plantation workers' unions provided an important first step in building union links throughout the tea chain. Following the meeting the All India Brooke Bond Employees' Federation, one of the participating unions, at its Federation Working Committee decided to initiate visits to tea gardens owned by Brooke Bond (a Unilever subsidiary) to discuss cooperation with the plantation workers' unions.

Source: 10F-UITA-IUL News Bulletin 1996, No. 1–2.

The key factor determining the success of collective bargaining is 'contract administration'. Both parties should understand the terms and conditions of the contract, explain it to all the workers at large, and build support for its effective administration. The factors hindering the effective functioning of the collective bargaining process include failure of employers to accept inevitability of trade unions, separatist tendencies of trade unions, failure of both parties in preparing for the process, unfair practices, and unequal strength of the parties (Exhibit 17.5).

EXHIBIT 17.5   Declaration of the Asia-Pacific trade unions

The trade unions of Asia-Pacific region, hereby adopt the following declaration:

'The Trade Unions are facing the challenges posed by the imperialist globalisation, and the Structural Adjustment Programme dictated by the trinity of World Bank, I.M.F and W.T.O. The economic policies based on Free Market economy have only helped the multinational corporations and monopolies leading to super profits for the corporate sector and increase in unemployment and poverty. The gap between the rich and poor within and between the countries has increased very fast.

In the organised sector, downsizing called 'right sizing', reduction of manpower through retrenchments and the so-called 'Voluntary' Retirement Schemes, hire and fire policy, attack on social security etc are resorted to, all on the plea of competitiveness and depicted as in the interest of consumer, though in reality these are done for the greed of the corporate sector for super profits. Small and medium industries cannot stand competition under the free market economy and face closures. This policy has affected even the financial sector and the retail trade. They further resorted to outsourcing to the ancillaries within the country and also to the ancillaries of the countries where cheap labour is available. Denationalisation, mergers and takeovers are taking place which also lead to the attack on the workers.

The organised sector is being dismantled and jobs are shifting to ancillaries and the unorganised sector; for

(Contd)

EXHIBIT 17.5   (Contd)

instance powerlooms, parts of engineering goods manufactured by small units are mostly on piece rate basis. The garment industry also comes under the same category.

In the developing countries, because of the backwardness the small and medium industries, the cottage and tiny industries, the hawkers and small retail traders and others do suffer.

The traditional unorganised sector which includes Agricultural workers, Hawkers, Beedi & Cigar, Handicrafts, Gem & Jewellery, Leather goods, Powerlooms, Rickshaw drivers, Headload workers, Brick Kilns, Fisheries etc. live on low wages, without security of service and with no social security or welfare schemes. Most of them are not organised in Trade Unions, hence lack collective bargaining capacity.

In most of the developing countries the right to organisation and collective bargaining are not implemented or large numbers are excluded. For instance Engineers, Technicians, Supervisors, Teachers and the Govt. Employees cannot organise Trade Unions and have no right to collective bargaining. In India the Supreme Court held recently that Govt. Employees have no right to strike and in Pakistan, formation of Trade Unions in Railways and certain special industries is banned. Even now Child Labour exists in a big way and bonded labour in concealed forms exists inspite of legislation which have several lacuna.

The Contractor workers, casual or temporary workers, the workers on time bound contract all come under the category of unorganized sector arising out of structural adjustment. Women are engaged more and more in the unorganized or the informal sector of economy.

- Equal wages for equal work are denied to women. The same is the position of casual and contract workers who get a fraction of wages of permanent workers doing the same job.
- The Labour laws whatever exist are not applicable in the Export Zones or the Economic Zones.
- The trade unions in the region, shall, in the coming period strive to organise the unorganised so that the workers, both in the organised and the unorganised sector together conduct struggles against the imperialist globalisation—against hunger and unemployment.
- Fight against the attack on organised sector.
- Fight for living wages, security of service and social security for the workers in unorganised sector with better living conditions.
- We further declare that we shall, in cooperation with all trade unions, irrespective of ideological differences, struggle for the implementation of the core labour standards.
- We declare that the Trade Unions in the Asia-Pacific region shall, unitedly with other trade unions in the respective countries, will campaign against the anti-working class policies being adopted by the Governments and shall demand the respective Govts. in these countries to shun these policies.
- We shall mobilise against the privatisation of public sector and the policies of globalisation and liberalization.
- We shall conduct struggles against the attack on the workers carried on through the policy of hire and fire and attack on social security.
- We shall conduct struggle for jobs for all; Social security for all; Legislation for security of service, social security and need based wages for workers in the unorganised sector.
- We shall organise rallies and demonstrations and wherever possible general strike to resist these impacts of the capitalist globalisation.
- We hereby resolve to observe a day, Asia-Pacific Solidarity Day on the 30th May, 2005 towards achieving: i) Full Employment ii) Security of service iii) Social Security for all iv) Implementation of social standards including core conventions.
- We are confident that an alternative is possible.

  Long live workers unity!
  Workers of the World unite, Unite!'

Source: www.wbtu.cz/docs/newdelhideclaration.doc, accessed on 16 September 2005.

COLLECTIVE BARGAINING IN INDIA

■ ■ ■
Collective bargaining in India has been growing mostly at the plant and organizational level and not at the industry level.

In India, collective bargaining has been growing along with the growth of trade unions and the first collective bargaining agreement was made in the textile industry of Ahmedabad. Collective bargaining has been growing rapidly in the post-independence scenario, happening mostly at the plant and organizational level and not at the industry level. The limited success of collective bargaining in our country can be attributed to the following factors:

- Problems with the unions such as absence of strong unions, multiplicity, and inter- and intra-union rivalries
- Lack of initiative by the government for the development of the process of collective bargaining
- Easy accessibility of adjudication leading to loss of sheen for collective bargaining
- Political interference in union matters and inter-party rivalry causing inter-union rivalry
- Negative attitude of managements

The National Commission of Labour has made the following recommendations for the success of collective bargaining:

- Limited intervention by the government and usage of compulsory adjudication as the last resort
- Strengthening the trade unions organizationally and financially by making appropriate amendments in the Trade Union Act, 1926 through various incorporations, such as
  - compulsory registration of trade unions,
  - enhancement of membership fee, and
  - reduction of external influence on union bodies and office bearers

Exhibit 17.6 discusses a case of favourable settlement and reinstatement of workers.

Future of Collective Bargaining in India

In India, the labour institutions are compatible with the government's officially promoted industrial pluralism and bilateral collective bargaining. The advent of economic liberalization has its effects on the union movement. The independent rank-and-file-led unions have come into

EXHIBIT 17.6   Sun Way and InterContinental hotels

In April 2004, when the IUF-affiliated Cambodian Tourism and Service Workers' Federation (CTSWF) took strike action to achieve the fair distribution of service charge, hotel owners undertook widespread dismissals. The most egregious case of this was at the Raffles Hotels in Siem Reap and Phnom Penh where over 300 workers were summarily dismissed for taking legal strike action. IUF affiliates around the world acted in solidarity, which coupled with a CTSWF campaign in defence of the dismissed workers, led to a favourable settlement and reinstatement in September 2004. However, during the dispute, other hotels in Cambodia took smaller, but still significant reprisals against union members undertaking legal industrial activity. On 6 and 7 November 2004 the IUF, in conjunction with the CTSWF, conducted an educational workshop with over 55 local union leaders to discuss the service charge campaign and future strategies for hotel unions in Cambodia, among other things. As part of the meeting's proceedings, union members from the Sun Way and Inter Continental Hotels in Phnom Penh, who were dismissed and suspended during the service charge dispute, were able to successfully return to work following solidarity actions from the CTSWF and IUF.

existence and engage in violent bargaining with the employers for securing substantial wage and non-wage benefits for workers. The employers on their part, for dealing with militant union leaders, have started adopting the strategy of 'outsourcing' from non-union locations. This in a way has led to decline in the growth of trade unions.

An analysis of 'monopoly' versus 'collective voice' framework, since independence, indicates that there has been rapid industrialization and minimum industrial strife in the collective voice framework. Further, the declining employment elasticities imply that more output can be attained with less employment, more so with capital intensive technologies. Unions oppose the introduction of such technologies because it reduces the employment elasticity in the production process.

Exhibit 17.7 provides insights on manpower availability, labour laws, industrial relations climate, and provisions for employing foreign nationals in the Indian state of Meghalaya.

EXHIBIT 17.7   Manpower availability

Meghalaya has a fairly large pool of skilled, semi-skilled, and unskilled labour. There is an adequate number of secretarial staff in most parts of the state. A fair number of management and technical personnel have qualifications from recognized professional institutions and universities of India.

Compensation Structure

Table 17.1 indicates the average range of compensation at various employee levels, in the medium-scale private sector organizations.

TABLE 17.1   Average range of compensation at various employee levels

Employee level	Average yearly compensation range (₹)
Top Management	10,000+
Middle Management	5,000–10,000
Junior Management	2,500–5,000
Supervisory	2,000–4,000
Secretarial/Clerical	1,500–3,000
Skilled Worker	1,500–3,000
Unskilled Worker	750–1,500

Source: North East Council (NEC)

It should be noted that the actual compensation paid may vary according to the company size and industry type as well as the skill, experience, length of service, etc., of the individual.

Besides salary and wages, a compensation package typically includes various fringe benefits, such as annual bonus, monthly contribution to Provident Fund, monthly house rent allowance, terminal gratuity, annual medical expenditure reimbursement or allowance, annual leave travel allowance, and accumulated leave encashment.

Labour Laws

Indian labour laws are applicable throughout the country. The state government may issue additional state rules under these laws from time to time. A brief overview of each of the major laws is provided here.

• The Factories Act of 1948 provides the rules regarding terms and conditions of employment in factories. This Act provides for welfare and personal security of labour by regulating working norms, working conditions,

(Contd)

EXHIBIT 17.7   (Contd)

health and safety to workers, etc. A similar provision has been made for the plantation workers in the Plantation Labour Act, 1965.

- The Minimum Wages Act, 1950 provides for the minimum wages to be paid to employees at the lowest level of an organization.
- The Maternity Benefit Act, 1961 provides benefits to women workers in the event of their pregnancy.
- The Employees State Insurance Act, 1948 ensures comprehensive health coverage for employees below a certain income level.
- The Payment of Bonus Act, 1965 imposes a statutory obligation on employees to pay a minimum bonus of 8.33% of the basic salary. The maximum bonus is 20% of the basic salary.
- The Payment of Gratuity Act, 1972 and the Employees Provident Fund and Family Pension Scheme, 1971 provide for retirement benefits and social security dues to the employees.
- The Industrial Employees Standing Order Act, 1946 specifies the disciplinary code for employees. Disputes are regulated by the Industrial Disputes (Amendment) Act of 1976. Direct collective bargaining or negotiation between employers and employees is widely practised.

Industrial Relations

The Trade Union Act, 1926 provides for the registration and operation of the trade unions. Membership in a trade union is not obligatory, but in practice most workers and office staff are enrolled as members of a union. The major trade unions are affiliated to political parties through the national trade union bodies.

The unions enter into binding contracts and settlement with the employers on behalf of the workers. Wages in the organized sector are left to the process of collective bargaining, conciliation, arbitration, and adjudication.

The industrial relations climate in the state is congenial. There is hardly any incidence of labour-related trouble.

Employing Foreign Nationals

Employment of foreign technicians for the supervision and training of Indian personnel or for other purposes connected to implementation of new projects does not require the prior approval of the Reserve Bank of India (RBI) provided their engagement conforms to certain prescribed conditions. However, permission is required from the RBI for the remittance of earnings made in India to foreign countries and from the Home Ministry if the stay in India is to be for more than three consecutive months.

Source: http://meghalaya.nic.in/industry/human.htm, accessed on 16 September 2005.

In several older sectors such as tea and jute plantations in eastern India and textiles in western India, the bargaining processes are under pressure as the inter-plant and inter-firm differences are becoming wider. Similar is the case with the Bureau of Public Enterprises, which sends guidelines for wage settlements to ministries. In Coal India, for example, employees in the better off units depend on the productivity levels. There have been similar moves in the banking sector too. For instance, the Indian Banks' Association (IBA), which coordinates the industry level collective bargaining process, has already indicated that the current wage settlement would be the last

■ ■ ■

In India, the critical aspects of collective bargaining system are under review, which include its coverage and scope and the demand for decentralized bargaining.

and in future the respective banks can decide the wage fixation depending on parameters such as productivity and profitability. This is in response to the demands from various public sector banks, which are demanding flexibility in compensation fitment to their employees in order to attract and retain the best human talent.

The two critical aspects of collective bargaining system are the expansion of the coverage and scope and addressing the pressure for decentralized

> ■ ■ ■
> The advent of the concept of HRM, which includes the basic premises of employee welfare, personalized attention, etc., eliminates the scope for union or collective bargaining.

bargaining. These tendencies are on account of various macro developments or parameters such as introduction of parallel production systems, sub-contracting of jobs, automation, flexibility, mergers and restructuring processes.

With regard to the demands for decentralized bargaining, the pressure is from better off units that have high levels of productivity and profitability. The employees' unions from these units would like to be rewarded better than the other units. The demand is due to the fact that the process of collective bargaining equalizes the profitable and not-so-profitable units and does not have the provision for rewarding higher level of productivity.

The other reason for demanding the decentralizing of the bargaining structure and expanding the scope and duration of labour contracts is to minimize the monopoly effects and inflexibilities in work rules, especially at micro levels. Another reason for reviewing the process of collective bargaining is that in spite of the low union density, by international standards, India loses more days every year than any other country on account of industrial conflict.

Another major factor for reduced importance of the role of trade unions and collective bargaining is the advent of the concept of HRM where the basic premises such as employee welfare, personalized attention, performance-based reward systems, etc., eliminate the scope for union or collective bargaining. The entry barriers to unions are even higher in the IT sector on account of proactive HRM practices.

The private corporate sector employs roughly 30% of formal workers in the country. In this sector, the pay fixation is determined by productivity and the unions are a party to the agreement of performance-based pay.

Exhibit 17.8 discusses a perspective on the right to strike by public employees.

EXHIBIT 17.8   Public employees and workers cannot forgo their right ro strike

---

The All India State Government Employees' Federation (AISGEF) notes with deep concern and anguish that the Division Bench of Supreme Court (SC) of the country, by their verdict on 21 July 2003 has not only upheld the arbitrary dismissal of about two hundred thousand state government employees and teachers who took part in the state-wide strike beginning on 2 July 2003, but highly justified the most autocratic, repressive measures of the Tamil Nadu government by terming the strike 'illegal' and stating that 'Jayalalitha government has sent a tough message that maladministration can be caused in this way.'

This is most unfortunate and obviously an open support for the most vindictive action against the employees and teachers by the political leadership of the government and bureaucracy, intending to suppress a justified collective action by the employees and teachers for redressal of their grievances when all other means of negotiated settlement failed. The Tamil Nadu government resorted to a drastic cut in the pensionary benefits and other dues of the employees and teachers that they earned through years of hard struggles.

AISGEF is shocked that the apex court instead of striking down the draconian ordinance, issued by the Tamil Nadu government arbitrarily amending the Tamil Nadu Essential Services Maintenance Act, 2002 at a time when the Tamil Nadu assembly was in session, gave it its strong approval.

This judgement of the SC justifies the action of the Tamil Nadu government in dismissing more than 2,00,000 employees and teachers and chargesheeting about 2,500 employees on the plea of so-called 'violence'. It also requests the Tamil Nadu government to consider reinstating the dismissed employees except those chargesheeted on the condition that the dismissed employees and teachers tender 'unconditional apology' for their action and give an undertaking not to resort to strike again. This is an utter humiliation of the employees and adds insult to the injury.

(Contd)

EXHIBIT 17.8 (Contd)

The apex court's assertion that Indian Constitution does not provide the government employees right to strike is nothing but justifying the British made Government of India Act, 1935 by which the British government treated the government employees of India as virtual slaves. The imperialist government did so while in their own country, UK, government employees were allowed the right to strike and even to contest elections on certain conditions.

In fact, the Constitution of India does not say which sections of the workers are eligible to strike. Article 19 guarantees fundamental rights for all and another article speaks of some restrictions, which the central government and the state governments have to consider and decide. Accordingly, the central and state governments framed the Government Servants' Conduct Rules at the Centre and in different states. The right to strike is a fundamental trade union right and the Indian Trade Union Act, 1926 and Industrial Disputes Act, 1947 deal with the right to form trade unions and collective bargaining by the workers.

The working class, in India and throughout the world, have established their rights through struggle and sacrifice. Whether industrial working class or government employees, they cannot forego their right to collective bargaining including the right to strike in furtherance of their legitimate interests whatever may be the circumstances. In the present case, in Tamil Nadu, the strike took place under compelling circumstances to restore their earned benefits that were arbitrarily cut down.

ILO, a tripartite body of the UN system, in its conventions 87, 98, and 154 has accepted these rights. Convention 151 meant for public service has specifically mandated that 'Public Employees shall have, as other workers, the Civil and Political rights which are essential for the normal exercise of freedom of association, subject only to the obligations arising from their status and the nature of the functions.'

ILO's convention is a tripartite decision—government, employer, and labour—and Government of India as a founder member of ILO cannot morally ignore it. Whether the Government of India has ratified these conventions or not is a different matter. The trade union movement has all through demanded ratification of this convention by the government and a go ahead to assert their rights.

The attacks made by the Tamil Nadu government on the employees and teachers is totally unprecedented in the history of India's trade union movement.

AISGEF strongly urges the Tamil Nadu goverment to withdraw all victimizations, dismissals, charge sheets, etc. and restore the arbitrarily cut pensionary and other benefits of the employees and teachers.

AISGEF urges all trade unions of the country and international trade unions to rise in strong protest against such a virulent attack on the trade union rights of the employees and teachers and to restore the snatched away economic benefits which have come in pursuit of the neo-liberal economic policy dictated by the World Bank and IMF. AISGEF strongly appeals to all trade unions of India to come out against such atrocities of the Tamil Nadu government and protect the trade union rights of the public employees and working class.

Source: www.tradeunionindia.org/miscellaneous/public_rights.htm, accessed on 16 September 2005.

COLLECTIVE BARGAINING IN THE ORGANIZED SECTOR

An important factor that is not much recognized, but still prevails in many organized sector units is fixing and revising wages through collective bargaining (Exhibit 17.9). The course of collective bargaining was influenced in 1948 by the recommendations of the Committee on Fair Wages, which reported that three levels of wages exist, that is, minimum, fair, and living.

■ ■ ■
More and more companies are placing less faith in productivity agreements and are instead looking at initiatives beyond collective bargaining.

These three wage levels were defined and it was pointed out that all industries must pay the minimum wage. The capacity to pay would apply only to the fair wage that could be linked to productivity. In addition to this the fifteenth Indian Labour Conference, a tripartite body, met in 1954 and defined precisely what the needs-based minimum wage was and how it could be quantified using a balanced diet chart.

This gave a great boost to collective bargaining; many organized sector trade unions were able to achieve reasonably satisfactory indexation and a system of paying an annual bonus. It is now a law that wage for the thirteenth month be paid as deferred wage to all those covered by the Payment of Bonus Act. The minimum bonus payable is 8.33% and the maximum is 20% of the annual wage.

COLLECTIVE BARGAINING—POLICIES AND PRACTICES

The managements in multi-location companies have started to decentralize the process of collective bargaining to leverage the local market conditions. The other perspective was that each distinct profit center should be treated separately and the bargaining strategy of the management should vary accordingly. A point that should be noted when comparing and contrasting unionized companies is that the frequency of employee representatives' meetings with management varied from twice a week to very rarely. These were used for formal discussions about grievances and procedural matters. In all, the important aspect regarding collective bargaining was that there was far less emphasis on achieving productivity gains through the ubiquitous mechanism of

EXHIBIT 17.9 Stress on collective bargaining for settling disputes

The secretary, Union Ministry of Labour, Dr P.D. Shenoy, has said that collective bargaining is the best method of settling disputes in the industry. He was delivering the 9th Balasubramaniam Memorial Lecture on 'labour–management collaboration: Means or hindrance to improve efficiency' organized by the Corporation Bank Officers' Organization, in Mangalore on Saturday.

Though collective bargaining has not been defined in the Industrial Disputes Act, it has come as an informal tool in settling disputes. Banking industry is known for settling disputes through collective bargaining. Dr. Shenoy also said that the third party steps in when there is no other way to settle the disputes. However, the mediator's role should be at a minimum level, and should be used only when required. Stressing the importance of human relationship, he said that 99% of any settlement depends on this aspect. Dr. Shenoy noted that a union in Corporation Bank was set up only after 65 years of the existence of the bank, and 50 year after the enactment of Trade Union Act. Stating that the unions have provided confrontation and cooperation to the bank, he said, "We have to move from confrontation to cooperation in the era of globalisation."

He said that suggestions and information provided by the unions are vital in the development of any institution. Describing globalization as a tiger, he said that to ride it one should tame it through cooperation. Dr Shenoy hoped that India would become an economic superpower by 2015. It has already become the world leader in the area of information technology, and is exporting skilled workforce. He congratulated the management and labour force of the bank for maintaining a cordial relationship and added that because of the cordial relationship, the bank adopted prudential norms much earlier.

The chairman and managing director of corporation Bank, Mr Cherian Varghese, who presided over the function said that stakeholders including shareholders and customers are the third and important element in the successful functioning of the organization. He said, 'In labour–management relation our commitment is to the shareholders and customers.' Stating that liberalization has put customers on the top, he said that their trust in the bank has played an important role in its growth. Because of the depositors' trust, the bank can borrow their money without any security. The labour and management should have mutual trust, he said, adding that their inter-dependence is vital for the bank's growth.

Source: The Hindu Business Line 2004, Internet Edn, Monday, 28 June.

productivity bargaining. More and more established companies, with few exceptions, have begun to place less faith in the continued pursuit of detailed productivity agreements and are instead looking at a wide span of initiatives beyond collective bargaining. In a way, the balance between industrial relations and 'new' human resource approaches has shown signs of adjustment.

Trade unions as a whole, both at national and workplace level, were relegated to the sidelines of most of the managerial initiatives. At most there were half-hearted attempts, which sounded like: *The unions were invited to the party, but they didn't seem to want to come. So, the party went ahead without them.* The companies had come up with more novel features such as mission, values, guiding principles, employee involvement, and potentially radical shake-up of the supervisors.

In fact, when we discuss the trade unions as 'partners', a key question that arises is that whom do we mean by 'the trade union'? Just as we have factions in managers, we have factions in trade unions too. There is an increased sense of tension between union representatives at the plant level and plant managers or local managers. Quite often, the plant level union representatives are criticized of cooperating with local managers ignoring the directives of central union leaders.

The Trade Union Act facilitates unionization both in the organized and unorganized sectors. It is through this law that the freedom of association, which is a fundamental right under the Constitution of India, is realized. The right to register a trade union, however, does not mean that the employer must recognize the union. There is in fact no law which provides for recognition of trade unions and consequently no legal compulsion for employers, even in the organized sector, to enter into collective bargaining.

Yet in reality, because of the strength of particular trade unions, there is fairly widespread collective bargaining, especially in the organized sector.

WORKERS' PARTICIPATION IN MANAGEMENT

The realization of workers' need for participation in the management is influenced by the following factors:

- Technology adoption leading to complexity in production process calls for increased worker cooperation.
- Employees are no longer treated as subservient, but are treated as equals.
- Growing influence of unions prevents exploitation of employees by the management.
- There are regulations and legislations that facilitate increased workers' participation in management (WPM).
- Higher levels of productivity and efficiency can only come through motivated and committed employees.

Objectives of Workers' Participation in Management

Globally the broad objectives of WPM are similar, but the specific objectives may vary from country to country depending on contractual factors such as political environment, economic development, and industrial relations. Gosep viewed WPM as a tool that can

- improve organizational efficiency and maintain cordial industrial relations;
- develop solidarity in the working community and bring out the latent skills of human resources;

- accede the respectable employee status both within the workers and also with the management in a humanitarian way; and
- facilitate self-development of workers.

The objectives of WPM in Germany include prevention of workers' exploitation, facilitating economic growth, and resolving labour management conflict in an amicable way. In UK, *joint committees* are used for discussing and bringing in changes in methods of production, improving the safety and welfare measure for employees, and resolving employee grievance and other problems in industrial relations.

In Israel, Histradrut engages in development of employees, nation building, and improvement in standard of living. The other forms of WPM include *Workers' Council in Yugoslavia*, *Joint Consultation* in Japan, and *Workers Assemblies* in China.

Workers Participation in Management in India

In India, the Industrial Policy Resolution, 1956, had advocated WPM as a step towards creating a socialistic pattern of society. The second five-year plan supported WPM for improving productivity of employees, involving employees in the decision-making process, and more importantly, meeting the employees' need for self-expression with the ultimate objective of maintaining cordial industrial relations. WPM facilitates the achievement of these objectives by providing challenging assignments to workers, increasing their responsibility consciousness, increasing the relevance of their work, permitting them to have a say in management decisions, improving employer–employee communication, and also worker–supervisor relationship.

WPM entered the Indian scene in the year 1920, when Mahatma Gandhi had suggested that workers should participate and contribute to the organization and also share its prosperity. He advocated a relationship characterized by friendship and cooperation between the workers and management. The Tata Iron and Steel Company (TISCO) had established joint committees in 1958.

An expert committee on the Companies Act and the Monopolies and Restrictive Trade Practices (MRTP) Act was set up by Government of India, under the chairmanship of Justice Rajinder Sachar, and the terms of reference among other things included suggesting of methods for improving WPM. The recommendations of the committee included worker's representation in the board of directors and allotment of equity to workers. Similarly, another Committee under the chairmanship of Ravindra Verma, the then Union Minister for Labour, was constituted to look into the various aspects, statutory and non-statutory schemes, and also recommend outlines or comprehensive schemes for WPM. The following are some of the key recommendations of the committee:

- Three-tier system of participation, that is, shop-floor, plant, and board levels
    - Legislation for covering all undertakings with 500 or more workers (public or private)
    - Provision for extending the scheme to enterprises with at least 100 workers
    - Usage of secret ballot for electing representative
    - Issue of not less than 10% equity to workers

> ■ ■ ■
> The second five-year plan supported WPM for improving productivity of employees and involving employees in decision-making with the objective of maintaining cordial industrial relations.

Based on the various schemes introduced between 1975 and 1977, the Government of India during the year 1983 formulated a comprehensive scheme for WPM in central public sector undertakings.

Forms of Workers' Participation in Management

The following are the various forms of WPM currently prevalent in the country:

- Works committee
- Joint management councils
- Joint councils
- Unit councils
- Plant councils
- Shop councils
- Workers' representation in management board
- Workers participation in capital share

The main features of the aforementioned councils include that every division or zone with 100 or more people shall have a joint council and the number of councils in the joint council would depend on factors such as types of services, in consultation with the recognized union. The members are to be actually engaged in the said region and would have a term of two years. In the event of mid-term vacation, the casual vacancy would be filled by nomination. The council would be headed by the chief executive officer (CEO) or regional head of the organization. It would have a secretary, who would assist in day-to-day activities, such as preparation of agenda and minutes, when deemed necessary or alternatively at least once in a quarter. The decisions are to be taken by the council on consensus basis only. The joint council would be used for resolving issues, unit level matters, skill development of employees, improving working conditions, examining the suggestions of workers, and awarding suitable awards.

Evaluation of WPM in India

A tripartite committee was constituted in September 1994 to examine and evaluate the success of WPM in the country. The committee after evaluation indicated that except for the government, the employees and employers have not taken the scheme seriously. The employee representatives were more interested in the betterment of workforce rather than addressing larger issues such as absenteeism and productivity. On the other hand, the employers seem to have neglected the joint management councils (JMCs) for decisions involving critical issues such as changes in production processes and employee redeployment. The following are some of the factors responsible for the failure of WPM in the country:

- Ideological differences and lack of proper participation
- Multiplicity of participative firms leading to duplication, redundancy, and wastage of time
- Industrial relations marked by lack of trust between the management and employees
- Improper attitude and lack of awareness among employees

To facilitate promotion of participative culture among Indian enterprises, it would be appropriate to ensure congenial work environment, committed approach from both parties, greater awareness for the scheme, setting of realistic objectives, making WPM complementary to collective bargaining, free flow of information, and more importantly carrying out the decision taken by WPM bodies.

QUALITY CIRCLES

Quality circles (QCs) are small groups of employees in a small work area or otherwise doing similar kind of work, who voluntarily meet regularly every week, for identifying, analysing, and resolving work-related problems. More importantly, they look at imperative issues such as quality

> **■ ■ ■**
> Quality circles are small groups of employees in a small work area doing similar kinds of work, who voluntarily meet regularly, to resolve work-related problems.

improvement and organizational performance. The employees come together voluntarily to form associations to contribute to the organization. The QCs owe their origin to Dr Kaoru Ishikawa, a Japanese scientist, who conceptualized and implemented QCs for improving productivity in Japan.

The main objectives of QCs include development and effective utilization of human resources, improving quality of products and services, cost reduction, satisfying workers' urge for participation and involvement, improving the employee morale, improving the supervisory and leadership skills, resolving problems in work environment, resolving conflicts, and more importantly tapping the dormant creativity of the workers.

The typical structure of QC consists of non-members and members. The hierarchy in an organization is at seven levels starting with the non-members, members, leader and deputy leader, facilitators, steering committee members, top management, and a coordinating agency. The leader and deputy leaders are elected by the QC members and the leader is generally the seniormost among them, who discharges functions such as conducting meetings, training, and motivating members.

The facilitator acts as a link between the QC leader and steering committee and among other things evaluates and reviews the QC operations. The steering committee is an apex level body, at plant level, and its functions include training of QC leaders, budgeting QC activities, linking QC activities to organizational goals, and growth. The coordinating agency coordinates the activities of steering committee. The QCs brainstorm on a problem or an issue, analyse the problem through date collection under the techniques, and come up with a solution based on a consensus.

The functioning of QCs can be made effective if members are made to realize that there is more than one way of resolving problems. Members can be encouraged to appreciate other member's ideas and they can be trained to arrive at solutions through consensus while avoiding interpersonal conflicts. In the following sub-sections (http://www.mahapwd.com/isoandqualitycircle/qc.htm), we would discuss the various aspects of quality circles in detail.

Introduction

People are the greatest assets of an organization as they help convert all other resources into utilities. However, management of 'people resources' has always been a complex problem, ever since the beginning of organized human activities. Several managerial responses have been developed to ensure better management of people.

A QC is one of the employee participation methods, which involves the development of skills, capabilities, confidence, and creativity of the people through the cumulative process of education, training, work experience, and participation. It also implies the creation of suitable work environment to create and sustain employee motivation and commitment towards work excellence. QCs develop and utilize the tremendous potential of people for improvement in product quality and productivity.

Origin

After the Second World War, the Japanese economy was in depression. Considering the disastrous effect of the war, Americans decided to help Japan in improving the quality standards of their products. General Douglas Mac Arthur, the then commander of the occupational forces in

Japan, took up the task of imparting quality awareness to the Japanese to help them improve their products as well as the reliability of the manufacturing systems including men, machines, and materials. By 1975, Japan attained leadership position in quality and productivity. This unique achievement in modern history attracted the attention of the rest of the world. Industrialists and politicians from all over the world started visiting Japan to know how they have achieved such magical results in a short span of time. The answer was the painstaking and persevering efforts of the Japanese leaders and workers as well as the evolving philosophy of small working groups called quality circles. Consequently, the QC concept was accepted all over the world as a very effective technique to improve the quality of work life.

Definition

A QC is a small group of 6 to 12 employees doing similar work who voluntarily meet together on a regular basis to identify improvements in their respective work areas. The group uses proven techniques to analyse and solve work-related problems that come in the way of achieving and sustaining excellence, for the mutual benefit of employees as well as the organization. It is 'a way of capturing the creative and innovative power that lies within the workforce'.

Philosophy

A QC is a people-building philosophy that encourages self-motivation to improve the working environment without any compulsion or monetary benefits. It represents a philosophy of managing people, especially those at the lower level, evolving a clearly defined mechanism and methodology for translating this philosophy into practice, and providing the required structure to make quality, a way of life.

This philosophy is likely to succeed where people are respected, are involved in decisions concerning their work life, and in environments where peoples' capabilities are looked upon as assets to solve work area problems.

The QC philosophy calls for a progressive attitude on the part of the management and its willingness to make adjustments, if necessary, in its style and culture.

If workers are prepared to contribute their ideas, the management must be willing to create a congenial environment to encourage them to do so.

Concept

The concept of QC is primarily based on the recognition of the value of the workers as human beings, their wisdom, intelligence, experience, attitude, and feelings. It is based on human resource management (HRM), considered as one of the key factors in the improvement of product quality and productivity. The following are the three major attributes of the QC concept:

- QC is a form of participatory management.
- It is a human resource development technique.
- It is a problem-solving technique.

Objective

The objectives of QCs are multi-faceted:

- Change in attitude:

- From 'I don't care' to 'I do care'
- Continuous improvement in the quality of work life through humanization of work

- Self-development:
  - Bring out the 'hidden potential' of people
  - People get the opportunity to learn additional skills
- Development of team spirit:
  - Individual vs team—'I could not do, but we did it'
  - Eliminate inter-departmental conflicts
- Improved organizational culture:
  - Positive working environment
  - Total involvement of people at all levels
  - Higher motivational level
  - Participatory management process

Structure

A QC has an appropriate structure for its effective and efficient performance. However, the structure varies from industry to industry and organization to organization. The structure of a QC consists of the following elements:

- *Steering committee*: This is at the top of the structure and is led by a senior executive. It includes representatives from the top management and the HR department. It establishes policies, plans, and directs the programme. Usually, the steering committee meets once in a month.
- *Coordinator*: A coordinator is a personnel or administrative officer who coordinates/supervises the work of the facilitators and administers the programme.
- *Facilitator*: A facilitator is a senior supervisory officer. The person coordinates the works of several QCs through the circle leaders.
- *Circle leader*: A circle leader is chosen from the lowest level of employees or supervisors. The person organizes and conducts circle activities.
- *Circle members*: The circle members are staff workers. They are the lifeblood of QCs. They should attend all meetings as far as possible, offer suggestions and ideas, participate actively in group process, and take training seriously with a receptive attitude. The roles of the steering committee, coordinator, facilitator, circle leader, and circle members are well-defined.

Launching Quality Circles

The major prerequisite for initiating QCs in any organization is the total understanding as well as complete faith in the participative philosophy, on the part of the top and senior management. In the absence of a strong commitment from the Chief Executive to support the QC movement, it would be inadvisable to attempt forming QCs. The launching of QCs involves the following steps:

- Expose middle level executives to the concept
- Explain the concept to the employees and invite them to volunteer as members of QCs
- Nominate senior managers as facilitators
- Form a steering committee
- Arrange training for coordinators and facilitators in the basics, approach, implementation,

techniques, and operation of QCs. Later, facilitators may provide training to circle leaders and circle members

- Fix the meeting schedule for the QC (preferably one hour a week)
- Formally inaugurate the QC
- Arrange the necessary facilities for the QC to meet and operate

Training

It is crucial to impart appropriate training to different sections of employees. Without a proper understanding of the real concept of QCs both the workers and management might view this philosophy with suspicion. Each group must be aware of the commitments and implications as well as the benefits of QCs. Such training comprises

- a brief orientation programme for the top management
- a programme for middle level executives
- training of facilitators
- training for circle leaders and members

Operation

The operation of QCs involves the following set of sequential steps:

- *Problem identification*: It involves identifying problems.
- *Problem selection*: It involves prioritizing and selecting the problems to be taken up first.
- *Problem analysis*: It involves clarifying and analysing the problem through basic problem-solving methods.
- *Generate alternative solutions*: It involves identifying/evaluating causes and generating possible alternative solutions.
- *Select the most appropriate solution*: It involves selecting the most appropriate solution by evaluating the alternative solutions in terms of investment and returns from the investment.
- *Prepare a plan of action*: It involves preparing a plan of action to convert solutions into reality by considering the 'who, what, when, where, why, and how' of solving problems.
- *Present solution to management circle*: It involves offering solutions to the management for approval by the members.
- *Implementation of solution*: It involves testing and implementing the recommended solution after evaluation by the management.

The following are the commonly used techniques to analyse and solve work-related problems:

- Brainstorming
- Pareto diagrams
- Cause and effect analysis
- Data collection
- Data analysis: The tools used for data analysis include the following
  - Tables
  - Bar charts
  - Histograms
  - Circle graphs
  - Line graphs
  - Scatter diagrams
  - Control charts

Organizations also expect the QCs to develop internal leadership, reinforce worker morale and motivation, and encourage a strong sense of teamwork.

Some of the benefits of QCs include higher quality, improved productivity, greater upward flow of information, broader and improved worker attitudes, job enrichment, and greater teamwork.

QCs often face problems such as unrealistic expectation of fast results, lack of management commitment and support, resistance by middle management, resentment by non-participants, inadequate training, lack of clear objectives, and failure to get solutions implemented.

It took more than two decades for the quality control concept to gain acceptance in India, after its introduction in Japan. This was due to the differences in the industrial context in the two countries. Japan laid emphasis on quality control for its survival in a competitive market. On the other hand, India had a reasonably protected sellers' market, with consequent lethargy towards efforts to improve quality and productivity. However, with the liberalization of the economy and privatization of infrastructure development, the quality control concept must now be treated as a necessity.

QCs are not limited to manufacturing firms alone, but are applicable to a variety of organizations that provide scope for group-based solution to work-related problems. QCs are relevant for factories, firms, schools, hospitals, universities, research institutes, banks, government offices, etc.

SUMMARY

Trade unions strive to improve the working conditions of workers through collective bargaining. Since the 1950s, the process of collective bargaining in India has progressed through four clear phases of trade union development. The International Labour Organization provides the framework for evaluating a country's compliance with freedom of association and effective recognition of the right to collective bargaining. Workers' participation in management (WPM), a part of the process of collective bargaining, involves participative and consultative decision-making between workers and management with regard to wages, working conditions, and the jobs of workers. WPM provides challenging assignments to workers, increases the relevance of their work, permits a say in management decisions, and leads to an overall improvement in the worker–supervisor relationship. In India, the Industrial Policy Resolution, 1956 was the first policy to advocate workers' participation in management. Works committee, joint management councils, and joint councils are among the major types of WPM in India. Quality circles, where employees come together voluntarily to form associations to contribute to the organization, are also a type of WPM. Activities of these groups include facilitating improvements in quality of products and services, bringing about cost reduction, and satisfying the workers' urge for participation and involvement.

■ ■ ■ ■ KEY TERMS

Animosity A hostile feeling or act

Arbitraries Established by a court or judge rather than by a specific law or statute

Authorization The power or right to give orders or make decisions

Dichotomy Division into two usually contradictory parts or opinions

Efficiency The quality of being efficient

Exploitation The act of employing to the greatest possible advantage

Harmony Agreement in feeling or opinion

Humanitarian Devoted to the promotion of human welfare and the advancement of social reforms

Industrial democracy A combination of administrative efficiency with genuine control by the people

Jurisprudence The branch of philosophy concerned

with the law and the principles that lead courts to make the decisions they take

Negotiate   To confer with another or others in order to come to terms or reach an agreement

Productivity   The rate at which goods or services are produced, especially output per unit of labour

Quality circles   Small group of employees in a small work area doing similar kind of work who voluntarily meet regularly to resolve work-related problems

Retreat   The process of going backward or receding from a position or condition gained

Solidarity   A union of interests or purposes or sympathies among members of a group

Stakeholder   Any party that has an interest in an organization. Stakeholders of a company include stockholders, bondholders, customers, suppliers, employees, etc.

Subservient   Subordinate in capacity or function

Tripartite   Composed of or divided into three parts

Unilateralism   A tendency of nations to conduct their foreign affairs individualistically, characterized by minimal consultation and involvement with other nations, even their allies

■ ■ ■ EXERCISES

Multiple Choice Questions

1. Which of the following functions of HRM deals with 'collective bargaining'?
   (a) Staffing
   (b) Forecasting
   (c) Employee-assistance management
   (d) Employee-relations management

2. A formal, systematic process that permits employees to complain about matters affecting them and their work is called
   (a) grievance procedure
   (b) collective bargaining
   (c) boycotts
   (d) arbitration

3. The second phase of trade union development is known as
   (a) period of substitution
   (b) period of economic stagnation and political instability
   (c) period of uneconomic development
   (d) none of these

4. Which of the following has been the single point agenda of the managements since the oneset of the industrial revolution?
   (a) Improving the productivity and functional efficiency
   (b) Improving the pay scales
   (c) Providing fringe benefits
   (d) Downsizing

5. Workers' participation in management tries to reduce the
   (a) dichotomy created by industrial revolutions
   (b) employee's ability to influence decisions
   (c) employee's responsibility to his/her own action
   (d) mental and emotional influence

Fill in the Blanks

1. Workers can participate in management decisions at the _____, _____, and _____ levels.

2. _____ is a two-party process, where both strive to arrive at an agreement for settling a dispute, devoid of animosity and mutual hatred.

3. _____, _____, and _____ are the three stages of collective bargaining.

4. The main objectives of quality circles include _____ and effective utilization of human resources.

5. The key factor determining the success of collective bargaining is _____.

Concept Review Questions

1. Define the nature and scope of collective bargaining.
2. Explain the process of collective bargaining.
3. Describe the role of collective bargaining in wage negotiation and employee welfare.
4. Evaluate the relevance of collective bargaining in the context of proactive HR policies.
5. What preparatory steps should be taken by unions and management for the success of collective bargaining?
6. What are the factors hindering the success of collective bargaining in India?

7. Explain the political influence on unions and its impact on collective bargaining process.
8. Examine workers participation in management (WPM) in India vis-à-vis the global scenario.
9. Identify the various factors affecting WPM.
10. Do you think its possible to align the objectives of WPM with the organizational objectives? Explain.
11. What methods can be adopted to avoid redundancy of levels in WPM?
12. Do you think the Government can be attributed for improving WPM in the country? Explain.
13. Explain the relevance of QCs to WPM.
14. Do you think QC is like a dinosaur, which is a part of history, or do you think it still has relevance? Explain.

Project Work

1. Collect data regarding collective bargaining in a sector and analyse its rate of success.
2. Analyse the role of Indian political parties in trade unions.
3. Collect data on the role of outsiders in trade unions vis-à-vis the educational level of workers in a specific industry.
4. Prepare a brief write up on evaluation of WPM in India.
5. Study WPM in a manufacturing environment.
6. Prepare an analytical report on the relevance of WPM to the IT industry.
7. Prepare a write-up on QC movement in India.
8. Analyse the QC movement in a service organization and suggest methods for its improvement.

■ ■ ■ | REFERENCES

Cimini, M. 1991(a), 'Collective bargaining in 1990: Search for solutions continues', *Monthly Labour Review*, January, Vol. 114, 1, pp. 19–33.

Cimini, M. 1991(b), 'Developments in industrial relations', *Monthly Labour Review*, December, p. 45.

Dwivedi, R.S. 2000, '*Industrial Relations in Indian Enterprises: Managing Human Resources*', Galgotia Publishing Company, New Delhi, pp. 461–506.

Dwivedi, R.S. 2000, *Managing Human Resources: Industrial Resources in Indian Enterprises*, Galgotia Publishing Company, New Delhi, pp. 405–52.

International Labour Organization 1997, *World Labour Report on Industrial Relations, Democracy, and Social Stability*, 1997–98, Washington, p. 283.

Mamoria, C.B., Satish Mamoria, and S.V. Gankar 2000, *Dynamics of Industrial Relations*, Himalaya Publishing House, New Delhi, pp. 545–78.

Rao, P. Subba 1999, '*Essentials of Human Resource Management and Industrial Relations*', Himalaya Publishing House, New Delhi, pp. 570–90, 630–56.

Virmani, B.R. (ed.) 1980, '*Workers' Participation in Management: The Focus*', Administrative Staff College of India, Hyderabad, pp. 14–58.

Quality circle—A way to quality improvement, http://www.mahapwd.com/isoandqualitycircle/qc.htm, accessed on 22 February 2010.

CASE STUDY 1 — Collective Bargaining in Shriram Logistics

Shriram Logistics was founded in the year 1930 in Hyderabad with just one branch for transportation of goods by road. The vision and values of the founder enabled the company to grow gradually into a pan-Andhra Pradesh organization with about 8 branches and an employee strength of 500. Slowly, the company expanded its operations into neighbouring states—Tamil Nadu, Karnataka, and Kerala by the 1970s. During the 1980s, the mantle was passed to the second generation and the company decided to scale up for pan-India operations. Though the union came into existence in the 1940s, it remained dormant due to the strong paternalistic approach of the founder. The chief executive officer (CEO) of the company also gave representation to workers in the board of directors.

The following are some of the changes introduced by the company in its operations during the early 1990s:

- It adopted the hub-and-spoke principle to support pan-India operations with 7 hubs—Kochi, Chennai, Hyderabad, Vijayawada, Mumbai, Nagpur, and Delhi.

- It expanded the fleet to both 7.5 and 10 tonner vehicles.
- It added cold containers to transport food (fish, ice creams, prawns, etc.) and processed agricultural items.
- It started employing outsourced and contract employees both in the hubs and in fleet, especially in areas such as truck loading, unloading, and cleaning.
- In order to reduce the capital expenditure, it rolled out the concept of franchises with the following aspects:
- The franchise would enter into an exclusive contract with the company.
- The company would partly fund the financing requirements of purchasing trucks by guaranteeing the business to the bank.

The trade union became aware of these developments and viewed them with suspicion. It felt that the aforementioned changes were aimed at reducing its influence. It felt that these measures were aimed at reducing salary costs and employee flexibility, which would have a serious impact on the welfare and job security of the employees.

Meanwhile, in the elections, the trade union elected a local Member of Legislative Assembly (MLA) as its President and this introduced the dimension of politics into the organization. In order to gain popularity, the newly elected President started instigating and spreading propaganda against the management.

There was another development as well. In one of the recent incidents, two outsourced trucks, which were transporting goods, met with an accident on the highway, and in both instances the driver and the cleaner of the trucks died on the spot. Since, the company had insured its employees against accidents, it contacted the insurance company and got compensation paid to the driver of one truck who was on its rolls. However, as the cleaner of the truck was on temporary rolls, the company passed on the responsibility to the outsourced agency.

In the case of the other truck, the company passed on the responsibility to the franchisee and did not pay any compensation to the bereaved families. The President of the trade union took this as an opportunity and instigated the employees for a strike to get compensation and employment to the families of the deceased. After a series of negotiations, the company agreed to pay ₹3 lakhs to each of the bereaved families, but did not agree to provide employment to their dependents.

Later, the union gave notice for wage settlement negotiations with the following agenda:

- The company would not employ any outsourced employees for its trucks.
- The company would take responsibility of the welfare of the franchise truck employees, in case of any mishap.
- The company would improve facilities at the hubs.
- The company would provide canteen facilities at the hubs at subsidized costs both for the company and franchisee employees.
- The company would revise salaries once in two years and increase salaries across all levels by 30%, as they were too low.

The Vice-President–HR of the company along with his team and the union representatives, after protracted negotiations, signed an agreement with the following aspects:

- The company would revise the salary of employees once in three years, with immediate revision of salaries prospectively with 12% hike.
- The company would ensure medical and accidental insurance of employees of franchise trucks.
- The company would improve facilities and provide subsidized foods at the hubs.
- Outsourcing would continue for segments such as cleaners and mechanics. However, the company will create a welfare corpus to provide facilities such as children education assistance.

Questions

1. Analyse the collective bargaining scenario in the company.
2. Do you think that the union is strong enough to ensure employee welfare?
3. Comment on the collective bargaining for the recent negotiations in the company.

The Battle in Seattle

Labour and environmental groups were the most vocal and influential of all the protesters on the streets of Seattle last week. Were they pursuing only their own protectionist interests or were they also, as they claimed, representing the cause of the defenseless workers and degraded environment in the developing world? To someone watching their strident advocacy from the perspective of the developing countries, the answer seemed to be clear—they were motivated more by their own self-interest than by altruistic or moral feelings toward the poor.

Take the question of labour standards—the real issue is not the observance of core standards such as freedom of association, formation of trade unions, collective bargaining and abolition of child or forced labour—the issue is whether the World Trade Organization (WTO) is the right forum and whether the trade rules are the right instrument to pursue objectives that are basically social, cultural, and political. Developing countries with vibrant and vocal democracies such as India, already cherish freedom of expression, collective bargaining and the like as inviolable rights, and they do not need to be told to pursue these objectives through the trade rules of the WTO. These countries already adhere to labour's core standards—not because of any linkage to trade or investment, but because of their governments' conviction that these are basic rights to be guaranteed in a well-functioning democracy. Those who want to link labour standards to the trade rules of the WTO have an ulterior motive, revealed time and again by the protesters themselves. The labour organizations of the United States and Europe have complained that the liberalization of trade and investment regimes will lure investment away from wealthy nations to countries where wages are low. However, low wages, the result of lower levels of national income, are the primary comparative advantage developing countries have, to attract investment and create jobs. This advantage will be destroyed if labour standards are linked to WTO rules. So, the protesters are not speaking on behalf of all workers, instead just those of industrialized nations.

As for child labour, India and other developing countries are seeking to eliminate it on their own volition and as a basic social objective. However, child labour exists for reasons much deeper and much more complex than are realized by the Seattle protesters. The fundamental reason is the acute poverty of the children's families. According to an earlier estimate, the abolition of child labour in India by 2010 would require 15–20 billion dollars. Is the West or anyone else ready to make available this magnitude of funds over the next 10 years to tackle this problem? It is a sinister assumption that child labour exists in poor countries in order to cut costs or to gain an advantage in international trade.

The Seattle protesters seem to have also forgotten that a large chunk of labour in poor countries, especially in agriculture is unorganized labour—not because rights to freedom of association or collective bargaining are denied, but because it best suits the workers' ethos and conditions. In what way can WTO rules or even ILO conventions handle unorganized labour? Will linking labour standards to trade rules not drive more and more labour to the unorganized sector to avoid the stringency of the trade disciplines? As for environ-mental issues, the protesters need to recognize that environmental degradation is being caused by two segments of people—the affluent and the poor or the greedy and the needy. The affluent are polluting the environment by excessive levels of consumption and the poor are forced into unsustainable practices due to poverty. The approach needed to tackle these two varieties is different, but trade rules applied in a simplistic manner can hardly solve the fundamental problems. Furthermore, several issues of concern to the developing world have received scant attention from the environmental lobbies. These include the implications of the patenting of life forms, not recognizing the contributions of indigenous and rural communities in terms of biodiversity, genetic resources, and traditional knowledge, the indiscriminate patenting of plants, medicines, and other products that are already well known in the third world, and the consequences of genetically engineered and patented seeds. Consider the result of WTO rules that deny developing nations the right to have automatic licensing on patented, but essential medicines. Yet that issue was not articulated by the protesters who seemed quite concerned about protecting rare species. Is the health of the poor a matter of lesser concern than the health of the turtles? Therefore, developing countries have strong reasons to believe that the push for linking labour and environmental issues to the trade rules of the WTO is not motivated by moral or ethical considerations. There is no factual evidence or economic logic to support assertions that if such a link is not forged, there will be a 'race to the bottom' around the world and host countries will deliberately lower standards in order to attract investment and enhance trade opportunities. There is, however, one perverse point on which the street protesters in Seattle and New Delhi seem to be united—from different viewpoints they both want the WTO to be closed. The former wants it to be closed if it does not expand its agenda to include labour and environmental standards and the latter wants the WTO to be closed if its agenda is expanded to include any new issues.

Good causes are often lost by pursuing wrong means.

Source: Adapted from http://www.indianembassy.org/policy/WTO/wto_india/battle_seattle_dec_ 05_99.htm, accessed on 23 August 2004.

Questions
1. Analyse the situation in Seattle.
2. Does WTO have a role in securing the rights of workers? Explain.
3. Analyse the role of trade unions in the Indian IT industry in the wake of the situation in Seattle.

CASE STUDY 3

Employee Participation—A Vital Aspect of Total Quality Management

Highly competitive and ever-changing markets demand greater flexibility and quicker response to ever-changing customer requirements. This has brought about innumerable changes in the method of operation and management of many companies. Conventional management methods focussed on officers or managers 'giving orders' versus workers 'taking orders'. They did not allow much room for competition. However, total quality management (TQM) enables companies to grow and stay highly competitive through highly organized and efficient methods. One of the most vital aspects of TQM is employee involvement. It encourages employees to use their expertise, skills, and creativity in day-to-day activities to improve the workplace and the goods or services they produce. A shift from the conventional management style to the participative style involves a lot of effort both by the employees and the management. In order to ensure successful implementation of participative management, the following three support systems can be considered: The organizational system, the interpersonal system, and the individual employees.

The organizational system focusses on changing the job responsibilities and roles of employees at all levels to correspond to the participative philosophy. The organizational system should be such that it facilitates improvement and teamwork

The interpersonal system focusses on encouraging employees to solve their own problems. Relevant knowledge should be preferred over status and collaboration should be given priority over competition.

The individual employees at all levels must update their skills and develop confidence to accept and carry out greater responsibilities. It is often seen that although managers are fully aware of the need to encourage the participation of their sub-ordinates, they are unaware of the methods to do so. Thus, employee involvement gets restricted to non-job-related issues like cafeteria menus and employee picnics. On the contrary, success of any improvement initiative requires massive involvement of employees in every problem that they face on the job front. They should be involved in data recording and analysis, besides care of gauges, tools, and machines. The best way to initiate employee participation is through an intense training on TQM principles including participative, group, data collection, and decision-making skills. Often employees hesitate to make suggestions and resist new methods for fear of losing their jobs. The transition from conventional management to participative management can be seen as a three-phase development process.

• In the first phase, the employees are encouraged to study and understand their jobs and immediate work areas thoroughly to develop suggestions for improving them.

- In the second phase, the employees are trained to develop skills to analyse problems and find solutions for them.
- In the third phase, the management can focus on the economic and business benefits gained through the employee inputs.

A look at the following cases shows how employee involvement resulted in increased quality, productive decision-making, and more efficient work methods. Springfield Remanufacturing Corporation in the US created a safety committee comprising of employees from all levels of the organization. The efforts of the empowered team resulted in a 69% reduction in recordable accidents and a 100% reduction in lost workday. Further, within a span of four years of implementation a 75% drop in insurance premiums was also recorded. In another case, the New York City Department of Parks and Recreation encouraged employee involvement in what were once management decision-making areas. The department was in need of information known only to the park workers. Ten teams were allotted projects on different areas of concern and one such area was the preventive maintenance of the department's vehicles. Employee inputs helped reduce the maintenance problems by over 50%. Inputs from another team resulted in the reduction of time card errors from 33% to 13%. The Internal Service Department of US implemented TQM and employee involvement to reduce customer complaints

and poor service delivery. One team at the Ogden service centre addressed the issue of tax-payer correspondence and within a year, savings of $5,77,986 were achieved after solving the problem. Other teams helped to solve the problems caused by incorrect data input. The total benefits achieved at the Ogden centre after employee participation amounted to $37,30,959. These case studies show that TQM and employee involvement are being successfully implemented not only in the manufacturing and service sectors, but also in public sector and non-profit organizations. Employees not only play a vital part in business reengineering, they also help to achieve cost savings, quality improvements, and customer satisfaction. The best way to achieve excellence in any business is to engage every mind involved to improve their surroundings.

Source: Adapted from http://www.themanagementor. com/kuniverse/kmailers_universe/manu_kmailers/ QM_employee2.htm, accessed on 23 August 2005.

Questions
1. Can you suggest some modifications for improving employee participation in the quality management practice being followed by the organization?
2. How can you bring in cultural change in the organization to facilitate participative management processes?
3. Do you think that the extent of reduction of number of lost workdays at Springfield Remanufacturing Corporation is unacceptable? Explain.
4. How can the organization improve the participation of employees in the teams?

Carris Reels

Vermont-based Carris Reels is an innovator when it comes to pairing employee ownership with significant employee participation in decision-making. Their employee–management committee brings together shop-floor workers and senior management to deliberate on major issues, which is an uncommon employee involvement technique even in the most participatory firms. Carris Reels has been recognized by the Boston Globe, ESOP Association, and National Center for Employee Ownership

as a pioneer in the field of employee ownership. Yet, since putting in place an employee stock ownership plan (ESOP) in 1994, the company has faced significant challenges, which are shared by many ESOP companies, including:

- Heightened expectations and some confusion about the changes that employee stock ownership might bring
- Desire to reconcile participation with the bottom line

- Perceived need for clarity and efficiency in decision-making processes

Since early 2001, the company has used the 'frontiers and boundaries' curriculum to help address these challenges. The employee–manage-ment committee worked with ownership associates to customize the 'zone charts'. A sub-committee completed charts to show the company's past, present, and several possible versions of the future. To begin moving towards the participation system they wanted, one plant used *Frontiers and Boundaries* advanced tools to document and improve their decision-making processes in dozens of specific decision areas and other plants followed. In addition to this, corporate headquarters used *Frontiers and Boundaries* decision reports to convey information on corporate decisions to local sites.

Before introducing the new system to the whole plant, the pilot site conducted training sessions only for the supervisors to ensure their comfort with it. 'That got it off to a good start,' says Dale Clary, the plant manager, 'and now supervisors are actually more comfortable that they have an instrument they can use to make sure they are doing things right.' At the same time, the plant management has been pleased to observe that ordinary employees have a very strong perception of their role in the decision-making process as 'alerters'. Every employee has been trained to know that they have the right and the responsibility to alert someone to a decision that they believe needs to be considered. 'The alerter role provides a basic and comfortable means of participation for everyone', says Clary. 'Everyone appreciates feeling involved and included,' he adds, 'and now we have a way to deal systematically with people's questions and concerns. It's made a huge difference'.

Source: Adapted from http://ownershipassociates.com/svcs_participation9.shtm, accessed on 23 August 2005.

Questions
1. Do you think the ESOP will bring in employee involvement and commitment? Explain.
2. Critically analyse the process adopted by Carris Reels for engaging employees.
3. Do you think training on new processes and systems will improve employee involvement in Carris Reels? Explain.
4. Do you think involvement of employees in designing new systems will bring in more employees? Explain.
5. Did the management make an attempt to really bring in employee involvement?

Managing Employee Safety and Health

Objectives

After studying this chapter, you will be able to understand
- the concerns about employee safety and health
- the various safety programmes and their evaluation
- the supervisor's role in workplace health and safety
- the major industrial accidents and occupational hazards
- the various health-related problems and remedies
- the various environmental legislations on health and safety

INTRODUCTION

Environmental pollution coupled with radiation, defective products, and unhealthy food cause an unknown number of illnesses. That is the bad news.

The good news is that our work and community environment has improved over the years and, today, one is far less likely to fall ill or die due to an accident or poisoning than in the past. The major reason is the increased attention to safety and health by both the government and the industry. Each employs an army of professionals to help increase the odds that one will survive in this complex—and dangerous—world.

Today, the concern for safety and health is a part of almost all jobs. The mechanic who fixes your car's brakes, the firefighter, the bus driver, even the plumber, each is concerned about safety and health to some degree.

Accidents can very quickly eat away profits—not to mention the morale and efficiency of employees. Reducing accidents in the workplace is an important part of remaining competitive in today's business climate.

Definitions

Let us now look at the definitions of some key terms:

Safety: It is a state of absence or freedom from risk of injury, accident, or dangerous occurrence.
Health: It is a state of complete physical, mental, and social well-being, not merely an absence of disease or injury.
Accident: It is an unplanned and uncontrolled event that has led to, or could have caused, injury to persons, damage to plants, or any other loss.

NEED FOR SAFETY

Regardless of the size of the enterprise, or how you chose to measure it, the safety of each and every employee is crucial to your organization's success. No matter how sophisticated the operations, activities, communication, and data processing systems are, they are designed, maintained, and operated by people.

The importance of having an emergency plan, disaster recovery plan, or business continuity plan to minimize the negative impact of potential natural or man-made disasters cannot be overlooked. The need for planning has been reinforced by the lessons learned in the aftermath of the terrorist attacks on 11 September 2001 and catastrophic natural events such as hurricanes, tornadoes, and earthquakes. However, the best plans are useless if a company does not initiate steps to protect the safety and health of its employees. Employees must come first for any business recovery operation to be effective.

The safety and protection of employees carries greater financial implications than many in corporate leadership roles recognize. It creates a ripple effect that can influence immediate and long-term costs.

The management also has a moral obligation to provide a safe work environment for the employees. Some companies have a full-time corporate safety staff. Each profit centre has an employee whose duties include overseeing safety at the local level. The person is usually involved in operations, conducts safety meetings, makes inspections, and is, preferably, a good communicator.

Although managers may take a good line about safety, their behaviour may convey a different message about its importance. Some managers may be so concerned about getting a job done that the employee assumes from the manager's anxiety that production is more important than safety, although that is not what the manager means at all. The end result is that the employee rushes the job, causes an injury or accident, and seems to be the cause of the problem, whereas it is the manager's behaviour that has actually been the catalyst for the employee's action.

SAFETY PROGRAMME

■ ■ ■
A good safety programme identifies and corrects hazards before an accident occurs and acknowledges outstanding performance.

A good safety programme identifies and corrects hazards before an accident occurs and acknowledges outstanding performance. Effective safety meetings and inspections with two-way communication between the management and the employees can help identity problems. Proper safety training needs to be imparted to employees to prevent accidents, and corrective action should be taken with an 'unsafe' employee, beginning with counselling, retraining, and progressive discipline, if necessary. The overall commitment by the management and the workforce is an important element of an effective safety programme.

Controlling costs is more important than ever if companies want to remain competitive. A strong safety programme is vital to reduce the number of accidents and, consequently, the costs incurred.

It may take longer to get a job done when all safety measures are in place. This means that supervisors must be allowed adequate time to accomplish a project in complete safety.

As part of company policy, employees should be made aware that they would be penalized or dismissed for failure to abide by the rules and to act responsibly about their own or their co-workers' health and safety.

■ ■ ■
To encourage the reporting of dangerous situations, a complaint procedure must be laid down and every employee must know it.

Setting Up a System for Complaints

Employees should be aware that they are expected to inform supervisors of unsafe workplace situations—near-miss incidents, and accidents due to malfunctioning of the machinery, and instances in which certain individuals follow unsafe practices and others condone this behaviour. To encourage the reporting of dangerous situations, a complaint procedure must be laid down and every employee must know it. A standard written format for such incidents can be created so that a record of the incident and the corrective action taken is kept.

Employees may feel uncomfortable about coming forward with the information because they may feel that it jeopardizes their positions. A procedure of anonymous reporting will circumvent this obstacle. A 'health and safety box', much like a suggestion box, can be used for such a purpose. The company's workforce should be informed of how the anonymous process works, how often it is checked, and how complaints and suggestions are handled.

Organizations should also establish an investigative procedure. Generally, the safety and health officer investigates allegations of safety violations thoroughly. Each complaint, anonymous or not, should be investigated and a report kept in file with the findings about its validity and what action, if any, was taken to remedy the situation.

Integrated Safety and Health Management System

■ ■ ■
An integrated safety and health management system will help reach all the goals set by the management for a business.

Every company must address the important issues of safety and health. While some companies have safety programmes, others have an integrated safety and health management approach.

An integrated safety and health management system will help reach all the goals set by the management for a business. Ask these simple sets of questions to discover where the business is on the programme vs system continuum:

- Are safety efforts primarily reactive to complaints or accidents?
- Does the management or the safety staff address issues one by one?
- Is awareness of regulations the concern of only a few individuals?

If the answers to these questions are 'yes', the business is safety-programme-oriented, reactive, and staff-driven.

- Is the safety staff accountable for defined activities and results?
- Does the safety staff continuously respond to complaints?
- Is there a safety manager?

If the answers to these questions are 'yes', the business is probably safety-programme-oriented and positioned to begin integrating safety and health concerns into its general business management.

- Are managers engaged and involved in safety- and health-related issues?
- Is the management held accountable?
- Are employees involved in the safety process?
- Is the company proactive in ensuring regulatory compliance?

If the answers to these questions are 'yes', the business probably has a safety and health management system in place, but it may not yet be integrated.

- Is the safety function consistently staffed, supported, and financed?
- Is the executive staff accountable for safety, and is their compensation affected by it?

- Is safety a core value of the business?
- Is safety a part of the strategic business plan?

If the answers to these questions are 'yes', then the company is well on its way to having an integrated safety and health management system.

Risk identification begins with situational assessment and analysis of data, followed by gap analysis. The elements of the analysis will most likely include

- leadership and administration
- employee selection, assessment, and placement
- orientation and training
- inspections
- incident reports, investigation, and analysis
- work rules, procedures, and permits
- health and wellness
- insurance and claims management
- purchasing and engineering controls
- communications and promotions
- regulatory compliance
- system evaluations

Setting standards includes developing customized initiatives, setting priorities, deploying strategies, and drafting timetables.

When the total safety and health management system and its integration into the business management system are evaluated, what are taken into account are the strengths, weaknesses, and opportunities from both an internal and external perspective. Internally, the system is evaluated against the standards set by the organization. Externally, the overall performance is compared to other benchmarks.

Communicating the Safety and Health Message

Any serious safety and health effort includes conveying readily understandable information to the employees about their responsibility in this respect. Some companies choose to host monthly training programmes emphasizing these issues, even going so far as to offer cardiopulmonary resuscitation and first-aid classes for all employees. Others release information through company publications and postings. Whatever the means of information, records need to be maintained detailing the communications, subjects covered, and when and how they were disseminated to employees.

Evaluation of Health and Safety Programmes

The evaluation of health and safety programmes is an integral part of any inspection. The following are the four basic elements that every work-site should have in place to protect employees from occupational hazards:

> ■ ■ ■
> The evaluation of health and safety programmes is an integral part of any inspection.

- management commitment and employee involvement
- work-site analysis
- hazard prevention and control
- health and safety training

This four-point work-place programme is designed to recognize and promote effective health and safety management as the best means of ensuring a safe and healthy workplace.

It must be stressed that a good written health and safety programme does not necessarily constitute a good programme. Effective implementation of the health and safety programme must be the focus of the evaluation. The areas to be reviewed during the inspection include formal training efforts, means of communication, avenues for employee participation, enforcement procedures, and disciplinary measures. Some basic questions to ask during employer and employee interviews include the following:

- Are the objectives clearly stated?
- Is the programme comprehensive?
- Are basic safety rules specified?
- Are disciplinary measures enforced when rules are not followed?
- Are there rules for housekeeping and general maintenance?
- Is personal protective equipment provided and used?
- Are the means of investigating accidents specified and followed?
- Are training sessions held?
- Is employee participation encouraged?
- Are there specified methods of employee participation?
- Are employees provided sufficient time to discuss health and safety issues?
- Are meetings scheduled on a regular basis for employees and company representatives to exchange information, and are records kept of these meetings?

ROLE OF THE SUPERVISOR

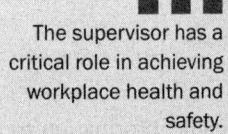

The supervisor has a critical role in achieving workplace health and safety.

The supervisor has a critical role in achieving workplace health and safety. Supervisors know the work practices and the employees they supervise and are in touch with the health and safety problems that can arise. They deal with issues raised by health and safety representatives, and can provide health and safety information and training to employees. Supervisors can also implement hazard control measures.

The following are some of the important roles of a supervisor:

- Ensuring that safety and health issues brought to his/her attention are resolved in a timely manner
- Walking routinely through his/her areas of responsibility and soliciting input from employees on safety and health issues
- Communicating to employees the status of safety items, that is, the results of inspections, of incident investigations, trending data, resolution of safety concerns, upcoming events, etc.
- Allocating the necessary resources to ensure the appropriate integration of safety measures with work tasks
- Participating in the development and communication of unit safety, health goals, and action plans
- Ensuring that the employees are represented on the unit level employee safety team and periodically attending the team meeting

- Ensuring that employees are aware of all the physical and chemical hazards in the workplace and how they are controlled to prevent injury
- Allowing employees to participate in inspections, investigations, hazard assessments, and safety reviews
- Organizing and personally attending monthly safety meetings
- Beginning safety meetings with safety share
- Ensuring that employees understand and can explain the following: stop work authority, discipline policy, safety policy, etc.
- Holding employees accountable for their safety contributions, and providing constructive feedback as needed throughout the year

The employer must provide the supervisor with appropriate training, information, and back-up support to be an effective force in preventing workplace injury and disease.

Planning Health and Safety Duties for Supervisors

The process of developing the health and safety expertise of supervisors is not difficult. It requires

- planning by senior management, with involvement from supervisors, and
- building health and safety duties into supervisors' job descriptions, with appropriate training and back-up mechanisms.

A good starting point in planning an effective role for supervisors is to define the health and safety duties of the supervisor and, indeed, of all levels of management.

By including a reference to health and safety duties in supervisors' job descriptions and by setting down specific duties in writing

- the importance of health and safety relative to other duties is stressed, and
- the stage is set for further planning on supervisor training and support mechanisms as well as on how health and safety is built into day-to-day supervisory duties.

Health and Safety Duties

The specific health and safety duties of supervisors will differ from one workplace to the next. They may include the following:

- Assisting in the implementation of policy procedures designed to provide and maintain a healthy and safe working environment
- Assisting with the identification of workplace hazards, particularly through routine inspections using prepared checklists
- Investigating accidents and incidents
- Participating in induction and ongoing training for employees
- Responding to issues raised by health and safety representatives
- Submitting statistics and reports on health and safety performance
- Participating in purchasing procedures designed to take health and safety into account
- Implementing procedures for the issue, use, storage, and maintenance of personal protective equipment
- Participating in emergency response arrangements for first aid, fire, and evacuation

■ ■ ■
The specific health and safety duties of supervisors will differ from one workplace to the next.

MAJOR INDUSTRIAL ACCIDENTS

■ ■ ■
External industrial accidents can be huge disasters and are caused by organizational errors, human factors, component failures, and deviation from operational conditions, etc.

Industrial accidents can be classified into two broad categories—external accidents that affect the environment around the factory and internal accidents that affect the people within the factory or work-site.

External industrial accidents can take the form of fires, chemical spills, discharge of toxic gases, and radiation. These types of accidents can be huge disasters. The causes of these industrial accidents include organizational errors, human factors, component failures, deviation from normal operational conditions, software defects, outside interference, and natural forces.

Internal industrial accidents can involve machines dealing with transmission, metalworking, woodworking, agriculture, construction, textile machines, tyre-making, food-making, printing, lifting equipment, etc., as well as pressure vessels, furnaces, refrigerators, hand tools, etc.

As per the International Labour Organization (ILO), a data bank on industrial accidents recorded 124 fatal accidents involving hazardous substances in the Asian region. Since more than 65% of them took place in only two countries and none in seven, it appears that many more occurred, but went unrecorded. Some of the more severe ones are mentioned in Table 18.1.

Early action should be taken by governments, employers', and workers' organizations to stem the rising number of accidents. In India, the Ministries of Labour and Environment are carrying out an extensive programme on major hazard control and a legislation for this purpose has been introduced. Malaysia has set up a unit for major hazard control within the Ministry of Human Resources. Indonesia and Thailand have taken steps to review the safety situation and identify major hazard installations. However, efforts have been scattered and unsystematic in most countries.

TABLE 18.1 Major industrial accidents in Asia (as per Indian Labour Organization)

Hazardous substance	Deaths	Injuries	Place and date of accident
Methyl isocyanate	>2,500	>2,00,000	Bhopal, India, 1984
Gunpowder	9	59	Seoul, Republic of Korea, 1987
Liquefied petroleum gas	35	15	Nagothane, India, 1990
Fireworks	40	60	Sungei Buloh, Malaysia, 1991
Ammonia	7	30	Dhaka, Bangladesh, 1991
Flammable chemicals	5	>200	Bangkok, Thailand, 1991
Gunpowder	63	52	Hubei, China, 1993
Reaction between hydrosulphate and sodium sulphide	15	25	Shenzen, China, 1993
Ethene	9	6	Beijing, China, 1997
Potassium chlorate	35	104	Chiang Mai, Thailand, 1999
Petrol	7	12	Chonburi, Thailand, 1999
Carbonyl chloride (phosgene)	1	101	Rayong, Thailand, 2000

■ ■ ■
Major accidents may be caused by human failures or errors, technical faults, or external forces.

Where a major hazard control system has been initiated, it needs to be improved, expanded, and completed. Major risks are recognized, but preventive laws are generally inadequate to cope with hazards and emergencies. The enforcement efforts of the governmental agencies concerned with the protection of workers, the public, and the environment are not properly coordinated.

Employers, workers, and the public are not fully aware of the damage that hazardous substances can cause. As a result, when a serious accident occurs, those involved are overwhelmed by its immediate effects, unable to grasp the full dimensions of its consequences. After the victims have been attended to and the incident brought under control, an assessment has to be made as to how to deal with the consequences of the accident and carry on with the tasks of repairing the damage, restarting the plant, and preventing a recurrence.

Major accidents may be caused by human failures or errors, technical faults, or external forces. Of these, the predominant cause is human failure on the part of not only the operators, but also maintenance personnel, supervisors, and plant and equipment designers and suppliers. Technical failures usually arise from human errors such as poor maintenance, overloading, and improper use of equipment. Therefore, attention should be directed more towards preventing human errors and failures at all levels.

Often, one event or condition can lead to a number of faults or failures, called common cause failures. A poorly trained and instructed operator is likely to take wrong action. If a company does not have a well-organized training programme, it is probably because its management does not consider safety a priority and does not devote adequate time and money to it. Both operator training and instruction as well as technical safety and maintenance of the installation tend to be neglected.

The most dangerous common cause failures are of organizational nature: poor commitment of the management to safety; lack of communication among departments, and inadequate instruction and information to workers. The higher a common cause failure is located in the management hierarchy, the more harm it can lead to. The management should be fully committed to plant safety and its commitment should be made known to all personnel.

Protest march against Dow Chemicals

Source: Yann, http://commons.wikimedia.org/wiki/File:Dow_Chemical_
banner,_Bhopal.jpg, accessed on 5 June 2012.

A serious accident has long-term effects at three levels: the enterprise, the people living in the vicinity, and the environment.

Immediate consequences The immediate consequences of a major accident may be large-scale death or injury, heavy damage to installations and buildings, and pollution and damage to the environment. While workers and installations are directly affected, serious accidents can also endanger the nearby population and environment.

Long-term consequences A serious accident has long-term effects at three levels: the enterprise, the people living in the vicinity, and the environment.

The enterprise is affected by

- adverse public reaction
- unfavourable publicity in the press and other media
- extensive repair or replacement, loss of production, interruption of supply to customers, and break in relations with them
- investigations by the judiciary, possibly generating further unfavourable publicity
- lawsuits resulting in severe punishment of the guilty
- indemnification of the victims and their relatives
- additional safety measures required by competent authorities
- increased insurance rates, expenses for recruitment and training of new personnel

As a result, the plant may have to be shutdown for a long time, perhaps even permanently.

People living in the vicinity of the accident may become permanently disabled or emotionally disturbed. Some chemical substances can cause illnesses that manifest themselves long after the actual exposure. Besides damage to property near the plant site, the property value itself may decline as people may not want to live near a potentially unsafe area.

Hazardous substances released in the accident may be detrimental to the environment, animals, and vegetation: crops may be ruined, water supply polluted, and land may not be suitable for grazing or cultivation for a long time.

System for Control of Major Accidents

The worst industrial accident ever, involving the catastrophic release of extremely toxic methyl isocyanate from a pesticide-manufacturing factory, occurred in Bhopal, India, on 3 December 1984, killing more than 2,500 people and affecting the health of several thousand people. The incident drew much attention to the problem of major hazards associated with the operation of certain chemical plants. In India, a strong need was felt to prevent the recurrence of such accidents by strengthening the country's occupational safety and health system. The Government initiated work to assess the existing safety measures in the chemical industry and to suggest remedial measures. The prevention and control of major accident hazards became a pressing issue.

Following the Bhopal gas tragedy in 1984, the Government of India initiated attempts to assess the existing safety measures in the chemical industry and suggest remedial measures.

At the request of the Government of India, the ILO sent a mission to India in April 1985 to identify and advise the government on the early priorities for establishing a system for controlling major accident hazards in the country. The mission, consisting of two experts, carried out a rapid survey of some representative chemical factories in different parts of India, assessed the prevailing situation in the chemical industry, and prepared a report.

The mission made the following recommendations:

- A list of hazardous chemicals and flammable gases should be established, each having a specific quantity such that any factory handling any substance above the stated quantity should be a major hazard works, by definition.
- An inventory of major hazard works should be obtained for each state.
- The list of hazardous chemicals and the inventory of the major hazard works should be maintained in a computerized data bank.

Initially, the Ministry of Labour implemented the ILO project on the establishment and initial operation of a system for controlling major accident hazards in twelve selected states. The immediate objective of the project was to strengthen the national system for preventing occupational accidents in certain industrial activities. This was done through identification, analysis, and control of industrial activities involving hazardous chemicals and processes that have the potential to cause major accidents.

The system for controlling major accident hazards in India, as established under the ILO project, consists of the following elements:

- Three-tier technical organization on major accident hazards control
- Rules for the control of major accident hazards
- Computerized data bank
- Strengthening of labour institutes and Inspectorates of Dock Safety
- Strengthening of the Inspectorates of Factories
- Training strategy

Three-tier Technical Organization

A three-tier technical organization, incorporating the national, regional, and state levels, was set up to control major accident hazards. At the national level, a multidisciplinary advisory division to control major accident hazards, staffed with relevant specialists, was set up in the Central Labour Institute, Mumbai. At the regional level, cells to control major accident hazards were set up in the three Regional Labour Institutes in Kolkata, Chennai, and Kanpur.

The advisory division and the cells function as resource centres for the control of major accident hazards. They also provide technical advice and guidance on hazardous chemicals to industry; investigate major accidents; inspect major accident hazard works; develop technical guidelines and training material; conduct specialized training programmes on the control of major accident hazards and on chemical safety to different target groups; and conduct studies and safety audits of hazardous operations.

> ■ ■ ■
> The advisory division and the cells function as resource centres for the control of major accident hazards.

Rules for the Control of Major Accident Hazards

Draft regulations on the control of major accident hazards were first prepared as model rules that were then notified to the states under the Factories Act of 1948. Through extensive consultations between the Ministry of Labour and the Ministry of Environment and Forests, these regulations were later harmonized with the draft rules prepared by the latter. The Ministry of Environment and Forests included the rules as the Manufacture, Storage, and Import of Hazardous Chemicals Rules, 1989 under the Environment (Protection) Act of 1986.

These rules to control major industrial accident hazards aim at preventing major accidents in certain industrial activities. In all, eleven authorities have been entrusted with the responsibility of enforcing the provisions in their respective fields. For example, the chief inspectors of factories were assigned the duty of enforcing the relevant provisions of the rules in factories and the chief inspector of dock safety assigned the same job in ports. These rules are also being included under their respective workplace-related legislation such as the Factories Act of 1948.

Computerized Data Bank

Computerized data banks, which have appropriate databases on the control of major accident hazards, were established in the Central Labour Institute and the three Regional Labour Institutes. These data banks enable the storage, retrieval, and dissemination of information. The databases so far created include the inventories of hazardous chemicals; the major accident hazard works/sites and the specialists in the field of major accident hazards control; the International Occupational Safety and Health Information Centre (CIS) database on occupational safety and health; the incidents involving major accident risk; and the details of the specialized training programmes conducted for the control of major accident hazards among the seven target groups within the enforcement authorities and industry. The databases on the inventories of hazardous chemicals, the major accident hazard sites/works, and the incidents of major risk are updated continuously.

Strengthening of Labour Institutes and Inspectorates of Dock Safety

The Central and the Regional Labour Institutes and the Inspectorates of Dock Safety have been strengthened by recruiting/deploying officers with qualifications and experience in chemical engineering to advise on chemical safety and the control of major accident hazards. The technical competence of these officers and other specialists has been developed by providing them with appropriate training, in India and/or abroad, in the control of major accident hazards. This has enabled the institutes and the Inspectorates of Dock Safety to develop technical guidelines and training materials, to carry out joint inspections with inspectors of factories, to perform studies and safety audits of hazardous operations, to conduct training programmes for the inspectors of factories, inspectors of dock safety, and technical personnel from the industry, and to provide technical advice to the major accident hazard sites/works.

Strengthening the Inspectorates of Factories

The Inspectorates of Factories of the states that have a considerable number of major accident hazard factories were strengthened with the recruitment of inspectors with chemical engineering qualifications. All the inspectors were trained in the control of major accident hazards abroad and/or in India. In addition, the inspectors were given specialized in-service training on inspecting major accident hazard sites. The criteria for prioritizing the major accident hazard sites were developed. The development of the technical competence of the inspectors and the provision of necessary instruments to the inspectorates have thus enhanced their ability to execute their tasks.

Training Strategy

Keeping in mind the emphasis laid in the project on training, a three-pronged training strategy was developed. The three focal points were to identify the target groups, to develop appropriate training material, and to conduct training programmes.

The target groups needing specialized training in the control of major accident hazards were identified. These included inspectors from the Inspectorates of Factories and Inspectorates of Dock Safety, senior executives, safety officers, workers who are members of safety committees, supervisory trainers from the major accident hazard works and port authorities, and trade union leaders at both the national and regional levels. Training manuals were developed to provide the background reading material needed by these training programme participants. There are manuals available now on the techniques of inspecting chemical plants and on the control of major accident hazards that are meant for the senior Inspectors of Factories, safety officers, supervisory trainers, and workers who are members of safety committees.

Over 100 specialized training programmes and seminars have been held, with nearly 3,500 participants from various target groups. A notable feature has been the input of several ILO experts on various aspects of the control of major accident hazards in these seminars and training programmes.

EMPLOYEE HEALTH—PHYSICAL AND MENTAL

Health can be subdivided into five basic types, namely, physical, emotional, social, spiritual, and intellectual. While physical health is perhaps the most commonly considered of these components, balancing all five is vital to achieving optimal health on the job and off it.

- *Physical health* refers to the body's physiological condition. Smoking, physical activity, alcohol, nutrition, and other lifestyle choices can all affect physical well-being.
- *Emotional health*, or the mental state of being, includes the stresses in a person's life, the person's reaction to stress, and the ability to relax and devote time to leisure activities. Growing evidence links emotional health to health care utilization, susceptibility to disease, and unhealthy lifestyle practices.
- *Social health* refers to the ability to get along with others, including family members, friends, co-workers, and neighbours.
- *Spiritual health* involves the condition of the spirit. Having a sense of purpose, being able to give and receive love, and feeling well disposed towards others are all manifestations of spiritual health. For some, religious faith may be included in this category as well.
- *Intellectual health* relates to achievements in life that occur through work, school, community service, or hobbies. The relationship between education and healthy lifestyle practices; unemployment and disease; socio-economic status and medical care utilization are all manifestations of the impact of intellectual health on overall health.

■ ■ ■
The impact of mental health problems in the workplace has serious consequences for individuals and for organizational productivity.

Mental health problems are among the most important contributors to the global burden of disease and disability. Of the ten leading causes of disability worldwide, five are psychiatric conditions: unipolar depression, alcohol use, bipolar affective disorder (manic depression), schizophrenia, and obsessive-compulsive disorder.

The burden of mental disorders on health and productivity throughout the world has long been profoundly underestimated. The impact of mental health problems in the workplace has serious consequences not only for the individuals whose lives are influenced either directly or indirectly, but also for enterprise productivity. Mental health problems strongly influence employee performance, rates of illnesses, absenteeism, accidents, and staff turnover.

The workplace is an appropriate environment to educate and raise individuals' awareness about mental health problems. For example, encouragement to promote good mental health practices, tools for recognition and early identification of the symptoms of problems, and establishment of links with local mental health services for referral and treatment can be offered. The need to demystify the topic and lift the taboos about the presence of mental health problems in the workplace, while educating the working population regarding early recognition and treatment will benefit employers in terms of higher productivity and reduction in direct and indirect costs. However, it must be recognized that some mental health problems need specific clinical care and monitoring as well as special considerations for the integration or re-integration of the individual into the workforce.

HEALTH PROBLEMS AND REMEDIES

There may be numerous types of health hazards for employees at the workplace. The major problems are discussed in detail here.

Noise

Continuous exposure to loud noise causes hearing loss. Exposure to noise, or unwanted sound, however, is far more than just a threat to our ears. William H. Stewart, former US Surgeon General, stated, 'Calling noise a nuisance is like calling smog an inconvenience. Noise must be considered a hazard to the health of people everywhere.' Studies have correlated noise with physiological changes in sleep, blood pressure, and digestion. Studies have also linked noise with a negative impact on the developing foetus.

According to noise expert Alice Suter, noise is one of the most common forms of sleep disturbance and when sleep disruption becomes chronic, adverse health effects are great. Studies show that exposure to noise is associated with rise in blood pressure. Studies have linked noise exposure with increased gastric emptying, peristaltic oesophageal contraction, as well as anxiety. Another study found an increase in the use of antacids and hypnotics, sedatives and antihypertensives in a noisy community, as compared to a quiet community.

Even noise that may not be at hazardous levels to our hearing can make us tense and angry. Consider how irritating the simple dripping of a faucet can be in the middle of the night, let alone more intrusive noises. Studies have found noise to be associated with increased aggression and less helpful behaviour.

Stress

Let us look at the following statements:

■ ■ ■
Job stress is defined as the harmful physical and emotional responses that occur when the requirements of the job do not match the capabilities, resources, or needs of the worker.

- One-fourth of the employees view their jobs as the number one stressor in their lives.

    –Northwestern National Life

- Three-fourths of the employees believe the worker has more on-the-job stress than a generation ago.

    –Princeton Survey Research Associates

- Problems at work are more strongly associated with health complaints than are any other life stressor—more so than even financial problems or family problems.

  –St. Paul Fire and Marine Insurance Co.

Job stress can be defined as the harmful physical and emotional responses that occur when the requirements of the job do not match the capabilities, resources, or needs of the worker. Job stress can lead to poor health and even injury.

The concept of job stress is often confused with challenge, but these concepts are not the same. Challenge energizes us psychologically and physically, and it motivates us to learn new skills and master our jobs. When a challenge is met, we feel relaxed and satisfied. Thus, challenge is an important ingredient for healthy and productive work.

Examples of individual and situational factors that can help to reduce the effects of stressful working conditions include the following:

- Balance between work and family or personal life
- A support network of friends and co-workers
- A relaxed and positive outlook.

Fortunately, research on job stress has greatly expanded in recent years. However, in spite of this attention, there is confusion about the causes, effects, and prevention of job stress.

Stress sets off an alarm in the brain, which responds by preparing the body for defensive action. The nervous system is aroused and hormones are released to sharpen the senses, quicken the pulse, deepen respiration, and tense the muscles.

Short-lived or infrequent episodes of stress pose little risk. However, when stressful situations go unresolved, the body is kept in a constant state of activation, which increases the rate of wear and tear to biological systems. Ultimately, fatigue or damage results, and the ability of the body to repair and defend itself can become seriously compromised. As a result, the risk of injury or disease escalates.

Many studies have looked at the relationship between job stress and a variety of ailments. Mood and sleep disturbances, upset stomach and headache, and disturbed relationships with family and friends are examples of stress-related problems that are quick to develop and are commonly seen in these studies. These early signs of job stress are usually easy to recognize. However, the effects of job stress on chronic diseases are more difficult to see because chronic diseases take a long time to develop and can be influenced by many factors other than stress. Nonetheless, evidence is rapidly accumulating to suggest that stress plays an important role in several types of chronic health problems—especially cardiovascular disease, musculoskeletal disorders, and psychological disorders.

Alcoholism

Alcoholism is a disease in which the person has an emotional or physical need for alcohol even though drinking hurts his or her life. It is a disease that cannot be helped by will power alone; it must be treated. If it is not treated, it will get worse and may ruin a person's family and social life, career, physical health, sense of worth and well-being, etc. Alcoholism is often called a family disease because it hurts the lives of family members and others who are close to the alcoholic. For the alcoholic to get well, family members must often take part in the treatment.

There is no one cause for alcoholism. A person's emotions, physical health, and upbringing can all play a part. Alcoholism runs in families, which suggests it may have a genetic cause.

An individual may also drink to get over difficult feelings or emotions that are caused by a treatable illness. Others may drink to lessen feelings of guilt, loneliness, or confusion.

People of any age can be alcoholics. They feel a physical need or craving for alcohol. They will develop serious health problems if the disease is not treated, and, if treated, can recover.

The symptoms are different for each person. Many or only a few of the following symptoms may be present:

Early stages
- drinking for relief from problems
- need for more and more alcohol to feel drunk
- 'blackouts'—not being able to remember events or blocks of time that happened while drinking
- hiding alcohol or sneaking drinks
- thinking more and more about alcohol
- planning activities around drinking

Middle to late stages
- drinking more than planned
- not admitting to having a drinking problem
- trying to control drinking by using mind games, such as deciding never to drink before noon
- breaking promises
- personality changes and mood swings
- drinking soon after a night's sleep

Late stages
- having severe withdrawal symptoms (symptoms when the body is no longer getting alcohol) such as delirium tremens (also known as the DTs or morning shakes).

Drug Abuse

The use of chemicals to alter the way we feel and see things is one of the oldest activities of the human race. However, a person's use of drugs, such as tobacco, cannabis, or heroin, can become uncontrolled. Even when the use of these drugs leads to serious physical and mental problems, the person may still not want to stop using them. If they decide to give up, they may find it is harder than they thought.

There are many different words used to describe drug use and addiction problems. Each drug has different patterns of use, intoxication, overdose, hangover, etc. For each drug, the term 'substance abuse' can cover different levels of use, including experimenting with use, bingeing, using large amounts without appearing intoxicated, using large amounts to get intoxicated, etc.

> ■ ■ ■
> Drug abuse has severe ramifications on the physical and mental health of the employee.

Drug abuse has severe ramifications on the physical and mental health of the employee. Therefore, all organizations should be concerned with the problem.

Cumulative Trauma Disorders

Most managers have now heard of cumulative trauma disorders (CTDs). As awareness of these illnesses grows, so probably will the frequency, unless preventive measures are taken. Pre-employment physical checks—to physically match the person with the job—are important in reducing the incidence of CTDs.

PREVENTIVE MEASURES, BENEFITS AND COMPENSATION

Preventive measures are categorized into three areas:

- Engineering
- Administrative
- Medical

Engineering precautions include using tools that can help reduce certain motions, and designing workstations to minimize awkward movements, such as lifting and turning at the same time. Rotating employees to different work-stations is an administrative control. Exercising before start-up and using braces that support the muscles are controls that can be adopted by most operations. Employees properly trained in lifting techniques can help limit back injuries. Some company physicians survey an operation and make recommendations on how to take proactive measures against CTDs.

Pre-employment examinations are helpful as long as the information is properly evaluated. Managers should review all medical reports before hiring a prospective employee.

Workers operating in extreme environments, such as freezers and coolers, can be especially prone to back strains. Going from a warm environment to very low temperatures can cause muscles to tighten. Stretching exercises can loosen muscles and make them more resistant to strains.

Health Benefits

An employer can provide health benefits for medical expenses (for example, purchasing medicines, and dental and eye problems) to both active employees and retired employees. Such a plan can be provided on an insured basis, a self-insured basis, or a combination of the two.

> ■ ■ ■
> An employer can provide health benefits for medical expenses to both active and retired employees on an insured or a self-insured basis, or a combination of the two.

There are no non-discrimination requirements if the plan is fully insured. That is, the employer can provide different or better insurance coverage to various groups of employees or retirees so long as the benefits are all provided through health insurance policies. However, if the plan is not fully insured, there can be no discrimination in favour of highly compensated employees (for example, a medical expense reimbursement plan that provides reimbursement for medical expenses that are not covered by the employer's insured medical plan).

Disability Insurance

Long-term disability benefits can be provided to employees depending on how the plan is structured. If the premiums for the coverage are not included in an employee's gross income, the benefits received by the employee are taxable. If, however, the premiums for the coverage are included in an employee's gross income, the benefits received by the employee are income tax-free.

Ergonomics

Often, the white-collar workplace overlooks safety issues and does not pursue ergonomic improvements until repetitive stress claims begin to accumulate.

Changes in physical surroundings can be accompanied by seminars or individualized training that emphasizes improved work habits. Tips and reminders can be incorporated in company newsletters, memos, or bulletins.

Besides good corporate citizenship, ensuring workers' safety and health is a matter of law and potential penalties. Criminal liability, including imprisonment and fines, can be incurred by employers who violate safety and health laws.

By starting on a course of promoting better occupational safety and health, employers put themselves in the most advantageous position for proving their intent (Exhibit 18.1).

Quality of Work Life

■ ■ ■

The quality of work life (QWL) is defined as the favourableness or otherwise of the job environment to the people.

The quality of work life (QWL) is defined as the favourableness or otherwise of the job environment to the people. Some definitions interpret it as the degree to which employees are able to meet their personal needs through their experience in the organization. The improvements in QWL are aimed at the enhancement of human dignity and growth by creating appropriate processes in which all the stakeholders, that is, management, unions, and employees, collectively work together to decide upon the workable actions and changes/improvement for achieving the twin objectives of improving the living standards of employees and also the efficacy of the organization. The general parameters used for determining the QWL are as follows:

- Adequate and fair compensation
- Safety and healthy working conditions
- Opportunity for developing skills and competencies
- Career progression opportunities
- Chances for social networking

Further, the specific issues being taken up by the trade unions with the personnel/IR personnel and, as identified by Klott, Mundick, and Schuster, are as follows:

- Compensation and job stability
- Occupational stress
- Organizational health programmes
- Alternative work schedules
- Participative management and control of work
- Recognition
- Congenial worker–supervisor relation
- Grievance redressal procedure
- Adequacy of resources
- Seniority and parity in promotions
- Employment on permanent basis

EXHIBIT 18.1   Industrial safety concerns in the ship breaking industry, Alang-India

Introduction

As part of an Integrated Coastal Zone Management Plan, it is necessary to review safety and related issues at the Alang and Sosia Ship Breaking Yard (ASSBY). ASSBY is located on the coast of Bhavnagar district and in the Gulf of Cambay, a distance of 56 km south from Bhavnagar city. This place has the best continental shelf available

(Contd)

EXHIBIT 18.1 (Contd)

for ship breaking in the whole of Asia. At the same time, it is known for the highest tidal level (10 meters) in the country. The vast expanse of intertidal zone gets exposed during ebb tide which makes it convenient for ship breaking activity, whereas the high tide makes it possible to accommodate big ships. The first ship breaking activity was started in 1983 at Alang. Today ASSBY boasts of the biggest ship-breaking yard in the whole of Asia with 182 plots carrying on this activity year round. Last year, ships worth 3.2 million tonnes were broken in this yard. With the facilitating measures in the budget, the ship breaking activity has the potential to achieve more tonnage.

Impact of ASSBY

The impact of any project will be different on different groups depending upon the way their lives and interests are affected by the project. Their attitudes to the project are shaped in response to the way the project affects them. There are basically four interest groups involved in the ship breaking activity. These include the Government of Gujarat through the Gujarat Maritime Board (GMB), the ship breaking management, the workers or labourers, and the villagers in the ASSBY area. All four groups are stakeholders. They have immensely benefited from the ship breaking industry. However, the sudden expansion of the ship breaking activity, a lack of trained management and manpower, and the unorganized nature of the industry have created some problems also. The problems of safety and the work environment in and around the yard are common for all the four stakeholders.

Issues

The Gujarat Ecology Commission has carried out a detailed study of ecological restoration at ASSBY. However, without going into the ecological details of the project, three basic issues can be mentioned: (a) issues causing ecological imbalance at Alang and in nearby areas, (b) issues causing impact on nearby villages and village infrastructure, (c) issues causing concern during ship breaking. The ship breaking activity itself is manual labour intensive and unorganised. It is necessary to bring advanced technology to this industry so that the rate of accidents can be reduced. The uproar on the Alang situation in the Western media is uncalled for, as the situation at Alang is within control and not beyond repair. What is required is a sustainable coastal zone management approach.

Neither Pakistan nor Bangladesh can compete with Alang. It is the ship breakers' entrepreneurship which has brought this development. However, if we do not take the necessary steps to solve the problems, we will lose Alang. All concerned parties will have to come together to solve the problems. Integrated coastal zone management is the key word for the development of Gujarat in the 21st century. It is time to develop a silver corridor on the coastal belt of Saurashtra, in place of the existing golden corridor. There will be many development pressures on marine resources, marine transportation, effluent discharge in marine area, and industrial pressures on coastal area. All these things call for an integrated coastal zone management (ICZM) approach.

The four stakeholders have different stakes in the ship breaking activity and try to influence the policy and programmes. Hence, an integrated plan can only be evolved after meaningful participation of all four stakeholders. The ship breaking activity, as it runs today, calls for much improvement. The industry, which is unorganized today, will earn more profit and long-term benefits if it is organized on scientific management lines, which incorporates a sustainable development philosophy. It is in the interest of the ship breakers that they cease to be fair weather friends and become scientific managers. The GMB should realize that the integrated coastal zone management is a multidisciplinary endeavour. It will have to take help from experts of different disciplines such as engineering, marine science, environmental science, sociology, and planning. The GMB will have to adopt a less rigid stance and call for the participation of all these experts.

There are around 24,000 direct workers and some 11,000 to 12,000 workers in allied activities in the ASSBY area. Of about 35,000 workers, according to one survey, only 0.55% belong to Gujarat. 99% of the workers are from other states, mainly from the backward and drought-prone regions of Orissa, Uttar Pradesh, and Bihar. This means that this is a migrant labour force. The Interstate Migrant Workman Act will have to be applied here. If this Act is applied, most of the problems of working and living conditions can be solved, because the ISMW Act

(Contd)

EXHIBIT 18.1 (Contd)

mentions accommodation, medical facilities, and even travelling allowance. Wages are not a problem for these workers, but the working and living conditions are hazardous and inhuman.

So far as the safety aspects are concerned, no standards are observed either by the workers or by the management. Of the 361 workers, according to the survey, 14 (3.88%) workers reported accidents, 11 workers (3.05%) sustained burns, and 14 workers (3.88%) reported injuries. Ten workers (2.77%) wear helmets, only one worker reported having gloves, two workers reported having shoes, and three workers reported having welding glasses.

Ship breaking labour is a semi-technical task. The survey mentions that 32 workers (8.62%) reported that they received some informal training, while the rest of them are untrained. Working hours are not decided. More than 50% of the workers reported that they work for between 8 and 12 hours. The state of industrial safety is found to be very poor as only a few plot owners provide safety equipment such as shoes, glasses, gloves, etc. The nozzles of gas cylinders create accidents due to heat and explosion. The oil remaining in fuel tankers also is a major cause of accidents. Fire accidents take place many times. As of today, the ship breaking industry falls under the Factory Act and they have to follow the Factory Act rules. There are various rules covering safety provisions mentioned in the Factory Act and these should be followed religiously. However, what is more important is the development of a safety-conscious mindset or culture for the ship breaking activity. All concerned stakeholders will have to come together to evolve such a safety-conscious mindset.

Source: Joshi, V. 1999, Industrial safety concerns in the ship breaking industry/Alang-India, *Wise Coastal Practices for Sustainable Human Development Forum*, http://www.csiwisepractices.org/read=85, accessed on 20 September 2005.

NATIONAL SAFETY COUNCIL OF INDIA

The National Safety Council of India (NSCI) is the apex body in India that looks into matters pertaining to safety in different industries. The activities of the council include collaboration with various international bodies, conducting various workshops, presenting annual awards to the industry for best safety practices, carrying out safety audit and risk assessment projects periodically, conducting specialized and implant training courses, publication of periodicals to communicate the importance of safety, and campaigning for awareness on safety through the annual National Safety Day/Week commencing 4 March (also the foundation day of NSCI).

LEGISLATION RELATED TO HEALTH AND SAFETY

The health- and safety-related rules of the Government of India have been presented in Table 18.2.

TABLE 18.2 Health and safety rules in India

Area	Details of Act/Legislation	Contents
General safety, health, and conditions of work	• Model Rules under the Factories (Amendment) Act, 1987 • The Factories Act, 1948, as amended by Act 20 of 1987, with exhaustive notes [1987]	It contains the rules issued under the authorities of the Factories Act vide amendments in 1987. The rules pertain to the recognition of competent persons, guidelines, records, and safety committees; site appraisals committees; health and safety policies; occupational health centres; ambulance; decontamination facilities; health records

(Contd)

TABLE 18.2 (Contd)

Area	Details of Act/Legislation	Contents
Industries and occupations	• Atomic Energy (Factories) Rules, 1996	The rules stipulate the safety and health rules applicable to nuclear energy establishments managed by the government and pertain to aspects such as inspection requirements; health requirements; excessive weights; eye protection; first aid; welfare facilities; medical examinations; working hours; noise protection; use of highly flammable liquids and flammable compressed gases; radioactive substances; lasers and optical radiation, etc.
Chemical safety	• The Insecticides Act, 1968	This Act contains guidelines regarding approval, inspection, law, licensing, list of chemical substances, notification of dangerous substances, prohibition of use, warning notices, etc.
Fires, explosions, and major hazards	• Control of Industrial Major Accident Hazards Rules, 1990 • Manufacture, Storage, and Import of Hazardous Chemicals Rules, 1989 (with Corrigendum, 1990) [1989]	These rules stipulate the definitions of relevant issues; general responsibilities of occupiers; notification of major accidents, industrial activities covered; collection, development and dissemination of information; notification of industrial activities; safety reports; preparation on on-site and off-site emergency plans; information to be given liable to be affected by major accidents, etc.
Physical hazards	• Atomic Energy (Control of Irradiation of Food) Rules,	These rules contain details pertaining to the modalities by which the food can be irradiated, as well as food irradiation licences and licence suspension, revocations, etc. It also contains the list of information elements that must appear in the licence request. The other aspects covered include radiological safety officer; monitoring of personnel, etc.

SUMMARY

The chapter begins with an introduction of health and safety and the need for safety measures in industries. This includes the disciplinary action and complaints redressal procedures, the developing of integrated safety and health management system, the importance of ergonomics, life insurance, health benefits, etc. The chapter attempts to briefly explain the quality of work life, the opportunity parameters, the specific issues of health and safety, the National Safety Council of India, etc.

The chapter ends with case studies to drive home the practical perspective and to test and improve the learning. The chapter has review questions followed by project assignments.

■ ■ ■ | KEY TERMS

Disability   A disadvantage or deficiency, especially a physical or mental impairment that interferes with or prevents normal achievement in a particular area

Discrimination   Treatment or consideration based on class or category rather than individual merit, partiality, or prejudice

Ergonomics   The applied science of equipment design, as for the workplace, intended to maximize productivity by reducing operator fatigue and discomfort

Irradiation   The use or application of ionizing radiation, especially in medical treatment and for the sterilization or preservation of food

Redressal Means of obtaining a remedy

Trauma An emotional wound or shock that creates substantial, lasting damage to the psychological development of a person

■ ■ ■ | EXERCISES

Multiple Choice Questions

1. Who is responsible for reducing unsafe working conditions and unsafe acts by employees in large facilities?
   (a) Chief executive officer
   (b) Chief safety officer
   (c) Occupational safety and health officer
   (d) Chief operations officer

2. Which of the following is a health hazard in the workplace?
   (a) Uncollected waste paper
   (b) Heavy object
   (c) Frayed crypt
   (d) All of these

3. Stress can affect not only your health, but also other aspects of your life. What else can be affected by stress?
   (a) Family relationships
   (b) Work performance
   (c) Your attention to safety
   (d) All of these

4. Which department enforces the standards set out in the Occupational Safety and Health Act?
   (a) Department of Health Services
   (b) Department of Labour
   (c) Department of Defense
   (d) Department of Financial Services

5. In an organization, which of the following is the best indicator of an effective safety and health programme?
   (a) Employees do not feel hesitant about sharing their problems
   (b) Employees feel motivated to perform well
   (c) Employees feel honoured that the organization is concerned about their problems
   (d) Employees do not suffer injuries and illnesses on a regular basis

Fill in the Blanks

1. Occupational health and safety refers to _____ and _____ dimensions of a workforce that result from the work environment provided by the organization.

2. Fires, chemical spills, discharge of toxic gases, and radiation are all forms of _____.

3. In India, _____ are carrying out an extensive programme on major hazard control and a legislation for this purpose has also been introduced.

4. The immediate objective of the _____ project was to strengthen the national system for preventing occupational accidents in certain industrial activities. This was done through identification, analysis, and _____ involving hazardous chemicals and processes that have the potential to cause major accidents.

5. The _____ institutes and the Inspectorates of Dock Safety have been strengthened by recruiting/deploying officers with qualifications and experience in chemical engineering to advise on chemical safety and the control of major accidental hazards.

Concept Review Questions

1. Explain the importance of managing employee safety and health hazards.

2. What are the issues involved in the safety and health aspects of employees?

3. Describe the importance of quality of work life and its relevance in the contemporary context.

4. Do you think that the broad and specific parameters indicated can be modified to meet the requirements of organizations?

5. Do you think health and safety measures have an effect on employee morale and motivation? If so, how?

6. Explain the proactive role played by the government in preventing occupational hazards.

7. Discuss the role of industrial legislation in preventing occupational hazards.

Project Work

1. Study the health and safety measures in a manufacturing company.

2. Prepare a report on health and safety measures in a service industry, preferably hospital, logistics, etc.
3. Prepare an analytical report on QWL and its relevance to the IT industry.
4. Conduct a survey on the adequacy of health and safety measures with the workers, management, and unions in a manufacturing company.

■ ■ ■ REFERENCES

Caudillo, J. 1995, 'Ergonomics and CTDs: The basics—cumulative trauma disorders', *Parks and Recreation*, June.

Fountain, M. 1991, 'Safety and health: whose job is it?', *Occupational Outlook Quarterly*, June.

Hofmann, D.A. and Lois, E.T. 2003, *Health and Safety in Organizations*, Jossey-Bass, Wiley Publishers, New Jersey, USA.

Hopps, D. 2000, 'Integrated approach—safety and health management', Fleet Owner, November.

Joshi, V. 1999, *Industrial safety concerns in the ship breaking industry*/Alang-India, http://www. csiwiseprac-tices.org/?read=85, accessed on 20 September 2005.

Rao, P. Subba 1999, *Essentials of Human Resource Management and Relation—Text Cases and Games*, Himalaya Publishing Company, New Delhi, pp. 653–57.

Rivenbark, L. 2004, 'Health and Safety in Organizations', *HR Magazine*, February.

Annual Activity Report October1999–March 2000, National Safety Council of India, www.aposho.org/about/AR16-India.htm, accessed on 23 August 2005.

CASE STUDY 1

Employee Safety in Indian Dynamites Limited

Indian Dynamites Limited, founded in 1975, is a subsidiary of a multinational corporation (MNC) located in Hyderabad. Over the years, the company has scaled its operations and has an employee strength of 5,000 across various units in the Hyderabad site.

The company manufactures chemicals used in the production of explosives. The company has an established track record of employee safety and health measures. This is significant due to the nature of its operations. The company has a chief labour officer and a safety officer to ensure compliance of the safety and security guidelines. Further, the company has implemented the following measures:

- Every new recruit has to go through mandatory training in safety, health, and security aspects.
- The tenured employee has to undergo refresher training in safety, health, and security for a half-day once in a quarter.
- All employees are required to get a 10-minute brief on safety, health, and security by their supervisors before they log in to their work every day.
- The supervisor has to ensure that each employee who logs in to production wears the safety kit provided to him/her.
- The tenured employees are to receive training to function as single points of contact (SPOCs) in the ratio of 1:500 employees.
- The company has recruited a doctor, who will be available in the small dispensary attached to the factory.
- The company has an ambulance, which is available round the clock.
- Every employee has to undergo mandatory health check once in a quarter.
- The company has provided medical insurance and group personal accident coverage to all its employees.
- Once in a quarter, the company will conduct a safety audit through an independent auditor. The auditor submits his report to the management committee.
- Based on the employee's feedback, the company has constituted an employee safety council consisting of safety SPOCs. A chief safety officer heads the council.
- The council periodically reviews the safety measures, collects feedback from the employees, and receives a copy of the employee safety audit report from the auditor.

Questions

1. Briefly analyse the employee safety measures at Indian Dynamites Limited.
2. Please study the safety practices in a chemical manufacturing unit in your neighbourhood and compare with those at Indian Dynamites Limited.
3. Suggest changes, if any, to the safety practices of the chemical manufacturing unit.

Unilever, UK: Safety in Action

CASE STUDY 2

Safety cannot be taken for granted. It can only be achieved with the wholehearted effort of everyone involved.

Unilever is committed to providing uniformly safe working conditions to employees worldwide. Safety at work is a primary business objective and the company's aim is to continually improve its performance in this key area. To achieve that, the concept of safety has to be embedded in the values and practices of everyone, everywhere.

Creating a safe workplace requires dual responsibility—of both the employer and the employee—in order to establish and improve standards.

Unilever companies throughout the world must comply with local safety legislation. In addition, Unilever mandates global internal standards in safety, health, and environment (SHE). It aims for continuous improvement in performance year on year.

High safety standards are an integral part of Unilever's culture. Many companies also set themselves the goal of achieving their country's nationally, and often internationally recognized safety standard. This was the case with Unilever South Africa's Boksburg twin factory site, which produces both powders and liquids for home and personal care (HPC) products as well as edible oils and margarines.

It scooped eight health and safety awards—the majority of prizes—at the National Occupational Safety Association (NOSA) awards in 2000. NOSA is an internationally recognized organization that focuses on excellence in occupational SHE risk management. Six of the site's staff received awards including the foods factory engineer Iain Reynard, who was cited as the 'health and safety personality of the year'.

Unilever South Africa subscribes to the NOSA SHE system and, as such, is required to be audited each year by NOSA professional auditors. The audit evaluates compliance with legislation as well as company SHE systems and practices, focusing on risk management. As a result of the audit, both factories on the Boksburg site received a NOSCAR (a NOSA 'Oscar'). This award is only given to companies that achieve 95% or more in their annual audit and which are proactive in risk assessments.

In order to improve its safety record, the Boksburg site changed its safety programme from being system driven to risk driven. 'We analyse the risks inherent in the manufacturing site and then apply the appropriate level of SHE intervention to mitigate the risk, either by physical changes or changes in people's behaviour,' explains Iain. For example, a slippery, hazardous staircase was made safer by covering the edges of the steps with a special non-slip strip.

The results of Boksburg's safety programme are impressive. By April 2001, both factories had beaten long-standing records: the foods factory had reached 1 million hours and the HPC factory just short of 3 million hours worked without a lost time accident (where an injury means a person cannot return to work the following day). As well as increasing the gap between lost time accidents, there is also a downward trend in minor accidents.

The benefits are many. Unilever South Africa has a reputation for being a safe company to work for. That in turn affects its corporate image positively and makes it a more attractive employer. With fewer incidents, there is a commensurate reduction in employee time off work, litigation, and compensation claims. Work continues uninterrupted and the factory remains a safe environment.

Perhaps the greatest benefit is the change in employee attitudes. Iain and Piet van Breda, the HPC factory engineer, regard all 1,485 employees as being members of the safety team. 'We have had total openness and honesty from people about what the factory's risks are,' Piet says. 'That has allowed us to tackle fundamental problems behind our systems.' National Safety Manager, Ailsa de Goede, also emphasizes that 'the success of any safety and health programme is the commitment of senior management in ensuring that all employees understand their SHE responsibilities'.

Unilever also believes that internal recognition for good safety performance is essential and has its own Occupational Safety Awards Scheme. In 2000 Unilever's Premier Safety Trophy was awarded to Hindustan Lever's factory in Kandla, India. The factory employs more than 500 people and produces over 90 personal products from toothpaste and soaps to skin creams and lotions. All staff are given safety training and the factory has an active safety committee.

The commitment to safety means that employees have achieved almost 6.5 million working hours without a lost time or 'restricted work-case' accident (where an injury means a person is fit to work, but undertakes light duties). Shrikant Bhide, Senior Vice-President–Supply Chain, for the region says, 'This is a highly complex factory and we identified safety as a key priority early on. Safety and quality go hand-in-hand. Quality starts with a workplace that is clean and safe.'

Making safety an issue in an office is far more difficult than in a factory. People believe offices are inherently safe places to work and, indeed, they are low risk. Nevertheless, accidents can happen. With that in mind, in 1998, Unilever's London office set itself new, internal standards and put in place a fresh programme to improve safety.

The aim has been to make all staff aware of safety. New employees spend half a day on fire, security, safety, health, and environment as part of their induction course. Safety stewards have been appointed around the building; a SHE committee has been formed

involving employee representatives; and safety has become an issue for consultative and steering committees to consider. 'We've raised the profile of safety and are altering the culture', explains Paul Haden, safety, health, and environment coordinator.

Changes in safety include the introduction of better equipment for high-risk tasks, such as cleaning the exterior windows on the multi-storey building, and introducing tools to make it easier for staff to lift or handle equipment. Small changes to simple tasks can make them much safer. For example, employees collecting drinks from the coffee bar are encouraged to carry no more than four cups and that too in a specially designed tray, thereby reducing the chances of spillages and burns.

As a result the office has seen a continuous reduction in accidents over the period 1997–2000. It also achieved a total of 1.5 million hours worked without a lost time accident, for which it received an internal safety award. This was the first time an office premises in Unilever received this accolade.

It is people who drive safety policies. Unilever works hard to instil safety as an important goal to which its employees are committed. Knowing that safety is not a finite point, all are encouraged to continually improve safety procedures and drive up the safety targets.

Source: http://www.unilever.comourvalues/environmentandsociety/casestudies/health/cik.asp, accessed on 20 September 2005.

Questions
1. Analyse the organizational culture in Unilever with specific relevance to the safety work conditions for the employees.
2. Critically analyse the various safety programmes that were conducted in Unilever.
3. Suggest changes in policies which can make health and safety measure attractive.

Health and Safety in MFI Furniture Group, UK

CASE STUDY 3

Health and safety lies at the heart of an organization's commitment to the people who work for it and its customers. This case study examines MFI's commitment to health and safety and shows how, in recent years, the company has successfully developed new approaches to auditing and

measuring health and safety performance standards in individual stores. MFI staff have been trained and given the responsibility to implement quality health and safety procedures at store level.

As a retailer, MFI is acutely aware that its business not only depends on attracting customers to its superstores to buy products, but that the safety of those customers is of great importance. In addition, MFI places great emphasis on the health and safety of its employees.

Importance of health and safety High standards of health and safety bring positive business benefits on three fronts:

Economic: The costs of accidents to a business can be crippling and can destroy the good reputation of the organization.

Statutory: With 186 MFI stores and over 75 Howden Joinery Depots, the MFI organization is regularly visited by Enforcement Officers working for local authorities to maintain health and safety standards. MFI needs to make sure it can always satisfy these officers that it is complying with the relevant acts of Parliament, regulations, and codes of practice. In addition, stores must have a fire certificate, which shows that MFI is complying with the requirements of county fire brigades. MFI seeks to more than satisfy each and every statutory requirement, which can be applied to its health and safety performance.

Morale: Every successful business needs a motivated workforce that is committed to the business and to improving its performance. MFI actively seeks to develop a partnership with its employees, showing a keen concern for their welfare in the workplace.

Organization of MFI supply chain The distribution of MFI furniture involves a network of links starting from Hygena, MFI's manufacturer. While Hygena is responsible for its own health and safety arrangements, MFI has a responsibility for any activity involving its own employees, for example, transporting furniture from the Hygena factories to MFI Home Delivery Centres. MFI even has to monitor the health and safety performance of contractors as part of a 'duty of care' even though kitchen and bedroom assembly takes place in the customer's own home.

Health and safety measures The Health and Safety at Work Act (1974) established a responsibility for both employers and employees to provide safe conditions at work. The employer's duty is to ensure, as far as it is reasonably practicable, the 'health, safety, and welfare at work of all employees'. The employee's duty is to take reasonable care to ensure both his or her own safety and the safety of others who may be affected by what he or she does or does not do.

MFI sets out responsibilities regarding health and safety in its employee handbook and produces a poster, which is displayed in prominent locations at all premises. The handbook also gives basic information about safety training, risk assessment, and consultation with management or support departments.

All retail staff must receive a safety induction within the first week of employment, carried out by a member of the management and assisted by a safety video specially produced for MFI.

Further safety training must then be given within the first two months of employment, covering the subjects of fire safety, manual-handling techniques and restrictions, and safety rules/procedures, which arise from a specific risk assessment covering each retail job. Training videos, overheads, and guidance are provided by the safety department to facilitate this task and one of the managers receives specific training on this local safety management role—called the safety coordinator role.

Incidents of customer or staff injuries resulting from the design of products are reported back to the safety department.

Recurring issues can then be passed on to a quality assurance manager who is a member of the Buying Department, so that they can be resolved with suppliers, or with MFI's merchandising section if the problem lies with display. For example, a loose rug can become a hazard if displayed on the floor of a showroom.

Care must also be taken in the design of racks, shelves, plinths, etc., used to display merchandise. Plinths must be very visible to avoid customers tripping; shelves must be secure so that they can withstand children who try to climb up them; and racks must be positioned and designed to avoid running children having head injuries from accidental contact. A key principle is to make showrooms 'kiddy-proof'.

As a dynamic retailer, MFI stores will need refitting on a regular basis, which may involve minor or major construction work being carried out during trading. For minor refit work, contractors must work within cordoned-off areas of the showroom. For major works, retailing operations take place away from the refit work. MFI works only with contractors it knows to be reliable and who have been involved in effective safety training.

Statutory requirements In addition to the Health and Safety at Work Act, MFI must abide by many law and safety regulations. Following the membership of UK in the European Union (EU), several sets of safety regulations have arisen from directives agreed by member states to ensure common standards of health and safety throughout Europe. Member states must introduce laws and regulations that comply with the EU directives.

Important examples include

- The Control of Substances (Hazardous to Health) Regulation (COSHH) 1994
- The Noise at Work Regulations 1989
- The Management of Health and Safety at Work Regulations 1992*
- The Manual Operations Regulations 1992*
- The Personal Protective Equipment at Work Regulations 1992*
- The Provision and Use of Work Equipment Regulations 1992*
- The Health and Safety (Display Screen Equipment) Regulations 1992*
- The Workplace (Health, Safety, and Welfare) Regulations 1992*
- The Reporting of Injuries, Diseases, and Dangerous Occurrences Regulations (RIDDOR) 1995
- The Construction (Design and Management) Regulations 1994
- The Construction (Health, Safety, and Welfare) Regulations 1996

One of the six sets of regulations simultaneously introduced from 1 January 1993, known generally as 'The Six-Pack'.

Apart from safety regulations, safety standards are also set out in codes of practice, guidance notes, and British or European standards which detail best practice.

The first hurdle to meeting all these standards is to keep abreast of changes as they take place. Only a small proportion of the total mass of regulations and standards will relate to any one business.

Safety advisers Each business must have the services of a competent safety professional—this has been made a legal requirement by the Management of Health and Safety at Work Regulations, 1992. The named person can be directly employed as a safety adviser or safety manager. In a smaller business, a safety consultant may be employed.

MFI uses a team of four safety advisers under the direction of one safety manager for its retailing business (MFI Furniture Centres Ltd) and its trade business (Howden Joinery Ltd). Following training, safety professionals have to keep up-to-date with legislative changes by

- reading journal articles
- attending regional health and safety meetings
- attending seminars and conferences on safety issues
- reading specialist safety bulletins and updates produced by information companies

Risk assessments Each MFI store is provided with a file of safety information including risk assessments, guidance documents, training overheads, etc. This is known as the 'risk assessment folder'. In addition, a health and safety documentation file, which is used to keep all records of staff safety training, safety bulletins, and equipment checks by contractors and visiting service engineers, is also supplied.

To ensure that all managers can clearly identify and remember the safety standards, which must be maintained in each store, MFI also supplies a safety audit document detailing and prioritizing requirements under the four section headings of fire safety, documentation, warehouse safety, and showroom safety. This document is also used by external safety auditors to check the stores' health and safety standards during an annual (unannounced) safety audit of every store. This audit is 'scored' across the four sections, using different priorities listed (A, B, or C) as a marking mechanism. A percentage score for each section and an overall percentage for each store are calculated.

Each store is expected to carry out checks regularly and to monitor performance. All MFI employees are expected to participate in making the checks and record the results in order to involve everyone in good health and safety practice. MFI's Safety Department has also devised questionnaires to check on the current understanding of employees at any one time.

Some examples of unsafe practices, which employees are instructed to avoid are as follows:

- Jumping off fork lift trucks before they come to a halt
- Climbing up warehouse racking, rather than using airport ladders, to pick customer orders
- Handling heavy boxes incorrectly
- Stacking shelves incorrectly or overloading
- Leaving items on the floor where people might trip over them

Health and safety policy   Policies provide working guidelines for employees to follow. MFI's safety policy has been continually updated and developed over time in response to changes in store layouts, distribution arrangements, changes in management structure, and changes in legislation.

The most recent major changes occurred in 1992 when some of the responsibilities for health and safety were moved from a centralized health and safety function to empowered store managers, who were made fully responsible for their own health and safety standards, supported by good quality safety training for management. At the same time, an auditing system was established, which made it possible for stock auditors to check the performance of stores compared to national norms. Cash prizes are awarded to stores that are able to exceed specified targets. These targets are established on the basis of previous performance. Stores are supplied with information on a regular basis on how they are performing compared to the targets set for them (enabling them to try to improve performance). Individual managers who are able to produce excellent health and safety results are recognized (named) in a special bulletin at the end of the financial year.

The MFI Safety Policy statement presents an overview of how it shares the task of ensuring good standards of health and safety within the business. Detailed policies are primarily contained within risk assessment documents, the safety audit documents, and associated guidance documents.

Safety bulletins are issued every one to two weeks. These draw attention to specific problems or concerns. The bulletins often carry requests for feedback from retail managers about potential safety problems. Safety policy is implemented through safety training of staff by management. It is also communicated during the training of management by the safety adviser team.

Safety bulletins (known as hotlines) are issued during the year, and risk assessment documents, which contain safety rules, are reviewed and redistributed to keep people up-to-date with changes.

National legislation, which is likely to impact businesses, is always published as a 'consultative document' before it becomes law. This gives organizations, such as MFI, the opportunity to voice their opinion about anything they are unhappy with. It also helps MFI to anticipate likely new changes. MFI belongs to the British Retail Consortium (BRC), which acts as an influential voice for the retail sector. Through membership of the BRC, MFI is given advance warning of new EU directives, which influence working practice.

Policy management   MFI's health and safety performance is monitored by the Safety Department. A monthly report is sent to the director responsible for health and safety and includes a tabulation of all customer accidents and 'most time' staff accidents, the number of hours lost through occupational sickness, and the number of visits by environmental health officers and fire officers. These statistics are compared with figures for the same period in the previous year.

MFI has been able to maintain a very good record of the accidents at work. In the period 1992–97, the reported accidents averaged 63 a year. With a total average workforce of approximately 5,500, this worked out at 1.1 compared with figures produced by the European Safety Agency of 4.5 for all European workers during 1993.

Improving performance   The essence of MFI's success in health and safety improvements is in having changed health and safety performance into something that could be quantified and measured.

MFI's safety standards follow the acronym SMART:

- Simple—the creation of simple audit questions that are easy to follow
- Measurable—a scoring system that allows direct comparisons
- Accountable—managers are made directly responsible for store performance
- Realistic—performance benchmarks are based on past performance
- Time related—scheduled safety checks and target staff training times

MFI has introduced a system to measure safety performance through its safety auditing programme. In the same way that retailers are set sales or profit targets, they are also set safety performance targets and are then rewarded via a bonus scheme if those targets are achieved.

Case summary   Health and safety has been successfully integrated into every manager's performance targets and this enables it to remain within his or her focus of attention. The responsibility for health and safety performance is clearly quoted in every manager's job description and is part of his/her quarterly performance appraisal criteria with the area manager.

Average audit scores for each retail area are calculated and ranked by the Safety Department so that regional managers of different areas can compare safety performance.

As standards improve, average scores also improve. Annual comparisons are made to ensure continuous improvement in safety standards. Many stores now achieve a score of 100 in one or two sections of their audit. A small number of stores have achieved a score of 100 in all sections. This helps encourage other stores to strive for excellence because these standards have been proved to be possible.

Questions

1. Analyse the health and safety conditions at MFI stores.
2. Critically analyse the health and safety measures that have been implemented by the management.
3. Do you think the safety measures are in tune with statutory requirements?
4. Explain the role of safety advisers in creating a conducive environment for health and safety.
5. Critically analyse the risk assessment methodology.
6. Briefly analyse the health and safety policy of the company.

Knowledge Management

Objectives

After studying this
chapter, you will be able
to understand
• the nature and
  resources of knowledge
• the various approaches
  to knowledge
  management
• the processes involved
  in managing knowledge
  workers
• the relationship
  between performance
  planning and
  knowledge
  management
• the impact of
  organizational culture
  and learning on
  performance
• innovation
  management in the
  context of information
  technology

INTRODUCTION

Organizations today are undergoing fundamental and radical changes in structure and management practices. The issues on which management practices are focused seem to be global competition, fast pace of technological change, and emergence of knowledge economy and knowledge workers. To cope with these issues, organizations need to become more flexible, dynamic, and agile to accommodate novelty, change, and innovation. Hence, in the present chapter we focus on three major challenges that organizations need to address immediately:

• Managing knowledge workers
• Performance improvement
• Technology and innovation management

Liberalization, privatization, and globalization have influenced all segments of the society. While the impact is minimal in some sectors, it is widespread in others. Business organizations in India, therefore, not only face competition from global players, but more so from the domestic players. Therefore, organizations need to be more innovative, competitive, and proactive in their endeavours. There is an urgent need to anticipate, advocate, and accelerate the change processes in the business environment and act accordingly. The gaps that demand attention in organizations, especially from HR functionaries, are talent gaps, knowledge gaps, and strategy gaps. It becomes essential, then, to redefine and transform HR practices from the traditional reactive approach to those that can anticipate business needs and provide solutions for them.

In the new millennium and information era, organizations have to compete on a global scale. Many executives and practising managers believe that firms around the world are facing unprecedented global competition. The advent of networked organizations means that organizations can no longer function in isolation within their economies; they have to function on a global scale.

■ ■ ■
Managements are finding it increasingly necessary to align their structures and culture to the requirements of knowledge management.

The traditional approach of spying on competitors or collecting information about them from the print media has given way to a Web-enabled world where information moves across the boundaries of not just organizations, but economies too. The information-driven competition has become even more pronounced because of informed customers. Research data also supports this belief.

The competitive advantage of workers in contemporary organizations is defined by their capabilities for knowledge management and managing knowledge workers. Managements are finding it increasingly necessary to align their structures and culture to the requirements of knowledge management.

Another issue of concern for modern organizations is to improve the performance at individual, group, strategic business unit (SBU), and organization levels. Performance management in an organization can only be perceived in the context of organizational strategy. The factors that affect performance management are the leadership, change phenomenon, culture, and learning processes in organizations.

More than a differentiating factor, technology has become an all-pervasive phenomenon. The profitability and performance of an organization is largely dependent on its ability to adapt and integrate technology with business processes/requirements through innovation.

GLOBALIZATION—IMPACT ON HRD

The twentieth century saw the advent of globalization. In simple terms, *globalization* can be defined as the process wherein the production and distribution of goods and services by organizations are not restricted within geographic boundaries (national frontiers). Following globalization, goods and services produced in one country are marketed in other countries too.

However, goods and services with trademark protection can be produced and marketed in the local country by multinational corporations (MNCs) or by agents authorized by them. For instance, the American MNCs Coke and Pepsi have a presence across the globe. They control the advertising and marketing efforts and produce on their own or through local authorized agents.

Human resource development (HRD) can be defined as the process encompassing a gamut of activities in an organization—manpower planning, recruiting, redeploying, training and development, management of performance, and providing for a satisfactory exit of employees. The entire set of activities are planned and managed keeping in view the goals and priorities of the organization.

The impact of organizational initiatives to gain or sustain market position in the context of global changes has a direct bearing on the HRD processes. HRD processes do not exist in isolation. Any proactive HRD functionary would be part of the strategic activities of the organization aimed at improving the bottom line, while maintaining or improving the market position. The HRD processes have their origin in the strategic activities and thus globalization has a direct impact on HRD in organizations.

■ ■ ■
Globalization is defined as the process wherein the production and distribution of goods and services by organizations are not restricted within geographic boundaries.

With competition increasing both at home and abroad, managers must find creative ways to deal with the competitive challenges they face. A classic example

> ■ ■ ■
> The HRD processes have their origin in strategic activities of an organization aimed at improving the bottom line, while maintaining or improving the market position.

of handling the challenges of globalization is that of Ford Motor Company, USA. Ford recognized very early that Asian and European markets offer a number of opportunities and turned them to its advantage.

Summarily, globalization means thinking globally, establishing manu-facturing facilities, procuring finance and human resources, and marketing throughout the world. It is a well-known fact that not only economies, but companies too globalize stage by stage. The methods generally adopted by organizations to follow the trends of globalization include exporting, licensing, contract manufacturing, joint ventures, mergers, and strategic alliances.

In business today, the world is the marketplace. With increased communication, transportation, networking, and financial flows, people, goods, capital, and information are moving around the globe like never before. We have become a part of the global village and there exists now a global economy where no organization is insulated from the effects of foreign markets and com-petition. Indeed, more companies are thinking of redesigning themselves for international competition and discovering ways to exploit the world. For example, Procter and Gamble is spreading its business to China, India, Russia, Brazil, and Israel. Similarly, Nestle, based in Switzerland, has a German chief executive officer (CEO) and gets more than 98% of its revenues from and has 95% of its assets outside Switzerland.

Global companies plan ventures not only in the national markets, but also in the global markets. They perceive factors, such as cost of labour, availability of skilled labour, and political and economic stability, for operations. Executives and employees are trained in worldwide operations. For example, employees in a global company based in India speak of London, New York, Singapore, and Tokyo as Indian businessmen speak of places within India. They make investments based on feasibility of worldwide projects, and procure raw materials, human resources, and other inputs from all over the world.

It is interesting to note that Mazda's sports car MX-5 Maita was designed in California, its prototype product created in England, assembled in Michigan and Mexico using advanced electronic components invented in New Jersey, fabricated in Japan by sourcing the finance from Tokyo and New York, and marketed worldwide.

The impact of globalization is felt by the society at large and consumers in particular. The advantages of globalization are in terms of free flow of capital and technology, increase in production and consumption of quality products, increase in jobs, and higher standards of living.

Global Marketplace

As a result of globalization, even organizations operating within the geographic boundaries of a particular country are affected by the trends prevalent in other parts of the world. The World Wide Web has come as a boon. It enables a remote service provider to offer his services to the farthest corner of the world. However, the premium is on quality and excellence. It also calls for understanding global markets, different buying habits of the people around the world, zero-defect performance, etc. Hence, individuals, businesses, and governments will have to evolve new rules for this emerging world.

Organizations particularly have to review their 4 Ps—product, price, promotion, and people. To understand the concept of the 4 Ps, let us take the example of firms in the IT industry. The

■ ■ ■
Increased salary
structures and
expectations of
employees are forcing
firms to adopt innovative
HR systems.

human resources here are highly mobile across countries and are, in a way, globalized. In a sense, though they appear to be global at the macro level, at the micro level, the local cultural factors cannot be set aside. The wages in Indian IT firms were once on the lower side, but with the active movement of employees, there has been a gradual change in salary structures. Another reason that is attributed by the experts to this change in salary structures is the rise of the Indian IT firms in the value chain; for example, firms that had started with mere focus on the Y2K problem have got into the area of providing turnkey solutions.

The increased salary structures and increased expectations/aspirations of the employees are forcing the HR functionaries of these firms to adopt innovative HR systems such as Employee Stock Options (ESOPs), performance management systems, and flexi-work hours. The scenario is not limited to Indian IT firms. It is also slowly expanding into other sectors such as the services sector that includes banking and finance firms. This is so because organizations in these sectors too are adopting IT for competitive as well as existential reasons, leading to an increasing number of their employees being IT professionals. This is forcing them to provide for HR systems at par with those in the IT industry. This is being done for the following reasons:

- To reduce the disparity between IT and non-IT professionals
- To decrease the attrition rates of IT professionals
- To integrate IT professionals into mainstream organizations
- To build tech-savvy organizations

Technological Revolution

It is an accepted fact that technological revolution will revolutionize lifestyles. Any technological transfer is beneficial both to the country that transfers the technology and to the country that receives the technology. While developed countries have adequate R&D funds, technological know-how, and necessary financial resources, they may not have the requisite facilities and markets.

Developing countries have bigger markets and increasing purchasing power, but scarce investment in resources and R&D. The operational constraints involve non-availability of foreign exchange, high cost of transfer, and problems of adapting to local conditions. Hence, the two aspects that draw our attention are R&D and HRD. The thrust areas in the development of HRD will be education and training of the employees to manage technology transfer.

The adoption of IT by organizations is a planned exercise and careful thought is required to prepare the employees for the purpose. Let us consider the banking sector in our country. The banks have taken up a series of steps as follows:

- Planning for tech-savvy manpower vis-à-vis IT implementation plans

■ ■ ■
The thrust areas in
HRD are education and
training of employees
to manage technology
transfer.

  - Training the trainers to meet the training requirements in the staff training colleges
  - Training the employees in a particular application, such as bank automation, before it is rolled out in the branches
  - Training the employees in relevant areas such as network management and IT security/audit

- Training the employees in business process reengineering and reengineered processes to derive maximum benefit from IT
- Training the employees on management information systems (circulars through intranets as against manual printed circulars, dissemination of information on bank products, services, strategies to the employees), statutory/periodical returns submission, etc.

All these steps substantiate the aspect that training and educating the employees before IT adoption in the organization is not just essential, but also critical to the IT initiatives if the organizations have to be successful.

Change in Employer and Employee Relations

■ ■ ■

The emergence of intellectual property rights and Internet marketing has changed the scene of industrial relations.

The emergence of intellectual property rights and Internet marketing has completely changed the scene of industrial relations. During 1995–99, the HR departments made three significant organizational structural changes— restructuring, downsizing, and performance-linked promotions. The nature of employment is either contractual or task-based. Hence, there is less of unionization and greater emphasis on performance.

New Work Environment

The new work environment would definitely be characterized as complex, semi-structured, performance-oriented, and focusing on high returns. Employees will experience a new sense of freedom as well as abundance of opportunities, and reap financial rewards. The emergence and management of knowledge workers would gain momentum. The emphasis would be on encouraging creativity, talent, knowledge, and performance.

In this chapter, we focus on the three most important challenges facing organizations in the twenty-first century: managing knowledge workers, technology transfer, and performance-improvement strategies.

KNOWLEDGE MANAGEMENT—A KEY EMERGING AREA

F.A. Hayek was among the first economists to note the importance of knowledge and its distribution for a well-functioning economy. Hayek argues that 'the economic problem of society...is not merely a problem of how to allocate 'given' resources—if 'given' is taken to mean given to a single mind ... it is rather a problem of how to secure the best use of resources known to any members of the society ... a problem of utilization of knowledge which is not given to anyone in its totality'.

Hayek's insight was that an organization's performance depends on the allocation of decision-making authority with the knowledge important to these decisions. It is obvious then that the opportunity set confronting an individual or a firm is a function of the individual's knowledge.

What is Knowledge?

According to Webster's Dictionary, knowledge is the fact or condition of knowing something with familiarity gained through experience or association. It may also be described as a set of models that describe various properties and behaviours within a domain or stored in organizational processes, products, facilities, systems, and documents.

■ ■ ■
Knowledge asset means knowledge regarding markets, products, technologies, and the organization that generates profits and value.

Though many definitions exist and are in vogue, we may conclude that knowledge refers to ideas or understanding, which an individual possesses, and those that are utilized effectively for goal realization. Further, it is very specific to the individual who creates it and interacts with it.

Knowledge asset, as applied to a business firm, means knowledge regarding the markets, products, technologies, and organization that a business owns or needs to own and which enable its business process to generate profits, value, etc.

Sources of Knowledge

There are two types of knowledge in any organization: formal or explicit knowledge and informal or implicit knowledge. Formal knowledge is that which is available in notes, manuals, reports, memos, and the like. Informal knowledge is that which is gathered and maintained through informal means, which is more crucial as it is in this context that the formal knowledge exists. The following are the major sources of informal knowledge:

- *Expert*: The main source should be a human expert as he or she already has the knowledge that is being sought by virtue of the position he or she occupies.
- *End user*: Interviews with the end user enable us to gain an overall view of the problem domain. The end user sees things from a high level and is able to consider all the major issues.
- *Multiple experts*: Another potential source whereby existing information may be cross-validated is always useful.
- *Literature*: Important information may be sourced from documents such as reports, books, regulations, and guidelines.

Importance of Knowledge in the Present-day Scenario

To appreciate why a knowledge-based concept of the firm can be useful for strategy formulation, let us consider some of the features that differentiate knowledge transfers from tangible goods transfers. In contrast to tangible goods, which tend to depreciate in value when they are used, knowledge grows when used and depreciates when not used. In today's world, companies derive most of their value from intellectual assets rather than physical assets.

When knowledge is shared, it best facilitates collaboration. An effective knowledge management programme should help a company do one or more of the following:

- Foster innovation by encouraging the free flow of ideas
- Improve customer service by encouraging the free flow of ideas
- Boost revenues by getting products and services to the market faster
- Enhance employee retention breaks by recognizing the value of employees' knowledge and rewarding them for it

■ ■ ■
The process of effectively managing the knowledge assets of an organization is called knowledge management.

- Streamline operations and reduce costs by eliminating redundant or unnecessary processes.

Further, a creative approach to knowledge management can result in improved efficiency, higher productivity, and increased revenues in practically any business function.

The challenge of deploying the knowledge assets of an organization to create competitive advantage becomes more crucial as:

- The marketplace is increasingly competitive and the rate of innovation is rising, so knowledge must evolve and be assimilated at an even faster rate.
- Corporations are organizing their businesses to be focused on creating customer value. Staff functions are being reduced as are management structures. There is a need to replace the informal knowledge management of the staff function with formal methods in customer-aligned business processes.
- Competitive pressures are reducing the size of the workforce which holds this knowledge.
- It takes time to experience and acquire knowledge. Employees have less and less time for this.
- A change in strategic direction may result in the loss of knowledge in a specific area. A subsequent reversal in the policy may then lead to a renewed requirement for this knowledge, but employees with that knowledge may not be there.
- Existing initiatives, such as business process reengineering and total quality management, have helped organizations become more efficient at what they do. However, they fail to make the best of the company's talent or help them differentiate themselves in the marketplace.
- By retaining knowledge as they downsize or restructure, organizations can save costly mistakes and avoid 'reinventing the wheel'.
- Companies can save millions annually by taking the knowledge from their best performers and applying it in similar situations elsewhere.

These and other benefits, such as improved customer service, faster problem solving, and more rapid adaptation to market changes have resulted from a focus on corporate knowledge.

The aforementioned reasons have convinced the business entities of today that their competitive advantage lies essentially in effectively managing their 'knowledge assets'. The process of effectively managing the knowledge assets of an organization is called knowledge management.

What is Knowledge Management?

A simple definition of knowledge management is that it is 'about connecting people to people and people to information to create competitive advantage'. In other words, it is the systematic process of finding, selecting, organizing, distilling, and presenting information in a way that improves an employee's comprehension in a specific area of interest. It helps an organization to gain insight and understanding from its own experiences.

Knowledge management is first and foremost a management discipline that treats intellectual capital as a managed asset. The primary tools applied in the practice of knowledge management are organizational dynamics, process engineering, and technology. These work together to streamline and enhance the flow of an organization's data, information, and knowledge and to deliver them to individuals and groups engaged in accomplishing specific tasks. It is about partnering technology with a corporate culture and business processes and using it as the vehicle to manage and deliver the business information and expertise of fellow workers to the most fundamental driver of business growth, the knowledge worker.

> ■ ■ ■
> The framework of the knowledge management initiative of any organization should cater to knowledge needs at all levels.

The framework of the knowledge management initiative of any organization should cater to knowledge needs at all levels—strategic, technical, and operational. Such a knowledge management framework should take care of the following:

- What are the knowledge assets a company possesses?
- Where is the knowledge asset?
- What does it contain?
- What is its use?
- What form is it in?
- How accessible is it?
- How can the knowledge add value?
- What are the opportunities for using knowledge assets?
- What would be the effect of its use?
- What are the current obstacles to its use?
- What would be its increased value to the company?
- What actions are necessary to achieve better usability and added value?
- How are actions to use the knowledge asset planned?
- How are the actions enacted?
- How to monitor actions?
- Has the use of the knowledge ensured added value?
- Did the use of it produce the desired value?
- How can the asset be maintained for this use?
- Did the use create new opportunities?

Approaches

The approaches to knowledge management can be categorized into three types.

- Mechanistic approach
- Cultural/behavioural approach
- Systematic approach

Each approach differs in its base. The assumptions and assessment of each may be summarized as shown in Table 19.1.

TABLE 19.1 Knowledge management and approaches

	Mechanistic	Cultural/behavioural	Systematic
Approach	It is characterized by the application of technology and resources to do better.	This approach focuses on innovation and creativity (the learning organization) rather than on leveraging existing explicit resources.	This approach is rational coupled with new ways of thinking.
Assumption	Accessibility to information is the key. Reuse of documents, intranet including networking technologies, groupware, etc., will make it work.	Behaviour, culture, and environment need to be changed and not just technology. The role of process is emphasized.	A systematic way of reviewing the processes, cultural patterns, and practices is needed.
Assessment	Unless 'experience' is combined in this model, it becomes yet another paper model.	Interplay of culture and organizational change may not be measured, cumulative, or replicable.	It has shown sustained positive results.

Process

The process of knowledge management covers information (both internal as well as external), experiences of the employees, and details of the systems/guidelines/process and procedures. The aim is to empower employees with the required information and knowledge in order to improve their performance and productivity.

The process of knowledge management consists of other sub-processes starting from identifying knowledge to retrieving and reusing organizational knowledge. The sub-processes may be broadly classified as follows:

- *Identification*: In this process, the knowledge that exists in various forms in, for instance, files, computers, conversations, minds of various people, etc., is identified. The entire process is long drawn and has to be democratic for its success. The best way for organizations to identify knowledge is to create teams of IT and respective departments, which can study the functioning of each department, identify the processes that generate data, and distinguish between the routine and repetitive activities and value adding activities.

- *Elicitation*: The next step is to retrieve the knowledge that is identified. As knowledge can be obtained directly and indirectly from available sources, the elicitation methods also vary. Appropriate systems need to be created to gather information. Some of these systems are interview, case study, protocols, simulation, prototyping, observation, and document analysis. In order to facilitate the acceptance of these methods, it is essential that employees from the respective functions/departments are involved in these exercises, for two reasons: first, to tap their in-depth knowledge; second, to train the employee for delegation of responsibility in the future.

- *Classification*: The third step is to classify the retrieved knowledge. The aim of this process is to put organizational knowledge into a form that makes it accessible to those who need it. Knowledge managers can categorize knowledge, describe it, map it, simulate it, and embed it in rules. Each of these has its own value and can be applied singly or in combination. Needless to say, new technologies make the prospects for these activities increasingly promising.

- *Storing*: The gathered knowledge has to be stored in such a way that it is readily and easily accessible. Building a robust infrastructure will allow knowledge to be leveraged through systems and technology platforms. It includes common communication, infrastructure, easy accessibility to knowledge sources, and having a common organizational vocabulary.

> ■ ■ ■
> Creating a sense of community within the organization is an important mechanism for enabling knowledge-creating cycles.

Besides these steps, creating a sense of community within the organization is an important mechanism for enabling knowledge-creating cycles.

Initiatives around the World

The following are some of the knowledge management initiatives taken by companies and practitioners worldwide. These initiatives reveal how companies create value from their intangible assets.

- National Bicycle Industrial Company Ltd, Japan, produces 'mass customized' bikes to the customer's exact height, weight, and colour preferences in a day. This is achieved through computer-aided designs and computer-integrated manufacturing, integrated with customer database. The organization has created a database of product designs that were developed internally by the R&D team. Further, it can also evaluate the product designs of the competitors against its own. The entire exercise has helped the company to be more aware of the design requirements from the customer's perspective and meet customer requirements. This has led to surge in sales and profits.

- Netscape, USA, has very close links with customers through the Internet. Customers are encouraged to report problems that enables the company to create new generations of software. This system has helped the organization to have a better understanding of the problems of the customers. By doing so, it has been able to provide data to its software development team to develop better software. The entire exercise has helped in developing shared and collective learning amongst the employees. It has also led to increased sales and revenues for the organization.

- Agro Corporation, USA, sells fertilizers and seeds. Data on farmer's soils are combined with weather forecasts and implementation on crops. The obtained analysis is sent back to the farmer through sales representatives to help farmers select the best combination of crops.

- 3M, USA, with 60,000 products from their own innovation process, tries to find a balance between creativity and conservatism. It values and encourages learning and risk taking, but managers are required to link continuous learning to revenues.

- McKinsey, the management consulting firm, has developed 'knowledge databases' that contain experiences from every assignment including names of team members and client revelations. Each team appoints a 'historian' to document the work.

- British Petroleum uses knowledge management as a means of drawing together talents from all over the organization. The company emphasizes transfer of tacit knowledge and has installed communication networks comprising videoconferencing, multimedia, and e-mail.

- Pfizer, Switzerland, has created competence models for recruiting treasury executives that call for knowledge building/sharing in addition to basic financial skills.

- Xerox, USA, provides convenient places where people can get together routinely to enhance cross-functional lines.

- Mitsushita, Japan, launched a company-wide policy to reduce yearly working time to 1,800 hours. Mitsushita created a promotion office with the task of facilitating experiments with the policy for one month by working 150 hours. Through such an experience employees got to know what 1,800 hours a year would be like.

The aforementioned examples of knowledge management in various organizations suggest that information and feedback, if obtained, processed, and made available to employees, would be able to invigorate the shared learning spirit and thereby contribute to improving employee performance as well as organizational performance.

- Companies that have applied knowledge management technologies have reported bottom-line business benefits.

- By introducing virtual teamworking using videoconferencing, British Petroleum has speeded up the solution of critical operative problems.

- By sharing the best practices among their semi-conductor plants, Texas Instruments has saved the equivalent of investing in a new plant.

- By sharing experience already in the company, but not known to the development leaders, Hewlett Packard now brings products to the market faster than before.

KNOWLEDGE WORK AND WORKER

The globalization of work and continuing advances in technology are changing the nature of the workforce. Information specialists called knowledge workers, equipped to maintain and expand the technological leadership role in the next century, are replacing blue-collar workers.

Knowledge workers, who are sometimes known by their professional speciality, for example, lawyer, doctor, programmer, information system designer, information specialist, librarian, teacher, and scientist, are also called gold-collar workers. Knowledge workers are also known for their special characteristics. They are people who can analyse, synthesize, and evaluate information and use that information to solve various problems.

A third way of describing knowledge workers is by their skills and abilities. People who are highly educated, creative, computer literate, and have portable skills that make it possible for them to move anywhere their intelligence or talent are needed. The employees in the IT industry are the best examples befitting this definition.

Knowledge workers basically use their intellect to transform ideas, products, services, and processes. They own the knowledge, utilize it, and still own it. Their main value to an organization is their ability to gather and analyse information and make decisions that will benefit the company. They are also involved in a continuous learning process as they are aware that knowledge has a limited shelf-life.

> ■ ■ ■
> Knowledge workers use their intellect to transform ideas, products, services, and processes.

Managing Knowledge Work

It is clear then that people possessing a certain type of knowledge, be it functional or otherwise, would certainly have an edge over those who do not possess it. These people may comprise a minority, but their expertise dominates over the majority. Another important aspect is that the performance of an individual, organization, industry, or country in acquiring and applying knowledge will increasingly become the key competitive factor for success and income. In the long run, societies will emerge as knowledge societies.

Some interesting characteristics associated with knowledge workers have emerged as a result of observations, which may be summarized as follows:

- Knowledge workers are eager to perform and they expect to be evaluated for their actual performance.
- They want that demands be made on them by knowledge rather than by bosses.
- They require a performance-oriented organization rather than an authority-oriented organization.
- Although they respect and acknowledge authority and responsibility within the hierarchical structure, they are also aware that knowledge work itself knows no hierarchy.

In a knowledge society, knowledge exists only in the form of an application. Knowledge in application is by definition highly specialized, which is why Plato and Socrates some 2,500 years ago refused to accept it as knowledge and considered it as 'techne' (skill).

Some knowledge work requires a fairly limited amount of knowledge, such as X-ray technology, for instance, while others might require a far more advanced theoretical knowledge, for instance, in business, whether in market research, product planning, designing systems, or advertising and promotion.

■ ■ ■
It is becoming increasingly necessary for employees to update their knowledge and skills to avoid redundancy.

What emerges is that whether knowledge exists in a highly complicated and advanced form or in a simplified form, it is specialized. In fact it is highly effective only when it is specialized. The shift that characterizes today's organizations is the focus on knowledge and knowledge worker. Hence, we have a new brand of people emerging in society and organizations. They are people who have understood and assimilated specialized knowledge, who are continuous learners, and are involved in the process of innovation in a different manner.

It is becoming increasingly necessary for employees to update their knowledge and skills to avoid redundancy. New technologies, which are taking over many of the routine tasks performed in the workplace, are directing workers towards the more complex tasks that require thinking, understanding, assimilating, new knowledge, and problem-solving. For instance, a new computer-guided system for finding defects in textiles does so with greater accuracy than humans and enables the work to be accomplished at a much faster speed. The time-saving aspects of new technologies not only free employees for more sophisticated tasks, but also increase pressure on them to develop new skills that will enable them to participate in the knowledge revolution that reflects the changing nature of the workplace.

What is obvious then is the change and challenge that the organizations will be facing in the near future. On the one hand, there is the demand for developing and maintaining knowledge management processes, models, etc., and on the other hand is the need to identify, retain, and motivate knowledge workers to gain competitive advantage.

Managing Knowledge Workers

Research indicates that organizations hire knowledge workers and leave them alone. They do not employ quality measurements, Six Sigma, reengineering, etc., or formally attempt to observe the flow of work. Further, they are not benchmarked, and there is no accountability for the money and time spent on their activities. Even if these assessments are attempted, the measurement yardsticks are varied and subtle.

The single greatest challenge executives will face over the next few years, according to Peter Drucker, is to learn how to manage knowledge workers. He observes that the vast majority of companies manage employees as though the companies still controlled the means of production. In knowledge organizations, however, it is each worker's knowledge and intelligence that combine to form the means of production. The organization cannot control or own that. A worker can leave at any time, taking the means of production with him or her. This leads Drucker to conclude that we must learn to lead and manage people in a new way. Companies need to learn to look at employees as assets to be valued rather than as costs. The value in a knowledge company lies in the minds of the employees more than it does in the machinery on the factory floor (Exhibit 19.1).

■ ■ ■
The value in a knowledge company lies in the minds of the employees more than it does in the machinery on the factory floor.

EXHIBIT 19.1 Pharmaceutical firms

Research scientists in the R&D units of pharmaceutical firms are given a totally free work environment. The chief executive/head of R&D does a periodic review of the focus areas of research, that is, diseases related to diabetes, cancer, etc., and provides information about the current treatment available and the trend of research (molecular/drug) being done elsewhere in the world. Based on these inputs, the scientists start their molecular research in groups. When they feel that enough work has been done and the results need to be tested, the head

(Contd)

EXHIBIT 19.1 (Contd)

of R&D, in consultation with the chief executive officer (CEO), makes plans for laboratory experiments, followed by live experiments on selected patients. The entire process could take between four and ten years, depending on the complexity of and peculiarities of the problem under research. In this kind of work environment, the organization cannot set targets in the manner of setting goals for a product marketing team. The scientists are knowledge workers, who expect a certain amount of freedom in terms of time and financial investment where the benefits/outcome cannot be expected on a quarter-to-quarter basis.

Knowledge workers are essentially investors. They make discretionary choices as to how and when their energies and skills may be invested in their companies. The decision to invest or apply the skill may be contingent on (a) ability, (b) motivation, and (c) opportunity available. Certain organizational characteristics such as job design, social interaction, leadership characteristics, and organizational culture play an important role in motivating the employees.

Organizations across different sectors are attempting to identify ways to manage knowledge workers. The methods being used include flexible work hours and environment, accommodation and furnishing arrangements for the employees and their families, opportunities for overseas scholarship, presentation of papers in conferences or workshops, holidays with family members, celebration of festivals/events, etc.

Few attempts have been made by theorists to provide a framework/system that would enhance the motivational levels of the knowledge worker. The employees in the future will be increasingly working in a knowledge-based environment where access to information and its availability will be a prerequisite. Since organizations are moving towards a flatter, leaner, and open system of functioning, there would necessarily be a smaller chain of command and fewer lines of authority to be crossed. In such a system, job responsibilities, expectations, and procedures need to be made available in real time for the knowledge worker to interact and make decisions (Exhibit 19.2).

> ■ ■ ■
> Organizations across different sectors are attempting to identify ways to manage knowledge workers.

Another vital requirement in managing the knowledge worker is developing an internal infrastructure in the communications area. This can be facilitated by email to all by way of virtual private networkers and cohesive distributed systems and having a standard organizational vocabulary.

EXHIBIT 19.2 The banking sector

In the banking sector, traditionally the view was 'Turn the page and learn the work'. The training, if any, was possible in the staff training colleges, nomination to which was based on the whims and fancies of branch managers/ regional managers to meet their training targets rather than on the training needs of employees. Moreover, the trainers in these colleges were quite often rejects from the fields, for which reason their level of contribution to the trainees' learning was questionable.

However, IT implementation has made a world of difference. The trainers now work in close coordination with the HR and IT departments on the number of employees to be trained in specific application packages and areas such as corporate marketing, retail banking, treasury, and network security. Further, the quality of trainers too has improved significantly for unless the trainers themselves have the expertise, they would not be able train the trainees. The lack of proper training can lead to disastrous consequences such as poor performance by the employees on the field.

Any piece of information or direction can be communicated instantly. Feedback can also be obtained immediately and can be monitored by performance reports and conveyed back to the employees. The knowledge worker would gain by this process and it would enhance their self-esteem.

Drucker stated that a knowledge worker shines in a team. Employee teams may be encouraged to meet, discuss, exchange, and build ideas, with no boundaries and constraints of operations. Coaching and mentoring may be the process involved. For instance, in the IT industry, most of the assignments are based on project teams. The project leader in these teams is more of a facilitator, who attempts to guide and coach the team members.

An open environment, easily accessible information or database, clarity in performance expectations and goals, and immediate feedback would enhance the self-esteem of the knowledge worker. This is why organizations such as Dr Reddy's have a set of corporate portals which provide their employees a whole gamut of information on product development, research development in their R&D wings, feedback from doctors regarding products, product information, etc, (Exhibit 19.3).

Boosting the productivity of the knowledge workers is the key to their company's survival and only limited progress has been made in addressing the problem, according to an analyst firm. This aspect is vindicated by the continuous hardships faced by HR professionals, who are constantly attempting to improve employee productivity through monetary and non-monetary incentives.

Boosting the motivation levels of knowledge workers is critical to their performance.

It is observed that knowledge workers tend to openly communicate the meaning of their work and are inclined towards information sharing. However, certain processes in the organization, such as operation of incentives, interfere in information sharing and might, at times, result in hoarding of information.

Hence, a company's best practices need to emphasize on relationships, collaboration, and professionalism and place less emphasis on formal performance measures. An interesting dimension that emerges is the fact that knowledge workers are committed to their work and objectives. Hence, the focus should be on processes and interactions. As the knowledge worker would be dwelling on ideas, reiterating, testing, etc., there needs to be a delinking of structure and facilitation for small group interactions. This aspect is evident from the process

EXHIBIT 19.3 Microsoft Corporation

As part of its Digital Dashboard initiative, Microsoft announced the availability of three toolkits to enable solutions for knowledge workers that deliver the right information at the right time. Available on the Web are Microsoft R Digital Dashboard Starter Kit, Outlook R 2000 Team Folder Wizard, and Team Productivity Update for Back Office Server 4.5. These three technologies make it easier for solutions providers and IT professionals to create 'Digital Dashboard' solutions and offer new tools for collaboration in Microsoft exchange and back office-based environments. First announced at the Microsoft Tech Ed 99 Conference, the Digital Dashboard initiative is a part of Microsoft's vision of knowledge workers without limits. This initiative focuses on how technology can help deliver a company's knowledge resources to an individual's desktop to support better decision-making.

of functioning in the software development teams in the IT industry, where the project leader and teams are briefed broadly about the project deliverables and time frames, and the working of modalities is left to the respective teams.

While assessing the performance of the knowledge worker, the focus needs to be on outcomes. The traditional scheduling of activities and working within the constraints of time act as hindrances. Essentially, the knowledge workers aim to be productive and enjoy their work, and a boss or manager needs to be sensitive to this and follow a non-interfering approach. The knowledge worker appreciates autonomy.

The HR functionaries in IT firms make it a point to train project leaders on these aspects. The project or team leaders, while guiding or coaching the team members, give an outline and leave the finer aspects to the developers in the team members.

Yet another related issue here is the time taken by the knowledge workers to complete tasks or innovate. There seem to be apparent individual differences in the speed and outcomes of performance. Hence, comparisons or stringent targets related to time may not be a desirable managerial aspect for the knowledge worker.

A knowledge worker's personality is typically an achievement-oriented one. They focus on commitments and expect others also to do so. On the other hand, promises made by the management or superiors are also taken seriously and they are expected to abide by them.

It goes without saying that knowledge workers will have to be paid satisfactorily, given that dissatisfaction with pay and benefits is a powerful demotivating factor. However, the incentives offered will vary.

The management of knowledge workers will need to be based on the assumption that the organization needs them more than they need the organization. They need to be handled delicately and sensitively as their mobility levels are high. They exhibit a lot of self-confidence and are interested to know the direction in which the organization is heading. They are willing to take responsibility and are interested in personal achievement. They also seek respect for the expertise in their field. Continuous education and training is what is expected of them. They prefer to make their own decisions within their sphere of competence. They seek the jobs where their abilities get manifested.

It is then obvious that organizations must create new employment patterns in order to satisfy a workforce that is utterly different from the uniform traditional workforce of the late twentieth century. Organizations may also take up wide participative management programmes, strengthen their communication channels, and make resources available for their employees.

> ■ ■ ■
> Knowledge workers need to be handled delicately and sensitively as their mobility levels are high.

In conclusion, it may be said that there is no single right way to manage people or organize a business. However, as knowledge workers will dominate the future workforce in organizations, the management must concentrate on how to retain, maintain, and motivate them.

PERFORMANCE PLANNING AND IMPROVEMENT

The process of planning the performance of the employees vis-à-vis the goals/objectives of the organization through continuous or gradual improvement can be termed as performance planning. The objective of the entire process is improvement of performance. Performance planning and improvement assume importance in the context of an organization's focus on performance enhancement.

■ ■ ■
Performance planning of the employees vis-à-vis the goals and objectives of the organization through continuous or gradual improvement can be termed as performance planning.

The ING-Vysya Bank (previously Vysya Bank Limited) implemented the Goal Oriented Performance Appraisal System (GOPAS) in the late 1990s to plan and improve employee performance. The following are the features of GOPAS:

- It aims at planning the performance of an employee for the ensuing financial year in advance.
- The performance targets are based on frank and open criteria.
- Performance is planned based on key performance areas.
- Planned performance is monitored on a quarterly basis.
- It includes aspects on training and learning needs.

In the twenty-first century, the importance of individual performance, in the organizational context, is more marked than ever before. Researchers ranging from various fields, such as organizational strategy, organizational design, organizational culture, organizational behaviour, and human resource management, have carried out extensive research, both normative and descriptive, on performance management through the control approach, the manipulative approach, and of late, the facilitative approach.

The researchers have carried out experiments in organizations to observe the effect of these parameters on performance and found a positive correlation. In fact, beginning from Henry Fayol, who had proposed the scientific principles of management for organizational performance improvement, where the underlying assumption was manipulation of human resources, to Hawthorne experiments, which were based on concern for human values, it can truly be said that there has been the advent of scientific approach towards understanding the factors affecting the performance of employees.

TECHNOLOGY AND INNOVATION MANAGEMENT

The early nineteenth century, which ushered in the industrial revolution, can be said to have brought the onset of technology revolution in the world. However, technology revolution has not been occurring in isolation. It is essentially characterized by interaction between transfer of innovation in technology and flexibility that could facilitate adaptability for better results.

■ ■ ■
The modern organization measures organizational effectiveness more in terms of return on talent (RoT) than return on investment (RoI).

Organizations, as sub-systems of the natural environment, cannot be an exception to this ever-evolving process. In the competitive scenario, organizations are in continuous quest for competence that would give them a competitive edge over the rest. A cursory glance at the practices of successful organizations, be they global, such as Microsoft, 3M, IBM, and CISCO, or local, such as Infosys, and Wipro, indicates that it is the 'speed of innovation' rather than innovation that makes the difference.

■ ■ ■
Organizational innovation is a new idea that leads to a tangible product, process, or procedure within the organization.

The modern organization would rely heavily upon talent and knowledge management and the effectiveness of the organization would be measured more in terms of return on talent (RoT) than return on investment (RoI). Hence, the emphasis would shift to the creation of a talent management system (TMS) that can effectively attract and retain talent.

The emphasis on talent is on account of two primary factors that have transformed the functioning of organizations, that is, innovation and information technology.

Any creative effort involves a certain amount of turbulence and, for organizations to be innovative, employees who can see things in a different perspective are required. Another major factor affecting the level of innovation in the organization is 'tolerance for failure' (ToF). Any new attempt or innovation cannot guarantee overnight success. This is particularly relevant in IT and pharma industries, where the level of product innovation is high. Albert Yu, Senior Vice-President of Intel's Microprocessor Products group and the person responsible for innovative engines of the semi-conductor superpower, is of the opinion that organizations would inevitably go through all the stages of grief—denial, anger, and acceptance—during the process of innovation. However, at the end of the transition, the organization would be rejuvenated and become mature in handling the crisis and increase its innovative capability in the process. Six things (Farren 2000) that are vital to an organization are as follows:

- A sense of purpose
- Leaders from core professions in the industry
- A research and development culture
- An emphasis on encouraging learning
- Sharing wealth
- Entrepreneurial mindset

Every innovation would lead to some perceptible change within the organization; hence, most often people tend to use these words interchangeably. Michael West and colleagues (West and Farr 1990; King and West 1987) have characterized organizational innovation as follows:

- A new idea cannot be called as innovation unless it leads to a tangible product, process, or procedure within the organization.
- It must be intentional rather than accidental.
- It must not be a routine change.
- It should be able to produce benefit to a part of or the entire organization or even to the society on a wider scale.
- It should be discernible and visible to the people at large.

The research questions addressed by occupational psychologists and compiled by Niegel King and Niel Anderson, (2003) are shown in Table 19.2.

Before we attempt to understand innovation, it would be useful for us to understand the research on creativity done by the psychologists. Parkhust (1999) in his attempt has given three definitions in terms of a creative person, product, or process.

Organizations can adopt several strategies for enhancing creativity through the following:

- Techniques for idea elicitation
- Brainstorming sessions for exploring or examining the exhaustible options in terms of ideas from the employees
- Online discussion groups and chats to facilitate exchange of ideas and debates among expert/ peer groups, etc.

TABLE 19.2 Creativity and organizations

Individual level	Group level	Organizational level
How should organizations select for creativity?	What are the characteristics of innovative work groups?	What are the causes and consequences of change?
Can training enhance creative performance at work?	What implications do social psychological theories of group processes have for understanding organizational innovation and change?	Is there an ideal structure, climate, or culture for innovation?
How is individual creativity related to organizational innovation?	How effective are team-building initiatives for promoting innovation?	Does the innovation process develop in clearly defined stages? How manageable is organizational change? What are the pros and cons of using internal and external change agents?

Organizations have been deploying various kind of tests such as the Kirton Adaptation Innovation inventory, 16PF, occupational personality questionnaire (OPQ), and Belbin Team Roles Inventory (BTRI). Apart from using western tools and techniques, Indian organizations have been attempting several methods such as outdoor exercises including task groups, trekking, and adventure sports such as rock climbing and rafting. These methods were proven to have developed team spirit among the employees, pulled down ego barriers, reduced monotony, and thus improved the creative and innovation skills of the employees. Research by psychologists on creative persons has indicated the following traits:

- Tolerance of uncertainty and ambiguity
- Self-confidence
- Unconventionality
- Originality
- Intrinsic motivation
- Above-average intelligence
- Determination to succeed

■ ■ ■
Indian organizations have been attempting several methods to develop team spirit and improve the creative and innovation skills of their employees.

According to the Gestalt School, creative problem-solving occurs when an individual discovers a hidden pattern that has not been seen before. Humanistic psychology is concerned with the individual human need for realization of complete potential (akin to the self-actualization need). Rogers (1954) described the motivation for creativity as stemming from a man's tendency to attain self-actualization.

Organizational Innovation and Social Groups

It is known from 'group' concepts that group norms exert profound pressure on the behaviour of individuals, more so in the context of organizations. Empirical research evidence has proved it beyond doubt that conformity with majority is related to group cohesiveness. The contrary

> ■ ■ ■
> The social identity theory propounded that group members tend to maintain a positive self-image by comparison with groups they identify as 'in-groups' rather than 'out-groups'.

research on 'minority influence' (Moscovici 1976) indicated that sometimes the minority would be able to change the position of the majority. Studies by Nemeth and Wachtler (1983) proved profound minority influence on the creativity in organizations.

The 'group polarization' phenomenon first researched by Stoner (1961) indicated that decisions after group consultation tend to be riskier than individual decisions. I. Janis (1972) described the same through the 'group think' concept where the concern of group members is more about protecting the group identity and the congenial atmosphere in the group rather than actually coming to optimal decisions. The social identity theory (Tajfel 1978, 1982; Hogg and Abrams, 1988) propounded that group members tend to maintain a positive self-image by comparison with groups they identify as 'in-groups' rather than 'out-groups'.

Nigel King and Neil Anderson (2003) in their studies on 'work group innovation' have discussed five principal research areas as follows:

- *Leadership*: It was observed that democratic and participative leadership style is found to promote group innovation. Manz, et al. (1989), based on data from seven innovations from the Minnesota Innovation Research Programme, have supported the contingency approach, based on requirements, as prescribing of one style is not feasible. In his study, Farris (1973) found that innovative teams were not those which were democratic, but those which had a moderate degree of control. N.R. Anderson and N. King (1991), in their article on 'Managing innovation in organizations', have proposed different styles of leadership for different phases of innovation (Table 19.3).

- *Group composition*: Team effectiveness is found to be higher when there is maximum interaction among team members and in case of a mismatch of preferences, the non-agreeing members would leave the job. As regards homogeneity vs heterogeneity, highly homogeneous groups are observed to be poor in innovation due to the 'group think' phenomenon, while a highly heterogeneous group may be at loggerheads with each other most of the time.

- *Group structure*: The structure of a group could be organic, where the approach to tasks is integrative, or mechanistic, where the approach is more of breaking down a task logically, without a holistic perspective. An organic group is found to be more innovative than a mechanistic group.

- *Group climate*: Nystrom (1990) defined climate as the collective 'feelings, attitudes, and behavioural tendencies which characterize organizational life'. The key factor affecting the climate

TABLE 19.3 Leadership and organizational innovation

Innovation phase	Leadership style	Manager's behaviour
Initiation	Nurturing	Encouraging safety and ideas, being supportive and open-minded, and ensuring a non-judgemental climate
Discussion	Developing	Obtaining opinions, evaluating proposals, agreeing and pushing to implement plans
Implementation	Championing/ validating	Convincing the concerned people about the proposal to obtain their commitment and ensuring participation in implementation
Routinization	Modifying	Checking the effectiveness and modifying/improving innovation

is the 'cohesion' in the group. Ideally, a semi-homogeneous or heterogeneous group is found to facilitate innovation.

- *Group longevity*: Groups with a short life-span would be focused on deliverables in the assigned task, while a long-standing group may become rigid due to set norms. Connie Gersicks found that new ideas do not evolve gradually, but happen on account of a 'quantum leap' in the developmental process.

Organizational Antecedents and Innovation

Researchers such as Rogers (1983) and Brown (1981) have done extensive research on the process of organizational innovation. The three important factors identified by King (1990) are:

- *Employees*: An organization that has participative, visionary, and/or transformational leaders coupled with supportive managers who are ready to act as change agents would have higher levels of innovation. Another aspect supporting the level of innovation are employees who are ready to support an 'idea champion'. Though not formally appointed as change agents, these employees find increasing number of co-workers who are 'idea champions'. These champions, with their high level of commitment, would be able to sell an idea across the organization and contribute to the success of the innovation.
- *Organizational structure*: John Child (1977) defined it as 'the formal allocation of work roles and administrative mechanisms to control and integrate work activities including those which cross organizational boundaries'. There has been substantial debate on organic vs. mechanistic structures of organizations. Burns and Stalker (1961), after extensive research on the characteristics of both structures, have concluded that an organic structure would support the initiatives of innovation in the organization due to in-built flexibility.
- *Organizational climate and culture*: After research on visible aspects, researchers shifted their focus to the intangible characteristics of an organization, such as the climate and culture, that nurture innovation in the organization. Nystrom (1990) defined organizational culture as 'the values, norms, beliefs embraced by the participants' and climate as 'the feelings, attitudes and behavioural tendencies' which characterize organizational life and may be operationally measured.

The climate supporting innovation must have features such as openness to change, risk-taking ability, and fault tolerance. As regards culture, researchers identify role cultures as bureaucratic in nature; power cultures as emphasizing status obedience and control; task cultures as a matrix structure with in-built flexibility and adaptability; and person cultures as emphasizing individual autonomy, decentralization, and informality. Each of them has its pros and cons and the extent of support each lends to innovation would be dependent on other organizational and environmental factors. As such, it would be tough to prescribe a normative structure for nurturing organizational innovation.

> ■ ■ ■
> The climate supporting innovation must have features such as openness to change, risk-taking ability, and fault tolerance.

Models of Innovation Process

There are several researchers who have described the various stages of innovation. Zaltman, et al. (1973) briefly described various stages in his model as shown in Table 19.4.

TABLE 19.4 Stages of innovation

Stage	Sub-stage
Initiation	Knowledge awareness: The organization becomes aware of the existence of an innovation, which it has the opportunity to utilize.
	Formation of attitudes: Members of the organization form and exhibit their attitudes to proposed innovation.
	Decision: The potential innovation is evaluated and the decision to proceed with the idea or abandon it is made.
Implementation	Initial implementation: First attempts to utilize the innovation are made, often on some sort of trial basis.
	Continued/sustained implementation: The innovation is routinized and becomes part of organizational life.

Thus, in our attempt to understand innovation in the organizational context, we have looked at various concepts including change, leadership, factors affecting organizational innovation, and models of innovation.

INFORMATION TECHNOLOGY AND ORGANIZATIONS

> ■ ■ ■
> There is a growing convergence of IT, knowledge management, and HR strategy with a view to building cohesive organizations.

Innovation in the traditional organizational context was a long-drawn process, involving a lot of time and effort apart from heavy expenditure for discovering an innovation, selling the idea across the organization, implementing, and routinizing it. The advent of IT with various tools and techniques has simplified the entire process.

Organizations in knowledge intensive as well as traditional industries are increasingly recognizing IT as a competitive weapon. They are discovering that with the help of IT, they can leverage organizational memory in terms of past experience and gain competitive advantage.

There is a growing convergence of IT, knowledge management, and strategy, with a view to building cohesive organizations, which are flexible, adaptive, and responsive, in accordance with environmental needs.

Traditionally, the IT infrastructure has been focusing on capturing the knowledge of experts in a central repository (Davenport and Prusak, 1998; Grover and Davenport, 2001). Employees, as users, tap the knowledge. The transformation in IT infrastructure over the last decade has turned employees into strategic partners. The shift in focus due to IT infrastructure has been from a functional work unit to process orientation. The IT infrastructure has enabled the channelizing of explicit knowledge throughout the organization to speed up the processes of strategy creation and implementation in several ways.

The emerging strategic requirements (Luiz Antonio Joia, 2003) has necessitated four major functions to be performed by the organization: (a) rapid decision-making, (b) integration of learning from experiments; (c) diffusion of learning across the organization; and (d) managing a portfolio of experiments. Antonio (2003) captured the knowledge management and IT requirements in the era of experimentation as shown in Table 19.5.

TABLE 19.5   Knowledge management and IT requirements

Strategic experimentation challenge	Knowledge management tool	Benefits/ outcomes	Examples of IT tools and applications	Future developments needed
Rapid decision-making	Visualization tools	Reduced decision time by allowing rapid visualization and prototyping as a basis for feasibility and go/no-go decision	Rapid prototyping, CAD, CASE tools	Real time display
	Group decision facilitation tools	Reduced decision time by allowing users to share knowledge asynchronously or in real time using rich media independent of geographic location	Group Support Systems (GSS), MS Meeting, Lotus Notes	Advanced multimedia and communication capabilities
	Knowledge representation	Intervention to identify individual mental models and to promote development of shared assumptions and goals	Decision Explorer	Repository of mental models to promote knowledge sharing
Rapid integration of learning from experiments	Decision histories	Learning requires the understanding of the original situation as well as the assumption, goals, and reasoning behind the decision to initiate the strategic experiment	Relational databases, Decision Support Systems (DSS)	Qualitative databases
	Group brainstorming and decision support	Capture and integration of knowledge using a wide variety of methods involved with the experiment	GSS using rich media, Decision Explorer	Multimedia enhanced communication facilitation
	Shared communication platforms	Efficient exchange of information and collaboration on individual documents and applications	Electronic mail, Net meeting, Workflow Management Systems, GSS, Lotus Notes, databases	Open platforms integrating multiple communications systems
Diffusion of learning from experiments throughout the organization	Knowledge maps or networks	Represents who knows what; allows rapid access to experts and expertise	Databases	Dynamic expertise coordination
	Repositories of case studies (learning histories) to identify	Compiles chronology of events and decisions; enables access to case histories; facilitates distribution of knowledge	Case-based expert systems, intranets, DSS	Case-based and focused search engines

(Contd)

TABLE 19.5 (Contd)

Strategic experimentation challenge	Knowledge management tool	Benefits/ outcomes	Examples of IT tools and applications	Future developments needed
	relevant precedent that sheds light on a particular problem			Neural networks
Management of a portfolio of experiments	Tools for monitoring experiment status	Provides continuous feedback about both qualitative and quantitative performance of strategic experiments	DSS, Content Analysis Applications	

Strategic Alignment of Information Technology

During the initial stages of IT implementation, managements allowed all-pervasive implementation of IT, without standardization, to facilitate acceptance and diffusion of IT skills among employees at large. However, as organizations moved up the value chain, they found it necessary to lay down a formal IT strategy that is aligned with the corporate IT strategy. The various steps initiated in the alignment process are as follows:

- Formulation of a formal IT strategy in alignment with corporate strategy
- Standardization of IT tools and applications
- Assessment of adherence to quality and standardization norms through periodic IT audit
- Safeguarding the corporate IT network and applications through network security measures

Another issue of debate for organizations in non-IT segments is whether to outsource the IT support, have the complete IT support in-house, or have a hybrid structure. In the era of core competence, non-IT firms are finding it increasingly convenient to outsource non-strategic functions. Even in HR, routine functions such as payroll processing, taxation, etc., are being outsourced.

IT and HR Strategy Integration

The IT strategy can be successful only when there is close coordination between the IT and HR functions. It is mandatory for the organization, before embarking upon implementation of IT plans, to ensure that the IT department is suitably staffed with employees possessing the required competence. More than other departments, the IT department has to coordinate with HR function to ensure staffing through the following steps:

■ ■ ■
Before embarking upon implementation on IT plans, it is mandatory for organizations to ensure that the IT department is staffed with employees who have the required competence.

- Recruitment of IT professionals at all levels
- Training and redeployment of existing employees
- Training and developing employees to get familiar with IT tools and applications
- Ensuring the commitment of the top management in the efforts through frequent communication and participation

IT and Workplace Design

Information technology has changed the layout and design of the workplace across organizations. We no longer see organizations piled up with huge volumes of paper, closely guarded for reasons of confidentiality. Instead, today we have sleek offices, in tune with the tastes of the new-generation employees. The advent of matrix structures has dismantled the huge executive cabins and given place to spacious work areas laid out with personal computers and, in some cases, cubicles that look alike for majority of employees. The seating arrangement is according to project teams—the team members and the team or project leaders are seated together. Physical communication has ceased to exist, except during the cafeteria breaks, as most of the communication is through e-mails, bulletin boards, and chats.

Employees are self-empowered for most of their requirements, such as leave, pay roll, etc. Information is displayed in the intranets, based on log-in and user IDs. Hence due to automation of workflow and empowerment on account of availability of information, most employee queries are addressed even before they arise. Networked organizations have gone ahead and implemented groupware solutions for workflow automation.

The workplace layout and designs are developed based on the following considerations (McCalmman 2000):

- How to manage knowledge and employees
- How to manage the interaction between people in numerous workplaces in synchronous/asynchronous patterns
- How to control organizations in a non-traditional manner
- How to manage closer relationships among the supplier, producer, and consumer (both on a B2C and B2B basis)
- How to manage the integration between the information networks of customers and suppliers

Virtual Organizations—The Reality

A virtual organization is a temporary network or a loose coalition of manufacturing and/or services that comes together for a specific business purpose and then disassembles when the purpose has been met (Christie and Levary 1998).

Virtual organizations share certain common features, such as use of IT for coordinating activities and the relatively loose coupling of multiple organizations, there remain various ways that such organizations can manifest (Evray and Niederman 2003). Researchers have identified various factors that contribute to the success of virtual organizations (Christie and Levary 1998):

A virtual organization is a temporary network of manufacturing and/or services that come together for a specific business purpose and disassembles when the purpose has been met.

- Focus on customer needs
- Choice of right partners with right core competence
- Win-win outcome for all participating organizations
- Protection of company's proprietary information
- New organization structure
- Trust
- Using power of information and communication
- Need for a new breed of leaders and employees

However, corporate leaders, based on their experience with technology, have raised a few concerns on information security due to interruption, interception, modification, and fabrication. Further, there are concerns on reliability, and the trade-offs involved in technology depend on the extent to which it can be deployed for non-virtual activities.

IT and Organizational Change

Information technology innovation cannot be explained as a contributor to organizational objectives or to the change process. IT innovation and organizational practice are considered as institutions in their own right. The interaction between them can be perceived as a dual process of institutionalization of IT and de-institutionalization of organizational structures and practices. Chrisanthi (2000) identified the following institutional elements of IT:

- The established view on the value of technology and knowledge as the axial principles for contemporary, 'post-industrial society' (Bell, 1973)
- A network of industries—including hardware manufacturers, telecommunication service providers, software producers, consultants, and units internal to 'user' organizations—which are creating, laying, maintaining, and further expanding a complex worldwide network of material resources and knowledge for technical information processing
- An elaborate set of professional expertise for the development and use of IT applications
- Sets of regulations for IT development and use, such as codes of ethical practice, copyright legislation, data protection acts, or freedom of information decrees
- Professional societies, such as Association for Computing Machinery (ACM) and International Federation for Information Processing (IFIP), promulgate standards of technology and practice

Technology and Organizational Learning

Information technology has completely transformed the world of organizational learning (OL). However, it requires a lot of planning to examine the readiness of the organization and also its requirements. The steps involved in implementing technology-enabled OL are as follows:

- Decide if the organization intends to purchase an off-the-shelf product or intends to develop it in-house.
- Decide the delivery options that can carry the OL to the employees at large.
- Identify the financial implications of the project.
- Plan to transform the organization into a learning organization irrespective of technology.
- Examine the technology update needs of the organization vis-à-vis the learning requirements.
- Evaluate training needs across the organization and the kind of technology that can support them.
- Study the readiness of the organization in terms of the mindset and attitudes of the organization.
- Evaluate the expertise available internally to develop and periodically update the content or alternately decide upon the sources from which it can be outsourced.
- Address the 'transfer of learning' issues through proper understanding of user requirements and also plan for action learning components in the e-learning process.
- Identify the resource persons who can be trained to be trainers.
- Decide the extent of support required from HR and IT departments for the entire process.

Thus, we have made a brief attempt to understand the roles of innovation and information technology in the process of organizational transformation. In the process, we have understood the role of organizational structure, processes in nurturing and supporting creativity and innovation in the organizations. More importantly, it has become clear that IT has played a major role in the entire process by facilitating organizational transformation and organizational learning.

SUMMARY

The chapter begins with the identification and description of the factors affecting the organizations in the twenty-first century. Subsequently, the impact of globalization on human resource development, knowledge management as an emerging tool, and the current state of knowledge management approaches and tools being implemented in organizations are dealt with. This is followed by examples of knowledge management implementation in international organizations. The chapter then proceeds to explain about knowledge workers, perspectives on managing knowledge workers with caselets for better understanding. In the following section, performance planning and improvement in the context of organizational strategy along with interrelated parameters, such as leadership, organizational culture, change, and learning, are analysed. The relation between HR strategy and performance, technology-based learning and performance, technology and innovation management in organi-zational context, methods of innovation and knowledge management, and IT requirements are also discussed. The chapter then proceeds to discuss the need for integration of IT and HR strategies vis-à-vis virtual organizations and aspects influenced by IT such as range and organizational learning.

■ ■ ■ | KEY TERMS

Cultural approach   An approach that focuses on innovation and creativity

Experts   Those who possess knowledge by virtue of the position they occupy

Knowledge   The condition of knowing something with familiarity gained through experience

Knowledge management   Connecting people and information to create competitive advantage

Knowledge workers   People who are equipped to maintain and expand technological leadership

Mechanistic approach   An approach characterized by the application of technology in resources to do better

Systematic approach   An approach that is rational, coupled with new ways of thinking.

■ ■ ■ | EXERCISES

Multiple Choice Questions

1. The following influence all segments of the society except
   (a) liberalization
   (b) privatization
   (c) globalization
   (d) training and development

2. The increased salary structures and expectations/aspirations of the employees are forcing the HR functionaries in Indian IT firms to adopt all of the following except
   (a) employee stock options (ESOPs)
   (b) performance management systems
   (c) flexible work hours
   (d) brain drain

3. Developing countries face constraints in the form of
   (a) scarce investment in resources and R&D
   (b) non-availability of foreign exchange
   (c) increased purchase parity
   (d) all of these

4. During the late 1990s, the HR departments made significant organizational structural changes, which included
   (a) restructuring
   (b) downsizing and performance-linked promotion

(c) rightsizing
(d) (a) and (b)
5. Knowledge management
   (a) treats intellectual capital as a managed asset
   (b) is sponsoring higher education for all workers
   (c) is training employees
   (d) is recruitment

Fill in the Blanks

1. The ultimate goal of knowledge management is to _____ with the required information and knowledge to improve their performance and productivity.
2. Knowledge workers, who are sometimes known by their professional specialty, are also called _____ workers.
3. It is extremely important for employees to update their knowledge and skills to avoid _____.
4. The _____ suggested that separation of the roles of chairman and CEO could lead to a conflict of interest between the actions in self-interest performed by managers and the ideals of the owner.
5. _____ is the process by which experienced employees share their knowledge through concepts and theories.

Concept Review Questions

1. Briefly explain the relevance of knowledge management in contemporary organizations.
2. What steps need to be initiated by the organization to integrate knowledge workers into the mainstream?
3. Explain the relevance of organizational strategy in performance management processes.
4. Analyse the various factors affecting performance management processes in the organization.
5. Explain the relevance of information technology to organizations.
6. Briefly outline the factors to be considered in the process of strategic alignment of information technology in organizations.

Critical Thinking Questions

1. Lal Chand Gupta, a first-generation entrepreneur, set up the ABC Corporation in 1941. The company began with manufacturing automobile spare parts and supplying them to leading manufacturers in the country. Over the years, they diversified into other industries such as textiles and consumer non-durables. Currently, the company has an annual turnover of ₹500 crore and its 1,800 employees are spread across four major locations in the country. Following the demise of Lal Chand Gupta in 2007, his eldest son Mohan Lal Gupta became the chairman and managing director (CMD) of the company.

Of late, the company has been losing its market share in all the industries in which it is operating. Mohan Lal Gupta has engaged a management consultant to analyse the working of the company and come up with suitable suggestions. After a thorough diagnosis, the consultant identified the following problems:

- The company has an aged workforce; the average age of its employees is 48 years.
- The machinery is outdated and requires immediate upgradation.
- The company should introduce information technology to network for management information system (MIS) and also coordinate the business processes.
- The company has to recruit professionals to change the organizational culture from paternalistic to modern.

If you were the CMD of the company, how would you respond to this situation?

2. Shrichand Industries is a leading bicycle manufacturer established in 1954 in Ludhiana. The promoter, Madan Kumar Ahuja, started the company with a small capital. By the early 1980s, the company grew to have a turnover of ₹120 crore. The strengths of the company include low-priced and robust bicycles and its brand, UNO cycle, signifies value for money to the consumers.

However, by the early 2000s, with the arrival of competitors, though the company grew, its market share reduced from 42% to 28% and the turnover stood around ₹202 crore. In 2011, Madan Kumar Ahuja's daughter, Ankita Ahuja, took over as the managing director (MD) of the company. She recruited Mukesh Jain, a young MBA from a leading management institute of the country, as marketing manager. Mukesh Jain did a market and competitor analysis and submitted a report-cum-action plan to the MD. The salient features of the plan are as follows:

- UNO cycle brand has been consistent in terms of market image of providing value for money and robust cycles to customers.
- It has not been able to launch new models since the year of inception.
- The competitors have been launching new models with style, finish, and additional features targeted at young customers.
- The company has to urgently reengineer its designs and launch new models targeted at young customers.
- Simultaneously, the company should also undertake brand-building activities through print and visual media for improving customer awareness and transforming the brand image.

- For the purpose of innovating its product, the company should leverage technologies such as CAD and computer-aided manufacturing (CAM).

If you were the MD of the comany, how would you respond to this situation?

Project Work

1. Discuss the case studies in the critical thinking questions section with your friends and arrive at an optimal solution.
2. Form a group and role-play these two case studies.
3. Study the profile of two companies, one from the services sector and the other from the consumer durables sector, and prepare an analysis based on the learning points in the chapter.
4. Prepare a case study on two industry leaders who have led the technology transfomation of their organizations.

■ ■ ■ | REFERENCES

Andersen, N.R. and King, N. 1991, 'Managing Innovation in Organizations', *Leadership and Organization Development Journal*, 12(4), pp. 17–21.

Borney, J. 1986, 'Organizational culture: Can it be a source of sustained competitive advantage?', *Academy of Management Review*, 11(3), pp. 656–65.

Child, J. 1972, 'Organizational structure, environment and performance: The role of strategic choice', *Sociology*, 6, pp. 1–22.

Deal, T.E. and Kennedy, A.A. 1982, *Corporate Cultures: The Rites and Rituals of Corporate Life*, Addison-Wesley, Reading.

Drucker, P. 1993, *Post-capitalist Society*, Harper Business, New York, p. 64.

Drucker, P.F. 1985, *Innovation and Entrepreneurship—Practice and Principles*, Harper & Row, New York.

Evans, J.S. 1991, 'Strategic flexibility and high technology maneuvers: A conceptual framework', *Journal of Management Studies*, January.

Eiesenharott, K.M. 1989, 'Agency theory: An assessment and review', *Academy of Management Review*, 14, pp. 57–74.

Hayek, F.A. 1945, 'The use of knowledge in society', *American Economic Review*, September, 35, pp. 1–18.

Hayes, Robert H. 1985, 'Strategic planning—forward in reverse?' *Harvard Business Review*, November–December, Vol. 63, 6, pp. 111–119.

Heracleous, L. and Devoge, S. 1998, 'Bridging the gap of relevance: Strategic management and organizational development', *Long Range Planning*, 31(5), pp. 732–44.

Heracleous, L. 2003, *Strategy and Organization: Realizing Strategic Management*, Cambridge University Press, Cambridge.

Kanter, R.M. 1983, *The Change Masters*, Simon & Schuster, New York.

Kiechel, Walter 1982, 'Corporate strategists under fire', *Fortune*, 27 December.

Nonaka, I. and Takeuchi, H. 1995, *The Knowledge Creation Company: How Japanese Companies Create the Dynamics of Innovation*, Oxford University Press, Oxford.

Peters, T. and Waterman, R. 1982, *In Search of Excellence*, Random House, New York.

Salanick, G.R. and Pfeffer J. Winter 1977, 'Who gets power—and how they hold on to it', *Organizational Dynamics*, 5, pp. 2–21.

Knowledge Management in Indisys Ltd

CASE STUDY 1

Indisys was started in 1975 by two budding Indian Institute of Technology (IIT) graduates in Bangalore, during the first generation of mainframe computers. The company got its first break by bagging a contract for business process support with C and C++ languages. The hard work and toil of its founders helped the company grow into a 1,000-employee-strong organization.

However, the big break for the company came along with other IT startups during Y2K projects, and the company grew into a 10,000-employee-strong organization.

The company continued to use the traditional word-of-mouth and classroom-based training approach. However, the company soon started discovering the pains of growth in the form of

- employee attrition;
- need to document the project learning and expertise;
- the constraints of traditional training methods; and
- fast changes in technology making it imperative for employees to upgrade their skills.

At this juncture, the company started research on knowledge management (KM) to support client requirements during knowledge transition and project management processes. The company started KM as a distinct practice. The first assignment for the Practice Head–KM was to revamp the entire learning architecture of Indisys.

The Practice Head, after a series of discussions with the chief people officer (CPO) and chief learning officer (CLO), decided to take the help of HR functionaries in understanding employee aspirations/expectations.

Simultaneously, the Practice Head asked his research team to study the emerging trends worldwide and to prepare a generic road map for KM rollout.

After a detailed study and research, the Practice Head along with the CPO and CLO suggested the following KM approach to the CEO:

- Create a core KM team.
- Assign a set of web developers who can support the project.
- Identify 2–3 single points of contact (SPOCs) for the project in each business area, who can support documenting the current processes and learning experiences.
- Roll out online self-certification courses in each project area.
- Upload the case studies in each project area to their e-learning portal.
- Train the HR team members to cascade the new initiative across the organization.
- Link the performance feedback to employee developmental plans and online courses.
- Encourage the research team to publish research papers in emerging technology areas and undertake pilot projects in different business areas.

Questions
1. Critically analyse the KM approach of Indisys.
2. Evaluate the pros and cons of the KM approach adopted by the organization.
3. Do you think KM can provide a competitive advantage to the organization in the marketplace?

Organizational Change and Information Technology

CASE STUDY 2

Modern Bank Limited was established in 1938 by Vasudev Mudaliar as a private bank. The bank grew to become a ₹100-crore business by 1944 and a ₹500-crore business by 1960. Vasudev Mudaliar was succeeded in the business by his sons. In 1974, an investor, Sudhakar Gupta, bought 51% equity in the bank and assumed charge as chairman.

The bank gradually expanded in the four southern states and grew to be a business worth ₹3,200 crore by 1985. In 1987, Sudhakar Gupta brought in Arvind Jain, a young MBA graduate, as the MD of the bank. Arvind Jain focused his energies on building the brand of the bank among the traditional segments and among the middle class. During his tenure, the bank recorded continuous business growth and by 1997, the bank's total business stood at ₹12,000 crore.

Arvind Jain was a fiery young man who essentially believed in turnaround performance. His style of leadership was autocratic and he believed that people around him should be committed to executing his orders rather than wasting time on debates and discussions. He formed a core group of top executives to strategize and monitor the implementation of action plans.

Being a traditional bank where hierarchy and authority were respected, it was not long before everyone adjusted to the new style of functioning. Everybody from the branch offices, regional offices, and the head office, religiously followed the orders of the top management. The result was a stupendous success. The bank became a force to reckon with among the private sector banks in southern India. Arvind Jain emphasized the following aspects:

- Recruiting top-notch professionals
- Reengineering the corporate brand of the bank
- Emphasizing marketing and business development
- A top-down approach in the decision-making process
- Adoption of technology for modernizing business operations

Along with the positive developments, there were a few negative aspects such as

- centralization of the bank's functioning
- formation of a coterie which wielded power in the bank
- emphasis on performance at any cost rather than on means
- frustration and disillusionment of the employees at large

Parallel with these developments, there were other developments too in the bank. Differences arose between the promoter Sudhakar Gupta and the MD Arvind Jain, which eventually led to the resignation and exit of the latter from the bank. A few of his faithful followers too resigned from the bank. The chairman, in consultation with the board, appointed a senior banking professional, Manoj Pillai, from an established public sector bank, as the MD of Modern Bank.

On assuming charge, Manoj Pillai reshuffled the top management and set up a new team at the corporate office. It was his belief that systems and procedures should take precedence over individuals in the bank, and that after goals are set, executives should be given freedom to perform.

A few hallmarks of his leadership and management approach in the bank were as follows:

- Streamlining systems and procedures
- Nurturing employees to strictly adhere to laid-down norms/systems
- Training of existing employees in core areas such as credit and audit.
- Recruiting and inducting young professionals, that is, MBA, M Com., etc., as management trainees into the bank to bring in fresh blood and enthusiasm
- Strengthening the training system for undertaking training and induction responsibilities
- Posting of successful line personnel as faculty in Staff Training Colleges to drive home the importance of training to the employees of the bank
- Continuing the technology upgradation processes undertaken during earlier review

However, the employees of the bank, especially the top and middle management, who were used to following the instructions and carrying out centralized decisions could not adjust to the new leadership approach. The top executives started perceiving the new leader as weak, due to lack of the charisma and strong drive that they had seen in the earlier leader. Further, the emphasis on reengineering the systems led to stagnation of product innovation and during the three years Manoj Pillai was with the bank, no product could be launched.

The bank slowly lost its market share and recorded a negative growth during the period 1997–2000. There was an interesting development in 1999, when the promoter offloaded a minor stake to a multinational bank. The changed business interest of the promoter led to further offloading of stake in favour of the multinational bank. As a result, the majority stake in the bank stood transferred to the multinational bank.

The new management undertook a series of measures to reengineer and redefine the brand image of the bank. These include

- upgrading the technology of the bank
- gearing up the bank for various technology initiatives such as core banking solutions, Internet banking, call centre, and help desk
- recruiting a new breed of professionals at all levels

and in all functional areas to cater to the needs of the bank

- implementing the performance planning and measurement approaches
- implementing cost to company (CTC) approach for all the middle and top management officials of the bank
- introducing voluntary retirement scheme (VRS) for employees found to be lacking in the new set of competence
- conducting massive exercise of rebranding and reengineering the product portfolio of the bank
- creating a core team of young professionals to continuously work on rebranding and product reengineering
- improving the learning infrastructure by networking the IT infrastructure with the existing training infrastructure to leverage the advantages

During the initial transformation period, the old genre of employees were frustrated by the higher compensation given to the new recruits as well as the importance accorded to them. This led to the exodus of a large number of employees through the voluntary retirement scheme. The remaining employees were in a state of confusion about the direction the bank was heading in.

In the meantime, the new management recruited an MD, Vikrant Advani, a senior banking professional with over 20 years of experience, to lead the bank, along with a new set of initiatives. After assuming charge, Vikrant Advani made it a point to personally interact with all senior executives. He communicated with all employees about the transformation process and the steps undertaken by the bank for the purpose.

As a step towards implementing the knowledge management process in the bank, the training department launched a whole set of initiatives with the help of the IT department as listed here.

- Setting-up of corporate intranet for the bank with built-in features such as bulletin boards and discussion and chat rooms
- Integrating the e-learning software with the Intranet to provide learning inputs to employees
- Identifying resource persons area-wise and making them available online to disseminate learning across the organization
- Collecting the critical experience of employees in various functional areas and presenting them as case studies for employees to learn
- Providing all the information and circulars related to various systems and procedures of the bank online to empower the employees with information
- Tying up with learning content providers for continuously updating the learning content

Questions

1. Analyse the case from the learning inputs in the chapter.
2. Do a SWOT analysis in terms of the technology and performance management areas for the bank.
3. Examine whether the technology transformation processes will lead to a change in organizational culture.
4. Do you feel that the bank is on the right track? Why?
5. Suggest steps for improving the knowledge management processes in the bank.
6. Do you think that e-learning should take precedence over traditional training in the bank?

Human Resource Accounting and Audit

INTRODUCTION

Organizations are increasingly finding it imperative to improve returns on investment, in order to stay competitive. Traditionally, accounting norms were viewed only from the financial perspective and were applied to all departments ranging from marketing, production, distribution, etc. Human resource management (HRM) was limited to salary and administration and, while doing so, it was analysed from the perspective of provisioning and expenditure.

However, in today's competitive scenario, it has become essential to analyse HRM activities and assess their contribution in a more systematic and methodical manner. The Indian industry has aggressively adopted various innovative systems, such as human resource (HR) audit and balanced scorecard, with a macro perspective of balancing performance management across all organizations. This chapter aims at the following:

- Introducing the theoretical framework behind concepts such as human resource accounting (HRA), HR audit, and balanced scorecard
- Explaining the strategic framework behind their implementation in international vis-à-vis the Indian context
- Presenting case studies to drive home the learning

Human Resource Audit

Human resource audit is the systematic assessment of an organization's HR service excellence. A good HR audit helps organizations to

- identify the HR programmes that are most important to achieving the organization's objectives
- find out how well the HR department is delivering these programmes
- benchmark HR work to ensure continuous improvement
- promote change and creativity

> ■ ■ ■
> HR audit is defined as the systematic assessment of an organization's HR service excellence and helps the organization to identify the HR programmes that are most important to achieve the organization's objectives.

- direct the focus of the HR staff to important issues
- bring HR closer to the line functions of the organization

Human Resource Accounting

Human resource accounting (HRA) is an information system that tells the management what changes have been occurring in the HR department of the business over a period of time. HRA also involves accounting for investment in people, their replacement costs, and the economic value of people in an organization.

Organizations can assess how much they can earn from an individual as the intellectual assets of a company are often worth three or four times the tangible asset value. Human capital provides valuable expert services, such as consulting, financial planning, and assurance services, which are in great demand.

In India, very few companies, for example, Bharat Heavy Electricals Limited (BHEL), Infosys, and Reliance Industries, have implemented HRA. Infosys, which started showing human resource as an asset in its balance sheet, has been reaping high market valuations. NIIT has been following a similar method called economic value addition (EVA), which helps assess the real value of an employee in the company.

BENEFITS OF HR PRACTICES

> ■ ■ ■
> The commitment of the employee is a complex factor dependent upon a host of factors.

Indian organizations have invested substantially in defining and implementing various processes and systems with a view to handling three main aspects, that is, competencies, commitment, and culture.

Competencies are not restricted to individuals, but are spread over teams, departments, divisions, and small business units (SBUs). They provide the lead and competitive edge to the organization.

The commitment of the employee is a complex factor dependent upon a host of factors, such as reward and recognition, developmental and learning opportunities, mentoring and fault-tolerance levels, etc., in the organization.

Culture is represented by the values and norms articulated and practised by the organization. It improves motivational levels and the commitment of the employees, and helps in instilling a sense of pride amongst the employees. The various instruments used for culture building in the organization include climate survey, value clarification exercises, and vision/mission workshops.

Organizations that inculcate good HR practices reap several benefits. These practices drive organizational growth. Some of the benefits are as follows:

- Capability to cope with leadership change in the organization
- Ability to exploit opportunities to their advantages
- Getting transformed into customer oriented and quality conscious organizations
- Transforming into learning organizations
- Training and developing their employees

> ■ ■ ■
> An audit helps an organization to assess its current position.

HR Audit

An audit helps an organization to assess its current position. It helps estimate what needs to be achieved to improve the HR function. The process involves a systematic review of all aspects of the HR function, typically with a checklist, in order to ensure that regulations and corporate policies are adhered to. The aim is to learn in the process or discover, but not to test. The basic premise is that there is always a scope for improvement.

A HR audit process will provide certain advantages to the organization, such as linking the HR strategy, reengineering the systems and processes, and improving the competency and functional efficiency of HR systems.

HR AUDIT

> ■ ■ ■
> Organizations undertake HR audits for various reasons depending on internal exigencies and requirements.

An HR audit is a comprehensive process, which begins with an understanding of the future business plans and corporate strategies of the organization. Some of the questions being raised during the process are as follows:

- What is the five-/ten-year plan of the organization?
- What competencies are needed to actualize these plans?
- What is the current level of organizational efficiency in terms of productivity, profitability, etc.?
- Does the organization have a learning culture? If not, how does it intend to build it?
- How are the various HR systems and subsystems being geared up to meet these requirements?

An HR audit examines the HR systems and subsystems in totality and in relation to various linkages and relationships with other aspects such as quality improvement processes and strategic planning. An HR audit basically has a business focus and foremost priority is accorded to business imperatives and prerequisites. It evaluates the HR strategy structure and systems and their appropriateness vis-à-vis the organizational requirements.

Organizations undertake HR audits for various reasons depending on internal exigencies and requirements. The reasons include

- making the HR function more business driven
- evaluating the HR systems and processes vis-à-vis the requirements of the organization
- improving the productivity and efficiency levels in the organization
- supporting the growth and expansion plans of the organization
- preparing the organization for probable change in leadership
- preparing the top management to set the strategic and long-term goals of the organization
- helping in transforming the style of management

Methodology

For a good HR audit, it is advisable to use a combination of methods.

The interviews can be scheduled hierarchically from the chief executive officer (CEO) to the HR chiefs, functional heads, the line managers, employees, etc., so that the auditors would be able to obtain a macro picture at the commencement of the audit and can subsequently relate the feedback from other constituents. Before conducting interviews, the auditors should be introduced to the people with whom they will be interacting.

During the process of observation, the auditors should attempt to look into various aspects, such as the physical layout, work environment, working conditions, amenities, and recreation facilities. During the meetings/discussions and transactions, the auditors should be able to select

> ■ ■ ■
> The auditors have to be competent in meeting and team management areas.

cross-functional teams, groups/teams from whom the feedback will be authentic and open. The auditors have to be competent in meeting and team management areas. The auditors can cross-check various aspects, such as the preparedness of the employees for the audit meetings, openness/receptivity to feedback, coordination of the meetings, interpersonal relations, and organizational conflicts.

Individual Interviews

The auditors/consultants begin their evaluation by means of one-to-one interviews with the top management and senior managers. This enables the auditors to understand the future plans of and the opportunities available for the company. Another reason is that these interviews help the auditors/consultants to understand the maturity of the top and senior management and also their style of management.

Group Interviews

When undertaking an HR audit in very large organizations, auditors may opt to obtain feedback from various segments of employees through group interviews. These groups may be selected on the basis of stratified sampling or random sampling methods. In some cultures, individuals may have inhibitions in giving feedback. In such cases, group interviews help to obtain feedback.

Workshops

In certain instances, the auditors may feel the necessity of replacing the individual and group interviews with large scale interactive processes (LSIP), with the number of participants ranging from 30 to 300. The participants may gather in a room to give a feedback on the HR function and systems. The participants work in small groups around various subsystems to make presentations of the SWOT analysis and the auditors record the feedback. The feedback could aid their audit process.

Questionnaires

The questionnaires can address the HR processes, such as career planning, work allocation, learning and developmental systems, and quality orientation. For the purpose of capturing the real picture, the auditors should do some homework before selecting various parameters in the questionnaire and assigning weighted averages to each of the items in the questionnaire depending on the organizational requirement. Another caution for the auditors is to sufficiently map all the key HR practices while designing the questionnaire. The auditors should also be conscious and empathetic while designing each of the parameters. Typically, some of the questionnaires design the items in the questionnaire with the OCTAPAC (openness, confrontation, trust, autonomy, proaction, authenticity, and collaboration) parameters.

> ■ ■ ■
> The auditors should also be conscious and empathetic while designing each of the parameters.

Dr Udai Pareek and Dr T.V. Rao have developed a questionnaire with over 250 items that takes around 90 minutes to complete. It can be administered individually or to a group. The individuals/groups are invited to assemble in a location and the objectives of the HR audit are explained to them and subsequently the questionnaire is provided to them for feedback. The questionnaire tries to assess various aspects, such as the competence of the HR staff, style of line managers, efficacy, and user friendliness in implementing various HR systems. The foremost benefit of the questionnaire is that it helps in benchmarking the systems and processes.

Observations

Auditors make it a point to visit the workplace, including the plant machinery room, canteen, and welfare amenities such as hospitals/schools being run by the management. These visits help the auditors assess the environment and the welfare orientation of the organization. Employees will not be giving their best to the organization unless they are provided with good surroundings and welfare amenities for themselves and their dependents. These observations are recorded with the help of a checklist.

Secondary Analysis

The analysis of secondary data gives a lot of insight into the state of affairs in an organization. For instance, an organization may have around 500 programmers in the J2E platform with a number of projects in that area. If the number of trained people is inadequate, it is an indication that the organization is not focusing upon building the competencies of the people working on the projects, leading to a possible drop in quality or standard.

The areas covered under the regulatory compliance audit include

- personal files and record keeping
- job descriptions
- compliance with the statutory requirements such as the Compensation Act, and rules regarding employees' state insurance (ESI), provident fund (PF), and gratuity

Challenges

An HR audit starts with an evaluation of the HR strategies, which either flow from or are aligned with the corporate strategies. However, in the absence of a correlation between the HR and corporate strategy, HR audit lacks direction and gets relegated to becoming a pure administrative and routine function.

The challenge in the IT and globalized era is to build and sustain world-class organizations. Irrespective of the specific strategy followed, organizations have to address the following challenges:

- Building and improving quality consciousness
- Striving to recruit and retain competent, creative, and committed employees
- Aligning the business processes with the technology infrastructure and leveraging it for competitive advantage
- Nurturing a creative and supportive work culture, which endanger professionalism and motivation among the employees
- Improving the responsiveness of the organization to environmental demands

■ ■ ■
An HR audit starts with an evaluation of HR strategies that either flow from or are aligned with corporate strategies.

- Retaining the flexibility and suppleness of the organization in spite of growth and development
- Training and developing the people through various interventions such as training, mentoring, and 360 degree feedback.
- Promoting learning orientation among the employees and facilitating the formation of informal networks to create a learning organization

Scope of HR Audit

Organizations undertake HR audits for many reasons:

- To ensure effective utilization of HR
- To review compliance with the laws and regulations
- To instil a sense of confidence in the HR department so that it is well-managed and prepared to meet potential challenges and opportunities
- To maintain or enhance the reputation of the organization in a community.

An audit examines the important aspects of the organization and its management, and is a means of identifying strengths, weaknesses, and areas where rectification may be warranted. An audit is done on a sampling basis. In a sampling, not every instance or situation can be examined.

An HR audit can be used by an organization for multiple purposes. Some of the more common reasons are as follows:

- To identify and address HR-related problems
- To seek out HR-related opportunities
- To conduct due diligence for mergers and acquisitions
- To support initial public offerings

How an audit is conducted is very often determined by its intended use. For instance, the type of audit used to ascertain HR practices may be significantly different from the type of audit used to support an initial public offering. Although the areas examined may be similar, the process used and the depth of inquiry will vary keeping in view the intended outcome.

AUDIT PROCESS

The HR audit process is conducted in different phases. Each phase is designed to build upon the preceding phase so that at the end of the audit, the organization has a very strong overview of the condition of the HR function. These phases include the following:

Pre-audit information   This phase involves acquiring and reviewing relevant HR manuals, handbooks, forms, reports, and other information. A pre-audit information request is forwarded to the client, who compiles the necessary information and submits it for a review to the auditors.

Pre-audit self-assessment   In order to minimize the time spent during the subsequent portions of the audit, a pre-audit self-assessment form is sent to the client. The self-administered 'yes/no' questionnaire asks a number of questions about current HR policies and practices.

The completion of this self-administered questionnaire allows auditors to identify key areas for focus during the HR audit.

On-site review   This phase involves a visit to the client's facility and interviews with the staff regarding HR policies and practices. A very in-depth HR audit checklist is completed.

Records review   A separate review is conducted of HR records and postings. Employee personnel files are randomly examined as well as compensation, employee claims, disciplinary actions, grievances, and other relevant HR related information are checked.

Audit report   The information gathered is used to develop an HR audit report. The audit report categorizes action needs into four separate areas, namely, (a) urgent and important (UI), (b) not urgent but important (NUI), (c) not urgent and not important needs (NNI)), and (d) important opportunities needs (IO) are sorted out. With the help of this classification scheme, the management can prioritize its steps.

■ ■ ■

Preparation for an Audit

> The completion of a self-assessment questionnaire significantly expedites the audit process and allows for better audit planning.

A comprehensive HR audit covers all areas of HR management, such as recruitment practices, training and development, compensation and benefits, employee and union relations, health, safety, and security, miscellaneous HR policies and practices—welfare, strategic HR issues, manpower planning/budgeting.

Besides classifying needs in each of these areas, the HR audit also cites relevant laws, cases, and research to support the recommendations.

Auditor engagement   If an internal resource is being used, it is better to appoint the resource formally with clarity on scope, and to select persons who are non-political or those who are not high in the hierarchy. Further, if internal resources are auditing, they must be given training in auditing.

Auditors must have access to relevant information contained in employee files, documents, manuals, handbooks, forms, reports, and other confidential documents of the organization. Auditors must be given unrestricted access to records, once they sign an agreement for confidentiality.

Data gathering   The completion of a self-assessment questionnaire significantly expedites the audit process and allows for better audit planning.

On-site access   The on-site part of the audit is most critical.

USING AUDIT FINDINGS

How does an organization use HR audit results? Since HR audit results are classified, an important aspect is already taken care of. Critical needs should be the first ones to be addressed. Organizations generally have three options for dealing with audit results.

■ ■ ■

> The HR audit helps an organization to assess where it currently stands, determine what it has to accomplish to improve its HR functions, systematically review all aspects of HR, and ensure that regulations and company policies are adhered to.

- Use the HR audit as a blueprint or action plan for addressing HR needs.
- Address as many needs as possible using the organization's internal expertise and resources.
- Contract out those need areas where internal expertise and resources are not available or do not fit in the core objectives of the organization.

An HR audit is much like an annual health check up and performs the same function for the organization. An audit helps an organization assess where it currently stands and determine what it has to accomplish to improve its HR functions. It involves systematically reviewing all aspects of human resources, usually with a checklist, and ensuring that the government regulations and company policies are being adhered to (Exhibit 20.1). The key to an audit is to remember that it is a tool to discover and not to test. There will always be room for improvement in every finding. A formal audit engagement letter is prepared, containing the objectives, scope, terms and conditions, time frame for completion, and remuneration for the auditor. A confidentiality agreement is also made between the auditor and the organization. This starts the formal process of auditing.

EXHIBIT 20.1   Quick HR audit checklist

Conducting an audit of your HR function can be a valuable exercise that can lead to a better understanding of the important role human resource management plays in your company. The following checklist can get you started.

Purpose of the Audit
- To look for potentially serious problems (land mines)
- To find areas needing improvement
- To document processes for use in merger or re-organization
- To address compliance issues

Sources of Data
- What do the written policies and procedures say?
- What do the HR managers say?
- What do the line managers say?

Basics
- How many employees are there in HR (and related departments, for example, training)?
- What is the organization chart for the HR department?
- What is the HR budget?

Recruitment
- How are candidates sourced?
- How are candidates selected?
- Are legal requirements met?
- Are the same processes used for all jobs in all locations?
- Are processes followed consistently?

Compensation and Benefits
- What are the different policy groups (for example, management, clerical, union)?
- How is the base pay policy set?
- What are the grading/job evaluation systems that are used?
- Are there up-to-date job descriptions?
- What variable pay practices are in place?
- How are pay increments decided?
- What is the benefit plan?
- Are the same processes used for all jobs in all locations?
- Are processes followed consistently?

Workforce Review
- Are there any critical skills shortages?
- Are there any critical succession issues?
- Is there anything unusual in the distribution of workers, age, gender, etc.?

(Contd)

EXHIBIT 20.1 (Contd)

- What are the processes that are used for workforce planning?
- What are the processes that are used for succession planning?
- Are the same processes used for all jobs in all locations?
- Are processes followed consistently?

Training and Development
- How much training is given?
- How is the training programme managed?
- Are there any staff development programmes?
- Are the same processes used for all jobs in all locations?
- Are processes followed consistently?

Industrial Relations
- What unions exist and what jobs are covered?
- What collective agreements are in place? When do these expire?
- How many grievances are there per year?
- Are there any outstanding grievances?

Legal
- Are processes in place to manage compliance issues for all relevant jurisdictions?
- Is there any outstanding litigation?
- Are the same processes used for all jobs in all locations?
- Are processes followed consistently?

HR Technology
- What technology is installed?
- How up-to-date is the technology?
- Is the data clean?
- Are there any important technology projects in progress?

Strategic HR
- Whom does the most senior HR person report to?
- How much interest does the top management have in HR issues?

Some Other Audit Techniques to Consider
- Audit of the corporate culture
- Competency audit of HR staff
- Metrics-based audit, using metrics such as those proposed by the Saratoga Institute
- Audit of customer satisfaction with HR

Source: http://www.councilofindustry.org/newsletter/january05/webnews_files/page0009.htm, accessed on 23 August 2005.

MODULES OF HR AUDIT

A comprehensive HR audit encompasses aspects such as legal compliance, compensation/salary administration, recruitment and orientation, training and development, employee relations, communications, file maintenance, policies and procedures, terminations, etc.

Recruitment and Selection Assessment Module

As a part of the audit, the auditors while assessing the recruitment and selection module will examine the following aspects:

- The existence of updated and accurate written policies and procedures to support the recruitment and selection processes
- A periodic review and an update on policies and procedures
- The communication of recruitment and selection policies to all concerned
- The budget and time frame for the recruitment for various positions
- The methods adopted for quality maintenance in the selection process

Performance Management Module

An important element of HRM, after recruitment and selection, is the management of performance. The HR auditors examine the following aspects:

- The maintenance and update of clearly defined performance plans
- The extent of documentation of performance plans by the employees
- The involvement of employees in the development of individual performance plans
- The communication of the performance evaluation process to the employees
- The methodologies for the identification of high performance and the evaluation of objective measures in performance
- The training of supervisors or feedback and counselling

Compensation Management Module

The HR auditors evaluating the compensation management examine the following aspects:

- The existence of clearly defined compensation plans and administative procedures
- Documentary support for salary actions relating to promotions, increases, demotions, etc.
- Written procedures addressing the statutory compliance requirements
- The procedures for examining compensation equity vis-à-vis similar positions in similar industries in the market
- The role of managers in compensation practices
- Documented incentive–award or incentive–compensation programmes and implementation plans

HR AUDIT—ACTION PLAN

The steps for improving the company's corporate HR function effectively are as follows:

- Define the role of the HR function in the context of the organization's current and future business plans.
- Create a system for cost-effective hiring.
- Develop programmes for the orientation and training of new employees.
- Develop and manage employee communication.
- Prepare key personnel policies and make it available to employees and also train the employees in policy adherence.
- Implement and install the human resource information system (HRIS).

ISSUES IN HR AUDIT

The methods of an HR audit can only be chosen based on the fundamental data relating to the familiarity of the auditor/consultant to the organization. Some of the issues to be addressed are as follows:

- Does the auditor have an idea of the business objectives of the organization?
- Is the auditor aware of the competitive dynamics and the relative position of the organization?
- Has the auditor developed sufficient knowledge about the business environment?
- Does the auditor have the competencies and skills required in understanding, tabulating, and analysing the feedback to be collected during the audit process?
- Does the auditor have the capability of clarifying the role expectations of various departments, executives, individuals, etc.?

LIMITATIONS OF HR AUDIT

> ■ ■ ■
> An HR audit does not give an evaluation of the individuals, but it essentially focuses upon units and systems.

Any audit is undertaken to evaluate the effectiveness of systems and procedures. The HR audit is not an exception. However, if the HR audit is held due to the directives/fancies of the CEO, it can lead to negative results. For instance, initially the top management may be very supportive of the HR audit process. However, when the feedback is continuously negative, they may become hostile and sometimes even aggressive with the auditors. Quite often the failure of an HR audit is on account of failure in the implementation of corrective action based on the feedback. There have been instances when the HR audit is used for a negative purpose, such as victimizing the HR department and removing some of the HR employees. HR audit should be voluntary and should be proactively undertaken by the management. There should not be any compulsion to conduct HR audit, in order to facilitate a fair and objective report generation.

An HR audit does not give an evaluation of the individuals, but it essentially focuses upon units and systems. However, if consultants so desire, they can give a formal feedback to the individuals.

BALANCED SCORECARD

Today, it has become essential for all the functional areas to get linked to corporate strategy. This requirement becomes more pronounced in the context of the HR function. It has been realized the world over, especially in the corporate world, that the human assets are the most valuable ones. To facilitate efficient performance, it is essential that job profiles should get linked to the corporate vision. It is in this context that the balanced scorecard has been formulated.

> ■ ■ ■
> A balanced scorecard provides an overall view of the organization's performance by integrating financial measures along with key performance indicators.

A balanced scorecard provides a framework for organizations to manage the implementation of strategy in an organization by linking the objectives, initiatives, and corresponding measures for evaluating success in the organizations. In brief, it provides an overall view of the organization's performance by integrating financial measures, along with key performance indicators, that is, the perspective of customers, internal business processes, organizational growth, learning, and innovation.

Robert Kaplan and David Norton developed the balanced scorecard as a performance measurement system. It evaluates organizational performance from various perspectives, that is, the perspectives of the customer, the business process, the learning measures apart from the user feedback, and the financial measures.

The financial perspective includes the operating income, return on capital employed (ROCE), and economic value added (EVA). The customer's perspective is measured through customer satisfaction, retention, and market share in target segments. The business process perspective includes cost, throughput, and quality. These are required for business processes such as procurement, production, and order fulfilment. The employee learning and growth is measured through employee satisfaction, employee retention, skill sets, etc.

The important aspects to be taken care of by organizations while devising the balanced scorecard are the objectives, measures/parameters for assessment, specific targets to be achieved, and more importantly the initiatives to be undertaken by the organizations.

The construction of an individual organization's balanced scorecard can be accomplished through a systematic process, by building consciences and clarity in terms of the translation of the business unit's machines and strategy into operational objective measures. Before the organization embarks upon the implementation of a balanced scorecard programme, it is essential to guide the senior management on issues such as the requirement and reason behind development and the adoption of the balanced scorecard in the business and also the conceptual backdrop. The steps involved in the process are as follows:

- Defining objectives and levels at the corporate level
- Linking corporate objectives to individual line of business (LOB) and measures
- Linking LOB objectives and measures to critical business processes

Need for the Scorecard

> ■ ■ ■
> The balanced scorecard is a comprehensive view of organizational performance focusing on vision and strategy.

The objective of every organization's measurement system is to motivate all employees to successfully implement the business unit's strategy.

The balanced scorecard is a comprehensive view of organizational performance with a focus on vision and strategy. To develop an effective balanced scorecard one should keep in mind the organization's vision and decide which strategies will lead to successful goal attainment. Thus, once a vision and subsequent strategy have been developed, the individual metrics—or vital signs—will emerge from that exercise quite naturally.

Building a Balanced Scorecard

The balanced scorecard framework and its information foundation can be created using the following ten steps:

- Building the business case
- Identifying strategies
- Identifying tactical objectives
- Identifying performance measurements
- Identifying data sources for calculating the measurements

- Creating a data warehouse to supply the data
- Selecting information technology to create the data warehouse
- Creating the balanced scorecard report
- Managing the strategy using the balanced scorecard
- Refining the tactical objectives in support of the strategy

Each of the ten steps is explained in further detail here.

Building the business case   It is critical to obtain executive support for the balanced scorecard approach to ensure that management support, resources, and strategic directions are made available. As with any strategic project, the first step in obtaining this support is to build a business case for implementing a balanced scorecard and data warehouse. The first step is to identify the experts and the key stakeholders, who should be involved in the design of the balanced scorecard, and to use their expertise to define the purposes and benefits of the project for documentation in the business case. The business case should also include a preliminary project budget and work plan.

The design team should include financial, operational, and clinical experts as well as information technology professionals. The team should be educated in the principles of the balanced scorecard and how a data warehouse can provide the required performance data.

Identifying strategies   The team should then identify specific business strategies that will achieve the purposes and benefits stated in the business case. For example, a healthcare organization's business case may include the goal of transforming its cardiology product line into a centre of excellence and marketing it as such to patients, physicians, and insurance carriers.

Identifying tactical objectives   The design team should then determine specific tactical objectives for these strategies using the four balanced scorecard perspectives on performance: financial, customer, internal process, and human resource. Some strategies will require that unique tactical objectives be developed. However, the balanced scorecard framework should include existing corporate tactical objectives that can help achieve almost any strategy (for example, increasing supply-chain efficiency).

Identifying performance measurements   For each new and existing tactical objective identified, the team should then determine outcome and driver measurements. The measurements will identify trends in the desired direction in the cause-and-effect relationships between drivers, performance outcomes, and the ultimate achievement of tactical objectives. The team should devise outcome and driver performance measurements that are effective in measuring the objective and will not require expensive or unfeasible data capture processes.

Identifying data sources   Much of the data needed to calculate the performance measurements may be obtained through the organization's existing information systems. Most of the financial measurements can be derived from the general ledger, accounts payable, grants management, and fixed-asset systems, and the remaining data often can be obtained from human resources, payroll, cost accounting, and budgeting systems. The existence of the required information in these numerous and disparate systems indicates the need for integrating it into a single source of information, that is, a data warehouse.

Because the goal of the balanced scorecard is to create views of the organization beyond the financial aspect, data regarding clinical care, external benchmarks, national performance indicators, and competitor market share are also required. Demographic, volume, insurance type, and clinical data based on coding (for example, International Classification of Diseases, ninth revision ICD-9, current procedural terminology (CPT), diagnosis related groups (DRG) are generally obtained from a patient billing or the medical record system. Demographics, market research, satisfaction survey results, severity and risk indexing, and quality-of-care measurements are not usually captured by traditional healthcare information systems and need to be purchased from a consulting firm, obtained through purchased software, or created using custom data collection methods.

Creating the data warehouse   A data warehouse is the information foundation for a specific analytical subject area—in this case, performance measurement. The many disparate information sources cited here need to be brought together, corrected, and organized into a data warehouse designed specifically for the analytical needs of performance measurement. The required data must be extracted from the various internal and external information systems and data sources. The disparate data must then be integrated, the data values standardized, and invalid data removed or corrected. The process and information technology to affect the extraction, integration, correction, and transformation of data are best supplied by information technology experts. The data are then loaded into the balanced scorecard data warehouse.

Selecting information technology   A work group made up of information technology professionals and experts in financial, clinical, and operational processes from the design team should evaluate the data warehousing software in the market. The group should determine the functionality needed and an acceptable price range, then select and purchase the appropriate software.

It is also necessary to evaluate and purchase decision support software, which includes the spectrum of tools that enables the creation and analysis of balanced scorecard reports. A growing selection of software is designed specifically for performance measurement analysis. These applications typically combine interactive data exploration capabilities with scorecard reports and 'dashboards' that graphically depict the performance measurements. To achieve higher levels of flexibility and customization, the organization may choose to create decision support capabilities using generic development tools.

Creating the balanced scorecard   The installation of hardware and software and the design for the balanced scorecard then need to be accomplished. For most uses, the balanced scorecard requires data extraction and measurement calculation routines. The prepared data should then be loaded into the performance measurement data warehouse. Finally, administrative and automated processes should be put into place so that the balanced scorecard can be updated periodically with more timely data, new measurements, and new analysis capabilities.

Managing the strategy   With the measurements shown on the balanced scorecard, the organization can respond to those objectives that have not been achieved and reinforce those that have been achieved. For example, if the percentage of population on the congestive heart failure critical pathway is decreasing, the team can work with the clinical staff to identify and rectify the root cause of this problem.

Refining and reusing After evaluating its first attempt at the balanced scorecard approach and refining its methodology where necessary, the team can add new corporate strategies to the balanced scorecard.

In the process of building a balanced scorecard, it is essential to define appropriate measurement architecture with the following steps:

- Selection of an appropriate organizational unit
- Identification of SBU/corporate linkages
- Build confidence on strategic objectives through interviews
- Synthesize the feedback from interviews and make it available to decision makers and the top management
- Hold an executive workshop to assign responsibility to individual executives
- Conduct subgroup meetings for dissemination down the line
- Select and design measures in aspects relating to core financial measures, core customer measures, core learning and growth measures
- Build the implementation plan after discussion, with time frame for each activity

Balanced Scorecard—Strategic Initiative

The balanced scorecard, which was originally meant to be an accurate performance measurement system, was subsequently used by researchers for achieving the following:

Strategy clarification A balanced scorecard helps in the conversion of strategic objectives at the organizational level into quantifiable measures for the members of the management and in the process helps in the development of consensus among the management team.

Communication of strategic objectives A balanced scorecard can be utilized for converting the macro objectives into operational objectives and to communicate them to the employees across the organization.

Planning and aligning strategic initiatives The organizational objectives are aligned with the department and group/team levels seamlessly across the organization.

Learning from feedback The management and the other members obtain feedback on implementation of strategy vis-à-vis the plan. Based on the feedback they evolve or modify the strategy for its successful implementation through the double-loop learning.

Management Information System and Balanced Scorecard

Traditionally the management information system (MIS) functions in all organizations by whatever name in finance/accounts functions. In the competitive scenario, organizations find it imperative to identify performance measures, which not only cover the finance-related indicators, but also the people-, learning-, and process-related indicators.

The key challenge in the balanced scorecard is to identify and articulate the vision, strategy, customer focus, market reality, issues related to people, and the need for long-term investments clearly for promoting innovations in the organization. For this purpose, the organization should have control mechanisms through appropriate MIS. To get objective factual data in the context of the implementation of the balanced scorecard, organizations should have the following in place:

- A definition of the balanced scorecard and an identification of the appropriate matrix for each function/group/individual
- Identification of the transaction systems that would provide the actual matrix.
- A definition of the process of converting the transaction data into the required matrix after analysis of the MIS
- Implementation of the required changes in systems and procedures

SUMMARY

The chapter begins with an overview of the emerging competitive scenario for organizations and the urgent need for HR activities to refocus in order to support organizational objectives. Organizations are finding it increasingly necessary to analyse HR practices through regular accounting and auditing procedures as are being made applicable to other financial organizations. Further, the chapter also covers the emerging scenario of linking HR deliverables to organizational deliverables through the balanced scorecard. It explains in detail the HR audit process and the prerequisites, the processes, procedures, and the methodology involved. It also explains the various modules of the HR audit, the areas and levels, the drawing up of the action plan, issues involved and their limitations. The chapter gives an overview of the concept of a balanced scorecard, its various perspectives, the steps involved, devising an appropriate architecture, strategic reasons for implementing it, the use of balanced scorecard for MIS purposes, etc. At the end, the chapter also provides case studies to reinforce the concepts discussed.

■ ■ ■ KEY TERMS

360 degree feedback   An effective means of gathering information about employees' behaviour and performance at work, including employees' relationships with others

Compensation   Something, such as money, given or received as payment or reparation, as for a service or loss

Correlation   A causal, complementary, parallel, or reciprocal relationship, especially a structural, functional, or qualitative correspondence between two comparable entities

Efficacy   Power or capacity to produce a desired effect

Framework   A set of assumptions, concepts, values, and practices that constitutes a way of viewing reality

Holistic   Emphasizing the importance of the whole and the interdependence of its parts

Incentive   An additional payment (or other remuneration) to employees as a means of increasing output

Prerequisites   Things or conditions that are required or necessary as a prior condition

Quantifiable   To determine or express the quantity

Stratified sampling   Sampling done in strata or layers

SWOT analysis   A very effective way of identifying strengths and weaknesses, and of examining the opportunities and threats faced

User-friendly   Making it easy for the user to make desired choices

Victimising   To subject to swindle or fraud

■ ■ ■ EXERCISES

Multiple Choice Questions

1. In the balanced scorecard, customer satisfaction, retention, and market share in target segments are all measures of

(a) customer's perspective

(b) financial perspective

(c) business process perspective

(d) learning and innovation

2. How do companies facilitate workforce diversity?

(a) Rely on external support systems for minority workers

(b) Encourage employees to challenge the beliefs and values of other employees

(c) Build in accountability through surveys and audits

(d) Reinforce traditional values

3. The HR audit process is conducted in

(a) three different phases

(b) six different phases

(c) four different phases

(d) five different phases

4. Which of the following methodologies is not a part of HR audit?

(a) Questionnaires   (b) Workshops

(c) Group interviews   (d) Videoconferenes

5. An information system that tells the management what changes have been occurring in the HR department of the business over a period of time is known as

(a) Human resource auditing

(b) Human resource accounting

(c) Balanced scorecard

(d) Performance management

Fill in the Blanks

1. _____ and _____ developed the balanced scorecard as a performance measurement system.

2. _____ is the systematic assessment of an organization's HR service excellence.

3. The questionnaires address HR processes such as career planning, work allocation, learning and developmental systems, and _____.

4. If the results of secondary data reveal that the number of trained people is inadequate, it is an indication that the organization is not focusing upon building the _____ working on the projects, leading to a possible drop in quality or standard.

5. The financial perspective of the balanced scorecard includes the _____, _____, and _____.

Concept Review Questions

1. Critically analyse the emerging scenario in the area of HR auditing in the country.

2. Prepare a case study on HR auditing at an organization of your choice.

3. Prepare a brief overview on the scenario of the implementation of the balanced scorecard by Indian organizations.

4. Give some suggestions for improving the effectiveness and also the implementation of the balanced scorecard by Indian organizations.

■ ■ ■ REFERENCES

Kaplan, R.S. and Norton, D.P. 1996, *The Balanced Scorecard: Translating Strategy into Action*, Harvard Business School Press, Boston, Massachusetts, pp. 50–57.

Karunakar, B. 2003, *Balanced Scorecard: Concepts and Experiences*, ICFAI University, Hyderabad, pp. 10–20.

Oliveira, J. 2001, 'The balanced scorecard: An integrative approach to performance evaluation', *Healthcare Financial Management*, May, pp. 89–97.

CASE STUDIES

Many organizations and enterprises have been working with HRA in a formalized and structured way for several years. Some of them have published their results. Other organizations and enterprises have carried out isolated HRA projects.

The five case studies presented here describe different aspects of the subject and cover the following: a private production enterprise, a public service provider, a private service provider, a public administrative organization, and a private production and retail enterprise (Table 20.1).

TABLE 20.1   Details of the case studies

Organization/enterprise	Country	Topic	Key performance indicators	Stakeholders	Media
Novo Nordisk	Denmark	Employment rehabilitation policy	Number of employees	Employees	Conferences, internal newsletters
Frederiksborg County	Denmark	The learning organization	Productivity index, days of absence, staff turnover, savings in money terms	Politicians, employees	Internal newsletters, book published by the external consultant
Skandia	Sweden	Intellectual capital	Value added per employee, number of contracts (total and per employee), training expense per employee, IT/administration expense	Investors, customers	Every six months in separate reports issued with annual or semi-annual financial reports, CD-ROM, Internet
Environmental Protection Agency	Denmark	Demographic description	Staff categories, staff turnover, absence due to sickness, number of employees attending courses	Politicians	Agency annual report
The Body Shop	UK	Surveys on personal learning and development	Days spent on work-based or course-based learning, employee satisfaction with support from The Body Shop	Employees, investors, customers	Comprehensive values report every two years

Novo Nordisk—Employment Rehabilitation Policy

Novo Nordisk is a Danish-based international group listed on the stock exchanges in Copenhagen, Zurich, London, and New York. Novo Nordisk develops, manufactures, and markets pharmaceutical products and industrial enzymes, and has approximately 14,000 employees.

As part of the company's staff policy, several years ago Novo Nordisk adopted the following rehabilitation policy: 'Those of Novo Nordisk's employees who, for reasons of ill health, are unable to manage their current job are, in so far as possible, to be guaranteed continued employment with Novo Nordisk.'

Guidelines have been laid down for the handling of rehabilitation cases establishing, for instance, that cases are to be handled as close to the employee's department as possible; which budget centre is to take on the rehabilitation costs; and what is to be done if the case cannot be resolved within the business area in question.

Novo Nordisk's compensation and labour relations department is following and charting developments in the area. Among its conclusions for 1997 are the following:

- The number of cases has decreased by 20% compared to 1996.
- Two out of three cases concerned women both in 1997 and 1996.
- Muscular and skeletal diseases still constitute the main reason for employment rehabilitation.
- There is no difference in the age or seniority of cases in 1997 compared to previous years. Women accepted for rehabilitation are slightly younger and have slightly less seniority than men.
- Fewer cases tend to be solved through voluntary early retirement.
- There is continued cooperation with external parties and the increased use of grants.

It is evident that most cases of rehabilitation arise in the basic production department, the finished goods area, and the laboratories.

In 1997, there were 93 new rehabilitation cases, equivalent to approximately 1% of the employees. Of these, approximately 60% were resolved at the beginning of 1998. The number of cases, in both absolute and relative terms, is down compared to 1996.

The outcome of cases resolved in 1997 is as follows:

- 33% continued in their own department of Novo Nordisk
- 25% continued in a different department of Novo Nordisk
- 33% took voluntary early retirement
- 9% were resolved in other ways

With this initiative, Novo Nordisk has assumed active social responsibility for its employees. Although no calculations are available, it must be assumed that this policy has had positive results for the employees in question, for the enterprise, and for society.

The individual employees who get the opportunity to continue his employment, for instance, in a less demanding job at Novo Nordisk, maintain their quality of life, since they keep their job and their social network. In addition, the individual secures a better financial situation by maintaining the job rather than receiving social welfare.

Without actively making an effort, Novo Nordisk would have suffered reduced efficiency due to more sick leaves taken and reduced performance in the longer term until the employee had to leave the company. In addition, more employees would have left the company, resulting in lost production during the period between one employee's resignation and another taking up the position, and the company would have suffered the direct costs relating to the hiring and training of more new employees.

For society, Novo Nordisk's policy will result in reduced costs, as the number of people on social security income will be lower. Due to the higher standard of living and quality of life for most employees, society will also have reduced expenses relating to the resulting effects on family and relatives.

Source: http://www2.trainingvillage.gr/download/publication/panorama/5085/chapter5_en.html, accessed on 24 August 2005.

Questions
1. Critically analyse the rehabilitation policy adopted by Novo Nordisk for the retention of its employees.
2. Can an HR audit provide a solution to the problems faced by the organization?
3. Would you suggest any corrective steps using the techniques/methodology of HR audits?

Frederiksborg County—A Better Working Life

Frederiksborg County Authority is one of the largest employers in Denmark with approximately 8,000 full-time employees. The workforce is divided into the social sector, the health sector, the educational, industrial and cultural sector, the technical administration, and the management department.

In 1994, the County Council decided to make an annual cutback of DKK 15 million on the service area—a significant amount. The County Council had two alternatives: to privatize cleaning and other functions or to take initiatives to keep the jobs in the public sector.

The problems in the public sector were identified as hierarchy, job demarcation, and the lack of decision-making powers for employees, who were in direct contact with the public. The public sector was

to become more open to cooperation and to take on new types of work in addition to its traditional tasks.

A project based on the concept of 'the learning organization' was launched. The idea behind the learning organization is that the ability to learn from previous experience—good or bad—and to incorporate new knowledge into the organization is crucial. The organization should strive to establish new frameworks and create an environment that supports knowledge sharing and dialogue beyond job demarcation lines, functions, projects, divisions, countries, etc. In other words, enterprises should focus on breaking down systems barriers and human barriers which undermine social relations, communication, knowledge sharing, dialogue, personal development, creativity, etc., and establishing organizational forms, systems, and structures that encourage the sharing of knowledge and experience and create an environment that stimulates individuals to seek knowledge and personal development.

In other words, the learning organization is about changing management systems, culture, and conduct, and introducing high-performance teams in order to create organizations prepared for change, that is, total enterprise integration.

The County's project was to create a better work environment, improve cooperation, and ensure greater delegation of responsibility and competency. The efficiency targets were expected to be met within the scope of this project, and the project included a major training programme which included, among other things, training the County's own employees to instruct one another. Great emphasis was placed on the operation of new employee teams and on enhancing the qualifications of low-skilled employees.

The key criteria of success included:

- *Good cooperation with the unions:* This is particularly relevant, as the project greatly affected job demarcation and the working conditions of employees. Despite the reduction in the number of employees, the unions maintained a constructive dialogue, thus influencing the future workplace, with greater emphasis on staff policy and on expanding the competency and responsibility of the employees.
- *Constructive cooperation with the training institutions*: It was a big challenge for the teachers to take part in a project to develop an organization rather than teach fixed syllabi.
- *Solving temporary problems with staff*: As large numbers of employees were in training during working hours, it was necessary during those periods to hire temporary staff for their positions.
- *Ensuring that enthusiasts were placed in key positions in the project*: It was paramount that the County management was committed and that the project enthusiasts kept faith in the learning organization concept as the right solution.

The success of this project can be highlighted by examples from two county institutions. The first example concerns a relief institution, where teams have been established and common values, rules, and norms implemented throughout the institution. This visionary process is aimed at creating a common goal, and the result is outstanding—for example, the number of relief days has been doubled without doubling staff. In concrete terms, this means that 100 families now receive relief with the same amount of resources previously sufficient for only 50 families.

This positive result has led to the institution developing new relief methods on its own initiative in a happy and creative atmosphere.

The second example is an institution, the residents of which were prone to violence. Previously, around 600 instances of residents hitting staff were reported annually. After the institution started working as a learning organization, the number of incidents reported fell to 60 a year. As a consequence, absence due to sickness among staff fell by one-third. Furthermore, due to the tough working conditions, the average employment period for staff at the institution before the start of the project was two years, in the first year, after the implementation of the project, there were no resignations.

Financial Evaluation of the Project

The project has not yet been completed, but the necessary annual DKK 15 million cutback has been achieved. The cutback has been achieved by removing job demarcation lines, thereby saving time and reducing staff. In addition, the improved working environment and job satisfaction has meant a marked reduction in absence due to sickness, which in turn has had a positive financial effect. Following the success, the County and the individual institutions are still working on setting up procedures for measuring the effects of the project, identifying key performance indicators, updated procedures, etc.

Communication

The County management group identified employees, the local management, and the County Council politicians as the target audience for communication regarding the project. The unions identified union members and others as the target audience for their communication.

One way of publicizing the project is by publishing brochures written in cooperation with the County management group. Another means of communication has been to participate in conferences, etc.

Source: http://www2.trainingvillage.gr/download/ publication/panorama/5085/chapter5_en.html, accessed on 24 August 2005.

CASE STUDY 3

Skandia—Reporting on Intellectual Capital

Skandia is one of Sweden's largest service companies and is listed on the Stockholm Stock Exchange. The company does domestic and international business in insurance, real estate, and banking. The company has been recognized for developing a concept for measuring and reporting on intellectual capital since 1994.

Reporting to the public has taken place twice a year since 1994, basically as reports issued with annual or half-yearly financial reports. Each new report, about 15 to 22 pages long, has focused on a special topic.

Skandia's reporting model, Navigator, is influenced by the concept of the balanced scorecard, which is an internal management tool.

Table 20.2 depicts the concept of Skandia's reporting model. For each of its business lines, Skandia reports on a number of focal points. For its subsidiary American Skandia, which provides variable annuities (unit-linked assurance) in the American market, the report as of 30 June 1997 was as shown in Table 20.2.

It can be seen that Skandia has developed a number of performance indicators for each of the five focal points and it reports consistently on these indicators every six months.

TABLE 20.2 Concept of Skandia's reporting model

Financial focus	1996	1995	1994*	1993*
Return on capital employed (%)	31.3	28.7	12.2	24.3
Operating result (MSEK)	579	355	115	96
Value added/employee (SEK 000s)	2,206	1,904	1,666	1,982
Return on capital employed (%)	31.3	28.7	12.2	24.3
Operating result (MSEK)	579	355	115	96
Value added/employee (SEK 000s)	2,206	1,904	1,666	1,982
Customer focus				
Number of contracts	1,33,641	87,836	59,089	31,997
Savings/contract (SEK 000s)	396	360	333	371
Surrender ratio (%)	4.4	4.1	4.2	3.6
Points of sale	33,287	18,012	11,573	4,805
Human focus				
Number of employees, full-time	418	300	220	133
Number of managers	86	81	62	N/A
Of whom, women	27	28	13	N/A
Training expense/employee (SEK 000s)	15.4	2.5	9.8	10.6

(Contd)

TABLE 20.2 *(Contd)*

Financial focus	1996	1995	1994*	1993*
Change in company's IT literacy (%)	N/A **	+2	+7	N/A
Process focus				
Number of contracts/employee	320	293	269	241
Administrative expenses/gross premiums written (%)	2.9	3.3	2.9	2.6
IT expense/administrative expense (%)	12.5	13.1	8.8	4.7
Renewal and development focus				
Share of gross premiums written from new	23.7	49.2	11.1	5.2
Increase in net premiums written (%)	113.7	29.9	17.8	204.8
Development expense/administrative expenses (%)	9.9	10.1	11.6	9.8
Proportion of staff under 40 years (%)	78	81	72	74

* *Accounting-based indicators for 1994 and earlier have not been recalculated in accordance with the new Swedish Insurance Annual Accounts Act, which took effect on 1 January 1996.*
** *New measurement method under development*

Questions

1. Critically analyse the concept of and reporting on the intellectual capital systematized by the Swedish group Skandia.
2. Does the report of Skandia have similarities with the balanced scorecard of Indian organizations?
3. Can we fine-tune the objectives related to the human focus for achieving better results?
4. Do you think it is also necessary for an organization to conduct the HR audit in the wake of the implementation of the balanced scorecard? If yes, please explain.

CASE STUDY 4

Environmental Protection Agency—Agency Annual Report

In 1995, the Danish government decided to launch projects designed to develop annual agency reports for a number of government agencies. The pilot scheme comprised 70 government agencies in 1996. Since 1997 the scheme has become compulsory for all government agencies meeting certain criteria of size and appropriation status. Annual agency reports should be closely linked to the budget for the year in question (the parliamentary appropriation).

The primary target group of the annual agency reports is the department of the relevant ministry, the Auditor General and the Public Accounts Committee as well as the Finance Committee and the Parliament. Secondary target groups include users of the services of the institution in question, the Ministry of Finance, the general public, labour-market organizations, other interest groups, and private suppliers of competing services.

The annual agency reports are prepared with public availability in mind. Among other places, similar high-quality accounts are found in Norway and Sweden. The main contents of the annual report are as follows:

- A narrative description of the agency as a whole, including its objectives and assignments, as well as its budgetary and financial situation, etc.
- Reliable reports on the financial and professional situation for the year, competition, etc., including
  - a description of financial and professional achievements
  - an explanation of the difference between budgeted and realized result
  - a description of activities carried out compared with goals set

– a basis for the assessment of financial con-sider-ations

– a basis for benchmarking with other govern-ment institutions

The standard contents of agency annual reports are as follows:

- Statement of revenue and expenditure
- Profit and loss analysis
- Staff and organization
- Grant statement
- Construction statement
- Environmental accounts (not required)

What is of interest for the purposes of this discussion paper is the requirement for a report on staff and organization. Such a report should cover the following:

- Staff time (in man-years) for the accounting year and the three previous years, and budget figures for the following year
- Absences due to sickness for the accounting year and the three previous years
- Staff turnover for the accounting year and the three previous years
- Overtime and additional work for the accounting year and the three previous years
- Description of the organizational structure and organizational chart
- Analysis and evaluation of development

As an example of how a Danish government agency has chosen to present its staff relations, part of the relevant section of the Danish Environmental Protection Agency's financial statements for 1996 is cited in the following.

Staff Policy

The primary aim of the staff policy of Danish Environmental Protection Agency (DEPA) is to create a basis to ensure that the Agency, as part of a political and administrative system, can perform current and future work assignments at a highly professional and resource-efficient level. The key words are readiness for change, adaptability, and flexibility. The Agency's main resource is its employees, and the staff policy is to recruit and keep qualified staff and to develop and enhance the motivation and qualifications of individual employees.

The staff policy is thus designed to ensure that the Agency's staff-mix and profiles are suitable for achieving the Agency's overall goals, strategies, and visions. In addition, the staff policy must fulfil the broad spectrum of demands, which the very varied professional staff make from their workplace.

The pivotal point of the Agency's staff policy is the annual appraisal reviews. A number of minor adjustments were made to the staff review concept at the end of 1996, based in part on a very positive external evaluation during the year and discussions at the Agency's Staff Conference. The Agency has implemented its staff policy in a number of agreements in the following main areas namely, recruitment, induction, skills development and career, mobility, working life and family life, working relations forums, working hours, work environment, etc.

Middle management consists mainly of academics with a social science degree. AC technicians comprise academics with technical degrees, that is, engineering, physics, agricultural science, pharmacy, veterinary science, etc. The category 'Other' comprises security staff, assistants, student workers, etc. The relative distribution of the Agency's employees at the end of 1996 shows the continuation of the long-term trend towards the expansion of the middle management and AC technician categories at the expense of the administrative staff (Table 20.3).

TABLE 20.3 Staff categories at DEPA

Staff category	Distribution, end 95	Distribution, end 96
Management (grade 37–39)	6.4%	6.2%
Consultants (35–36)	2.7%	3.5%
Middle management	22.3%	24.6%
Academic technicians (AC)	31.7%	32.6%
Administrative staff	31.2%	28.6%
Other	5.7%	4.5%
Total	100.0%	100.0%

Table 20.4 details the engagement and resignation of permanent staff during the period, including job rotation to and from other agencies within the ministerial area and to and from the Environmental Protection Agency.

TABLE 20.4 Staff turnover (permanent staff only) at DEPA

	1995	1996
Engagements	60	69
Resignations	43	43
Gross staff turnover as % of man-years	28%	28%

The average number of days of absence due to sickness within the public sector in 1995 was 7.1 days per employee. In Table 20.5, absence due to sickness is calculated in terms of man-years, and the average absence data is thus not immediately comparable. Using an estimated average number of employees with the Agency in 1995, the Agency's average number of days of absence due to sickness is approximately one day per employee above the public sector average for 1995, while the estimated average per employee in 1996 was reduced to approximately 6.8 days (that is, below the 1995 public sector average).

TABLE 20.5 Absence due to sickness at DEPA

	1995	1996
Number of man-years	372	397
Number of days of absence	3,217	2,857
Number of days of absence per man-year calculated as number of days of absence on weekdays due to sickness	8.6	7.2

Skill Development and Supplementary Training

The handling of day-to-day work assignments in the Danish Environmental Protection Agency places great demands on the staff. As mentioned earlier, one of the principal objectives of the staff policy is to develop and enhance the motivation and qualifications of each employee from a quality control perspective as well as with a view to securing and recruiting staff.

The most important skill development is in the form of in-house training for varying types of work.

The Agency seeks to enhance the skill profiles of individual employees through diverse tasks that have professional and personal development potential. The Agency has a tradition of giving each employee personal responsibility and, as much as possible, of letting employees follow a case from start to finish. In addition to workplace training, employees' skills are developed through various forms of supplementary training such as secondment, participation in courses, etc. The supplementary training of individual employees is set out at the appraisal reviews. The course-based supplementary training of the Environmental Protection Agency is planned and coordinated in the Central Supplementary Training Committee.

Supplementary training includes the Ministry's compulsory basic training course for new employees, as well as the selection of courses common to the ministerial area. In 1996, 313 of the Agency's employees attended 884 courses. In comparison, 267 Agency employees attended 606 courses in 1995. In 1996, an overhaul of the ministry's common supplementary training system was launched with a view to establishing a new basic training programme, technical courses, and a modular super-structure. Supplementary training activities within the Environmental Protection Agency in 1996 included the following:

- Implementation of a special supplementary training programme for employees on international assignments
- Implementation of a specialized accounting course for administrative staff
- Continued implementation of a special supplementary training programme for IT super users
- A special programme in connection with the Project Electronic Workplace for all employees

The increasing number of international assignments undertaken by the Agency has necessitated the institution of a supplementary training programme for employees on international assignments. In addition to assignments under the auspices of the European Union (EU), the Scandinavian countries and other international forums, the Agency has since 1991 undertaken assignments under the auspices of the Danish Ministry of Foreign Affairs related to environmental assistance to Central and Eastern Europe and certain developing countries. The international project work, in particular, places new demands on its employees, which the Agency seeks to address with the special programme for employees on international assignments.

In 1996, the Environmental Protection Agency continued its implementation of a staff administration system. This system rationalizes staff administration and helps achieve a more systematized staff development.

As the previous paragraphs demonstrate, the presentation is very open, incorporating policies and details from the staff interview programme, benchmarking on sickness, etc. The presentation includes a significant amount of specific data.

Source: http://www2.trainingvillage.gr/download/publication/panorama/5085/chapter5_en.html, accessed on 24 August 2005.

Questions

1. Critically analyse how the Danish Environmental Protection Agency has utilized legal requirements for reporting on 'staff and organization' to measure a number of HRA performance indicators and for benchmarking other agencies.
2. Do the main contents emphasized upon in the annual report have a close resemblance to the balanced scorecard?
3. Which approach do you think is more appropriate for the HR audit or the balanced scorecard?
4. Explain the relevance of the balanced scorecard to the organization.
5. Can an audit of HR projects reduce the turnover and absenteeism by identifying the causes for these issues and arriving at some solutions?

CASE STUDY 5

The Body Shop—Use of Surveys

The Body Shop is an international chain, which makes and sells skin and hair care products and has over 1,500 branches in 47 markets throughout America, Europe, and Asia. Most of the shops and branches are owned by franchisees. The main headquarter is located in Little Hampton, England. The founders and main shareholders of The Body Shop, Anita and Gordon Roddick, have committed themselves and The Body Shop to sustainable development. That includes, among other things, the measurement of social performance and the carrying out of the processes of social and ethical auditing.

In 1997, The Body Shop published their second 'Values Report', a comprehensive 220-page report. This report includes comments on the pursuit of social and ecological changes regarding employees, franchisees, customers, suppliers, shareholders, community, environment, and animal protection. The section on employees is 40 pages long and covers topics such as company aims, progress on environmental targets and performance relating to employees, employee consultation, employee views, occupational safety and health, animal protection performance standards relating to employees and new targets.

The 27-page section on employee views covers a number of topics including views on The Body Shop's mission and values, learning and development, career development, diversity and equal opportunities, communication, work satisfaction, working for The Body Shop, pay and benefits, and The Body Shop's actions in response to the social audit. Each of the subsections includes figures (tables and graphs) apparently taken from the files of the HR departments, results from comprehensive surveys in 1995 and 1997, and comments (quotations) from the employees.

The following quotation is taken from the section on Personal Learning and Development:

Following a company-wide reorganisation in 1994, a formal unit responsible for learning and development activities across all head office divisions was established within the Human Resources function to facilitate a more cohesive approach to training and learning and development in all head office and supply areas. By mid-1995 the Learning and Development unit had grown from one full-time training manager to a team of seven. In early 1997, it was decided that the Learning and Development unit should be established as an independent department and report to the newly established executive post of Stakeholder Development. The Learning and Development department now employs seven Learning and

Development experts as well as a team of five support staff. In addition to these, there were 13 full-time UK positions directly related to retail training activities. These were mostly field-based trainers offering in-store support to both company and franchised shops.

The Learning and Development department continued to reinforce the new approach to training, which was developed and introduced during 1995. The learning and development strategy adopted by the Company emphasizes the employees' assumption of more proactive responsibility for their own development, especially regarding proposals for development plans, and actively encourages them to seek learning opportunities.

The Body Shop published a Rough Guide to Learning in 1995. During the 1995/97-audit cycle, key initiatives launched by the Learning and Development team included the setting up of three learning centres across the head office sites that allow employees to access a wide and varied range of information at the time most convenient for them. Within the first year, 371 people visited the centres.

The 'Learning is of Value to Everyone' (LOVE) scheme, which is aimed at supporting personal rather than professional development initiatives of staff by subsidizing associated costs up to £100 a year, was extended from the supply division to the rest of the company. Between August 1996 and February 1997, 380 people availed themselves of the opportunity to learn something new.

A senior management programme and a number of other managerial and supervisory development programmes were developed and implemented during the audit cycle. Key programmes include five supervisory programmes (43 participants); management skills programme (29 participants); and the first-ever comprehensive senior management development programme (16 participants). Other initiatives have included developing a programme called 'Sharing the Vision', which is offered to senior managers who have joined the company during the last two years and which fosters greater understanding of the company's social and environmental agenda (46 managers participated between 1995 and 1997). Fourteen managers have also attended a programme, designed by The Body Shop in conjunc-

tion with other partners, called 'New Ways of Thinking and Working' at a leading management training centre at Roffey Park.

Prompted by the first social audit results, the Learning and Development unit explored the issue of professional qualifications further. The first employee survey results regarding how the company encourages employees to gain qualifications were moderate. The issue was explored in focus groups and discussed with the operational HR areas of the company. Subsequently, new policy and guidelines were introduced to clarify what support was available for those wishing to pursue further education and gain qualifications.

In the absence of a company-wide recording and monitoring system at the departmental level regarding learning and development activities undertaken by employees, the social audit survey in 1997 continued to solicit information on the learning and development activities of the employees.

Rather surprisingly, the recalled number of days spent on work-based learning has declined since 1995. Thirty five percent of all respondents recalled not having spent any time on work-based learning in contrast to 31% in 1995, and percentages in other categories also showed a slight downward trend (Table 20.6). From Table 20.6 it is clear that employees in the company-owned shops spend much more time on work-based learning—for example, coaching, job swap, reading, training videos, team building sessions, secondment, etc.—compared to those employed in other key areas of the business, especially to those working in the supply division.

The number of recalled days spent on course-based learning was slightly mixed compared to 1995 (Table 20.7). Although the number of employees who could not recall any courses attended decreased by 2% and the number of employees having spent more than 10 days on courses increased by 1%, the situation remained largely the same as in 1995. A slightly different divisional picture emerged compared to work-based learning: company shop employees are well above the average in categories from one to five days of courses, but below average in six days and above courses; the situation is reversed in the supply areas.

TABLE 20.6   Number of days spent on work-based learning in twelve months

No. of days	1995 Total	1997 Company shops	Supply	Offices	Total
None	31%	18%	46%	37%	35%
1–2 days	28%	34%	18%	30%	27%
3–5 days	18%	18%	14%	17%	16%
6–10 days	11%	12%	11%	8%	10%
More than 10 days	12%	14%	9%	7%	10%

TABLE 20.7   Number of days spent on course-based learning in twelve months

No. of days	1995 Total	1997 Company shops	Supply	Offices	Total
None	44%	39%	51%	36%	42%
1–2 days	25%	34%	16%	27%	25%
3–5 days	17%	14%	15%	19%	16%
6–10 days	8%	7%	9%	9%	8%
More than 10 days	5%	3%	8%	8%	6%

In addition, the social audit survey continued to ask employees whether they had any professional qualifications and whether they were currently studying for a work-related qualification. The results show that 17% of all respondents had qualifications, compared to 11% in 1995; 21% were studying for a qualification, and 10% of these maintained that this was work-related. The survey further queried how The Body Shop supported those studying for a work-related qualification; the breakdown of the support provided is summarized in Figure 20.1.

The questionnaire explored the levels of satisfaction regarding a wide range of different aspects of personal learning and development. The following provides an overview of the key results.

Percentage of those studying for a work-related qualification

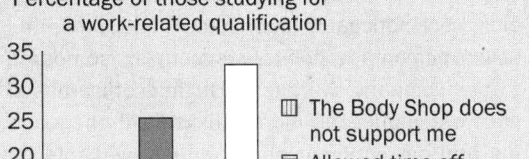
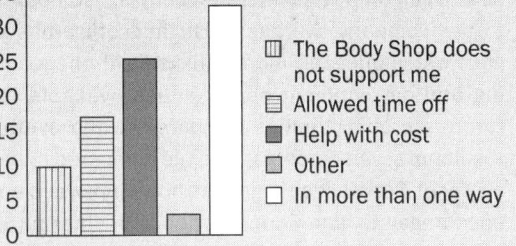

The Body Shop does not support me
Allowed time off
Help with cost
Other
In more than one way

FIGURE 20.1   The Body Shop support for work-related qualifications

In general, an upward trend can be observed in the levels of satisfaction regarding personal learning and development. The biggest increase is related to the way The Body Shop was perceived to encourage employees to obtain qualifications; the overall level of satisfaction increased from 14% in 1995 to 24% in 1997. The response was similar in all key areas of the business. However, employees in the supply division expressed more dissatisfaction compared to other parts of the company (four percentage points higher than the average) and employees in the office areas expressed lower levels of dissatisfaction compared to the overall results (five percentage points lower than the average). As mentioned earlier, prompted by the results of the first survey, the company introduced a policy and specific guidelines on the support extended to those wishing to obtain work-related qualifications. In addition, a number of in-house programmes leading to a qualification and tailored to the company's needs were introduced during 1995–97. At the end of the audit period, 114 people were participating in such courses.

Similarly, a positive trend can be observed regarding more general attitudes toward opportunities to receive training to improve skills for current jobs (satisfaction level up by four percentage points); opportunities for personal development and growth in the company (up by five percentage points); and learning and development opportunities available for future opportunities in the company (up by six percentage points). In general, the results from company shop and office-based staff resonated with the overall trends of improved satisfaction levels. However, the results from the supply division were noticeably lower (down nine, nine, and seven percentage points, respectively, compared to the company averages). Further, office-based staff were noticeably more satisfied with the learning and development opportunities available for future job opportunities compared to the overall result (up seven percentage points compared to the average). Satisfaction regarding how employees are encouraged to gain work experience in other parts of the company improved only slightly compared to 1995, remaining the lowest-scoring learning and development tool. The whole area of secondments and work experience is currently under review, and no comprehensive company-wide guidelines exist at the moment, although there has been an increase in the number and types of secondments offered.

In contrast, the views of the employees on how new employees are welcomed and trained on joining the company improved by five percentage points, office-areas being close to the average increase, company shop employees expressing the highest satisfaction levels (14 percentage points higher than the average), and supply division employees expressing far lower levels of satisfaction (17 percentage points lower than the average). The development of the two-day company-wide induction programme offered to all head office and supply division employees continued during 1995–97. A new welcome pack was designed for all new starters and a 'buddy scheme' introduced, whereby new starters are linked to a partner to help them settle in.

The survey explored attitudes on general training in human resource-related issues for the first time. The results were moderate, with only 22% expressing satisfaction and 43% not expressing an opinion either way. This is an area of training that has been undertaken in an ad hoc way and through a number of approaches; the results reinforce the need for a more structured process. The survey also explored attitudes to appraisals for the first time. The overall view regarding how appraisals are carried out received one of the top scores amongst learning and development issues (53% either satisfied or very satisfied). Similarly, satisfaction levels were amongst the top scores regarding the outcomes of appraisals (51% either satisfied or very satisfied). However, this clearly leaves room for improvement, considering that appraisals are encouraged to be an opportunity for a two-way discussion for identifying mutual development needs. Results from different areas of the business were similar, with company shops leading the way slightly.

As the example illustrates, the management of The Body Shop regularly carries out very extensive surveys among its employees. The results of the surveys are compared to results of previous surveys as well as (although not in this example) to internal objectives and external benchmarks.

Employee surveys have gained significant prominence in the past decade and must be considered a permanent tool in HRA.

Questions
1. Critically analyse how the Body Shop performs employee surveys and uses this tool to communicate the Group's policies to its employees and to develop new policies in cooperation with employees.
2. Why do you think the number of work-based learning days have declined?
3. Critically analyse the HR practices of the organization from the statistics presented in the case.
4. Don't you think the HR audit would be a duplication of effort and that the organization should focus instead upon using the results of the survey for initiating steps or suitable policies?

HR Accounting and Audit in South Indian Cements Ltd

South Indian Cements Ltd was founded during the year 1980 as a private limited company. It grew organically and inorganically and expanded its footprints across all the four southern states, that is, Andhra Pradesh, Karnataka, Tamil Nadu, and Kerala. The company, which had an initial turnover of ₹50 crore, clocked a turnover of ₹5,000 crore by the year 2005.

The company also decided to expand its reach to the eastern, western, and northern parts of the country. However, for expansion, it wanted to raise capital (equity) from the stock markets.

The chief executive officer (CEO) of the company called for a review meeting to discuss the related issues with the management team. One of the critical issues that came up during the meeting was the need to conduct HR accounting and audit. For this purpose, the company decided to appoint an external consultant who would support it in the process.

The Vice-President–HR, Vice-President–Quality, and Vice-President–Finance were given the responsibility of identifying the consultant for the assignment. After a long search, the team appointed Niven Associates, who have considerable experience in HR accounting and audit, with the following objectives:

- Conduct a detailed audit of all the HR processes.
- Identify process inefficiencies and suggest changes to improve their functional capability.
- Do a detailed accounting of all human resources and value them, as the valuation would be included in the balance sheet of the company.

Niven Associates asked for the following:

- List of employees and their experience, qualification, and compensation details
- The process maps and guidelines for all the HR processes
- A single point of contact (SPOC), with whom they could coordinate their assignment. The Vice-President–HR appointed an employee, Aditya Sandilya, as the SPOC.

After receiving the required information, they sought permission to interact with a list of employees for a random sample audit on process and performance feedback for the HR function.

After a detailed audit, the consulting team gave suggestions for improvement. The team suggested changes for cost optimization and process turnaround times (TATs) reduction. They also valued the human resources based on parameters such as level, qualifications, and skill sets, which were converted into financials, based on their annual cost to company (CTC). The total amount was valued as the human capital of the organization.

Questions

1. Analyse the HR accounting and audit process in South Indian Cements.
2. Analyse the benefits of these processes to the organizations.
3. Compare the practices in South Indian Cements with those in other organizations.

Leadership, Values, and Corporate Social Responsibility

Objectives

After studying this chapter, you will be able to understand
- the definition and importance of leadership
- the approaches to leadership
- values and their relevance in today's context
- the Indian ethos in management
- corporate social responsibility (CSR) and business environment

LEADERSHIP

Leadership may be defined in terms of a totality of functions performed by executives as individuals and as a group. 'Leadership is interpersonal influence exercised in a situation and directed through a communication process, towards the attainment of a specialized goal or goals.' Thus, leadership is the process of influencing the activities of an individual or a group of individuals for goal achievement in a given situation. The leadership process comprises three factors—the leader, the follower, and other variables.

An analysis of the definition of leadership brings out certain basic characteristics. These are as follows:

- Leadership is basically a personal quality. This quality motivates individuals to follow the leaders.
- A leader tries to influence individuals to behave in a particular way.

> ■ ■ ■
> Leadership is the process of influencing the activities of an individual or a group of individuals for goal achievement in a given situation.

- The relationship between the leader and individuals (followers) arises out of working for a common goal.
- Leadership is a continuous process of influencing behaviour.
- Leadership is exercised in a particular situation. The situation variables also affect the effectiveness of leadership.

Importance of Leadership

Leadership is an important factor in making an organization successful. Without a good leader, an organization cannot function effectively. Since the organization is basically a deliberate creation of human beings or certain specified objectives, the activities of its members need to be directed in a certain way. The importance of good leadership can be summarized as follows:

- *Motivating employees*: As discussed earlier, motivation is necessary for work performance. The higher the motivation, the better the performance. A good leader motivates the employees to perform better. Good leadership in the organization itself is a motivating factor for the individuals.

- *Creating confidence*: A good leader creates confidence in his/her followers by directing them, advising them, and getting good results in the organization through them. Once an individual, with the help of a leader, attains high efficiency, he/she tries to maintain it as he/she acquires a certain level of confidence regarding his/her ability. Sometimes, in the absence of good direction, individuals fail to recognize their qualities and capabilities.

- *Building morale*: Morale is expressed as the attitude of the employees towards the organization and the management and their voluntary cooperation in offering their services to the organization. High morale leads to high productivity and organizational stability. Good leadership promotes employee morale ensuring high productivity and stability in the organization.

Thus, good leadership is essential in all aspects of managerial functions whether it is motivation, communication, or direction. Good leadership ensures success in the organization.

LEADERSHIP THEORIES

Many research studies, particularly by behavioural scientists, have been carried out to find out how a leader can be effective. Is their success due to their personality, their behaviour, the types of followers they have, or the work conditions, or is it a combination of these? However, no satisfactory answers have been found. Various theories or approaches on leadership have been propounded, the prominent among these being the trait theory, the behavioural theory, and the situational theory.

Trait Approach

Trait is defined as a relatively enduring quality of an individual. The trait approach seeks to determine 'what makes a successful leader' from the leader's own personal characteristics. The trait approach leadership studies were quite popular between 1930 and 1950. Leaders of eminence were selected and their characteristics studied. The hypothesis was that people having certain traits could become successful leaders. Various research studies have specified traits for successful leadership emphasizing the various aspects of intelligence, attitudes, personality, and biological factors. Stogdill has presented a review of such studies. According to him, various trait theories suggest that a successful leader should have: (a) physical and constitutional factors (height, weight, physique, energy, health, appearance); (b) intelligence; (c) self confidence; (d) sociability; (e) will (initiative, persistence, ambition); (f) dominance and (g) surgency (talkative, cheerfulness, geniality, enthusiasm, expressiveness, alertness, and originality). In a later study, Ghiselli has found supervisory ability, achievement motivation, self-actualizing, intelligence, self-assurance, and decisiveness as the qualities related with leadership success.

> ■ ■ ■
> Trait is defined as a relatively enduring quality of an individual.

> ■ ■ ■
> The trait approach gives the indication that leaders should have certain personal characteristics and the management can develop such qualities through training and development programmes.

Critical Analysis

This approach does not consider the whole environment that makes a leader—trait may be only one factor. Moreover, no generalization can be drawn about the traits that account for leadership, as there are considerable variations in traits established by various researchers. In brief, this approach has the following problems:

- A generalization of traits required for a successful leader cannot be made. This is evident by various researches conducted on leadership traits.
- No evidence has been given about the degree of the various traits required, because people have had various traits in different degrees.
- Measuring the traits is a problem. Though there are various tests to measure personality traits, however, no definite conclusions can be drawn.
- Many people with the traits specified for a leader did not make good leaders.

This approach, however, gives the indication that leaders should have certain personal characteristics. The management can develop such qualities through training and development programmes.

Behavioural Approach

This approach emphasizes that strong leadership is the result of effective role behaviour. Leadership is shown more by a person's acts than by his or her traits. Though traits influence acts, they are also affected by followers, goals, and the environment in which these occur. Thus, four basic elements—leaders, followers, goal, and environment—affect each other in determining leadership behaviour. Leadership acts may be viewed in two ways. Some acts are functional (favourable) to leadership and some are dysfunctional (unfavourable). The dysfunctional acts are the inability to accept the ideas of subordinates, a display of emotional immaturity, poor human relations, and poor communications. A leader uses three skills—technical, human, and conceptual—to lead his/her followers. Technical skill refers to a person's knowledge and proficiency in any type of process or technique. Human skill is the ability to interact effectively with people and build a team. Conceptual skill deals with ideas and enables a manager to deal successfully with abstractions, to set up models, and devise plans. The behaviour of a manager in a particular direction will make him a good leader, while the opposite of this would discard him as a leader. Setting goals, motivating employees to achieve goals, raising the level of morale, building team spirit, communicating effectively, etc., are the functional behaviours of a successful leader.

■ ■ ■
The behavioural approach emphasizes that strong leadership is the result of effective role behaviour and leaders use three types of skills—technical, human, and conceptual—to lead their followers.

The basic difference between trait approach and behavioural approach is that the former emphasizes some particular trait to be possessed by a leader, while the latter emphasizes a particular behaviour by him. It is true that favourable behaviour provides greater satisfaction to the followers and the leader is easily recognized, however, this approach suffers from one weakness. A particular behaviour may be effective at a time, while at other times this may not be so. This means the time factor becomes a vital element and it has not been considered here.

Situational Approach

This approach focuses on the situation in which leadership is exercised. Since 1945, much emphasis in leadership research has been given to the situations that surround the exercise of leadership. The contention is that leadership may be successful in one situation while in others it may not.

According to a research conducted by the Ohio State University, the four situational variables that affect the performance of leadership are as follows:

> ■ ■ ■
> The situational approach focuses on the situation in which leadership is exercised and contends that leadership may be successful in one situation while in others it may not.

- Cultural environment
- Differences between individuals
- Differences between jobs
- Differences between organizations

Cultural environment Culture is a man-made social system of belief, faith, and value. Culture may interfere with rational production efficiency by requiring actions unnecessary or unrealistic from a rational point of view, but necessary from the cultural point of view. Thus, leadership should be directed to influence the behaviour of the followers in the context of culture.

Differences between individuals Human behaviour is a result of the combination of antecedent factors. Besides, for any given aspect of behaviour there may be many contributing factors, not causative in nature.

Differences between jobs People in an organization perform different types of jobs. The importance of placing individuals in jobs that they can do satisfactorily stems from four different considerations—economic, legal, personal, and social. Different job conditions influence leadership behaviour differently.

Differences between organizations Various organizations differ on the basis of their size, age, ownership pattern, objectives, complexity, managerial pattern, cultural environment, etc. In different types of organizations, leadership processes tends to differ. For example, leadership behaviour will be different in military or government administration as compared to business organizations.

The limitations of this approach are as follows:

- This theory emphasizes the leadership ability of an individual in a given situation. Thus, it measures his/her present leadership potentialities. Whether this individual will fit into another situation is not answered by this theory.
- Organizational factors become helpful or form constraints to a great extent to an individual leader in exercising his/her leadership. Thus, it is difficult to measure his/her personal abilities as a good leader.
- The theory does not emphasize the process by which good leaders can be made in an organization. Thus, it puts a constraint over the leadership development process.

Eclectic Approach

Sanford has developed the eclectic approach to leadership. He contends that leadership depends upon the traits of a leader, the situational variables, and the type of followers. These three factors should be integrated to study the leadership pattern. In fact, this is not a new theory, but an integration of various theories.

GROUP AND EXCHANGE THEORIES OF LEADERSHIP

The group theories of leadership have their roots in social psychology. The classic exchange theory, in particular, serves as an important basis for this approach. This means simply that the leader

Exchange theories propose that group members make contributions at a cost to themselves and receive benefits at a cost to the group or other members.

brings more benefits/rewards than burdens/costs to the followers. There must be a positive exchange between the leaders and followers in order for group goals to be accomplished. Chester Barnard applied such an analysis more than a half-century ago to managers and subordinates in an organizational setting. More recently, this social exchange view of leadership was summarized as follows: Exchange theories propose that group members make contributions at a cost to themselves and receive benefits at a cost to the group or other members. Interaction continues because members find the social exchange mutually rewarding. This statement emphasizes that leadership is an exchange process between the leader and his/her followers. Social psychological research can be used to support this notion of exchange.

Fiedler's Contingency Model of Leadership Effectiveness

This model discusses the relationship between a leadership style and the favourableness of the situation. Fiedler described situational favourableness in terms of three empirically derived dimensions:

- The leader–member relationship, which is the most critical variable in determining the favourableness of situations,
- The degree of task structure, which is the second most important input into the favourableness of the situation, and
- The leader's position power obtained through formal authority, which is the third most critical dimension of the situation.

Situations are favourable to the leader if all three of the aforementioned dimensions are high. In other words, if the leader is generally accepted and respected by the followers (high first dimension), if the task is very structured and everything is 'spelled out' (high second dimension), and if a great deal of authority and power are formally attributed to the leader's position (high third dimension), the situation is favourable. If the opposite exists (if the three dimensions are low), the situation will be very favourable for the leader. Fielder was convinced through his research that the favourableness of the situation in combination with the leadership style determines effectiveness.

Fiedler was convinced through his research that the favourableness of the situation in combination with the leadership style determines effectiveness.

Path–Goal Leadership Theory

Another widely recognized theoretical development is the path–goal theory. In essence, the path–goal theory attempts to explain the impact that leader behaviour has on subordinate motivation, satisfaction, and performance. The theory incorporates four major types or styles of leadership:

The path–goal theory attempts to explain the impact that leader behaviour has on subordinate motivation, satisfaction, and performance.

- *Directive leadership*: This style is similar to that of the Lippitt and White authoritarian leader. Subordinates know exactly what is expected of them, and the leader gives specific directions. There is no participation by subordinates.
- *Supportive leadership*: The leader is friendly and approachable and shows a genuine concern for subordinates.

- *Participative leadership*: The leader asks for and uses suggestions from subordinates, but makes independent decisions.
- *Achievement-oriented leadership*: The leader sets challenging goals for subordinates and shows confidence that they will attain these goals and perform well.

CHARISMA

Charisma is a Greek word meaning a divinely inspired gift. In the study of leadership, charisma is a special quality of leaders whose purposes, powers, and extraordinary determination differentiate them from others.

Definitions of charisma and charismatic leadership:

- A devotion to the specific and exceptional sanctity, heroism, or exemplary character of an individual person and of the normative patterns revealed or ordained by that person.
- Endowment with the gift of divine grace.
- The process of influencing major changes in the attitudes and assumptions of organization members, and building commitment for the organization's objectives.
- Leadership that has a magnetic effect on people.
- It is a combination of individualized consideration, intellectual stimulation, and inspirational leadership—a component of transformational leadership.

Charisma: A Relationship between the Leader and the Group Manager

A key dimension of charismatic leadership is that it involves a relationship or interaction between the leader and the people being led. Furthermore, the people accepting the leadership must attribute charismatic qualities to the leader. Charismatic leadership is possible under certain conditions. The beliefs of the team members must be similar to those of the leader, and an unquestioning acceptance and affection for the leader must exist. The group members must willingly obey the leader and they must be emotionally involved both in the mission of the charismatic leader and in their own goals. Finally, the followers must have a strong desire to identify with the leader.

> ■ ■ ■
> A key dimension of charismatic leadership is that it involves a relationship or interaction between the leader and the people being led.

Effects of Charisma

A charismatic leader, according to House, is any person who brings about certain outcomes to an unusually high degree. The nine charismatic effects are as follows:

- Group members' trust in the correctness of the leader's beliefs
- Similarity of the group members' beliefs to those of the leader
- Unquestioning acceptance of the leader
- Affection for the leader
- Willing obedience to the leader
- Identification with and emulation of the leader
- Emotional involvement of the group members or constituents in the mission
- Heightened goals of the group members

- Feeling on the part of group members that they will be able to accomplish or contribute to the accomplishment of the mission

Charisma and transformational leadership are closely intertwined. As we look specifically at the characteristics of charismatic and transformational leaders, we note that many of these characteristics apply to leaders in general.

- *Vision*: A charismatic leader offers an exciting image of where the organization is headed and how to get there. A vision is more than a forecast because it describes an ideal version of the future of an entire organization or an organizational unit.
- *Masterful communication skills*: To inspire people, the charismatic leader uses colourful language and exciting metaphors and analogies.
- *Ability to inspire trust*: Group members and constituents believe so strongly in the integrity of charismatic leaders that they will risk their careers to pursue the chief's vision.
- *Ability to make group members feel capable*: One technique for helping group members feel more capable is to enable them to achieve success on relatively easy projects. The leader then praises the group members and gives them more demanding assignments.
- *Energy and action orientation*: Like entrepreneurs, most charismatic leaders are energetic and serve as a model for getting things done on time.
- *Emotional expressiveness and warmth*: A key characteristic of charismatic leaders is the ability to express feelings openly.
- *Willingness to take personal risk*: Charismatic leaders are typically risk takers, and risk taking adds to their charisma.
- *Use of unconventional strategies*: Part of being creative is to use unconventional strategies to achieve success. The charismatic leader inspires others by formulating unusual strategies to achieve important goals.
- *Self-promoting personality*: Charismatic leaders are hardly diffident; they toot their own horns and allow others to know how important they are. Richard Branson, for example, has relied on self-promotion to help build his empire.
- *Propensity to emerge during crises*: Early formulations of charismatic leadership emphasized that the charismatic leader arises in response to a crisis.
  - *Minimum internal conflict*: Charismatic leader are confident and determined that they are right, even through setbacks. They appear to have less internal conflict between their emotions, impulses, and feelings than most other people. As they are convinced they are right, they experience less guilt and discomfort in reprimanding group members.

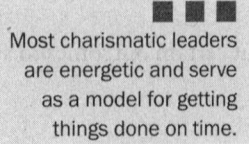
Most charismatic leaders are energetic and serve as a model for getting things done on time.

Charismatic Leader Theories

Although the charismatic concept or charisma goes as far back as the ancient Greeks and is cited in the Bible, its modern development is often attributed to the work of Robert House. On the basis of the analysis of political and religious leaders, House suggests that charismatic leaders are characterized by self-confidence and confidence in subordinates, high expectations from subordinates, ideological vision, and the use of personal example. Followers of charismatic leaders identify with the leader and the mission of the leader, exhibit extreme loyalty to and confidence in the leader, emulate the leader's values and behaviour, and derive self-esteem from their relationship with the leader.

Because of the effects that charismatic leaders have on followers, the theory predicts that the performance of the followers will be beyond expectations. Moreover, the followers will have a strong commitment to the leader and his/her or her mission. House and his colleagues provide some support to the charismatic theory, but as with other leadership theories, complexities are found and more research is needed.

Effective transformational leaders share the following characteristics:

- They identify themselves as change agents.
- They are courageous.
- They believe in people.
- They are value driven.
- They are lifelong learners.
- They have the ability to deal with complexity, ambiguity, and uncertainty.
- They are visionaries.

> ■ ■ ■
> House suggests that charismatic leaders are characterized by self-confidence, confidence in subordinates, high expectations from subordinates, ideological vision, and the use of personal example.

LEADERSHIP STYLES

Leadership styles are the patterns of behaviour, which a leader adopts in influencing the behaviour of his/her followers (subordinates) in the organizational context. These patterns emerge in the leader as he/she begins to respond in the same fashion under similar conditions; he/she develops habits that become somewhat predictable to those who work with him/her. The dimensions of leadership styles are (a) power dimension where the superior uses varying degree of authority; (b) employee or task orientation; and (c) motivation.

Power Dimension

According to this dimension, there are three leadership styles:

- Autocratic leadership
- Participative leadership
- Free-rein leadership

> ■ ■ ■
> Leadership style is the pattern of behaviour that leaders adopt in influencing the behaviour of their followers in the organizational context.

Autocratic Leadership

This is also known as the authoritarian, directive, or monotheistic style. In this style, the managers centralize the decision-making power in themselves. They structure the complete work situation for their employees and employees do what they are told. Here, the leadership may be negative because the followers are uniformed, insecure, and afraid of the leaders' authority. There are three categories of autocratic leaders:

> ■ ■ ■
> In case of autocratic leadership, the leaders centralize decision-making power in themselves.

- *Strict autocrat*: The leader follows autocratic styles in a very strict sense. The method of influencing the subordinate's behaviour is through negative motivation, that is, by criticizing subordinates, imposing penalty, etc.,

- *Benevolent autocrat*: The leader also centralizes the decision-making power in himself, but the motivation style is positive. The leader can be effective in getting efficiency in many situations. Some people perform better under a strong authority structure and they derive satisfaction from this kind of leadership.
- *Incompetent autocrat*: Sometimes, superiors adopt an autocratic leadership style just to hide their incompetence, because in other styles they may be exposed before their subordinates.

The main advantages of the autocratic technique are as follows:

- There are many subordinates in an organization who prefer to work under a centralized authority structure and strict discipline. They get satisfaction from this style.
- It provides strong motivation and reward to a manager exercising this style.
- It permits very quick decisions as a single person takes most of the decisions.
- Less competent subordinates also have the scope to work in the organization as they do negligible planning, organization, and decision-making.

The disadvantages of this style are as follows:

- Team members dislike it especially when it is strict and when the leader lacks motivational skills.
- Employees lack motivation. Frustration, low morale, and conflict develop in the organization jeopardizing the organizational efficiency.
- There is more dependence and less individuality in the organization. As a result, development of future leaders in the organization is hindered.

Participative Leadership

This style is also called democratic, consultative, or ideographic. Participation is defined as the mental and emotional involvement of a person in a group situation that encourages him to contribute to and share responsibility in group goals. A participative manager decentralizes the decision-making process. Instead of taking unilateral decisions, he or she emphasizes consultation and participation of the subordinates.

The various benefits of real participative management are as follows:

- It is a highly motivating technique for employees, as they feel elevated when their ideas and suggestions are given weight in decision-making.
- The employee's productivity is high because they are party to the decision. Thus, they implement the decisions wholeheartedly.
- They share the responsibility with the superior and try to safeguard him also.
- It provides organizational stability by raising morale. Further, leaders are also prepared to take organizational positions.

The common methods adopted are democratic functioning, supervision, production, committees, suggestion programmes, and multiple-management. However, this style has the following limitations:

■ ■ ■
A participative manager decentralizes the decision-making process.

- The complex nature of an organization requires a thorough understanding of its problems, which lower level employees may not be able to do. As such, participation does not remain meaningful.

- Some people in the organization want minimum interaction with their superiors or associates. For them, the participation technique is discouraging instead of encouraging.
- Participation can be used covertly to manipulate employees. Thus, some employees may prefer the open tyranny of an autocrat as compared to the covert tyranny of a group.

Free-rein Leadership

■ ■ ■
Free-rein style is rarely used in business organizations as the contribution of the manager is almost nil.

Free-rein or laissez faire technique means giving complete freedom to subordinates. In this style, the manager determines the policy, programmes, limitations, or actions once and the entire process is left to the subordinates. Group members perform everything and the manager usually coordinates with outside agencies to bring information and material which the group needs.

This style is suitable to certain situations where the manager can leave a choice to his/her group. It helps subordinates to develop independent personalities. However, the contribution of the manager is almost nil. It tends to permit the different units of an organization to proceed at cross purposes and the result can be chaos. Hence, this style is very rarely used in business organizations.

Likert's Management System

Rensis Likert and his associates have studied the patterns and styles of managers for three decades and have developed certain concepts and approaches important to understanding leadership behaviour. He has given a continuum of four systems of management.

Likert's four systems of management in terms of leadership styles may be referred to as exploitative autocratic (system 1), benevolent autocratic (system 2), and participative (system 3). He ascribes this mainly to the extent of participation in management and the extent to which

■ ■ ■
Likert states that leadership must be such that it ensures maximum probability that in all interactions and relationships each member views the experience as supportive and builds and maintains a sense of personal worth and importance.

the practice of a supportive relationship is maintained. He states that leadership and the other processes of an organization must be such as to ensure the maximum probability that in all interactions and in all relationships with the organization, each member in the light of his/her background, values, desires, and expectations, will view the experience as supportive and one which builds and maintains his/her sense of personal worth and importance.

Likert has also isolated three variables, which are representative of his total concept of system 4. These are (a) the use of supportive relationships by managers, (b) the use of group decision-making and group methods of supervision, and (c) high-performance goals.

Employee Production and Employee Orientation

An attempt was made to study leadership behaviour by locating clusters of characteristics that seemed to be related to each other and various indicators of effectiveness. The studies identified two concepts, which were called employee orientation and production orientation. The employee-orientation concept stresses the relationship aspects of jobs. It emphasizes that every individual is important and takes interest in everyone accepting his/her individuality and personal needs. The production-orientation concept emphasizes the production and technical aspects of

Low structure and high consideration	High structure and high consideration
Low structure and low consideration	High structure and low consideration

FIGURE 21.1 Management styles based on structure and consideration

jobs and employees are considered as tools for accomplishing the jobs. This is parallel to the authoritarian concept of leadership behaviour.

■ ■ ■
The employee-orientation concept emphasizes that every individual is important and takes interest in everyone accepting his/her individuality and personal needs.

At almost the same time, the leadership studies initiated by the Bureau of Research at the Ohio State University attempted to identify the various dimensions of leader behaviour. Initiating structure refers to the leader's behaviour in delineating the relationship between himself or herself and the members of the work group and in endeavouring to establish well-defined patterns of organization. The channels of communication refer to behaviour indicative of friendship, mutual trust, respect, and warmth in the relationship between the leader and the members of his/her staff. The research studies also show that initiating structure and consideration are two separate distinct dimensions and not mutually exclusive.

The four quadrants show the various combinations of initiating structure and consideration (Figure 21.1). In each quadrant, there is a relative mixture of initiating structure and consideration and a manager can adopt any one style.

Managerial Grid

One of the most widely known approaches of leadership styles is the managerial grid developed by Blake and Mouton. They emphasize that the leadership style consists of factors of both the task-oriented and relation-oriented behaviour in varying degrees. Their concern for the leadership style has been used to convey how managers are concerned about people or production, rather than how much production is getting out of the group. Thus, it does not represent real production or the extent to which human relationship needs are being satisfied. Concern for production means the attitude of superiors towards a variety of things such as the quality of policy decisions, procedures and processes, creativeness of research, quality of staff services, work efficiency, and the volume of output. Concern for people includes the degree of personal commitment towards goal achievement, maintaining the self-esteem of workers, responsibility based on trust, and satisfying interpersonal relations. The managerial grid identifies four leadership styles based on these two factors found in organizations as shown in Figure 21.2.

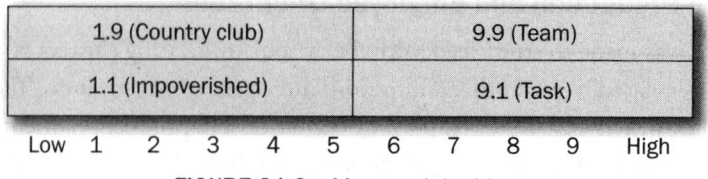

FIGURE 21.2 Managerial grid

Blake and Mouton have described the styles as follows:

- The exertion of minimum effort is required to get work done and sustain organization morale.
- Thoughtful attention to the needs of people leads to a friendly and comfortable organization atmosphere and work tempo.
- Efficiency results from arranging work in such a way that human elements have little effect.
- Adequate performance through the balance of work requirements and the maintenance of satisfactory morale.
- Work accomplished is from committed people with interdependence through a common stake in the organization's purpose and with trust and respect.

Each style points out the relative contents of concern for production or people and implies that the most desirable leader behaviour is 9.9 (maximum concern for production and people). In fact, Blake and Mouton have developed training programmes that attempt to change managers towards 9.9 management styles.

The managerial grid is a useful device for managers to identify and classify managerial styles. It helps them understand why they get the reaction that they do from their subordinates. It can also suggest some alternative styles that may be available to him/her.

However, it does not explain why a manager fails in one part or the other of the grid. What a manager's style is will be influenced by many factors, including the superior, the kind of subordinates he/she supervises, and the situation in which he/she finds himself.

Successful Leadership vs Effective Leadership

An individual attempts to affect the behaviour of another through the exercise of leadership. The response of the other person (subordinate) may either be compatible with the expectations of the leader or otherwise. Further, the compatible response may be the result of either the impact of the leader's appropriate style or because of position power. In case of the former, the leader is effective as the subordinate sees his/her own needs being accomplished by satisfying the goals of the organization and the leader. In the latter case, the leader is successful in getting compatible behaviour, but this has been done because of his/her position. In this case, the leader is successful but not effective. Thus, a distinction can be made between successful and effective leadership.

Success has to do with how the individual or group behaves; effectiveness describes the internal shape or predisposition of an individual or a group and thus is attitudinal in nature. An individual

interested only in success tends to emphasize his/her position power and uses close supervision. On the other hand, if he/she intends to be effective, he/she will depend on his/her personal power characterized by more general supervision. Position power can be delegated downward in the organization; personal power cannot be delegated, but is generated upward from below through follower acceptance. The success or effectiveness is not an 'either...or' position; rather these can be in the form of a continuum ranging from very successful to very unsuccessful or very effective to very ineffective.

Thus, a manager can be successful, but ineffective having only a short run of influence over the behaviour of others. On the other hand, if a manager is both successful and effective, his or her influence tends to lead to a long run of productivity. However, it should be emphasized that a successful and effective framework is a way of evaluating the response to a specific behavioural response and not of evaluating performance over a period of time. Total performance is the result of a host of factors and not of leadership alone; hence it can be evaluated in the light of these factors.

Leadership Skills

Today, leadership theories and practices recognize the importance of skills—how leaders behave and perform effectively. Both styles and roles/activities are closely related to skills and can be used as a point of departure for the discussion of skills. First, some of the commonly recognized leadership skills are identified; then, training, job redesign, and behavioural management skills are suggested as effective leadership techniques.

A list of suggested leadership skills critical to success in the global economy includes the following:

- *Cultural flexibility*: In international assignments, skills refer to cultural awareness and sensitivity. In domestic organizations, the same skill could be said to be critical for success in light of increasing diversity. Leaders must have skills not only to manage, but also to recognize and celebrate the value of diversity in their organizations.
- *Communication skills*: Effective leaders must be able to communicate in written form, orally, and non-verbally.
- *HRD skills*: Since human resources are so much a part of leadership effectiveness, leaders must have human resource development (HRD) skills of developing a learning climate, designing and conducting training programmes, transmitting information and experience, assessing results, providing career counselling, creating organization change, and adapting learning materials.
- *Creativity*: Problem solving, innovation, and creativity provide the competitive advantage in today's global marketplace. Leaders must not only be creative themselves and possess the skills, but also provide a climate that encourages creativity and assists their people to be creative.

■ ■ ■
Leadership skills critical to success in a global economy include
- cultural flexibility
- communication skills
- HRD skills
- creativity
- self management and learning

- *Self management of learning*: This skill refers to the need for the continuous learning of new knowledge and skills. In this time of dramatic change and global competitiveness, leaders must undergo continuous change themselves. They must be self-learners.

Whetten and Cameron provide a more empirical derivation of effective leadership skills. On the basis of an interview study of more than 400 highly effective managers, the ten skills most often identified are given in Table 21.1.

TABLE 21.1   Ten important skills of leaders

• Verbal communication (including listening)	• Delegating
• Managing time and stress	• Setting goals and articulating a vision
• Managing individual decisions	• Self-awareness
• Recognizing, defining, and solving problems	• Team-building
• Motivating and influencing others	• Managing conflict

Follow-up studies and related research have found skills similar to these ten skills. Through statistical techniques, the results of the various research studies were combined into the following four categories of effective leadership skills:

- Participative and human relations (for example, supportive communication and team-building)
- Competitiveness and control (for example, assertiveness, power, and influence)
- Innovativeness and entrepreneurship (for example, creative problem-solving)
- Maintaining order and rationality (for example, managing time and rational decision-making)

Entrepreneurial Leadership Style

A general picture emerges of a task-oriented and charismatic leader. Entrepreneurs drive themselves and others relentlessly, yet their personalities inspire others.

Entrepreneurs and 'intrapreneurs' often use a leadership style that incorporates the following behaviours.

- *Strong achievement motive*: Entrepreneurs have stronger achievement motives than most managers. Building a business is an excellent vehicle for accomplishment.
- *High degree of enthusiasm and creativity*: Related to the achievement need are enthusiasm and creativity. The entrepreneur's enthusiasm in turn makes him persuasive. As a result, entrepreneurs are often perceived as charismatic. Some entrepreneurs are often so emotional that they are regarded as eccentric.
- *Tendency to act quickly when opportunity arises*: Entrepreneurs are noted for seizing opportunities when they arise. When a deal is on the horizon, they push themselves and those around them extra hard.
- *Constant hurry*: Entrepreneurs and intrapreneurs are always in a hurry. When engaged in one meeting, their minds typically begin to focus on the next meeting. Their flurry of activity rubs off on group members and those around them.
- *Visionary perspective*: Entrepreneurs and intrapreneurs, at their best, are visionaries. They see opportunities that others fail to observe. Specifically, they have the ability to identify a problem and arrive at a solution.
- *Dislike of hierarchy and bureaucracy*: Entrepreneurs are not ideally suited by temperament to working within the mainstream of a bureaucracy. Many successful entrepreneurs are people who were frustrated by the constraints of a bureaucratic system. Intrapreneurs, by definition, fair reasonably well into a bureaucracy. Yet, they do not like to be restrained by tight regulations.
- *Preference for dealing with external customers*: One of the reasons why entrepreneurs and intrapreneurs have difficulty with bureaucracy is that they focus their energies on products, services, and customers, rather than on employees. Some entrepreneurs are gracious to customers and moneylenders, but brusque with company insiders.

Management by Values

'There is indeed a need to rekindle old principles and ethical values, which, alas, have too often been ignored or neglected in recent years in the belief that quicker profits and greater accumulation of wealth will be the result', says J.R.D. Tata.

Values

> ■ ■ ■
> Managers at all levels are expected to have a strong and noble character based on basic human values. Value orientation and holistic management will enable a manager to lead a better life.

It is an accepted fact that human beings spend two-thirds of their life doing some work/activity or the other. To work is an innate need, an inborn propensity, characteristic of human beings. Activity is not only an important aspect in life, but it is essential for health and growth. Not only is there a fundamental need for activity, but it is through such activity that every form of life adjusts itself to its environment. Sometimes activity is engaged in for its own sake; sometimes it is reflexive and often purposive in that it is engaged in with an end, object, or purpose in mind, which is important to us.

The formal setting where these purposive activities are carried out may be termed as organizations. An organization comes into existence to achieve its objectives/goals. These goals may be long term or short term. The goals determine the structure in an organization vis-à-vis the number, type of people, etc. The structure determines the position and the hierarchical relationships among people.

It is an accepted fact that human beings spend two-thirds of their life in organizations. The interaction between an individual and an organization is an interesting phenomenon. Both aim at development. An individual's interpretation of his/her growth and development indicates task accomplishment and achieving success and competence. On the other hand, the organization aims at increased turnover and growth.

These aspects may be realized by the management process. It may be said that managers may be guided by values. The managers at all levels are expected to have a strong and noble character based on basic human values. Oriented values and holistic management will enable a manager to lead a much better life qualitatively. It will bring greater happiness when it is translated into societal benefit in the form of running an organization or any other field of human activity.

Hence, the following sections present an overview of the importance of values in life, of the Indian ethos for management, and also help identify the aspects of management by values.

Importance of Values in Life

Values are called '*gunas*'. The mental contents of a good person are called moral and ethical values. These are also referred to as *Daivi Sampatti* or divine qualities. Some of these qualities are fearlessness, courage, purity of mind and heart, integration of thought, action and behaviour, generosity, empathy, love and affection, forbearance, control of mind, non-violence, fairness, charity, modesty, loyalty, vigour, cheerfulness, integrity, etc.

A manager with these values has a state of mind, which is in equanimity. Such a person can mobilise his/her energies and those of others around him and help accomplish wonders.

The importance of moral values is recognized in the concept of dharma in India. The Bhagavad Gita says '*Yad Yad Acharati Sreshthah, Tat Tat ev Ithera Tanah, Sa Yat Pramanam Kuruthat, Lokah tad anuvarthatha*'. The path trodden and the practices followed by the noble person (leader) are followed by all other men. The leader (noble person) sets high standards of conduct, which the whole world adopts, accepts, and follows.

It is then clear that the leader of the enterprise by his/her conduct and practice would set forth certain principles, which manifest the value system.

■ ■ ■
The human values establish business values such as service, communication, excellence, credibility, innovation, creativity, and coordination and enhance the reputation and goodwill of the organization.

Values thus serve the process of transforming the level of consciousness to pure high levels. They help us to distinguish between the *preya* (the pleasant) and the *shreya* (the good)—between the desired and the undesirable, the delectable and the electable.

Our effectiveness at work is tied to exercising intrinsic human values, that is, moral and ethical values. These human values establish business values such as service, communication, excellence, credibility, innovation, creativity, and coordination. Human values help in self-development, maintaining good interpersonal interactions, and reducing conflicts and disputes. They also enhance the reputation and goodwill of the organization.

Ethics and values must be an integral part of the management and work culture. In the process of exclusively pursuing material well-being, we have threatened both the physical environment and the ethical moral fabric of our society. We have created unwanted stresses and strains, unrest and loneliness in the human mind and an adverse organizational work life. Hence, the development of people, not only of their skills, but also of their moral, ethical, and spiritual values now becomes a necessity.

According to Peter Drucker (2004), 'The final proof of the sincerity and seriousness of a management is uncompromising emphasis on integrity of character. ...it is character through which leadership is exercised. It is the character that sets the example and is imitated.'

Spirituality is the essence of our Indian genius and wisdom. It is the source of our national vitality. The vitality of Indian wisdom and culture lies in its creative endeavour, in spiritual science, thought, and practice. We need to maintain this creative and positive attitude for the progress and development of India and humanity as a whole.

Indian Ethos for Management

The Indian ethos for management means the application of principles of management as revealed in our ancient wisdom and described in the Upanishads and the Gita. The Indian ethos is based on Indian scriptures: (a) *Srutis* (e.g., the *Upanishads, the Gita*) and (b) *Smritis* (e.g., the *Puranas*). Indian thought provides the eternal knowledge of creation and the cosmos and man recognizes the close interrelation between the spiritual and worldly life of a human being.

As per the Indian ethos, all work is worthy and honourable. This is called dignity of work. All work is considered as a valuable means for purifying our mind and ego, as well as for gaining money, power, fame, and name. Work is worship of the divine within and without.

■ ■ ■
The Indian ethos of management stress that a management with a proper combination of values and skills can assure harmony and progress in an organization and it also contributes to the development and growth of the society.

The divine element in the individual (as a core or substratum) is only a portion of the universal or cosmic consciousness (pure consciousness). The sublime Indian concept offers a secure base for mutual trust, cooperation, teamwork, living and working for the public benefit, and other such noble ideas of organizational and societal life.

The Indian ethos puts much greater emphasis on values—human and ethical. Knowledge is not power, character is real power and wealth. Values must be combined with skills. Only then can we have effective and efficient management, enriched quality of work life in the organization, and enriched quality of human life.

Character is based on divine values and these are based on wisdom. Therefore, Indian thought regards wisdom as the balance. Internalization alone enables one to cultivate moral and ethical values and improve our character and quality as a human being. A manager with an enriched quality of mind and heart can deliver effective management.

The management that has a proper combination of values and skills can assure harmony and progress in its own organization and contribute towards the healthy development and growth of society. This is the unique contribution of the Indian ethos.

Some salient ideas and thoughts of the Indian ethos in management as revealed by our scriptures:

- *Atmano mokhardham, jagat hitaya cha*: All work is an opportunity for doing good to the world and thus gaining materially and spiritually in our lives.
- *Acheyet dana manabhayam*: Worship people not only with material things, but also by showing respect to their ever-present divinity within.
- *Yagah kamasu kaaushalam; satvam yoga nehyate*: He who works with a calm and even mind achieves the most.
- *Parasparam bhavayantah sreyah param bhavapsyathah*: By mutual cooperation, respect, and fellow feeling, all of us will enjoy the highest good—both material and spiritual.
- *Parapar devo bhav*: Regard the other person as a divine being. All of us have the same consciousness, though our packages or containers are different.

Thus, it may be seen that management by values is not an unknown phenomenon in India. India recognized the importance of values in organizations and life centuries ago.

VALUE SYSTEMS—PAST AND PRESENT

For all living creatures, action is inevitable. Having been born, man cannot escape from work and Vedanta says man has to work to attain 'abhyudaya' (worldly excellence) within the ambit of dharma and also strive to attain 'nihsreyasa' (spiritual excellence). Vedanta finds an honoured place for all desires and wages of man from the material and the sensory to the moral, ethical, aesthetic, and transcendent in its concept of *purusharthas*, that is, values sought after by *purusha* or man. These are dharma, *artha*, *kama*, and *moksha*.

The word 'kama' refers to craving and satisfaction at the sensory level. 'Artha' is the instrument of satisfaction of *kama*. Dharma, which means the ethical sense, helps to discipline and regulate the pursuit of the first and second. Human values in management and administration proceed from the *purushartha* of dharma. The ultimate *purushartha* to be attained by man is *moksha*—self-realization.

> ■ ■ ■
> In Indian ethos, the profit motive of an organization should subserve the service motive. Business is considered an instrument for creating wealth and welfare and is to be pursued through ethically worthy means.

The need to attain perfection or excellence in work is an attempt to satisfy one's need for self-actualization. Such a person, while seeking excellence, will not be looking for the results of his/her action, which fulfil his/her lower order needs, but will strive for self-realization. Like an individual striving to achieve *purushartha*, an organization, which is nothing but a corporate individual, should also have a corporate dharma. Of course, profit making remains one of its motives, but it should subserve the service motive. Today, business is considered an instrument for creating wealth and welfare, functioning for socially desirable goals, through result-oriented enterprises. It has to be pursued through ethically worthy means, resulting in generation of healthy, wholesome individuals who would carry positive values and impulses into their community.

The early days of the second millennium had some marked similarities with the socio-political forces shaping our life today. Around 1000 AD, Islam was spreading fast, China had a booming economy, and Europe was a struggling economy scarred by nationalism. Religion held sway over moral behaviour; compliance with a moral code was obligatory, and straying from the code could mean death. The daily life of man consisted of 'religious observance', dutiful work, and family obligations. Ethical behaviour guided both personal and working lives.

Halfway through the second millennium, three major events took place and changed the long-held moral convictions.

- The explorations of seagoing Europeans changed ideas about the shape and extent of the world and subsequently its place in the universe.
- The dominance of the Roman Catholic Church was challenged by the reformation and with it emerged new concepts of morality.
- The concept of moral choice and freedom of thought and behaviour sowed the seeds of humanism and transformed the concept of work—work to achieve the desired lifestyle.

In the second quarter of the millennium, the Industrial Revolution transformed agricultural seeds into manufacturing employees and also brought in new social roles—customers and shareholders. Gradually, over the 20th century, the roles of the employee, customer, and shareholder merged into a new role—that of the stakeholder. This century also witnessed the emergence of business ethics.

The operations of business enterprises affect a wide spectrum of stakeholders. The shareholders, suppliers, consumers, local community, and society at large are affected by the way an enterprise functions. There has been a growing acceptance of the plea that businesses should be socially responsible. A business enterprise, which makes use of the resources of the society and depends on society for its functioning, should discharge its duties and responsibilities in enhancing the welfare of the society of which it is an integral part. Corporate management has to meet the rising expectations of not merely the shareholders, but all stakeholders while adhering to ethical practices and a code of conduct, which must meet international standards. All societies are governed by principles of ethics and values are governed by the principles of ethics and they hold the values dear. Companies need to adhere to such values to serve the objectives of the society.

Values, then, are not a repeat of the actual conduct, but are a system of criteria by which conduct is judged and sanctions applied. Functionally, it is a set of principles whereby conduct is directed and regulated. It also acts as a guide for individuals and the social group.

In an organization, the mission statements proclaim the values nurtured and sought in the future. It serves as a beacon in the functioning of the organization to move from where it is to where it ought to be.

Peter and Waterman (1982) give a crystallized list of the values of some excellent American companies:

- Belief in being the best

- Belief in the importance of details of execution
- Belief in the importance of people as individuals
- Belief in superior quality and service
- Belief that most members of the organization should be innovators
- Belief in the importance of informality to enhance communication
- Explicit belief in and recognition of the importance of economic growth and profits

Hopstede and Bond (1988) studied the value of the orientation of people in Singapore, Taiwan, South Korea, Hong Kong, and Japan and incorporated a new dimension—Confucian Dynamism. The component values of this dimension include the importance of persistence, relationship by status, thrift and a sense of shame, and the relative unimportance of personal steadiness and stability, dignity, respect for tradition, and reciprocation of greetings, etc. It was also found that culture in the form of dominant values is a necessary condition for economic growth.

The following is the list of values in force in the Matsushita Electric Company in Japan:

- National service through industry
- Fairness
- Harmony and cooperation
- Struggle for betterment
- Adjustment and assimilation
- Gratitude

In India, gradually more and more companies are emerging with formal statements of values and benefits. We quote here two examples—one from the public sector and the other from a private sector company. The public sector firm has the following list of values in circulation:

- Foremost is customer satisfaction
- Employees, being the most important resource, must be treated with respect and dignity
- Integrity, fairness, and equality in business dealings
- Positive encouragement to creativity and innovation
- A strong belief in quality and excellence
- An ethos of discipline and commitment
- Mutual loyalty and prosperity for vendors and suppliers
- Contribution to a clean environment and quality of life

In another successful private sector company, the following list of values were articulated:

- Ensure customer satisfaction.
- Seek excellence in what you do.
- Set high standards of ethics.
- Foster creativity and innovation.
- Avoid all discrimination.
- Contribute to the benefit of society.
- Respect the dignity of each individual.

Chakraborty (1998) offers the following enumeration of the value system, which is valid for the Indian psyche in the Indian management context. These are values rooted deep in the structure of the Indian culture and society.

■ ■ ■
Advances in the spheres of transport, business communication, and information are creating interdependent global economies. There is also a need to evolve sound patterns of economic and social organizations as well as human behaviour.

- Individuals must be respected—because of the transcendent, divine enrichment in them.
- Cooperation and trust
- Jealousy to be avoided
- *Chitta shuddhi* or purification of the mind—with the noble thoughts of compassion, friendliness, humility, gratitude, etc.
- Top quality product service
- Work is worship
- Containment of greed
- Ethical and moral soundness
- Self-discipline and self-restraint—because they conserve energy, strengthen will-power, create trust, and confer dignity
- Customer satisfaction
- Creativity
- Inspiration to give
- Reunification and detachment

Today, we are living in a world of unprecedented change. Developments in science and technology are forcing organizations everywhere to adjust and adapt to the fast-changing environment. Advances in the sphere of transport, business communication, and information are creating interdependent global economies. It is not impossible to alleviate disease, ignorance and poverty with the resources of science and technology. We also need to evolve sound patterns of economic and social organizations as well as human behaviours. It means that organizations need to be guided morally in their obligations towards customers, employees, shareholders, suppliers, regulators, and the community at large.

Moral behaviour with respect to customers will include

- providing goods and services, which meet the claims of the producer and deliverer
- charging prices that do not exploit customers and yet yield a reasonable return on investment
- ensuring that the explicit/implicit contracts between both the parties are sustained

In relation to employees, moral behaviour will ensure that, among other things, corporate values include

- providing a fair reward for services rendered
- protection from avoidable hazards
- giving opportunities for individuals to make an optimum contribution to the success of the organization from which stakeholders will benefit

When it comes to owners, be they shareholders or sole proprietors, moral behaviour will take account of

- adding value by ethical means
- avoiding actions that will bring individual owners to ill repute undeservedly
- forewarning owners of potential changes that may harm their reputation and/or investment

> ■ ■ ■
> In the emerging social order, management ceases to be a career discipline and must be taken as a developmental process where the management approach has to be focused upon the development of man and society.

For suppliers, it is essential that, in its moral behaviour, the purchasing company

- avoids placing the supplier in jeopardy by taking undue advantage of relative power
- selects suppliers on the basis of merit, rather than criteria that harms the other stakeholders
- forewarns suppliers in good time of changes in the purchasing policy that are likely to have an adverse effect on their business

When it comes to regulators (whose role, in part, is to monitor the moral behaviour of companies within their remit), it is essential that

- they are supplied with accurate data
- issues of ethics that are likely to need their judgement are brought to their attention as soon as possible
- both parties perceive the relationship as that of a partnership rather than that of police and suspect

Turning to the concept of communities—local, national, and global—as stakeholders, moral behaviour comes into play in matters such as

- contributing to communal care
- safeguarding the ecology
- enhancing the awareness of the duties of the citizens of the three types of communities

According to Tom Chapell (1993) business, ethical value, and social responsibilities are not contradictory. An enterprise adopting value-driven management can manage for profit and also assure the common good. Such an enterprise represents business with a soul. A company can be reoriented to make it possible for others to live according to their true values and aspirations.

However, of late, there seems to be an erosion of some values and a transition from contentment to avariciousness; from selflessness to selfishness; from duties to rights; from patience to haste; from humility to arrogance; from discipline to indulgence; from metaphysical to physical; from emotional purity to intellectual sharpness; from spirit to matter.

If an attempt is made to reverse the transition, changes need to be introduced at the behavioural and intellectual levels. A reversal may be highlighted using symbols, rituals, etc., which will indicate the changes made. It may be said that values are concerned with truth, not novelty and admit the superiority of only the spiritual over the social and secular.

In the emerging social order, management ceases to be a career discipline; it must be taken as a developmental process. The management approach has to be focused upon the development of man and society and not merely to train and retain a worker. The worker has to be made 'soul-conscious' to believe that he/she is being guided by his inner being to serve the divine through his/her work and behaviour.

Explicit reference to human attitudes, values, and life styles in future management thought will make management profoundly humanistic. It will deal with human aspirations and potentialities and will integrate them into the underlying matters of the global approach. In its ultimate nature, it will be scientific and spiritual at the same time.

CORPORATE SOCIAL RESPONSIBILITY

■ ■ ■
Corporate social responsibility is defined as the continuing commitment of businesses to behave fairly and responsibly and contribute to economic development, while improving the quality of life of the workforce and the community at large.

According to corporate social responsibility (CSR) an enterprise is accountable for its impact on all relevant stakeholders. It is continuing the commitment of the business to behave fairly and responsibly and contribute to economic development, while improving the quality of life of the workforce and their families, as well as of the local community and society at large.

By expressing their social responsibility, companies are affirming their role in social and territorial cohesion, quality, and environment. Through production, employment relations, and their investments, companies are able to influence employment, the quality of jobs and the quality of industrial relations, including respecting fundamental rights, equal opportunities, non-discrimination, the quality of goods and services, health and the environment.

Ultimately, CSR can only be taken on by the firms themselves. However, it can also pose challenges to policy makers to develop or adapt policies and legislation, in order that they may support and promote the awareness of the business case for CSR.

Social partners also play a crucial part in the wider implementation of CSR. Any company strategy towards CSR based on an integrated and balanced approach to economic, social, and environmental factors requires innovative thinking, new skills, and a closer involvement of the social partners.

Evolution

The state has traditionally taken on the responsibility of providing the national institutional framework to promote both economic progress and equitable social development. However, the ability of the government to fulfil this responsibility is increasingly being challenged by the forces of globalization that are disconnecting networks of production and institutional financial frameworks within the nation state. Overall, liberalization has strengthened the private sector, as the lowering of trade investment and financial barriers has increased the scope and the mobility of transnational corporations. Evidence is found, for example, in the steady increase in foreign direct investment flows in recent years. As corporations extend their operations across boundaries in a global market, their activities increasingly fall outside the regulatory reach of individual states. Today, most individual governments have only a limited capacity to hold global private sectors accountable to legal and ethical standards, including assurances that corporations contribute to or at a minimum do not undermine the values of equity, social justice, human rights, and environmental protection.

■ ■ ■
As corporations extend their operations across boundaries in a global market, their activities increasingly fall outside the regulatory reach of the individual states.

Most transnational corporations, while often retaining their headquarters in the major cities of industrialized countries, have established mass production facilities on an immense scale in the countries with weak regulatory institutions, where labour costs are lower and the monitoring of labour, the environment, and other standards is less well established. Most countries have welcomed direct foreign investment and the growth of transnational corporations has had a direct and wide-reaching impact on the economic and social conditions of a significant share of their populations.

The extent to which transnational corporations now operate outside the regulatory framework of any particular country brings to the fore, fundamental questions regarding the obligations or responsibilities of the private sector for promoting general economic growth and social progress, and for maintaining and promoting standards and norms of ethical behaviour. Apart from contributing to the economic progress of a country through the creation of income and employment, what more should the private sector do? Should a society expect the private sector to care about and contribute to a larger common good? Are such expectations reasonable and can they be achieved? Do they impose too heavy a burden on the private sector? Do they shift too much authority from governments?

It is regularly argued that the primary motivation of corporations should be to make a profit for shareholders, and that responsibility for ensuring that political, economic, and social objectives are met should rest solely with governments. Corporations, it is argued, should be required to obey laws and regulations, pay taxes, and maintain labour and environmental standards as they exist, but cannot be responsible for solving social problems, achieving full employment, or eradicating poverty. Yet, it can also be argued that the private sector has both a practical need and a certain ethical responsibility for the well-being of the environment in which it operates, based on its own needs for economic and social stability in which to operate, its needs for a skilled and healthy workforce, and the benefits it obtains from reduced governmental regulation. It could be argued that expanding markets are only sustainable if they are complemented by a social response to ensure a certain degree of equity. At the level of the individual enterprise, it could similarly be claimed that with wealth comes certain responsibilities. Thus, the private sector in general and transnational corporations in particular might find it in their interests to accept a greater responsibility for promoting an environment conducive to their continuing success.

These opposing views lie in the heart of the current global debate on CSR, a debate that has intensified in recent years as a result of the growing attention paid to the social impact of globalization and economic and financial liberalization. The increase in power and influence of corporations has sparked a reaction asking them to accept commensurately greater responsibilities. This reaction has come particularly, but not exclusively, from organizations of civil society, which are working to ensure that corporate activities are socially and environmentally sustainable. The growing public demand for enhanced CSR has been amplified by the current policy orientation in many industrialized countries, which has reduced the role of the public sector in the economic and social spheres of the society; by the increasingly large and unpredictable private capital flows across national boundaries, which have substantially reduced the leverage of governments, particularly of developing countries, in controlling their economic fate; and by the unprecedented period of strong economic growth in large parts of the industrialized world, which has resulted in the spectacular growth of corporate wealth, benefits, and influence in political decision-making.

This reaction in turn, created a counter response, particularly, but not exclusively, from developing countries, which fear the imposition of new forms of conditionality and see CSR as a new form of protectionism and a hindrance to their development. Many argue that at their stage of development, their primary advantage lies in the low wages and flexible regulation that they can offer to entice direct foreign investment by transnational corporations. They view calls for greater CSR as thinly veiled attempts to limit their competitiveness and their economic development, and regard it as a luxury affordable mainly by the wealthy countries. They are joined by many corporations, which are often reluctant to be bound or committed by a concept that they view as unclear in its definitions and implications, and see it as one that is imposed upon them by a force of public opinion that is essentially amorphous and potentially hostile.

Definition

There are probably as many definitions of CSR, as there are stakeholders involved in the issue. At its most basic level, corporate responsibility is concerned with the relationships that a company maintains with its shareholders, clients, suppliers, creditors, and employees, as well as with the communities in which it operates. Corporations are responsible for ensuring that their day-to-day operations produce a selected range of products and services in the most efficient and economical manner, and for producing a profit in the process. Corporations are responsible for obeying all relevant laws and regulations, for paying taxes and for reporting accurately their operations. These are areas that directly affect a company's operations and for which it is the primary factor. The concept of CSR goes much further, involves many more stakeholders and includes activities that might extend far beyond the day-to-day operations of the individual company.

What groups can be regarded as stakeholders in a particular company? Who defines who is a stakeholder? Is it the company or a political authority that decides who has a stake in its operations, or is the concept of stakeholder self-selecting? Traditionally, the term 'stakeholder' has been used to include management, shareholders, workers, customers and suppliers, as well as individuals who operate outside the direct cycle of daily business. Examples of indirect stakeholders include the relatives of workers who depend on their income; people living in the vicinity of a company who are concerned about the effects of a company's operations on the quality of the air they breathe and the water they drink; workers in industries that supply inputs to the company needs or who sell products the company makes; or the politicians dependent on company tax payments to support local services. Stakeholders can be even more broadly identified as those individuals or groups that have an interest or take interest in the behaviour of a company both within and outside its normal mode of operation. They may be members of consumers' groups or non-governmental 'watchdog' organizations that have chosen to scrutinize a company's behaviour, even though they might not be directly affected by that behaviour. They might, therefore, help to establish what the code of social responsibility for a particular company entails or at least how they perceive it, even if they are not directly able to influence the company's adherence to that code. Stakeholders' interests can be represented in an organized form. Employers' organizations, trade unions, non-governmental organizations, consumers' groups, investors, and local communities all represent, or aim to represent, certain interests of the stakeholders. At other times, stakeholder interests are expressed in less organized forms, including demonstrations, protests, or boycotts. The spread of communication technologies, including the Internet, has encouraged the mushrooming of such non-organized expressions of stakeholder interests around the world.

Are there degrees of interest among different stakeholders, and how close to the actual operations of a company does a stakeholder have to be for his or her opinion to matter? What role does the media play? To what extent should various stakeholders be included in corporate decision-making, and what kinds of processes are needed for them to be able to participate effectively in decision-making? What degree of involvement by stakeholders is appropriate? Should, for instance, local communities have a say in a company's decision to lay off workers or to move jobs out of the community? Small local businesses will surely suffer from the loss of income attributable to increased unemployment, but to what extent—if at all—should a company consider these roll-on effects in its decision-making?

CSR, therefore, involves the establishment of a dialogue between a company and its stakeholders. The term 'corporate citizenship' often refers to the action a company takes to become actively engaged in dialogue and to set policies on issues of direct social impact for one or more of its stakeholders. Good corporate citizens not only engage in discussions with stakeholders, but they also make an attempt to respect and comply with the concerns of the stakeholders. Compliance with those concerns can thus be made into a 'social contract' between a company and the society in which it operates.

While there is little agreement about the exact scope and depth of the social responsibility of companies, a number of common minimum elements of social responsibility may be identified. The first element would be that companies must comply with the laws and regulations of the country in which they operate and attempt to follow internationally agreed standards in such areas as labour, human rights, and environmental protection. The second element would be for companies to undertake philanthropic activities where they operate, including donating money, time or staff for benevolent causes. Companies sometimes put such actions forward as a proof of a commitment to social responsibility.

No business wants its reputation or product brand damaged by the disclosure of any negative behaviour, act, or accident. Many companies have recognized the need to develop a statement of CSR and to put in place a corporate communications and public relations strategy. Beyond this, more companies are seeing the benefits of associating with social concerns. The growth of the concept of 'cause-related marketing' in business theory and practice is a case in point: to create a strategic position and marketing discipline that links a company and its products to a social cause, it is helpful to bolster relationships with key stakeholders, enhance brand value, increase sales, and differentiate similar products in a competitive marketplace while providing benefit to a cause or an issue. This could lead to the misperception that a company engaged in cause-related marketing is a socially responsible company. Social responsibility should extend beyond compliance with the law, beyond philanthropy, and beyond public relations.

In a globalized world, CSR has become more complex. As companies have been increasingly involved in international trade and investment, their participation in dialogue with stakeholders has become an important element in a truly global corporate citizenship. The social contract of an individual corporation could, therefore, very well consist of a number of subcontracts, one for each host society in which it operates. Globalization has expanded the set of stakeholders far beyond the immediate community in which the company has its headquarters. In a developing country production facilities of a garment producing company, for example, workers, their families, and their communities all represent new stakeholders' groups. Does the 'social contract' a company might establish at home also extend beyond national boundaries to affect the company's behaviour in other countries? If a transnational corporation operates in many countries to produce and market its products, how many social contracts does it enter into? Should it maintain one standard to be applied internationally or should it develop separate standards that are appropriate to local circumstances? Should consumers in one country help to determine a company's behaviour in other countries? Some consumer groups have proved effective in raising public attention and have become important forces in determining the orientation, coverage, and assessment of the codes of conduct of companies. Who, ultimately, defines the standards of behaviour of the company?

Ways in which CSR is Exercised

Most initiatives towards establishing a corporate strategy for social responsibility are laid down in codes of conduct. A code of conduct can generally be defined as a written policy or statement of principles intended to serve as the basis for a commitment to socially responsible behaviour. As codes of conduct are mostly defined and developed by companies themselves, they generally do not carry any legal or regulatory obligation. They tend to be statements of principle that a company or an industry voluntarily follows.

Although the largest number of initiatives to enhance CSR has been undertaken by the private sector itself, representatives of governments have sometimes participated in alliances of business associations, non-governmental organizations, and other stakeholder groups, and their participation has stimulated a broader range of support for the initiatives taken. One example of an initiative that benefited from extensive government participation and endorsement at the national level was the 1996 Apparel Industry Partnership in the United States (mainly concerned with setting criteria for the global sourcing of United States transnational corporations in the clothing and footwear industries). Another was the 1998 Ethical Trading Initiative in the United Kingdom and Northern Ireland, a grouping of non-governmental organizations and business representatives established to provide a forum for discussion, training, and dissemination of best practices, and now receiving financial support from the government of the United Kingdom.

Social Responsibility vs Business

The issue of CSR remains perplexing to many who continue to be convinced that the goal of a business is only to increase profits. Yet, if we look around, we notice that in countries, such as Germany and Japan, with high trust or consensual practices, a much broader view is adopted and applied. The main question asked in these countries is 'who is the corporation responsible and accountable to'. In those countries, employees and customers tend to be equal partners with investors. In addition, the environment is also considered to be an important partner in many companies in Scandinavia. A survey of executive attitudes towards stakeholder capitalism conducted by the Japanese Ministry of Finance revealed an interesting contrast between France, Japan, and the United States.

Arguments For and Against Social Responsibility

The classical view of Milton Freidman about social responsibility is:

'What does it mean to say that 'business has responsibilities'? Only people can have responsibilities. A corporation is an artificial person and in this sense may have artificial responsibilities, but 'business as a whole cannot be said to have responsibilities, even in this vague sense...what does it mean to say that the corporate executive has a 'social responsibility' in his capacity as businessman?'

If these statements are not pure rhetoric, it must mean that the corporate executive is to act in some way that is not in the interest of his/her employees. Freidman says that economists argue that today's manager's primary responsibility is to operate the business in the best interest of stockholders. Because the stockholders' single concern is financial return, managers should not suggest spending their organization's money and resources for social good. If they do so, they undermine the market mechanism as well. Because socially responsible actions usually reduce profit and dividends, stockholders lose. If prices go up to pay for our social actions, our customers lose. Moreover, consumers reject higher prices, and then sales drop. For this reason, the company will lose.

Analysis of Freidman's View

When Freidman recommends that business managers seek only to 'increase profit' and make as much money as possible', he is not suggesting that they ignore ethical responsibilities. He does not endorse any of the sceptical positions. Rather, he argues for the normative position, and claims that in pursuing the maximization of profits one is doing what is ethically required. Business managers ought to increase profits because, objectively, this is the ethically correct thing to do.

On moral issues, Freidman offers the following principle to guide the action of individual business managers:

In a free enterprise or a private property system, a corporate executive is an employee of the owners of the business. He/she has a direct responsibility to his/her employers. That responsibility is to conduct the business, in accordance with their desire, which generally will be to make as much money as possible while conforming to the basis rules of the society, both those embodied in law and those embodied in ethical custom.

Freidman's ethical position is quite radical. He tells us that in principle an individual in business must always make the decision that will increase profit, but what increases the profit? For example:

- The stock market will view the socially responsible company as less risky and open to public criticism, which is why social responsibility will improve company's stock price in the long term.
- Business organizations usually have enough money, resources, technical experts, and managerial talent to support social projects.
- People consider social goals very important.

Accountability to Stakeholders

This is the information age. One cannot sweep things under the rug anymore. What corporations do—positive or negative—is immediately known around the world. Investors and consumers are empowered by information. This transparency of business practices means that CSR is no longer a luxury, but a requirement.

A narrow focus on products and services, brands and logos, revenues and margins, is no longer enough. In the emerging global economy, companies will also be judged on the basis of environmental stewardship, employee relations, diversity, community relations, and human rights. If a company cannot communicate in these terms—if it cannot manage its reputation to these requirements—then it cannot compete and it will not prosper. Consumers want to know what is inside a company. They want to do business with companies they can trust and believe in.

CSR is nothing more than corporations becoming accountable to all their stakeholders—not just shareholders, but employees, customers, the communities in which they do business, the people downriver and downwind who drink and breathe and inhabit the ecosystem that each corporation touches, for good or for bad.

The emerging, information-based global economy will demand transparency and sustainability. Businesses can no longer succeed at the expense of their employees, the community or the environment. CSR is a business strategy designed for an economy where economic, environmental, and social goals are positively interwoven.

Positive Correlation between CSR and Business Success

An emerging body of literature and other data suggests a positive correlation between CSR and business success. The following are some examples:

- The Dow Jones Sustainability Group Index has found that companies that focus on a 'triple bottom line' of economic, environmental, and ethical sustainability outperform other companies in the stock market. The Index found that the six best environmental performers in the chemicals industry outperform the six lowest performers by 9.2% per year in annual return.
- A 1999 Cone Roper study found that 68% of customers would 'have no problem' paying more for a product that is linked to a good cause.
- A two-year study by the Performance Group, a consortium of seven companies—Volvo, Unilever, Monsanto, Imperial Chemical Industries, Deutsche Bank, Electrolux, and the German insurer Gerling—concluded that improving environmental compliance and developing environment-friendly products can enhance company earnings per share, increase profitability, and also be important in wining contracts or investment approval in emerging markets.
- A 1999 study, cited in Business and Society Review, showed that 300 large corporations found that companies that made a public commitment to rely on their ethics codes outperformed companies that did not do so by two to three times, as measured by market value added.
- A 1997 DePaul University study found that companies with a defined corporate commitment to ethical principles do better financially (based on annual sales/revenues) than companies that don't.
- In 1997, Coca-Cola experienced a 490% increase in the sales of its products at 450 WalMart stores during a six-week campaign with Mothers against Drunk Driving, in which the company donated a portion of its sales to the organization.
- At the request of IBM, UCLA professor David Lewin studied 156 companies to determine the link between corporate philanthropy and significantly higher returns on assets or financial investments. Lewin concluded that corporate philanthropy can, over time, enhance business performance.
- A Wirth Worldwide survey found two out of three Americans saying that if there is 'a suspicion' that a certain product harms the environment or endangers public health, they would avoid the product, 'even if there is no scientific evidence that it causes any harm' (The Green Business Letter 2000).
- The 1997 Access Omnibus Survey by Business in the United Kingdom found that 86% of consumers said they have a more positive image of a company if they see it 'doing something to

make the world a better place'. Sixty-four per cent said that cause-related marketing 'should be a standard part of a company's business practices'.

A 1999 Millennium Poll of 25,000 citizens across 23 countries conducted by Environics International Ltd, in cooperation with The Prince of Wales Business Leaders Forum and the Conference Board, concluded 'public pressure on companies to play broader roles in society will increase significantly over the next few years'. Among its findings, the poll found that: 90% of the people surveyed want companies, to focus on more than profitability; 60% of the people, in forming impressions of companies, focus on corporate citizenship ahead of brand reputation or financial factors; 40% said they responded negatively to or talked negatively about companies they perceived as not being socially responsible; 17% reported actually avoiding the products of companies they perceived as not being socially responsible.

General ideas about social responsibility need to be translated into specific actions. Socially responsible companies can adopt social programmes, set social goals, honour stakeholder interests, and seek optimum profits rather than maximum profits.

SUMMARY

The chapter begins with an attempt to define the various perspectives of leadership, the importance of leadership, the various theories and styles of leadership, the difference between a successful and unsuccessful leader, various skills of successful leadership and the entrepreneurial kinds of leadership. In the segment on management by values, values and their importance are explained both generally and also in the context of life. A brief explanation of the Indian ethos, Vedic texts, comparative perspectives of value systems of the present and the past with a brief highlight on the Hopstede theory, and a cultural assessment of values and the Indian research, especially by Dr. Chakraborty, have also been given. In the segment on corporate social responsibility (CSR), the basic facets of CSR have been explained and the need for improvement of CSR has also been explained, especially in the context of the global scenario, followed by an explanation of various ways in which CSR could be extended. The accountability to stakeholders has been explained in brief as also the positive correlation between CSR and business success.

■ ■ ■ | KEY TERMS

Articulating   Composed of distinct, meaningful syllables or words, as human speech

Contingency   An event that may occur, but that is not likely or intended; a possibility

Decisiveness   Having the power to decide; conclusive

Ecology   The science of the relationships between organisms and their environments

Emulation   Effort or ambition to equal or surpass another

Entice   To attract by arousing hope or desire; lure

Equanimity   The quality of being calm and even-tempered; composure

Fanatic   A person marked or motivated by an extreme, unreasoning enthusiasm, as for a cause

Imperceptibly   Impossible or difficult to perceive by the mind or senses

Monotheistic   The doctrine or belief that there is only one God

Rekindle   To revive or renew

Self-actualizing   To develop or achieve one's full potential

Self-assurance   Having or showing confidence and poise

Transnational corporation   Relating to or involving several nations or nationalities

■ ■ ■ | EXERCISES

Multiple Choice Questions

1. Which of the following refers to the right to make decisions, direct the work of others, and give orders?
   (a) Leadership
   (b) Authority
   (c) Delegation
   (d) Management

2. According to which of the following leadership styles, leadership is a set of abilities that allows the leader to recognize the need for change, to create a vision to guide that change, and to execute that change effectively?
   (a) Transformational
   (b) Charismatic
   (c) Autocratic
   (d) Transactional

3. According to which of the following theories, leaders may use different styles with different members of the same work group?
   (a) Path–goal leadership
   (b) Vroom–Jago–Yetton model
   (c) Leader–member exchange theory
   (d) Situational leadership theory

4. Continuing commitment of businesses to behave fairly and responsibly and contribute to economic development, while improving the quality of life of the workforce and the community at large is known as
   (a) corporate governance
   (b) corporate social responsibility
   (c) business strategy
   (d) business ethics

5. A Cone Roper study found that 68% of customers would 'have no problem' paying more for a product that is linked to a good cause. This is an example of
   (a) charity
   (b) social service
   (c) corporate social responsibility and business success correlation
   (d) all of these

Fill in the Blanks

1. A leader is likely to be considered a failure if _____ _____

2. _____ and values must be an integral part of the management and work culture.

3. A high degree of _____ and _____ are related to entrepreneurial leadership style.

4. The _____ is a useful device for managers to identify and classify managerial styles; it suggests some alternative styles that may be available to them.

5. In case of _____, the leaders centralize decision-making power in themselves, and such leadership can be negative.

Concept Review Questions

1. Define the various styles of leadership.
2. Explain the various approaches to leadership.
3. Does leadership have an impact on organizational performance? If so, explain.
4. Explain the relevance of values in today's context.
5. Do you think we should adopt the Indian ethos or should we be guided by western values in the globalized scenario? Substantiate your stand.
6. Discuss the various factors influencing the value system of an organization.
7. Discuss the evolution of corporate social responsibility (CSR) in India.
8. Analyse the relationship between CSR and business strategy.
9. Compare and contrast the international trends with the Indian trends in CSR.

Project Work

1. Prepare an analytical report on some of the leading Indian corporate leaders.
2. Study the leadership styles in an organization of your choice and review it in the context of organizational performance.
3. Prepare a case study on the evolution of one leading IT firm in the country.
4. Prepare a comparative report on the leadership styles in the IT industry vs the manufacturing sector.

■ ■ ■ REFERENCES

Bass, B.M. 1990, 'From transactional to transformational leadership: Learning to share the vision,' *Organizational Dynamics*, Winter 1990, pp. 19–31.

Barrow, J.C. 1976, 'Worker performance and task complexity as causal determinants of leader behaviour style and flexibility,' *Journal of Applied Psychology*, vol. 61, pp. 433–40.

Bass B.M. 1985, *Leadership and Performance Beyond Expectations*, Free Press, New York, pp. 54–61.

Bernard, M.B. 1990, *Bass and Stogdill's Handbook of Leadership*, 3rd Edn, Free Press, New York, p. 11.

Blake, R. and Mouton, J.S. 1978, 'Should you teach there's only one best way to manage?', *Training HRD*, April 1978, p. 24.

Blake, R. and Mouton, J.S. 1981, 'Management by grid principles or situationalism: Which?', *Group and Organization Studies*, December, pp. 439–55.

Chapell, T. 1993, *The Soul of a Business: Managing for Profit and the Common Good*, Bantam Books, New York.

Conger, J.A. 1993, 'Personal growth training: Snake oil or pathway to leadership?' *Organizational Dynamics*, Summer, pp. 19–30.

Davis K. and Newstrom J. 1985, *Human Behaviour at Work: Organizational Behaviour*, 7th Edn, McGraw Hill, New York, pp. 160 –82.

Drucker, P.F. 2004, *The Daily Drucker*, HarperCollins, New York.

Fiedler, F.E. and Mahar L. 1979, 'The effectiveness of contingency model training: A review of the validation of leader match,' *Personnel Psychology*, Spring, p. 46.

Fiedler F.E, Chemers, M.M., and Mahar, L. 1976, *Improving Leadership Effectiveness: The Leader Match Concept*, Wiley, New York.

Gary, A.Y. 1981, *Leaderships in Organizations*, Prentice Hall, Englewood Cliffs, p. 70.

Hersey, P. and Blanchard, K.H. 1982, *Management of Organizational Behaviour*, 4th edn, Prentice-Hall, Englewood Cliffs.

Kirkpatrick, S.A. and Locke E.A. 1996, 'Direct and indirect effects of three core charismatic leadership components of performance and attitudes,' *Journal of Applied Psychology*, vol. 81, no. 1, pp. 36–51.

Likert, R. 1967, *The Human Organization*, McGraw-Hill, New York, pp. 3–11.

Miner, J.B. 1975, 'The uncertain future of the leadership concept: An overview,' In Hunt J.G. and Larson L.L. (Eds) *Leadership Frontiers*, Kent State University, Comparative Administration Resources Institute, Kent, pp. 197–208.

Whetten, D.A. and Cameron, K.S. 1991, *Developing Management Skills*, HarperCollins, New York, p. 8.

White, B.J. 1994, 'Developing leaders for the high-performance workplace,' *Human Resource Management*, Spring 1994, p. 163.

CASE STUDY 1

Leadership Challenges in Canaracola Company

Canaracola was founded in the year 1985 to manufacture soft drinks under the brand Cancola. The soft drink was manufactured and marketed in two flavours, that is, lime and orange. From an initial turnover of ₹10 crores in 1985, the company achieved a turnover of ₹500 crore by the year 2005. During the annual business review conference of the organization, the chief executive officer (CEO) made a proposal to outsource the manufacturing to local players from a strategic perspective. However, it was decided that distribution, brand building/advertising, and marketing would be controlled by the organization.

Further, to control the quality of the product manufactured by local players, it was decided that in every local player's manufacturing plant, the company would station a quality assurance manager (QAM), who would be recruited and placed on the company rolls.

After a detailed business review, the company decided to appoint five local manufacturers in all five regions of the country during the year 2006. It also decided to restructure its operations to include the newly approved QAM in the structure. Further, for strategic and operational reasons, it was decided that QAMs would be recruited at the level of Senior Manager and they would directly report to the Vice-President–Quality at the corporate office.

As per the revised plan, the HR, in coordination with the Vice-President–Quality, recruited one QAM for each of the outsourced manufacturing plants. Before deployment, the newly hired QAMs were inducted into the organization and trained in quality assurance aspects. However, after the commencement of work by the QAMs, it was observed that there were some issues in quality with the manufacturer located in the western region. The Vice-President reviewed the situation and advised for improved vigilance on the part of QAMs.

However, the problems continued and the Vice-President during a surprise inspection found out that the QAM in the site was not adhering to the prescribed quality checks. He gave an oral warning to the QAM and advised him to be alert in performing his duties. However, the issues resurfaced again. The Vice-President ordered for background verification details of the QAM from the HR department and found out that the QAM

was working with a competitor. He ordered the vigilance head to do a further study and track the QAM. The vigilance head found that the QAM had integrity issues in his earlier job, but the HR executive had overlooked it as a minor flaw and hired him.

The issues were discussed and the Vice-President–HR and Vice-President–Quality decided that the QAM be terminated with immediate effect as a measure of zero tolerance on integrity issues. Further, the Vice-President–HR also terminated the HR executive, who had not studied the background verification report before recommending the QAM for recruitment. The Senior Manager–Recruitment was issued a stern warning as well.

Questions
1. Analyse the case from the leadership and value perspectives.
2. Do you think that the organization is strong in its value orientation?
3. Are the actions taken by the company against the QAM, HR executive, and Senior Manager–Recruitment in sync with its value orientation? If yes, justify your answer.

Lisa's Story

CASE STUDY 2

'Lisa's Story' is a case study about Lisa starting a small business and her team-building adventures.

Starting a Small Business

After leaving high school, Lisa held several jobs including secretarial, administration, and customer service positions. These jobs were satisfactory; however, Lisa yearned for something better. She wanted to become a manager and felt that she could perform a manager's position as well as any of the managers she had worked for in the past.

Lisa finally landed a manager's job in the financial services area. This was her big chance to prove how she could manage a busy department of a metropolitan finance business.

Lisa did not think it would be all that hard as her previous bosses were fairly average performers and they seemed to be able to get along well in their orga-

nizations. She thought, 'to be a manager it was just common sense, right...?'

There was a lot more to being an effective manager than using one's common sense. Lisa had to endure a steep learning curve and understand that management was more difficult than she had imagined.

The hardest thing Lisa found was getting people to do things. Lisa thought that as she was the manager people would do as she told them, given that Lisa's own experience was that she always carried out her manager's instructions. Anyway, she fumbled her way through learning to be a manager for about five years.

Lisa tried a number of approaches from being strict and in control to being laid back, and all possible styles in between. Being overly strict and continually pushing the staff did not work very well and created resentment, just like being too friendly and accommodating only generated slack systems and low work output.

Her natural tendency was to be a bit of a 'controller' as she followed the example of some of the managers she had encountered in her early years of working.

Lisa finally came to the conclusion that her way of managing people did not work very well. After pondering her management issues for a few days, Lisa decided to take action and speak to her boss, David.

On Monday morning she walked into David's office, sat down and immediately started talking about something completely different! Lisa could not share her innermost feelings with him. She did not want to appear weak and silly after he had been a long time supporter of Lisa and had given her the opportunity of the job in the first place. Now, several years after getting the job, she felt stressed and thought she could not control the people in her team.

The situation came to a head on Thursday afternoon as Lisa was trying to convince her team member, Patricia, that customers must be spoken to in a friendly way with respect and not treated as a number in the system. The discussion became heated and Lisa could not understand why her team member had 'refused' to acknowledge the importance of customer service. Lisa fumed 'Patricia is the one with the problem...right?'

Soon afterwards, David came into her office, closed the door and sat down. David said that he had overheard the shouting and had been observing Lisa's behaviour for some time. Lisa immediately started to defend her actions and David listened.

After she had had her say, David told Lisa about his experiences as a manager and how it took him a long time to develop the necessary skills to manage the organization.

David suggested that Lisa would make a good manager, but she needed to learn how her team members thought about their work and how to develop good communication and trust between the people in her team. He asked Lisa about her life outside of work.

Tears filled her eyes and fell to her cheeks as Lisa told him of the problems she was having at home and explained to David about the split in her family. After half an hour or so Lisa felt better as she had unloaded a huge burden from her mind by sharing her problems with David.

As time passed, Lisa gradually learned that to be a successful working manager, she needed to lead her team as well as be a cooperative and supportive team member.

Also, that the skills of management are developed on the job, where it counts. Lisa stayed with the firm for another year then made the decision of starting a small business of her own.

Starting a small business is next!

Source: http://www.smallbusiness-teambuilding.com/startingasmallbusiness.html, accessed on 20 September 2005.

Questions

1. Do you think formal education has any correlation with leadership? Discuss this in Lisa's context.
2. Critically analyse the leadership qualities of Lisa vis-à-vis that of an effective manager.
3. Do you think the superior–subordinate relationship has an impact on grooming employees as effective leaders? If so, discuss it in Lisa's context.

CASE STUDY 3

Leadership Development that Works: Aon Consulting

Retaining and developing top talent is critical. Companies often spend thousands of dollars and commit extensive resources to leadership development programmes. Too often, however, these programmes do not deliver the promised results.

The Situation

An organization in the technology industry needed an innovative solution to replace its traditional leadership development programmes. It was undergoing significant changes, and its existing programmes were not delivering the desired return on investment (RoI).

Aon Consulting responded to this client's needs by creating *Horizons™*, a leadership development programme built on best practices and years of experience identifying and developing high potential leaders. The programme has now grown into a family of leadership development programmes. Each programme leverages leading edge assessment and behavioural-change techniques to ensure participant development and demonstrable improvements in job performance over time. Three programmes reflect the emerging business challenges facing different groups within the organization:

- LEAD develops leaders and high potentials.
- HR Catalyst develops HR professionals.
- Technical Catalyst develops technical professionals.

Aon Consulting conducts programmes around the world in languages such as Japanese, Mandarin, Korean, German, Hindi, and French. The ISO 9001: 2001 certified assessment centre operations team ensures that each programme is delivered flawlessly and achieves the desired results. In addition, the team successfully handles programme logistics to further enhance participants' experience and lighten the administrative burden on clients.

Source: Aon Consulting FORUM, December 2004/January 2005, http://www.aon.com/about/publications/pdf/issues/2004_forum_dec_jan_tsc.pdf, accessed on 20 September 2005.

Questions

1. Analyse leadership development as a motivational tool for employee retention or reduction of employee attraction in the context of this case study.
2. Can we analyse the return on investment on the efforts towards leadership building and the results in terms of performance variance?
3. Critically examine the time frame indicated in the case study vis-à-vis the expectation of grooming effective leaders.
4. Can you suggest any changes in the projects of the company for making the entire programme more effective?

Woolworths Group in Asia

CASE STUDY 4

Woolworths Group is principally a UK retailer focused on the home, family, and entertainment sector. During 2003–04, through the Corporate Social Responsibility (CSR) Committee, Woolworths Group has continued to work to understand the positive and negative impact of its business.

With increased direct sourcing from manufacturers and factories in developing nations, it is now in a better position to influence environmental factors within its supply chain. Woolworths Group Asia Limited (WGAL)'s buying office in Hong Kong has already made a significant step forward in determining priorities for continuous improvement and establishing long-term business partnerships throughout Asia.

When it was known that factory audits are pre-arranged visits, consideration was given to using routine product inspection visits as an opportunity to complete a brief, unannounced check on factory conditions. The quality assurance (QA) team within WGAL developed a simple procedure for inspectors to complete a summary report, focusing on the key elements of its Environmental and Ethical Code of Conduct. Since the launch of this procedure in October 2003, over 150 reports have been completed, which allow the company to monitor changes more effectively and provide added due diligence.

Woolworths Asia Facts and Figures

- Number of containers (TEUs) shipped: 17,697 (+8% year on year)
- Number of purchase orders processed: 16,207 (+66% year on year)
- Number of letters of credit raised: 2,244 (–12% year on year)
- Number of products managed: 5,708 (+10% year on year)
- Number of ports used to ship: 44 ports in 25 different countries
- Number of suppliers used: 361
- Number of factories used: 783
- Number of products inspected: 4,625

Woolworths Asia provides consistently better cost prices through

- better negotiation
- working with factories rather than trading companies
- removing agents and importers (where they are not adding value)
- making it easier to work with Woolworths Asia than any other importer/supplier
- educating and helping to develop the buying team
- understanding the real cost of products and negotiating bottom up
- working closely with suppliers and forecasting requirements regularly
- managing stock held by suppliers in order to reduce lead times to shipment

Positive Agent for Change

Through its supplier questionnaire, Woolworths is able to identify legal and ethical issues where, either a factory will be ineligible for appointment or it is possible to address the problems the company find so that an appointment can be made or an existing relationship can be continued.

This ongoing stewardship of the supply chain is a vital element of Woolworth's QA team's mission of ensuring that the company's guiding principles are upheld wherever possible. It also provides Woolworths with the opportunity to be a positive influence in improving conditions in some of the markets where goods are sourced.

At the end of 2003, one of its suppliers proposed sourcing electrical goods from a Hong Kong business, which owns a Factory in Dongguan City in mainland China. The QA team arranged for the factory to be audited and it was found that it did not comply with a number of critical failure points.

Factory in Manila, Philippines

An established source for Woolworths' children's clothing moved to new factory premises in Manila towards the end of 2002. Woolworths' QA team paid a visit to the factory and identified several issues concerning safety and the general working environment, for example there was

- only one entrance/exit for the office and production sections
- an accumulation of obsolete and dirty machinery
- unguarded machinery and cooling fans
- inadequate lighting and generally poor housekeeping standards.

As a result of this visit, corrective action was issued and a commitment was obtained from its supplier to make necessary changes.

Aluminium Picture Frame

India is a growing source of inspiration for Woolworths, and it is essential that the company develop its understanding of the potential to manufacture chosen products there. Picture frames are manufactured in the Moradabad region, which traditionally produces handcrafted brass and aluminium wares. Picture frame—along with a vase and dish—is a typical product that can be sourced from the region.

These picture frames are made from molten aluminium, sand-casted in a traditional Indian way, and polished by hand in a factory that they have been working with for over a year. Traditionally, the industry has always been regarded as dirty, and, therefore, health and safety considerations have always been a concern, so, at the start of its relationship with the supplier Woolworths' QA team conducted a full audit to ensure that all of our quality, environmental, and ethical minimum standards were being met. Despite being approved for the minimum acceptable criteria, several issues were identified that the company believed could be improved upon. An action plan was agreed upon at the time, to facilitate improvements to the factory's working environment, including increased use of personal protective equipment, better air ventilation in the polishing rooms, and modifications to their fire extinguishers and exits.

A year on, a follow-up audit confirmed that the identified improvements were being implemented, and a further set of actions was highlighted and agreed upon with the management. The success of purchasing products from this part of the world is dependent upon the supplier's willingness to work with Woolworths to improve areas of concern.

Source: http://www.woolworthsgroupplc.com/csr/index.cfm and http://www.nottingham.edu.my/business/csrasia/CSR_CaseStudies_9.htm, accessed on 20 September 2005.

Questions
1. Briefly explain the evaluation of CSR in Woolworths Group.

2. Critically analyse the positive agent for change in CSR in Woolworths Group.

3. Analyse in brief the country-wise CSR initiatives by Woolworths Group.

4. Do you think the attempts reflect Woolworths Group's positive orientation towards CSR?

CASE STUDY 5

WWF and the APP Partnership—A Lesson Learnt

The agreement between World Wildlife Fund (WWF) and Asian Pulp and Paper (APP) in 2003 was touted by some as the next big thing in corporate–NGO relationships, and as a cop-out by others.

WWF had for some time been aggressively pursuing corporate partnerships and had, in some ways, led the pack in what was then a burgeoning area. The criticisms came from those in the not-for-profit sector who saw that the organization was getting too close to, and allowing itself to be associated with, a company many consider to be among the worst in sustainability terms in the region.

For the company's part, it too drew some flak. By entering into a relationship with WWF, was it reneging on what some would call its hard-line business agenda? Was it endeavouring to exploit the civil sector to further its own commercial agendas? Could it be trusted to extend a helping hand to an icon like WWF, without holding a knife in the other?

Whatever the basis for the partnership, it broke down in February 2004. The reasons for the breakdown, given the partnership's high profile and test-case status in Indonesia and the region, contain salient lessons for all non-governmental organizations and corporations here and elsewhere as corporate-NGO partnerships become more mainstream and goals-focused.

The basis of the agreement was an attempt by WWF to put an end to the massive logging of native forests in Indonesia, APP's base, and other parts of the South East Asia region. APP and its parent, Sinar Mas, were and are a major logger in the region and might be seen as a vital centre of influence in the efforts to help put an end to rampant logging, illegal or otherwise.

The company saw reason to work with the WWF as it could see its name being muddied and, as it entered a major refinancing phase, its ability to attract capital being eroded by an extended risk profile brought about by its perceived sustainability weaknesses.

The approach of the company to Ethical Corporation's repeated requests to discuss the issue give an indication of its discomfort. Numerous messages were left with the company's director of sustainability and stakeholder engagement, Alan Aidrie, but were not returned. This may tell us something. It would have been unlikely the company would have been so reluctant to speak before the relationship with WWF broke down. It would appear now to be something of an embarrassment.

So, without APP's input, the only detail on this case can be offered by WWF. This is, in itself, an instructive matter for all NGOs seeking engagement with major corporations.

WWF and APP signed their agreement in August 2003. The central document was a letter of intent, in which the company agreed to four points of convergence with the WWF: the protection of forests with conservation values; legal compliance, including legal wood sourcing; resolution of social conflicts; and long-term sustainability.

The most significant part was that the company accepted WWF's request to put forward a sustainability action plan to be approved by WWF. It was the company's failure to provide an adequate action plan that led to the deal being cancelled in February.

WWF Indonesia director, Nazir Foead, says the company simply failed to present a plan for sustainable operation that the organization could accept. 'The company provided a plan in which there were question marks on the data and statistics used,' he said. Most importantly, WWF was concerned that the company put forward an unsatisfactory assessment of its operations and thus its targets were lacking.

Foead says the company was not planting or regenerating enough. According to its sustainability plan,

APP would still be using 85% native forest fiber for two years. This raised questions about where those resources would be found, for logging at that rate was not sustainable in Indonesia.

WWF had hoped the company would commit to replacing 'degraded' forest with plantations, but Foead says APP was assessing too much forest as degraded, in order to justify clearing it of native wood to make way for plantations.

As the company continues its attempts to develop a capitalization package with banks and other lenders, it remains to be seen to what extent that influence will affect the company's future.

Source: www.nottingham.edu/mg, *accessed* on 20 August 2005.

Questions

1. Critically analyse the global movement towards CSR especially in the context of WWF and industry partnership.
2. Do you think the success of CSR would vary based on the contextual factors? If so, explain in brief.
3. Critically analyse the reasons for the failure of CSR in the activities of WWF as detailed in the case study.
4. Briefly analyse the role of NGOs in enforcing CSR by corporate houses.

Bovince—A Small- and Medium-sized Enterprise

Bovince, a small and medium-sized enterprise (SME), has put corporate social responsibility (CSR) into practice. Bovince is a family-run printing business in a deprived area in the east of London, specializing in poster printing, bus shelter, and advertising panels. The company is run by Managing Director Peter Rosen, whose zeal for CSR issues comes from a deep personal conviction and a desire to make a difference, not only for the company's stakeholders, but also for the company's profitability. His enthusiasm has inspired two other key members of his staff who now drive CSR with him. The trickle-down of their ideas into the rest of the staff (numbering more than 60) is in itself inspiring. Bovince is also one of the few SMEs to have produced a social report. This and other activities led it to receive the Queen's Award for industry in 2001.

The activities of the enterprise started with a focus on waste paper management, and moved on to embrace the following:

- *Staff learning programme*: The Kaizen continuous improvement programme enhanced the performance and the working practices of the technicians considerably.
- *Improved culture*: Staff turnover is very low and the average length of service is 10 years.
- *Reputation*: The company recycles waste, produces drawing paper for local schools, as well as redirects old stock from suppliers. Tony Blair recently invited Peter Rosen to a meeting on business regeneration. Funding from a whole battery of governmental and local authority sources flows into the company.
- *Recruitment*: As a result of its efficiency, the company offers higher than average salaries to its staff.
- *Productivity*: Health and safety issues are crucial. Bovince has dramatically cut the number of days lost through illness or injury. For example, the film processor developer was formerly delivered as a liquid in drums, which were difficult to handle. A move to a powdered form—which was more expensive—cut down storage space, spillages, and injuries, because the containers were much smaller.
- *Environmental issues*: The company moved to computer-based processing of the graphics sent in by their clients, resulting in a huge reduction in the use of photographic film and in the subsequent amount of waste.
- *Customers*: Bovince's engagement with CSR, as a marketing instrument, will help the company to expand into Europe.

Two limitations, which must also be acknowledged, are:

- Bovince's CSR activity takes a lot of management time.

- The company's clients are primarily advertising companies, which are not convinced that adopting CSR makes Bovince a better supplier.

Rosen remains positive: 'CSR is good for my business and brings a challenge that we all enjoy. Our CSR activity motivates my staff, helps the environment and positively affects our bottom line.'

Source: www.accaglobal.com/pdfs/members_pdfs/ publications/csr03.pdf, accessed on 20 August 2005.

Questions

1. Briefly analyse the CSR initiatives by SMEs, especially Bovince.

2. Critically analyse the activities undertaken by Bovince as part of its CSR.

3. Do you think that the scope/activities can be extended to overcome the limitations?

International HRM

Objectives

After studying this chapter, you will be able to understand
- the concept of international HRM (IHRM)
- the impact of global processes and cultural diversity on HR strategies
- the international aspects of recruitment and selection, training, rewards, and appraisal management
- the contemporary issues in IHRM

INTRODUCTION

There has been a paradigm shift between the way business was conducted prior to the globalization and the way it is conducted now. Globalization resulted in integration of markets, emergence of new markets (e.g., China and India), increase in foreign direct investment (FDI), and cross-border assimilation of production and services. For organizations, both local and multinational corporations (MNCs), it opened up new opportunities and challenges unheard of before. Organizations now operate in a rapidly expanding and highly competitive global business environment. MNCs have grown in number, and their impact on the state is evident.

Globalization paved the way for mergers, acquisitions, and strategic alliances, which caused changes in the organizational structures. The acquisition of Corus by Tata and Arceler Steel by Mittal was a significant event for Indian MNCs. Advances in technology and telecommunication also added a new dynamics to the global business environment. Managing people in the new scenario became a significant issue. The new business environment demanded a deeper understanding of human issues apart from the financial concerns.

With the spread of business across borders, the need for international managers became very evident. The success and failure of firms largely depends on strategies, practices, and policies.

A multinational corporation is a firm/company that is based in one country and manufactures goods or provides services in different countries.

However, in the global business environment, organizations cannot negate the dependence on people with cross-cultural skills. Since management of employees of diverse cultures in offices worldwide depends on the availability of people with international exposure and experience, the interest in the study of IHRM and cross-cultural management grew. IHRM also became part of management education. Corporations not only began hiring people with cross-cultural competencies, but also started redesigning their existing HR policies to suit the needs of people from different cultures.

INTERNATIONAL HRM AND ITS ROLE

> ■ ■ ■
> IHRM deals with the issues related to the use of human resources of organizations across countries.

The interest in studying the ways in which organizations manage their human resources across different national contexts resulted in the introduction of the concept of IHRM. The international context adds extra complexity to the management of people as compared to a purely national setting. IHRM deals with issues that organizations face while conducting business across borders. It involves studying the HRM strategies, policies, and practices that global firms pursue to manage a diverse workforce. Morgan defines IHRM as the interplay among the three dimensions, namely, attitude of human resources, types of employees, and country of operation.

The duality of culture (its pervasiveness as well as its uniqueness) impacts global business strategies and HRM. It was observed that the MNCs with distinctive IHRM policies, procedures, and competencies can realize higher profits by applying them in markets where local competitors lack similar competencies. Demands to become locally responsive with suitable HR practices arise from consumer tastes and preferences, social norms, and the extent to which government controls business in a country.

HR activities are determined by, and influence, organizational factors. Hence, IHRM would involve structural changes to aid international growth, realize adaptive control and coordination mechanisms, and plan appropriate operations to be used in various markets. Further, the effect of the different HRM approaches need to be studied in IHRM as it is the people who play the critical role in all organizational operations. Effective management of the employees from different cultural backgrounds is crucial to achieve optimum performance. Hence, recruitment and selection activities in an international business environment assumes significance. MNCs are required to address the issues regarding competencies of a global manager, examine earlier examples of expatriate failure, and identify crucial factors to be attended to before sending for or accepting an international assignment. Further, IHRM also involves designing selection criteria for international assignments, managing dual-career couples, and female expatriates.

Dimensions of IHRM

Two basic dimensons of IHRM have emerged from meta-analysis of research in the area of IHRM. These are *standardization* and *knowledge networking*. While the first dimension involves the study of uniformity of international HR strategies, structure, and policies, the second dimension focuses on internal communication and coordination mechanisms used to support the creation and diffusion of ideas/experiences.

High standardization would mean IHRM characterized by highly integrated HR strategies and procedures, whereas low standardization would mean IHRM characterized by locally developed (and implemented) HR strategies and practices. There are companies that are constantly trying to balance this integration and localization of HR (and business) strategies. These companies develop appropriate communication and coordination mechanisms to achieve the fine balance between the two strategies. These mechanisms help organizations to identify cases where IHRM standardization is possible as well as those where local responsiveness is possible. Knowledge networking refers to the development of this intelligence among corporations. For example, companies such as Toyota, Suzuki, Samsung, Philips, TCS, and McDonalds have practised knowledge networking to excel and grow. Unilever, a multinational FMCG, is one company that has been strategically managing its knowledge assets.

IHRM and Employee Relations

The concept of employee relations is critical as the premise of IHRM is built on it. Three alternative approaches focus on the impact of global processes on domestic employment relations. These are the economic globalization approach, the institutionalist approach, and the integrated approach.

■ ■ ■
The three approaches on the impact of globalization on domestic employment relations are economic, institutionalist, and integrated.

The *economic globalization approach* predicts that international markets operate in accordance with universal principles and will cause a convergence of national employment relations.

The *institutionalist approach* contends that global forces are more fluid in their dynamics and will result in 'divergent' power struggles.

The *integrated approach* suggests that both global economic trends and domestic institutions are important in structuring national patterns of employment relations.

The central theoretical argument of the integrative model is that IHRM should be explicitly related to the MNC's global business strategy and that its changing forms must be understood in relation to the strategic evolution of the MNC.

RESEARCH AND EMERGENCE OF DIFFERENT APPROACHES TO IHRM

Studies on international and comparative issues in mainstream HRM consider the subject of IHRM from a number of different perspectives. Dowling, Welch, and Schuler (1999), have identified three broad approaches emerging in the field of IHRM:

- Earlier studies examining human behaviour in organizations with an international perspective, which emphasized a cross-cultural approach
- Studies that seek to describe, compare, and analyse HRM in different countries
- Studies that concentrate on aspects of HRM in MNCs

However, it is difficult to identify a unifying approach to the IHRM concept in the literature. Many of the earlier studies in IHRM have merely dealt with the management of high-level expatriate managers instead of the broader issues concerning HRM in MNCs. In recent years, studies have focused on recruitment and selection, training and development, performance appraisal, and compensation of expatriates. Human and financial costs of poor performance or failure of expatriates on international assignments highlight the criticality of IHRM. Studies have also attempted to explain the benefits and methods of cross-cultural training of expatriates. However, very few studies have concentrated on a unifying approach by studying organizational, management, HR, and industrial relations (IR) issues emanating from the internationalization of business.

■ ■ ■
An expatriate is someone who works in a different country, but is a national of another country where his/her firm is headquartered in.

HR Systems across Cultures

When we add the dimension of cultural diversity to HRM, it explores the international aspects of recruitment and selection, rewards, training and development, and performance appraisal, as well as the issue of repatriation.

The global company rests on the effective management of multicultural work teams that represent diverse competencies, varying levels of experience, and different cultural backgrounds. This implies that in the context of IHRM, the simple function of staffing (HR planning, recruitment, and selection) becomes a critical factor for organizational growth.

Similarly, compensation and rewards management requires managers to be familiar with the foreign country's employment law, preferred benefits, and currency fluctuations. Further, irrespective of the business strategy, training and development interventions in MNCs include cross-cultural training and enhancement of competencies associated with global leadership.

Studies suggest that performance appraisal is the preferred way to ensure that employee competencies, behaviour, and motivation are performed effectively in the host/other country. Studying appraisal systems in the context of IHRM raises interesting questions regarding performance criteria for an individualistic, task-oriented expatriate transferred to, for example, a more collectivist and a relationship-oriented subsidiary.

COMPARATIVE HRM

Defined as the systematic investigation of HRM practices in two or more countries to increase knowledge and understanding that has analytic rather than descriptive implications, comparative HRM has played a crucial role for firms conducting business across borders. The need to explore cross-border HR practices, presence and role of trade union organizations, and prevalence of non-standard employment patterns, all become important while understanding the role of an HRM function. The variations highlight the uniqueness of HR practices across countries and imply that HRM has to be understood through different cultural paradigms. For example, the selection of people must match organizational needs and be within the national institutional regulations. Managers need to be cognizant of the complexities of intercultural phenomena and ethnocentric issues.

There is a need for MNCs to do a thorough study and gain understanding of the practices prevalent in the host country before introducing the HR practices of the parent country. They must deliberate before adapting those practices to avoid a catastrophe. Research reveals that there are significant differences in the use of non-standard employment contracts defined as part-time, short-term, and temporary agency work, and independent contracting across countries. For example, China's foreign-owned enterprises (FOEs) operating under 'socialist capitalism' have provided a new context to manage the Chinese employment relationship. A review of whether Chinese HR practices are becoming more 'westernized', given the logic of market-driven capitalism, would yield useful knowledge.

Earlier studies have identified high systemic rigidities and weak individual-level motivational effects arising from traditional South Korean employment practices that are traditionally based on seniority. However, recent studies have identified change in employment practices.

In India, the World Bank and the International Monetary Fund (IMF) made it necessary for the Indian government to change from a regulated 'mixed economy' to a 'free market economy'. Such a change had its own implications on the business of overseas firms operating here as well as on Indian firms. Even within a country, variations can be found in HR practices. However, a comparative study of HRM practices in Indian public and private sector organizations reveals that they are more similar than different.

The 1980s stereotypical model of Japanese management attracted considerable attention. The *Japanization* phenomenon centred on core elements—flexibility, quality, and minimum waste. The quality movement that started from Japan led the entire world towards adopting unique practices, which were scientific and strived for zero defect/error. Following the financial crisis of 1997, Japanese companies too were forced to take a relook at their HR practices across the globe.

An organization that manages people in different institutional, legal, and cultural circumstances has to be aware not only of HR practices that are allowed/not allowed in various countries/regions of the world, but also of the various cost-effective management practices. For example, a performance appraisal system, which depends on US-style openness between a manager and a subordinate, where both employees are expected to frankly express their opinions on the work performed by the other, may work in some European countries. However, the same appraisal system is unlikely to fit with the 'greater hierarchical assumptions' and 'loss-of-face' fears of oriental cultures.

There has always been a debate among practitioners and researchers regarding universal HRM policies and best practices. Exhibit 22.1 outlines the key aspects of this debate.

IHRM ISSUES IN STRATEGIC AND ORGANIZATIONAL CHANGE

When two industry giants engage in a merger or acquisition, they find it extremely hard to create and sustain value over time. Mergers and acquisitions involve successful integration of two independent organizational cultures and systems. Two examples could be mentioned here: the acquisition of Chrysler Corporation by Daimler Benz in 1998 and the acquisition of the Jaguar Land Rover by Tata Motors in March 2008. In August 2007, the Chrysler group was sold to Cerberus Capital Management, a private equity firm. Two years later, in April 2009, Chrysler

EXHIBIT 22.1 The convergence/divergence debate

A common theme in the comparative HRM literature has been 'convergence' and 'divergence' in HR practices that came into prevalence after globalization.

Studies suggest that divergence of HR practices in Asian economies does not constitute convergence to an anglo-centric HRM ideal-type model. Changes in HR strategies and practices within an MNC are influenced by changes in the business environment and industry best practices. However, the gaps between universalism versus national culture and HR practices are evident. The sheer differences in economies, national institutional profiles, and cultures get in the way of claims for convergence.

HR professionals need to adopt a global orientation in their activities. This is important for HR people working in the giant MNCs as well as in small and medium-sized enterprises (SMEs). The liberal economic environment of the 21st century, fewer restrictions on labour movement, and the advent of new technology have made it possible for even start-up enterprises to operate internationally almost as soon as they are established. International organizations, today, are not limited to the private sector. Many international organizations such as those in the UN family, the Organization for Economic Cooperation and Development (OECD), the World Health Organization (WHO), the regional trade bodies, charities, and religious groups have employees who work across borders (Brewster and Lee 2006).

LLC filed for bankruptcy and subsequently was rescued by a financing of US $6.6 billion by the federal US government. Tata Motors has problems post acquisition of Jaguar in the UK. In 2009, it got into a conflict with the UK government over the relative financial responsibilities during the global economic recession.

International Assignments: Need and Issues

The main reasons why MNCs need their managers to take international assignments can be outlined as follows:

■ ■ ■

International assignments
help to fill the skill/
knowledge gap, provide a
training ground, and aid
in change management.

- Staffing: filling the skills gap, new units/offices/SBUs, technology and knowledge transfer
- Management development: training and development purposes, developing common corporate values and culture
- Organizational development: change management, transfer of knowledge, competence, procedures, and practices

While the positives of international assignments could be the excitement and thrill of conducting business deals in foreign locations, staying in top hotels, duty-free shopping, business class travel, etc., the negatives of prolonged stay could be multifarious. In the subsequent few paragraphs, we discuss various HR issues and problems in international assignments.

Compensation-related issues   Compensation-related issues are one of the major types of issues that companies face while sending employees on international assignments. Employees have to deal with various issues related to home and family, chaos in work arrangements (especially if there are issues pending at the local level), travel logistics, and lapses, which can prove to be quite stressful. Apart from all these, health concerns due to poor/irregular diet, lack of sleep, etc., can lead to long-term illnesses. Adapting to the host culture may become problematic for employees, if only a limited cultural training has been provided before the assignment.

International managers must be able to examine the complexities that arise when firms move from compensation at the domestic level to compensation in an international context. Here, to detail the key components of international compensation is critical to ensure employee satisfaction. During international assignments, the problem of taxation, the cost of living data, and the problem of compensation management become difficult areas to handle, making it necessary for organizations to keep track of the recent developments and global compensation issues.

Training related issues   Training aims to improve skills and attitude, whereas development aims to increase abilities for a future position or a job. An international assignment provides an opportunity for both training and development, and has a strategic role in international business operations. The role of training in preparing and supporting personnel on international assignments is important. Various training issues one needs to understand here include expatriate adjustment and on-assignment performance. Importance of pre-departure training programmes, such as cultural awareness, preliminary visits, and language skills along with relocation assistance, are critical for on-the-job performance. Managing multicultural teams also requires appropriate sensitivity training.

Apart from traditional expatriate assignments, IHRM also includes training and development aspects relating to short-term assignments, non-standard assignments, and international business travel as well.

Career issues The training of employees and proper management of their international assignments lead to a successful post-assignment stage. Once the assignment is over, re-entry to the previous/original position raises issues for both the expatriate and the MNC. IHRM examines and addresses the process of re-entry or repatriation, job-related issues, family and social factors that affect re-entry, and work adjustment. Further, companies always want to analyse the return on investment (ROI) and knowledge transfer from such international postings/assignments. This necessitates designing of a repatriation programme to smoothen the process of re-entry and career continuation.

FUTURE ISSUES IN IHRM

Considering global economic and political issues, cost management, recruitment and selection, employee retention, and supporting organizational policies have been identified as the key focus areas for IHRM.

While managers may be more concerned about the operational and administrative matters, researchers may want to explore more strategic issues. Selecting and retentaining employees, developing global capabilities, managing performance, and managing change have been the major concerns for organizations operating in different nations. Changing assumptions and expectations of employees due to socio-economic changes is one major factor that necessitates the need to study IHRM more closely.

Over the years, expatriate management has been the prime focus of IHRM research. However, organizations must give more emphasis to the strategic issues in future to grow and sustain themselves against competition. Changes in the organization structure would be required to manage such issues. Since work patterns are now more region-centric or geo-centric, cultural issues would continue to be an important area of IHRM research. Global HR policies would be required to be more future-centric, flexible, and constantly evolving in nature. Communication would be more complex, and networking would be more prominent in the future.

SUMMARY

The domain of IHRM spans social, cultural, and economic boundaries. In this chapter, we discussed the evolution of IHRM, the importance and relevance of research in the field of IHRM, and multiple issues that are associated with business across borders. The chapter highlights the role of IHRM in organizations, and discusses its two dimensions, namely, standardization and knowledge networking. When we study the HR systems and practices of two or more nations, we enter the domain of comparative HRM. The section on comparative HRM outlines how this became important for organizations.

The convergence and divergence debate dominates IHRM literature and would continue to be so. The chapter emphasizes the need to understand the uniqueness of HRM rather than taking sides with convergence or divergence of practices. Further, the chapter explains various HR issues, such as those related to compensation, training, and career, which need to be addressed properly for a successful international assignment. The chapter concludes by discussing future issues in IHRM from the perspective of practitioners and researchers.

■ ■ ■ | KEY TERMS

Comparative HRM A systematic investigation of HRM policies and practices across organizations operating in two or more countries

Convergence vs divergence The debate on the need for a common model for best practices in management across cultures/countries, or appreciation of their uniqueness and development of multiple approaches/practices

International HRM Study of the issues related to HR practices, policies, and strategies that organizations adopt to manage operations across two or more countries

Knowledge networking Internal communication and coordination mechanisms used to support the creation and diffusion of ideas/experiences

■ ■ ■ | EXERCISES

Multiple Choice Questions

1. International human resource management (IHRM) deals with managing human resources across
   (a) different states
   (b) different companies
   (c) different industries
   (d) different national contexts

2. Morgan defines IHRM as the interplay among the following dimensions:
   (a) Human resource attitude
   (b) Types of employees
   (c) The country of operation
   (d) All of these

3. Internal communication and coordination mechanisms used to support the creation and diffusion of ideas/experiences is the focus area of
   (a) comparative HRM
   (b) IHRM
   (c) knowledge networking
   (d) standardization

4. The approach that predicts that international markets operate in accordance with universal principles and will result in a 'convergence' of national employment relations is called
   (a) institutionalist approach
   (b) economic globalization
   (c) integrated approach
   (d) knowledge networking

5. The duality of culture (its pervasiveness, yet its uniqueness) impacts
   (a) global business strategies
   (b) types of employees
   (c) HRM strategies

   (d) HR activities

Fill in the Blanks

1. IHRM involves studying the HRM _____, _____, and practices that global firms pursue in response to the internationalization process.

2. Demands to become locally responsive with suitable HR practices arise from _____, social norms, and the extent to which government controls business in a country.

3. Two basic dimensions of IHRM that have emerged from meta-analysis of research in the area of IHRM are _____ and _____.

4. In India, the World Bank and the International Monetary Fund made it necessary for the Indian government to change from a regulated 'mixed economy' to a _____.

5. A systematic investigation of HRM policies and practices across organizations operating in two or more countries is known as _____.

Concept Review Questions

1. Outline the factors contributing to the evolution of IHRM.

2. Why do you think organizations would require managers with multicultural experience?

3. How do you see cultures affecting business decisions/actions?

4. How have globalization and cultural diversity contributed to the increased relevance of IHRM?

5. What are some basic issues that people may face during international assignments while working for a global organization?

6. How is compensation an important aspect during and after an international assignment?

Project Work

1. An MNC may face numerous problems because of the huge cultural and legal differences between the countries that it operates in. Visit websites, gather data from secondary sources, and analyse them. Prepare a report with your findings on how these MNCs manage operations across nations.

2. Visit research databases and collect articles on IHRM. Go through them and find out what would be the future direction for organizations if they wish to excel in a multicultural or multi-ethnic environment.

■ ■ ■ | REFERENCES _____

Bartlett, C.A. and Ghoshal, S. 1989, *Managing across Borders: The Transnational Solution*, Harvard Business School Press, Boston, MA.

Black, J.S. 1990, 'The relationship of personal characteristics with the adjustment of Japanese expatriate managers', *Management International Review*, 30, 2, pp. 119–34.

Boxall, P. 1995, 'Building the theory of comparative HRM', *Human Resource Management Journal*, 5(5), pp. 5–17.

Brewster, Chris, 2002, *Globalizing HR*, Chartered Institute of Personnel and Development, London.

Brewster, C. and Lee, S. 2006, 'HRM in not-for-profit international organizations: Different, but also alike', in H. H. Larsen and W. Mayrhofer (Eds), *European Human Resource Management*, Routledge, London.

Brewster, C.J. and Larsen, H.H. 2000, *Human Resource Management in Northern Europe*, Blackwell, Oxford.

Brouthers, K.D., Brouthers, L.E., and Werner, S. 2008, 'Resource-based advantages in an international context', *Journal of Management*, 34, 2, pp. 189–217.

Bush, V.D., Rose, G.M., Gilbert, F., and Ingram, T.N. 2001, 'Managing culturally diverse buyer-seller relationships: The role of intercultural disposition and adaptive selling in developing intercultural communication competence', *Journal of the Academy of Marketing Science*, 29, 4, pp. 391–404.

Carpenter, M., Sanders, W.G., and Gregersen, H. 2001, 'Building human capital with organizational context: The impact of international assignment experience on multinational firm performance and CEO pay', *Academy of Management Journal*, 44, 3, pp. 493–511.

Chang, S.J. and Rosenzweig, P. 2001, 'The choice of entre mode in sequential foreign direct investment', *Strategic Management Journal*, 22, 8, pp. 747–76.

Chen, G. and Starosta, W. 2000, 'The development and validation of the intercultural communication sensitivity scale', *Human Communication*, 3, pp. 1–15.

Clarke, C. and Hammer, M.R. 1995, 'Predictors of Japanese and American managers job success, personal adjustment, and intercultural interaction effectiveness', *Management International Review*, 35, 2, pp. 153–70.

Dowling, Peter J., Welch, Denice E., and Schuler, Randall S. (1999), *International Human Resource Management*, ITP, Southwestern College Publishing, Cincinnati.

Engardio, P., Bernstein, A., and Kripalani, M. 2003, 'The new global job shift', *Business Week*, 3 February.

Harris, H., Brewster, C., and Sparrow, P. 2001, *Globalization and HR: A literature review*, CIPD, London.

'Research note: World investment report 2004—the shift towards services', *Transnational Corporations* 13(3), UNCTAD, pp. 87–124.

Sparrow, P., Brewster, C., and Harris, H. 2004, *Globalizing Human Resource Management*, Routledge, London.

'Special report: A survey of globalization and tax', 2000, *The Economist*, 354 (8155), 29 January pp. 1–18.

Stiles, P. 2006, 'The human resource department: Roles, coordination and influence', In G. Stahl and Bjorkman (Eds) *Handbook of Research in International HRM*, Edward Elgar, London.

'The world's view of multinationals', *The Economist*, 354 (8155), 29 January, pp. 21–22.

Trends International 2001, 'Foreign investment: Belgium favourite', Belgium, April, 3, pp. 42.

Vaill, P. 1989, *Managing as a Performing Art: New ideas for a world of chaotic change*, Jossey-Bass, San Francisco.

http://www.shvoong.com/humanities/1805814-problems-issues-international-hr-mgt, accessed on 12 February 2012.

CASE STUDY

Managing across Borders

With its headquarters in Singapore, Priya Foods Limited is a leading fast food chain in South Asia. Over the last ten years, the company has grown tremendously and has acquired or partnered with leading food chains in the Middle East and Europe. The top management team has ensured growth of the organization by recruiting skilled people and using aggressive selling strategies to capture market from other leaders in fast food retail.

With menus that offer a wide range of options to fit the needs of the multiple cultures in which Priya outlets operate, the company provides hygienic food at reasonable prices. As part of the growth strategy, Priya outlets concentrate across highways, suburbs, and expressways rather than city centres. The strategy is to attract travellers, who would be keen to try new things as long as they are fresh, hygienic, and not expensive. Further, the wide variety of items on the menu would help them to decide easily for the entire family as well. As the visitors at these locations may not be too particular about fine dining facilities, the strategy allows companies to optimize space requirements, and incur less cost on establishments as compared to that in the city.

As part of its expansion plans, Priya has recently acquired a UK-based food retail giant in a mega deal. It has decided to rebrand and merge the acquired food chain with Priya within six months. The management at Priya has decided to use an ethnocentric approach, and send its own management team to UK to lead this changeover and rebranding exercise. As several crucial measures are to be planned and delivered, they have also hired management consultants specializing in such rebranding exercises.

Some managers have expressed the desire to move to the UK, and take part in this changeover process. Some of them even want to stay there for a longer time, which is encouraging, as more than half of the employees of the acquired company have left post acquisition.

The main challenges for Priya's management are multidimensional:

- Most of the managers have never worked in UK.
- All managers need to be fluent in UK English and understand the local preferences.
- A large number of local staff are to be recruited for UK operations.
- Managers need to be flexible to move between countries.
- Managers need to devise compensation plans that are comparable and comply with company's norms.

Questions

1. What kind of difficulties do you envisage in managing the acquired UK company?
2. As a consultant, suggest ways to facilitate smooth changeover and to develop appropriate compensation policies.

Answer Key

Chapter 1: Nature and Concept of HRM

Multiple Choice Questions
1. (b)   2. (c)   3. (a)   4. (c)   5. (c)

Fill in the Blanks
1. Performance planning
2. the success of an organization
3. Michael Porter
4. focus dimension
5. long-term process

Chapter 2: HRM in a Dynamic Environment

Multiple Choice Questions
1. (a)   2. (d)   3. (c)   4. (d)   5. (a)

Fill in the Blanks
1. Increased profit
2. retention strategy
3. control costs
4. psychological contract
5. collective engagement

Chapter 3: Strategic Human Resource Management

Multiple Choice Questions
1. (b)   2. (c)   3. (d)   4. (a)   5. (d)

Fill in the Blanks
1. cost leadership, innovation
2. outside the area
3. valuable
4. internal, HR strategy
5. technical HR

Chapter 4: Human Resource Planning

Multiple Choice Questions
1. (a)   2. (b)   3. (d)   4. (b)   5. (d)

Fill in the Blanks
1. Markov analysis
2. demand and supply
3. Redeployment plans
4. Short-term HR planning
5. Regression analysis

Chapter 5: Job Analysis and Design

Multiple Choice Questions
1. (c)   2. (a)   3. (a)   4. (c)   5. (b)

Fill in the Blanks
1. Job rotation
2. Job description
3. Job evaluation
4. Job analysis
5. Herzberg, job enrichment

Chapter 6: Recruitment and Retention

Multiple Choice Questions
1. (a)   2. (d)   3. (a)   4. (c)   5. (a)

Fill in the Blanks
1. retain valuable human resource
2. to attract qualified candidates and not unqualified ones
3. Walk-ins, employee referrals
4. Internal source of recruitment
5. Careful planning

Chapter 7: Employee Selection

Multiple Choice Questions
1. (b)   2. (d)   3. (a)
4. (a)   5. (a)   6. (a)

Fill in the Blanks
1. selection ratio
2. weighted application blank
3. leniency
4. stress interviews
5. Intelligence, achievement

Chapter 8: Placement Procedures

Multiple Choice Questions
1. (c)   2. (c)   3. (c)   4. (c)
5. (d)   6. (d)   7. (c)

Fill in the Blanks
1. Downsizing, lay-off
2. Exit interview
3. Job enlargement

4. dismissal
5. public, private

Chapter 9: Career Development

Multiple Choice Questions
1. (a)   2. (c)   3. (d)   4. (d)   5. (d)

Fill in the Blanks
1. Anne Roe, occupation
2. tentative, realistic
3. achievements
4. loyalty, commitment
5. full-time traditional manner

Chapter 10: Training and Development

Multiple Choice Questions
1. (d)   2. (a)   3. (d)
4. (d)   5. (a)   6. (d)

Fill in the Blanks
1. Role playing
2. the training and development
3. both are similar PA methods
4. the objectives of performance enhancement
5. educated

Chapter 11: Developing Managers

Multiple Choice Questions
1. (c)   2. (c)   3. (c)   4. (b)   5. (d)

Fill in the Blanks
1. knowledge development
2. competitive environment
3. ineffective
4. E-learning
5. Careful designing

Chapter 12: Need and Importance of Performance Appraisal

Multiple Choice Questions
1. (a)   2. (b)   3. (b)   4. (b)   5. (c)

Fill in the Blanks
1. halo effect
2. performance appraisal
3. forced distribution
4. checklist appraisal

5. permanent change

Chapter 13: E-HRM

Multiple Choice Questions
1. (b)   2. (c)   3. (a)   4. (c)   5. (a)

Fill in the Blanks
1. automate
2. performance management metrics
3. training
4. transparency
5. Competency management

Chapter 14: Employee Motivation, Incentive Plans, and Fringe Benefits

Multiple Choice Questions
1. (d)   2. (b)   3. (b)   4. (b)   5. (a)

Fill in the Blanks
1. job enlargement
2. valence, instrumentality, expectancy
3. affiliation, power, achievement
4. employee stock ownership plan (ESOP)
5. lack of praise, recognition

Chapter 15: Compensation Packages and the Wages and Bonus Act

Multiple Choice Questions
1. (a)   2. (c)   3. (c)   4. (d)   5. (b)

Fill in the Blanks
1. Employee equity
2. key class matching
3. job analysis
4. job worth
5. Job classification

Chapter 16: Industrial Relations and Issues

Multiple Choice Questions
1. (a)   2. (b)   3. (a)   4. (d)   5. (a)

Fill in the Blanks
1. chief executive officer
2. economic
3. Information and communication technology (ICT)
4. competency, commitment, culture
5. staff turnover

Chapter 17: Collective Bargaining and Workers' Participation in Management

Multiple Choice Questions

1. (d)   2. (a)   3. (b)   4. (a)   5. (a)

Fill in the Blanks

1. shop floor, departmental, board
2. Collective bargaining
3. Identification, negotiation, contract administration
4. development
5. contract administration

Chapter 18: Managing Employee Safety and Health

Multiple Choice Questions

1. (b)   2. (d)   3. (d)   4. (b)   5. (d)

Fill in the Blanks

1. physiological, psychological
2. external industrial accidents
3. the Ministries of Labour and Environment
4. ILO, control
5. central and the regional labour

Chapter 19: Knowledge Management

Multiple Choice Questions

1. (d)   2. (d)   3. (d)   4. (d)   5. (a)

Fill in the Blanks

1. empower employees
2. gold-collar
3. redundancy
4. agency theory
5. Externalization

Chapter 20: Human Resource Accounting and Audit

Multiple Choice Questions

1. (a)   2. (c)   3. (d)   4. (d)   5. (b)

Fill in the Blanks

1. Robert Kaplan, David Norton
2. Human resources audit
3. quality orientation
4. competencies of the people
5. operating income, return on capital employed (ROCE), economic value added (EVA)

Chapter 21: Leadership, Values, and Corporate Social Responsibility

Multiple Choice Questions

1. (a)   2. (a)   3. (c)   4. (b)   5. (c)

Fill in the Blanks

1. the followers stop sharing their issues with him/her
2. Ethics
3. enthusiasm, creativity
4. managerial grid
5. authoritarian, directive, or monotheistic style

Chapter 22: International HRM

Multiple Choice Questions

1. (d)   2. (d)   3. (c)   4. (b)   5. (a)

Fill in the Blanks

1. strategies, policies
2. consumer tastes and preferences
3. standardization, knowledge networking
4. free market economy
5. comparative HRM

Index

Related Titles

ORGANIZATIONAL CHANGE AND DEVELOPMENT

Dipak Kumar Bhattacharyya, Professor, Xavier Institute of Management, Bhubaneswar | 9780198066460

Organizational Change and Development is aimed at postgraduate students specializing in human resources and strategy. Providing a strong conceptual foundation of the subject, the book takes the readers through all the processes and stages of change, as seen and experienced worldwide.

Key Features
• Discusses organizational development experiences in several Indian and international organizations such as Wal-Mart, Lehman Brothers, Godrej, and Indian Ordnance Factories
• Provides appendices on guidelines for organizational change, sample of a dashboard, and organizational health survey

CROSS-CULTURAL MANAGEMENT

Shobhana Madhavan, Associate Professor, Amrita School of Business, Amrita Vishwa Vidyapeetham, Coimbatore | 9780198066293

Cross-cultural Management—Concepts and Cases is a comprehensive textbook designed for postgraduate degree/diploma students of business management and practising managers. It explains how culture impacts international management in the areas of communication, negotiations, organizational behaviour, and human resource management.

Key Features
• Discusses cross-cultural management in today's corporate India with a wide variety of Indian/Asian examples—making this text relevant to today's global India
• Provides important tips on business etiquette and key information regarding doing business in several countries, ranging from Brazil to Nigeria

PRODUCTION AND OPERATIONS MANAGEMENT, 2/E

Kanishka Bedi, Vice-President (Executive Education) and Associate Professor, U21 Global Graduate School, Singapore | 9780195690873

This completely revised edition of *Production and Operations Management* adopts an application-oriented approach to the subject.

Key Features
• Includes detailed coverage on Bureau of Indian Standards (BIS), Agmark grading, ISO 9000, ISO 14000, and COPC-2000 in the chapter on quality management
• Provides hands-on applications of various models, such as the transportation model, using MS Excel, MS Project, and SPSS
• Provides numerous solved examples, classroom-tested cases, and end-chapter problems with critical thinking elements and interesting activities such as group discussions and outdoor projects

INDUSTRIAL RELATIONS

C.S. Venkata Ratnam, Ex-Director, International Management Institute, New Delhi | 9780195671087

The book provides in-depth coverage of the four key components of industrial relations: the conceptual foundations, the institutional structure and policy framework, the role of government, and industrial relations in unionized organizations.

Key Features
• Explores the emerging issues in industrial relations, such as labour law reform, employment security and management of redundancies, and technological change and industrial relations
• Examines the challenges faced by business organizations in industrial relations

---

Other Related Titles

• 9780195683592 Tanuja Agarwala: *Strategic Human Resource Management*
• 9780195698718 Haldar: *Human Resource Development*
• 9780195693379 Deb and Kohli: *Performance Management*
• 9780195698374 Bhattacharyya: *Compensation Management*